STATISTICS IN
HEALTH ADMINISTRATION

Volume II

Advanced Concepts and Applications

Colin M. Lay, Ph.D.
Robert W. Broyles, Ph.D.

University of Ottawa

AN ASPEN PUBLICATION®
Aspen Systems Corporation
Germantown, Maryland
London, England
1980

Library of Congress Cataloging in Publication Data (Revised)

Broyles, Robert W.
Statistics in health administration.

Lay's name appears first on the t.p. of v. 2.
Includes index.

CONTENTS: v. 1. Basic concepts and applications.
v. 2. Advanced concepts and applications.
1. Health services administration—Statistical methods.
2. Statistics. I. Lay, Colin M., joint author. II. Title
RA409.R85   362.1'068   79-23280
ISBN 0-89443-153-6 (v. 1)
ISBN 0-89443-166-8 (v. 2)

Library of Congress Catalog Card Number: 79-23280
ISBN: 0-89443-166-8

Printed in the United States of America

1 2 3 4 5

Table of Contents

Preface

The primary objectives of this text are to study selected statistical techniques that may be used when examining phenomena influenced by several variables and to illustrate the applicability of these techniques to problems confronting health care administrators. Statistics deals with the analysis of random and systematic variations. Multivariate statistics relates the fluctuation in a dependent variable to the systematic effect of one or more independent, or predictor, variables.

Potential applications abound in many areas of health care management. Financial management, cost analysis, planning, economic analysis, quality control, and patient or facility scheduling are examples of areas where multivariate statistical analysis can provide important insights into problems. As an application in planning, we might argue that the use of health services by a specific population is influenced by: (1) the economic and sociodemographic characteristics of that population, (2) the incidence of specific diseases or injuries, (3) the severity of the diseases and injuries presented, (4) the supply of health services in the area, and (5) an array of factors depicting the characteristics of health providers in the service area. Similarly, the costs of hospital operation will depend on: (1) the volume of care provided, (2) the size of the hospital, (3) the primary function served by the hospital, (4) the severity of presenting conditions, (5) the prescribing pattern of physicians to whom hospital privileges have been extended, (6) the mix of patients admitted to the institution, and (7) the patterns of treatment of the various diseases. When analyzing these and other similar phenomena, the health administrator must use statistical techniques that are applicable to multivariate analyses.

Material Covered in This Text

The statistical techniques that have been selected for discussion in this text are analysis of variance, correlation, and covariation as well as simple and multiple linear regression analysis. An understanding of the material presented in this work requires a basic knowledge of fundamental statistical concepts as presented in Volume I of the companion text, *Statistics in Health Administration: Basic Concepts and Applications.*

The present text follows directly from our earlier work, in that the final chapter of the companion text is devoted to an assessment of differences among multiple proportions. Recognizing that a proportion is simply a special form of the arithmetic mean, the first statistical technique described in this work is *analysis of variance,* a statistical tool that permits an assessment of the differences among the means of several groups defined by a single independent variable. This is referred to as *one-way analysis of variance* (ANOVA). In addition, this text also examines two-way ANOVA without interaction, two-way ANOVA with interaction, factorial ANOVA, and fixed and random models of analysis of variance.

An understanding of analysis of variance prepares one for the use of correlation and regression analysis, which may be employed to assess the relationship between two or more variables. In this regard, there are many situations in which the health administrator is required to examine a variable that is influenced by several other factors. For example, the control of costs requires an understanding of the relationship between costs and the volume of care provided by the institution and other relevant factors. Simple or multiple regression analysis aids the health care manager in examining the determinants of cost behavior. Similarly, quality of care is increasingly an important issue in health care management, and multiple regression allows the assessment of the simultaneous impact of several factors on the outcomes experienced by similar patients.

Simplifying the Concepts

After several years of teaching quantitative methods to students of health administration, the authors have found that simple matrix algebra may be used to simplify the expression of many computational formulas found in beginning courses in basic statistics. We find it very useful in the early chapters of the text, and absolutely necessary in the discussion of multiple regression. We have found that this usefulness extends beyond statistics to financial management and planning. Thus, we have included a discussion of matrix algebra in Chapter 1 of this work. Students who are not familiar with matrix algebra should review Chapter 1.

Our experience has been that students grasp the material much more easily when they think in terms of matrix algebra. They are able to reduce a forest of mathematical symbols to a few basic matrix operations. Formulas are easily understood and relate closely to the underlying statistical concepts. The computations are easily carried out, either using a hand calculator or an appropriate computer package.

Throughout this text, we introduce simplified examples from the health care field to illustrate the use of the selected statistical tools. In our opinion, a hand calculator is necessary for carrying out the computations. However, we realize that most *real world* problems require the analysis and manipulation of large sets of data. In fact, the manager frequently requires more than the use of a hand calculator.

Statistical Analysis and the Use of Computers

The study of the statistical techniques discussed in this work can be a sterile academic exercise unless tools are provided to handle the large amounts of data that confront the administrator. Computer packages for carrying out the repetitive computations are necessary, and we have chosen two of the most appropriate. Our use of matrix algebra is complemented by a computer language known as APL (A Programming Language). APL can be used as a language to reinforce the matrix algebra implementation of computing formulas. In addition, programs are available, both in the text and from commercial APL suppliers, to carry out the statistical analysis. Secondly, one of the most widely used statistical analysis packages called SPSS (Statistical Package for the Social Sciences) is featured in this text.

APL

Several computer languages have been developed in recent years allowing the analyst to employ the computer to perform the operations of matrix algebra, and APL (A Programming Language) is the foremost of these languages. APL is primarily an interactive language that permits the user to express ordinary arithmetic, algebra, and matrix algebra in simplified terms. The results of computations are immediately available to the user, avoiding the turnaround time problem associated with batch computer systems. Since some readers may not be familiar with APL, a thorough introductory discussion of this programming language is presented in Chapter 2. APL is presented as an adjunct to the main examination of statistical concepts and techniques. As a result, the manager or the student who wishes to may ignore the APL sections.

APL has become very popular since 1970 for use in the analysis of quantitative management problems in private industry. Statistical, financial management, and planning programs (sometimes called models) are widely available and easily adaptable to the specific requirements of any user. Programs are easily developed to meet the novel requirements of any industry. (Program development and debugging is much easier in APL than in such well-known languages as COBOL, BASIC, FORTRAN, and PL/1).

Because of the growing emphasis on operations research, planning, and management engineering in the health care industry, APL is certain to gain recognition as a valuable tool in hospitals and planning agencies. APL is widely available on a monthly rental basis from time-sharing computer service bureaus in North America and Europe. Unlike many computer systems a very small investment suffices for an extensive trial, and the benefits are potentially great. Microcomputers using APL were introduced in the late 1970s, and they are also inexpensive.

SPSS

The Statistical Package for the Social Sciences (SPSS) is probably the most popular and most widely available statistical analysis package. Although no statistical package is easy to use, SPSS is simpler to use than the other major package considered, namely, the Biomedical Computer Programs (BMDP). We believe that SPSS may be employed by the statistical novice or the intermediate user, while BMDP is perhaps more appropriate for the advanced user. Since many readers may not be familiar with the fundamentals of SPSS, an introduction to the use of this statistical package is presented in Chapter 3. SPSS is used as an adjunct to Chapters 4, 7, and 8 in the discussions of analysis of variance and correlation. However, it becomes the major instructional vehicle in Chapters 11, 12, and 13, in the discussion of the use of multiple regression. An understanding of SPSS is important.

SPSS is becoming more familiar to hospital data processing departments as they become more deeply involved with statistical analysis. For those who are not familiar with this language a thorough introduction is contained in Chapter 3. SPSS can be used on virtually all medium and large-scale computers. It may be most readily accessible to any hospital or planning agency through rental of time *as needed* from a computer service bureau or an affiliated university. Instruction and assistance with the use of SPSS is usually available from computer center consultants. Often specialists in SPSS provide extensive consulting and application services. When renting computer time only a small investment of personal familiarization time is necessary. Programming expertise is *not necessary* for the use of SPSS, but it may be helpful for establishing systems to perform selected statistical analyses on a routine (say monthly) basis. A hospital management engineering, financial management, or planning department could profitably train a person in the use of SPSS, in order to assist managers and planners during the initial stages of use.

Though this work is structured so that the reader may disregard the coverage of APL and SPSS he or she should understand that separately, or together, these languages make statistics an *important tool* for the manager and the planner. They are widely available on an inexpensive, pay-as-you-go basis. They are easy to learn and easy to use, and they facilitate expanding use with increasing understanding and confidence. The increasing requirement for quantitative information in health care management makes statistical analysis imperative. Either or both of these tools can be very helpful.

Organization of the Text

To assist the users of this text, each chapter has been subdivided into several sections. At the beginning of each chapter we present a set of performance objectives as well as a map to the chapter indicating those sections which: (1) present elementary explanations of concepts, principles and algebraic equations; (2) treat concepts and procedures at a slightly higher level of mathematical sophistication (i.e., the expression of computational equations using the notation and operations of matrix algebra); (3) consider supplementary applications of statistical analysis to problems of health care management; (4) consider the use of SPSS and APL to perform required calculations; and (5) present additional problems for solution.

The use of this text may be tailored to the interests of the reader with the guidance of the following classification of the sections appearing in each of the chapters. (Each section has been assigned a letter code, which is listed in the chapter map.)

CODE	*EXPLANATION*
A	Introduction and Explanation of Concepts
B	Development of Algebraic Formulas
C	Development of Computational Equations Using Matrix Algebra
D	Sections Dealing with the Application of SPSS
E	Sections Dealing with the Application of APL
F	Supplementary Applications to Health Care Management
G	Problems for Solution

Those portions labelled A and B represent an introduction to statistical concepts and techniques as applied to health care management. The focus of the sections labelled C is on the development of a slightly *more advanced but simpler* expression of computational equations. The portions grouped into the D and E categories are intended to enhance the application of statistics in solving real world problems by illustrating the usefulness of the computer as a managerial tool. Finally, sections grouped in the F and G categories are intended to enhance the user's ability to use statistics in addressing problems that confront the health care manager. Note that problems whose solutions appear in the text are preceded by an asterisk.

The Users of this Text

We anticipate that this work will be useful to health care practitioners, students of health administration, and to instructors who teach statistics to students of health care administration. That the *administrator* of the health care facility is subjected to increasing pressures to contain costs and to improve the efficiency of operations, requires no documentation. In response to these demands, the manager of the health care facility is forced to increase the use of the scientific approach in the decision-making/problem-solving process. Such an approach, however, requires a fundamental knowledge of multivariate statistical analysis. Thus, this text has been designed to provide the administrator with an understanding of the appropriate techniques as well as their application to practical situations found in most health care facilities. The examples used to illustrate the statistical techniques are expressed in terms of simplified practical problems. However, to enhance the usefulness of multivariate statistical analysis in solving real world problems, the administrator is encouraged to consider those sections in which computer applications are examined.

Most *students* face the study of statistics with a certain amount of trepidation that is usually related to difficulties experienced previously in the study of mathematics. On the other hand, most students recognize that an understanding of statistics is required for the study of health administration. Concerning the fear usually expressed by beginning students in statistics, the mathematical proofs and derivations have been presented at the lowest level which, in the author's opinion, is consistent with achieving an understanding of modern statistics. In this sense, this text seeks to provide the student with the understanding and skills required for a successful career in health administration.

The authors believe that this work is tailored to the needs of the *instructor* who is responsible for a second statistics course devoted to multivariate statistical analysis for students in health care administration. The companion text, *Statistics in Health Administration: Basic Concepts and Applications*, is suitable for the first course. In the authors' opinion, for students who will be taking the second course, it is appropriate to utilize the matrix algebra sections of the first course because they become necessary when finally arriving at the discussion of multiple regression. For those students who may wish to proceed to health care financial management, research, planning or health economics, the time devoted to understanding basic and multivariate statistics with matrix algebra will be repaid when moving on to more advanced work in statistical analysis or econometrics. In such courses and texts, matrix algebra is assumed. Similarly, the computer applications should be emphasized in the second course and preferably in the first course as well.

For those students who do not wish to become statisticians, economists, or researchers, we believe that careful attention to the basics of matrix algebra will pay dividends because many of the formulas are much easier to understand, both in the study of variance and standard deviation and in analysis of variance and regression analysis. Furthermore, many concepts in budgeting and financial management are more simply expressed in matrix algebra and easily implemented in APL. In our opinion, most students find matrix algebra easier to understand and manipulate than the usual forest of summation signs and subscripts. This leads to a happier and more productive teaching and learning experience.

Glossary of Terms

Finally, a glossary of statistical terms has been added, adapted from *Dictionary/Outline of Basic Statistics* by Freund and Williams, published in 1966 by McGraw-Hill (now out of print). We hope that this glossary will clarify the statistical terms which are encountered in practice as well as in this book.

Colin M. Lay
Robert W. Broyles
Ottawa, Ontario
March 1980

Acknowledgments

As with any large task a number of people have contributed to make the final product a reality. Our wives, Marjorie and Rita, and our children, Steven, Andrew, and Erin have patiently accepted our long hours of work. Micheline Leblanc has diligently deciphered our handwriting, and typed many drafts and revisions. Our students in the MHA Programme have used the books in draft form, and have made many valuable suggestions about the presentation of the material.

Our editors at Aspen, Mike Brown and Margot Raphael, and their staffs have put in many hours of work with us to refine and improve the manuscript. They have helped us to achieve books which we believe to be of exceptionally high quality, well worth the effort.

We acknowledge Biometrika Trustees, Hafner Press, and Butterworths Publishers, Ltd. for granting permission to reprint statistical tables and McGraw-Hill Book Company for the glossary. The rest of the material constitutes our own selection, presentation, reworking and extension of material which is widely known in basic statistics. We must of course accept responsibility for any errors which may remain, and indicate our great debt to the many statisticians upon whose work we have drawn.

Part I

Fundamentals

Chapter 1

Basic Summation Notation and an Introduction to Matrix Algebra

Objectives

After completing this chapter you should be able to:
1. Use variables, subscripts and summation notation.
2. Define the terms scalar, vector, matrix, and transpose.
3. Create and use scalars, row and column vectors, and matrices.
4. Perform matrix addition and subtraction, and give the conformability condition for these operations.
5. Perform scalar, vector and matrix multiplication, and give the conformability condition for multiplication.
6. Calculate the determinant and inverse of a 2×2 matrix.
7. Create an identity matrix, and show that $\mathbf{A}\mathbf{A}^{-1} = \mathbf{A}^{-1}\mathbf{A} = \mathbf{I}$ for a 2×2 matrix $\mathbf{A}$.
8. Solve a system of two simultaneous linear equations, using matrix algebra.

Who Needs This Chapter

This chapter provides an introduction to those aspects of basic matrix algebra which are necessary for understanding the material presented in later chapters. Those with little or no previous experience with matrix algebra will need to work carefully through this chapter.

Note that *most* of the material in this chapter is identical to the material in Appendix B of *Statistics in Health Administration (Volume I): Basic Concepts and Applications*. Section 1.5 has been added to introduce the inverse of a matrix and its use in the solution of a set of linear equations. The inverse is important in the study of regression analysis in Part III of

3

the book. Problems related to the inverse have been added to the problem set at the end of the chapter. They are questions 4(i), 5(d) and (e), 6(c) and (d), 13, 14 and 15.

Chapter Map

Section 1.1 deals with basic algebra and summation notation and has been assigned the letter code B.

All other sections of the chapter are labeled C.

A limited knowledge of mathematics is required for an understanding of statistics as presented in this book. A thorough examination of the principles that underlie statistics would require a knowledge of mathematical subjects that are normally taught in advanced courses to students majoring in mathematics. However, our objectives and hence our prerequisites, are far more modest. At most, the mathematics required for an understanding of statistics as presented here consists of basic college algebra, including basic matrix algebra. Indeed, a knowledge of high school algebra will probably provide a sufficient foundation for understanding the subject matter presented in this work.

The primary purpose of the discussion in this chapter is to provide a brief review of certain key mathematical skills on which portions of this text are predicated. We shall discuss basic subscript and summation notation as well as the fundamental operations of matrix algebra.

1.1 SUMMATION NOTATION[B]

Since all of the formulas that we examine in this book are applicable to different sets of data, we represent the values, measurements, or observations to which these equations apply by general symbols such as x, y, or z. Without a slight modification, however, we encounter serious problems because there are not enough letters in the alphabet to accommodate our needs. For example, if we wanted to represent the length of stay associated with each patient hospitalized in Canada and the United States during the past ten years by a different letter, it becomes clear that we would use all the letters of the alphabet without accommodating even a small fraction of our data. For this reason, we employ subscripts when referring to specific observations or values contained in a set of data. To illustrate the use of subscripts, suppose we selected five hospitalized patients from institution A and recorded the length of stay experienced by each. We might symbolize the set of data reflecting the lengths of stay associated with these patients by the symbols x_1, x_2, x_3, x_4, and x_5. Similarly, if we selected five patients from institution B and recorded the length of stay associated with each of these individuals, we might symbolize the resulting set of data by y_1, y_2, y_3, y_4, and y_5. When referring to any one of these observations in general, we shall follow the convention of employing the notations x_i or y_j where i and j are variable subscripts having the values 1, 2, 3, 4, and 5 in this example.

Observe that the above symbolization is arbitrary. Rather than referring to the two sets of data by x and y, we could have used any other letter or symbol. Similarly, instead of employing the letters i and j as variable subscripts, we could have used other letters such as k, l, and m. As a general rule, it is customary to use different letters to refer to different kinds of measurements and different subscripts to refer to different individuals or items. For example, suppose that the supply items held by a given institution have been ordinally ranked in terms of annual usage. We might refer to the ninth and tenth items appearing on the list by x_9 and x_{10}, respectively. Similarly, suppose that a set of patients has been ordinally ranked in terms of usage of a particular service. In this example, we might let x_3, y_3, and z_3 represent the age, sex, and marital status of the third patient appearing on the list.

Given this understanding, let us now introduce the symbol Σ (Greek sigma), which is a mathematical notation that will simplify formulas involving large sets of numerical data. By definition, we write

$$\sum_{i=1}^{n} x_i = x_1 + x_2 + \cdots + x_n \qquad (1.1.1)$$

Hence, the symbol $\sum_{i=1}^{n} x_i$ refers to the summation of x's having the subscripts 1, 2, ..., n. Accordingly, we might write

$$\sum_{i=1}^{n} x_i^2 = x_1^2 + x_2^2 + \cdots + x_n^2 \qquad (1.1.2)$$

or

$$\sum_{i=1}^{n} x_i y_i = x_1 y_1 + x_2 y_2 + \cdots + x_n y_n \qquad (1.1.3)$$

Since summation plays a central role in many of the equations that appear in this work, it will be helpful to examine some of the fundamental rules that pertain to this operation. By and large, these rules, three of which are presented next, are easy to understand and to prove.

The *first* rule simply states that the sum (or difference) of two or more terms is equal to the sum (or difference) of their respective summations. In the case of three variables, this rule may be expressed symbolically by

$$\sum_{i=1}^{n} (x_i + y_i + z_i) = \sum_{i=1}^{n} x_i + \sum_{i=1}^{n} y_i + \sum_{i=1}^{n} z_i \qquad (1.2)$$

If we wished to express subtraction rather than addition, we would have done so by introducing minus signs rather than plus signs on both sides of the equation.

The *second* basic rule states that the sum of the products between some constant, k, and a variable, x_i, is equal to the constant times the summation of the variable. Thus, the second rule may be expressed by

$$\sum_{i=1}^{n} kx_i = k \sum_{i=1}^{n} x_i \tag{1.3}$$

which is proven as follows:

$$\sum_{i=1}^{n} kx_i = kx_1 + kx_2 + \ldots + kx_n$$

$$= k(x_1 + x_2 + \cdots + x_n)$$

$$= k \sum_{i=1}^{n} x_i$$

The *third* rule is that the summation of a constant, k, from 1 to n is equal to the product of n and k. Thus, the third rule may be expressed by

$$\sum_{i=1}^{n} k = nk \tag{1.4}$$

which is proven by noting that

$$\sum_{i=1}^{n} k = k + k + \ldots + k$$

$$= kn$$

where the number of k's is equal to n.

1.2 FUNDAMENTAL MATRIX OPERATIONS[C]

Many of the algebraic expressions which we examine in this text are greatly simplified by the use of matrix notation and operations. Expressing algebraic formulas in matrix notation serves to:

1. facilitate the computational work associated with many statistical techniques;

2. reduce or eliminate the need to memorize complicated algebraic expressions;
3. provide a better understanding of the fundamental logic and concepts of modern statistics;
4. provide the basis for understanding the mechanics of computer-based programs for performing desired calculations and statistical tests.

With these advantages in mind, the objective of this section is to introduce the uninitiated to the fundamentals of matrix algebra.

1.2.1 A General Description[C]

A matrix is a rectangular array or table of numbers that have been arranged in rows and columns. As such, a matrix is a device that is used to organize and present numerical data so that they may be manipulated mathematically with ease. One of the primary advantages of employing matrix notation is that the algebra of matrices provides a means of organizing data and simplifying a large number of complicated manipulations.

Consider first the aspect of a matrix as an aid in organizing data. Suppose we are provided with information concerning the number of days of hospital care used by patients of differing ages during the past three years. Suppose further that the information is originally conveyed to us in tabular form as in Table 1-1.

Table 1-1 Use of Service by Age of Patient during the Period 1978–1980

| Age | Days of Care Utilized Year | | |
	1978	1979	1980
0–15	80,000	82,000	86,000
16–44	60,000	65,000	68,000
45–64	50,000	56,000	62,000
65+	90,000	92,000	85,000

These data may be written in matrix notation as follows:

$$
\begin{bmatrix}
80,000 & 82,000 & 86,000 \\
60,000 & 65,000 & 68,000 \\
50,000 & 56,000 & 62,000 \\
90,000 & 92,000 & 85,000
\end{bmatrix}
$$

Observe that the position of an element determines its meaning. For example, the element 56,000, which appears in the third row and the second column, represents the number of days of care used by patients in the age category 45–64 during 1979. Thus, a given row represents the use of service by the corresponding age group during the three-year period, while a given column reflects the use of service by all age groups during the corresponding year.

Given this general description, let us now consider the notation for describing a matrix. We already know a matrix is an array of numbers arranged in rows and columns. It is identified by enclosing the data in square brackets. The individual entries in a matrix are referred to as elements or terms of the matrix. In this text we follow the convention of denoting matrices by uppercase boldface letters and the elements of the matrix by lowercase italic letters. Thus, we might write

$$
\mathbf{A} =
\begin{bmatrix}
a_{11} & a_{12} & a_{13} \\
a_{21} & a_{22} & a_{23}
\end{bmatrix}
$$

where $\mathbf{A}$ is a 2×3 matrix. In this case, the expression "2×3" is read "2 by 3" and means that there are 2 rows and 3 columns in the matrix. In general, a matrix with r rows and k columns is referred to as a *matrix of order* $r \times k$ (r by k).

Observe that the elements of matrix $\mathbf{A}$ may be expressed generally by the term a_{ij}. Here, the first subscript, i, refers to the row in which the element appears, while the second subscript, j, indicates the column in which the term appears. For example, the element a_{12} appears in the first row and second column of the matrix while the term a_{23} appears in the second row and third column of the matrix. In this way, the subscript attached to an element locates its position in the matrix.

By way of contrast, a matrix consisting of a single column is referred to as a *column vector* and is represented by a lowercase and boldface letter.

For example,

$$\mathbf{x} = \begin{bmatrix} 1 \\ 2 \\ 3 \end{bmatrix}$$

is a column vector of order 3. Similarly, a matrix consisting of a single row is called a *row vector* and we shall use a "prime" (') to indicate a row vector. For example,

$$\mathbf{y}' = \begin{bmatrix} 1 & 2 & 3 & 4 \end{bmatrix}$$

is a row vector of order 4. Alternatively, we might have referred to **x** as a matrix of order 3 × 1 and **y**' as a matrix of order 1 × 4. The "prime" symbol is often called "transpose" and **y**' is read "**y** transpose."

A single number such as 3, 1/50, or −12 is called a *scalar*. Here we might think of a scalar as a matrix of order 1 × 1.

1.2.2 Matrix Addition [C]

Having described matrices in general terms, we now consider the basic arithmetic operations of matrix algebra. Beginning with the operation of addition, we may write

$$\mathbf{A} = \begin{bmatrix} -1 & 6 & 7 \\ 9 & 14 & 12 \end{bmatrix} \quad \text{and} \quad \mathbf{B} = \begin{bmatrix} 5 & -3 & 6 \\ 10 & 14 & 8 \end{bmatrix}$$

The addition of these two matrices is given by

$$\mathbf{A} + \mathbf{B} = \begin{bmatrix} (-1 + 5) & (6 - 3) & (7 + 6) \\ (9 + 10) & (14 + 14) & (12 + 8) \end{bmatrix} = \begin{bmatrix} 4 & 3 & 13 \\ 19 & 28 & 20 \end{bmatrix}$$

Thus, the matrix representing the sum of **A** and **B** is formed by adding each element in matrix B to the corresponding element of matrix A.

Obviously, matrix addition is possible only when the two matrices involved are of the *same order*. That is, two matrices may be added if and only if they have the *same number of rows and columns*.

1.2.3 Matrix Subtraction[C]

If we write the matrices **A** and **B** as

$$\mathbf{A} = \begin{bmatrix} 20 & 16 & 10 \\ 14 & 18 & 6 \end{bmatrix} \quad \text{and} \quad \mathbf{B} = \begin{bmatrix} 5 & 8 & 4 \\ 7 & 9 & 2 \end{bmatrix}$$

the matrix operation of subtraction may be illustrated by

$$\mathbf{A} - \mathbf{B} = \begin{bmatrix} (20-5) & (16-8) & (10-4) \\ (14-7) & (18-9) & (6-2) \end{bmatrix} = \begin{bmatrix} 15 & 8 & 6 \\ 7 & 9 & 4 \end{bmatrix}$$

Thus, we find that the difference between two matrices is found by sub-tracting each element in matrix B from the corresponding element of matrix A. As in the case of matrix addition, matrix subtraction is possible if and only if the two matrices involved are of the same order.

1.2.4 Matrix Multiplication[C]

Referring to matrix addition, it can be easily shown that

$$\mathbf{A} + \mathbf{A} = 2\mathbf{A}$$

Extending this finding to the case in which there are $\lambda\mathbf{A}$'s in the summation, where λ is the Greek letter lambda, we find that

$$\mathbf{A} + \mathbf{A} + \cdots + \mathbf{A} = \lambda\mathbf{A} \tag{1.5}$$

This result applies to any value of λ and constitutes the definition of *scalar multiplication*. When we multiply the matrix **A** by a scalar, every element in **A** is multiplied by λ. For example, letting $\lambda = 3$ and

$$\mathbf{A} = \begin{bmatrix} 1 & 2 & 3 \\ 4 & 5 & 6 \end{bmatrix}$$

we find

$$3\mathbf{A} = 3\begin{bmatrix} 1 & 2 & 3 \\ 4 & 5 & 6 \end{bmatrix} = \begin{bmatrix} 3 & 6 & 9 \\ 12 & 15 & 18 \end{bmatrix}$$

Scalar multiplication is the simplest form of matrix multiplication.

We now turn attention to multiplication operations involving *vectors* and then consider the multiplication of matrices. Suppose we wrote

$$\mathbf{x}' = [12 \quad 10 \quad 6]$$

and

$$\mathbf{a} = \begin{bmatrix} 7 \\ 4 \\ 3 \end{bmatrix}$$

The product $\mathbf{x}'\mathbf{a}$, which is written as

$$\mathbf{x}'\mathbf{a} = [12 \quad 10 \quad 6] \begin{bmatrix} 7 \\ 4 \\ 3 \end{bmatrix}$$

is given by

$$\mathbf{x}'\mathbf{a} = 12(7) + 10(4) + 6(3) = 142$$

This example illustrates the procedure for obtaining $\mathbf{x}'\mathbf{a}$. Observe that $\mathbf{x}'\mathbf{a}$ is obtained by multiplying each element of $\mathbf{x}'$ by the corresponding element of $\mathbf{a}$ and summing the resultant products.

Consequently, if

$$\mathbf{x}' = [x_1 \quad x_2 \quad \cdots \quad x_n] \text{ and } \mathbf{a} = \begin{bmatrix} a_1 \\ a_2 \\ \vdots \\ a_n \end{bmatrix}$$

then

$$\mathbf{x}'\mathbf{a} = x_1 a_1 + x_2 a_2 + \cdots + x_n a_n \qquad (1.6.1)$$

$$= \sum_{i=1}^{n} x_i a_i \qquad (1.6.2)$$

The similarity between this result and that of Equation (1.1.3) should be readily apparent. Also observe that the product of $\mathbf{x'a}$ is possible if and only if the vectors $\mathbf{x'}$ and $\mathbf{a}$ have the same number of elements.

Having described vector multiplication, we may now consider *vector-matrix products*. If we defined the row vector $\mathbf{x'}$ as

$$\mathbf{x'} = [5 \quad 10 \quad 20]$$

and the matrix $\mathbf{A}$ as

$$\mathbf{A} = \begin{bmatrix} 5 & 4 & 6 \\ 6 & 2 & 12 \\ 10 & 7 & 9 \end{bmatrix}$$

The product $\mathbf{x'A}$ is written as

$$\mathbf{x'A} = [5 \quad 10 \quad 20] \begin{bmatrix} 5 & 4 & 6 \\ 6 & 2 & 12 \\ 10 & 7 & 9 \end{bmatrix}$$

and we calculate $\mathbf{x'A}$ as follows:

$$\mathbf{x'A} = [5(5) + 10(6) + 20(10) \quad 5(4) + 10(2) + 20(7) \quad 5(6) + 10(12) + 20(9)]$$

$$= [285 \quad 180 \quad 330]$$

Observe that the first element of the product vector is given by

$$[5 \quad 10 \quad 20] \begin{bmatrix} 5 \\ 6 \\ 10 \end{bmatrix} = 285$$

while the second element is given by

$$[5 \quad 10 \quad 20] \begin{bmatrix} 4 \\ 2 \\ 7 \end{bmatrix} = 180$$

Finally, the third element of the product vector is found by

$$[5 \quad 10 \quad 20] \begin{bmatrix} 6 \\ 12 \\ 9 \end{bmatrix} = 330$$

Observe that the elements of this vector are derived in the same way as the product $x'a$. Here, however, we used each successive column of A as the vector a. Thus, the product $x'A$ is obtained by repetitions of the product $x'a$, where the vector a is represented by successive columns of the matrix A.

Multiplying two matrices can now be explained as a repetitive series of vector multiplications. To obtain the product of two matrices, say A and B, we need only think of matrix A as consisting of a series of row vectors, and matrix B as consisting of a series of column vectors. We assert that

$$AB = C$$

where:

$$A = \begin{bmatrix} 1 & 5 & 7 \\ 6 & 12 & 8 \end{bmatrix}$$

$$B = \begin{bmatrix} 3 & 5 & 8 \\ 2 & 4 & 11 \\ 6 & 9 & 2 \end{bmatrix}$$

$$C = \begin{bmatrix} c_{11} & c_{12} & c_{13} \\ c_{21} & c_{22} & c_{23} \end{bmatrix}$$

The element c_{11} of the product matrix C is obtained by multiplying the *first column* of B by the *first row* of A; thus, the *first row* of A times the *first column* of B yields

$$c_{11} = [1 \quad 5 \quad 7] \begin{bmatrix} 3 \\ 2 \\ 6 \end{bmatrix}$$

$$= 1(3) + 5(2) + 7(6)$$

$$= 55$$

Similarly, the element c_{12} of the product matrix is obtained by multiplying the first row of **A** by the second column of **B**; thus,

$$c_{12} = \begin{bmatrix} 1 & 5 & 7 \end{bmatrix} \begin{bmatrix} 5 \\ 4 \\ 9 \end{bmatrix}$$

$$= 1(5) + 5(4) + 7(9)$$

$$= 88$$

The element c_{13} is obtained by multiplying the first row of **A** by the third column of **B**; thus,

$$c_{13} = \begin{bmatrix} 1 & 5 & 7 \end{bmatrix} \begin{bmatrix} 8 \\ 11 \\ 2 \end{bmatrix}$$

$$= 1(8) + 5(11) + 7(2)$$

$$= 77$$

Using the second row of **A**, we repeat the process in order to obtain the elements c_{21}, c_{22}, and c_{23} of the product matrix **C** as follows:

$$c_{21} = \begin{bmatrix} 6 & 12 & 8 \end{bmatrix} \begin{bmatrix} 3 \\ 2 \\ 6 \end{bmatrix}$$

$$= 6(3) + 12(2) + 8(6)$$

$$= 90$$

$$c_{22} = [6 \quad 12 \quad 8] \begin{bmatrix} 5 \\ 4 \\ 9 \end{bmatrix}$$

$$= 6(5) + 12(4) + 8(9)$$

$$= 150$$

$$c_{23} = [6 \quad 12 \quad 8] \begin{bmatrix} 8 \\ 11 \\ 2 \end{bmatrix}$$

$$= 6(8) + 12(11) + 8(2)$$

$$= 196$$

To summarize this example, we may express the multiplication of the matrices **A** and **B** by

$$\mathbf{AB} = \begin{bmatrix} 1 & 5 & 7 \\ 6 & 12 & 8 \end{bmatrix} \begin{bmatrix} 3 & 5 & 8 \\ 2 & 4 & 11 \\ 6 & 9 & 2 \end{bmatrix}$$

which yields

$$\mathbf{AB} = \begin{bmatrix} 1(3)+5(2)+7(6) & 1(5)+5(4)+7(9) & 1(8)+5(11)+7(2) \\ 6(3)+12(2)+8(6) & 6(5)+12(4)+8(9) & 6(8)+12(11)+8(2) \end{bmatrix}$$

$$= \begin{bmatrix} 55 & 88 & 77 \\ 90 & 150 & 196 \end{bmatrix}$$

Several additional comments concerning matrix multiplication are important. First, it should be obvious that

*the product **AB** is permitted if and only if the number of elements appearing in each row of **A** is equal to the number of elements appearing in each column of **B**. This implies that the number of columns in **A** must equal the number of rows in **B**.*

Although we were able to obtain the product **AB** in terms of our example, the product **BA** does not exist. A second point concerning matrix multiplication is worthy of note. As seen above, when a matrix of order 2 × 3 was multiplied by a matrix of order 3 × 3 the product matrix was of the order 2 × 3. In general, we might express this relation in the form

$$\mathbf{A}_{r \times k} \mathbf{B}_{k \times m} = \mathbf{P}_{r \times m} \tag{1.7}$$

which allows us to ascertain the conformability of **A** and **B** for multiplication as well as the order of their product.

> *At the heart of many of the calculations that we perform in this text is a special form of matrix multiplication. We frequently encounter the term* **X′X**, *which is the multiplication of the matrix* **X** *by its transpose.*

In general, the transpose of matrix **A** is the matrix whose columns are the rows of **A**. This implies that the order of the elements must be retained when deriving the transpose of a matrix. For example, if

$$\mathbf{A} = \begin{bmatrix} 1 & 7 & 10 \\ 6 & 4 & 14 \end{bmatrix}$$

the transpose of **A** is given by

$$\mathbf{A}' = \begin{bmatrix} 1 & 6 \\ 7 & 4 \\ 10 & 14 \end{bmatrix}$$

We find that

$$\mathbf{X} = \begin{bmatrix} 1 & x_1 \\ \vdots & \vdots \\ 1 & x_i \\ \vdots & \vdots \\ 1 & x_n \end{bmatrix}$$

and its transpose play a central role in the computational work of Chapter 4 in Volume I. At this point in the analysis, however, it is only necessary to verify that:

$$\mathbf{X'X} = \begin{bmatrix} 1 & \cdots & 1 & \cdots & 1 \\ x_1 & \cdots & x_i & \cdots & x_n \end{bmatrix} \begin{bmatrix} 1 & x_1 \\ \vdots & \vdots \\ 1 & x_i \\ \vdots & \vdots \\ 1 & x_n \end{bmatrix}$$

$$\mathbf{X'X} = \begin{bmatrix} n & \sum_{i=1}^{n} x_i \\ \sum_{i=1}^{n} x_i & \sum_{i=1}^{n} x_i^2 \end{bmatrix} \tag{1.8}$$

The derivation of this important result should be clearly understood.

1.3 THE DETERMINANT OF A MATRIX[C]

We turn our attention now to an operation that is appropriate for *square matrices* (i.e., matrices of order $r \times r$), which leads to a *scalar* value known as the *determinant*. This operation is of importance when finding the *inverse* of a matrix, which plays a role in the counterpart of division in matrix algebra, as well as in calculating measures of the variance exhibited by a set of data. In the following discussion we shall limit our analysis to a 2×2 matrix, since the calculation of the determinant and the inverse of higher order matrices is more easily accomplished by simple computer programs.

In this book, we represent the determinant of a matrix $\mathbf{A}$ by $|\mathbf{A}|$. The value of the determinant for a 2×2 matrix is the product of its diagonal terms less the product of the off-diagonal terms. Thus, if

$$\mathbf{A} = \begin{bmatrix} a_{11} & a_{12} \\ a_{21} & a_{22} \end{bmatrix}$$

the determinant of $\mathbf{A}$ is

$$|\mathbf{A}| = a_{11}a_{22} - a_{12}a_{21} \tag{1.9}$$

where a_{11} and a_{22} are the diagonal elements of the matrix, while a_{12} and a_{21} are its off-diagonal elements. To illustrate, suppose that

$$\mathbf{A} = \begin{bmatrix} 7 & 10 \\ 4 & 20 \end{bmatrix}$$

The determinant of **A** is given by

$$|\mathbf{A}| = 7(20) - 4(10)$$

$$= 100$$

Returning for a moment to Equation 1.8 we find that

$$|\mathbf{X'X}| = n\Sigma x_i^2 - (\Sigma x_i)^2 \qquad (1.10)$$

which when multiplied by $\lambda = 1/n^2$ yields

$$\lambda|\mathbf{X'X}| = \frac{n\Sigma x_i^2 - (\Sigma x_i)^2}{n^2} \qquad (1.11)$$

1.4 THE INVERSE OF A MATRIX[C]

The determinant plays a central role in deriving the inverse of a matrix. In previous sections we discussed the arithmetic operations of addition, subtraction, and multiplication. However, we have not discussed division because, in its usual sense, this operation does not exist in matrix algebra. In order to perform the operation of "division" in matrix algebra, it is necessary to derive the *inverse* of a matrix. The inverse of the matrix **A** is usually denoted by the symbol $\mathbf{A}^{-1}$, which is read as "A inverse," "A to the minus one," or "the inverse of **A**." As shown next, the inverse of a matrix is useful when solving a system of linear equations.

The use of the inverse in solving an algebraic expression may be illustrated by the following example. If we were given the algebraic expression

$$ax = b \qquad (a \neq 0)$$

we could solve for x as follows:

$$\frac{1}{a}(ax) = \frac{1}{a}b = a^{-1}b$$

Hence,

$$x = a^{-1}b$$

where a^{-1} is used to represent $1/a$.

Let us now modify this example and show how we might derive the simultaneous solution for two linear equations. For example, let

$$6x_1 + 4x_2 = 360$$

$$4x_1 + 16x_2 = 480$$

These equations could be solved simultaneously by substitution. In terms of our example, we find:

$$6(120 - 4x_2) + 4x_2 = 360$$

Hence, we find that $x_1 = 48$ and $x_2 = 18$.

However, we could have expressed this system in matrix notation as follows:

$$\begin{bmatrix} 6 & 4 \\ 4 & 16 \end{bmatrix} \begin{bmatrix} x_1 \\ x_2 \end{bmatrix} = \begin{bmatrix} 360 \\ 480 \end{bmatrix}$$

Letting

$$\mathbf{A} = \begin{bmatrix} 6 & 4 \\ 4 & 16 \end{bmatrix}$$

$$\mathbf{x} = \begin{bmatrix} x_1 \\ x_2 \end{bmatrix}$$

$$\mathbf{b} = \begin{bmatrix} 360 \\ 480 \end{bmatrix}$$

this system of equations could be expressed as:

$$Ax = b \tag{1.12}$$

which has the solution:

$$x = A^{-1}b \tag{1.13}$$

Thus, in order to find the simultaneous solution to this system of linear equations, it is necessary to premultiply the column vector **b** by the inverse of **A**.

The *inverse* of **A** is defined as a matrix whose product with **A** is the identity matrix. Referring to the next illustration, the identity matrix **I** is defined by:

$$I = \begin{bmatrix} 1 & 0 \\ 0 & 1 \end{bmatrix}$$

Observe that

$$AI = A = IA$$

and

$$AA^{-1} = I \tag{1.14}$$

In terms of our example, we let

$$A^{-1} = \begin{bmatrix} c_{11} & c_{12} \\ c_{21} & c_{22} \end{bmatrix}$$

$$A = \begin{bmatrix} a_{11} & a_{12} \\ a_{21} & a_{22} \end{bmatrix} \quad \text{and} \quad I = \begin{bmatrix} 1 & 0 \\ 0 & 1 \end{bmatrix} .$$

Substituting we find:

$$\begin{bmatrix} a_{11} & a_{12} \\ a_{21} & a_{22} \end{bmatrix} \begin{bmatrix} c_{11} & c_{12} \\ c_{21} & c_{22} \end{bmatrix} = \begin{bmatrix} 1 & 0 \\ 0 & 1 \end{bmatrix} \tag{1.15.1}$$

Our problem is to find the values of A^{-1} such that Equation 1.15.1 is satisfied. Expanding Equation 1.15.1, we find:

$$a_{11}c_{11} + a_{12}c_{21} = 1 \qquad (1.15.2)$$

$$a_{21}c_{11} + a_{22}c_{21} = 0 \qquad (1.15.3)$$

$$a_{11}c_{12} + a_{12}c_{22} = 0 \qquad (1.15.4)$$

$$a_{21}c_{12} + a_{22}c_{22} = 1 \qquad (1.15.5)$$

If we multiply Equations 1.15.2 and 1.15.3 by a_{21} and a_{11}, respectively, we obtain:

$$a_{21}a_{11}c_{11} + a_{21}a_{12}c_{21} = a_{21}$$

$$a_{11}a_{21}c_{11} + a_{11}a_{22}c_{21} = 0$$

Solving for c_{21} yields:

$$c_{21} = \frac{-a_{21}}{a_{11}a_{22} - a_{21}a_{12}}$$

Recalling that $|A| = a_{11}a_{22} - a_{21}a_{12}$, we find:

$$c_{21} = \frac{-a_{21}}{|A|}$$

Employing a similar procedure, we obtain:

$$c_{12} = \frac{-a_{12}}{|A|}$$

$$c_{11} = \frac{a_{22}}{|A|}$$

$$c_{22} = \frac{a_{11}}{|A|}$$

After substituting these values, we find:

$$\mathbf{A}^{-1} = \frac{1}{|\mathbf{A}|} \begin{bmatrix} a_{22} & -a_{12} \\ -a_{21} & a_{11} \end{bmatrix} \qquad (1.16)$$

Even though the results expressed by Equation (1.16) only pertain to a 2×2 matrix, we shall make extensive use of this formula in subsequent chapters. Returning to our example, the determinant of **A** is found by:

$$|\mathbf{A}| = 6(16) - 4(4)$$

$$= 80$$

The inverse of **A** is found to be:

$$\mathbf{A}^{-1} = \frac{1}{80} \begin{bmatrix} 16 & -4 \\ -4 & 6 \end{bmatrix} = \begin{bmatrix} .20 & -.05 \\ -.05 & .075 \end{bmatrix}$$

Thus, the simultaneous solution to the system of linear equations is:

$$\begin{bmatrix} x_1 \\ x_2 \end{bmatrix} = \begin{bmatrix} .20 & -.05 \\ -.05 & .075 \end{bmatrix} \begin{bmatrix} 360 \\ 480 \end{bmatrix}$$

$$\begin{bmatrix} x_1 \\ x_2 \end{bmatrix} = \begin{bmatrix} 48 \\ 18 \end{bmatrix}$$

Observe that $x_1 = 48$ and $x_2 = 18$, which agrees with the results obtained earlier.

1.5 THE IMPORTANCE OF MATRIX ALGEBRA IN THIS TEXT[C]

The material presented in this chapter covers only the most basic aspects of matrix algebra. It is essential that the user of this text understand this material before attempting the matrix (C) portions of later chapters. The use of matrix notation simplifies many expressions in later chapters. It is well worth the user's time to become familiar with the operations and their meaning.

Problems for Solution[G]

1. *Let*

$$\mathbf{A} = \begin{bmatrix} 1290 & 6512 & 736 \\ 4303 & 8206 & 1020 \\ 5672 & 1927 & 2001 \end{bmatrix}$$

$$\mathbf{B} = \begin{bmatrix} 926 & 5200 & 230 \\ 3000 & 9000 & 800 \\ 6260 & 1700 & 2200 \end{bmatrix}$$

Find

(a) **A + B**
(b) **A − B**

2. *Let*

$$\mathbf{A} = \begin{bmatrix} 12 & 14 & 16 \\ 30 & 50 & 10 \\ 8 & 7 & 9 \\ 4 & 6 & 1 \end{bmatrix} \qquad \mathbf{B} = \begin{bmatrix} 1 & 3 & 2 & 6 \\ 4 & 2 & 6 & 1 \\ 5 & 5 & 7 & 4 \end{bmatrix}$$

Find

(a) **A·B**
(b) **B − A**
(c) Does **A·B = B·A**?

3. *Let*

$$\mathbf{A} = \begin{bmatrix} 1 & 3 & 6 \\ 2 & 7 & 9 \\ 8 & 3 & 4 \end{bmatrix} \qquad \mathbf{B} = \begin{bmatrix} 2 & 6 \\ 12 & 10 \\ 20 & 1 \end{bmatrix}$$

Find

(a) $\mathbf{A} \cdot \mathbf{B}$
(b) $\mathbf{B} \cdot \mathbf{A}$
(c) Does $\mathbf{A} \cdot \mathbf{B} = \mathbf{B} \cdot \mathbf{A}$?

4. *Given:*

$$\mathbf{A} = \begin{bmatrix} 3 & 5 \\ 7 & 8 \end{bmatrix} \qquad \mathbf{B} = \begin{bmatrix} 4 & 2 & 12 \\ 9 & 3 & 6 \end{bmatrix}$$

$$\mathbf{x}' = \begin{bmatrix} 1 & 6 \end{bmatrix}$$

Calculate:

(a) $\mathbf{AB}$
(b) $\mathbf{BA}$
(c) $|\mathbf{A}|$
(d) $\mathbf{A}'\mathbf{A}$

(e) $\mathbf{B}'\mathbf{B}$
(f) $\mathbf{BB}'$
(g) $\mathbf{x}'\mathbf{B}$
(h) $\mathbf{x}'\mathbf{Ax}$

(i) $\mathbf{A}^{-1}$

5. *Given:*

$$\mathbf{A} = \begin{bmatrix} 4 & 6 \\ 3 & 2 \\ 7 & 1 \end{bmatrix} \qquad \mathbf{B} = \begin{bmatrix} 2 & 4 & 5 & 7 \\ 3 & 2 & 7 & 5 \end{bmatrix}$$

Calculate:

(a) $\mathbf{AB}$
(b) $\mathbf{BA}$
(c) $\mathbf{A}'\mathbf{A}$

(d) $\mathbf{A}^{-1}$
(e) $(\mathbf{A}'\mathbf{A})^{-1}$

6. *Given:*

$$X = \begin{bmatrix} 1 & 3 \\ 1 & 7 \\ 1 & 4 \\ 1 & 9 \\ 1 & 6 \\ 1 & 5 \\ 1 & 8 \end{bmatrix} \quad y = \begin{bmatrix} 6 \\ 3 \\ 9 \\ 10 \\ 12 \\ 8 \\ 7 \end{bmatrix}$$

Calculate:

(a) $X'X$

(b) $X'y$

(c) $(X'X)^{-1}$

(d) $(X'X)^{-1}X'y$

7. *Given:*

$$X = \begin{bmatrix} 1 & 2 & 4 & 9 \\ 1 & 7 & 6 & 5 \\ 1 & 3 & 1 & 8 \\ 1 & 9 & 9 & 6 \\ 1 & 5 & 2 & 4 \end{bmatrix} \quad y = \begin{bmatrix} 6 \\ 3 \\ 9 \\ 10 \\ 8 \end{bmatrix}$$

Calculate:

(a) $X'X$

(b) $X'y$

8. Suppose that we are provided with the following information concerning the number of physicians by specialty and age in each of two regions.

Region I

| | Medical Specialty | | |
Age	General Practice	Surgery	Internal Medicine
30–39	400	60	190
40–49	800	240	30
50–59	110	52	70
60–69	30	3	6

Region II

| | Medical Specialty | | |
Age	General Practice	Surgery	Internal Medicine
30–39	212	83	364
40–49	350	612	87
50–59	62	316	79
60–69	14	4	12

Using matrix notation, determine the number of physicians in these two regions (separately and together) by age and type of medical specialty.

9. Using the information provided in problem 8, determine whether Region I has a greater or a fewer number of physicians by age and medical specialty than Region II.

10. Suppose that we are provided with the following information concerning the number of restricted activity days per person per year experienced by 1,000 males who were grouped by age and family income.

	Family Income		
	Under	6,000–	$15,000
Age	$6,000	$14,999	and Over
10–29	20	17	18
30–49	35	29	21
50–69	42	37	36

Also suppose that the corresponding data for females were as follows:

	Family Income		
	Under	$6,000–	$15,000
Age	$6,000	$14,999	and Over
10–29	12	9	3
30–49	28	27	15
50–69	37	25	27

Using matrix notation determine:
  (a) The number of disability days per person per year for males and females by age and family income.
  (b) Whether males experienced a greater or a lesser number of disability days per person per year by age and family income than females.

11. Assume that our institution provides services S_1, S_2 and S_3 in the medical management of diagnostic conditions M_1, M_2, M_3 and M_4. On the basis of historical records, suppose further that management has estimated the total service requirements by diagnosis for the coming period as follows:

	Service		
Condition	S_1	S_2	S_3
M_1	1,200	1,300	20
M_2	800	600	400
M_3	500	480	150
M_4	0	370	230

Also suppose that the number of manhours of labor of type L_1, L_2, L_3 and L_4 are employed in producing each unit of service S_1, S_2 and S_3 as follows:

	Labor			
Service	L_1	L_2	L_3	L_4
S_1	1.3	.5	0	.1
S_2	2.1	1.2	2.3	1.0
S_3	0	0	1.5	2.6

What is the total amount of labor by type of labor that we expect to employ during the coming period (for each diagnostic condition and in total)?

12. If the wages paid to L_1, L_2, L_3 and L_4 are $7.00, $6.00, $9.00 and $4.00 per hour respectively, what is the total wage bill in problem 11 above?

13. For each of the following **A** matrices show that $A^{-1}A = AA^{-1} = I$.

(a) $A = \begin{bmatrix} 7 & 3 \\ 4 & 6 \end{bmatrix}$

(b) $A = \begin{bmatrix} -3 & 1 \\ 2 & 4 \end{bmatrix}$

(c) $A = \begin{bmatrix} 7 & 15 \\ 15 & 50 \end{bmatrix}$

14. Show that when $|\mathbf{B}| = 0$, $\mathbf{B}^{-1}$ does not exist.

(a) $\mathbf{B} = \begin{bmatrix} 3 & 7 \\ 6 & 14 \end{bmatrix}$

(b) $\mathbf{B} = \begin{bmatrix} -4 & -12 \\ 7 & 21 \end{bmatrix}$

(c) $\mathbf{B} = \begin{bmatrix} 3 & -9 \\ 18 & -54 \end{bmatrix}$

15. Use matrix algebra to solve the following systems of two linear equations:

(a) $3x_1 + 2x_2 = 7$
       $4x_1 - 7x_2 = 15$

(b) $-5x_1 + 3x_2 = 14$
       $6x_1 - 8x_2 = -5$

(c) $-9x_1 - 5x_2 = 4$
       $7x_1 + 2x_2 = -3$

(d) $8x_1 - 7x_2 = 12$
       $-5x_1 + 3x_2 = 11$

Chapter 2

An Introduction to Computers and the Use of APL

Objectives

Upon completion of this chapter you should be able to:
1. Define the terms hardware and software.
2. Name the major components of computer hardware.
3. Name two examples of software.
4. Describe a card, and tell its importance.
5. Punch data into cards.
6. Describe APL and its usefulness.
7. Use APL in calculator mode for the following:
    a. type in data and correct typing errors;
    b. perform ordinary scalar arithmetic;
    c. create and use scalar variables;
    d. create and use vectors and matrices for ordinary scalar arithmetic;
    e. use the RHO operator for reshaping and for determining shape;
    f. use subscripts to define portions of vectors or matrices;
    g. perform row, column, and matrix summation;
    h. perform vector and matrix multiplications;
    i. transpose a matrix;
    j. create an identity matrix;
    k. find the determinant and inverse of a matrix;
    l. use matrix inversion and multiplication to solve a system of linear equations.
8. Differentiate between variables, functions, workspaces and libraries in APL.

Who Needs This Chapter

This chapter provides a brief introduction to the use of APL. Those with no or little experience in the use of APL should work carefully through this chapter.

Note that *most* of the material in this chapter is identical to the material in Appendix C of *Statistics in Health Administration (Volume I): Basic Concepts and Applications*. However, Section 2.8 differs from the corresponding section of the companion volume, through the inclusion of material on identity matrices, matrix inversion, and solution of systems of linear equations.

Chapter Map

Sections 2.1, 2.2 and 2.3 contain a nontechnical introduction to computers and have been assigned letter code A.

Sections 2.4 to 2.10 deal with the use of APL and are labeled E. Additionally Sections 2.6, 2.7 and 2.8 require knowledge of basic matrix algebra and are labeled C.

In this work we emphasize the use of computers in carrying out the computations for statistical analysis. In particular, we suggest the use of "A Programming Language" (APL) and the SPSS Batch System (Statistical Package for the Social Sciences), which are relatively easy to use and are widely available both to the student and to the administrator of the health care facility.

To use a computer for performing statistical analyses the student must have a basic understanding of:

1. what a computer is;
2. what APL is and how to use it;
3. what SPSS is and how to use it.

2.1 WHAT A COMPUTER IS[A]

A computer is a machine that stores and processes both numeric and nonnumeric data and can both receive the data from and return the results to humans. It is often called an *information processing* machine, and in this text we are particularly interested in the processing of numbers for statistical purposes.

A computer consists of a set of physical devices collectively called the *hardware* of the system. The hardware by itself is like a car without a driver. The directions for processing the data to make information are stored as programs, and collectively these programs are called *software.* To be useful, then, a computer system requires both hardware and software.

The hardware consists of input devices, a central processing unit (CPU), and output devices. Figure 2-1 represents the flow of information from input devices through the CPU to output devices. Historically, the card reader has been the major device through which data are *first* put (entered) into the machine. Subsequently, data stored on magnetic tapes, disks, or drums could feed data to the CPU. Since the mid-1960s the relative importance of cards has diminished as key-to-tape or key-to-disk systems have become popular for initial recording of data, replacing keypunching (key-to-card) systems. This replacement has occurred primarily where the volume of data is great enough so that the low unit costs of storing data on tape or disk, and the greater speed of entry into the computer, offset the low cost of keypunches and cards, which are relatively bulky for storage and slow for reading.

The CPU stores the programs (software) and the data to be processed. APL is an example of *a programming language* and a set of programs allowing the computer to interpret lines typed on a time-sharing terminal

Figure 2-1 Hardware Devices and Flow in Information through a Computer

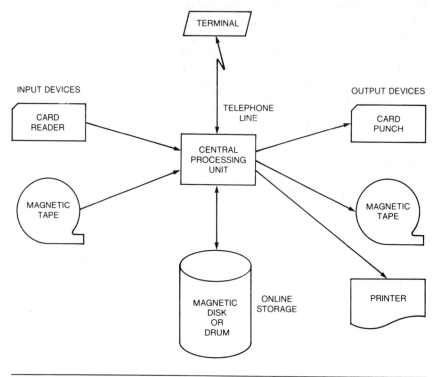

(e.g., a typewriter connected by telephone line to the computer). Also, programs may be written in APL and stored for later use. Thus, APL is one example of software and SPSS is another. However, SPSS has a rather different focus. SPSS consists of a large number of coordinated programs that can be instructed to perform specific statistical analyses on data represented as variables. SPSS is much more efficient at statistically analyzing large volumes of data, but APL has a much broader scope of application than just statistical analysis.

In both cases the CPU stores the programs and the data, and it also controls the operation of the entire computer. The active program (written in APL, or part of the SPSS system) consists of a very large number of instructions that are to be *executed* (carried out) one after another. The CPU controls the execution of instructions by fetching, interpreting, and performing one instruction at a time, sequentially, at very high speed. The types of instructions include reading data through an input device, copying data, performing basic arithmetic, comparing numbers, selecting alternative courses of action on the basis of the results of the comparison ($A > B$, $A = B$, $A < B$), and writing the results on some output device. Instructions are arranged so that the same sequence of operations is performed for each group of input data (a record representing a case, which may be one patient, one hospital, etc.). This arrangement of instructions to be repeated time and again is called a *loop*, and this term reinforces the idea of the cyclic nature of the basic statistical calculations being performed.

The results of the operations are *written* onto some output device, such as a printer. Other output devices include the printing portion of the time-sharing terminal, or magnetic tape or disk units, and microfilm devices. Magnetic tapes and disks are often used for long-term storage of data (and programs) because they can be used for input as well as output, and are reliable for long-term storage.

In order to use the computer, the person must know where to find the card reader and printer or the terminal(s) and must know how to use them. They may be located at the main computer center or at a remote site. Details of hours of operation, obtaining an account number, preparing the data, and submitting and retrieving a job, or logging-on to and signing-off the system must be known as well. All of this information is more or less unique to the individual university or hospital because of the tremendous variety of different types of computers and their physical arrangements.

For our purposes in this book the availability of APL makes the computer an APL machine, while SPSS makes an SPSS machine. Section 2.4 and Chapter 3 provide a description and instructions for the use of each of these two machines. First, however, a discussion of cards and card punching.

2.2 CARDS: PREDOMINANT BUT DYING-OUT [A]

Dr. Herman Hollerith of the U.S. Bureau of the Census invented and used cards for the Census of 1890. A company he founded became one of the parents of IBM. Hollerith cards were used extensively for 50 years before the birth of computers and were used as the prime information storage media for unit record or tabulating machines, which were electromechanical sorting, calculating, summarizing, printing, and punching machines.

Cards are still used in many university computer centers because of their versatility, ease of use, and relatively low cost. (Student labor is not counted at its true value.)

Figure 2-2 shows a Hollerith card with the numbers 0–9 and the letters A–Z punched into it. Notice the black spaces where holes have been punched. A card has spaces for holes arranged as a 12 by 80 matrix. Each *column* can store a single character, and the 12 rows are called *punches.* There are 10 *numeric punches* (0–9), and above them 2 *zone punches.* Numbers are represented by numeric punches *only,* while the letters have one zone and one numeric. Notice that the letters A through I have a 12-zone punch, while J through R have an 11-zone punch, and S through Z have a zero-zone punch. Thus, the zero punch is used in both capacities—numeric and zone.

2.3 PUNCHING DATA INTO CARDS[A]

The most commonly used keypunch on university campuses is the IBM model 029, introduced in the mid-1960s, which replaced the 026. A newer model was introduced in the early 1970s, but it is less suitable for university use. We concentrate on the model 029, but many non-IBM university computer centers still use the 026.

The keypunch machine occupies the space of a small office desk, with the card mechanisms rising above the surface about 12 inches. The ON/OFF switch is underneath the right-hand side of the desk. On the upper right (above the desk) is the spring loaded input card hopper. The cards are fed one at a time down to the card path, passing to the left first through the punching station, then the reading station and finally being stacked in the hopper on the upper left. Figure 2-3 shows the general flow.

The operator controls the feeding and punching from a keyboard console placed at the front of the desk just below the card path. There is sufficient room for source documents beside the console. The normal alphabetic keys and space bar are found in their standard places, but there is only an alphabet of capitals. The shift position is called *numeric shift,* and the numbers are in a quasi-adding-machine arrangement towards the right-hand side of the alphabetic keys. The numeric shift meaning (numbers and special characters) of each key is shown on the key.

There are various control keys and levers that differ from a standard electric typewriter. The keys are *FEED, REGister, RELease, DUPlicate,* and *NUMeric* shift. (Disregard ALPHA shift.) The levers are located in a row above the keys. They include *CLEAR, AUTOmatic FEED, PRINT* (on/off), and others that are not important to us.

There is a column indicator associated with a program drum, which is located above the card path between the punch and read stations. The drum is accessed through a swing down door, and the indicator is (poorly) visible through a window in the door.

Figure 2-2 A Punched Card Showing the Numbers and the Alphabet and
the Zone and Numeric Punches

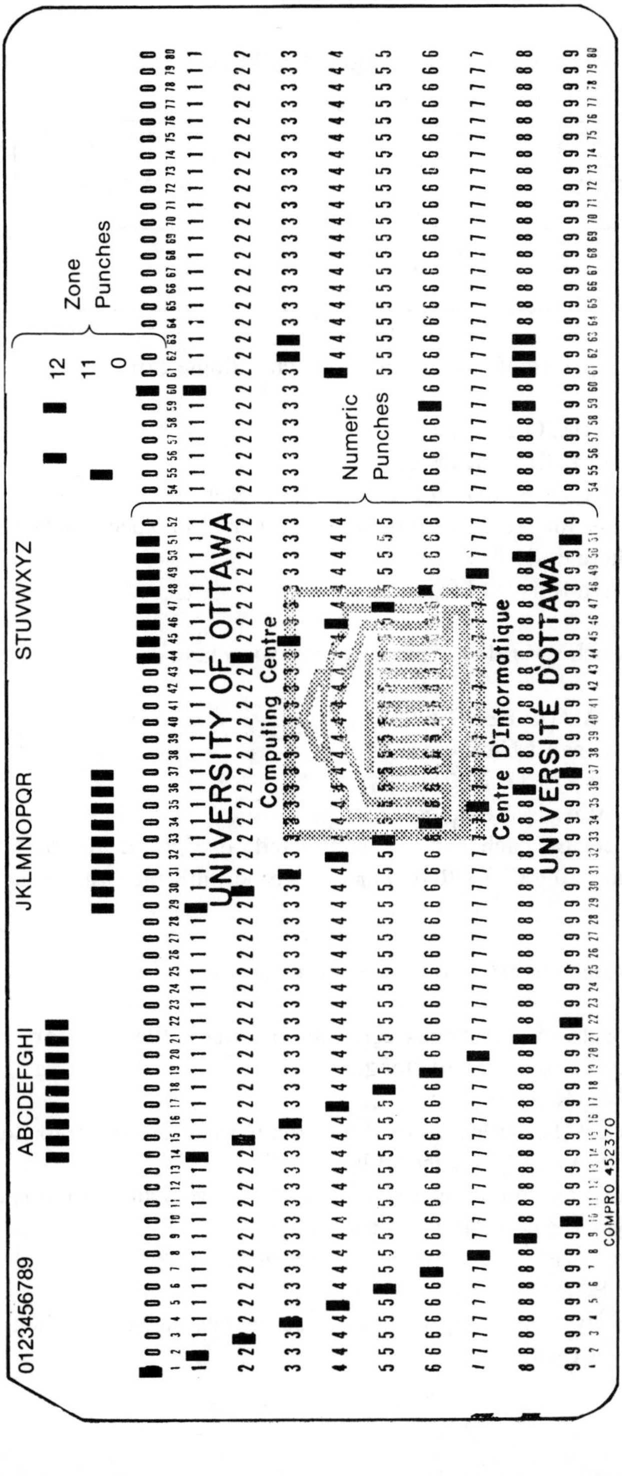

Figure 2-3 Flow of Cards through a Key Punch

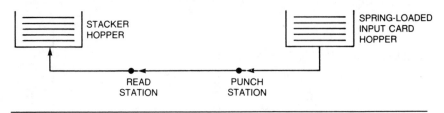

The sequence of operations to punch a single card is:

1. Set AUTO FEED off.
2. Lift the CLEAR lever.
3. Press the FEED and then the REG key.
4. Type the desired alphabetic, numeric, or special characters as and where desired.
5. When finished lift the clear lever.

To punch several cards in sequence you must:

1. Set AUTO FEED on.
2. Lift the CLEAR lever.
3. Press FEED, FEED.
4. Type desired data on card.
5. RELease each card as completed, except for the *last* card, which should be CLEARed. For every card until the last repeat steps 4 and 5.

To correct an error in a card you must:

1. Locate the erroneous columns and mark the necessary correction to be visible while punching.
2. CLEAR the path.
3. Insert the erroneous card into the path before the read station.
4. FEED and REGister a blank card.
5. Press and hold down DUPlicate until the error column is reached.
6. Type the corrections as necessary.
7. DUPlicate the rest of the card if necessary.
8. CLEAR the path.
9. Verify that the correction was indeed accurate, then destroy the error card.

PLEASE THROW OUT ALL USED CARDS, GATHER AND SAVE UNUSED ONES, and LEAVE THE WORKSTATION NEAT AND TIDY.

2.4 BASIC APL FOR STATISTICAL ANALYSIS[E]

APL stands for "A Programming Language," which was developed by Kenneth Iverson of IBM in the early 1960s. APL is a high-level computer programming language intended to make it easy for people to use computers in an interactive (or conversational) mode. It allows easy and powerful manipulation of both numeric and nonnumeric data. APL is intended both for the naive nonprogrammer and for the sophisticated advanced programmer who is responsible for designing complex models, as well as for all classes of users between these two. No matter who you are, APL is for you, and you can find it very helpful in many management situations where numbers have to be treated mathematically.

APL is designed to operate first and foremost as an interactive language, which permits the user to enter a line on a computer terminal. In turn, the computer interprets the request entered by the user, carries out the request immediately, and returns the requested information. This form of operation is known as CALCULATOR mode or EXECUTION mode. Indeed, an APL system is a far more powerful calculator than the most expensive hand calculators sold. APL also has a very powerful and simple means of creating, modifying, and saving FUNCTIONS, which allows more complex operations than can be specified on a single line. While in FUNCTION DEFINITION mode, the user types a series of lines that are stored for later interpretation and execution. The user can enter as much of a function as is desired at the moment and then switch to execution mode and try it out. Functions can be constructed (i.e., created, modified, and enlarged) interactively, extremely rapidly, and with far greater productivity than with normal programming languages.

APL is extremely useful for constructing management models that can be used to solve problems too large for hand calculators, or that may be too small to be worth the effort of programming in any other language. APL can also be used in the financial management of hospitals for implementing demonstration or prototype information systems for management. APL is an interpretive language and as such this language is less efficient in its use of the computer than are other languages such as COBOL, PL/1, and FORTRAN. Thus, if there is to be a great deal of use of a program written in APL over an extended period of time, it may be worthwhile to translate it into a more efficient language. In the translation process it will become evident that while COBOL is far more efficient in the execution of individual computer instructions, it is far less efficient in the use of the programmer's time. APL requires far less space and fewer instructions to express the required processing than does COBOL. One of the main advantages of developing a prototype program in APL is that development and modification are rapid, simple, and not very costly, and also that the prototype provides precise specifications for the eventual replacement program.

2.4.1 The APL Keyboard [E]

In order to use APL the user must be able to enter both instructions and data for processing. Information is typed on a keyboard that is very similar to an ordinary office typewriter. The layout of an APL keyboard is shown in Figure 2-4. All APL keyboards are very similar, but some have extra characters defined, and/or different placement of the backspace, attention, return, and tab keys and the power and other control switches.

Experienced typists will immediately note the important similarities to and differences from ordinary keyboards. The similarities are:

1. The placement of all letters is identical to normal typewriters.
2. The numbers are located on the top row as in normal typewriters.

The differences are:

3. All letters print only as capitals and must be typed in lowercase (not shifted) mode.
4. The number one (1) is given its own key, whereas most typists are accustomed to using the lowercase L (i.e., 1).
5. The punctuation characters comma (,) and period (.) are placed normally, but only in lowercase. Their uppercase versions are the semicolon (;) and the colon (:), respectively.
6. The question mark (?) is an uppercase Q.
7. The apostrophe (') is an uppercase K, and is often referred to as a *single quote*, while there is no double quote quotation mark.

The carriage return, backspace, and tabulate keys are shown in the diagram, but their placement varies from terminal to terminal.

THE REMAINING SYMBOLS ARE SPECIAL CHARACTERS FOR APL. In particular, the user should note:

8. The four arithmetic operators addition ($+$), subtraction ($-$), multiplication ($\times$), and division ($\div$) are on the 2nd and third keys

Figure 2-4 APL Keyboard

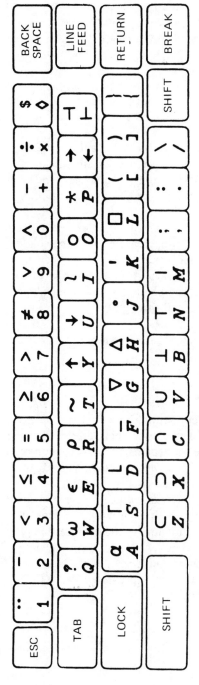

Courtesy of I.P. Sharp Associates

from the right on the top row,* while exponentiation is represented by an asterisk (*), which is the uppercase P.

9. The letter O has as its uppercase a large circle (O), while the letter J has a small circle (o), and all of these are different from the number zero (0).

10. There are round brackets ((and)) for arithmetic expressions, as the uppercase of square brackets ([and]), which are used for subscripts in referencing elements in arrays (about which there will be more later).

11. APL distinguishes between the negative symbol (¯), which is printed raised and is the uppercase 2, and the subtraction symbol (−), which is the uppercase of the plus sign and is printed in the center of the line between the two numbers, variables, or expressions to be subtracted.

12. The uppercase I has the Greek letter iota (ι), which is different from the single quote (' uppercase K) and the solidus, or vertical bar (|), which is the uppercase M.

13. The underscore character (__) is the uppercase F.

14. The arithmetic comparison operator symbols are located on the uppercase numbers 3 through 8.

The other special characters are introduced and explained as the need arises in the text.

2.4.2 Data in APL$^{(E)}$

APL is capable of representing numeric, character, and logical data with much greater ease for the user than many other languages. (It is not necessary to predefine the type of any particular piece of data. APL keeps track of the messy details, and, as experienced programmers know, the details are sometimes very messy.)

A beginner can get by with numeric data and ignore other types until they become necessary. York University's version of APL (which we use here) stores numbers with up to 16 significant digits. So do most other versions. Integer numbers (... ¯3, ¯2, ¯1, 0, 1, 2, 3, 4 ...) and real numbers (with a decimal point) can be represented. Extremely large or extremely small numbers are represented in EXPONENTIAL (i.e., scientific) notation. For example,

---

*Some terminals do not have the ◇ key shown beyond these two. It is optional and is not discussed in this work.

$1.45629E^-16$ means $.00000000000000145629$

while

$2.35741E18$ means 2357410000000000000

both of which have too many digits to be expressed any other way.

To type a number in APL one types all of the digits (in proper order from left to right) with a negative sign in the leftmost position if required, and a decimal point in the proper position if required. Commas are not permitted when entering a number, but can be provided when the computer is printing out a number. (The computer can be instructed to put the commas in, but people are not allowed to do so, because the comma is used for something special.) The first blank space marks the end of the number, as does a carriage return. A carriage return is required at the end of every line of input and is represented in the following pages by Ⓡ.

A hand calculator has one or several memories (technically called *registers*) in which to store numbers between or during calculations. All computer programs, including APL, accomplish the same thing by defining VARIABLES. A very large number of variables can be defined, and this makes computer programs much more versatile than even the most advanced hand or printing calculators (in 1978, that is). A variable is given a name of 1 or more characters, of which YORK APL (the version on our computer) pays attention to only the first 8. Any alphabetic or numeric character, which may be underscored, or the character Δ can be used in the variable name. The first character must not be numeric or Δ.

The ASSIGNMENT or SPECIFICATION operator (←) is used to assign a numeric value to a variable. This is shown by an example inside the following program fragment and small fragments of APL programs are shown similarly (Exhibit 2-1), wherever required.

Exhibit 2-1

```
A←3 Ⓡ
PATIENTN←74593102 Ⓡ
```

To find out what numeric value has been stored in (assigned to) a variable, merely type the name of the variable. The computer will type the value on the next line. (See Exhibit 2-2.)

Exhibit 2-2

```
               A  Ⓡ
        3
               FATIENTN Ⓡ
        74593102
```

Note that the user's typing starts at the seventh column of the page, because APL moves in six spaces on a new line when it is waiting for the user to start something new. If no value has been assigned to a variable, the computer will instead type a "VALUE ERROR" message. This is shown in Exhibit 2-3, where B has not yet been defined by assigning something to it.

Exhibit 2-3

```
                    B  Ⓡ
        B
        ?  VALUE  ERROR
```

2.4.3 APL as a Calculator[E]

As indicated earlier, a beginner finds it easiest to start using APL in the calculator mode. APL has a large number of OPERATORS defined, and this makes it an extremely powerful language. However, we start with the basic arithmetic operators. Addition, subtraction, multiplication, and division are represented by $+$, $-$, $\times$, $\div$, respectively. Examples of simple operations are shown next in Exhibit 2-4.

Exhibit 2-4

```
             3+4  Ⓡ
        7
             3×4  Ⓡ
        12
             3-4  Ⓡ
        ⁻1
             3÷4  Ⓡ
        .75
             4÷3  Ⓡ
        1.333333333
```

Several operations can be carried out on one line, but there is a feature of APL to be noted that is different from almost all other computer languages. APL interprets and carries out all operations requested starting from the right-hand side of the line and working progressively to the left. The results of the rightmost (first) operation are used as part of the second. This may be modified by the use of round parentheses. Operations within parentheses are performed, and the result is used with the operator to the right of the parentheses. The right to left rule makes APL dramatically different from all other common programming languages, and the parentheses are the only modification to the rule. Once the user is accustomed to the rule, it poses no problem. In the example demonstrated in Exhibit 2-5, there are intermediate results whose values are 10, 15, and 18 but which are not printed out by APL. The first two lines state the problem to APL and show the reply. The others are presented only for purposes of illustration of the intermediate stages.

Exhibit 2-5

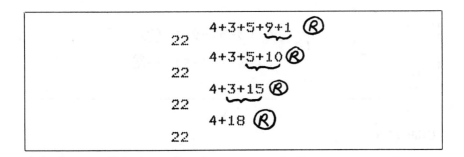

A novice might have trouble with subtraction (or division) the first time, but the rule is still the same. (See Exhibit 2-6.)

On the other hand, to get what one would normally have expected from Exhibit 2-6 it is necessary to rephrase the problem as shown in Exhibit 2-7. A modified problem can be given to the computer if parentheses are used to change the order of execution. (See Exhibit 2-8.) Variables can be used in place of numbers as shown in Exhibit 2-9.

Exhibit 2-6

$$
\begin{array}{l}
\quad\ \ 4-3-5-\underbrace{9-1}\ \ \text{(R)} \\
{}^-2 \\
\quad\ \ 4-3-\underbrace{5-8}\ \ \text{(R)} \\
{}^-2 \\
\quad\ \ 4-\underbrace{3-\ {}^-3}\ \ \text{(R)} \\
{}^-2 \\
\quad\ \ 4-6\ \ \text{(R)} \\
{}^-2
\end{array}
$$

Exhibit 2-7

$$
\begin{array}{l}
\quad\ \ 4+{}^-3+{}^-5+{}^-9+{}^-1\ \ \text{(R)} \\
{}^-14
\end{array}
$$

Exhibit 2-8

$$
\begin{array}{l}
\quad\ \ 4-(3-5)-9-1\ \ \text{(R)} \\
14 \\
\quad\ \ (4-3)-(5-9)-1\ \ \text{(R)} \\
6
\end{array}
$$

Exhibit 2-9

$$
\begin{array}{l}
\quad A \leftarrow 4\ \ \text{(R)} \\
\quad B \leftarrow 3\ \ \text{(R)} \\
\quad C \leftarrow 5\ \ \text{(R)} \\
\quad D \leftarrow 9\ \ \text{(R)} \\
\quad XYZ \leftarrow A+B+C+D+1\ \ \text{(R)} \\
\quad XYZ\ \ \text{(R)} \\
22 \\
\quad A-B-C-D-1\ \ \text{(R)} \\
{}^-2
\end{array}
$$

2.5 VECTORS, MATRICES, AND ARRAYS IN APL(E)

So far, only SCALAR numbers have been used in the examples, but APL can perform operations on sets of numbers with equal facility, and THIS IS ONE OF THE ADVANTAGES TO COME FROM THE USE OF APL. A scalar number is a single number; a VECTOR is a set of numbers in a single row or column; a MATRIX is a rectangular 2-dimensioned table of numbers; and an ARRAY is the generalization of a matrix to 3, 4, or more dimensions.

A set of two or more numbers typed on a single line is a vector and can be assigned to a variable, as shown in Exhibit 2-10. (By this stage the novice should be accustomed to pressing carriage return and we drop the use of ⑬.)

Exhibit 2-10

```
        M←2 3 5 1 9 4
        M
2   3   5   1   9   4
        N←1 4 3
        N
1   4   3
```

Vectors can be CATENATED (i.e., joined) to make a longer vector using the RAVEL operator (,). A very long vector can be entered as a series of shorter vectors, which are to be catenated to form the long one. (See Exhibit 2-11.)

Exhibit 2-11

```
        Q←M,N
        Q
2   3   5   1   9   4   1   4   3
        M,N
2   3   5   1   9   4   1   4   3
```

Alternatively, we might enter a portion of a long vector on the line then extend it onto one or more subsequent lines, as shown in Exhibit 2-12.

Exhibit 2-12

```
        N←N,4 2 5 7
         N
    1  4  3  4  2  5  7
```

It is important to be able to find out how long a vector is, and the RHO operator (ρ) operating MONADICALLY on a vector gives us the size or length of the vector as in Exhibit 2-13. (When operating on a matrix or an array it tells us the shape.)

Exhibit 2-13

```
         M
    2  3  5  1  9  4
         N
    1  4  3  4  2  5  7
         ρM
    6
         ρN
    7
         ρM,N
    13
         M,N
    2  3  5  1  9  4  1  4  3  4  2  5  7
```

Note that unlike all previous operators, ρ is shown working on only one operand. This use is called the *monadic form of* ρ. All others have been DYADIC (e.g., 4 + 3) with the operator having one operand on the right and one on the left. Most operators can be used either monadically or dyadically and they usually mean different things when used in the two different ways.

When ρ is used dyadically it RESHAPES the vector on the right-hand side as specified by the vector operand on the left-hand side. To create a matrix with 2 rows and 3 columns from the vector **M** we must reshape it. (See Exhibit 2-14.)

Exhibit 2-14

```
      M
2   3   5   1   9   4
      ρM
6
      2  3  ρM
          2                    3                    5
          1                    9                    4


      XYZ←3  2  ρM
      XYZ
          2                    3
          5                    1
          9                    4
```

Note that the first monadic use of ρ on a matrix gives the shape of the matrix, and the second application gives the number of dimensions. (See Exhibit 2-15.) (The output of ρ is a vector, which is operated on by the second ρ, and so on!)

Exhibit 2-15

```
              ρXYZ
      3   2
              ρρXYZ
      2
              ρρρXYZ
      1
```

2.5.1 Creation of Matrices and Vectors

The operator ρ, in its reshaping use, creates a new vector, matrix, or array out of the elements of the vector operand on the right-hand side according to the shape specifications of the left-hand side vector operand. Each of these vectors may have 1 or more elements. In the first example in Exhibit 2-14, **M** had 6 elements and was reshaped into a 2 × 3 matrix as specified by the vector (2   3). RHO operates by copying as many elements (i.e., 3) as necessary to create the first row, and then as many more (again 3) as necessary to create the second row. In the second example in Exhibit 2-14, XYZ was to be created with order (shape) 3 × 2. The first 2 elements became the first row, the next 2 the second row, and the last 2 the third row.

RHO copies as many elements from the right-hand vector as are necessary to create the reshaped matrix. The necessary number of elements can be determined by multiplying the elements of the shape specification vector. If the right-hand vector has more elements than are required, only the necessary ones are copied. For example, we can create a 2 × 2 matrix from M, and we can create a 3 × 4 matrix from M, N. (See Exhibit 2-16.)

Exhibit 2-16

```
     M
 2   3   5   1   9   4
     2   2  ρM
         2                   3
         5                   1
     M,N
 2   3   5   1   9   4   1   4   3   4   2   5   7
     3   4ρM,N
         2               3               5               1
         9               4               1               4
         3               4               2               5
```

In the 2 × 2 matrix the first 4 out of the 6 elements were copied, and in the 3 × 4 matrix the first 12 out of the 13 elements were copied.

If the right-hand vector has too few elements, the reshaping copies all elements that are available and then starts recopying from the beginning, as shown in Exhibit 2-17. RHO always copies exactly the number of elements that are needed.

We can create a vector of any required size by copying elements from an original vector. The original vector may have 1 or more elements, as before, and the newly created vector may have the same number or more or fewer elements. The following examples show that we can expand an original single (scalar) number (e.g., 1 or 0) into a vector of any desired length. We can also use RHO to extract (copy) a short vector from the left portion of a longer vector, or we can expand a short vector into a longer one. (See Exhibit 2-18.)

Exhibit 2-17

```
      M
 2   3   5   1   9   4
     2  4ρM
          2              3              5              1
          9              4              2              3
```

Exhibit 2-18

```
              4ρ1
        1   1   1   1
              6ρ0
    0   0   0   0   0   0
              6ρ1 2 3 4
    1   2   3   4   1   2
              3ρ1 2 3 4
    1   2   3
              1,(4ρ0)
    1   0   0   0   0
```

2.5.2 Creation of a Matrix of Data

When it is desirable to enter data as a matrix, we enter the data as a long vector and reshape the vector using ρ. The data may be entered as one long vector with the elements of the first row followed by the elements of the second row, and so on. An alternative that is often very useful is to type a vector for each row, assigning each vector to a variable with a meaningful name. These vectors can be catenated in the proper order and then reshaped into the desired matrix. For example, in Table 1-1 of Chapter 1 we used an example of the days of hospital care used by patients of different age groups in the three years 1978 to 1980. Each row represents an age group and each column a year. We type the rows of data, assigning them to variables with labels A15, A44, A64, and A65, where the As mean age, and the numbers indicate which age range is included in the vector. Each vector has 3 elements because there are 3 years. The variables are catenated and reshaped to create the matrix USE. (See Exhibit 2-19.)

Exhibit 2-19

```
A15← 80000  82000  86000
A44← 60000  65000  68000
A64← 50000  56000  62000
A65← 90000  92000    85000


USE←4 3 ρ A15, A44,A64,A65
USE
80000        82000        86000
60000        65000        68000
50000        56000        62000
90000        92000        85000
```

2.5.3 Use of Subscripts

In Chapter 1 we used small numeric subscripts to indicate which element of the matrix we are examining. In APL we can use subscripts to display or change one or several elements from a matrix. For any dimension of a vector, matrix, or array one or more subscripts can be specified. Square brackets are used to enclose the subscripts, and the list of subscripts for each dimension is given as a vector, with the vector for the rows preceding and separated by a semicolon from that for the columns. Omission of the specification of subscripts for·either dimension is used to indicate that all of the subscripts for that dimension are to be used.

In Exhibit 2-20 the first example calls for the single element from the intersection of row 1 and column 2. The second calls for all of row 1. The third calls for elements 2 and 3 of row 3. The fourth one calls for all of column 3. The last one calls for a submatrix of four elements from the intersection of rows 1 and 4 with columns 2 and 3.

2.5.4 Differentiation Between Column and Row Vectors

We know already that in matrix algebra there are column vectors and row vectors and that the difference between them is important. However, in APL we do not need to worry about differentiating because APL automatically takes care of that for us. We had a column vector x and a row vector y', but in APL we just call them X and Y, and their use as column or row vectors is interchangeable. (See Exhibit 2-21.)

Exhibit 2-20

```
          USE[1;2]
     82000
          USE[1;]
     80000   82000   86000
          USE[3;2 3]
     56000   62000
          USE[;3]
     86000   68000   62000   85000
          USE[1 4;2 3]
        82000         86000
        92000         85000
```

Exhibit 2-21

```
            X← 1 2    3
            X
      1   2  3

            Y← 1    2  3  4
            Y
      1   2  3  4
```

2.6 BASIC OPERATIONS ON VECTORS AND MATRICES[C]

In Chapter 1, Sections 1.2.2 and 1.2.3 discussed matrix addition and subtraction. Simple scalar addition or subtraction of corresponding elements can be performed for vectors and matrices of the same order. In Exhibit 2-22 we show the APL versions of the examples used in those sections. In each case we first create the matrices; we then display them in order to check for errors; and finally, we request and perform the desired addition or subtraction. The results must, of course, be identical to those obtained earlier.

Note that a comment can be typed on any line by starting the line with the combination symbol ၉, which is "∩ backspace o". A comment is included only for the person who eventually reads the printout, as an expla-

Exhibit 2-22

```
     A    ADDITION OF MATRICES

    A←2 3 ρ ¯1 6 7   9 14 12
    A
         ¯1              6              7
          9             14             12

    B←  2 3 ρ 5 ¯3 6     10 14 8
    B
          5             ¯3              6
         10             14              8

    A+B
          4              3             13
         19             28             20




     A    SUBTRACTION OF MATRICES

    A←  2 3 ρ   20 16 10   14 18 6
    B←  2 3 ρ    5 8 4    7 9 2
    A
         20             16             10
         14             18              6
    B
          5              8              4
          7              9              2
    A-B
         15              8              6
          7              9              4
```

nation from the person who originally typed the information. The APL system ignores comments entirely.

It is often useful to be able to find the sum of the elements of a vector, or of the rows or columns of a matrix. The operator $+/$ finds the summation of a vector or the sums of the rows of a matrix. The operator $+\!\!\!/$ may be used to find the sums of the columns of a matrix. In Exhibit 2-23, **A** is as

Exhibit 2-23

```
       A
          ¯1                 6                7
           9                14               12

       A1←¯1 6 7
       A2←9 14 12

       A     +/   SUMS ALONG A VECTOR OR ALONG
                  A ROW OF A MATRIX

       +/A1
  12
       +/   A2
  35
       +/   A
  12   35


       A   +/ SUMS DOWN THE COLUMNS OF A MATRIX
       A   +/ BACKSPACE ¯

       +⌿ A
   8   20  19
```

previously defined, and **A1** and **A2** are typed in separately, but contain the same elements as the rows of **A**. The operations of $+/$ and of $+\neq$ are demonstrated.

Scalar multiplication of a matrix produces an element by element multiplication, as shown in Exhibit 2-24. Similarly, we could add (or subtract from, or divide by) a *scalar* to (every element of) a matrix.

Matrix algebra defines special operations called *vector* and *matrix multiplication*. In Chapter 1 we defined the multiplication of vectors of equal length as first the multiplication of pairs of corresponding elements, followed by the addition (or summation) of all of the products. We first show these two steps separately in APL. After defining **X** and **A**, APL allows us to perform an ordinary *scalar* multiplication of *corresponding elements* and to print the results immediately. In the next line we reperform the multiplication, but this time we also sum using $+/$ to obtain

Exhibit 2-24

```
  A    SCALAR MULTIPLICATION OF A MATRIX

  A ← 2 3 ρ  1 2 3   4 5 6
  A
       1           2           3
       4           5           6

  3×A
       3           6           9
      12          15          18
```

the vector product, which is a single number, a scalar. The last line shows a new operator, $+.\times$, which APL has defined as the *vector* or *matrix multiplication* operator. It performs the multiplication and summation operations and prints the final result only. Sometimes the user may want to see the intermediate stage of the pair products. In these situations we simply take $X \times A$ as well as $X +.\times A$, as in Exhibit 2-25.

Exhibit 2-25

```
        A    VECTOR-VECTOR MULTIPLICATION

        X← 12 10 6
        A←   7  4   3

        X×A
    84  40  18

        +/ X×A
   142
        X+.×A
   142
```

After considering vector-vector multiplication we defined vector-matrix multiplication as a series of vector-vector multiplications. In Exhibit 2-26 we name the row vector **XT**, where the **T** reminds us of *transpose* to emphasize that it is conceptually a row vector. We define **A** and then

Exhibit 2-26

```
        ⍝    VECTOR-MATRIX MULTIPLICATION

        XT← 5 10 20
        A←3 3 ρ    5 4 6    6 2 12    10 7 9

        XT
  5   10  20
        A
              5            4            6
              6            2           12
             10            7            9
  .
        XT+.×A[;1]
  285
        XT+.×A[;2]
  180
        XT+.×A[;3]
  330

        XT+.×A
  285   180   330
```

multiply **XT** times each of the columns of **A** using $+.\times$ to show the step-by-step development of the product **X'A**. The last line demonstrates that $+.\times$ is applicable to vectors and matrices.

In the preceding example, much of the material is included for explanatory purposes only. Stripped to the bare essentials, the example of vector-matrix multiplication is shown in Exhibit 2-27.

Once the user understands the concept of vector-matrix multiplication, APL performs the calculation reliably and quickly.

Exhibit 2-27

```
        XT←5    10     20
        A←  3  3 ρ    5 4 6    6 2 12    10 7 9
        XT+.×A
  285   180   330
```

The process of vector-vector and vector-matrix multiplication may be extended to accommodate to matrix-matrix (or just plain matrix) multiplication. We present the APL approach in Exhibit 2-28, showing only the data plus the essential APL operation. The example is the same as that used in the original presentation of matrix multiplication, in Section 1.2.4.

Exhibit 2-28

```
A←  2 3 ρ  1 5 7 6 12 8
B ← 3 3 ρ  3 5 8 2 4 11    6 9 2
A
      1           5           7
      6          12           8
B
      3           5           8
      2           4          11
      6           9           2
A+.×B
     55          88          77
     90         150         196
```

Note that conformability for multiplication requires that the number of columns of the left-hand matrix be the same as the number of rows of the matrix on the right. This leads to vector multiplications, where the vectors have the same lengths as required. In Exhibit 2-29 the order of **B** and **A** is reversed and they are not conformable. Therefore, **BA** is not defined, and APL types an error message to the user.

2.7 THE X TRANSPOSE X MATRIX[C]

As indicated in Chapter 1, Section 1.2.4, the matrix $X'X$ plays a key role in many of the statistical formulas described in this text. For the

Exhibit 2-29

```
              B+.×A
      B+.×A
        ? LENGTH ERROR
```

purposes of using APL we introduced the transposition operator, which is ⍉ and is typed as o backspace \. (Note that o is the uppercase of the letter O.)

While APL does not differentiate between row and column vectors, it does keep track of the rows and columns of matrices. Transposition copies the original rows and makes them columns in the new matrix. The original columns become rows in the process. Transposition is the monadic use of the operator ⍉. In Exhibit 2-30 we create the matrix **A**, transpose it calling the result **AT** (for **A**-transpose) and then multiply to obtain **A'A**.

Exhibit 2-30

```
A← 2 3 ρ   1 7 10    6 4 14
AT← ⍉A
ATA←AT+.×A
ATA
      37           31           94
      31           65          126
      94          126          296
```

Exhibit 2-31 shows a situation in which the first row of **X'** is all 1s. The reader should verify that the result follows the pattern shown in Equation (1.8) in Chapter 1, Section 1.2.4.

Exhibit 2-31

```
XT← 2 6   ρ   (6ρ1),    7 3 9   11 5 3
XT
      1        1      1       1       1      1
      7        3      9      11       5      3
X←⍉XT
XT+.×X
      6       38
     38      294
```

2.8 THE MATRIX INVERSE AND ITS APPLICATIONS[C]

In this volume we use the determinant of a square matrix for calculations for variance and analysis of variance. However the determinant is also important in the definition of the inverse of the matrix which is used in regression analysis. The definitions of the determinant and inverse are covered in Chapter 1. In this section we show the calculation of determinants and inverses using APL.

2.8.1 The Determinant of a Matrix

A determinant is a scalar which can be calculated only for a square matrix, and is defined as the sum of terms which are products of elements of the matrix, where half of the terms have negative signs. For a 2×2 matrix

$$\mathbf{A} = \begin{bmatrix} a_{11} & a_{12} \\ a_{21} & a_{22} \end{bmatrix}$$

the determinant is defined as

$$|\mathbf{A}| = a_{11}a_{22} - a_{21}a_{12}$$

For larger matrices many terms are involved, and computer programs use special formulas which result in faster calculations. In Exhibit 2-32 DET is such a program, adapted from Katzan (1970). It is used to find the determinants of two matrices.

Exhibit 2-32

```
              A← 2 2 ρ  7 10  4 20
              A
                  7                10
                  4                20
              DET  A
        100

              B← 2 2 ρ 7 10 28 40
              B
                  7                10
                 28                40
              DET  B
        4.97379915E‾14
```

The determinant of **A** can be verified easily using the formula given above. When the determinant of **B** is checked by hand it is found to be zero, but the program has produced a value which is only approximately zero, .0000000000000497 ... This is because the computer program is more general than the formula above, and the computer uses binary rather than decimal arithmetic. For matrix **B** this leads to a small round-off error which did not occur for **A**. When the determinant of a matrix is zero the matrix is said to be *singular.* This is of importance when working with regression analysis.

Although hand calculation of determinants of matrices of order 3, 4 or larger is possible, the use of APL is infinitely easier.

2.8.2 The Identity Matrix

As discussed in Section 1.4 the identity matrix is a special square matrix (of any size) which has only 1s on the main diagonal and 0s elsewhere. An identity matrix of order 3 is

$$\mathbf{I} = \begin{bmatrix} 1 & 0 & 0 \\ 0 & 1 & 0 \\ 0 & 0 & 1 \end{bmatrix}$$

Exhibit 2-33 shows the simplest APL approach to creating an identity matrix. One of order 3 is shown. The first two lines show the creation of a vector consisting of a 1 and three 0s. The next line shows the APL command to reshape that vector into a 3 × 3 matrix. The reshaping process on which this is based was discussed in Section 2.5.1.

More generally, for an identity matrix of any size, say *n*, the second line of Exhibit 2-34 shows the appropriate command. (This can easily be defined as a function, for those who care to do so.)

Exhibit 2-33

```
        1,3ρ0
  1   0   0   0
        3 3 ρ 1,3ρ0
           1              0              0
           0              1              0
           0              0              1
```

Exhibit 2-34

```
N←4
I←(N,N) ρ 1,Nρ0
I
    1         0         0         0
    0         1         0         0
    0         0         1         0
    0         0         0         1
```

2.8.3 The Inverse of a Matrix

A square matrix with a non-zero determinant has an inverse which is a square matrix of the same order, as discussed in Section 1.4. The product of a matrix and its inverse is always the identity matrix of the same order. For example if A is square and $|A| \neq 0$ then

$$A^{-1}A = AA^{-1} = I$$

In Exhibit 2-35 we recall the matrix A defined in Exhibit 2-32. First we show its determinant, use the APL inversion operator ⊞ (which is □ backspace ÷) to obtain A^{-1}, and show that the result of multiplying AA^{-1} is the identity matrix.

Exhibit 2-35

```
      A
           7        10
           4        20
      DET A
100
      ⊟A
         .2       ⁻.1
       ⁻.04       .07

      A+.× ⊟A
           1  ⁻1.387778781E⁻17
  ⁻1.387778781E⁻17           1
```

In Exhibit 2-36 we recall the matrix **B** defined in Exhibit 2-32. Its determinant is zero, and attempting to find its inverse results in a domain error (division by zero).

Exhibit 2-36

```
            B
                 7           10
                28           40
            DET B
        4.9737991SE¯14

               ⊞  B
       ⊞  B
       ? DOMAIN ERROR
```

In Exhibit 2-37 we create a larger matrix **A**, and find its determinant and inverse. Because of the varying lengths of the numbers the inverse is rather

Exhibit 2-37

```
    A← 3 3 ρ    3 4 7    ¯1 2 ¯5    7 2 ¯3
    A
           3           4           7
          ¯1           2          ¯5
           7           2          ¯3
    DET A
  ¯252

       ⊞ A
  ¯1.587301587E¯2   ¯.1031746032    .1349206349
   .1507936508    .2301587302   ¯3.174603175E¯2
  6.349206349E¯2  ¯.0873015873   ¯3.968253968E¯2


       '999990.999999'  $  ⊞A
  ¯0.015873      ¯0.103174      0.134920
   0.150793       0.230158     ¯0.031746
   0.063492      ¯0.087301     ¯0.039682
```

difficult to interpret, and we finish by showing the printing of the inverse controlled by the use of the York APL format control operator $ (S backspace |). The left operand of $ is a *control string* (a character vector specifying the number of digits to be printed before and after the decimal point. Other features are allowed in this control string but we ignore them here.

Exhibit 2-38 shows a singular matrix of order 3, its determinant, and the attempt to find its inverse.

Exhibit 2-38

```
        A←  3 3 ρ    3 4 7      ¯1 2 ¯5      6 8 14
        A
            3          4          7
           ¯1          2         ¯5
            6          8         14
        DET  A
    7.993605777E¯15


        ⌹  A
    ⌹  A
    ?  DOMAIN ERROR
```

2.8.4 Systems of Linear Equations

In Section 1.4 we discussed the solution of a system of simultaneous linear equations of the form:

$$Ax = b$$

for which the solution has the form:

$$x = A^{-1}b$$

Exhibit 2-39 shows the solution of the original example using APL.

The reader should note that the product of a matrix and its inverse is always the identity matrix. (See Exhibit 2-40.)

The solution of a system of 3, 4, or more linear equations using APL is just as simple, although hand calculations become extremely tedious and error-prone. For four equations **A** is of order 4 × 4 and **B** is of length 4. The APL solution of such a system is painless, and is shown in Exhibit 2-41. At-

Exhibit 2-39

```
A←   2   2   P   6   4     4   16
B←  360   480
X←  (⌹A)     +.×   B
X
48   18
```

Exhibit 2-40

```
(⌹A)    +.×     A
          1             0
          0             1
```

Exhibit 2-41

```
A←  3  4  7  12    ¯1  2  ¯5  15    7  2  ¯3  ¯1     6  9  3  10
A←   4  4    P    A
A
       3              4           7           12
      ¯1              2          ¯5           15
       7              2          ¯3           ¯1
       6              9           3           10
B←    17   10   9   12
X←  (⌹A)     +.×     B
X
2.038437002   ¯1.428548644    .4256778309    1.13492823
```

tempting to solve this system by hand and calculator methods should dispel any lingering doubts about the power of APL.

2.9 PROCEDURES FOR USING APL[E]

2.9.1 Turning on APL: The Process of Logging-On

Most APL systems are run on a computer system shared by many users, and known as a *time-sharing system*. APL users usually are located anywhere from a few hundred feet to a few hundred miles from the computer, and they use some form of telephone line to send information back and forth from the computer to the user's terminal. Either the terminal may be a typewriter-like device that prints information on paper, or it may be a television-like screen called a *cathode ray tube* (CRT) with a typewriter keyboard, which displays information on the face of the screen.

The most important skill to learn for using APL is how to establish a connection with the APL system, a procedure often called *logging-on* or *signing-on*. The exact details vary from one system to another, and from one type of terminal to another. The user must first turn on the power switch for the terminal and perhaps also on a coupler, which connects the telephone line to the terminal. The telephone line may be connected directly and permanently to the computer, or the user may have to use a normal dial-up telephone, calling the computer and placing the telephone handset into a special receptacle on the acoustic coupler. Specific instructions will be provided by the computer center providing the APL service.

A few companies are providing small stand-alone APL computers that do not depend on any other devices except the wall plug for electricity. The manufacturer provides the necessary instructions for turning the machine on.

If the user is using a time-sharing system an identification (log-on) ritual is necessary before the computer will allow the user to do anything. The computer center personnel must know to whom to send the bill! The log-on also protects the user from unauthorized persons who might wish to use the computer or to gain access to the data stored in the files in the memory of the machine. Unauthorized access to data is especially sensitive in a health care environment. Therefore, the user must take great pains to ensure that the passwords and lock codes remain secret. The exact sequence and details of identifying yourself to the computer vary considerably but include typing an account code and a secret password or lock code. If everything is acceptable the computer will type a welcome message. If something is incorrect the computer may allow the person to try again, or it may disconnect the line.

> *For each different system the user will have to ask the account representative or consultant how to establish the connection and how to sign on.*

2.9.2 Turning Off APL: The Process of Logging-Off

Logging- or signing-off is the second most important skill that must be learned. Fortunately, it is usually rather simple.

First, the user should consider whether anything in the active workspace needs to be)SAVEd, as a file or as a total workspace. If so, the appropriate command(s) must be issued.

Then the user types)OFF. The computer will respond with a goodbye message, perhaps indicating the cost of performing the computer work during the session, and other information.

Finally, the user should turn off the appropriate power switches and hang up the telephone if a dial line was being used.

2.9.3 Erasing Typing Errors

The third most important thing to know when using APL is how to erase the inevitable typing errors that occur. The method of erasure depends on the terminal being used. On an IBM 2741 terminal the procedure is to backspace to the erroneous character, press the attention (ATTN) button, wait for the computer to space up 1 line, and point to the error, before retyping from that point. On a wide class of other terminals, known as ASCII terminals (including DIABLO types and DECWRITER types) the procedure is to backspace to the error, and press LINEFEED followed by CARRIAGE RETURN. The computer retypes the initial correct portion of the line, and the user can continue typing from that point.

A variety of other procedures are possible, and the user must find out the appropriate one from the account representative or consultant.

2.9.4 Libraries, Workspaces, and Files

Each user account is either allocated a certain maximum amount of storage space on the disk files, or pays for whatever space is used. The relatively permanent storage is called a LIBRARY and is stored on magnetic disks, where it is available whenever the user wants it. The library space is limited and must be carefully managed. Old data and programs should be)DROPped.

The information in use while signed-on is called the ACTIVE WORKSPACE. The active workspace contains two types of information: FUNCTIONS and VARIABLES. The active workspace has a name, as does every function and variable. The active workspace name is CONTINUE, unless the user has specified otherwise. The command to change the active workspace name is)WSID followed by a blank and a 1 to 8 character *name*. When issued without a name the command is a question and the computer replies with the current name.

A FUNCTION is a collection of APL commands that the user can perform by typing the name of the function. A function may require 0, 1, or 2 variables (known as OPERANDS) to be typed as well, depending on the definition of the function. A function can be defined by entering FUNCTION DEFINITION MODE under the control of the ∇ (DEL) character. Programming is beyond the scope of this text, and persons interested in learning to program in APL should consult a standard text, such as the one by Katzan (1970), and the APL supplier's manual for particular details.

A VARIABLE may be a numeric scalar, vector, matrix or array, or it may be a character string which is treated by APL is if it were a vector of single characters. A variable has a name, and can be created or redefined by assigning a value or values to it. Its current value can be displayed by typing its name.

The active workspace may contain functions or variables or both. The functions contained can be listed by typing)FNS. The variables contained can be listed by typing)VARS. A copy of the active workspace can be stored in the library by typing)SAVE. The variable A can be saved by typing)SAVE A. A function can be saved similarly. The contents of a library can be displayed by typing)LIB or)LIB, *library* (for the library of some other user.) Users are generally identified by a four-digit user number, and the author's number on the University of Ottawa system is 3176, and is used in many of the examples in the text when something specific must be retrieved from the library. (There is nothing sacred about that particular number, and a user on a different system would use his/her own number.)

To obtain a workspace, function, or variable from a library the user types)LOAD *name* or)LOAD *name, library* if the desired library is different from the one under which the user is logged-on. The user may drop something from only his/her own library by typing)DROP *name*. A function or variable may be removed from the active workspace by typing)ERASE *name*.

2.10 CONCLUSION[E]

Two important points should be obvious throughout the text.

1. MATRIX ALGEBRA SIMPLIFIES THE EXPRESSION OF MANY STATISTICAL FORMULAS COMPARED TO THEIR EXPRESSION IN ORDINARY ALGEBRA.
2. APL ASSISTS IN CARRYING OUT COMPUTATIONS THAT OTHERWISE BECOME VERY TEDIOUS. THIS ALLOWS

THE USER TO FOCUS MORE CLEARLY ON THE PERFORM-
ANCE OF PROCEDURES, RATHER THAN BECOMING
BOGGED DOWN IN THE MECHANICAL ASPECTS OF THE
ARITHMETIC.

An analogy to the relationship between a driver and a car may be useful
here. A car driver does not need to consciously consider how the motor,
drive shaft, and wheels function in order to be able to drive a car. In fact,
it is possible to drive a car without any appreciation of what a motor is or
how it works. However, a driver who is completely ignorant about the
internal operation of a car is likely to get into trouble much more easily
than a driver who is familiar with the way a car works. An expert racing
driver/owner is quite likely to be extremely familiar with all aspects of
the car's construction, operation, maintenance, and repair.

Our objective in this text is to prepare health care managers and students who have a fairly thorough understanding of basic statistics as
currently applied in health care management and research. Those who
wish to become experts will leave this work far behind, but we hope that
it can provide a useful first step for such people. We hope that our students will be able to use basic statistics wisely enough to avoid the many
pitfalls that await the unwary. We believe that our approach using basic
matrix algebra and APL allows the user to understand the mechanics of
the calculations, without being overwhelmed by summation symbols and
subscripts that are the usual presentation in basic statistics texts. This
then allows them to concentrate on the nature of the statistical analysis
they are performing rather than the complexity of the arithmetic.

REFERENCES

Gilman, L., and Rose, A. J. *APL: An Interactive Approach,* 2nd rev. ed. New York: John
Wiley & Sons, 1976.

Katzan, H. Jr. *APL Programming and Computer Techniques.* New York: Van Nostrand
Reinhold, 1970.

Problems for Solution

The reader with access to an APL terminal should work carefully through the examples of this chapter, and then through the examples and problems of Chapter 1.

Chapter 3

An Introduction to SPSS

Objectives

After completing this chapter you should be able to:
1. Define the terms case, variable and value.
2. Draw and describe a diagram showing the flow of the process of preparing the computer inputs for analysis.
3. List the types of SPSS control cards and give examples of each type.
4. Write SPSS control cards and data cards on coding sheets, for later punching.

Chapter Map

All sections of this chapter are labeled D.

The SPSS Batch System consists of special purpose computer software for performing statistical analysis. It provides a means of performing statistical analyses with little or no pain. Some people believe that statistics is necessarily painful, but even for those people, SPSS is relatively painless.

In SPSS the individuals (people, hospitals, departments, etc.) being studied are referred to as *cases*. For each case the known attributes are called *variables*. All things known about the individuals are represented as values of these variables. The SPSS system consists of a set of programs and a control language. The control language allows the user to: (1) describe the external format of raw data variables; (2) enter the data into the computer; (3) perform calculations on variables thereby transforming them or creating new variables; (4) group values of any variable (e.g., to create age ranges); (5) select for analysis cases that meet specified conditions (e.g., males only, or males over age 30); and (6) specify which statistical procedures are to be performed and the variables involved.

The SPSS capabilities relevant to readers of this book include analysis of variance (ANOVA), Pearson correlation, and linear and multiple regression. More basic types of statistical analysis are used in Volume I. Beyond the scope of this volume, there are more advanced analytical techniques described in the *SPSS* manual, such as factor analysis, discriminant analysis and canonical correlation. Mastery of the material covered in the present volume aids substantially in understanding these more advanced techniques.

SPSS is a system designed for use in the batch-processing mode, but another system called SCSS has also been developed, where the C indicates *conversational,* for use in the time-sharing mode.

3.1 STATISTICAL STUDIES: HOW TO USE SPSS

In any research study BEFORE starting the study or collecting ANY data it is important to have a good design, beginning with the objectives (possibly formal statistical hypotheses), continuing to include the methods of data collection, and ending with the proposed methods of analysis of the data as well as the way that the analysis will lead to answers to the questions. That a complete proposal/design be prepared and reviewed by others is important, because a number of pitfalls await the unwary. Undesigned studies often lead to a late realization that not enough, or too many, or the wrong data have been collected.

If not enough or the wrong data have been collected, the appropriate questions cannot be answered. If data for too many variables have been collected, the inexperienced researcher quickly finds that SPSS (or any other package) can easily produce an astonishing mound of paper full of irrelevant analyses tending to distract and confuse the researcher as well as hiding the appropriate analyses, if they exist. It is *easy* to generate *hundreds* or *thousands* of tables, unless careful thought is given ahead of time to which few tables will answer the questions being asked. In a large number of irrelevant tables the researcher will surely find that up to 10 percent of them are statistically significant. Any significant but irrelevant results are called *spurious*. Also, the amount of time spent preparing cards for analyzing such a large number of variables can be truly overwhelming, especially when viewed in retrospect. The lack of a carefully thought out design, including a specification of the expected analysis, can easily lead to disaster.

3.1.1 Preparation for Data Analysis Using SPSS

Before commencing the actual analysis of data using SPSS (or any other package for that matter) three processes must be completed: (1) the collected data must be converted to machine (computer) readable form; (2) the SPSS commands required to process the data must be prepared; and (3) the JCL (Job Control Language) cards must be prepared to tell the computer to read in the data and use the SPSS package. These are parallel processes and can be carried out in any order. During the analysis phase, however, the third and especially the second steps listed above will have to be repeated. Errors in the analysis and insights resulting from the analysis often lead to the use of new procedures and tests.

Figure 3-1 shows the flow of the processes required for preparation of the computer inputs for processing by SPSS. Note that the upper branch deals with the data preparation, while the logically parallel branch deals with the SPSS programming. The data collection branch assumes an interview situation with data being recorded on a response sheet for later keypunching. Other types of studies would have a different process in the top branch, especially if the data were already on machine readable media.

Note that the data and the SPSS/JCL statements must be checked to verify their accuracy. SPSS can be used to help in the process of checking the accuracy of the data. The procedures are described below, but a two-step error checking process is required. The FREQUENCIES procedure can help detect unexpected values of the study variables, and in a second step the SELECT IF and LIST CASES procedures can identify the individual offending cases, which can then be investigated and corrected.

3.1.2 Getting to Know SPSS

The SPSS system has excellent user-oriented documentation in the form of three books: (1) the *SPSS Primer* by Klecka, Nie, and Hull; (2) the main

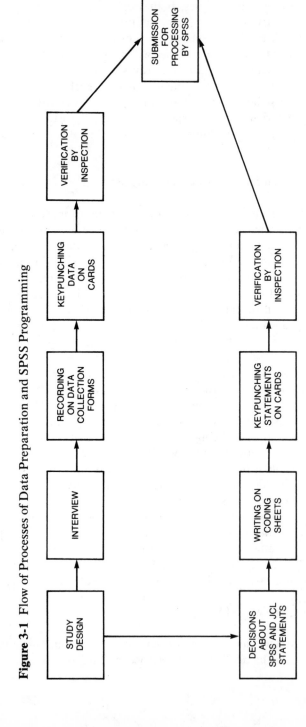

Figure 3-1 Flow of Processes of Data Preparation and SPSS Programming

manual *Statistical Package for the Social Sciences* 2nd edition, by Nie, et al.; and (3) *SPSS Update: New Procedures and Facilities for Releases 7 and 8* (all of which are published by McGraw-Hill). The primer is oriented to the novice. It covers only the most frequently used statistical procedures and suppresses some of the advanced details of these procedures. The main manual covers the full details of all available procedures in version 6 of the system, while the *SPSS Update* shows the changes and additions to versions 7 and 8 of the system. For the serious user, SPSS, Inc. has published *SPSS Statistical Algorithms.*

The novice, with little or no computer knowledge, should read the introductory sections of both the primer (Chapters 1, 2, 3, 4, and Appendix A) and the main manual (Chapters 1, 2, and 3). The person with computer experience (say FORTRAN) can dispense with the primer.

SPSS classifies control cards into *procedure* cards, which call for carrying out some statistical operation, and all others called *nonprocedure* cards. It is useful to further categorize the latter into:

1. Job Description;
2. Data Definition and Retrieval;
3. Data Modification;
4. Task Control;
5. End of Job.

In any run the SPSS deck must contain at least one card from all groups except Data Modification. The Data Definition, Data Modification, and Task Control groups have a variety of choices that make SPSS both a powerful and flexible data analysis system.

The *Job Description group* contains RUN NAME, TASK NAME, and COMMENT cards. The RUN NAME card is required as the first card in each SPSS run, while the TASK NAME card is optional but may be used with any procedure card. The COMMENT card allows the user to include explanatory information in the listing of the SPSS program without any impact on the operations being performed. The RUN NAME card is described in Chapter 7 of the primer and all of these cards are described in Chapter 6 of the manual.

The *Data Definition and Retrieval group* includes cards that describe the raw input data, or variables which have been created by data modification cards, and cards for naming, saving, and retrieving SPSS system files. The *format of raw input data must be described* either by a DATA LIST card or by a pair of VARIABLE LIST and INPUT FORMAT cards. The DATA LIST is easier to use. The(se) card(s) *must* be accompanied by an INPUT MEDIUM and an N OF CASES card. When raw input data are being used (rather than a saved file) then the READ INPUT DATA card must follow[1] the first procedure card and its associated OPTIONS and STATISTICS cards. When a saved file is used, then the GET FILE card must be used instead of the READ INPUT DATA, but in a different place. Optionally the MISSING VALUES card can be used to control processing in many procedures where cases should be ignored if they are missing part of the data, and the VAR LABELS and VALUE LABELS cards allow provision of information that will make the printed tabular results of analyses more meaningful to the reader. These cards are described in Chapter 5 of the primer and Chapter 4 of the manual.

The *file creation and retrieval* part of the Data Definition group consists of the FILE NAME, SUBFILE LIST, RUN SUBFILES, SAVE FILE, and GET FILE cards. These cards allow the creation and use of SPSS system files with all data definition information. System files are necessary for advanced work and are useful for teaching examples where the volume of data definition cards would obscure the procedures being presented. The file cards are covered in Chapters 4, 5, and 7 of the manual.

The *Data Modification* cards are optional but often extremely useful for creating new variables as transformations or combinations of input variables, or for changing the forms of variables so they are more convenient for the analysis desired. As an example, patient age is often of interest but different groupings of ages may be desired for certain analyses. Age should always be collected in years (where possible) and then transformed by means of a RECODE statement to obtain desired groups. In other situations age and sex might be believed to interact so that a single variable may be desired to distinguish among young, middle-aged, and old males and females. That variable can be created by a combination of RECODE and IF, or RECODE and COMPUTE statements. The RECODE statement is described in Chapter 6 of the primer, and all three are described in Chapter 8 of the manual. The DO REPEAT and END REPEAT cards provide a time-saving extension to these data modification cards, which is described in the manual and in the version 7 update.

The *Task Control* cards include all of the available procedure cards, along with the OPTIONS and STATISTICS cards (as defined for each procedure), the READ INPUT DATA card, and the RUN SUBFILES card. Chapter 5 of the manual and Chapter 7 of the primer describe the use of all of these cards, while Chapters 8 to 11 of the primer cover specific procedures. The manual has a much more extensive coverage of procedures in Chapters 14 to 26; however the statistical topics covered in this text go only as far as Chapter 22 of the manual.

The *end of job* card in every SPSS run is the FINISH card and it must always be included.[2]

3.1.3 SPSS Batch Job Submission

Three types of cards must be punched by the user to submit SPSS jobs for processing. These are:

1. Job Control Language (JCL) cards;
2. Data cards;
3. SPSS cards.

The *JCL cards* provide information to the operating system (OS) software, which controls the sequencing of jobs from one user to the next. The user's account number and identification are first, followed by cards indicating the system to be used (SPSS), and the form and location of input and output datasets. These JCL cards have limited flexibility in format, and the novice user is counselled to use the layout(s) specified in the examples in the text (as modified by the instructor), and to have the correctness checked by some more experienced user before submission to the computer.

The layout of the *data cards* must be determined by the student as part of the problem solution, but there are no restrictions on the decisions about which columns may or may not be used for data. (The first two columns of a data card must never contain either // or /*, since these are indicators for JCL cards.)

The layout of the *SPSS cards* must follow the rules specified in the manual or the primer, with special attention paid to distinguishing columns 1–15 (the control field) from columns 16–80 (the specification field). The control field is used in SPSS to identify the type of card (RUN NAME, DATA LIST, data modification, procedures, OPTIONS, STATISTICS, etc.), while the specification field is used to provide the necessary information to complete the specification of the operation requested in the control field. The student must locate the details of SPSS card control fields and specifications in either the primer or the manual.

The examples used in this book show listings of cards that have been used to *run* the programs. Included are JCL, data, and SPSS cards. For the JCL only the account number and programmer name need to be changed on the JOB card. The programmer name may be longer or shorter, but there must be no blanks left between the name and the MSGLEVEL and CLASS parameters (see Figure 3-2, second card).

Data may be submitted to SPSS in two general ways:

1. as raw input data,
2. as an SPSS system file.

Figure 3-2 Deck Setup for Running SPSS with Input Data on Cards (University of Ottawa)

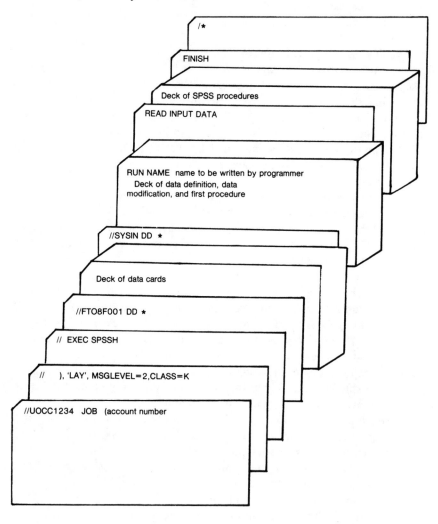

Figure 3-3 JCL and SPSS Cards for Input Data on Cards

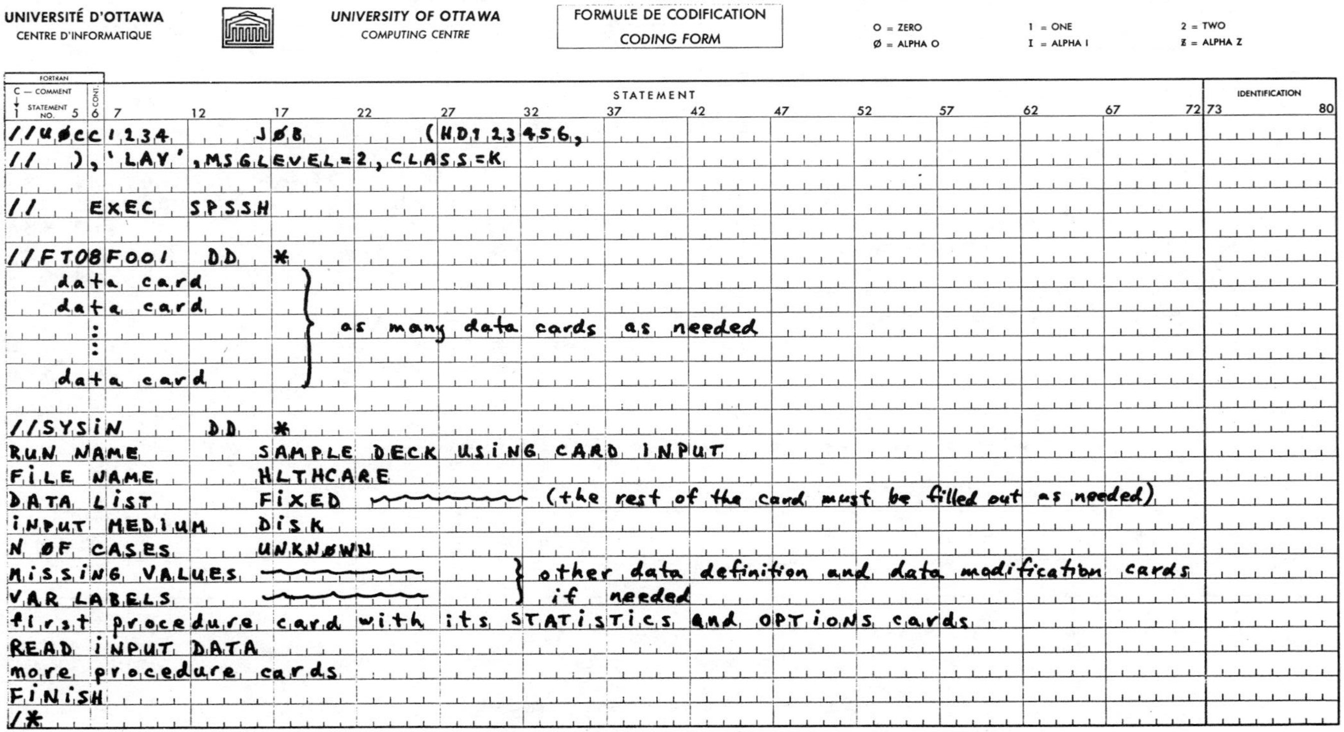

UNIVERSITÉ D'OTTAWA
CENTRE D'INFORMATIQUE

UNIVERSITY OF OTTAWA
COMPUTING CENTRE

FORMULE DE CODIFICATION
CODING FORM

0 = ZERO   Ø = ALPHA O
1 = ONE   I = ALPHA I
2 = TWO   Z = ALPHA Z

```
//uØCC1234.      JOB      (HD123456,
//  ,'LAY',MSGLEVEL=2,,CLASS=K,
//  EXEC  SPSSH
//FT08F001  DD  *
  data card
  data card
 ....            as many data cards as needed
  data card
//SYSIN  DD  *
RUN NAME       SAMPLE DECK USING CARD INPUT
FILE NAME      HLTHCARE
DATA LIST      FIXED _____ (the rest of the card must be filled out as needed)
INPUT MEDIUM   DISK
N OF CASES     UNKNOWN
MISSING VALUES _____  } other data definition and data modification cards
VAR LABELS                 if needed
first procedure card with its STATISTICS and OPTIONS cards
READ INPUT DATA
more procedure cards
FINISH
/*
```

Figure 3-4 JCL and SPSS Cards Using SPSS Saved System File

UNIVERSITÉ D'OTTAWA
CENTRE D'INFORMATIQUE

UNIVERSITY OF OTTAWA
COMPUTING CENTRE

FORMULE DE CODIFICATION
CODING FORM

O = ZERO
Ø = ALPHA O
1 = ONE
I = ALPHA I
2 = TWO
Z = ALPHA Z

FORTRAN: C — COMMENT, STATEMENT NO. (1–5), CONT. (6), STATEMENT (7–72), IDENTIFICATION (73–80)

```
//UØCC1234    JØB       (HD123456,
//   ),'LAY',MSGLEVEL=2,CLASS=K

//   EXEC   SPSSH
//FT03F001   DD   UNIT= ~~~~ definition of location of SPSS saved system file

//SYSIN      DD   *
RUN NAME        SAMPLE RUN USING AN SPSS SAVED FILE
GET FILE        file name previously used on a SAVE FILE card

CØMPUTE         ~~~ }
RECØDE          ~~~ }
IF              ~~~ } data modification and data definition cards
VAR LABELS      ~~~ }      if needed
VALUE LABELS    ~~~ }
MISSING VALUES  ~~~ }

procedure cards with OPTIONS and STATISTICS cards

FINISH
/*
```

Raw input data may be punched in cards or stored on magnetic tape or disk. Although SPSS allows data cards to be inserted in the SPSS deck immediately following the READ INPUT DATA card, the preferred method is to insert them following a JCL card (//FT08F001 DD *), which is used to mark the beginning of data cards.[2] Raw data on tape or disk require a different format of the FT08 card. Presented in Figure 3-2 is a deck of cards that is ready for submission to the computer. Figure 3-3 illustrates the same information as it would appear on a coding sheet. Note that, for tape or disk input of the raw data, the * on the FT08 card would be replaced by information describing the tape or disk dataset, its location, and the conditions of its use, and there would then be no data cards in the input deck.

In some cases it is desirable to have partially processed data stored as an SPSS system file. Presented in Figure 3-4 are the JCL and SPSS cards that are required to process such a system file. Note that the GET FILE card replaces the following cards:

1. FILE NAME
2. DATA LIST (or VARIABLE LIST and INPUT FORMAT)
3. INPUT MEDIUM
4. N OF CASES
5. READ INPUT DATA

Also if no further data modifications or transformations are desired, the COMPUTE, RECODE, IF, MISSING VALUES, VAR LABELS, and VALUE LABELS cards are not required.

Use of an SPSS system file instead of raw data requires a slight modification in the JCL. In this case, an FT03 card replaces the FT08 card.

In conclusion, this chapter has provided an introduction to the use of SPSS for a novice. The SPSS manual and primer are excellent user-oriented documents and every reader should have access to one or both. Their use is necessary to provide an understanding of what can be done, or what has been done in an example in the text. In this work we do not even *try* to give a complete explanation of the SPSS details.

NOTES

1. The READ INPUT DATA card is optional under some circumstances in Version 8.
2. Version 8 allows more flexibility.

Part II

Analysis of Variance

Chapter 4

One-Way
Analysis of Variance

Objectives

After completing this chapter, you should be able to:
1. Define the sums of squares components model for one-way ANOVA.
2. Define the structural model for one-way ANOVA.
3. Calculate the necessary sums of squares using:
   a. definitional equations
   b. computational equations
   c. matrix notation equations
4. Construct the ANOVA table.
5. Test for significance.
6. Use appropriate APL and SPSS programs to perform one-way ANOVA.

Chapter Map

Section 4.1 introduces the basic concept of ANOVA and has been assigned the letter code A.

Sections 4.1.1, 4.1.2, 4.1.3, 4.2, and 4.3 define the basic algebraic expressions and have been assigned the letter code B.

Section 4.4 and its subsections present the one-way ANOVA equations in matrix notation and have been assigned the letter code C.

Section 4.5 demonstrates an additional application to health care management and has been assigned the letter code F.

Section 4.6 explains the use of SPSS programs for performing one-way ANOVA and has been assigned the code D.

Section 4.7 explains the use of APL and has been assigned the code E.

4.1 INTRODUCTION TO ANALYSIS OF VARIANCE[A]

In Chapter 12 of the companion text, *Statistics in Health Administration*, Volume I, we examined the methods by which the difference between the means of two groups might be evaluated statistically. The purpose of the discussion in this chapter is to consider the problem of determining whether observed differences among the means of three or more samples are attributable to chance or whether there are significant differences among the means of the corresponding populations. For example, we might be interested in determining whether there are: (1) significant differences in the effectiveness of three different drugs that may be used in the treatment of a given condition, (2) significant differences among the average lengths of stay associated with several institutions, or (3) significant differences in the average daily costs of three or more institutions.

4.1.1 The Basic Model[B]

By way of illustration, suppose we are interested in examining the average lengths of stay associated with four institutions, which we designate as A_1, A_2, A_3, and A_4. Assume further that we select three patients from each of the institutions and obtain the following information pertaining to their lengths of stay:

Institution A_1: 10, 14, 6
Institution A_2: 9, 13, 5
Institution A_3: 8, 12, 4
Institution A_4: 9, 9, 6

The means of these four samples are 10, 9, 8, and 8, respectively, and we wish to determine whether the differences among these four means are significant or whether they can be attributed to chance. This situation is portrayed graphically in Figure 4-1, where each point appearing in the chart corresponds to a length of stay experienced by a patient in one of the four institutions. The horizontal lines appearing in this graph correspond to the mean stays associated with the four institutions. Thus, we see there is not only variation in the three lengths of stay associated with each institution, but there is also variation among the mean stays of these four hospitals. Letting μ_1, μ_2, μ_3, and μ_4 represent the true average lengths of stay associated with the four institutions, the null hypothesis we wish to test may be expressed as:

$$\mu_1 = \mu_2 = \mu_3 = \mu_4$$

Figure 4-1 Length of Stay by Institution

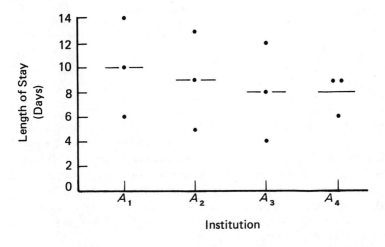

The alternate hypothesis we wish to examine is that the four means are not equal.

We will discover that it is desirable to express the four means to be compared as follows:

$$\mu_1 = \mu + \alpha_1 \tag{4.1.1}$$

$$\mu_2 = \mu + \alpha_2 \tag{4.1.2}$$

$$\mu_3 = \mu + \alpha_3 \tag{4.1.3}$$

$$\mu_4 = \mu + \alpha_4 \tag{4.1.4}$$

Observe that in this example, μ is given by:

$$\mu = \frac{\mu_1 + \mu_2 + \mu_3 + \mu_4}{4} \tag{4.2}$$

We shall refer to μ as the *grand mean*, while the α's are referred to as the *treatment effects*. Employing this notation, we are able to express the null hypothesis $\mu_1 = \mu_2 = \mu_3 = \mu_4$ in the form:

$$\alpha_1 = \alpha_2 = \alpha_3 = \alpha_4 = 0 \tag{4.3}$$

while the alternate hypothesis is that *not* all the α's are zero (i.e., that two or more α's are nonzero). The preceding expressions can be summarized in the form of a *structural model* for the mean of hospital i:

$$\mu_i = \mu + \alpha_i \qquad\qquad (4.4)$$

where i may assume the values 1, 2, 3, or 4.

The logic underlying the examination of the null hypothesis $\mu_1 = \mu_2 = \mu_3 = \mu_4$ is as follows. If the differences between these means are small and attributable to chance, the null hypothesis cannot be rejected. On the other hand, if the differences among the means are so large that they cannot be attributed to chance, the null hypothesis may be rejected in favor of the alternate hypothesis. These considerations suggest that we require a precise measure of the *differences among means* as well as a decision criterion by which we may evaluate the null hypothesis.

Recall that when examining the variance of a sample of the numbers $x_1, \ldots, x_i, \ldots, x_n$, we employ the term $\sum_{i=1}^{n} (x_i - \bar{x})^2$ in the numerator of the equation by which we compute s^2. Following a similar procedure, we might measure the differences among the means by calculating their variance relative to the grand mean, which in this example is given by:

$$\frac{10 + 9 + 8 + 8}{4} = 8.75 \text{ days}$$

Let us represent each patient's observed length of stay by x_{ik}, where the subscript i refers to the institution (A_i), and the subscript k refers to the patient within the hospital.

Let us further represent the number of samples by p (4 institutions in this case) and the number of observations per sample by n (3 patients per institution). Let us represent the mean for sample i by:

$$\bar{x}_{i.} = \frac{1}{n} \sum_{k=1}^{n} x_{ik} \qquad\qquad (4.5)$$

The *dot* indicates that the subscript k has been eliminated by summation. The mean of all the samples can be represented similarly by $\bar{x}_{..}$. Finally, let us represent the variance of the means by $s_{\bar{x}}^2$, where the subscript $\bar{x}$ indicates that we are dealing with means. We can calculate the variance of the means by:

$$s_{\bar{x}}^2 = \frac{\sum\limits_{i=1}^{p} (\bar{x}_{i.} - \bar{x}_{..})^2}{p - 1} \qquad (4.6)$$

And for our example,

$$s_{\bar{x}}^2 = \frac{(10 - 8.75)^2 + (9 - 8.75)^2 + (8 - 8.75)^2 + (8 - 8.75)^2}{4 - 1}$$

$$\cong .92$$

4.1.2 Two Estimates of Population Variance[B]

We saw in Figure 4-1 that there are considerable differences between the lengths of stay experienced by the individual patients as well as variation among the mean stays of the four institutions. Consider, for example, institution A_4 where the deviations about the mean stay of 8 days are given by $(9 - 8)$, $(9 - 8)$, and $(6 - 8)$. Concerning the variability in the lengths of stay within each of the institutions, we assume that the populations from which the samples were selected may be approximated by the standard normal curve having equal variances, which we designate by σ^2.

If we now combine this assumption with the assumption that the null hypothesis $\mu_1 = \mu_2 = \mu_3 = \mu_4$ is true, we may assume that these four samples were selected from the same population having the mean μ and the variance σ^2. Recall that, for large populations, the standard error of the mean is given by $\sigma_{\bar{x}} = (\sigma/\sqrt{n})$. Now, let us use $s_{\bar{x}}^2$, which in our example was found to be .92, as an estimate of $\sigma_{\bar{x}}^2$. This implies:

$$s_{\bar{x}}^2 = \frac{\sigma^2}{n} \qquad (4.7)$$

which allows us to estimate σ^2, the common variance of the population from which we assume the samples were selected. Thus, we find that the

first estimate of $\sigma^2 = ns_{\bar{x}}^2$ (4.8)
$$\cong 3(.92) = 2.76$$

If σ^2 were known, we could compare $n(s_{\bar{x}}^2)$ with the population variance directly, and reject the null hypothesis if $n(s_{\bar{x}}^2)$ were found to be much larger than σ^2. This is so because such a finding would suggest that the variation among the means is greater than what would be expected from the variability of the population. As a consequence, if $n(s_{\bar{X}}^2)$ is much larger than σ^2, we can not attribute differences among the means to chance variation.

Unfortunately, however, σ^2 is not known and we are forced to obtain a second estimate of the common population variance with existing data. Having assumed that the samples came from the same population, we may use the mean of the *within* sample variances as our second estimate of σ^2. Referring to our example, recall that we had four samples, the variances of which we now designate by s_1^2, s_2^2, s_3^2, and s_4^2. The second estimate of the common variance σ^2 is then given by:

$$\text{Second estimate of } \sigma^2 = \frac{s_1^2 + s_2^2 + s_3^2 + s_4^2}{4} \tag{4.9}$$

$$= \frac{1}{4}\left[\frac{(10 - 10)^2 + (14 - 10)^2 + (6 - 10)^2}{3 - 1}\right.$$

$$+ \frac{(9 - 9)^2 + (13 - 9)^2 + (5 - 9)^2}{3 - 1}$$

$$+ \frac{(8 - 8)^2 + (12 - 8)^2 + (4 - 8)^2}{3 - 1}$$

$$+ \left.\frac{(9 - 8)^2 + (9 \cdot - 8)^2 + (6 - 8)^2}{3 - 1}\right]$$

$$= 12.75$$

4.1.3 Comparing the Two Estimates: The F Statistic [B]

We now have two estimates of σ^2. The first estimate is based on the variation *among* the means of the four samples, which was found to be:

$$n \cdot s_{\bar{X}}^2 = 3(.92) = 2.76$$

The second estimate of σ^2 was based on the variation *within* the samples, which was found to be:

$$\frac{s_1^2 + s_2^2 + s_3^2 + s_4^2}{4} = 12.75$$

Comparing these two estimates, we can assert that if the first is much larger than the second, it is reasonable to reject the null hypothesis. If the null hypothesis is not true, we would expect the variation *among* the means to be much larger than the variation *within* the four samples, since the first estimate would reflect the differences among the means as well as chance variation. The second estimate, which is based on variation within the samples, reflects only chance variation.

To provide a systematic basis of comparing the two estimates of σ^2, we shall employ the *variance ratio*:

$$F = \frac{\text{Sample variance among the means}}{\text{Sample variance within the samples}} \qquad (4.10)$$

If the null hypothesis is true (i.e., $\mu_1 = \mu_2 = \mu_3 = \mu_4$) and the samples come from normal populations having a common variance σ^2, the sampling distribution of this statistic is the F distribution.

Tables for $\alpha = .05$ and $.01$, respectively, and a description of the use of the F tables, are included in Appendix C.

We reject the null hypothesis if the computed value of F exceeds F_α. If we compare the means of p samples of size n, the corresponding degrees of freedom (df) in the numerator and denominator are $(p - 1)$ and $p(n - 1)$, respectively. Observe that the denominator is an estimate of σ^2, which is based on $p(n - 1)$ independent deviations from the mean. This becomes clear when one recognizes that there are $(n - 1)$ independent deviations in each of the p samples.

Returning to our example, the value of $F_{.05} = 4.07$ for $(p - 1) = 4 - 1 = 3$ and $p(n - 1) = 4(3 - 1) = 8$ degrees of freedom. The calculated value of F is given by:

$$F = \frac{2.76}{12.75} \cong .22$$

Clearly, $F < 1.0 < F_{.05}$ and the null hypothesis cannot be rejected. Thus, even though there are differences among the average lengths of stay, the variations within the samples are also large and we therefore conclude that the observed differences in the mean stays could be attributed to chance.

We have just described the most important elements of analysis of variance in the simplest fashion possible. In the next section we consider the problem of examining differences among p means in a more rigorous fashion.

4.2 ONE-WAY ANALYSIS OF VARIANCE[(B)]

The basic approach taken in the analysis of variance is to partition the total variability in a set of data into two components, each of which reflects a specific source of variation.

In terms of the patient length of stay example introduced in the previous section, the two sources of variation might be: (1) actual differences among the mean stays of the four institutions, which is referred to as the *treatment effect*; and (2) chance variation, which in problems of this kind, is called *experimental error*. Thus, the task before us is to partition the total variation to reflect the treatment effects and the experimental error. This leads to the mathematical *identity*

Total Variation = Treatment Effect + Experimental Error

which is referred to as the *variance components* or *sums of squares components* model. The measure of total variation that we shall employ is called the *total sum of squares, SS(T)*, which is given by the *definitional* equation

$$SS(T) = \sum_{i=1}^{p} \sum_{k=1}^{n} (x_{ik} - \bar{x}_{..})^2 \qquad (4.11)$$

where: x_{ik} = observation k contained in sample i for $i = 1, 2, \ldots, p$, and $k = 1, 2, \ldots, n$ for each sample

$\bar{x}_{..}$ = the grand mean or the mean based on all np observations, and the dots represent the fact that the subscripts have been eliminated by summation.

The data collection design for this study may be viewed as a set of vectors comprising a two-dimensional matrix or table. As shown in Figure 4-2, one of the dimensions is represented by the matrix rows and this dimension is called the *treatment*. If we displayed the hospitals in our study along the rows, they would be regarded as the treatments. The other dimension in such a matrix refers to the *observations* within each of the treatments. In terms of our example, the columns contain information

Figure 4-2 Data Collection Design Matrix for Patient Length of Stay

		Patients		
		1	2	3
			(Subscript k)	
Institutions (Treatment) (Subscript i)	1	10	14	6
	2	9	13	5
	3	8	12	4
	4	9	9	6

depicting the use of service by the first, second, and third patients in each of the institutions. Each *element* of the matrix represents either one piece of information that must be collected, or one observation to be made. As an example, consider the element a_{11} in the data matrix. In this case, observe that this element represents the length of stay (LOS) experienced by the first patient in institution A_1. Each cell of the design represents the group of n observations that belong together, because there is no (apparent) way of differentiating among them. (In Chapter 5 we extend this design matrix concept to include more dimensions beyond the treatment.) In this example, there are $4 \times 3 = 12$ patients for whom data must be collected. In general, there are pn observations to be made in a design involving one-way analysis of variance (ANOVA).

Observe that if we divide Equation 4.11 by $(np - 1)$, we obtain the variance of the total set of data and, as a result, $SS(T)$ is interpreted in much the same way as a sample variance.

Letting $\bar{x}_{i.}$ represent the mean of sample i, we begin with the definition

$$SS(T) = \sum_{i=1}^{p} \sum_{k=1}^{n} (x_{ik} - \bar{x}_{..})^2$$

which, after appropriate manipulation, becomes the identity:

$$SS(T) = n \sum_{i=1}^{p} (\bar{x}_{i.} - \bar{x}_{..})^2 + \sum_{i=1}^{p} \sum_{k=1}^{n} (x_{ik} - \bar{x}_{i.})^2 \quad \textbf{(4.12)}$$

which is the basis of a one-way ANOVA. The derivation of this equation may be found in more advanced texts (e.g., Winer 1971). We can see that Equation 4.12 partitions the total sum of squares into two components. The first term, $n \sum_{i=1}^{p} (\bar{x}_{i.} - \bar{x}_{..})^2$, is a measure of the variation *among* the means. If we divide the first term by $p - 1$, we obtain the quantity that we referred to earlier as $n \cdot s_{\bar{x}}^2$. Similarly, the second term, $\sum_{i=1}^{p} \sum_{k=1}^{n} (x_{ik} - \bar{x}_{i.})^2$, represents a measure of the variation *within* the individual samples. If we divide $\sum_{i=1}^{p} \sum_{k=1}^{n} (x_{ik} - \bar{x}_{i.})^2$ by $p(n - 1)$, we obtain the mean of the sample variances that was used earlier in the denominator of the F statistic.

> *We shall refer to the component that measures* variation among the means *as the* treatment sum of squares, $SS(TR)$, *while the term that measures* variation within the samples *will be referred to as the* error sum of squares, $SS(E)$.

With regard to the error sum of squares, the word *error* refers to the experimental error corresponding to what is meant by "chance".

As mentioned previously, Equation 4.12 may be represented by the sums of squares components model, which is the identity:

$$SS(T) = SS(TR) + SS(E) \qquad (4.13)$$

The definitional formulas for the sums of squares components model are:

$$SS(T) = \sum_{i=1}^{p} \sum_{k=1}^{n} (x_{ik} - \bar{x}_{..})^2 \qquad (4.14.1)$$

$$SS(TR) = n \sum_{i=1}^{p} (\bar{x}_{i.} - \bar{x}_{..})^2 \qquad (4.14.2)$$

$$SS(E) = \sum_{i=1}^{p} \sum_{i=1}^{n} (x_{ik} - \bar{x}_{i.})^2 \qquad (4.14.3)$$

Note that these three equations are the components of Equation 4.12. The first and third are very similar to each other, with the difference being the $\bar{x}_{..}$ and $\bar{x}_{i.}$, which represent the overall mean and the mean for treatment i, respectively.

Returning to our numerical example, we obtain the various sums of squares as follows:

$$SS(T) = (10 - 8.75)^2 + (14 - 8.75)^2 + (6 - 8.75)^2$$
$$+ (9 - 8.75)^2 + (13 - 8.75)^2 + (5 - 8.75)^2$$
$$+ (8 - 8.75)^2 + (12 - 8.75)^2 + (4 - 8.75)^2$$
$$+ (9 - 8.75)^2 + (9 - 8.75)^2 + (6 - 8.75)^2$$
$$= 110.25$$
$$SS(TR) = 3 ((10 - 8.75)^2 + (9 - 8.75)^2 + (8 - 8.75)^2 + (8 - 8.75)^2)$$
$$= 8.25$$
$$SS(E) = (10 - 10)^2 + (14 - 10)^2 + (6 - 10)^2$$
$$+ (9 - 9)^2 + (13 - 9)^2 + (5 - 9)^2$$
$$+ (8 - 8)^2 + (12 - 8)^2 + (4 - 8)^2$$
$$+ (9 - 8)^2 + (9 - 8)^2 + (6 - 8)^2$$
$$= 102$$

Hence, we find:

$$SS(TR) + SS(E) = 8.25 + 102 = 110.25 = SS(T)$$

In order to test the null hypothesis $\mu_1 = \mu_2 = \cdots = \mu_p$, which may also be expressed as $\alpha_1 = \alpha_2 = \cdots = \alpha_p = 0$, against the alternate hypothesis that the treatment effects are not all zero, we compare $SS(TR)$ with $SS(E)$ by means of an appropriate F statistic. To systematize the calculation of the appropriate F statistic, it is customary to present the necessary work in an analysis of variance table similar to Table 4-1. Here it will be observed that the first column indicates the source of variation (total, treatment, and experimental error), while the second column indicates the number of degrees of freedom (df) on which the respective sums of squares (SS) are based. The fourth column indicates the mean sums of squares (MS), which is simply the sums of squares divided by the corresponding number of degrees of freedom. The last column of the table indicates the F statistic, which is the ratio of the two mean squares. Also observe that the mean square terms are identical to the two estimates of σ^2 that were employed earlier and that the degrees of freedom corresponding to the numerator and denominator of the F statistic are $(p - 1)$ and $p(n - 1)$, respectively.

Returning to our example, we would construct the analysis of variance table as shown in Table 4-2.

Table 4-1 Model Analysis of Variance Table: One-Way ANOVA

Source of Variation	df	SS	MS	F
Treatment	$p-1$	$SS(TR)$	$MS(TR) = \dfrac{SS(TR)}{p-1}$	$MS(TR)$
Error	$p(n-1)$	$SS(E)$	$MS(E) = \dfrac{SS(E)}{p(n-1)}$	
Total	$pn-1$	$SS(T)$		

Table 4-2 One-Way Analysis of Variance Table for Patient Length of Stay

Source of Variation	df	SS	MS	F
Treatment (A_i)	3	8.25	2.75	.22
Error	8	102.00	12.75	
Total	11	110.25		

Here, as before, the computed value of F (.22) is compared with the value of $F_{.05}$ for $(p-1) = 3$ and $p(n-1) = 4(3-1) = 8$ degrees of freedom, which was found earlier to be 4.07. Since $.22 < 4.07$, we cannot reject the null hypothesis.

It is appropriate for the reader to practice the computation of one-way ANOVA using one or more problems at the end of this chapter. At this point, these problems should be practiced using the *definitional* formulas already presented, and later using the *computational* formulas in Section 4.3, and the matrix algebra formulas in Section 4.4.

4.3 COMPUTATIONAL ALGEBRAIC FORMULAS FOR ONE-WAY ANOVA[B]

As might be imagined, the calculation of the sum of squares can be quite tedious and it is convenient to employ expressions that simplify the computational work. Letting $T_{i.}$ denote the total of the observations associated with treatment i (i.e., the sum of the observations in sample i)

and $T_{..}$ denote the grand total of all the data, we may write the computational formulas:

$$SS(T) = \left(\sum_{i=1}^{p} \sum_{k=1}^{n} x_{ik}^2 \right) - \frac{1}{pn} T_{..}^2 \qquad (4.15.1)$$

$$SS(TR) = \frac{1}{n} \cdot \sum_{i=1}^{p} T_{i.}^2 - \frac{1}{pn} T_{..}^2 \qquad (4.15.2)$$

and, by subtraction:

$$SS(E) = SS(T) - SS(TR) \qquad (4.15.3)$$

As for Equations 4.14.1–4.14.2, the derivations of 4.15.1–4.15.3 may be found in more advanced texts.

Returning to our example, we can arrange these simplified formulas as shown in Table 4-3.

Thus, we find

$$T_{..} = 105; \sum_{i=1}^{p} \sum_{k=1}^{n} x_{ik}^2 = 1,029; \quad \text{and} \quad \sum_{i=1}^{p} T_{i.}^2 = 2,781$$

and substituting appropriately we find:

$$SS(T) = 1,029 - \frac{1}{4(3)} (105)^2 = 110.25$$
$$SS(TR) = \frac{1}{3} \cdot 2,781 - \frac{1}{4(3)} (105)^2 = 8.25$$

and, by subtraction,

$$SS(E) = 110.25 - 8.25 = 102$$

These results are identical to those obtained in Table 4-2.

You should recognize that the concepts of one-way ANOVA are defined by Equations 4.14.1 through 4.14.3, but that it is often easier to compute $SS(T)$, $SS(TR)$, and $SS(E)$ using Equations 4.15.1 through 4.15.3 arranged in the format of Table 4-3.

The problems at the end of this chapter should be redone at this point using the computational formulas.

Table 4-3   Table for Arranging Simplified ANOVA Calculations

	x_{ik}	x_{ik}^2	$T_{i.}^2$
Institution A_1	10	100	
	14	196	
	6	36	
Subtotal ($T_1.$)	30		900
Institution A_2	9	81	
	13	169	
	5	25	
Subtotal ($T_2.$)	27		729
Institution A_3	8	64	
	12	144	
	4	16	
Subtotal ($T_3.$)	24		576
Institution A_4	9	81	
	9	81	
	6	36	
Subtotal ($T_4.$)	24		576
Grand Totals	105	1,029	2,781

4.4 TRANSLATION TO MATRIX ALGEBRA[C]

The authors have found that most students of analysis of variance have great difficulties in remembering the required formulas because they are complex. Both sets of Equations 4.14 and 4.15 involve one or two summation signs in each equation. These summation signs obscure the essential nature of ANOVA. This is particularly true when the concepts are extended to two-way ANOVA as in Chapter 5.

Fortunately, matrix algebra simplifies the expression of these summations substantially. We begin by expressing the concept of variance in matrix notation, then proceed to one-way ANOVA.

4.4.1 Variance Expressed in Matrix Notation[C]

Let us introduce a new example for Section 4.4. Let us assume we have data for the number of laboratory tests for each of four patients in three hospitals:

Hospital A:	14	12	13	14
Hospital B:	10	9	11	10
Hospital C:	7	8	6	7

The average number of tests for hospital A is:

$$\frac{1}{4}(14 + 12 + 13 + 14) = 13.25$$

For B the average is 10, while for C it is 7, and the overall mean is 10.083. To find the variance within any one of the hospitals, we employ the general formula:

$$s^2 = \frac{\sum\limits_{k=1}^{n}(x_k - \bar{x})^2}{n - 1} \tag{4.16.1}$$

By algebraic manipulation it is easy to derive the computational formula

$$s^2 = \frac{1}{n - 1}\left[\sum_{k=1}^{n} x_k^2 - \frac{\left(\sum\limits_{k=1}^{n} x_k\right)^2}{n}\right] \tag{4.16.2}$$

For hospital B this gives:

$$s_B^2 = \frac{1}{4 - 1}\left[(10^2 + 9^2 + 11^2 + 10^2) - \frac{1}{4}(10 + 9 + 11 + 10)^2\right]$$

$$= \frac{1}{3}\left[402 - \frac{1}{4}(40)^2\right]$$

$$= \frac{1}{3}[402 - 400]$$

$$= \frac{2}{3}$$

$$\cong .6667$$

If we let the matrix

$$\mathbf{X} = \begin{bmatrix} 1 & x_1 \\ 1 & x_2 \\ \vdots & \vdots \\ 1 & x_n \end{bmatrix} \quad \text{and} \quad \mathbf{X}' = \begin{bmatrix} 1 & 1 & \cdots & 1 \\ x_1 & x_2 & \cdots & x_n \end{bmatrix}$$

where $\mathbf{X}$ (and $\mathbf{X}'$) are comprised of a vector of 1s and a vector containing observations on x_i. Thus we know that

$$\mathbf{X}'\mathbf{X} = \begin{bmatrix} n & \Sigma x \\ \Sigma x & \Sigma x^2 \end{bmatrix} \quad \text{and} \quad |\mathbf{X}'\mathbf{X}| = n\Sigma x^2 - (\Sigma x)^2$$

where $|\mathbf{X}'\mathbf{X}|$ is the determinant of $\mathbf{X}'\mathbf{X}$ as defined in Chapter 1. Using these results:

$$s^2 = \frac{1}{n(n-1)} |\mathbf{X}'\mathbf{X}| \qquad (4.16.3)$$

Notice that s^2 is

$$\frac{\text{Sum of Squares}}{(n-1)}$$

and therefore

$$\text{Sum of Squares} = \Sigma(x - \bar{x})^2 = \frac{1}{n} |\mathbf{X}'\mathbf{X}|$$

Therefore, to find the sum of squares for any set of data, define a matrix with a column vector of 1s and a column vector of the data. Although any letters could be used, let us assume for the moment that there are n data elements, and that we call the matrix $\mathbf{X}$. This allows us to state:

$$\text{Sum of Squares} = \frac{1}{n} |\mathbf{X}'\mathbf{X}| \qquad (4.17)$$

For hospital B of our example

$$\mathbf{X}' = \begin{bmatrix} 1 & 1 & 1 & 1 \\ 10 & 9 & 11 & 10 \end{bmatrix} \quad \text{and} \quad \mathbf{X}'\mathbf{X} = \begin{bmatrix} 4 & 40 \\ 40 & 402 \end{bmatrix}$$

As a result, we find:

$$\text{Sum of Squares for } B = \frac{1}{4} \begin{vmatrix} 4 & 40 \\ 40 & 402 \end{vmatrix}$$

$$= \frac{1}{4} [4(402) - (40)^2]$$

$$= 402 - \frac{1}{4} (40)^2$$

$$= 2$$

Then

$$s_B^2 = \frac{\text{Sum of Squares for } B}{n - 1}$$

$$= \frac{2}{3} \cong .6667$$

as before.

4.4.2 One-Way ANOVA in Matrix Notation[C]

From the definitional formulas 4.14.1–4.14.3 we see that

$$SS(T) = \sum_{i=1}^{p} \sum_{k=1}^{n} (x_{ik} - \bar{x}_{..})^2$$

and

$$SS(TR) = \sum_{i=1}^{p} (\bar{x}_{i.} - \bar{x}_{..})^2$$

If we were to create a matrix $\mathbf{X}$ out of a vector of 1s and a vector of x_{ik} data elements (np of them), so that

$$\mathbf{X}' = \begin{bmatrix} 1 & 1 & 1 & 1 & 1 & 1 & \cdots & 1 & \cdots & 1 \\ x_{11} & x_{12} & x_{13} & x_{14} & x_{21} & x_{22} & \cdots & x_{ik} & \cdots & x_{34} \end{bmatrix}$$

then

$$\mathbf{X'X} = \begin{bmatrix} np & \Sigma x \\ \Sigma x & \Sigma x^2 \end{bmatrix}$$

and $SS(T) = \dfrac{1}{np} \, |\mathbf{X'X}|$

Similarly, if we create a matrix $\mathbf{Y}$ out of a vector of 1s and a vector of the $p = 3$ treatment means, $\bar{x}_{i.}$, so that

$$\mathbf{Y'} = \begin{bmatrix} 1 & 1 & 1 \\ \bar{x}_{1.} & \cdot \, \bar{x}_{2.} & \bar{x}_{3.} \end{bmatrix}$$

then

$$\mathbf{Y'Y} = \begin{bmatrix} p & \Sigma\bar{x}_{i.} \\ \Sigma\bar{x}_{i.} & \Sigma\bar{x}_{i.}^2 \end{bmatrix}$$

From Equation 4.14.2 we find:

$$SS(TR) = n \sum_{i=1}^{p} (\bar{x}_{i.} - \bar{x}_{..})^2$$

and, as a result,

$$SS(TR) = \frac{n}{p} \, |\mathbf{Y'Y}|$$

This allows us to state the ANOVA equations in matrix form as:

$$SS(T) = \frac{1}{np} \, |\mathbf{X'X}| \qquad (4.18.1)$$

$$SS(TR) = \frac{n}{p} \, |\mathbf{Y'Y}| \qquad (4.18.2)$$

$$SS(E) = SS(T) - SS(TR) \qquad (4.18.3)$$

4.4.3 Laboratory Tests Example in Matrix Notation[C]

First we restate the data for the number of laboratory tests for the patients in the three hospitals as follows:

					Means
Hospital A:	14	12	13	14	13.25
Hospital B:	10	9	11	10	10
Hospital C:	7	8	6	7	7

To obtain $SS(T)$ we create $\mathbf{X}$, so that

$$\mathbf{X}' = \begin{bmatrix} 1 & 1 & 1 & 1 & 1 & 1 & 1 & 1 & 1 & 1 & 1 & 1 \\ 14 & 12 & 13 & 14 & 10 & 9 & 11 & 10 & 7 & 8 & 6 & 7 \end{bmatrix}$$

Applying Equation 4.18.1, we see that

$$SS(T) = \frac{1}{12} |\mathbf{X}'\mathbf{X}| = \frac{1}{12} \begin{vmatrix} 12 & 121 \\ 121 & 1305 \end{vmatrix}$$

$$= \frac{1}{12} [12(1305) - (121)^2]$$

$$= 1305 - \frac{1}{12} (14641)$$

$$\cong 84.9167$$

To obtain $SS(TR)$ we create $\mathbf{Y}$, such that

$$\mathbf{Y}' = \begin{bmatrix} 1 & 1 & 1 \\ 13.25 & 10 & 7 \end{bmatrix}$$

from which we find:

$$SS(TR) = \frac{4}{3} |\mathbf{Y}'\mathbf{Y}| = \frac{4}{3} \begin{vmatrix} 3 & 30.25 \\ 30.25 & 324.5625 \end{vmatrix}$$

$$= \frac{4}{3} [3(324.5625) - (30.25)^2]$$

$$= 1298.25 - 1220.0833$$

$$= 78.1667$$

Finally,

$$SS(E) = SS(T) - SS(TR)$$
$$\cong 84.9167 - 78.1667$$

$$= 6.75$$

We may now complete the ANOVA table for this problem, as shown in Table 4-4.

The critical test value of $F_{.01}$ for 2 and 9 degrees of freedom is 8.02. Therefore, the computed value of F for this problem far exceeds the critical value, and we reject the null hypothesis, concluding that there are significant differences in the number of laboratory tests received by patients in the three hospitals.

To ensure a thorough understanding of this material, the student should rework the example of Section 4.4 using the definitional and computational formulas of Sections 4.2 and 4.3. In addition, the student should also rework the example of Section 4.1.1 using matrix notation formulas. Finally, the problems at the end of this chapter may now be reworked using matrix notation.

4.5 APPLICATIONS TO HEALTH CARE MANAGEMENT[F]

The techniques described in this chapter are applicable to those situations in which management wishes to examine the differences between three or more means. As such, the use of analysis of variance in health

Table 4-4 ANOVA Table for Laboratory Tests Example

Source	SS	df	MS	F
Treatment (Hospitals)	78.1667	2	39.08335	52.11
Error	6.75	9	.75	
Total	84.9167	11		

care management is almost without limit. In this section, we simply describe situations in which one-way ANOVA is appropriate in a managerial setting.

That hospitals are reimbursed on a cost basis is well known. As a result, the fee structure of the hospital should reflect differences in the costs of each service provided by the institution. Thus, when evaluating the fee structure of the hospital, management might be interested in examining differences in the incurred costs when each service in a well-defined set of services is provided. Suppose that on the basis of historical information we are able to identify the following costs associated with four different occasions on which the services S_1, S_2, S_3, and S_4 were provided.

Service	Occasions			
	1	2	3	4
S_1	$8.00	$9.50	$10.00	$10.50
S_2	10.00	12.00	14.00	16.00
S_3	4.50	5.00	6.50	8.00
S_4	1.50	3.40	5.00	5.50

Without additional information, management could evaluate the differences in the average costs of providing the services S_1, S_2, S_3, and S_4 using one-way ANOVA.

4.6 USE OF THE SPSS BATCH SYSTEM FOR ONE-WAY ANOVA[D]

An understanding of the calculations we have demonstrated for performing analysis of variance thus far is necessary for a good conceptual grasp of ANOVA. However, when performing ANOVA on a large set of data the computational work is considerable and may be prohibitive. This difficulty may be overcome by using one of several computer packages, which eliminates the burden of computation. Here, we present two of the simple SPSS procedures that are useful for performing one-way ANOVA: BREAKDOWN and ONEWAY. We defer discussion of the major procedure, ANOVA, to Chapter 7 in order to utilize the concepts presented in that chapter.

Figure 4-3 presents the cards required to enter the data for the length of stay example first introduced in Section 4.1.1. The first three cards contain Job Control Language (JCL), which is standard for invoking SPSS.

Figure 4-3 SPSS Cards for Performing One-Way ANOVA

```
//UOCC3568      JOB        (HD123456,
//  ),'COLIN M. LAY',MSGLEVEL=2,CLASS=K
//  EXEC SPSSH
//FT08F001   DD   *
10 1
14 1
 6 1
 9 2
13 2
 5 2
 8 3
12 3
 4 3
 9 4
 9 4
 6 4
//SYSIN   DD   *
RUN NAME          ONE-WAY ANOVA DEMONSTRATION - LOS DATA
INPUT MEDIUM      DISK
N OF CASES        UNKNOWN
DATA LIST         FIXED/ 1 LOS 1-2, INST 4
VAR LABELS        LOS,PATIENT LENGTH OF STAY/
                  INST,INSTITUTION WHERE PATIENT TREATED/
BREAKDOWN         TABLES = LOS BY INST
STATISTICS        1
READ INPUT DATA
ONEWAY            LOS BY INST(1,4)/
STATISTICS        1,3
FINISH
/*
```

The fourth JCL card (//FT08F001) introduces the data set. There are two pieces of data for each of the 12 observations, and these are described by the DATA LIST card. Length of stay (LOS) is contained in columns 1 and 2 of each card, and the institution where the patient was treated (INST) is contained in column 4.

The procedure BREAKDOWN (*SPSS,* pp. 249–66) focuses on describing the overall sample and its components in terms of sum, mean, variance, and standard deviation of the dependent variable and the number of observations. The dependent variable in this example is length of stay, and the subsamples are identified by the independent variable, institution, which must be nominal or ordinal. The general (simplest) mode of operation of BREAKDOWN is presented, but the integer mode is more efficient, and the interested reader should refer to the SPSS manual. The general mode for this example is requested by:

BREAKDOWN   TABLES = LOS BY INST

and the STATISTICS card calls for an ANOVA table to be produced. BREAKDOWN can handle several independent variables, but this procedure can only produce a one-way analysis of variance. Therefore, in a different example with several independent variables, BREAKDOWN could be used to produce a hierarchical (tree-like) description of the sample and the subsamples, but would produce only a one-way ANOVA table for the first variable specified after the "BY", if STATISTIC 1 were specified. The output for our simple example is shown in Figure 4-4. The first page of output shows the sum, mean, standard deviation, variance, and number of cases for the entire sample and each subsample, while the sums of squares and the ANOVA table are presented on the second page. If the independent variable had been comprised of only two categories, SPSS would have automatically replaced the analysis of variance by a *t*-test of the difference between the two means.

The ONEWAY (*SPSS*, pp. 422–33) procedure that is requested following the READ INPUT DATA card is a second example of the performance of one-way ANOVA. This procedure is limited to one-way ANOVA, but it has a number of extra capabilities that make it more attractive than BREAKDOWN.

In Figure 4–3 the performance of the analysis of variance is requested by:

ONEWAY   LOS BY INST (1,4)/

which differs from the specification of BREAKDOWN by the *required* addition of the lowest and highest integer values (1,4) of the independent variable, INST. The slash (/) at the end of the line indicates the end of the specification of the dependent and independent variables, and the beginning of one of the other facilities of the procedure. These other facilities are beyond the scope of this chapter and their discussion is deferred to Chapter 6.

STATISTICS 1 requests a set of statistics for each group or subsample identified by the independent variable. These include: the group number, number of cases, mean and standard deviation of the group, standard error of the mean, minimum and maximum observed values of the dependent variable, and the 95 percent confidence interval for the mean of the group.

The output of this procedure is shown in Figure 4-5. The ANOVA table is shown first, followed by the statistics requested by the STATISTICS card.

Most APL systems have analysis of variance programs included, and in our system the program (function) to perform one-way ANOVA is called ANOVA2 (the choice of the number for the name is unfortunately not very meaningful). Referring to Exhibit 4-1 the program is stored in the ANOVPRAC workspace in library 3176 (Appendix E). This workspace

Figure 4-4 BREAKDOWN Ouput for One-Way ANOVA

```
ONE-WAY ANOVA DEMONSTRATION - LOS DATA
FILE  NONAME  (CREATION DATE = 04/18/79)                                    04/18/79        PAGE  2

- - - - - - - - - - - - - -  D E S C R I P T I O N   O F   S U B P O P U L A T I O N S  - - - - - - - - -
CRITERION VARIABLE   LOS    PATIENT LENGTH OF STAY
  BROKEN DOWN BY     INST   INSTITUTION WHERE PATIENT TREATED
- - - - - - - - - - - - - - - - - - - - - - - - - - - - - - - - - - - - - - - - - - - - - - - - - - - -

VARIABLE                CODE   VALUE LABEL        SUM        MEAN      STD DEV    VARIANCE     N
FOR ENTIRE POPULATION                         105.0000     8.7500     3.1659     10.0227    ( 12)

INST                    1.                     30.0000    10.0000     4.0000     16.0000       3
INST                    2.                     27.0000     9.0000     4.0000     16.0000       3
INST                    3.                     24.0000     8.0000     4.0000     16.0000       3
INST                    4.                     24.0000     8.0000     1.7321      3.0000       3

TOTAL CASES =   12
```

```
ONE-WAY ANOVA DEMONSTRATION - LOS DATA                                       04/18/79        PAGE  3
CRITERION VARIABLE LOS

- - - - - - - - - - - - - -  A N A L Y S I S   O F   V A R I A N C E  - - - - - - - - - - - - - - - - -

VARIABLE                CODE   VALUE LABEL        SUM        MEAN      STD DEV   SUM OF SQ      N
INST                    1.                     30.0000    10.0000     4.0000     32.0000       3
INST                    2.                     27.0000     9.0000     4.0000     32.0000       3
INST                    3.                     24.0000     8.0000     4.0000     32.0000       3
INST                    4.                     24.0000     8.0000     1.7321      6.0000       3
WITHIN GROUPS TOTAL                           105.0000     8.7500     3.5707    102.0000    ( 12)
```

```
*************************************************************************
*                                                                       *
*             A N A L Y S I S   O F   V A R I A N C E                    *
*                                                                       *
*   SOURCE           SUM OF SQUARES   D.F.   MEAN SQUARE     F     SIG.   *
*                                                                       *
*   BETWEEN GROUPS        8.250        3        2.750      0.216  0.8828 *
*                                                                       *
*   WITHIN GROUPS       102.000        8       12.750                    *
*                                                                       *
*          ETA = 0.2736        ETA SQUARED = 0.0748                      *
*                                                                       *
*************************************************************************
```

Figure 4-5 Output of SPSS Procedure ONEWAY (Simplest Features)

```
ONE-WAY ANOVA DEMONSTRATION - LOS DATA                                    04/18/79        PAGE  5
FILE   NONAME   (CREATION DATE = 04/18/79)
- - - - - - - - - - - - - - - - - - O N E W A Y - - - - - - - - - - - - - - - - - - - - - -

     VARIABLE  LOS          PATIENT LENGTH OF STAY

                                      ANALYSIS OF VARIANCE

            SOURCE            D.F.    SUM OF SQUARES   MEAN SQUARES   F RATIO    F PROB.

     BETWEEN GROUPS            3          8.2500         2.7500        0.216     0.8828

     WITHIN GROUPS             8        102.0000        12.7500

     TOTAL                    11        110.2500
```

GROUP	COUNT	MEAN	STANDARD DEVIATION	STANDARD ERROR	MINIMUM	MAXIMUM	95 PCT CONF INT FOR MEAN
GRP01	3	10.0000	4.0000	2.3094	6.0000	14.0000	-0.0633 TO 19.9350
GRP02	3	9.0000	4.0000	2.3094	5.0000	13.0000	-0.9367 TO 13.9300
GRP03	3	8.0000	4.0000	2.3094	4.0000	12.0000	-1.9367 TO 17.9366
GRP04	3	8.0000	1.7321	1.0000	6.0000	9.0000	3.6973 TO 12.3027
TOTAL	12	8.7500	3.1659	0.9139	4.0000	14.0000	6.7385 TO 10.7615

```
TESTS FOR HOMOGENEITY OF VARIANCES

     COCHRANS C = MAX. VARIANCE/SUM(VARIANCES) =  0.3137,  P =  0.970  (APPROX.)
     BARTLETT-BOX F =                             0.417,  P =  0.741
     MAXIMUM VARIANCE / MINIMUM VARIANCE =        5.333
```

Exhibit 4-1

```
        )LOAD ANOVFRAC,3176
SAVED  17,09/ 79,107/ 9416

        A← 10 14 6      9 13 5      8 12 4      9 9 6
        AA←Q (4 3)  P A
        AA
            10              9              8              9
            14             13             12              9
             6              5              4              6


        ANOVA2 AA

             1              3             10              0
             2              3              9              0
             3              3              8              0
             4              3              8              0
             3           8,25           2,75    ,2156862745
             8            102          12,75              0
            11        110,25    3,570714214              0
```

must be)LOADed before we can enter the data. Using the example of the
lengths of stay from Section 4.1, we type the data as a vector and assign it
to **A**. We then reshape it into a matrix and transpose it, so that each column
of **AA** represents the treatments (hospitals). (ANOVA2 requires that the
data be entered in column form.) As usual, printing the matrix allows us to
check for any typing errors that might have occurred.

The program is requested to work on **AA** by typing 'ANOVA2 AA'.

The first p (4) rows of output give the treatment numbers in the first
column, the numbers of observations in the second column, and the
averages for the treatments (hospitals) in the third. The fourth column is
filled with zeros (for the programmer's convenience of creating the results
as one large matrix).

The next three rows give the F table with the treatment, error, and total
sources of variance. In this part of the matrix the first column gives the
numbers of degrees of freedom, and the second the sums of squares. The
third column gives the treatment mean square (2.75), the error mean
square (12.75), and the square root of the error mean square (3.5707).
The fourth column is used only for the F ratio.

In Exhibit 4-2 we start to show the use of APL for solving the one-way
ANOVA using matrix algebra. The data have already been entered as the

Exhibit 4-2

```
        A
 10    14   6   9   13   5   8   12   4   9   9   6
       PA
 12
       XT← (2 12)  P  (12P1),A
       X←⍉XT
       PX
 12   2
       PXT
  2   12
       )DIGITS 3
WAS   10
       XT
  1    1   1   1    1   1   1    1   1   1   1   1
 10    14   6   9   13   5   8   12   4   9   9   6
       )DIGITS 10
WAS    3
```

Exhibit 4-3

```
       XTX←XT  +.×  X

       M←'99,999,990.99'
       M $ XTX
          12.00              105.00
         105.00            1,029.00

       DET XTX
 1323
       DETXTX←DET XTX
       P←4
       N←3

       SST←  (1÷P×N)  ×  DETXTX
       SST
 110.25
```

vector **A**, and it is used with a row vector of 1s to form the matrix **XT** (**X** transpose) which is itself transposed to obtain **X** [remember that (**X**')' = **X**]. The command ')DIGITs 3' is used to force APL to print only three significant digits, which is a sufficient number in this case to allow printing **XT** in as short a line as possible. The normal number of digits printed is 10, and we reset it to 10 after printing *XT*.

In Exhibit 4-3 we calculate the total sum of squares, *SST*, starting with the matrix multiplication which gives *XTX* (which is **X**'**X**), and its printing under format control (M$XTX). As discussed in Chapter 2, the function DET finds the determinant of any square matrix, such as *XTX* for which the value is 1323. P, N, and DETXTX are used in finding *SST* by means of Equation 4.18.1.

In Exhibit 4-4 we calculate the treatment sum of squares, *SSTR*. First we find the mean LOS for the 4 hospitals (MEANS) and then create *YT* and *Y*, with a vector of *1's* and the vector of means. This is followed by the

Exhibit 4-4

```
     MEANS←(+/AA)÷N

     YT←(2 4) ρ (4ρ1),MEANS
     YT
         1            1            1            1
        10            9            8            8

     Y←⍉YT
     YTY←YT +.× Y
     M2←'99,990.9999'

     M2 $ YTY
     4.0000      35.0000
    35.0000     309.0000

     DETYTY ← DET YTY
     DETYTY
 11

     SSTR←(N÷P)×DETYTY
     SSTR
 8.25
```

Exhibit 4-5

```
    SSE←SST-SSTR
    SSE
102

    MSTR←SSTR÷P-1
    MSTR
2.75

    MSE←SSE÷P×(N-1)
    MSE
12.75

    F←MSTR÷MSE
    F
.2156862745
```

multiplication to obtain YTY $(\mathbf{Y}'\mathbf{Y})$. The determinant is taken as DET YTY and used in Equation 4.18.2 with n/p to find $SSTR$.

Exhibit 4-5 shows the calculations for the error sum of squares as $SST-SSTR$. The final entries illustrate the appropriate mean sums of squares, and the F ratio for one-way ANOVA.

This completes the discussion of the use of the computer for performing one-way analysis of variance. At this point the student may work out one or more of the examples or problems at the end of the chapter using SPSS. To perform the matrix operations in APL the program DET must be available (see Appendix E). The user should check with a statistics consultant or an APL supplier to determine the availability of ANOVA2 or its equivalent.

BIBLIOGRAPHY

Katzan, H., Jr. *APL Programming and Computer Techniques.* New York: Van Nostrand Reinhold, 1970.
Nie, N. H.; Hull, C. H.; Jenkins, J. G.; Steinbrenner, K.; and Bent, D. H. *SPSS: Statistical Package for the Social Sciences*, 2nd ed. New York: McGraw-Hill, 1975.
Winer, B. J. *Statistical Principles in Experimental Design.* New York: McGraw-Hill, 1971.

Problems for Solution[G]

1. A random sample of 5 employees from each of 3 departments in the hospital shows the following numbers of days absent over the past year:

   Radiology: 3 2 4 1 2
   Laboratory: 2 4 3 3 2
   Housekeeping: 4 5 6 4 3

   Testing at the .05 level, are the differences among the departments significant?

2. A random sample of 4 family medicine physicians (with approximately the same total patient load) practicing in 4 different cities, shows the following number of referrals in a given month:

   City A: 13   15   12   14
   City B: 17   16   19   19
   City C: 10   14   12   11
   City D: 8   6   9   10

   Testing at the .01 level, are there significant differences among the referral volumes in the different cities?

3. A random sample of operating room times (minutes) for a particular operative procedure at 5 different hospitals shows:

   Hospital I: 35   30   39   32
   Hospital II: 42   47   41   38
   Hospital III: 29   32   37   30
   Hospital IV: 48   46   42   44
   Hospital V: 28   33   39   34

   Testing at the .05 level, are the differences among the hospitals' patterns of operating times significant?

Chapter 5

Two-Way Analysis
of Variance

Objectives

After completing this chapter, you should be able to:

1. Differentiate between one-way and two-way analysis of variance (with and without interaction).
2. Describe the concept of interaction and how interaction can alter or mask the main effects of the variables being studied.
3. Define the structural model and null hypotheses for each type of ANOVA.
4. Define the data collection design matrix for each type of ANOVA.
5. Define the sums of squares components model for each type of ANOVA.
6. Perform the calculations for two-way analysis of variance (with and without interaction), display the results in an ANOVA table, and test the components for significance.
7. Use APL to perform two-way ANOVA.

Chapter Map

In this chapter the introductory sections with letter code A include 5.1, 5.2, 5.2.2, 5.3, and 5.3.1.

The sections using ordinary algebra in the development of formulas (code B) include 5.2.1, 5.2.3 through 5.2.5.1, and 5.3.2 through 5.3.6.

Matrix algebra formulas are developed and used in Sections 5.2.6, 5.2.7, and 5.3.7, and these sections have been assigned code C.

Section 5.4 and all of its subsections are devoted to the use of APL and have been assigned code E.

5.1 INTRODUCTION(A)

In Chapter 4 we studied one-way ANOVA and used it to determine whether there are differences among the means of three or more groups. In basic statistics, inferences can be made about the differences between the means of only two groups. One-way ANOVA extends this capability to accommodate three or more groups. In this chapter we extend the analytical tools to investigate differences among groups classified on the basis of two or more *factors* that might cause variation.

In one-way ANOVA we examined the effects of differences among groups classified on one dimension, which we called the *treatment effect*. We saw that the treatment factor could be the group of hospitals studied, or a group of departments within a hospital, or a group of operative procedures. The treatment factor is sometimes called the *independent* variable, while the variation being studied is a property of the *dependent* variable. In the first example presented in Chapter 4, the dependent variable was the length of stay in the hospital for each of several patients. In the second example, the dependent variable was the number of lab tests for each patient. In each of these two examples, the *unit of analysis*, or the *case*, is the individual patient.

In Chapters 5 and 6 we examine the effects of two or more factors (or independent variables) on the variability in the dependent variable. The tools we describe are two-way and factorial analysis of variance.

Two-way ANOVA deals with two factors, while factorial ANOVA deals with two or more factors. Two-way ANOVA with interaction is the simplest form of factorial ANOVA. In two-way or factorial analysis, each case must be classified on each of the dimensions (factors or independent variables), and the dependent variable must be measured as before. The factors might be hospital and type of illness, as in the first example in this chapter; or department and category of employee; or type of physician and type of practice setting; or type of illness and presence or absence of infection; and so on, for two-factor experiments. A three-factor experiment might have department, category, and sex of employee; or type of physician, type of illness, and infection status; and so forth, as the independent factors. The dependent variable might be length of stay, or number of lab tests, or number of days of sick leave taken, or number of referrals, or cost of treatment, or many other phenomena of interest, depending on the objectives of the study.

5.2 TWO-WAY ANOVA WITHOUT INTERACTION(A)

Let us return to the example of patient length of stay introduced in

Section 4.1. In this illustration, the length of stay was recorded for three patients in each of four institutions as follows:

Institution A_1: 10, 14, 6
Institution A_2: 9, 13, 5
Institution A_3: 8, 12, 4
Institution A_4: 9, 9, 6

We saw earlier that the average lengths of stay in the four institutions were 10, 9, 8, and 8 days, respectively.

When we examined the mean stays of the four institutions, we found that the differences among the average lengths of stay were not significant. Recall that the differences were not significant, because there was considerable variation within the four samples resulting in a large experimental error. Since this value appeared in the denominator of the F statistic, the resulting variance ratio was too small to be significant.

Now, suppose that the first value associated with each institution is associated with a patient who was hospitalized with acute appendicitis; the second value is associated with a patient who was hospitalized with arteriosclerotic heart disease; and the third value is associated with a patient hospitalized with an acute respiratory infection. This specification adds a new dimension to our experiment. We now find that the mean stay associated with all patients hospitalized with acute appendicitis, which is represented by the subscript a, is:

$$\bar{x}_a = \frac{10 + 9 + 8 + 9}{4} = \frac{36}{4} = 9 \text{ days}$$

while the mean stay associated with all patients hospitalized with arteriosclerotic heart disease, which is represented by the subscript hd, is:

$$\bar{x}_{hd} = \frac{14 + 13 + 12 + 9}{4} = \frac{48}{4} = 12 \text{ days}$$

Similarly, the mean stay experienced by patients hospitalized with an acute respiratory infection, which is represented by the subscript r, is:

$$\bar{x}_r = \frac{6 + 5 + 4 + 6}{4} = \frac{21}{4} = 5.25 \text{ days}$$

This new dimension implies that a portion of the unexplained variance in the one-way analysis, $SS(E)$, may be attributable to the different conditions for which the patients were hospitalized.

This suggests that we should have performed a two-way analysis of variance in which the total variability in the length of stay data is partitioned into *three* components. The first component reflects differences due to one variable, which we referred to as *treatments* (i.e., factor A, which is defined as the different institutions in our example), while the second component reflects differences attributable to a second variable, factor B, which we refer to as *blocks* (i.e., the conditions for which patients were hospitalized). The third component contains the unexplained variation and is referred to as the *experimental error*. The terms *treatments* and *blocks* are historical remnants because of the development of ANOVA in agricultural research on the effectiveness of different seed treatments.

Before proceeding further, it is necessary to point out that there are essentially two different approaches to the analysis of two-variable experiments. The approaches depend on whether the interaction between two variables, A and B, can be measured, or not. We consider first the situation in which no interaction can be measured, and then we return to an analysis of the two variables, A and B, with interaction in the next section.

5.2.1 The Structural Model for Two-Way ANOVA Without Interaction[B]

The first major task in two-way analysis of variance is to specify the hypotheses to be examined. Let us simplify the task by letting μ_{ij} correspond to the true mean of treatment i and block j. Thus, in terms of our example, μ_{ij} corresponds to the true mean stay of institution i and condition j. As a result, we may express the true mean stay of institution i and condition j by the structural model:

$$\mu_{ij} = \mu + \alpha_i + \beta_j \qquad (5.1)$$

As before, μ is the grand mean or the mean of all x_{ij} while the α_i are the treatment effects. Accordingly, we refer to the β_j as the block effects. We use p as the maximum number of treatment categories, and q as the maximum number of block categories. In two-way ANOVA *without* interaction there is only *one* observation for each combined category of treatment and block, so that $n = 1$. Therefore, there are pq observations or cases in total.

We may now write the two null hypotheses we wish to examine as:

$$H_{01}\colon \alpha_1 = \alpha_2 = \cdots = \alpha_p = 0 \qquad \textbf{(5.2.1)}$$

$$H_{02}\colon \beta_1 = \beta_2 = \cdots = \beta_q = 0 \qquad \textbf{(5.2.2)}$$

The alternative to the first of the null hypotheses is that some of the treatment effects, α_i, are not equal to zero. Similarly, the alternative to the second hypothesis is that some of the block effects, β_j, are not equal to zero. However, regardless of the truth of the null hypotheses, it is necessary that $\Sigma_i\, \alpha_i = 0$ and $\Sigma_j\, \beta_j = 0$ (exactly), since $(1/pq)\, \Sigma_i\, \Sigma_j\, \mu_{ij} = \mu$.

5.2.2 The Design Matrix for Two-Way ANOVA(A)

As with one-way analysis of variance, the data collection design can be shown as a matrix. There are 2 dimensions, institutions and disease categories, but only 1 patient is observed for each combination. As shown in Figure 5-1, we define the 4 rows of the matrix by the institutions and the 3 columns by the disease categories. In this case, there are $4 \times 3 = 12$ patients to be observed. In general, pq observations are required if there is 1 observation per cell in the design.

5.2.3 Definitional and Computational Formulas(B)

The two null hypotheses to be tested are $H_{01}\colon \alpha_i = 0$ for all values of i, and $H_{02}\colon \beta_j = 0$ for all values of j. The first of these corresponds to the

Figure 5-1 Data Collection Design Matrix for Two-Way ANOVA for Patient LOS

		1 (*a*)	2 (*hd*)	3 (*r*)
Institutions	A_1			
	A_2			
	A_3			
	A_4			

treatment effect in one-way analysis of variance, but the formulas for $SS(T)$ and $SS(TR)$ must be modified slightly (see Winer or Kirk for the detailed development). Given that each treatment mean is based on q observations, the total and treatment sums of squares are given by:

$$SS(T) = \sum_{i=1}^{p} \sum_{j=1}^{q} (x_{ij} - \bar{x}_{..})^2 \qquad (5.3.1)$$

$$SS(TR) = q \sum_{i=1}^{p} (\bar{x}_{i.} - \bar{x}_{..})^2 \qquad (5.3.2)$$

respectively. The equations are structurally identical to 4.14.1 and 4.14.2, but several differences should be noted. First, references to subscript k in Equation 4.14.1 have been replaced by references to subscript j in Equation 5.3.1. Further, since the number of elements in each treatment is nq, where n is 1, the n that appears in Equation 4.14.2 is replaced by q in Equation 5.3.2.

In order to test the second of the null hypotheses, we require a quantity that is similar to $SS(TR)$ but measures the variation of the means obtained for the various blocks (e.g., the means of 9, 12, and 5.25 days obtained for the three different conditions) instead of the variation in the means obtained for the different treatments. Such a measure may be defined by:

$$SS(B) = p \sum_{j=1}^{q} (\bar{x}_{.j} - \bar{x}_{..})^2 \qquad (5.3.3)$$

$$SS(E) = SS(T) - SS(TR) - SS(B) \qquad (5.3.4)$$

Note that $\bar{x}_{.j}$ corresponds to the mean of block j, and p corresponds to the number of treatments. Also note that $SS(B)$ is structurally similar to $SS(TR)$.

Equations 5.3.1 through 5.3.4 represent the definitional formulas for two-way analysis of variance without interaction, and the purpose of the following discussion is to present the computational expressions that are employed when calculating the components $SS(T)$, $SS(TR)$, $SS(B)$, and $SS(E)$. Let $T_{i.}$ refer to the total for treatment i, $T_{.j}$ represent the total for block j, and $T_{..}$ represent the grand total for all observations. After substituting n for q and k for j into Equations 4.15.1 and 4.15.2, the computational formulas for $SS(T)$ and $SS(TR)$ in two-way analysis of variance without interaction are given by Equations 5.4.1 and 5.4.2, shown next, while Equations 5.4.3 and 5.4.4 give $SS(B)$ and $SS(E)$, respectively.

$$SS(T) = \sum_{i=1}^{p} \sum_{j=1}^{q} x^2_{ij} - \frac{1}{pq} T^2_{..} \qquad (5.4.1)$$

$$SS(TR) = \frac{1}{q} \sum_{i=1}^{p} T^2_{i.} - \frac{1}{pq} T^2_{..} \qquad (5.4.2)$$

$$SS(B) = \frac{1}{p} \sum_{j=1}^{q} T^2_{.j} - \frac{1}{pq} T^2_{..} \qquad (5.4.3)$$

$$SS(E) = SS(T) - SS(TR) - SS(B) \qquad (5.4.4)$$

Observe that the error sum of squares here is not the same as that in one-way ANOVA. As we will see in our example, $SS(T)$ and $SS(TR)$ are computationally and numerically identical to one-way ANOVA, which implies that

$$SS(E, \text{one-way}) = SS(B) + SS(E, \text{two-way}) \qquad (5.5)$$

Equation 5.5 shows that the inclusion of a second factor, which is represented by the various disease categories in our example, permits a more precise examination of the first factor, which was represented by the different institutions.

5.2.4 The ANOVA Table: Two Way without Interaction[B]

Systematizing our computational work as before, it is convenient to construct a two-way analysis of variance table with no interaction as shown in Table 5-1. Substituting q in place of n, the degrees of freedom for $SS(T)$ and $SS(TR)$ are obtained as before. The number of degrees of freedom associated with the block effect is $(q - 1)$, while the error degrees of freedom is $(q - 1)(p - 1)$. The reader should verify that the degrees of freedom specified in the table are additive. In the significance test for the *treatment* effects, the degrees of freedom associated with the numerator and denominator of the F statistic are $(p - 1)$ and $(q - 1)(p - 1)$, respectively. Similarly, the degrees of freedom in the numerator and denomi-

Table 5-1 Model Two-Way Analysis of Variance Table: No Interaction

Source of Variation	df	SS	MS	F
Treatment	$p - 1$	$SS(TR)$	$MS(TR) = \dfrac{SS(TR)}{p - 1}$	$\dfrac{MS(TR)}{MS(E)}$
Block	$q - 1$	$SS(B)$	$MS(B) = \dfrac{SS(B)}{q - 1}$	$\dfrac{MS(B)}{MS(E)}$
Error	$(q - 1)(p - 1)$	$SS(E)$	$MS(E) = \dfrac{SS(E)}{(q - 1)(p - 1)}$	
Total	$qp - 1$	$SS(T)$		

nator of the F statistic by which the significance of the *block* effects are evaluated are $(q - 1)$ and $(q - 1)(p - 1)$, respectively.

5.2.5 Patient LOS Example: Two-Way ANOVA without Interaction[B]

In the patient LOS example, the totals are: for the Institutions, $T_{i.}$: 30, 27, 24, and 24; for the Diseases, $T_{.j}$: 36, 48, and 21; and overall, $T_{..} = 105$; while $\sum^p_{i=1} \sum^q_{j=1} x^2_{ij} = 1029$. Thus, using the computational expressions previously presented, we find:

$$SS(T) = 1029 - \frac{1}{12} (105)^2 = 110.25$$

$$SS(TR) = \frac{1}{3} (900 + 729 + 576 + 576) - \frac{1}{12} (105)^2 = 8.25$$

$$SS(B) = \frac{1}{4} (36 + 48 + 21) - \frac{1}{12} (105)^2 = 91.5$$

$$SS(E) = 110.25 - 8.25 - 91.5 = 10.5$$

Note that $SS(T)$ and $SS(TR)$ are identical to the values calculated in Chapter 4 and that the one-way ANOVA $SS(E)$ was 102, which is the sum of $SS(B)$ and $SS(E,$ two-way).

5.2.5.1 The ANOVA Table for Patient LOS[B]

Let us now turn our attention to the analysis of the variance table corresponding to our example shown in Table 5-2. Considering the treatment effects first and letting $\alpha = .05$ as the level of significance, we find that the value of $F_{.05}$ for 3 and 6 degrees of freedom is 4.75, which exceeds 1.57. Hence, the null hypothesis concerning the equality of the mean stays associated with the four institutions cannot be rejected. However, when we consider the block effects, we find that the value of $F_{.05}$ for 2 and 6 degrees of freedom is 5.14, which is exceeded by the calculated F value of 26.14. Thus, we reject the null hypothesis that the block effects are zero and conclude that there is a difference in the mean stays experienced by patients hospitalized with acute appendicitis, arteriosclerotic heart disease, and acute respiratory infections.

Note that when the block effect is identified separately, the error sum of squares and mean square are substantially smaller than they were in the one-way ANOVA. A reduction in the value of $MS(E)$ leads to a larger F value for the treatment effect, which, in our example, is still insignificant.

At this point, the reader should establish mastery of this material by constructing an analysis of variance table for either or both of Problems 1 and 2 at the end of this chapter.

Table 5-2 Two-Way Analysis of Variance Table for Patient LOS

Source of Variation	df	SS	MS	F
Treatment (Institution)	3	8.25	2.75	1.57
Block (Disease Category)	2	91.50	45.75	26.14
Error	6	10.50	1.75	
Total	11	110.25		

5.2.6 Two-Way ANOVA without Interaction: Matrix Notation [C]

As in one-way ANOVA, matrix notation can be used to simplify the expression of the sums of squares equations. Here we use notation that is compatible with and extends the matrix operations presented in Chapter 4. We create three matrices $\mathbf{X}$, $\mathbf{Y}$, and $\mathbf{Z}$ so that: $\mathbf{X}$ is of order $pq \times 2$ and contains a vector of 1s and a vector of all the raw data; $\mathbf{Y}$ is of order $p \times 2$ and contains a vector of 1s and a vector of treatment means; and, $\mathbf{Z}$, is of order $q \times 2$ and contains a vector of 1s and a vector of block means. Thus, we find:

$$\mathbf{X}' = \begin{bmatrix} 1 & 1 & \cdots & 1 & \cdots & 1 \\ x_{11} & x_{12} & \cdots & x_{ij} & \cdots & x_{pq} \end{bmatrix} \text{ with } pq \text{ elements/row} \quad (5.6.1)$$

$$\mathbf{Y}' = \begin{bmatrix} 1 & 1 & \cdots & 1 & \cdots & 1 \\ \bar{x}_{1.} & \bar{x}_{2.} & \cdots & \bar{x}_{i.} & \cdots & \bar{x}_{p.} \end{bmatrix} \text{ with } p \text{ elements/row} \quad (5.6.2)$$

$$\mathbf{Z}' = \begin{bmatrix} 1 & 1 & \cdots & 1 & \cdots & 1 \\ \bar{x}_{.1} & \bar{x}_{.2} & \cdots & \bar{x}_{.i} & \cdots & \bar{x}_{.q} \end{bmatrix} \text{ with } q \text{ elements/row} \quad (5.6.3)$$

The formulas for the sums of squares are:

$$SS(T) = \frac{1}{pq} \, |\mathbf{X}'\mathbf{X}| \qquad (5.7.1)$$

$$SS(TR) = \frac{q}{p} \, |\mathbf{Y}'\mathbf{Y}| \qquad (5.7.2)$$

$$SS(B) = \frac{p}{q} \, |\mathbf{Z}'\mathbf{Z}| \qquad (5.7.3)$$

$$SS(E) = SS(T) - SS(TR) - SS(B) \qquad (5.7.4)$$

The fact that these are identical to the definitional formulas presented earlier is easily verified. The reader should note the pattern of p's and q's carefully. In each case the *denominator* is given by the length of the vector of data.

5.2.7 Patient LOS Example Using Matrix Formulas[C]

For the patient length of stay example the raw data matrix is:

$$\mathbf{X'} = \begin{bmatrix} 1 & 1 & 1 & 1 & 1 & 1 & 1 & 1 & 1 & 1 & 1 & 1 \\ 10 & 14 & 6 & 9 & 13 & 5 & 8 & 12 & 4 & 9 & 9 & 6 \end{bmatrix}$$

from which we find:

$$\mathbf{X'X} = \begin{bmatrix} 12 & 105 \\ 105 & 1029 \end{bmatrix}$$

Applying Equation 5.7.1 yields:

$$SS(T) = \frac{1}{12} |\mathbf{X'X}| = \frac{1}{12}(12 \times 1029 - 105^2) = 110.25$$

The matrix of treatment (hospital) means is:

$$\mathbf{Y'} = \begin{bmatrix} 1 & 1 & 1 & 1 \\ 10 & 9 & 8 & 8 \end{bmatrix}$$

from which we find:

$$\mathbf{Y'Y} = \begin{bmatrix} 4 & 35 \\ 35 & 309 \end{bmatrix}$$

An application of Equation 5.7.2 yields:

$$SS(TR) = \frac{3}{4} |\mathbf{Y'Y}| = \frac{3}{4}(4 \times 309 - 35^2) = 927 - 918.75 = 8.25$$

The matrix of block (disease) means is:

$$\mathbf{Z'} = \begin{bmatrix} 1 & 1 & 1 \\ 9 & 12 & 5.25 \end{bmatrix}$$

from which we obtain:

$$\mathbf{Z'Z} = \begin{bmatrix} 3 & 26.25 \\ 26.25 & 252.5625 \end{bmatrix}$$

An application of Equation 5.7.3 yields:

$$SS(B) = \frac{4}{3} |\mathbf{Z'Z}| = \frac{4}{3} (3 \times 252.5625 - 26.25^2)$$

$$= 1010.25 - 918.75$$
$$= 91.5$$

Finally, after substituting appropriately into Equation 5.7.4, we obtain:

$$SS(E) = 110.25 - 8.25 - 91.5$$
$$= 10.5$$

These results are identical to those found in Section 5.2.4, and can be used to construct the ANOVA table (Table 5-2).

At this stage the reader should use the matrix formulas to reformulate and solve Problems 1 and 2 at the end of the chapter.

5.3 TWO-WAY ANALYSIS OF VARIANCE: INTERACTION[A]

We now turn attention to the second of the two approaches to two-way analysis of variance. In this section we consider situations in which the interaction of the two variables can be measured. In analyzing such situations we usually replicate all or part of the experiment and employ factorial analysis of variance to detect the interactive effects as well as the main effects of the two factors considered.

To illustrate this technique, let us consider a slightly different example. Suppose that the data presented in Table 5-3 represent the number of laboratory procedures provided by three institutions to similar inpatients who have been admitted with the four conditions that have been identified for analysis. In this situation, we wish to examine: (1) differences in the use of laboratory services that are attributable to the different medical conditions, (2) differences in the use of laboratory services that are attributable to the different institutions, and (3) differences in use that are attributable to the interaction between the different institutions and medical conditions.

Table 5-3 Data for Laboratory Tests Example

Condition (Factor A) (Treatments)		Institution (Factor B)		
		(B_1)	(B_2) (Blocks)	(B_3)
Pregnancy	(A_1)	1, 3, 5	6, 4, 7	8, 9, 10
Malignant Neoplasm	(A_2)	4, 7, 5	7, 8, 9	2, 5, 6
Trauma	(A_3)	1, 2, 4	3, 7, 6	1, 4, 5
Appendicitis	(A_4)	2, 1, 5	1, 2, 4	8, 9, 11

In connection with the interactive effect, it is quite possible for one of the institutions to treat the more serious conditions and, as a result, provide a different quantity of laboratory services in diagnosing and monitoring the presenting conditions relative to the other institutions.

5.3.1 The Data Collection Design Matrix[A]

The model for data collection can be represented by a matrix with p rows for treatments, q columns for blocks, and n observations per cell. For our laboratory example, there are $p = 4$ conditions (treatments), $q = 3$ institutions (blocks), and $n = 3$ patients (observations) per cell. The design is diagrammed in Figure 5-2.

Figure 5-2 Data Collection Design Matrix for Laboratory Tests Example

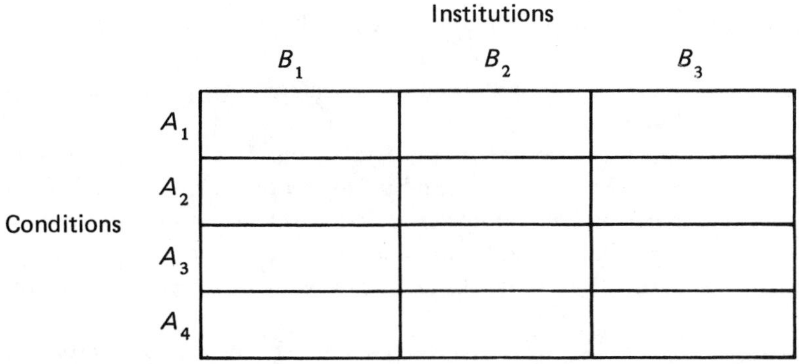

5.3.2 The Structural Model: Two-Way ANOVA with Interaction[B]

We may now write the true mean corresponding to treatment i and block j in the form of the structural model:

$$\mu_{ij} = \mu + \alpha_i + \beta_j + \alpha\beta_{ij} \tag{5.8}$$

where μ and the α's and the β's are defined as before, while the $\alpha\beta$'s correspond to the interactive effects. Thus, in addition to the null hypotheses

$$H_{01}: \alpha_1 = \alpha_2 = \cdots \alpha_p = 0 \tag{5.9.1}$$

and

$$H_{02}: \beta_1 = \beta_2 = \cdots \beta_q = 0 \tag{5.9.2}$$

we also test the null hypothesis that there is no interaction between the two variables:

$$H_{03}: \alpha\beta_{11} = \alpha\beta_{12} = \cdots = \alpha\beta_{pq} = 0 \tag{5.9.3}$$

Note that the treatment effects *must* sum to zero (i.e., $\sum_i \alpha_i = 0$), as must the block effects ($\sum_j \beta_j = 0$), and the interaction effects ($\sum_i \sum_j \alpha\beta_{ij} = 0$).

5.3.3 Algebraic Notation: Two-Way ANOVA with Interaction[B]

In developing the structural model, the null hypotheses, and the definitional and computational equations we use the following notation:

1. x_{ijk} represents observation k associated with treatment i and block j.
2. $T_{ij.} = \sum_{k=1}^{n} x_{ijk}$ represents the total of the n observations associated with the cell corresponding to treatment i and block j. (The *dot* subscript indicates that the corresponding subscript has been eliminated by summation.)
3. $\bar{x}_{ij.} = (1/n) T_{ij.}$ represents the mean of the n observations of treatment i and block j.
4. $T_{i..} = \sum_{j=1}^{q} \sum_{k=1}^{n} x_{ijk}$ represents the total of the qn observations associated with treatment i.

5. $\bar{x}_{i..} = (1/qn) T_{i..}$ represents the mean of the qn observations associated with treatment i.
6. $T_{.j.} = \Sigma_{i=1}^{p} \Sigma_{k=1}^{n} x_{ijk}$ represents the total of the pn observations associated with block j.
7. $\bar{x}_{.j.} = (1/pn) T_{.j.}$ represents the mean of the pn observations associated with block j.
8. $T_{...} = \Sigma_{i=1}^{p} \Sigma_{j=1}^{q} \Sigma_{k=1}^{n} x_{ijk}$ represents the grand total of all observations.
9. $\bar{x}_{...} = (1/pqn) T_{...}$ represents the grand mean.

5.3.4 The Sums of Squares Model and Equations[B]

For two-way ANOVA with interaction, we add another component to the sums of squares model, which becomes:

$$SS(T) = SS(TR) + SS(B) + SS(TRB) + SS(E) \qquad (5.10)$$

where $SS(T)$, $SS(TR)$, $SS(B)$, and $SS(E)$ are defined as before and $SS(TRB)$ represents the interactive effect between the two factors being considered.

The algebraic definitions of each component comprising the sums of squares model for two-way analysis of variance with interaction are as follows:

Component	Definitional Equation	
$SS(T) =$	$\displaystyle\sum_{i=1}^{p} \sum_{j=1}^{q} \sum_{k=1}^{n} (x_{ijk} - \bar{x}_{...})^2$	(5.11.1)
$SS(TR) =$	$\displaystyle qn \sum_{i=1}^{p} (\bar{x}_{i..} - \bar{x}_{...})^2$	(5.11.2)
$SS(B) =$	$\displaystyle pn \sum_{j=1}^{q} (\bar{x}_{.j.} - \bar{x}_{...})^2$	(5.11.3)
$SS(TRB) =$	$\displaystyle n \sum_{i=1}^{p} \sum_{j=1}^{q} [\bar{x}_{ij.} - (\bar{x}_{i..} + \bar{x}_{.j.} - \bar{x}_{...})]^2$	(5.11.4)
$SS(E) =$	$SS(T) - SS(TR) - SS(B) - SS(TRB)$	(5.11.5)

(See Winer or Kirk for the detailed development.)

The definitional equation for $SS(T)$ appears to be self-explanatory, but the other expressions deserve further comment. Recall from our discussion of two-way analysis of variance without interaction that $SS(TR)$ and $SS(B)$ were defined as

$$q \sum_{i=1}^{p} (\bar{x}_{i.} - \bar{x}_{..})^2$$

and

$$p \sum_{j=1}^{q} (\bar{x}_{.j} - \bar{x}_{..})^2$$

respectively. In the case of two-way analysis of variance with interaction, we must account for the number of observations appearing in each of the cells of the design matrix. As shown previously, this is accomplished by multiplying the sum of the squared deviations by n, which corresponds to the number of observations appearing in the combinations of treatments and blocks.

Concerning the definitional form of $SS(TRB)$, note that $(\bar{x}_{i.} + \bar{x}_{.j} - \bar{x}_{..})$ represents the difference between the sum of the means corresponding to treatment i and block j and the grand mean $\bar{x}_{..}$. Recalling that $\bar{x}_{ij}$ is the mean of the n observations corresponding to treatment i and block j, we find that $(\bar{x}_{ij} - (\bar{x}_{i.} + \bar{x}_{.j} - \bar{x}_{..}))$ indicates the magnitude of variation in $\bar{x}_{ij}$ relative to the difference between $\bar{x}_{i.} + \bar{x}_{.j}$ and $\bar{x}_{..}$. Thus, by squaring $(\bar{x}_{ij} - (\bar{x}_{i.} + \bar{x}_{.j} - \bar{x}_{..}))$, summing over all i treatments and j blocks, and multiplying by n, for the number of observations for each combination, we obtain a measure of the interaction between the two variables.

The total, treatment, and block sums of squares are calculated in the same way as in the case of two-way analysis of variance, but we now write the computational formulas as follows:

Component	Computational Formulas	
$SS(T) = \sum\limits_{i=1}^{p} \sum\limits_{j=1}^{q} \sum\limits_{k=1}^{n} x^2_{ijk} - \dfrac{1}{pqn} T^2_{...}$		(5.12.1)

$$SS(TR) = \frac{1}{qn} \sum_{i=1}^{p} T^2_{i..} - \frac{1}{pqn} T^2_{...} \qquad (5.12.2)$$

$$SS(B) = \frac{1}{pn} \sum_{j=1}^{q} T^2_{.j.} - \frac{1}{pqn} T^2_{...} \qquad (5.12.3)$$

$$SS(TRB) = \frac{1}{n} \sum_{i=1}^{p} \sum_{j=1}^{q} T^2_{ij.} - \frac{1}{pqn} T^2_{...} - SS(TR) - SS(B) \qquad (5.12.4)$$

$$SS(E) = SS(T) - SS(TR) - SS(B) - SS(TRB) \qquad (5.12.5)$$

5.3.5 The ANOVA Table: Two-Way with Interaction[B]

The model analysis of variance table is presented in Table 5-4. Note that each cell of the design has n observations, and therefore $(n - 1)$ degrees of freedom. Since there are pq cells, the error mean square has $pq(n - 1)$ degrees of freedom.

We conclude that the variation among the cell means $\bar{x}_{ij.}$ attributed to the treatment, block, and interaction effects is not significant unless the computed value of F is greater than $F_{.05}$ or $F_{.01}$ for: $(p - 1)$ and $pq(n - 1)$ degrees of freedom; $(q - 1)$ and $pq(n - 1)$ degrees of freedom; or $(q - 1)(p - 1)$ and $pq(n - 1)$ degrees of freedom, respectively.

Table 5-4 Model Table for Two-Way Analysis of Variance with Interaction

Source of Variation	df	SS	MS	F
Treatment	$p - 1$	$SS(TR)$	$MS(TR) = \dfrac{SS(TR)}{p - 1}$	$\dfrac{MS(TR)}{MS(E)}$
Block	$q - 1$	$SS(B)$	$MS(B) = \dfrac{SS(B)}{q - 1}$	$\dfrac{MS(B)}{MS(E)}$
Interaction	$(q - 1)(p - 1)$	$SS(TRB)$	$MS(TRB) = \dfrac{SS(TRB)}{(q - 1)(p - 1)}$	$\dfrac{MS(TRB)}{MS(E)}$
Error	$pq(n - 1)$	$SS(E)$	$MS(E) = \dfrac{SS(E)}{pq(n - 1)}$	
Total	$pqn - 1$	$SS(T)$		

5.3.6 Calculations and ANOVA Table for the Laboratory Tests Example[B]

In order to use the computational formulas 5.12, we need to calculate all $T_{ij.}$, $T_{i..}$, $T_{.j.}$, and $T_{...}$ values. It is convenient to display these calculations in a matrix of totals as shown in Table 5-5.
Then the sums of squares can be calculated as follows:

$$SS(T) = 1{,}204 - \frac{1}{4 \cdot 3 \cdot 3} (182)^2$$

$$= 1{,}204 - 920.11$$

$$= 283.89$$

$$SS(TR) = \frac{1}{9} (53^2 + 53^2 + 33^2 + 43^2) - 920.11$$

$$= 950.666 - 920.11$$

$$= 30.56$$

$$SS(B) = \frac{1}{12} (40^2 + 64^2 + 78^2) - 920.11$$

$$= 981.67 - 920.11$$

$$= 61.56$$

$$SS(TRB) = \frac{1}{3} (9^2 + 17^2 + 27^2 + 16^2 + 24^2 + 13^2 + 7^2 + 16^2 + 10^2$$

$$+ 8^2 + 7^2 + 28^2) - 920.11 - 30.56 - 61.56$$

$$= 1{,}134 - 920.11 - 30.56 - 61.56$$

$$= 121.77$$

$$SS(E) = 283.89 - 30.56 - 61.56 - 121.77$$

$$= 70.00$$

The analysis of variance is shown in Table 5-6.

Table 5-5 Cell and Marginal Totals for Laboratory Tests Example

	Institutions			
	B_1	B_2	B_3	Total
Conditions A_1	9	17	27	53
A_2	16	24	13	53
A_3	7	16	10	33
A_4	8	7	28	43
Total	40	64	78	182

Table 5-6 Two-Way ANOVA Table with Interaction: Laboratory Tests Example

Source of Variance	df	SS	MS	F
Treatments (Conditions)	3	30.56	10.19	3.49
Blocks (Institutions)	2	61.56	30.78	10.55
Interaction	6	121.77	20.30	6.96
Error	24	70	2.92	
Total	35	283.89		

Since $F_{.05}$ equals 3.01 for 3 and 24 degrees of freedom, 3.40 for 2 and 24 degrees of freedom, and 2.51 for 6 and 24 degrees of freedom, we find that all of the null hypotheses are rejected at the level of significance, $\alpha = .05$.

5.3.7 Two-Way Analysis of Variance with Interaction: Matrix Notation[C]

Equations 5.11.1 through 5.11.5 may be expressed using matrix notation as follows:

$$SS(T) = \frac{1}{pqn} |\mathbf{X'X}| \quad \text{where} \quad \mathbf{X'} = \begin{bmatrix} \cdots & 1 & \cdots \\ \cdots & x_{ijk} & \cdots \end{bmatrix} \quad \text{(5.13.1)}$$

and there are pqn elements in each row

$$SS(TR) = \frac{qn}{p} |\mathbf{Y'Y}| \quad \text{where} \quad \mathbf{Y'} = \begin{bmatrix} \cdots & 1 & \cdots \\ \cdots & \bar{x}_{i..} & \cdots \end{bmatrix} \quad \text{(5.13.2)}$$

and there are p elements in each row

$$SS(B) = \frac{pn}{q} |\mathbf{Z'Z}| \quad \text{where} \quad \mathbf{Z'} = \begin{bmatrix} \cdots & 1 & \cdots \\ \cdots & \bar{x}_{.j.} & \cdots \end{bmatrix} \quad \text{(5.13.3)}$$

and there are q elements in each row

$$SS(TRB) = \frac{n}{pq} |\mathbf{W'W}| \quad \text{where} \quad \mathbf{W'}$$

$$\mathbf{W'} = \begin{bmatrix} \cdots & 1 & \cdots \\ \cdots & [\bar{x}_{ij.} - (\bar{x}_{i..} + \bar{x}_{.j.} - \bar{x}_{...})] & \cdots \end{bmatrix} \quad \text{(5.13.4)}$$

and there are pq elements in each row

The reader should verify the results presented in Table 5-6 using the matrix operations specified previously. Also, the reader should note the simple patterns of p's, q's, and n's in the matrix formulas.

Because the interaction terms must sum to zero, the form of $\mathbf{W'W}$ is special. The off-diagonal elements must be zero, and this requirement will be violated only if an error has been introduced by rounding during the calculation of the averages ($\bar{x}_{...}$, $\bar{x}_{ij.}$, $\bar{x}_{i..}$, or $\bar{x}_{.j.}$). In such a case, the sum will be very small.

5.4 APL FOR TWO-WAY ANOVA[E]

5.4.1 Use of ANOVA2 for Two-Way ANOVA without Interaction[E]

The approach to computing two-way ANOVA is very similar to that of one-way ANOVA, and is shown in Exhibit 5-1. First, the workspace

Exhibit 5-1

```
A←   10 14 6     9 13 5     8 12 4     9 9 6
AA←Q(4 3) ρ A
AA
     10           9          8          9
     14          13         12          9
      6           5          4          6

ANOVA2   AA

     1           3         10          0
     2           3          9          0
     3           3          8          0
     4           3          8.         0
     3        8.25         2.75  .2156862745
     8         102        12.75          0
    11      110.25   3.570714214          0


ANOVA2   QAA

     1           4          9          0
     2           4         12          0
     3           4          5.25       0
     2        91.5        45.75      21.96
     9       18.75   2.083333333          0
    11      110.25   1.443375673          0
```

ANOPRAC is loaded from library 3176 (Appendix E). The data are entered by typing the vector **A** as described in Chapter 4. The vector is reshaped and transposed to create the matrix **AA** as previously. At this point, the program ANOVA2 may be applied separately to **AA** and to $(\mathbf{AA})'(\mathbf{Q}\,\mathbf{AA})$ to obtain $SS(T)$ and $SS(TR)$ from one, and $SS(T)$ and $SS(B)$ from the other. $SS(T)$ is the same in both cases (110.25), whereas

$$SS(E) = SS(T) - SS(TR) - SS(B)$$
$$= 110.25 - 8.25 - 91.5$$
$$= 10.5$$

This allows the user to construct the two-way ANOVA table as in Table 5-2.

5.4.2 APL as a Matrix Desk Calculator: Two-Way without Interaction[E]

The use of APL as a matrix desk calculator requires the following steps:

1. Create **XT** and **X, YT** and **Y**, and **ZT** and **Z** (Exhibit 5-2).

Exhibit 5-2

```
        ⍴  A:   CREATE XT,  X; YT,  Y;   ZT,  Z

        P←4
        Q←3
        PQ←P×Q

        XT←(2,PQ)⍴(PQ⍴1),A
        X←⍉XT

        YB←(1÷Q)×+/AA

        YT←(2,P)⍴(P⍴1),YB
        Y←⍉YT

        ZB←(1÷4)×  +/AA
        ZT←(2,Q)⍴(Q⍴1),ZB
        Z←⍉ZT


        )DIGITS 3
WAS  10

        XT
     1    1    1    1    1    1    1    1    1    1    1    1
    10   14    6    9   13    5    8   12    4    9    9    6

        )DIGITS 10
WAS   3

        YT
              1            1            1            1
             10            9            8            8

        ZT
              1            1            1
              9           12         5.25
```

2. Calculate $SS(T) = \dfrac{1}{pq} |\mathbf{X'X}|$ (Exhibit 5-3).

Exhibit 5–3

```
    A   B:  CALCULATE SST FROM XT AND X

    XTX← XT +.× X
    DETXTX← DET XTX
    SST← (1÷PQ) × DETXTX
    SST
110.25
```

3. Calculate $SS(TR) = \dfrac{q}{p} |\mathbf{Y'Y}|$ (Exhibit 5-4).

Exhibit 5–4

```
    A   C:  CALCULATE SSTR


    YTY← YT +.× Y
    DETYTY← DET YTY
    SSTR← (Q÷P) × DETYTY
    SSTR
8.25
```

4. Calculate $SS(B) = \dfrac{p}{q} |\mathbf{Z'Z}|$ (Exhibit 5-5).

Exhibit 5–5

```
    A   D:  CALCULATE SSB


    ZTZ← ZT +.× Z
    DETZTZ← DET ZTZ
    SSB← (P÷Q) × DETZTZ
    SSB
91.5
```

5. Calculate $SS(E) = SS(T) - SS(TR) + SS(B)$ (Exhibit 5-6).

Exhibit 5-6

```
        A   E:       CALCULATE  SSE


        SSE← SST - (SSTR + SSB)
        SSE
     10.5
```

6. Calculate mean squares and F ratios (Exhibit 5-7).

Exhibit 5-7

```
     A   F:    CALCULATE MEAN SQUARES AND F RATIOS


     MSTR← SSTR÷(P-1)
     MSB← SSB÷(Q-1)
     MSE←SSE÷(P-1) x (Q-1)

     MSTR
  2.75
     MSB
  45.75
     MSE
  1.75

     F←(MSTR , MSB) ÷ MSE
     F
  1.571428571   26.14285714
```

5.4.3 APL for Two-Way ANOVA with Interaction[E]

The implementation of the set of matrix algebra Equations 5.13.1 through 5.13.4 in APL is straightforward, but rather lengthy. The demonstration of the matrix approach is perhaps less useful than the demonstration of the previous levels. Because of the lengthiness of the procedure, it was programmed in APL and the function is titled AN2WAYIN, where the components of the name mean ANOVA, 2WAY, with INteraction. The steps for using AN2WAYIN are given in Table 5-7.

The use of AN2WAYIN with the data for the Laboratory Tests example is shown in Figure 5-3. First, all observations for each condition are typed into 4 vectors, A1 to A4. These are then catenated and shaped into the matrix LABTESTS, which is printed out for visual verification. The program is called by typing AN2WAYIN LABTESTS. The remainder of the page is printed by the computer. Note that information concerning the design matrix and the cell means, as well as the ANOVA table, is produced without calculated values of *F*. The *F* values are omitted for reasons discussed in the next chapter.

As a convenience for those users who might wish to program AN2WAYIN for themselves, a listing is included in Appendix E. Listings for DET and DATETIME are also found in Appendix E.

Table 5-7 Steps for Two-Way ANOVA Using AN2WAYIN

A. User Steps
   —1. Load ANOVPRAC from 3176
      (contains the program AN2WAYIN).
    2. Type in vectors.
    3. Form data matrix for data collection design with a name for the problem.
    4. Call for the program to analyze the data by typing AN2WAYIN.
B. Program Performs the Following Steps
    1. Create **X** matrix:

$$\mathbf{X}' = \begin{bmatrix} \cdots & 1 & \cdots \\ \cdots & x_{ijk} & \cdots \end{bmatrix}$$

  2. Find

$$SS(T) = \frac{1}{pqn} \, |\mathbf{X}'\mathbf{X}|$$

  3. Create treatment means matrix **Y**:

$$\mathbf{Y}' = \begin{bmatrix} \cdots & 1 & \cdots \\ \cdots & \bar{x}_{i..} & \cdots \end{bmatrix}$$

Table 5-7 continued

    4. Find

$$SS(TR) = \frac{qn}{p} |Y'Y|$$

    5. Create block means matrix Z:

$$Z' = \begin{bmatrix} \cdots & 1 & \cdots \\ \cdots & \bar{x}_{.j.} & \cdots \end{bmatrix}$$

    6. Find

$$SS(B) = \frac{pn}{q} |Z'Z|$$

    7. Create interaction means matrix W:

$$W' = \begin{bmatrix} \cdots & 1 & \cdots \\ \cdots & [\bar{x}_{ij.} - (\bar{x}_{i..} + \bar{x}_{.j.} - \bar{x}_{...})] & \cdots \end{bmatrix}$$

    8. Find

$$SS(TRB) = \frac{n}{pq} |W'W|$$

    9. Calculate $SS(E) = SS(T) - (SS(TR) + SS(B) + SS(TRB))$
   10. Calculate degrees of freedom and mean squares.
   11. Print the analysis of variance table.

BIBLIOGRAPHY

Kirk, R. *Experimental Design: Procedures for the Behavioral Sciences.* Monterey: Brooks/Cole, 1968.

Winer, B. J. *Statistical Principles in Experimental Design.* New York: McGraw-Hill, 1971.

Figure 5-3 Two-Way ANOVA with Interaction Using AN2WAYIN

```
       )LOAD ANOVPRAC,3176
SAVED 10.18/ 79.108/ 9192
    A1← 1 3 5   6 4 7   8 9 10
    A2← 4 7 5   7 8 9   2 5 6
    A3← 1 2 4   3 7 6   1 4 5
    A4← 2 1 5   1 2 4   8 9 11


    LABTESTS← (4 3 3) ρ A1,A2,A3,A4
    LABTESTS
        1        3        5
        6        4        7
        8        9       10

        4        7        5
        7        8        9
        2        5        6

        1        2        4
        3        7        6
        1        4        5

        2        1        5
        1        2        4
        8        9       11

    AN2WAYIN LABTESTS

TWO WAY ANALYSIS OF VARIANCE WITH INTERACTION

DATE: 4/18/79      TIME: 10:21:45


4   TREATMENTS (ROWS IN DESIGN MATRIX)
3   BLOCKS (COLUMNS IN DESIGN MATRIX)
12  CELLS IN DESIGN MATRIX
3   CASES PER CELL


CELL MEANS
    3.000      5.667      9.000
    5.333      8.000      4.333
    2.333      5.333      3.333
    2.667      2.333      9.333


GRAND MEAN   5.055555556
```

```
ANOVA TABLE WITHOUT F-VALUES
SOURCE              SUMS OF SQUARES    DF    MEAN SQUARES

TREATMENT              30.5555556       3    10.1851852
BLOCK                  61.5555556       2    30.7777778
INTERACTION           121.7777778       6    20.2962963
ERROR                  70.0000000      24     2.9166667
TOTAL                 283.8888889      35
```

```
CALCULATE APPROPRIATE F-VALUES
DEPENDING ON INTERACTION SIGNIFICANCE
AND DATA MODEL OF FIXED, RANDOM OR MIXED EFFECTS
```

Problems for Solution[G]

1. Assume that three hospitals collaborate on a study of frequency of radiology by each randomly selecting one patient chart in each of five problem areas, and extracting the number of x-rays for the problem in question. Are there significant differences?

	Peptic Ulcers	Heart Disease	Broken Leg	Lung Cancer	Spinal Curvature
Hospital H_1:	3	4	2	4	7
H_2:	2	4	1	5	5
H_3:	4	5	2	6	9

2. A metropolitan ambulance service has four dispatch locations. In a study of response times, the following data were obtained on the basis of random sampling of a single call during each half of each shift one day.

Response Times in Minutes

Dispatch Location	Midnite 4 AM	4 AM 8 AM	8 AM Noon	Noon 4 PM	4 PM 8 PM	8 PM Midnite
1	4	3	5	6	7	3
2	3	4	4	3	5	4
3	2	3	4	2	4	4
4	2	2	3	4	5	3

Are the differences significant?

3. A random sample of 3 patients admitted for 4 different diagnoses (A, B, C, D) was taken for 2 physicians. The number of prescriptions written for each patient was counted.

Physician	Diagnosis	Patients' Prescriptions		
1	A	11	7	3
	B	12	10	8
	C	8	6	4
	D	10	6	2
2	A	12	8	4
	B	6	4	2
	C	17	14	11
	D	3	1	0

a) Performing 1-way ANOVA only, are there differences among physicians?

b) Performing 1-way ANOVA only, are there differences among diagnosis categories?

c) Performing 2-way ANOVA with interaction, do the previous conclusions change? Explain.

d) Draw the data collection design matrix for this study.

e) Write the structural model appropriate for this study.

4. The laboratory director was interested in the productivity of the lab on a particular type of test, and measured the number of samples processed per hour during 7 normal "busy" times, for 2 of the technicians. The data follow:

Tech. 1   91   80   71   74   85   85   72
Tech. 2   58   70   80   77   79   71   58

Is there a difference between the technicians? Use both the method of difference between means, and that of this chapter. Compare t^2 and F.

5. The data for the previous problem are drawn from a large study in which the technicians were using three different machines (A, B, C) for the test. The complete set of data is as follows:

Tech.	Mach.	Samples Processed per Hour					
1	A	91 80 71	74 85 85	72 79 95	86 95 71	82 80 73
	B	86 84 93	86 84 87	90 82 90	76 88 99	80 85 92
	C	71 77 71	77 79 79	71 82 87	88 70 76	88 88 89
2	A	79 62 71	81 78 66	65 63 71	80 67 74	62 61 82
	B	58 70 80	77 79 71	58 79 62	79 72 67	73 75 74
	C	81 86 87	87 78 81	69 85 73	76 69 73	71 82 76

a) Is there a difference between technicians?
b) Is there a difference among machines?
c) Do the differences depend on which technician uses which machine?
d) Draw the data collection design matrix for this study.
e) Write the structural model appropriate for this study.

Chapter 6

Factorial Analysis of Variance

Objectives

Upon completion of this chapter you should be able to:

1. Describe the extension of two-way ANOVA with interaction to factorial ANOVA.
2. Write the sums of squares components and structural models and write the null hypotheses for a three-factor design.
3. Draw both forms of the data collection design matrix for a three-factor model.
4. Draw a graph of the means in a one-way or a two-way ANOVA experiment, and interpret the graph as indicating main effects and/or interaction effects.
5. Relate the interpretation of the graph to significance testing for the problem.
6. List the advantages of two-way and factorial designs over one-way designs.

Chapter Map

Only Section 6.2, which uses basic algebra and has been assigned the letter code B, goes beyond the simplest levels of presentation.

All other sections have been assigned the letter code A.

6.1 THE NEED FOR SEVERAL FACTORS(A)

Thus far in Chapters 4 and 5 we have discussed analysis of variance (ANOVA) designs that allow us to test for differences among the means of three or more groups of observations with either one or two independent variables, referred to as *factors*. We indicated that one-way ANOVA is more powerful than the *t*-test for differences between means because ANOVA allows the testing of more than two means simultaneously, but with only one independent factor. Two-way ANOVA is more powerful because there are many situations where two factors acting simultaneously are associated with variance components in the dependent variable. Adding the interaction component to the two-way model gives more precise specification of the sources of variance in the dependent variable.

In many situations we realize that a number of factors may be acting simultaneously to cause variation in the dependent variable, and the objective of the remainder of this work is to describe tools that are available for dealing with relatively complex situations. The tools that we will examine are factorial analysis of variance, covariance and correlation, and multiple regression. Factorial ANOVA is particularly suited to situations where the independent variables (factors) are either nominal or categorized, while correlation and multiple regression can handle nominal variables but are more particularly suited to interval and ratio scale independent (predictor) variables.

6.2 BASIC FACTORIAL DESIGNS(B)

A simple extension of the laboratory tests two-way ANOVA with interaction model would add one more independent variable to include age (measured in ranges of 0 to 19 years, 20 to 29 years, 30 to 39 years, and 40 years and over). Then factor A would be condition, with 4 levels; factor B would be institution, with 3 levels; and factor C would be age, with 4 levels. The basic structural model for the mean value of any cell would show the *main effects* for all three factors as α (alpha), β (beta), and γ (gamma), as well as all two-way interactions and the three-way interaction. The form of the structural model equation is:

$$\mu_{ijg} = \mu + \alpha_i + \beta_j + \gamma_g + \alpha\beta_{ij} + \alpha\gamma_{ig} + \beta\gamma_{jg} + \alpha\beta\gamma_{ijg} \qquad (6.1)$$

where:

μ_{ijg} = the mean for cell ijg
μ = the overall mean as before
α, β, γ = combinations of the three factors

The null hypotheses are:

$$H_{0\alpha}: \quad \alpha_i = 0 \quad \text{for all values of i (conditions)}$$
$$H_{0\beta}: \quad \beta_j = 0 \quad \text{for all values of j (institutions)}$$
$$H_{0\gamma}: \quad \gamma_g = 0 \quad \text{for all values of g (ages)}$$
$$H_{0\alpha\beta}: \quad \alpha\beta_{ij} = 0 \quad \text{for all combinations of } i \text{ and } j$$
$$H_{0\alpha\gamma}: \quad \alpha\gamma_{ig} = 0 \quad \text{for all combinations of } i \text{ and } g$$
$$H_{0\beta\gamma}: \quad \beta\gamma_{jg} = 0 \quad \text{for all combinations of } j \text{ and } g$$
$$H_{0\alpha\beta\gamma}: \alpha\beta\gamma_{ijg} = 0 \quad \text{for all combinations of } i, j, \text{ and } g$$

The alternatives to these hypotheses would be that two or more factors within any of the hypotheses are nonzero. The set of constraints on the α, β, and γ and interaction term values are similar to the constraints discussed in Chapters 4 and 5. They are:

$$\sum_i \alpha_i = 0, \quad \sum_j \beta_j = 0, \quad \sum_g \gamma_g = 0, \quad \sum_i \sum_j \alpha\beta_{ij} = 0,$$

$$\sum_i \sum_g \alpha\gamma_{ig} = 0, \quad \sum_j \sum_g \beta\gamma_{jg} = 0, \quad \text{and} \quad \sum_i \sum_j \sum_g \alpha\beta\gamma_{ijg} = 0.$$

In words, for each hypothesis, the sum of the terms *must* be zero.

The *sums of squares components model* for a three-factor design is:

$$SS(T) = SS(A) + SS(B) + SS(C) + SS(AB) + SS(AC) + SS(BC)$$
$$+ SS(ABC) + SS(E) \tag{6.2}$$

We note that the addition of a third factor has added four more components to the sums of squares model. Thus, the three-factor model provides even greater accuracy in the determination of the sources of variation in the dependent variable (assuming that three independent variables are relevant).

The cells of the data collection design matrix form a three-dimensional matrix when a three-factor model is being tested. The design matrix for the suggested extension of the laboratory tests model is shown in Figure 6-1. However, drawing such a matrix is rather difficult, and the mean values for the cells are usually presented as a series of two-dimensional tables as shown in Figure 6-2. Note that the mean value in each cell is based on n observations, and if n were 5 then this design would imply $4 \times 3 \times 4 \times 5$, or 240, observations must be collected. If n were larger, and more realistic for significance testing, the number of observations would be correspondingly larger.

The ANOVA table for this example would be constructed as shown in Table 6-1. The sources of variation are partitioned into the factor main effects and interaction effects, as well as error and total. As before, the error

Figure 6-1 Data Collection Design Matrix for Expanded Laboratory Tests Model

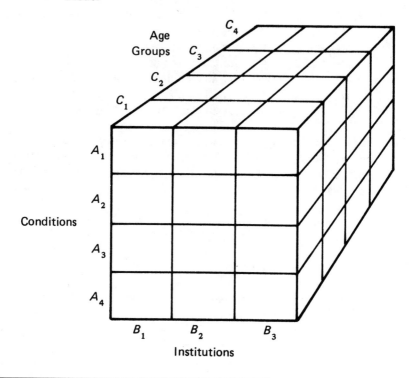

sum of squares is derived from the sum of squares components model, Equation 6.2, and is given by:

$$SS(E) = SS(T) - SS(A) - SS(B) - SS(C) - SS(AB) - SS(AC)$$
$$- SS(BC) - SS(ABC) \tag{6.3}$$

Only one of the F ratios has been shown in the table, because the discussion of fixed, random, and mixed factors designs of the next chapter must be extended and applied to this situation. If fixed factors are assumed, then the F ratios are simple, with $MS(E)$ in the denominator in all cases. However, the situation is somewhat more complex if mixed or random factors are assumed, and expert advice should be sought during the *design phase* for such a study.

Figure 6-2 Mean Values for Cells in Data Collection Design Matrix

C_1

	B_1	B_2	B_3
A_1	$\bar{X}_{111\cdot}$	$\bar{X}_{121\cdot}$	$\bar{X}_{131\cdot}$
A_2	$\bar{X}_{211\cdot}$	$\bar{X}_{221\cdot}$	$\bar{X}_{231\cdot}$
A_3	$\bar{X}_{311\cdot}$	$\bar{X}_{321\cdot}$	$\bar{X}_{331\cdot}$
A_4	$\bar{X}_{411\cdot}$	$\bar{X}_{421\cdot}$	$\bar{X}_{431\cdot}$

C_2

	B_1	B_2	B_3
	$\bar{X}_{112\cdot}$	$\bar{X}_{122\cdot}$	$\bar{X}_{132\cdot}$
	etc.		

C_3

	B_1	B_2	B_3
	$\bar{X}_{113\cdot}$	$\bar{X}_{123\cdot}$	$\bar{X}_{133\cdot}$

C_4

	B_1	B_2	B_3
	$\bar{X}_{114\cdot}$	$\bar{X}_{124\cdot}$	$\bar{X}_{134\cdot}$

Table 6-1 ANOVA Table for Expanded Laboratory Tests Model

Source	SS	df	MS	F
Main Effects				
A (Conditions)	SS(A)	3	MS(A) = SS(A)/3	
B (Institutions)	SS(B)	2	MS(B) = SS(B)/2	
C (Age Groups)	SS(C)	3	MS(C) = SS(C)/3	
Interaction Effects				
AB	SS(AB)	6	MS(AB) = SS(AB)/6	
AC	SS(AC)	9	MS(AC) = SS(AC)/9	
BC	SS(BC)	6	MS(BC) = SS(BC)/6	
ABC	SS(ABC)	18	MS(ABC) = SS(ABC)/18	MS(ABC)/MS(E)
Error	SS(E)	239 − 47 = 192	MS(E) = SS(E)/192	
Total	SS(T)	240 − 1 = 239		

If a *four*-factor design were postulated, then the preceeding discussion must be extended to accommodate:

$$\binom{4}{1} = 4 \text{ main effects} \qquad : A, B, C \text{ and } D$$

$$\binom{4}{2} = 6 \text{ two-way interactions} \quad : AB, AC, AD, BC, BD, \text{ and } CD$$

$$\binom{4}{3} = 4 \text{ three-way interactions} : ABC, ABD, ACD, \text{ and } BCD$$

$$\binom{4}{4} = 1 \text{ four-way interaction} \quad : ABCD$$

Finding significant three- or four-way or higher order interactions is extremely rare. However, the use of the factorial ANOVA model permits an examination of all main effects and interactions, as well as the pooling of nonsignificant interactions into the error sum of squares. This allows an examination of all factors and interactions that would appear to be potentially important in explaining the variation in the dependent variable.

6.3 ADVANTAGES OF FACTORIAL ANOVA[A]

There are four main advantages to using factorial designs in management research:

First, researchers can manipulate and control two or more *variables simultaneously.* This is important because in many situations more than one variable has an influence on outcomes of interest (dependent variable), and an examination of these variables one at a time is incomplete and may be misleading.

Second, attribute variables, e.g., age, sex, marital status, presence or absence of infection, job category, etc.) cannot be manipulated by the researcher, but their impact on the outcome of interest can be measured. (We speak of *controlling* for the impact of age or sex, and so forth, while studying the effects of other variables.) Such an examination requires an understanding of causal analysis, as well as partial correlation and partial regression coefficients, which are considered in Chapter 12.

Third, factorial ANOVA (and multiple regression) is *more precise* than one-way ANOVA because any systematic effect of the second, third, fourth and other factors, and their interactions, are extracted from the error sum of squares. If there *is* something significant, larger *F* values are likely to result when using factorial ANOVA than when using one-way ANOVA.

Fourth, researchers are able to enrich their models by developing hypotheses and performing tests for interactive effects. Sometimes interactions may mask main effects, ensuring that *only factorial* analysis of variance can detect the effects that are present. Multiple regression has the same capabilities, when interaction terms are included, as do some other tools in the field of pattern recognition.

The advantages of factorial ANOVA and multiple regression are similar for other types of statistics. For example, analysis of proportions theory has been developed (not covered in this text) that allows the researcher to study the joint and interactive effects of several independent variables. The emphasis on multivariate statistics of all types reflects the growing realization that many phenomena are very complex, and that simple one-way statistics can no longer be considered as completely adequate.

6.4 GRAPHICAL DISPLAY OF MAIN EFFECTS AND INTERACTIONS[A]

The remaining chapters of this work deal with the analysis of data in complex situations with tools that summarize a large amount of data. It is always useful to present diagrams that help to abstract the essence of the relationships being examined. A large number of situations in medical care have been simplified by the use of graphical presentation of the data along with the numerical values. For example, a number of common lab tests are presented in the form of *profiles,* where the patient's results are plotted on a scale that includes the *normal* ranges. A number of hospital management engineering reporting systems provide a time-based (monthly or weekly) plot of departmental performance indices, which allow the managers to evaluate how well they are doing relative to their own previous levels. In many other situations, data are presented in graphic form only because there are too many numbers to allow comprehension in any other way. For example, EEG and ECG studies produce results in the form of a tracing, although in recent years there have been concerted efforts to computerize the analysis of these patterns, ultimately requiring a conversion of tracings into numbers.

6.4.1 Display of Main Effects(A)

Referring to the example of Section 4.1, in which we examined the lengths of stay by institution, recall that we constructed a scatter diagram that portrayed each patient's length of stay (LOS). As shown in Figure 4-1, each patient was plotted as a point, while the mean LOS for each institution was indicated by a horizontal bar. The mean LOS for each of the institutions is plotted in Figure 6-3 to illustrate the essence of the relationship among the means. The means are connected by a line to emphasize the relationship, and later in this section we use several lines to emphasize different variables. It is possible to test the pattern of the means to see if there is either a *linear* or a *polynomial* trend (an option in the SPSS procedure ONEWAY), which may be meaningful if the independent variable is measured on an ordinal scale.

Figure 6-3 Mean Length of Stay by Institution

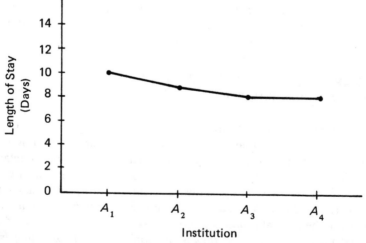

The diagram suggests that there is a difference among the means, but not a large one. However, only the F test can demonstrate whether or not the relationship is significant. The computed F value of .22 found in Section 4.1 was obviously insignificant, and, as a result, the relationship displayed in Figure 6-3 is not statistically significant.

However, in Section 5.2 we examined the same data recognizing that one patient in each institution had each of three conditions, appendicitis, heart disease, and respiratory infection, denoted by subscripts a, hd, and r, respectively. The data are replotted in Figure 6-4 to show the differences among the LOS experiences for the different conditions as well as differences in the lengths of stay associated with the institutions. Each line represents the LOS experience for one condition across institutions. The shape of the lines is very similar to the shape of the line presented in Figure 6-3, but the separation of the lines suggests a difference among conditions that is stronger than that among institutions. The two-way analysis of variance indicated that the differences in the lengths of stay among *conditions* are significant. On the other hand, when we compared the computed value of F (i.e., $F \cong 1.6$) with the tabular value of F for the appropriate degrees of freedom, we found that the differences in the lengths of stay among *institutions* were not statistically significant.

It is important to note that the statistical analysis and the graphic portrayal of the relationship are used in a complementary fashion.

Figure 6-4 Length of Stay by Institution and Condition

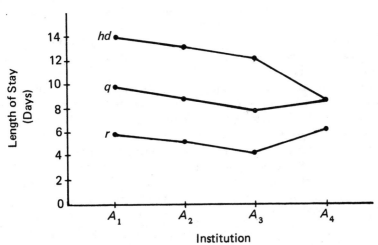

The graph may suggest the existence of a relationship, but the statistical analysis must be performed to determine whether the relationship is significant or whether the observed differences must be attributed to random fluctuations.

6.4.2 Investigation and Display of Interactions[A]

We have suggested in earlier sections that the study of the effects of two or more independent variables (factors) on the values of the dependent variable should investigate both main effects and interactions, and that either or both may be significant. In this section we examine the graphic technique introduced in the previous section to illustrate the effects of interactions. *We use the criterion of converging or intersecting line segments in the graph to suggest the presence of interactions.*

To plot the lines it is necessary to start with the table (matrix) of mean values of each cell in the design matrix. Differences due to main effects can be seen by examining the means of the rows and columns of the matrix, if two factors are being studied, or the relevant planes, if a third factor is being studied.

6.4.2.1 Nosocomial Infections Example[A]

The first example of plotting and investigating for interaction is drawn from an investigation in the area of disease costing, which examined the extra cost of treatment for patients who became infected while in the hospital. Hospital-acquired (nosocomial) infections are common enough to be troublesome, and it is alleged that hospital stays are longer and that treatment costs are higher for patients acquiring nosocomial infections. Since treatment cost has been seldom studied in detail in the past, the *disease costing* approach of collection and analysis of data reflecting all services provided to patients for their treatment has been proposed and was used in a study at the Ottawa General Hospital (Heidemann 1975).

After investigation of the frequency of various types of infection and the types of patients becoming infected, female patients undergoing Caesarian Section or Total Abdominal Hysterectomy with or without hospital-acquired Urinary Tract Infection (UTI) were selected for study. An analysis of the cost of providing care to these patients was performed. In this study, the direct patient care was represented by the use of surgical services, laboratory tests, x-rays, and nursing services, while indirect patient care was represented by the services provided by the dietary, housekeeping, administration, and maintenance departments. The costs of providing direct patient care to each patient was given by the product of price and the quantity of services used, while the costs of the indirect services were allocated in proportion to the patient's length of stay. Using these figures, a total treatment cost was obtained for each patient in the study population.

Sixty randomly selected patients were studied with 15 patients in each cell of the design matrix. The design matrix is shown in Figure 6-5. The treatment cost data for these patients has been stored in the matrix FCTINFCT in workspace ANOVPRAC in library 3176 (Appendix E). The analysis of the data is shown in Figure 6-6. The first two rows of FCTINFCT are Caesarian Section patients' costs (no UTI then UTI-Cells 1 and 2). Rows 3 and 4 are for Hysterectomy patients.

Because of considerations discussed in Chapter 7, the program does not calculate F values. For our analysis we calculate F values for *treatment, block,* and *interaction* using $MS(E)$ as the divisor, giving 3.57, 7.00 and .07, respectively. When the calculated F values are compared with a critical value of 4.01 for $F_{.05}$, we find that only the infection (block) effect is significant.

The mean costs for the four groups of patients are presented graphically in Figure 6-7. From the diagram it appears that Hysterectomy patients cost more to treat than Caesarian Section patients, and infected patients cost more than noninfected. The latter difference appears stronger than the former. The line segment for Hysterectomy patients is almost parallel (has the same slope as) to that for Caesarian Section patients, which suggests that there is little or no interaction. The tests of significance presented earlier indicate that only the main effect for the infections is significant.

6.4.2.2 LABTESTS Example[A]

A second example is drawn from the Laboratory Tests example used in Section 5.3. The mean numbers of lab tests are shown in Table 6-2 and are graphed in Figure 6-8.

Figure 6-5 Data Collection Design Matrix for Nosocomial Infection Treatment Cost Study

INFECTION

		No UTI	UTI
	Caesarian Section	Cell 1	Cell 2
PROCEDURE			
	Hysterectomy	Cell 3	Cell 4

Figure 6-6 Analysis of Variance for Nosocomial Infection Study

```
)LOAD ANOVPRAC,3176
SAVED 10:18/ 79.108/ 9192

    '99990.99'  $  .005+FCTINFCT

558.63  602.82  634.96  657.20  681.72  686.78  694.13  694.24  699.76  700.13  718.36  743.37  744.41  805.45  807.13
609.58  629.06  642.45  701.18  724.75  788.60  802.34  899.09  914.42  918.77  928.00  928.68  935.95  1196.31  1245.47

582.30  606.44  649.90  652.25  708.79  782.91  787.41  789.41  804.34  862.80  912.90  919.09  959.02  984.28  1229.99
610.51  675.28  682.24  690.70  707.01  708.69  750.34  776.60  915.15  993.42  1043.17  1144.93  1259.49  1475.71  1786.01

    AN2WAYIN FCTINFCT


TWO WAY ANALYSIS OF VARIANCE WITH INTERACTION

DATE:  4/18/79    TIME: 10:27:27

2  TREATMENTS (ROWS IN DESIGN MATRIX)
2  BLOCKS (COLUMNS IN DESIGN MATRIX)
4  CELLS IN DESIGN MATRIX
15 CASES PER CELL

CELL MEANS
  695.273   857.643
  815.455   947.950

GRAND MEAN  829.0803333


ANOVA TABLE WITHOUT F-VALUES
SOURCE           SUMS OF SQUARES      DF      MEAN SQUARES

TREATMENT        166,146.5979267      1       166,146.5979267
BLOCK            326,045.8680067      1       326,045.8680067
INTERACTION        3,347.1576600      1         3,347.1576600
ERROR          2,609,684.1342000     56        46,601.5023964
TOTAL          3,105,223.7577933     59


CALCULATE APPROPRIATE F-VALUES
DEPENDING ON INTERACTION SIGNIFICANCE
AND DATA MODEL OF FIXED, RANDOM OR MIXED EFFECTS
```

Figure 6-7 Mean Treatment Costs for Infected and Noninfected Patients by Procedure

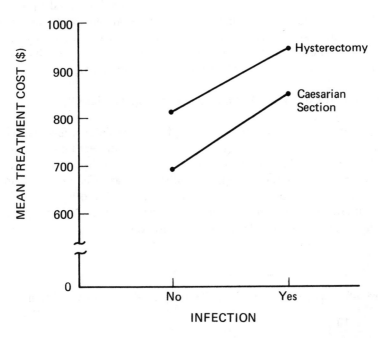

Referring to Table 6-2, observe that the column of means shows the differences among the conditions while the row of means shows the differences among the hospitals. In this example, the main effect of the hospitals is more noticeable than that for the conditions.

Table 6-2 Mean Numbers of Laboratory Tests by Hospital and Condition

Conditions	Hospitals			Mean
	B_1	B_2	B_3	
A_1 Pregnancy	3	5.67	9	5.89
A_2 Malignant Neoplasm	5.33	8	4.33	5.89
A_3 Trauma	2.33	5.33	3.33	3.66
A_4 Appendicitis	2.67	2.33	9.33	4.78
Mean	3.33	5.33	6.50	5.05

The most striking aspect of Figure 6-8 is the extreme lack of parallelism of the lines, and these results suggest very strong interaction. The situation concerning the main effects is much less obvious, although hospital B_1 tends to have fewer lab tests than the other two. Differences among conditions are not clear from the diagram. However, when we refer to the analysis of variance presented in Table 5-6, and the conclusions drawn there, we see that the effects due to conditions, hospitals, and interaction are all significant.

6.4.3 Examples of Types of Main Effects and Interactions[A]

Presented in Figure 6-9 are six examples of simple experiments. Three demonstrate main effects only and the others show different kinds of interaction. Figure 6-9(a) shows a main effect due to factor A, but no effect due to factor B or due to interaction. Figure 6-9(b) shows an effect due to factor B only. Figure 6-9(c) shows main effects due to factors A and B, but no effects due to interaction. In these first three examples the lines are either parallel, or coincide, and this indicates a lack of interaction.

Figure 6-8 Mean Numbers of Lab Tests by Hospital and Condition

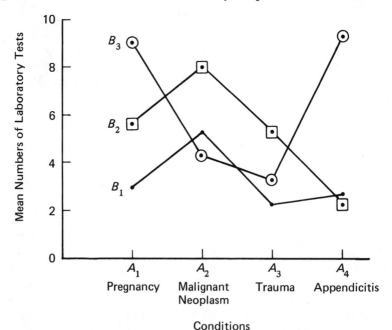

Figure 6-9 Examples of Lack of Interaction and Types of Interaction

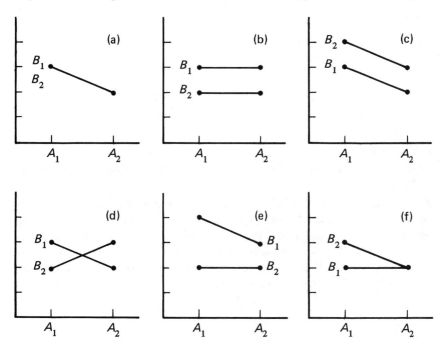

The next three examples presented in Figure 6-9 illustrate two types of interaction: symmetric and nonsymmetric. Figure 6-9(d) shows symmetric interaction that is completely dominant. In this case, there is no main effect due to either factors A or B, and only a factorial approach will isolate relevant differences. Figures (e) and (f) show nonsymmetric interactions. In these figures there are main effects due to factors A and B, but they are much stronger in Figure 6-9(e) than in Figure 6-9(f). The nonparallel lines provide us with an indication of the interactive effects.

See Kerlinger (1973) and Winer (1971) for further discussions of graphing and interactions.

BIBLIOGRAPHY

Heidemann, E. "The Financial Impact of Hospital Acquired Infection." Master's Research Project, School of Health Administration. University of Ottawa, August 1975.

Kerlinger, F. N. *Foundations of Behavioral Research,* 2nd ed. New York: Holt Rinehart and Winston, Inc., 1973.

Winer, B. J. *Statistical Principles in Experimental Design.* New York: McGraw-Hill, 1971.

Problems for Solution[(G)]

1. Graph the means of any of the supplementary problems solved in Chapters 4 and 5. Interpret the graphs in light of the significance testing performed previously.

2. We wish to investigate the differences in sick leave days "taken" by four types of nursing personnel (registered nurses, graduate nurses, nursing aides and orderlies) belonging to two different unions in five different hospitals. Draw the data collection design matrix. Assuming that at least 10 people per cell are to be included, how many observations must be made? Why is it likely to be difficult to fill all the cells?

Chapter 7

Advanced Topics in Analysis of Variance

Objectives

After completing this chapter, you should be able to:

1. Estimate the components of the structural model for one-way or two-way ANOVA, including treatment, block, and interaction effects.
2. Establish and evaluate contrasts of means (comparisons of pairs or groups of means).
3. Differentiate between fixed and random factors models.
4. Understand and construct a table showing the expected value of mean squares for a two-factor model.
5. Perform and interpret tests of significance for the fixed, mixed, and random two-factor models.
6. Understand and use a computer package to perform factorial analysis of variance.
7. Understand the relationship between research design and orthogonality.

Chapter Map

The material presented in this chapter is somewhat complex and should be considered as advanced reading.

Brief portions of Sections 7.1, 7.2, 7.5, and 7.6 present introductory material and have been assigned the letter code A.

The majority of the material in Sections 7.2, 7.4, and 7.5 utilizes ordinary algebra and has been assigned the letter code B.

Section 7.3 utilizes both ordinary and matrix algebra and has been assigned both letter codes B and C.

Section 7.7 demonstrates the use of SPSS and has been assigned the letter code D.

161

7.1 INTRODUCTION [A]

In Chapters 4 through 6 we have considered the basic models of analysis of variance, ranging from one-way to factorial ANOVA. We have examined the equations, basic significance testing, use of the computer, and graphing of means. In this chapter, we extend the presentation and investigate the components of the structural model, comparisons among means, as well as some problems of interpretation of both *fixed* and *random* models, which pose traps for the novice. A major objective is to ensure that the reader appreciates the limits of the understanding gained thus far, as well as the nonstatistician manager's need for competent statistical consulting in any situations beyond the simplest.

7.2 ESTIMATING THE COMPONENTS OF THE STRUCTURAL MODEL [A]

In this section and in the next, we examine two methods of making specific comparisons of interest in analysis of variance studies. In this section, we examine the α's, β's, and γ's of the structural models, comparing individual group means to the *overall mean*. In the next section, we examine the differences between pairs of means (or among groups of means) by forming and testing what are called *contrasts*. Contrasts specifically ignore the overall mean and therefore answer a very different kind of question than do the components of the structural model.

7.2.1 Estimation of Treatment Effects for One-Way ANOVA [B]

In Chapter 4, we indicated that the structural model for one-way ANOVA is that the mean for any one group, μ_i, can be expressed as a deviation from the overall mean, μ. This can be expressed as:

$$\mu_i = \mu + \alpha_i \qquad (7.1.1)$$

with the requirement:

$$\Sigma \alpha_i = 0 \qquad (7.1.2)$$

The unknown population grand mean, μ, is estimated by the overall mean of the samples, $\bar{x}_{..}$, while the means of the individual samples, μ_i, are estimated by $\bar{x}_{i.}$.

Solving Equation 7.1.1 for α_i, and using the estimates of the population means, we see that the estimate of the individual treatment effect is:

$$\alpha_i = \bar{x}_{i.} - \bar{x}_{..} \qquad (7.2)$$

If we return to the patient length of stay example of Section 4.1, we recall that three patients were sampled in each of four institutions. The overall average length of stay was 8.75 days, and the averages for the individual institutions were 10, 9, 8, and 8 days, respectively. Thus, in this example, our estimates for the α's are:

$$\alpha_1 = \bar{x}_1. - \bar{x}.. = 10 - 8.75 = 1.25 \text{ days}$$
$$\alpha_2 = 9 - 8.75 = .25 \text{ days}$$
$$\alpha_3 = 8 - 8.75 = -.75 \text{ days}$$
$$\alpha_4 = -.75 \text{ days}$$

We interpret these results as showing that on the average, patients in institution 1 stayed 1.25 days longer than the average of the four institutions; those in institutions 2 stayed .25 day longer; and those in institutions 3 and 4 stayed .75 day shorter than the group average.

In Chapter 4 we performed the analysis of variance and obtained an F value of .22, which (being < 1) is insignificant. The null hypothesis was:

$$H_0: \alpha_1 = \alpha_2 = \alpha_3 = \alpha_4 = 0$$

Based on the analysis of the data, this null hypothesis must be retained, and the calculated values for the α's must, regretfully, be ignored. The overall F test is the only one that is possible for the examination of the components of the structural model. Subsidiary tests *are* possible when we turn to the examination of contrasts in Section 7.3. However, we first examine the structural model for two-way ANOVA with interaction.

7.2.2 Estimating the Components of the Structural Model for Two-Way ANOVA with Interaction [B]

The structural model for two-way ANOVA with interaction is:

$$\mu_{ij} = \mu + \alpha_i + \beta_j + \alpha\beta_{ij} \qquad \text{(7.3.1)}$$

where:

$$\sum_i \alpha_i = 0 \qquad \text{(treatment effects)} \qquad \text{(7.3.2)}$$

$$\sum_j \beta_j = 0 \qquad \text{(block effects)} \qquad \text{(7.3.3)}$$

$$\sum_i \sum_j \alpha\beta_{ij} = 0 \qquad \text{(interaction effects)} \qquad \text{(7.3.4)}$$

The individual observations are represented by x_{ijk}, cell means by $\bar{x}_{ij.}$, treatment means by $\bar{x}_{i..}$, block means by $\bar{x}_{.j.}$, and the grand mean by $\bar{x}_{...}$. The estimates of the components are given by:

$$\alpha_i = \bar{x}_{i..} - \bar{x}_{...} \qquad\qquad\qquad (7.4.1)$$

$$\beta_j = \bar{x}_{.j.} - \bar{x}_{...} \qquad\qquad\qquad (7.4.2)$$

and by substituting these values into Equation 7.3.1 and solving for $\alpha\beta_{ij}$, we obtain

$$\alpha\beta_{ij} = \bar{x}_{ij.} - (\bar{x}_{i..} + \bar{x}_{.j.} - \bar{x}_{...}) \qquad (7.4.3)$$

Let us return to the laboratory tests example of Section 5.3. In that example, the number of laboratory tests was recorded for each of 3 patients, for each of 4 conditions (Pregnancy, A_1; Malignant Neoplasm, A_2; Trauma, A_3; and Appendicitis, A_4), in each of 3 institutions (B_1, B_2, and B_3). The cell, treatment, block, and grand means are given in Table 7-1.

The ANOVA results gave F values of 3.49, 10.55, and 6.96 for conditions, institutions, and interaction, respectively. Comparing the calculated values against the appropriate $F_{.05}$ values, we found that all of these effects were significant. From the data in Table 7-1 it is possible to calculate the estimates of the components of the structural model. First, the α_i's are found as follows:

$$\alpha_1 = \bar{x}_{1..} - \bar{x}_{...} = 5.889 - 5.056 = .833$$
$$\alpha_2 = .833$$

Table 7-1 Cell and Marginal Averages for Laboratory Tests Example

| Conditions | Institutions | | | |
	B_1	B_2	B_3	Average
A_1	3	5.667	9	5.889
A_2	5.333	8	4.333	5.889
A_3	2.333	5.333	3.333	3.667
A_4	2.667	2.333	9.333	4.778
Average	3.333	5.333	6.5	5.056

$$\alpha_3 = -1.389$$
$$\alpha_4 = -.278$$

Here, it will be observed that the sum of the treatment effects is equal to $-.001$ rather than zero, as required by Equation 7.3.2. In this case, the observed error is caused by rounding. Turning attention to the block effects, we find:

$$\beta_1 = \bar{x}_{.1.} - \bar{x}_{...} = 3.333 - 5.056 = -1.723$$
$$\beta_2 = .277$$
$$\beta_3 = 1.444$$

On the basis of these calculations, we find that $\Sigma_j \beta_j = -.002$ rather than zero, as required by Equation 7.3.2. As before, the observed error is a consequence of rounding our calculations to 3 decimals. Finally, the interactive effects represented by $\alpha\beta_{ij}$ are given by:

$$\alpha\beta_{ij} = \bar{x}_{ij.} - (\bar{x}_{i..} + \bar{x}_{.j.} - \bar{x}_{...})$$

Returning to our example, we find:

$$\alpha\beta_{11} = 3 - (5.889 + 3.333 - 5.056)$$
$$= -1.166$$
$$\alpha\beta_{12} = 5.667 - (5.889 + 5.333 - 5.056)$$
$$= -.499$$
$$\alpha\beta_{13} = 9 - (5.889 + 6.500 - 5.056)$$
$$= 1.667$$

Similarly, the reader should verify:

$\alpha\beta_{21} = 1.167$	$\alpha\beta_{22} = 1.834$	$\alpha\beta_{23} = -3.000$
$\alpha\beta_{31} = .389$	$\alpha\beta_{32} = 1.389$	$\alpha\beta_{33} = -1.778$
$\alpha\beta_{41} = -.388$	$\alpha\beta_{42} = -2.722$	$\alpha\beta_{43} = 3.111$

As will be recalled, Equation 7.3.4 requires that the sum $\Sigma_i \Sigma_j \alpha\beta_{ij}$ must equal zero. In terms of our example, the reader should verify that $\Sigma_i \Sigma_j \alpha\beta_{ij} = .004$ and that the disparity between the results obtained previously and those specified by Equation 7.3.4 is a result of rounding errors. Since all of the null hypotheses were rejected, we were able to conclude that: (1) one or more of the α_i's are significantly different from zero, (2) one or more of the β_j's are significantly different from zero, and (3) one or more of the $\alpha\beta_{ij}$'s are significantly different from zero. However, we are not able to say which of the α's, β's, or $\alpha\beta$'s, differ from zero or whether all of these terms differ from zero. On the other hand, given $\Sigma\alpha_i = 0$, we know that if one of the α_i is not equal to zero, then at least one of the other α_i must be nonzero. The same reasoning applies to the β_j's and to the interactive effects represented by the $\alpha\beta$'s. Note that because of these relationships a further set of requirements is imposed, namely, that $\Sigma_i \alpha\beta_{ij} = 0$ for each j and $\Sigma_j \alpha\beta_{ij} = 0$ for each i.

7.3 COMPARISONS AMONG TREATMENT MEANS[B, C]

The second method of describing observed differences in treatment effects involves a comparison or *contrast* between two or more treatment means. When we compare two or more treatment means, the difference obtained allows us to examine a portion or *component* of the treatment sum of squares, and to test the component for statistical significance. A comparison or contrast between two treatment means is defined as the absolute value of the difference between the two means. Thus, $|\bar{x}_{1.} - \bar{x}_{2.}|$ defines the comparison or contrast between the means of treatments 1 and 2.

Comparisons among several treatment means may be constructed in a number of different ways. The most commonly employed approach is to compare the differences among all possible pairs. When this procedure is followed, there are $(k/2)$ possible tests to be performed. Returning to the patient length of stay example of Section 4.1 in which we examined four hospitals, the comparisons are as follows:

$$\bar{x}_{1.} - \bar{x}_{2.}, \bar{x}_{1.} - \bar{x}_{3.}, \bar{x}_{1.} - \bar{x}_{4.}, \bar{x}_{2.} - \bar{x}_{3.}, \bar{x}_{2.} - \bar{x}_{4.}, \text{ and } \bar{x}_{3.} - \bar{x}_{4.}$$

Other types of contrasts include an examination of one mean as compared with the average of the others. For example, we might wish to examine the contrasts given by:

$$\bar{x}_{1.} - \frac{\bar{x}_{2.} + \bar{x}_{3.} + \bar{x}_{4.}}{3} \quad \text{or} \quad \bar{x}_{2.} - \frac{\bar{x}_{1.} + \bar{x}_{3.} + \bar{x}_{4.}}{3}$$

The choice of the type and number of comparisons to be made depends on the original expectations and the hypotheses that led to the experiment or the collection of the data. When reaching decisions concerning the number and type of contrasts that will be constructed, the interpretation or the meaning of the results is the most important factor to be considered.

However, there are only a certain number of *independent* tests that can be performed on a given set of data and, with a large number of tests, the probability of one or more independent tests resulting in a rejection of the null hypothesis H_0 becomes rather large. For m independent tests and with $\alpha = .05$, the probability of committing at least one Type I error is given by $1 -$

$.95^m$. For example, the probability of committing a Type I error when one test is performed is given by $1 - .95$, or $.05$. However, when three tests are performed the probability of committing a Type I error becomes $1 - .95^3$, or $.143$, and when five tests are performed the probability is $1 - .95^5$, or $.226$. In general, a comparison or a contrast for four means assumes the form:

$$c_1\bar{x}_{1.} + c_2\bar{x}_{2.} + c_3\bar{x}_{3.} + c_4\bar{x}_{4.} \qquad (7.5)$$

where $\Sigma\, c_i = 0$. Observe that Equation 7.5 is a linear function of the $\bar{x}_i$'s subject to the requirement that $\Sigma\, c_i = 0$. As an example, suppose $c_1 = 1$, $c_2 = -1$, and $c_3 = c_4 = 0$. When these values are substituted for c_1, c_2, c_3, and c_4 into Equation 7.5 we obtain:

$$(1)\bar{x}_{1.} + (-1)\bar{x}_{2.} + (0)\bar{x}_{3.} + (0)\bar{x}_{4.} = \bar{x}_{1.} - \bar{x}_{2.}$$

which we recognize as a comparison between $x_{1.}$ and $x_{2.}$. Conversely, if $c_1 = 1$, $c_2 = -1/3$, $c_3 = -1/3$, and $c_4 = -1/3$, we find that Equation 7.5 becomes:

$$(1)\bar{x}_{1.} + \left(-\frac{1}{3}\right)\bar{x}_{2.} + \left(-\frac{1}{3}\right)\bar{x}_{3.} + \left(-\frac{1}{3}\right)\bar{x}_{4.}$$

As a result, we obtain:

$$\bar{x}_{1.} - \frac{\bar{x}_{2.} + \bar{x}_{3.} + \bar{x}_{4.}}{3}$$

which we recognize as a comparison between $\bar{x}_{1.}$ and the average of $\bar{x}_{2.}$, $\bar{x}_{3.}$, and $\bar{x}_{4.}$.

The definition of a contrast may be expressed quite simply in matrix notation. Let

$$\bar{\mathbf{x}} = \begin{bmatrix} \bar{x}_{1.} \\ \bar{x}_{2.} \\ \vdots \\ \bar{x}_{p.} \end{bmatrix} \qquad \text{and} \qquad \mathbf{c}' = [c_1 \quad c_2 \quad \cdots \quad c_p]$$

Thus, a contrast is defined by:

$$\mathbf{c'\bar{x}} \qquad (7.6)$$

As mentioned earlier, it is possible to construct only a limited number of contrasts before a new one becomes redundant with previous comparisons. The set of independent contrasts is referred to as the *set of orthogonal contrasts*, where the term *orthogonal* means unrelated or independent. More specifically, if we have a set of contrasts c_1, c_2, c_3, ..., c_p,

$$c_1 \text{ and } c_2 \text{ are orthogonal if } c_1'c_2 = 0$$

The entire set of contrasts is orthogonal if all pairs are also orthogonal (e.g., $c_1'c_2 = 0$, $c_1'c_3 = 0$, $c_1'c_4 = 0$, $c_2'c_3 = 0$, etc.).

As an example of this discussion, let us assume:

$$c_1' = [-3 \quad -1 \quad 1 \quad 3]$$

$$c_2' = [\ 1 \quad -1 \quad -1 \quad 1]$$

$$c_3' = [\ 1 \quad 1 \quad -1 \quad -1]$$

In this example, we find:

$$c_1'c_2 = (-3 + 1 - 1 + 3) = 0$$

and

$$c_2'c_3 = (1 - 1 + 1 - 1) = 0$$

which implies that c_1 and c_2 as well as c_2 and c_3 are orthogonal. However,

$$c_1'c_3 = (-3 - 1 - 1 - 3) = -8$$

which implies that c_1 and c_3 are *not orthogonal*. In this example, then, only two of the three contrasts are orthogonal.

We stated at the beginning of this section that a contrast defines a component of the sum of squares for treatments [i.e., a component of $SS(TR)$]. This component can be tested for significance. The component is defined as:

$$SS(\mathbf{c}) = \frac{n(\mathbf{c}'\overline{\mathbf{x}})^2}{\mathbf{c}'\mathbf{c}} \text{ with 1 degree of freedom} \qquad [7.7]$$

where $\mathbf{c}$ is a contrast of $\overline{\mathbf{x}}$ and there are n observations per treatment. Two components of $SS(TR)$ are orthogonal if their contrasts are orthogonal as evidenced by:

$$\mathbf{c}_1'\mathbf{c}_2 = 0$$

Note that a treatment sum of squares with $(p - 1)$ degrees of freedom can be divided into $(p - 1)$ orthogonal components. Usually there are many different ways of obtaining the $(p - 1)$ orthogonal components. Orthogonal components are, by definition, independent and additive, which implies that each component *explains* or *absorbs* a different portion of the variation. Conversely, it is possible to obtain an indefinitely large number of nonorthogonal contrasts, and these components are neither additive nor independent.

To illustrate this point, let us return to the numeric example in which we were interested in examining differences in the mean stays of the four institutions. Perhaps the simplest set of contrasts involves the differences among pairs of mean stays. In this situation, there are $\binom{4}{2} = 6$ possible contrasts, which are identified as follows:

$$\overline{x}_{1.} - \overline{x}_{2.}, \overline{x}_{1.} - \overline{x}_{3.}, \overline{x}_{1.} - \overline{x}_{4.}, \overline{x}_{2.} - \overline{x}_{3.}, \overline{x}_{2.} - \overline{x}_{4.}, \text{and} \overline{x}_{3.} - \overline{x}_{4.}$$

Employing the notation developed previously, these contrasts may be defined by:

$$\mathbf{c}_1' = [1 \quad -1 \quad 0 \quad 0]$$

$$\mathbf{c}_2' = [1 \quad 0 \quad -1 \quad 0]$$

$$\mathbf{c}_3' = [1 \quad 0 \quad 0 \quad -1]$$

$$\mathbf{c}_4' = [0 \quad 1 \quad -1 \quad 0]$$

$$\mathbf{c}_5' = [0 \quad 1 \quad 0 \quad -1]$$

$$\mathbf{c}_6' = [0 \quad 0 \quad 1 \quad -1]$$

In this situation, there are six possible contrasts, but only certain pairs are orthogonal to each other. They are either $\mathbf{c}_1$ and $\mathbf{c}_6$, or $\mathbf{c}_2$ and $\mathbf{c}_5$, or $\mathbf{c}_3$ and $\mathbf{c}_4$.

The student should verify that all other pairs are not orthogonal (e.g., $c_1'c_2 = 1$).

The procedures for testing the difference between two means for statistical significance were discussed at length in Volume I. However, we have seen that only certain pairs of such tests involve independent contrasts when considering the observed differences between the mean stays of the four institutions. Note that it is possible to construct a third and more complex contrast that is independent of the other two in any pair. For example, c_1 and c_6 would both be orthogonal to

$$c_7' = [.5 \quad .5 \quad -.5 \quad -.5].$$

In the final analysis, only pairs of simple contrasts may be constructed when examining the differences among the mean stays of the four hospitals. One such pair of contrasts is:

$$c_1 : \bar{x}_1 - \bar{x}_2 = 10 - 9, \text{ or } 1$$

which is independent of the contrast

$$c_6 : \bar{x}_3 - \bar{x}_4 = 8 - 8, \text{ or } 0$$

As a consequence, these two contrasts may be tested for statistical significance. Obviously, c_6 is not significant and the investigator might more profitably investigate the contrasts specified by c_2 and c_5. Observe that statistical tests concerning the four contrasts that remain after the first two have been chosen provide no new information.

There are several approaches we might follow when specifying the number and type of contrasts that are to be examined in a given situation. On the one hand, we might examine *all* possible contrasts, in which case we are likely to obtain a large number of highly repetitive results that may be significant or nonsignificant (Kirk 1968; Winer 1971).[1] On the other hand, we might select the number and type of contrasts within the context of the specific hypotheses we wish to examine. For obvious reasons, the second basis for determining the number and type of contrasts to be examined is the preferred approach.

7.3.1 Example of Orthogonal Additive Contrasts and the Treatment Sum of Squares[B, C]

Let us assume that the data in the matrix HEART, presented in Figure 7-1, represent lengths of stay for heart disease patients in six hospitals (A, B,

Figure 7-1 ANOVA for Heart Disease Patients' Lengths of Stay

HEART

17	16	10	8	7	9
13	14	9	9	8	6
16	17	11	12	10	8
12	13	8	6	6	5
15	12	6	7	8	6
17	14	7	6	9	9
16	18	6	8	6	7

ANOVA2   HEART

1	7	15.14286	0	
2	7	14.85714	0	
3	7	8.142857	0	
4	7	8	0	
5	7	7.714286	0	
6	7	7.142857	0	
5	494.9762	98.99524	27.65721	
36	128.8571	3.579365	0	
41	623.8333	1.891921	0	

..., F). The overall one-way analysis of variance has been performed using the program ANOVA2. The calculated $SS(TR)$ and $SS(E)$ are 494.9762 and 128.8571 with 5 and 36 degrees of freedom, respectively, which gives an F value of approximately 27.66. The $F_{.05}$ value is in the range $2.45 < F_{.05} < 2.53$, which implies that the differences among the hospitals are highly significant. But which differences are significant, and which differences contribute most to the $SS(TR)$?

Let us assume that hospitals A and B are teaching hospitals, and that the major research hypothesis was that heart disease patients experience longer lengths of stay in teaching hospitals. From the ANOVA2 output we see that there appear to be large differences between the means of the teaching and nonteaching hospitals. The vector of mean stays (rounded to 3 decimals) is:

$$\bar{x}' = [15.143 \quad 14.857 \quad 8.143 \quad 8.000 \quad 7.714 \quad 7.143]$$

A contrast vector that will compare the average of the teaching to the average of the nonteaching hospitals is:

$$c_1' = [.5 \quad .5 \quad -.25 \quad -.25 \quad -.25 \quad -.25]$$

The research question can be answered by investigating the significance of the contrast $c_1'\bar{x}$. Performing the vector multiplication and extending the accuracy of calculations to 4 or 5 decimal digits, as necessary, gives:

$$c_1'\bar{x} = 7.25$$

where the mean for A and B is 15 and that for C, D, E, and F is 7.75. The significance of this contrast can be investigated starting with Equation 7.7, which gives the component of $SS(TR)$ attributable to the contrast. Thus, the sum of squares given by:

$$SS(c_1) = \frac{n(c_1'\bar{x})^2}{c_1'c_1} = \frac{7(7.25)^2}{.75}$$

$$= 490.58333$$

is equivalent to $MS(c_1)$ and has 1 degree of freedom. We may now construct an F ratio of the form:

$$F_{c_1} = \frac{MS(c_1)}{MS(E)} = \frac{490.58333}{3.57965}$$

$$= 137.06$$

for which the critical level lies in the range $4.08 < F_{.05} < 4.17$. Obviously, the difference between the means of the teaching and nonteaching hospitals is highly significant, and the research hypothesis is accepted.

Let us now demonstrate that the independent components of $SS(TR)$, as obtained using orthogonal contrasts, are additive. Since the treatment sum of squares has 5 degrees of freedom, statistical theory states that only 5 orthogonal contrasts may be constructed. In terms of our research hypothesis, we found that one of the contrasts is given by:

$$\mathbf{c_1}' = [.5 \quad .5 \quad -.25 \quad -.25 \quad -.25 \quad -.25]$$

which implies that four additional contrasts must be specified. Given that the specification of our problem requires a dichotomy of both teaching and nonteaching hospitals, we are fortuitously forced to examine contrasts that reflect these two components. As a result, we may examine pairwise differences and obtain three simple orthogonal contrasts, which are given by:

$$\mathbf{c_2}' = [1 \quad -1 \quad 0 \quad 0 \quad 0 \quad 0]$$

$$\mathbf{c_3}' = [0 \quad 0 \quad 1 \quad -1 \quad 0 \quad 0]$$

$$\mathbf{c_4}' = [0 \quad 0 \quad 0 \quad 0 \quad 1 \quad -1]$$

Finally, an orthogonal contrast of the average of C and D with the average of E and F is given by:

$$\mathbf{c_5}' = [0 \quad 0 \quad .5 \quad .5 \quad -.5 \quad -.5]$$

At this point in the analysis, the student should verify that $\mathbf{c_1}'\mathbf{c_2}$, $\mathbf{c_1}'\mathbf{c_3}$, $\mathbf{c_1}'\mathbf{c_4}$, $\mathbf{c_2}'\mathbf{c_3}$, and so on, are all equal to zero which, of course, demonstrates orthogonality.

Having specified five orthogonal contrasts, we may now demonstrate that the corresponding sums of squares are additive. We have already calculated $SS(\mathbf{c_1})$ as follows:

$$SS(\mathbf{c_1}) = \frac{n(\mathbf{c_1}'\bar{\mathbf{x}})^2}{\mathbf{c_1}'\mathbf{c_1}} = \frac{7(7.25)^2}{.75} = 490.58333$$

Similarly, we find:

$$SS(\mathbf{c_2}) = \frac{7(.286)^2}{2} = .286286$$

$$SS(\mathbf{c_3}) = \frac{7(.143)^2}{2} = .0715715$$

$$SS(\mathbf{c_4}) = \frac{7(.571)^2}{2} = 1.1411435$$

$$SS(\mathbf{c_5}) = \frac{7(.643)^2}{1} = 2.894143$$

The sum of $SS(c_2)$ to $SS(c_5)$ is 4.393144, and by adding $SS(c_1)$ we obtain 494.97647. This should be identical, but it differs from $SS(TR) = 494.9762$ by only .00027, which is caused by rounding errors in the calculations.

Since each sum of squares has 1 degree of freedom, these values are also mean squares, and after dividing by $MS(E) \cong 3.579$, we find that only the F ratio for c_1 is greater than 1. As a consequence, the difference represented by c_1 is the only contrast that is statistically significant. Stated differently, we conclude that there are no significant differences within the groups of teaching and nonteaching hospitals.

7.4 TESTS FOR HOMOGENEITY OF VARIANCE [B]

An assumption underlying the null hypothesis for the analysis of variance is that all of the individual samples are drawn from the same population and that the variance of the population may be estimated by the average of the sample variances. Under the assumption that the samples come from the same population, the variances should be roughly equal. If the variances are not nearly equal, there may be a bias in the corresponding F test, which may preclude the possibility of reaching a valid conclusion.

Several tests of the homogeneity assumption have been proposed. The simplest, which was proposed by Hartley (Winer, 1971, pp. 92-94), is to create a special F ratio of the maximum and minimum variances of the p samples. This ratio is given by:

$$F_{max} = \frac{\text{Largest of } p \text{ treatment variances}}{\text{Smallest of } p \text{ treatment variances}} \qquad (7.8)$$

Once computed, this variance ratio is then compared with specially tabulated values for p and $(n - 1)$ degrees of freedom (see Winer, 1971).

A similar test proposed by Cochran (Winer, 1971, pp. 94-95) is defined as the ratio of the largest sample variance to the sum of the sample variances:

$$C = \frac{\text{largest } s_i^2}{\Sigma s_i^2} \qquad (7.9)$$

The 95th and 99th percentiles for the distribution of the coefficient C, which is not an F statistic, is given by Winer, and the SPSS procedure ONEWAY calculates the probability $(1 - \alpha)$ for this test.

A third, more powerful but more complicated, test is known as the *Bartlett-Box test*. The statistic and its significance level are also calculated by the SPSS procedure ONEWAY.

7.5 INFERENCE IN FIXED AND RANDOM FACTORS MODELS[A]

In our discussion of ANOVA in Chapters 4 through 7, we assumed that the values of the dependent variable were derived from a random sample selected from each of all the possible levels of the categories into which one or two independent variables might be grouped. In this regard, the dependent variable is always measured in terms of a ratio or interval scale. For example, depending on the nature of our study, the dependent variable might be treatment costs, the number of laboratory procedures used, or a measure of employee morale. On the other hand, the independent variables included in our analysis are usually categorical in nature. For example, sex, marital status, department, disease category, type of surgical procedure, and type of employee are truly nominal variables. Note that independent variables may also be ordinal, interval, or ratio variables that have been grouped into various categories. For example, depending on the nature of the study, we might group the independent variable into various age ranges, salary ranges, or years of experience.

In most of the situations encountered in health care administration, the potential independent variables have many categories and, as a result, it might be necessary to limit the number of categories included in the study. For example, the independent variables in a study of the effects of working conditions on employee morale might include: the different types of working conditions, the different departments, and different hospitals. Perhaps only two or three different working conditions are contemplated for the experiment, but most large hospitals have from 30 to 60 departments and there are thousands of hospitals that could potentially be included in such an experiment.

In our discussion of ANOVA in Chapters 4, 5, and 6, we assumed that all levels of the independent variables are represented in the experiment. If only a few levels are possible, it is feasible to perform the experiment. On the other hand, if many levels are possible, the required number of observations may become excessive. In this regard, recall that for p levels of factor A (treatment), q levels of factor B (block) and n observations in each cell of the data matrix, npq observations are required. Thus, as p and q increase, the number of observations increases rapidly.

Let us assume that there are P departments and Q hospitals in our hypothetical study. In terms of the formulas developed in Chapter 5, we assume that $p = P$ and $q = Q$. Such an assumption leads to a *fixed factors* model. We know that large values of P and Q lead to the gathering of excessive amounts of data and we may decide to limit the number of categories for study, so that $p < P$ and $q < Q$. If we restrict our conclusions to the p departments and to the q hospitals, we still have a *fixed factors* model. However, if we randomly select the p departments and q hospitals from larger populations, then these factors are *random*, and we may wish to generalize our conclusions beyond the bounds of the study. If we restrict our study to the hospitals in one city and randomly select the departments, then one factor is fixed and the other is random. In such a situation, we refer to the mode of analysis as a *mixed* model.

7.5.1 Inference for Fixed Factors Models [B]

Tests of statistical significance are relatively simple for a fixed factors model. Recall that when performing a two-way analysis of variance with interaction, the corresponding F ratios are given by $MS(TR)/MS(E)$, $MS(B)/MS(E)$, and $MS(TRB)/MS(E)$. These ratios are then compared with the tabular value of F_α for the appropriate degrees of freedom when performing tests of significance. In this section, we shall return to the problem involving the use of laboratory service (introduced in Section 5.3) and examine the test of significance for the fixed factors incorporated in this example. We then consider the statistical examination of random factors models and mixed factors models.

The analysis of variance table that was originally constructed when examining the use of laboratory services is reproduced here as Table 7-2. Here, a column indicating the level of significance (α), has been added for the F tests and that the calculated values of the F ratio are equal to or greater than F_α for the α levels shown for the appropriate number of degrees of freedom. Also recall that the smaller the value of α, the greater the level of significance. An inspection of this table reveals that the F ratios for the treatment, block, and interactive effects are all significant at the .05 level. However, these results pertain to a fixed factor model and cannot be generalized beyond the four conditions and three hospitals. We find in Section 7.5.3 that generalization is possible by changing the basic assumptions, but that the results are more conservative.

7.5.2 Expected Values of Mean Squares [B]

In this section we shall ignore the theoretical development of the expected values of the mean square terms pertaining to a fixed factors model. Rather, we simply present the expected values of the mean square terms and, on the

Table 7-2 ANOVA Table for LABTESTS Using Fixed Factors Model

Source	SS	df	MS	F	α
Treatment (Conditions)	30.56	3	10.19	3.49	.05
Block (Hospitals)	61.56	2	30.78	10.55	.01
Interaction	121.77	6	20.30	6.96	.01
Error	70.00	24	2.92		
Total	283.89	35			

basis of this discussion, we shall illustrate the problems that arise when performing tests of significance. A theoretical treatment of these issues is given in Winer (1971). In this section, we consider first, the results obtained when a one-factor model is employed (i.e., one-way ANOVA) and then consider two-factor models.

For a one-factor design, recall that the components of the sums of squares model are given by:

$$SS(T) = SS(TR) + SS(E)$$

and that $MS(TR) = SS(TR)/(p - 1)$ and $MS(E) = SS(E)/p(n - 1)$. Also recall that the structural model is:

$$\mu_i = \mu + \alpha_i$$

with the null hypothesis $H_0 : \alpha_i = 0$ for all i. We have said that $MS(E)$ and $MS(TR)$ are independent estimates of σ_e^2 if the null hypothesis that all α_i are zero is true. Under the alternate hypothesis ($\alpha_i \neq 0$), the expected values of the mean squares can be expressed as follows:

$$E[MS(E)] = \sigma_e^2 \qquad (7.10.1)$$

$$E[MS(TR)] = \sigma_e^2 + n\sigma_\alpha^2 \qquad (7.10.2)$$

The quantities σ_e^2 and σ_α^2 **cannot** be measured directly, while the terms $MS(E)$ and $MS(TR)$ are calculated using the formulas presented in Chapter 4. If the null hypothesis is true, $\sigma_\alpha^2 = 0$, and $E[MS(E)] = E[MS(TR)]$. However, a significant F ratio of the form $MS(TR)/MS(E)$ implies that $\sigma_\alpha^2 \neq 0$.

Fortunately, for a one-factor design the form of the F test is the same for both a fixed factor and for a random factor model. Unfortunately, for a two

(or more)-factor design the situation is more complex, because the expected values of the mean squares have more terms in the expression.
With respect to a two-factor design, we assume:

---

1. $\mu_{ij} = \mu + \alpha_i + \beta_j + \alpha\beta_{ij}$ (7.11)

2. For each cell, n out of N possible observations were selected randomly.

3. For factor A (treatments), p out of P levels were chosen randomly.

4. For factor B (blocks), q out of Q levels were chosen randomly.

Note that we are changing our notation here from TR, B, and TRB to A, B, and AB, respectively.
The expected values of the mean squares are expressed as:

$$E[MS(A)] = \left(1 - \frac{n}{N}\right)\sigma_e^2 + n\left(1 - \frac{q}{Q}\right)\sigma_{\alpha\beta}^2 + nq\sigma_\alpha^2 \qquad (7.12.1)$$

$$E[MS(B)] = \left(1 - \frac{n}{N}\right)\sigma_e^2 + n\left(1 - \frac{p}{P}\right)\sigma_{\alpha\beta}^2 + np\sigma_\beta^2 \qquad (7.12.2)$$

$$E[MS(AB)] = \left(1 - \frac{n}{N}\right)\sigma_e^2 + n\sigma_{\alpha\beta}^2 \qquad (7.12.3)$$

$$E[MS(E)] = \left(1 - \frac{n}{N}\right)\sigma_e^2 \qquad (7.12.4)$$

Usually $n \ll N$ and therefore $(1 - n/N) \cong 1$, and the first term in each of the expressions on the right-hand side is approximately σ_e^2. As before, the mean squares are calculated using the appropriate formulas, but the σ^2 **cannot** be calculated directly.

7.5.3 Tests of Significance [B]

Arising from Equations 7.12.1 through 7.12.4 are two types of considerations for performing tests of significance. First is the question of whether the A and B factors are fixed or random, and second is the effect of the interaction term (AB) on the tests concerning the main effects of the factors.

Let us first examine the effect of fixed and random factors. If A is a fixed factor, then $p = P$ because all levels of A have been included. Similarly, if B is fixed then $q = Q$. If the levels of the factors are randomly chosen, it is assumed that $p \ll P$ and $q \ll Q$, respectively.

These assumptions play an important part in determining the form of the expected values of $MS(A)$ and $MS(B)$. The type of factor A determines the expression for factor B, and vice versa. The reason for this is that p/P appears in the second term of $E[MS(B)]$, and q/Q appears in the second term of $E[MS(A)]$. If factor A is *fixed* we find that $(1 - p/P) = (1 - 1) = 0$, and 7.12.2 becomes:

$$E[MS(B)] = \sigma_e^2 + np\sigma_\beta^2 \qquad (7.13.1)$$

However, if factor A is *random*, $p \ll P$ and $(1 - p/P) \cong 1$, and Equation 7.12.2 assumes the form:

$$E[MS(B)] = \sigma_e^2 + n\sigma_{\alpha\beta}^2 + np\sigma_\beta^2 \qquad (7.13.2)$$

Therefore, if factor A is *fixed*, the appropriate ratio to examine factor B is given by:

$$F_B = \frac{MS(B)}{MS(E)} \qquad (7.14.1)$$

because

$$E(F_B) = \frac{E[MS(B)]}{E[MS(E)]} = \frac{\sigma_e^2 + np\sigma_\beta^2}{\sigma_e^2} = 1 + \left(\frac{np}{\sigma_e^2}\right)\sigma_\beta^2 \qquad (7.14.2)$$

which tests the null hypothesis $\sigma_\beta^2 = 0$.
However, if factor A is *random*, then the appropriate ratio is:

$$F_B = \frac{MS(B)}{MS(AB)} \qquad (7.14.3)$$

because

$$E(F_B) = \frac{E[MS(B)]}{E[MS(AB)]} = \frac{\sigma_e^2 + n\sigma_{\alpha\beta}^2 + np\sigma_\beta^2}{\sigma_e^2 + n\sigma_{\alpha\beta}^2} = 1 + \frac{np}{\sigma_e^2 + n\sigma_{\alpha\beta}^2}\sigma_\beta^2$$

(7.14.4)

which examines the hypothesis that $\sigma_\beta^2 = 0$.

The preceding discussion suggests that the appropriate test for examining the statistical significance of the interactive effect is always

$$F_{AB} = \frac{MS(AB)}{MS(E)}$$ (7.14.5)

However, the appropriate test for examining the significance of the main effects exerted by factors A and B depends on the fixed or random nature of B and A, respectively. In this case, the nature of factor B controls the test employed for factor A, and vice versa.

7.5.4 Fixed Model[B]

When calculating the expected values of the mean squares, Equations 7.12.1 through 7.12.4 reduce to the four special cases presented in Table 7-3. If both factors are fixed or if our sample represents the universe and we do not care to generalize beyond the sample, the F tests are simple and are based on the first column of Table 7-3. The expected value of the F ratio for factor A is:

$$E[F_A] = \frac{E[MS(A)]}{E[MS(E)]} = \frac{\sigma_e^2 + nq\sigma_\alpha^2}{\sigma_e^2}$$ (7.15)

The null hypothesis is $H_{0\alpha}: \sigma_\alpha^2 = 0$; and $E[F_A] = 1$, if $H_{0\alpha}$ is true. The others are similar. Therefore, for *both factors fixed* the F ratios should be calculated as:

$$F_A = \frac{MS(A)}{MS(E)}, F_B = \frac{MS(B)}{MS(E)}, F_{AB} = \frac{MS(AB)}{MS(E)}$$ (7.16)

7.5.5 The Effects of Interaction[B]

The other columns of Table 7-3 provide the basis for examining the effects of significant interaction when dealing with mixed or random models. In

Table 7-3 Expected Values of Mean Squares for Fixed, Mixed and Random Two-Factor Designs

	FIXED	MIXED	MIXED	RANDOM
	Both Fixed	A Fixed B Random	A Random B Fixed	Both Random
$E[MS(A)]$	$\sigma_e^2 + nq\sigma_\alpha^2$	$\sigma_e^2 + n\sigma_{\alpha\beta}^2 + nq\sigma_\alpha^2$	$\sigma_e^2 + 0 + nq\sigma_\alpha^2$	$\sigma_e^2 + n\sigma_{\alpha\beta}^2 + nq\sigma_\alpha^2$
$E[MS(B)]$	$\sigma_e^2 + np\sigma_\beta^2$	$\sigma_e^2 + 0 + np\sigma_\beta^2$	$\sigma_e^2 + n\sigma_{\alpha\beta}^2 + np\sigma_\beta^2$	$\sigma_e^2 + n\sigma_{\alpha\beta}^2 + np\sigma_\beta^2$
$E[MS(AB)]$	$\sigma_e^2 + n\sigma_{\alpha\beta}^2$	$\sigma_e^2 + n\sigma_{\alpha\beta}^2$	$\sigma_e^2 + n\sigma_{\alpha\beta}^2$	$\sigma_e^2 + n\sigma_{\alpha\beta}^2$
$E[MS(E)]$	σ_e^2	σ_e^2	σ_e^2	σ_e^2

these cases, the appropriate F test for the main influence of factors A and B depends on either the significance or nonsignificance of the interactive effect. In this section, we consider first the situation in which both A and B are random.

7.5.5.1 Random Model [B]

As before, to examine the significance of the interactive effect, the null hypothesis is given by $H_{0_{\alpha\beta}}: \sigma_{\alpha\beta}^2 = 0$. The appropriate F ratio assumes the form:

$$F_{AB} = \frac{MS(AB)}{MS(E)} \tag{7.17.1}$$

since

$$E[F_{AB}] = \frac{E[MS(AB)]}{E[MS(E)]} = \frac{\sigma_e^2 + n\sigma_{\alpha\beta}^2}{\sigma_e^2} \tag{7.17.2}$$

An inspection of Equation 7.17.2 reveals that, if the null hypothesis is true, the expected value of F_{AB} is unity. Conversely, if there is real interaction between A and B, the expected value of F_{AB} is greater than unity.

Consider next F_A and F_B. With respect to F_A, the ratio

$$\frac{MS(A)}{MS(E)}$$

is inappropriate since

$$E(F_A) = \frac{E[MS(A)]}{E[MS(E)]} = \frac{\sigma_e^2 + n\sigma_{\alpha\beta}^2 + nq\sigma_\alpha^2}{\sigma_e^2} \tag{7.17.3}$$

depends on both $\sigma_{\alpha\beta}^2$ and σ_α^2. On the other hand, if there is a significant interactive effect, the ratio

$$F_A = \frac{MS(A)}{MS(AB)} \tag{7.17.4}$$

is appropriate since

$$\frac{E[MS(A)]}{E[MS(AB)]} = \frac{\sigma^2 + n\sigma_{\alpha\beta}^2 + nq\sigma_\alpha^2}{\sigma^2 + n\sigma_{\alpha\beta}^2} \tag{7.17.5}$$

In this case, Equation 7.17.5 examines the null hypothesis, which is given by $H_{0_\alpha}: \sigma_\alpha^2 = 0$. Similarly, if the interactive effect is significant, the test for factor B is given by:

$$F_B = \frac{MS(B)}{MS(AB)} \qquad (7.17.6)$$

Conversely, *if the interactive effect is not significant*, we simply pool $SS(E)$ and $SS(AB)$ to obtain:

$$MS(E + AB) = \frac{SS(E) + SS(AB)}{df_E + df_{AB}} \qquad (7.17.7)$$

As a consequence, the appropriate F tests are given by:

$$F_A = \frac{MS(A)}{MS(E + AB)} \quad \text{and} \quad F_B = \frac{MS(B)}{MS(E + AB)} \qquad (7.17.8)$$

7.5.5.2 Mixed Model [B]

For the *mixed models*, with significant interaction, one of the main effects is compared with $MS(E)$, and the other with $MS(AB)$. With A fixed and B random,

$$F_A = \frac{MS(A)}{MS(AB)} \quad \text{and} \quad F_B = \frac{MS(B)}{MS(E)} \qquad (7.18.1)$$

are the appropriate tests. On the other hand, when B is fixed and A is random, the ratios

$$F_A = \frac{MS(A)}{MS(E)} \quad \text{and} \quad F_B = \frac{MS(B)}{MS(AB)} \qquad (17.18.2)$$

represent the appropriate statistical tests. As before, if the interactive effect is not significant, the sums of squares for error and interaction are pooled.

7.5.5.3 Example: Random Model—LABTESTS [B]

In the laboratory tests example used in Sections 5.3 and 7.5.1, the number of lab tests were counted for patients with different conditions in different hospitals. For the fixed model where we did not want to generalize beyond the confines of the experiment, we found significant interaction and significant main effects (see Table 7-2).

However, if we use the random model, because we wish to generalize for all conditions and all hospitals, we test first the interaction and then the main effects. The significance of the interaction is tested by $F_{AB} = 20.3/2.92 = 6.95$, which is significant at the .01 level for 6 and 24 degrees of freedom. This finding forces us to evaluate $F_A = MS(A)/MS(AB) = 10.18/20.3$, which is less than 1 and therefore not significant. F_B is tested as $MS(B)/MS(AB) = 30.73/20.3 \cong 1.52$ with 2 and 6 degrees of freedom. Comparing the tabular value of F at the .05 level of significance with the computed F value, we find that the main effect is not significant.

Therefore, in the random model for the LABTESTS example, the interaction is significant but the main effects are not. Therefore, we cannot say that all hospitals (B) differ among themselves, nor that all conditions (A) differ among themselves, but we can say that the number of lab tests does depend on the *particular combination* of condition and hospital. This is a much more conservative result than we found for the fixed factors model for these data.

7.5.5.4 Example: Mixed Model—LABTESTS [B]

Let us suppose that we wish to view the results of the experiment from the perspective of all conditions in those three hospitals [i.e., conditions (A) random, but hospitals (B) fixed].

The appropriate F ratios are:

$$F_{AB} = \frac{MS(AB)}{MS(E)} = \frac{20.3}{2.92} \cong 6.95 \qquad \text{which is significant, as before}$$

$$F_A = \frac{MS(A)}{MS(E)} = \frac{10.18}{2.92} \cong 3.49 \qquad \text{which is significant at the .05 level}$$

$$F_B = \frac{MS(B)}{MS(AB)} = \frac{30.78}{20.3} \cong 1.52 \qquad \text{which is not significant}$$

Therefore, we conclude that these three hospitals do not differ significantly among themselves in the number of lab tests performed, but that there are significant differences among all the conditions, and that the number of lab tests also depends on the combination of the particular condition and the hospital.

7.5.5.5 Example: Mixed Model—Nosocomial Infection Treatment Cost Study [B]

In the Heidemann study used in Section 6.4.2.1, the treatment costs for 60 patients undergoing Hysterectomy and Caesarian Section were investigated

to determine the treatment cost impact of hospital-acquired (nosocomial) infections. The ANOVA table for the study is reproduced as Table 7-4.
For this example, we consider the procedure factor random and the infection factor fixed. The two procedures were selected from a number of different possibilities, while infection is a yes/no type of variable.
Examining the interactive effects first, we find:

$$F_{AB} = \frac{MS(AB)}{MS(E)} = \frac{3,347}{46,601} < 1.0$$

and therefore the interaction is not significant. Pooling the interaction and error sums of squares yields:

$$SS(E + AB) = 2,609,684 + 3,347 = 2,613,031$$
$$df(E + AB) = 56 + 1 = 57$$
$$MS(E + AB) = 45,842.6$$

Thus, for surgical procedures we find that $F_A = MS(A)/MS(E + AB) =$ 166,146.6/45,842.6 $\cong$ 3.62 with 1 and 57 degrees of freedom, which is not significant at the .05 level of confidence. Similarly, for infections we find that $F_B = MS(B)/MS(E + AB) = 326,045.9/45,842.6 \cong 7.11$ with 1 and 57 degrees of freedom, which is significant at the .01 level of confidence.

On the basis of these findings, we conclude that there is no significant interaction between procedure and infection, and that there is no significant difference between the procedures. However, these results suggest that there is a significant difference in the treatment costs of noninfected and infected patients.

7.5.6 Conclusions—Fixed and Random Factors[A]

While the computations for significance tests for the fixed model are the simplest, the situation of the experiment more often fits the mixed or random

Table 7-4 ANOVA Table for Nosocomial Infection Treatment Cost Study

Source	SS	df	MS
Surgical Procedure (*A*)	166,146.60	1	166,146.60
Infection (*B*)	326,045.90	1	326,045.90
Interaction (*AB*)	3,347.16	1	3,347.16
Error	2,609,684.10	56	46,601.50
Total	3,105,223.80	59	

model. There is less likelihood of finding significance using the mixed or random model. This guarantees that we are more conservative in extending our findings beyond the actual data that was collected.

7.6 BALANCED DESIGNS AND ORTHOGONALITY (A)

The analysis of variance models we have examined thus far have all assumed equal n's in each cell. The (independent) factors are assumed to be unrelated (orthogonal) to each other, and orthogonality is partially assured by having an equal number of observations in each cell. Orthogonality is completely assured in a pure experiment by the random assignment of equal numbers of subjects to each cell so that only the experimental factors will influence the outcomes. However, in the managerial application of ANOVA, there are many characteristics that are determined by the subjects and not by the management researcher. For instance, associated with patients and employees are attributes such as age, sex, marital status, education level, job category, illness category, and so forth, which the researcher may want to study or *control*. Any relationship among these attribute variables may affect the values of the dependent variable, and the management researcher should select a stratified random sample to avoid problems as much as possible.

If the researcher is unable to obtain an equal number of subjects for each cell, the design is termed *unbalanced*, and there is an artificially created dependence among the so-called independent factors. This leads to difficulty in computation, although the Winer text gives appropriate formulas. However, it also leads to difficulties when interpreting the *meaning* of the results, and the approach that is often used is that of multiple regression coupled with the various approaches to significance testing as discussed in Chapter 12 of this work, and in Chapter 22 of the SPSS manual.

7.7 USE OF THE SPSS BATCH SYSTEM (D)

SPSS performs analysis of variance in a number of related procedures. Several of these, namely BREAKDOWN, ONEWAY, and ANOVA are designed for one-way, two-way, or factorial analysis of variance as discussed in Chapters 4 through 7. (The other procedures are designed for regression and other techniques.) BREAKDOWN and ONEWAY were described in Chapter 4, but two features of ONEWAY were not considered until this chapter, namely, CONTRAST and tests for homogeneity of variance. The use of the CONTRAST and homogeneity features is discussed in Section 7.7.1. The main analysis of variance program is ANOVA, and its use is described in Section 7.7.2.

Figure 7-2 SPSS Cards for Performing ONEWAY ANOVA with Contrasts

```
//    ),'COLIN M. LAY',MSGLEVEL=2,CLASS=K
//    EXEC    SPSSH
//FT08F001    DD   *
17 1
13 1
16 1
12 1
15 1
17 1
16 1
16 2
14 2
17 2
13 2
12 2
14 2
18 2
10 3
 9 3
11 3
 8 3
 6 3
 7 3
 6 3
 8 4
 9 4
12 4
 6 4
 7 4
 6 4
 8 4
 7 5
 8 5
10 5
 6 5
 8 5
 9 5
 6 5
 9 6
 6 6
 8 6
 5 6
 6 6
 9 6
 7 6
//SYSIN DD *
RUN NAME            HEART DISEASE - LENGTH OF STAY
INPUT MEDIUM        DISK
N OF CASES          UNKNOWN
DATA LIST           FIXED / 1 LOS 1-2  INST 4
VAR LABELS          LOS, PATIENT LENGTH OF STAY/
                    INST, INSTITUTION WHERE PATIENT TREATED/
ONEWAY              LOS BY INST (1,6)/
                    CONTRAST = .5 .5 -.25 -.25 -.25 -.25/
                    CONTRAST = 1 -1/
                    CONTRAST = 0 0 1 -1/
                    CONTRAST = 0 0 0 0 1 -1/
                    CONTRAST = 0 0 .5 .5 -.5 -.5/

STATISTICS          1,3
FINISH
/*
```

7.7.1 SPSS Procedure ONEWAY (D)

The use of ONEWAY was described in Chapter 4, but it is reconsidered here because of its handling of topics covered earlier in this chapter. Section 7.3 dealt with contrasts, and the example employed in Section 7.3.1 was introduced to illustrate the use of ONEWAY. Also, the tests for homogeneity of variance described in Section 7.4 were requested as part of the output. Figure 7-2 shows the set of cards necessary for performance of ONEWAY. The reader should verify that the CONTRASTS requested are those originally used in Section 7.3.1.

The output for this procedure is shown in Figure 7-3. The first page contains the ANOVA table and the requested group statistics, while the second page evaluates the requested contrasts and shows the tests for homogeneity of variance. Note that the contrasts are tested on two bases. The first basis involves situations in which the assumption of homoscedasticity is satisfied. In these situations, the population variances are averaged. The second basis involves those situations in which one or more of the three tests concerning homoscedasticity indicate that the assumption of equal variance is violated. In these situations, more complex formulas with separate variance estimates are appropriate, and these formulas are not covered in this text. The user must decide whether to use the contrast evaluation based on pooled (homogeneous) variance or separate (nonhomogeneous) variance estimates, after examining the homogeneity tests requested by statistic 3.

The other facilities provided by SPSS for ONEWAY are beyond the scope of this work, but are listed here for reference purposes. Seven approaches to a posteriori contrasts are provided by the RANGES facility, and tests for linear, quadrantic, or higher order trends of the sample means are provided by the POLYNOMIAL facility.

7.7.2 SPSS Procedure ANOVA (D)

The major SPSS procedure for carrying out analysis of variance is named ANOVA and is described in Chapter 22 of the SPSS manual (pp. 398–433). ANOVA is compatible with the other SPSS procedures in that a dependent variable and a list of up to five independent variables are specified. This means that each observation must have a value for the dependent variable and for each independent variable. The independent variable values must be integers, and the minimum and maximum values must be specified. This method of providing data to SPSS makes the data format incompatible with most classical analysis of variance programs, because they are arranged to read in all n values of the dependent variable for cell 1 of the design matrix, and then for cell 2, cell 3, and so on, until all dependent variable data for all

Figure 7-3 Output from SPSS Procedure: ONEWAY Showing Contrasts

```
HEART DISEASE - LENGTH OF STAY                                          04/18/79        PAGE  2
FILE   NONAME   (CREATION DATE = 04/18/79)
- - - - - - - - - - - - - - - - - - - - - - - - - - - - - - - - - - - - - - - - - - - - - - - - -

VARIABLE  LOS      PATIENT LENGTH OF STAY

- - - - - - - - - - - - - O N E W A Y - - - - - - - - - - - - -

                            ANALYSIS OF VARIANCE

            SOURCE             D.F.     SUM OF SQUARES    MEAN SQUARES    F RATIO    F PROB.

   BETWEEN GROUPS               5          494.9763         98.9952       27.657     0.0000
   WITHIN GROUPS               36          128.8570          3.5794
   TOTAL                       41          623.8333

                         STANDARD    STANDARD
GROUP     COUNT     MEAN     DEVIATION    ERROR    MINIMUM    MAXIMUM    95 PCT CONF INT FOR MEAN

GRP01       7     15.1429    1.9518    0.7377    12.0000    17.0000    13.3378 TO 16.9480
GRP02       7     14.8571    2.1931    0.8289    12.0000    18.0000    12.8289 TO 16.9540
GRP03       7      8.1429    1.9518    0.7377     6.0000    11.0000     6.3378 TO  9.9540
GRP04       7      8.0000    2.0817    0.7868     6.0000    12.0000     6.0748 TO  9.9252
GRP05       7      7.7143    1.4960    0.5654     6.0000    12.0000     6.2307 TO  9.9979
GRP05       7      7.1429    1.5736    0.5948     5.0000     9.0000     5.6875 TO  8.5982

TOTAL      42     10.1667    3.9007    0.6019     5.0000    18.0000     8.9511 TO 11.3622

VARIABLE  LOS      PATIENT LENGTH OF STAY

CONTRAST COEFFICIENT MATRIX

            GRP01 GRP02 GRP03 GRP04 GRP05 GRP06

CONTRAST 1   0.5   0.5  -0.3  -0.3  -0.3  -0.3
CONTRAST 2   1.0  -1.0   0.0   0.0   0.0   0.0
CONTRAST 3   0.0   0.0   1.0  -1.0   0.0   0.0
CONTRAST 4   0.0   0.0   0.0   0.0   1.0  -1.0
CONTRAST 5   0.0   0.0   0.0   0.0   0.5  -0.5

                      POOLED VARIANCE ESTIMATE                 SEPARATE VARIANCE ESTIMATE
           VALUE    S. ERROR   T VALUE   D.F.   T PROB.     S. ERROR   T VALUE   D.F.   T PROB.

CONTRAST 1  7.2500   0.6193    11.707    36.0   0.000       0.6501    11.152    20.8    0.000
CONTRAST 2  0.2857   1.0113     0.283    36.0   0.779       1.1096     0.257    11.8    0.801
CONTRAST 3  0.1429   1.0113     0.141    36.0   0.888       1.0785     0.132    12.0    0.897
CONTRAST 4  0.5714   1.0113     0.565    36.0   0.576       0.8207     0.696    12.0    0.499
CONTRAST 5  0.6429   0.7151     0.899    36.0   0.375       0.6776     0.943    22.3    0.355

TESTS FOR HOMOGENEITY OF VARIANCES
COCHRANS C = MAX. VARIANCE/SUM(VARIANCES) = 0.2239, P = 1.000 (APPROX.)
BARTLETT-BOX F =                                0.255, P = 0.937
MAXIMUM VARIANCE / MINIMUM VARIANCE =           2.149
```

cells have been entered. The classical method of data entry was chosen to resemble the tabular calculations shown for one-way ANOVA in Section 4.2 of this book. The SPSS method does not require the data to be in any specific order, and it was chosen because SPSS actually uses a multiple regression formulation of the ANOVA problem, which allows the computational treatment of both equal and unequal sample sizes in the cells. SPSS allows performing *analysis of covariance*, an extension of regular analysis of variance,

---

Figure 7-4 SPSS Cards for Performing Analysis of Variance

```
//UDCC3576       JOB       (HD123456,
//    ),'COLIN M. LAY',MSGLEVEL=2,CLASS=K
//    EXEC    SPSSH
//FT08F001    DD   *
 1  1  1
 3  1  1
 5  1  1
 6  1  2
 4  1  2
 7  1  2
 8  1  3
 9  1  3
10  1  3
 4  2  1
 7  2  1
 5  2  1
 7  2  2
 8  2  2
 9  2  2
 2  2  3
 5  2  3
 6  2  3
 1  3  1
 2  3  1
 4  3  1
 3  3  2
 7  3  2
 6  3  2
 1  3  3
 4  3  3
 5  3  3
 2  4  1
 1  4  1
 5  4  1
 1  4  2
 2  4  2
 4  4  2
 8  4  3
 9  4  3
11  4  3
//SYSIN    DD   *
RUN NAME          ANOVA DEMONSTRATION - LABORATORY TESTS
INPUT MEDIUM      DISK
N OF CASES        UNKNOWN
DATA LIST         FIXED/ 1 TESTS 1-2, COND 4, INST 6
VAR LABELS        TESTS, NUMBER OF LAB TESTS FOR EACH PATIENT/
                  COND, CONDITION FOR WHICH PATIENT TREATED/
                  INST, INSTITUTION WHERE PATIENT TREATED/
VALUE LABELS      COND (1)PREGNANCY (2)MAL.NEOPLASM
                  (3)TRAUMA (4)APPENDICITIS
ANOVA             TESTS BY COND (1,4), INST (1,3)
STATISTICS        1
READ INPUT DATA
FINISH
/*
```

Figure 7-5 SPSS Output for ANOVA Demonstration

```
ANOVA DEMONSTRATION - LABORATORY TESTS

FILE   NONAME   (CREATION DATE = 06/15/78)

* * * * * * A N A L Y S I S   O F   V A R I A N C E * * * * * * * * * * * * * *
            TESTS    NUMBER OF LAB TESTS FOR EACH PATIENT
         BY COND     CONDITION FOR WHICH PATIENT TREATED
            INST     INSTITUTION WHERE PATIENT TREATED
* * * * * * * * * * * * * * * * * * * * * * * * * * * * * * * * * * * * * * * *
```

SOURCE OF VARIATION	SUM OF SQUARES	DF	MEAN SQUARE	F	SIGNIF OF F
MAIN EFFECTS	92.111	5	18.422	6.316	0.001
COND	30.556	3	10.185	3.492	0.031
INST	61.556	2	30.778	10.552	0.001
2-WAY INTERACTIONS	121.778	6	20.296	6.959	0.000
COND INST	121.778	6	20.296	6.959	0.000
EXPLAINED	213.889	11	19.444	6.667	0.000
RESIDUAL	70.000	24	2.917		
TOTAL	283.889	35	8.111		

```
36 CASES WERE PROCESSED.
 0 CASES ( 0.0 PCT) WERE MISSING.

* * * M U L T I P L E   C L A S S I F I C A T I O N   A N A L Y S I S * * *
            TESTS    NUMBER OF LAB TESTS FOR EACH PATIENT
         BY COND     CONDITION FOR WHICH PATIENT TREATED
            INST     INSTITUTION WHERE PATIENT TREATED
* * * * * * * * * * * * * * * * * * * * * * * * * * * * * * * * * * * * * * * *

GRAND MEAN =   5.06
```

VARIABLE + CATEGORY	N	UNADJUSTED DEV'N ETA	ADJUSTED FOR INDEPENDENTS DEV'N BETA	ADJUSTED FOR INDEPENDENTS + COVARIATES DEV'N BETA
COND				
1 PREGNANCY	9	0.83	0.83	
2 MAL.NEOPLASM	9	0.83	0.83	
3 TRAUMA	9	-1.39	-1.39	
4 APPENDICITIS	9	-0.28	-0.28	
		0.33	0.33	
INST				
1	12	-1.72	-1.72	
2	12	0.28	0.28	
3	12	1.44	1.44	
		0.47	0.47	
MULTIPLE R SQUARED			0.324	
MULTIPLE R			0.570	

which is beyond the scope of this work. However, it is a capability that does not alter or interfere with regular analysis of variance.

The regular output of the ANOVA procedure is a normal ANOVA table, and, by calling for STATISTIC 1, the user can obtain a Multiple Classification Analysis (MCA) table. The MCA table merely contains the estimates of the α_i's, and β_j's from the structural model of the ANOVA problem as described in Section 7.1 of this text. It also allows production of the statistics Eta and Eta^2, which are related to R and R^2 in the multiple regression model described in Chapter 10.

Figure 7-4 presents the cards required to perform the ANOVA on the data for the laboratory tests problem used in much of this chapter. Three variables are used in the analysis: The dependent variable is TESTS, which was defined as the number of laboratory tests for each patient; the two independent variables (factors) are COND, the condition for which the patient is treated, and INST, the institution where the patient is treated. The ANOVA procedure statement is:

ANOVA   TESTS BY COND (1, 4), INST (1, 3)

and a multiple classification analysis is called for by STATISTIC 1. Figure 7-5 shows the output of the procedure. Since the ANOVA table is standard, it does not need any further explanation, except to say that the F statistics are calculated for the fixed model, and the significance column gives the α level for each F test. In the Multiple Classification table the α and β components of the structural model are presented as *unadjusted deviations*.

NOTES

1. The texts by Kirk and Winer discuss a number of variations of testing all possible simple contrasts to avoid this problem. These methods are included in the RANGES facility for the SPSS procedure ONEWAY. However, these tests are beyond the scope of this work. See also the references by Ryan (1959 and 1960) and Scheffé (1953).

BIBLIOGRAPHY

Kirk, R. *Experimental Design: Procedures for the Behavioral Sciences.* Monterey: Brooks/Cole, 1968.
Ryan, T. "Multiple Comparisons in Psychological Research." *Psychological Bulletin* LVI (1959): 26-47.
Ryan, T. "Significance Tests for Multiple Comparisons of Proportions Variances and Other Statistics." *Psychological Bulletin* LVII (1960): 318-328.
Scheffé, H. "A Method for Judging All Contrasts in the Analysis of Variance," *Biometrika* XL (1953): 87-104.
Winer, B. J. *Statistical Principles in Experimental Design,* New York: McGraw-Hill, 1971.

Problems for Solution[(G)]

1. For the problems solved at the end of Chapter 5, assume a mixed and then a random model and retest for significance under the changed assumptions.

2. For one or more of the problems of Chapter 4, choose an appropriate set of orthogonal contrasts. Compute the contrasts, the sums of squares, and significance. Estimate the components of the structural model.

3. Solve one or more of the problems of Chapters 4 and 5 using SPSS.

Part III
Regression Analysis

Chapter 8

Covariation and Correlation

Objectives

After completing this chapter, the student should be able to:
1. Understand the nonparametric test of association;
2. Understand the concept of covariation;
3. Calculate the covariance between two variables;
4. Understand and calculate the correlation coefficient;
5. Perform tests concerning the correlation coefficient.

Chapter Map

Section 8.1 introduces the basic concepts of covariation and correlation and has been assigned the letter code A.

Sections 8.2, 8.3, 8.3.1, 8.4, 8.4.1, and 8.5.3 introduce basic algebraic expressions and have been assigned the letter code B.

Sections 8.3.2 and 8.4.2 illustrate the use of matrix algebra to calculate correlation and covariance and have been assigned the letter code C.

Section 8.5 (with all its subsections) illustrates the use of SPSS to compute and test correlations and has been assigned the letter code D.

Section 8.6 (with all its subsections) illustrates the use of APL and has been assigned the letter code E.

8.1 INTRODUCTION[A]

There are many situations in which management wishes to examine the association or the relationship between two or more variables. For example, we might wish to examine the relationship between factors such as cost and the provision of service, use of care and family income, the provision of care and resource use, the use of care and different coinsurance charges, and so forth.

The purpose of this chapter is to describe several techniques that may be used to measure the extent to which two variables are associated or related. Specifically, we shall examine a nonparametric measure of association as well as the concepts of covariation and correlation. In addition to providing a measure of the association between two variables, the concepts of covariation and correlation also provide the basis for regression analysis, which is introduced in the next chapter.

For purposes of future illustration, suppose that we are interested in the physiological development of children and that the information presented in Table 8-1 is available to us. We will see that these data provide the basis for estimating the extent to which the age, height, mass, and sex of the child are associated.

If we were initially interested in the association between age and height, we might begin our examination of the association between these two variables by constructing a scattergram as shown in Figure 8-1. An inspection of the scattergram suggests that there is a strong positive relationship between these two variables. That is, as the variable age assumes larger values, the values assumed by the variable height also increase, and our task is to express this association numerically.

8.2 THE QUADRANT TEST FOR ASSOCIATION[B]

One approach to measuring the strength of the relationship between these variables is to divide the scattergram into four quadrants with the origin located at the intersection of the *median* age and height. We then count the number of points in each of the four quadrants.

As shown in Figure 8-2(a), if there are an equal number of points in each of the four quadrants, there would be no indication of a relationship between the variables. On the other hand, a substantial concentration of points in quadrants 1 and 3 indicate a positive relationship, while a substantial number of points in quadrants 2 and 4 indicate a negative relationship between the two variables. These situations are portrayed in Figures 8-2(b) and 8-2(c).

Table 8-1 Data for Physiological Development Study

Child	Age (Years)	Height (Centimeters)	Mass (Kilograms)	Sex
Mary	10	145	40	F
Jim	5	105	20	M
John	3	100	16	M
Jane	6	95	20	F
Agnes	4	95	17	F
Alan	3	80	15	M
Joseph	15	170	64	M
William	12	150	45	M
Brenda	10	135	40	F
David	9	145	45	M
Ephraim	14	140	50	M
Fred	15	150	66	M
Greta	10	120	39	F
Harold	6	115	27	M
Ina	3	90	13	F
Cheryl	11	125	42	F
Suzanne	9	125	31	F
Richard	7	120	25	M
Grace	8	130	30	F
David	7	100	23	M
Sally	13	160	57	F

Recognizing that the quadrants are defined by the *median* (middle) age and height, it is possible to count the number of points appearing in only one quadrant. For example, if we have 22 points and let $\alpha = .01$, a largest quadrant count of 9 or more points is required to demonstrate an association between the two variables. This may be observed in Figure 8-3 where a positive relation between the two variables has been displayed. Observe that 11 points appear to the right and to the left of the vertical median line. In addition, 11 points appear above and below the horizontal median line. We could also have looked at the smallest number of points occurring in any of the quadrants. A table for the limits for either the smallest or the largest number of points is reproduced in Appendix E. The observed number must be either less than the lower limits or larger than the upper limits.

This procedure is referred to as a *nonparametric* test because we require no assumptions concerning the kind of distribution or relationship. For

Figure 8-1 Scattergram of Height and Age—Physiological Development Study

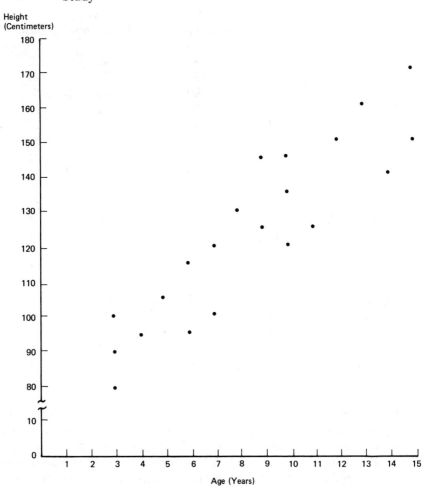

Figure 8-2 Scattergrams of No, Positive and Negative Relationships

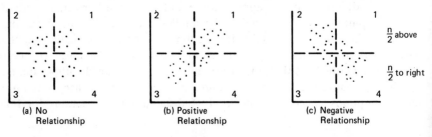

Figure 8-3 Sample Scattergram for Nonparametric Testing for Significant Association

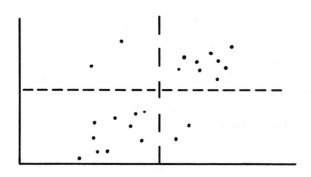

more information about this and related tests see the book by Quenouille (1952).

8.3 COVARIANCE[B]

As implied by its name, covariance measures the extent to which the values of two variables vary together. Here, we observe that if two variables, say x and y, are related so that the large values of x are associated with the large values of y, for any point (x_i, y_i) the deviations $(x_i - \bar{x})$ and $(y_i - \bar{y})$ are both likely to be of the same sign. As a consequence, most of the products $(x_i - \bar{x})(y_i - \bar{y})$ will be positive. In such a situation, we say the covariance between x and y is positive. Conversely, if the variables x and y are related so that the large values of x are associated with small values of y and vice versa, the deviations $(x_i - \bar{x})$ and $(y_i - \bar{y})$ are likely to be of the *opposite* sign. As a result, the product $(x_i - \bar{x})(y_i - \bar{y})$ will likely be negative. In this case, the variables x and y are said to exhibit negative covariance.

8.3.1 Algebraic Expressions for Calculating Covariance[B]

In general, the covariance between two variables, x and y, is defined by

$$\text{Cov}(x, y) = \frac{\Sigma(x - \bar{x})(y - \bar{y})}{n - 1} \tag{8.1}$$

Returning to our example and letting "h" represent height and "a" represent age, we may calculate Cov(h, a) as follows:

$$\text{Cov}(h,\ a) = \frac{\Sigma(h - \bar{h})(a - \bar{a})}{n - 1} \qquad (8.2)$$

If we assume that the data are distributed normally, we observe that the product $(h - \bar{h})(a - \bar{a})$ for a point in quadrant 1 will be positive. However, the product that corresponds to a point in quadrant 2 will be negative. Therefore, a positive covariance would indicate a positive relationship, while a negative covariance would indicate a negative relationship. Obviously, a zero covariance would indicate no relationship between the two variables. The sign of Cov(h, a) associated with each of the four quadrants constructed earlier is shown in Figure 8-4.

Recall that $\Sigma(x - \bar{x})^2$ was employed in the formula by which we calculated the variance (Var) of the random variable x and when this term was expanded and reduced, we obtained $\Sigma x^2 - (1/n)(\Sigma x)^2$. This result permits us to assert that

$$\Sigma(h - \bar{h})(a - \bar{a}) = \Sigma ha - \frac{1}{n}(\Sigma h\,\Sigma a)$$

Substituting $\Sigma ha - (1/n)(\Sigma h\Sigma a)$ for the product $\Sigma(h - \bar{h})(a - \bar{a})$ in Equation 8.2 we obtain:

$$\text{Cov}(h,\ a) = \frac{1}{n - 1}\left[\Sigma ha - \frac{1}{n}(\Sigma h\,\Sigma a)\right] \qquad (8.3)$$

Figure 8-4 Positive and Negative Covariance by Quadrant

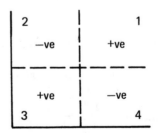

8.3.2 Calculating Covariance: Matrix Notation[C]

Returning to our earlier work on variance, if we let

$$X = \begin{bmatrix} 1 & x_1 \\ & \\ & \\ 1 & x_i \\ & \\ & \\ 1 & x_n \end{bmatrix}$$

such that

$$X'X = \begin{bmatrix} n & \Sigma x \\ \Sigma x & \Sigma x^2 \end{bmatrix}$$

we obtained the results:

$$\Sigma(x - \bar{x})^2 = \frac{1}{n} |X'X|$$

which implied:

$$\mathrm{Var}(x) = \frac{1}{n(n-1)} |X'X|$$

Making use of this fact, let us return to our numeric example and modify the matrix X by adding observations on h as follows.

$$X = \begin{bmatrix} 1 & a_1 & h_1 \\ 1 & a_2 & h_2 \\ 1 & a_3 & h_3 \\ . & . & . \\ . & . & . \\ . & . & . \\ 1 & a_n & h_n \end{bmatrix}$$

In this formulation, the h's represent heights and the a's represent ages. If we then calculate the product

$$\mathbf{X'X} = \begin{bmatrix} n & \Sigma a & \Sigma h \\ \Sigma a & \Sigma a^2 & \Sigma ha \\ \Sigma h & \Sigma ha & \Sigma h^2 \end{bmatrix}$$

we obtain enough information to estimate the covariance of height and age as well as Var(age) and Var(height). This is shown below

$$\text{Cov(height, age)} = \frac{1}{n(n-1)} \begin{vmatrix} n & \Sigma a \\ \Sigma h & \Sigma ha \end{vmatrix} \qquad (8.4)$$

$$\text{Var(height)} = \frac{1}{n(n-1)} \begin{vmatrix} n & \Sigma h \\ \Sigma h & \Sigma h^2 \end{vmatrix} \qquad (8.5)$$

$$\text{Var(age)} = \frac{1}{n(n-1)} \begin{vmatrix} n & \Sigma a \\ \Sigma a & \Sigma a^2 \end{vmatrix} \qquad (8.6)$$

Using the data presented in Table 8-1 to perform these calculations, we obtain:

$$\mathbf{X'X} = \begin{bmatrix} n & \Sigma a & \Sigma h \\ & \Sigma a^2 & \Sigma ha \\ & & \Sigma h^2 \end{bmatrix}$$

$$= \begin{bmatrix} 21 & 180 & 2{,}595 \\ & 1{,}844 & 24{,}000 \\ & & 333{,}125 \end{bmatrix}$$

Observe that $\mathbf{X'X}$ is symmetrical and, as a result, the bottom half of the matrix is easily obtained.

Referring to Equation 8.4 and substituting appropriately we find:

$$\text{Cov(height, age)} = \frac{1}{21 \times 20}(21 \times 24{,}000 - 2{,}595 \times 180)$$

$$= \frac{1}{420} \times (504{,}000 \quad - \quad 467{,}100)$$

$$= 87.857$$

Similarly, after substituting appropriately into Equations 8.5 and 8.6 we obtain:

$$\text{Var(height)} = \frac{1}{420} \times (21 \times 333{,}125 \quad - \quad 2{,}595^2)$$

$$= 622.857$$

$$\text{Var(age)} = \frac{1}{420} \times (21 \times 1{,}844 \quad - \quad 180^2)$$

$$= 15.057$$

A moment's reflection will reveal that the absolute value of the computed covariance between two variables cannot exceed the greatest variance of the two variables for which we seek to establish a relationship. Also note that the maximum possible value of the covariance becomes larger as the values of the variances increase. In this regard, the limits on the value of the covariance term are $+\infty$ and $-\infty$, depending on the nature of the data. As a result, the covariance gives the direction, but not the strength, of the relationship between the variables.

8.4 CORRELATION[B]

The *correlation coefficient* not only indicates the direction of the relationship between two variables, but also indicates the strength of the relationship, as standardized for the size of the variances of the variables. The correlation coefficient is defined by

$$r = \frac{\text{Cov(height, age)}}{\sqrt{\text{Var(height)} \cdot \text{Var(age)}}} \qquad (8.7)$$

An inspection of Equation 8.7 will reveal that the correlation coefficient is the ratio of the covariance and the geometric mean of the variances of the two variables. We can show that the theoretical limits of the correlation coefficient are $r = \pm 1$. Thus, two correlation coefficients are comparable indicators of the strength of relationships, regardless of the variables involved. As before, we distinguish between samples and populations when dealing with correlation coefficients. Sample values are usually represented by the letter r and the theoretical or population values are represented by ρ (rho).

Since $1/n(n-1)$ is a common factor in the definitions of variance and covariance, this term is eliminated in the computational formula. Returning to our example, we find that the correlation between height and age is given by:

$$r_{ha} = \frac{\begin{vmatrix} n & \Sigma a \\ \Sigma h & \Sigma ha \end{vmatrix}}{\sqrt{\begin{vmatrix} n & \Sigma h \\ \Sigma h & \Sigma h^2 \end{vmatrix} \cdot \begin{vmatrix} n & \Sigma a \\ \Sigma a & \Sigma a^2 \end{vmatrix}}} = \frac{36{,}900}{\sqrt{261{,}000 \times 6{,}324}} = .9072$$

This finding may be interpreted to mean that there is a very strong positive association between age and height. As will be described in more detail later, the values assumed by two variables that are highly related exhibit little variability about a straight line with a positive or a negative slope. The values of weakly correlated variables have a greater scatter.

8.4.1   Significance of Correlation[B]

As seen previously, the correlation coefficient may vary between $+1$ and -1, but this information does not tell us whether the correlation or association between two variables is significant. On the basis of statistical theory, we compute the standard error (Std Err) of r as:

$$\text{Std Err}(r) = \sqrt{\frac{1 - r^2}{n - 2}} \qquad (8.8.1)$$

which permits us to compute a t statistic of the form:

$$t = \frac{r}{\text{Std Err}(r)} = r\sqrt{\frac{n - 2}{1 - r^2}} \qquad (8.8.2)$$

The value of t, as computed by Equation 8.8.2, is then compared with the tabular value of t for $(n-2)$ degrees of freedom. The decision criterion for testing

$$H_0: r = 0$$

against

$$H_a: r < 0, \quad r > 0, \quad \text{or} \quad r \neq 0$$

remain unchanged from our earlier discussion.

8.4.2   The Correlation Matrix[C]

In this section, we consider the possibility of encountering more than two variables for which we wish to compute correlation coefficients that depict the relationship between all pairs and display our results in a matrix called the *correlation matrix*. Suppose we are interested in the correlation among the set of variables that we label $x_1, \ldots, x_k$. Suppose further that these variables are associated with some unit of analysis such as the patient, the hospital, a city, and so forth. If we then selected a sample of n patients, n hospitals, or n cities, we would create a data matrix of the form:

$$\mathbf{X} = [1 \mid \mathbf{X}_1 \mid \mathbf{X}_2 \mid \cdots \mid \mathbf{X}_k] \tag{8.9}$$

where each partition is a column vector containing n elements that represent observations or measurements on the variables being examined. Thus, each row represents a case and each column represents a variable. As before, we calculate:

$$\mathbf{X}'\mathbf{X} = \begin{bmatrix} n & \Sigma x_1 & \Sigma x_2 & \cdots & \Sigma x_k \\ \Sigma x_1 & \Sigma x_1^2 & \Sigma x_1 x_2 & \cdots & \Sigma x_1 x_k \\ \Sigma x_2 & \Sigma x_1 x_2 & \Sigma x_2^2 & \cdots & \Sigma x_2 x_k \\ \cdot & \cdot & \cdot & \cdot & \\ \cdot & \cdot & \cdot & & \cdot \\ \cdot & \cdot & \cdot & & \\ \Sigma x_k & \Sigma x_1 x_k & \Sigma x_2 x_k & & \Sigma x_k^2 \end{bmatrix} \tag{8.10}$$

which is symmetric and of order $k + 1$. The matrix given by $\mathbf{X}'\mathbf{X}$ is frequently referred to as the *cross product* matrix when analyzing the correlations among multiple variables.

On the basis of these findings, we are able to compute the variances and the covariances of all the variables. We may summarize these results in a symmetric matrix that we call $\mathbf{C}$. This matrix is found to be:

$$
C = \begin{bmatrix}
\text{Var}(x_1) & \text{Cov}(x_1x_2) & \text{Cov}(x_1x_3) & \cdots & \text{Cov}(x_1x_k) \\
\text{Cov}(x_1x_2) & \text{Var}(x_2) & & & \text{Cov}(x_2x_k) \\
\text{Cov}(x_1x_3) & & \text{Var}(x_3) & & \text{Cov}(x_3x_k) \\
\vdots & & & \ddots & \vdots \\
\text{Cov}(x_1x_k) & & \cdots & & \text{Var}(x_k)
\end{bmatrix} \qquad (8.11)
$$

Now consider only the elements $\text{Var}(x_1)$, $\text{Var}(x_2)$, ..., $\text{Var}(x_k)$, which appear along the diagonal of the matrix C. Taking the square root of each to obtain the standard deviation, employing the results to create a diagonal matrix, and inverting the resulting matrix we obtain:

$$
S^{-1} = \begin{bmatrix}
\dfrac{1}{s_1} & & & & 0 \\
& \dfrac{1}{s_2} & & & \\
& & \dfrac{1}{s_3} & & \\
& & & \ddots & \\
0 & & & & \dfrac{1}{s_k}
\end{bmatrix} \qquad (8.12)
$$

Noting that the transpose of S^{-1} is S^{-1} (because it is diagonal), the product $S^{-1}CS^{-1}$ results in the matrix R, which is also symmetric. Here, we find:

$$
R = \begin{bmatrix}
r_{11} & r_{12} & r_{13} & r_{14} & \cdots & r_{1k} \\
r_{12} & r_{22} & r_{23} & r_{24} & \cdots & r_{2k} \\
r_{13} & & r_{33} & r_{34} & \cdots & r_{3k} \\
r_{14} & & & r_{44} & \cdots & r_{4k} \\
\vdots & & & & \ddots & \vdots \\
r_{1k} & & & & & r_{kk}
\end{bmatrix} = S^{-1}CS^{-1} \qquad (8.13)
$$

where: $r_{11} = r_{22} = r_{33} = \cdots r_{kk} = 1.000$

The correlation matrix is extremely important, and we shall return to it in Chapter 10 where we discuss multiple regression.

8.5 USE OF SPSS TO COMPUTE AND TEST CORRELATIONS[D]

Once the concept of correlation as a measure of association is understood, prepackaged computer programs are used in order to perform the required calculations. Calculating the correlation between two variables with up to 30 observations is feasible with a hand calculator. However, such a task is quite tedious and when there are ten or more variables, as is fairly common, the required calculations are excessive. We noted before that the extensive use of statistics, at the level of analysis of variance and beyond, only became common with the advent of electronic computers.

Correlation is central to a number of types of analyses in the SPSS system, but there are several programs described in Chapter 18 of the SPSS manual (pp. 276–300), which deal specifically with correlation. These programs are:

1. PEARSON CORR
2. NONPAR CORR
3. SCATTERGRAM

Of these, NONPAR CORR deals with ordinal data rather than the interval/ratio scale data assumed by Pearson correlations. Two types of rank order correlations are computed by NONPAR CORR, the Spearman rho (r_s), and the Kendall tau (τ). We shall only consider PEARSON CORR and SCATTERGRAM in the following discussion.

8.5.1 Data Entry for SPSS: The Physiological Study[D]

Preparing data that is to be analyzed by the SCATTERGRAM, PEARSON CORR, or any other procedure that might be desired, is a simple matter. Referring to the physiological development study introduced earlier, the data for each child would be punched into a single card and each card would have the same format. Ignoring the variable names, punching the original data pertaining to the variables AGE, HEIGHT, and MASS as well as recoding SEX so that males are assigned the value 0 and females are assigned the value 1, the card format is as follows:

Variable	Columns (right justified)
AGE	1-2
HEIGHT	5-7
MASS	9-10
SEX	12

Recall that the term *right justified* means that the last unit or digit of the number must be in the right-hand column defined for the field. If necessary, blank columns (or zeros) are inserted to the left of the number. Figure 8-5 shows a complete set of cards for performing the SPSS procedures for this chapter. The cards with the data for the children are inserted between the //FT08F001 and //SYSIN cards. The DATA LIST card defines the format for SPSS to read the data cards. The format for this card is as follows:

DATA LIST   FIXED/1 AGE 1-2, HEIGHT 5-7, MASS 9-10, SEX 12

The remaining portions of Figure 8-5 are described as needed in the following sections.

8.5.2 SCATTERGRAM[D]

The procedures SCATTERGRAM and PEARSON CORR have a slightly different focus. SCATTERGRAM is used to construct one or a series of scattergrams, each of which employs two variables. Among the available statistics appearing on the page following the diagram is the Pearson correlation coefficient. Unless the user specifies scale ranges for the X and Y axes, the program automatically calculates scales that use all the space available on the diagram. The scale values are printed above and below as well as to the left and right of the plotting area. In addition, the user may also control the scales directly, which results in plots of different sets of data that may be compared directly. Moreover, by directly controlling the scales, it is possible to examine a selected portion of the data.

As employed in Figure 8-5, the simplest form of the SCATTERGRAM procedure card is:

SCATTERGRAM   AGE TO SEX

Such a card produces a series of two variable diagrams in which data pertaining to AGE-HEIGHT, AGE-MASS, AGE-SEX, HEIGHT-MASS, HEIGHT-SEX, and MASS-SEX are plotted. For a list in this format there

Figure 8-5 SPSS Cards for Carrying Out Correlations, Covariances, and SCATTERGRAMS

```
//UDCC2068    JOB    (HD123456,
//            ),'COLIN M. LAY',MSGLEVEL=2,CLASS=K
//    EXEC   SPSSH
//FT08F001  DD  *
10 145 40 1
 5 105 20 0
 3 100 16 0
 6  95 20 1
 4  80 17 1
 3  80 15 0
15 170 64 0
12 150 45 0
10 135 40 1
 9 145 45 0
14 140 50 0
15 150 66 0
10 120 39 1
 6 115 27 0
 3  90 13 1
11 125 42 1
 9 125 31 1
 7 120 25 0
 8 130 30 1
 7 160 57 1
//SYSIN DD  *
RUN NAME        CORRELATION AND COVARIANCE  DEMONSTRATION - PHYSIOLOGICAL STUDY
INPUT MEDIUM    DISK
N OF CASES      UNKNOWN
DATA LIST       FIXED/ 1 AGE 1-2, HEIGHT 5-7, MASS 9-10, SEX 12
PEARSON CORR    AGE TO SEX
STATISTICS      1,2
COMMENT         STATISTIC 1 CALLS FOR MEANS AND STANDARD DEVIATIONS FOR EACH
                VARIABLE
                STATISTIC 2 CALLS FOR CROSS PRODUCT DEVIATIONS AND COVARIANCE TO
                BE PRINTED OUT
READ INPUT DATA
PEARSON CORR    AGE TO MASS WITH SEX
OPTIONS         3
COMMENT         OPTION 3 CAUSES A 2-TAIL TEST OF SIGNIFICANCE
                OTHERWISE (DEFAULT OPTION) A 1-TAIL TEST IS PERFORMED
SCATTERGRAM     AGE TO SEX
OPTIONS         7
STATISTICS      ALL
COMMENT         OPTION 7 CAUSES AUTOMATIC SCALING ON THE AXES TO GET
                INTEGER VALUES ALONG THE AXES
FINISH
/*
```

are $\binom{n}{2}$ or $n!/(n-2)!2!$ diagrams produced. Since the range of the scale has not been specified by the above SCATTERGRAM procedure card, automatic scaling is in effect.

Values of the first variable appearing in each pair are plotted on the vertical scale while the values of the second variable appear on the horizontal scale. The first scattergram, and the associated statistics are shown in Figure 8-6.

To produce diagrams for only selected variables, the keyword "WITH" may be used. For example, to plot MASS against the other variables in the analysis, the required statement is as follows:

SCATTERGRAM   MASS WITH AGE, HEIGHT, SEX

Such a statement would generate only three diagrams. To obtain a plotting of HEIGHT with AGE and SEX as well as a plotting of MASS against the other variables, the following statement is required:

SCATTERGRAM   MASS WITH AGE, HEIGHT,
                SEX/HEIGHT WITH AGE, SEX

To control the scale of the plot, the lowest and highest values desired for a variable must be enclosed in parentheses following the name. The scales are divided horizontally and vertically into 10 divisions with 11 values printed to include the first and last values. To obtain scales that are easy to read and interpret, the lowest and highest values appearing on the plot should be small integers (0 to 10), simple fractions (e.g., .2, .25, .5, .75) powers of 10 (e.g., ... 10^{-2}, 10^{-1}, 10^{0}, 10, 10^{2}, ...) or the product of an integer or fraction with a power of 10. The scale intervals are chosen in a similar fashion. For example, the minimum and maximum observed as well as the minimum and maximum suggested scale values for the physiological development study are shown in Table 8-2. These scale intervals would be specified as follows:

SCATTERGRAM   MASS(0, 100) WITH AGE(0, 20),
                HEIGHT(0, 200), SEX(0, 5)

As in most procedures, the options available in SCATTERGRAM include label printing and handling of missing data. The more specific options are:

Option 4: suppression of rectangular grid lines
Option 5: printing of diagonal grid lines
Option 6: two-tailed test of r, if statistic 3 is chosen

Figure 8-6 Printout Produced by SCATTERGRAM—AGE versus HEIGHT

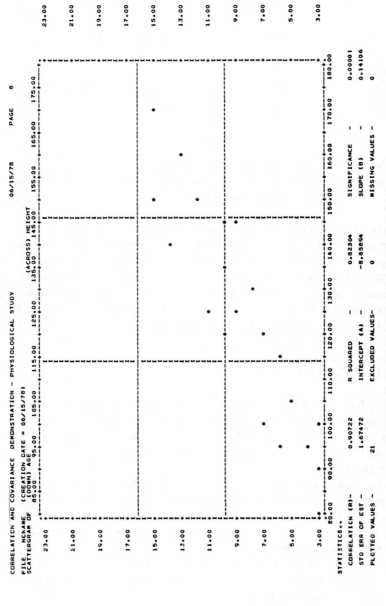

Table 8-2 SCATTERGRAM Scaling for Physiological Study

	Observed Values		Suggested Scale		Scale Interval
Variable	Min	Max	Min	Max	
AGE	3	15	0	20	2
HEIGHT	80	170	0	200	20
MASS	13	66	0	100	10
SEX	0	1	0	5	0.5

Option 7: integer values automatic scaling
Option 8: printing a subset of cases (the first n) if there is not enough workspace to hold all cases.

Statistics available in SCATTERGRAM include the Pearson r as well as four statistics that relate to linear regression analysis (discussed in the next chapter). Specifically, statistics 1 and 3 call for the Pearson r and its significance to be calculated; statistic 2 calls for r^2, which is the proportion of variation shared by the variables and is related to the goodness of the regression line. Statistics 4, 5, and 6 call for the standard error of estimate, the Y intercept, and the slope of the regression line. These latter topics are considered in Chapter 9.

8.5.3 PEARSON CORR[B]

The focus of PEARSON CORR is on the Pearson correlation coefficients for the group of variables specified as well as an examination of the significance of these coefficients. The procedure can print the correlation matrix in two formats as well as punch the correlation matrix on cards or write it on a disk or a tape file.

The usual output for PEARSON CORR includes the entire symmetric correlation matrix with the correlation coefficient, the number of cases on which it is based, and its level of significance for each pair of variables for which calculations are requested. It is also possible to print only the nonredundant portion of the triangular matrix to save both printing time and space. However, the format is such that it is more difficult to interpret and is only useful when avoiding printing time which is required when dealing with extremely large groups of variables.

The procedure card has two different forms. The first of these forms is referred to in SPSS as the matrix form and the other, for lack of a better name, is referred to in this text as the "WITH" or the *redundant* form.

The matrix form is usually specified when an entire square symmetric correlation matrix is desired. As an example of the matrix form used in Figure 8-5 consider:

PEARSON CORR   AGE TO SEX

which will generate a 4 by 4 correlation matrix as shown in Figure 8-7.

The *redundant* or the WITH form can also be made to compute and print the same matrix, but each of the coefficients will be calculated separately which results in more than twice as many coefficients as in the case of the matrix form. The procedure card for the "WITH" form has the format:

PEARSON CORR   AGE TO SEX WITH AGE TO SEX

This format causes every variable in the first list to be correlated with every variable appearing in the list following the word WITH. This procedure is most useful when printing only a small portion of the correlation matrix. All n_1 by n_2 coefficients are calculated. Another example in which only four coefficients will be calculated is given by:

PEARSON CORR   AGE, HEIGHT WITH MASS, SEX

The options available in PEARSON CORR include the handling of missing data as well as the more specific options listed next:

Option 3: two-tailed test of significance (instead of a one-tailed test)
Option 4: punching or writing the correlation matrix onto an external medium such as cards, tape, or disk for later use as an input to other procedures
Option 5: suppression of the number of cases and significance from the printout
Option 6: printing only nonredundant coefficients

In addition, statistic 1 calls for means and standard deviations to be printed, while statistic 2 adds the cross products in deviation form as well as the covariance matrix.

8.6 USE OF APL TO CALCULATE CORRELATIONS[E]

8.6.1 APL as a Matrix Desk Calculator[E]

The first subsection shows the use of APL to implement the matrix operations used in Sections 8.3 and 8.4 to calculate covariances and corre-

Figure 8-7 SPSS—PEARSON CORR Output

```
STATISTICAL PACKAGE FOR THE SOCIAL SCIENCES                                    06/15/78        PAGE  1
SPSS FOR OS/360, VERSION H, RELEASE 7.0, MARCH 1977

DEFAULT SPACE ALLOCATION..    ALLOWS FOR..      75 TRANSFORMATIONS
WORKSPACE     52500 BYTES                      300 RECODE VALUES LAG VARIABLES
TRANSPACE      7500 BYTES                      1200 IF/COMPUTE OPERATIONS

        RUN NAME        CORRELATION AND COVARIANCE DEMONSTRATION - PHYSIOLOGICAL STUDY
        INPUT MEDIUM    DISK
        N OF CASES      UNKNOWN
        DATA LIST       FIXED/ 1 AGE 1-2, HEIGHT 5-7, MASS 9-10, SEX 12

THE DATA LIST PROVIDES FOR  4 VARIABLES AND  1 RECORDS ('CARDS') PER CASE. A MAXIMUM OF  12 COLUMNS ARE USED ON A RECORD.

LIST OF THE CONSTRUCTED FORMAT STATEMENT..
(F2.0,2X,F3.0,1X,F2.0,1X,F1.0)

        PEARSON CORR    AGE TO SEX
        STATISTICS      1,2
        COMMENT         STATISTIC 1 CALLS FOR MEANS AND STANDARD DEVIATIONS FOR EACH
                        VARIABLE
                        STATISTIC 2 CALLS FOR CROSS PRODUCT DEVIATIONS AND COVARIANCE TO
                        BE PRINTED OUT

***** PEARSON CORR PROBLEM REQUIRES    288 BYTES WORKSPACE *****

        READ INPUT DATA

AFTER READING    21 CASES FROM SUBFILE NONAME  .  END OF FILE WAS ENCOUNTERED ON LOGICAL UNIT # 8


CORRELATION AND COVARIANCE DEMONSTRATION - PHYSIOLOGICAL STUDY                  06/15/78        PAGE  2

FILE  NONAME  (CREATION DATE = 06/15/78)

VARIABLE     CASES              MEAN            STD DEV
AGE            21             8.5714            3.8804
HEIGHT         21           123.5714           24.9571
MASS           21            34.5238           16.1078
SEX            21             0.4762            0.5118

VARIABLES    CROSS-PROD DEV    VARIANCE-COVAR    VARIABLES    CASES    CROSS-PROD DEV    VARIANCE-COVAR
AGE          1757.1429          87.8571          AGE          MASS       1210.7143         60.5357
HEIGHT        -1.7143           -0.9857          HEIGHT       MASS       7480.7143        374.0357
SEX          -15.7143           -0.7857          MASS         SEX         -16.2381         -0.8119

- - - - - - - P E A R S O N   C O R R E L A T I O N   C O E F F I C I E N T S - - - - - - - - - - - - -

                AGE          HEIGHT         MASS          SEX

AGE          ( 1.0000)     ( 0.9072)     ( 0.9685)     (-0.0432)
             S=0.001       S=0.201       S=0.001       S=0.426

HEIGHT       ( 0.9072)     ( 1.0000)     ( 0.9304)     (-0.0615)
             S=0.201       S=0.001       S=0.201       S=0.396

MASS         ( 0.9685)     ( 0.9304)     ( 1.0000)     (-0.0985)
             S=0.001       S=0.201       S=0.001       S=0.336

SEX          (-0.0432)     (-0.0615)     (-0.0985)     ( 1.0000)
             S=0.426       S=0.396       S=0.336       S=0.001

(COEFFICIENT / (CASES) / SIGNIFICANCE)        (A VALUE OF 99.0000 IS PRINTED IF A COEFFICIENT CANNOT BE COMPUTED)
```

lations. Subsection 8.6.2 demonstrates the use of two simple programs to do the same thing.

In Exhibit 8-1, the workspace CORRPRAC is loaded from library 3176 (Appendix F). It contains the programs that are used to operate on the data. Then in four lines the vectors **H**, **A**, **M**, and **S** are defined, representing height, age, mass, and sex, respectively. They are defined in groups (of 3) so as to validate their accuracy. Finally, their lengths are checked.

In Exhibit 8-2, **XT** (which stands for **X**$'$) is formed as a 5 by 21 matrix, and is printed to help verify its correctness. (A hint for verifying its correctness is to check the columns, since the typing was done by rows.) Finally, **X** is assigned as the transpose of **XT**, and the shapes of the two matrices are verified.

In Exhibit 8-3, **XTX** (**X**$'$**X**) is calculated and printed. It can be used to check the accuracy of the partial matrix shown in Section 8.3.2.

In Exhibit 8-4, the value of $L = 1/21 \times 20$ is calculated, and is used as the scalar multiplier. Then a portion of **XTX** is extracted, and it is assigned to **AH**. It consists of those elements found at the intersections of rows 1 and 3 with columns 1 and 2. It yields:

$$\mathbf{AH} = \begin{bmatrix} n & \Sigma a \\ \Sigma h & \Sigma ah \end{bmatrix}$$

Note that there are two assignments. First the submatrix is assigned to **AH**, which is then assigned to the quad ($\Box$) symbol which causes it to be printed on the terminal immediately.

The determinant and covariance, DETAH and COVAH respectively, are calculated and printed similarly.

In Exhibit 8-5, the age submatrix is extracted and its determinant (DETAA) and variance (VARA) are calculated and printed. Height is handled similarly (DETHH and VARH). Finally, the correlation of age and height (RAH) is calculated and printed.

8.6.2 The Use of Stored Covariance and Correlation Programs[E]

While calculation of covariances and correlations employing APL as a matrix calculator is useful for grasping the matrix concepts, it soon becomes boring, and programs are useful to proceed with the statistics rather than the calculations.

Two programs, COV and CMRT, have been created to perform covariance calculations (COV) as well as correlations and t-tests (CMRT). (They are included in the workspace CORRPRAC.) Their use is shown in Figure

Exhibit 8-1

```
)LOAD CORRPRAC,3176
SAVED 14.43/ 79.107/ 6272

H+145 105 100   95 95 80   170 150 135   145 140 150   120 115 90   125 125 120   130 100 160
A+10  5   3      6  4  3    15  12  10      9  14  15    10   6   3    11   9   7     8   7  13
M+40  20  16    20 17 15    64  45  40     45  50  66    39  27  13    42  31  25    30  23  57
S+1   0   0      1  1  0     0   0   1      0   0   0     1   0   1     1   1   0     1   0   1

21  ?H
21  ?A
21  ?M
21  ?S
```

Exhibit 8-2

```
      XT← 5 21 ρ (21ρ1),A,H,M,S
      )DIGITS 4
WAS 10
      XT
  1   1   1   1   1   1   1   1   1   1   1   1   1   1   1   1   1   1   1   1   1
 10   5   3   4   6   3  15  12  10   9  14  15  10   6   3  11   9   7   8   7  13
145 105 100  95  95  80 170 150 135 145 140 150 120 115  90 125 125 120 130 100 160
 40  20  16  20  20  15  64  45  40  45  50  66  39  27  13  42  31  25  30  23  57
  1   0   0   1   1   0   0   0   1   0   0   0   1   0   1   1   1   0   1   0   1

      X←⍉XT
      ρX
21 5
      ρXT
5 21
      )DIGITS 10
WAS 4
```

Exhibit 8-3

```
    XTX ←  XT  +.×   X
    ρXTX
 5  5
    XTX
        21         180        2595         725          10
       180        1844       24000        7425          84
      2595       24000      333125       97070        1220
       725        7425       97070       30219         329
        10          84        1220         329          10
```

Exhibit 8-4

```
        L←1÷21×20
        L
     2.380952381E‾3

        □←AH←XTX[1 3;1 2]
            21            180
          2595          24000

        □←DETAH ←  DET AH
     36900
        □←COVAH ←  L×DETAH
     87.85714286
```

Exhibit 8-5

```
        DETAA← DET XTX[1 2;1 2]
        □←VARA←L×DETAA
     15.05714286

        □←DETHH← DET XTX[1 3;1 3]
     261600
        □←VARH←L×DETHH
     622.8571429
        □←RAH←DETAH÷(DETAA×DETHH)*1÷2
     .9072178063
```

```
Figure 8-8  The Use of Correlation and Covariance Programs

        Y←WYt+4 21 ρ A,H,M,S
        )DIGITS 4
WAS 10
        YT
        10    5    3    6    4    3   15   12   10    9   14   15   10    6    3   11    9    7    8    7   13
       145  105  100   95   95   80  170  150  135  145  140  150  120  115   90  125  125  120  130  100  160
        40   20   16   20   17   15   64   45   40   45   50   66   39   27   13   42   31   25   30   23   57
         1    0    0    1    1    0    0    0    1    0    0    0    1    0    1    1    1    0    1    0    1

        )DIGITS 10
WAS 4

        CMRT Y

CORRELATION MATRIX
 1.000   0.907   0.969  ⁻0.042
 0.907   1.000   0.930  ⁻0.061
 0.969   0.930   1.000  ⁻0.097
⁻0.042  ⁻0.061  ⁻0.097   1.000

T-VALUES FOR DF= 19
  0.000    9.401   16.956   ⁻0.187
  9.401    0.000   11.066   ⁻0.268
 16.956   11.066    0.000   ⁻0.430
 ⁻0.187   ⁻0.268   ⁻0.430    0.000

VALUES OF R AND T ARE ALSO AVAILABLE WITH FULL PRECISION

'999990.99999' $ COV Y
 15.05714   87.85714   60.53571  ⁻0.08571
 87.85714  622.85714  374.03571  ⁻0.78571
 60.53571  374.03571  259.46190  ⁻0.81190
⁻0.08571  ⁻0.78571  ⁻0.81190   0.26190
```

8-8. For programs such as these the *vector of 1s must not be included*, so the matrix **Y** is created, and its transpose **YT** is printed. *CMRT Y* calls for correlations and *t*-tests. Age, height, and mass are seen as highly significantly correlated, whereas sex has an insignificant slightly negative correlation with the others. *COV Y* calls for their covariances. Finally, the function definitions and instructions are included in Appendix F for those who may be interested.

BIBLIOGRAPHY

Quenouille, M. H., *Associated Measurements*, London, Butterworths Scientific Publications, 1952.

Problems for Solution[(G)]

1. For each of the following scattergrams indicate whether the correlation is high, low, or 0, and whether it is positive (+ve) or negative (−ve). (i.e., +ve High, +ve Low, 0, −ve Low, or −ve High).

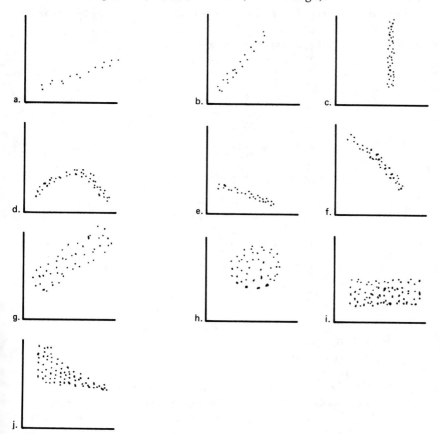

2. For the first six children in the example of Section 8.1, using a calculator find the correlations of height and mass, and height and sex. Are they significant? Do they make sense? State the substantive questions and the conclusions in words.

3. Type the data for the study into APL as shown in Section 8.6.1 and create the matrices **XT** and **X**.
   a. Print the data matrix **X**.
   b. Calculate and print **XTX**.
   c. Calculate the variances, covariances, and correlations of Age, Height, and Mass, carrying out the matrix and determinant operations, step by step.
   d. Use CMRT to find the entire correlation matrix.
   e. Are the correlations of the three variables significant?
   f. State the substantive hypotheses and the conclusions in words.

4. Use SPSS procedure PEARSON CORR to carry out the calculations required for Question 3. Obtain the scattergrams for the three pairs of variables using SCATTERGRAM.

5. Assume that **X** and **X'** have data for three variables, a, b, and c that are the 2nd, 3rd, and 4th vectors, respectively.

$$
\mathbf{X'} =
\begin{bmatrix}
1 & 1 & 1 & 1 & 1 & 1 & 1 & 1 & 1 & 1 & 1 & 1 & 1 & 1 & 1 \\
21 & 43 & 34 & 45 & 25 & 36 & 21 & 75 & 34 & 67 & 89 & 30 & 21 & 35 & 36 \\
43 & 56 & 78 & 34 & 12 & 45 & 56 & 67 & 78 & 35 & 47 & 24 & 38 & 15 & 45 \\
76 & 54 & 86 & 43 & 52 & 75 & 65 & 54 & 45 & 56 & 34 & 24 & 78 & 56 & 34
\end{bmatrix}
$$

$$
\mathbf{X'X} =
\begin{bmatrix}
15 & 612 & 673 & 832 \\
612 & 30886 & 28457 & 32042 \\
673 & 28457 & 35807 & 38697 \\
832 & 32042 & 38697 & 50676
\end{bmatrix}
$$

   a. What are the variance and standard deviation of a?
   b. What is the covariance of a and c?
   c. What is the correlation of a and b?

6. Assume that both the nursing and housekeeping departments keep records of the number of hours worked in each ward each week, and of the number of patient bed-days and lab test requisitions as well. For the week of March 3–9 the following data were obtained:

Ward No.	1	2	3	4	5	6	7	8	9	10
Patient Bed-Days	105	147	245	175	210	252	203	154	140	196
Lab Tests	150	175	200	150	145	250	200	160	120	150
Hours Worked Housekeeping	26	37	62	44	52	63	50	39	35	50
Nursing	300	588	857	525	903	1008	709	473	495	903

a. What are the correlations and covariances among the variables?
b. Are the correlations significant for $\alpha = .05$?
c. Do the correlations agree with intuition?
d. What should the null hypotheses be about these correlations?

Chapter 9

Linear Regression Analysis

Objectives

After completing this chapter, the student should be able to:
1. Understand the basic concept of regression.
2. Calculate regression estimates.
3. Perform ANOVA for linear regression.
4. Understand, compute, and interpret the coefficient of determination, the coefficient of correlation, and standardized regression coefficients.
5. Construct confidence intervals for regression coefficients.
6. Perform tests of significance using regression coefficients.
7. Construct confidence intervals for y and $\hat{y}$.

Chapter Map

Sections 9.1 and 9.2 (and all its subsections) present the basic concepts of regression analysis and have been assigned the letter code A.

Sections 9.3, 9.5, 9.5.1, 9.5.3, 9.6, 9.7, 9.7.2, and 9.7.3 introduce basic algebraic expressions and have been assigned the letter code B.

Sections 9.4, 9.5.2, 9.5.4, 9.7.3.2 and 9.8 express computational equations using matrix notation and have been assigned the letter code C.

Sections 9.7.1, 9.7.3.1, and 9.7.3.3 have *ordinary* and *matrix* algebra formulas in parallel and have been assigned the letter codes B and C.

9.1 INTRODUCTION[A]

Many of the problems confronting management require a forecast or a prediction concerning the value that will be assumed by a variable of interest. For example, when developing the institution's budget, management requires a prediction concerning the level of operations as well as the personnel, consumable supplies, and capital required to carry out the expected rate of activity. Such forecasts provide the basis for developing an operational statement of expectations, while an application of predicted factor prices to anticipated resource use provides the basis for the development of a budget expressed in financial terms. As another example, management may be interested in predicting the impact of a change in the institutional fee schedule on the use of care or the impact of changes in the demographic composition of the population at risk on the use of care. These are only a few of the many situations in which predictions are required in the management of the health care facility.

In this chapter and the chapters that follow we examine the basic concepts underlying regression analysis as well as the usefulness of this technique for explanation, prediction, and control in health care management. We already know that covariance and correlation analyses permit us to measure the extent to which two variables are associated or related and we shall employ these techniques in this chapter to develop the fundamental concepts of regression analysis.

Regression analysis is a useful managerial tool for examining the statistical relationship between two or more variables in order to predict the value of one variable from known or assumed values of the other, or others. We shall see that regression analysis may be used to reach conclusions concerning hypotheses about the relationship between two variables while controlling for other factors included in the analysis.

In this chapter, we shall limit our discussion to an examination of the relationship between two variables, say x and y. We may express the relationship by the general form:

$$y = f(x) \tag{9.1}$$

which means that y is some function of x. Here, we refer to y as the *dependent variable* and to x as the *independent* or *predictor variable*. We further assume that the association between x and y can be expressed by a linear equation. Our main task, then, is to examine a method of estimating the linear relationship between these two factors so that we can predict the value of y for known or assumed values of x and examine hypotheses concerning the relationship between x and y.

9.2 BASIC CONCEPTS OF REGRESSION ANALYSIS[A]

There are three basic measures used in simple (bivariate) correlation and regression analysis: (1) line of average relationship, (2) standard error of the estimate, and (3) the coefficient of correlation. Each of these is described briefly in this section, while the remainder of the chapter is devoted to a further discussion of these concepts and their use in regression analysis.

9.2.1 Line of Average Relationship[A]

The line that expresses the relationship between two variables is called the *line of average relationship,* or more commonly, the *regression line.* Perhaps the most commonly used equation to express this relationship is of the form:

$$y_i = b_0 + b_1 \times x_i \qquad (9.2)$$

where b_0 is the y-intercept and b_1 is the slope of the line. Here, b_0 and b_1 are numeric constants and are called the *regression coefficients* of the equation. Once these constants are known, we may substitute known or assumed values of x into the linear equation and solve for y. Thus, for each known or assumed value of the independent variable x, we are able to predict the corresponding value for the dependent variable y. The term *linear equation* indicates that a *straight line* is formed by plotting all pairs of values of x and y that satisfy Equation 9.2.

9.2.2 The Standard Error of the Estimate[A]

The *standard error of the estimate* (s_{yx}) is a measure of the extent to which the individual observations are scattered about the regression line. If the observations are close to the regression line, s_{yx} will be small. On the other hand, if the observations are widely scattered about the line, s_{yx} will be large. Thus, s_{yx} is in effect the *standard deviation* of values of the dependent variable (y) about the regression line, and is expressed in terms of the units in which the dependent variable is measured.

9.2.3 Coefficient of Correlation[A]

The third basic concept underlying regression analysis is the correlation coefficient discussed in Chapter 8. Recall that the coefficient of correlation is a single numeric value expressing the extent to which two variables are related. We have seen that the values assumed by r range from -1 to $+1$.

When $r = +1$ or -1 all the points lie on the straight line and we say that there is *perfect correlation* between the two variables. Obviously, $r = -1$ indicates *negative correlation*, while $r = +1$ indicates *positive correlation*. When r is close to zero, we say that the relationship between x and y is weak or nonexistent.

9.3 SIMPLE REGRESSION ANALYSIS[B]

To demonstrate the general procedure used in estimating the constants for a straight line, suppose we are interested in examining the relationship between age and the use of physician services, as measured by the number of doctor's office visits per person per year. Assuming we wish to predict use of care in terms of age, the dependent variable in our analysis (y_i) is the number of doctor's office visits and the independent (predictor) variable (x_i) is age. In examining this relationship, suppose we are provided with a set of paired observations $(x_1, y_1), \ldots, (x_i, y_i), \ldots, (x_n, y_n)$ where x_i represents the age of patient i and y_i corresponds to the use of physician care by patient i. For purposes of illustration, our methods will be based on the information introduced in Table 9-1 where the number of doctor's office visits (y_i) and the age (x_i) associated with each of 11 patients have

Table 9-1 The Number of Doctor's Office Visits versus Age of Patient

Patient	Number of Doctor's Office Visits (y_i)	Age of Patient (Years) (x_i)
1	1	5
2	3	20
3	3	35
4	1	15
5	5	50
6	3	16
7	4	40
8	6	47
9	2	18
10	3	23
11	5	30

been presented. If we plot these data as shown in Figure 9-1, it is evident that few, if any, of the points fall on a straight line even though the pattern formed by the dots may be represented by a straight line. An inspection of the scattergram suggests that the relationship between use of ambulatory care and age might be represented by a linear equation of the form:

$$y_i = b_0 + b_1 x_i + e_i \qquad (9.3)$$

where e_i is a random variable representing the difference between the actual and predicted values of y.

Theoretically, it is possible to construct an infinite number of lines in the space defined by the axes x and y. Some of these lines will provide a good fit to our data, while other lines are such poor fits that they may be excluded from consideration. However, we must then choose from among those lines that appear to provide a good fit to our data, a single line that best fits the data. In order to do so, we require a criterion by which we may select the best of these lines.

Figure 9-1 Scattergram of Patients' Numbers of Doctor's Office Visits per Year versus Age

Number of visits

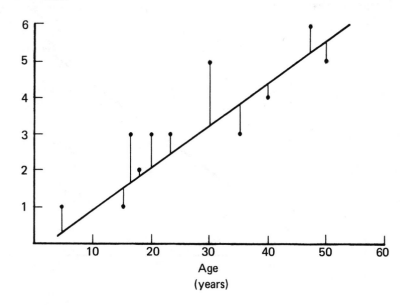

Age
(years)

The criterion we shall employ in selecting the line providing the best fit for our data is called *least squares*. A straight line fitted by the least squares method gives a best fit to the data, since it minimizes the sum of the squares of the vertical deviations from the points to the line (the e_i's) in Figure 9-1. Returning to our numeric example, consider point D of Figure 9-2. The coordinates of point D are actually (15,1). However, if we read the number of visits associated with the patient who is 15 years of age, we find the corresponding predicted value is approximately 1.5 visits per year. Thus, the error we make when predicting this patient's use from the line is $-.5$ visits, which is the difference between the actual number of visits (1 visit per year) and the estimated number of visits (1.5 visits per year). We see from Figure 9-2 that there are 11 such errors corresponding to the 11 data points. The least squares criterion we employ in estimating the line that best fits the data requires that the sum of squares of the errors must be minimized. For any line drawn through the point $(\bar{x}, \bar{y})$ the sum of the deviations about the line will be zero, since some of the deviations will be positive and others will be negative. However, if we square the deviations before summing, there are no negative terms. Therefore, the *criterion of least squares* is that *the sum of the squared deviations should be minimized.*

Figure 9-2 Deviation of the Predicted Number from the Actual Number of Visits

Number of visits

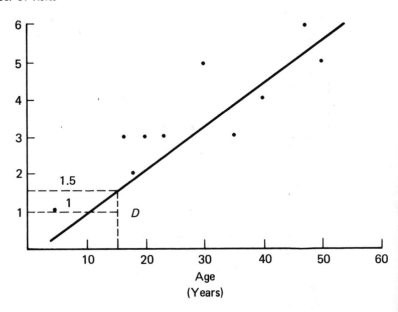

Let us now consider the method of calculating the constants b_0 and b_1 as well as the term e_i, which appear in Equation 9.3. The derivation of the computational equations for estimating the values of b_0 and b_1 are presented in a number of standard texts on statistics and econometrics (e.g., Draper and Smith 1966; Johnston 1972) and we merely state these equations here. We estimate the slope of the regression line first, and the computational form by which the coefficient b_1 is estimated follows:

$$b_1 = \frac{\Sigma x_i y_i - (\Sigma x_i)(\Sigma y_i)/n}{\Sigma x_i^2 - (\Sigma x_i)^2/n} = \frac{n\Sigma x_i y_i - \Sigma x_i \Sigma y_i}{n\Sigma x_i^2 - (\Sigma x_i)^2} \qquad (9.4)$$

Observe that this equation is equivalent to:

$$b_1 = \frac{\Sigma(x_i - \bar{x})(y_i - \bar{y})}{\Sigma(x_i - \bar{x})^2} = \frac{\mathrm{Cov}(x, y)}{\mathrm{Var}(x)} \qquad (9.5)$$

Concerning the estimation of b_0, observe that once we have calculated b_1, we may substitute its value in Equation 9.2. If we also substitute $\bar{x}$ for x_i and $\bar{y}$ for y_i in Equation 9.2, we obtain:

$$\bar{y} = b_0 + b_1\bar{x} \qquad (9.6)$$

which allows us to solve for b_0 as follows:

$$b_0 = \bar{y} - b_1\bar{x} \qquad (9.7)$$

Draper and Smith and Johnston show that the constant b_0 can be estimated by:

$$b_0 = \frac{(\Sigma y_i)(\Sigma x_i^2) - (\Sigma x_i)(\Sigma x_i y_i)}{n(\Sigma x_i^2) - (\Sigma x_i)^2} \qquad (9.8)$$

Regarding the calculation of the error term, e_i, it is necessary to differentiate between the observed value of y and the predicted value of the dependent variable, which we now represent by $\hat{y}_i$. From Equation 9.3 we know that the observed value of y may be expressed in the form:

$$y_i = b_0 + b_1 x_i + e_i \qquad (9.9.1)$$

On the other hand, predicted values of the dependent variable are obtained from:

$$\hat{y}_i = b_0 + b_1 x_i \qquad (9.9.2)$$

If we substitute $\hat{y}_i$ for $b_1 + b_1 x_i$ in the first of these two expressions, we obtain

$$y_i = \hat{y}_i + e_i \qquad (9.9.3)$$

As a consequence, the error term e_i is found by:

$$e_i = y_i - \hat{y}_i \qquad (9.9.4)$$

As implied earlier, then, the error term e_i for $i = 1, \ldots, n$ is simply the difference between the observed and predicted values of the independent variable.

Returning to our example, we find that Equations 9.4 and 9.8 require the calculation of $\sum_{i=1}^{n} x_i$, $\sum_{i=1}^{n} y_i$, $\sum_{i=1}^{n} x_i^2$, and $\sum_{i=1}^{n} x_i y_i$. These values are computed as shown in Table 9-2. Thus, we have $n = 11$, $\Sigma x_i = 299$,

Table 9-2 Tabular Computations for Linear Regression

	x_i	y_i	x_i^2	$x_i y_i$
	5	1	25	5
	20	3	400	60
	35	3	1,225	105
	15	1	225	15
	50	5	2,500	250
	16	3	256	48
	40	4	1,600	160
	47	6	2,209	282
	18	2	324	36
	23	3	529	69
	30	5	900	150
Totals	299	36	10,193	1,180

$\Sigma y_i = 36$, $\Sigma x_i^2 = 10{,}193$, and $\Sigma x_i y_i = 1{,}180$. After making the appropriate substitutions into Equations 9.4 and 9.5, we may calculate the estimates of b_0 and b_1 as follows:

$$b_1 = \frac{1{,}180 - (299)(36)/11}{10{,}193 - (299)^2/11}$$

$$= \frac{201.45455}{2{,}065.6364}$$

$$= .0975266 \cong .098$$

$$b_0 = \frac{(36)(10{,}193) - (299)(1{,}180)}{11(10{,}193) - (299)^2}$$

$$= \frac{366{,}948 - 352{,}820}{112{,}123 - 89{,}401}$$

$$= \frac{14{,}128}{22{,}722}$$

$$\cong .622$$

Alternatively, we could have calculated b_0 using Equation 9.7. Had we followed this procedure, it would have been necessary to calculate $\bar{x}$ and $\bar{y}$ as follows:

$$\bar{x} = \frac{299}{11} = 27.1818, \qquad \bar{y} = \frac{36}{11} = 3.2727$$

Substituting $b_1 = .097$, $\bar{x} = 27.1818$, and $\bar{y} = 3.2727$ into Equation 9.7 we find

$$b_0 = 3.2727 - .0975266(27.1818)$$

$$= .6217508 \cong .622$$

Thus, specializing Equation 9.9.2,

$$\hat{y}_i = .622 + .098\, x_i \qquad\qquad \textbf{(9.10)}$$

provides the estimate of the relationship between use of ambulatory care and age, which may be used to predict the number of doctor's office visits in terms of the age of the patient. As an example, consider the estimated number of doctor's office visits used by patient 8 who is 47 years old. Substituting $x_8 = 47$ we get:

$$\hat{y}_8 = .622 - .098(47)$$

$$= 5.228$$

Thus, the error committed when estimating the use of ambulatory care by Equation 9.10 is $6 - 5.228$, or .772. Therefore, using Equation 9.9.4,

$$e_8 = y_8 - \hat{y}_8 = .772$$

9.4 LINEAR REGRESSION EXPRESSED IN MATRIX NOTATION[C]

We know that matrix notation simplifies the expression of the required computations for analysis of variance. In this section we apply matrix notation to simplify the expression of the calculations for estimating b_0 and b_1. We shall discover a need to rely heavily on the familiar concept of $X'X$.

Recall that for observation i the value of the dependent variable y_i was defined by:

$$y_i = b_0 + b_1 x_i + e_i$$

This equation implies that for the observations $1, \ldots, i, \ldots, n$, we have a set of equations of the form:

$$y_1 = b_0 + b_1 x_1 + e_1$$

$$y_2 = b_0 + b_1 x_2 + e_2$$

$$\vdots \qquad\qquad \vdots$$

$$y_i = b_0 + b_1 x_i + e_i$$

$$\vdots \qquad\qquad \vdots$$

$$y_n = b_0 + b_1 x_n + e_n$$

Using the following definitions:

$$\mathbf{y} = \begin{bmatrix} y_1 \\ y_2 \\ \cdot \\ \cdot \\ \cdot \\ y_i \\ \cdot \\ \cdot \\ \cdot \\ y_n \end{bmatrix}, \quad \mathbf{X} = \begin{bmatrix} 1 & x_1 \\ 1 & x_2 \\ \cdot & \cdot \\ \cdot & \cdot \\ 1 & x_i \\ \cdot & \cdot \\ \cdot & \cdot \\ \cdot & \cdot \\ 1 & x_n \end{bmatrix}, \quad \boldsymbol{\epsilon} = \begin{bmatrix} e_1 \\ e_2 \\ \cdot \\ \cdot \\ e_i \\ \cdot \\ \cdot \\ \cdot \\ e_n \end{bmatrix}$$

and

$$\mathbf{b} = \begin{bmatrix} b_0 \\ b_1 \end{bmatrix}$$

We may rewrite this system of equations in matrix notation as:

$$\mathbf{y} = \mathbf{Xb} + \boldsymbol{\epsilon} \qquad (9.11)$$

where: **y** is a column vector of n observations of the dependent variable, with estimated values represented by $\hat{\mathbf{y}}$

x is an $n \times 2$ matrix in which the second column consists of the n observations of the independent variable that correspond to y_1, $y_2, \ldots, y_i, \ldots, y_n$

$\boldsymbol{\epsilon}$ is a column vector consisting of the n deviations $y_i - \hat{y}_i$ for $i = 1$, $\ldots, n$

b is a column vector of the coefficients b_0 and b_1, which are to be estimated by the least squares method.

Also observe that **Xb** is a column vector with n elements as well, which we may see by expanding Xb as follows:

$$\mathbf{Xb} = \begin{bmatrix} 1 & x_1 \\ 1 & x_2 \\ \cdot & \cdot \\ \cdot & \cdot \\ 1 & x_i \\ \cdot & \cdot \\ \cdot & \cdot \\ \cdot & \cdot \\ 1 & x_n \end{bmatrix} \begin{bmatrix} b_0 \\ b_1 \end{bmatrix} = \begin{bmatrix} b_0 + b_1 x_1 \\ b_0 + b_1 x_2 \\ \cdot \\ \cdot \\ b_0 + b_1 x_i \\ \cdot \\ \cdot \\ \cdot \\ b_0 + b_1 x_n \end{bmatrix}$$

In terms of our example, we find:

$$\mathbf{Xb} = \begin{bmatrix} 1 & 5 \\ 1 & 20 \\ 1 & 35 \\ \cdot & \cdot \\ \cdot & \cdot \\ \cdot & \cdot \\ 1 & 30 \end{bmatrix} \begin{bmatrix} .622 \\ .098 \end{bmatrix} = \begin{bmatrix} .622 + .098 \times 5 \\ .622 + .098 \times 20 \\ .622 + .098 \times 35 \\ \cdot \\ \cdot \\ \cdot \\ .622 + .098 \times 30 \end{bmatrix} = \begin{bmatrix} 1.112 \\ 2.582 \\ 4.052 \\ \cdot \\ \cdot \\ \cdot \\ 3.562 \end{bmatrix}$$

These results suggest that $\mathbf{Xb}$ is a vector containing the predicted values of $\mathbf{y}$, namely $\hat{\mathbf{y}}$.

From Draper and Smith and the Johnston texts we find that the least squares criterion leads to a set of *normal equations*:

$$b_0 n + b_1 \Sigma x_i = \Sigma y_i \tag{9.12.1}$$

$$b_0 \Sigma x_i + b_1 \Sigma x_i^2 = \Sigma x_i y_i \tag{9.12.2}$$

These normal equations may be expressed in matrix notation by:

$$\mathbf{X'Xb} = \mathbf{X'y} \tag{9.12.3}$$

where:

$$\mathbf{b} = \begin{bmatrix} b_0 \\ b_1 \end{bmatrix} \qquad \mathbf{X} = \begin{bmatrix} 1 & x_1 \\ \cdot & \cdot \\ \cdot & \cdot \\ 1 & x_i \\ \cdot & \cdot \\ \cdot & \cdot \\ 1 & x_n \end{bmatrix} \qquad \text{and} \qquad \mathbf{y} = \begin{bmatrix} y_1 \\ \cdot \\ \cdot \\ y_i \\ \cdot \\ \cdot \\ y_n \end{bmatrix}$$

Thus, the solution for $\mathbf{b}$ is given by:

$$\mathbf{b} = (\mathbf{X'X})^{-1} \mathbf{X'y} \tag{9.13}$$

This is an important result and should be committed to memory.

From Chapter 2 we know the inverse of a 2×2 matrix may be computed as follows. Letting

$$A = \begin{bmatrix} a & b \\ c & d \end{bmatrix}$$

then A^{-1} is given by:

$$A^{-1} = \frac{1}{ad - bc} \begin{bmatrix} d & -b \\ -c & a \end{bmatrix} = \frac{1}{|A|} \begin{bmatrix} d & -b \\ -c & a \end{bmatrix}$$

Returning to the inverse of $X'X$, we know:

$$X'X = \begin{bmatrix} n & \Sigma x \\ \Sigma x & \Sigma x^2 \end{bmatrix}$$

Thus, applying Equation 9.14, we find the inverse of $X'X$ is:

$$(X'X)^{-1} = \frac{1}{|X'X|} \begin{bmatrix} \Sigma x^2 & -\Sigma x \\ -\Sigma x & n \end{bmatrix} \tag{9.15.1}$$

$$= \frac{1}{n\Sigma x^2 - (\Sigma x)^2} \begin{bmatrix} \Sigma x^2 & -\Sigma x \\ -\Sigma x & n \end{bmatrix} \tag{9.15.2}$$

Making use of the preceding equations, let us return to our example and show how b_0 and b_1 are computed using matrix operations. In this case, we let

$$X = \begin{bmatrix} 1 & 5 \\ 1 & 20 \\ 1 & 35 \\ 1 & 15 \\ 1 & 50 \\ 1 & 16 \\ 1 & 40 \\ 1 & 47 \\ 1 & 18 \\ 1 & 23 \\ 1 & 30 \end{bmatrix} \quad \text{and} \quad y = \begin{bmatrix} 1 \\ 3 \\ 3 \\ 1 \\ 5 \\ 3 \\ 4 \\ 6 \\ 2 \\ 3 \\ 5 \end{bmatrix}$$

Thus,

$$\mathbf{X'X} = \begin{bmatrix} 11 & 299 \\ 299 & 10{,}193 \end{bmatrix} \quad \text{and} \quad \mathbf{X'y} = \begin{bmatrix} 36 \\ 1{,}180 \end{bmatrix}$$

and

$$|\mathbf{X'X}| = 11(10{,}193) - (299)^2$$

$$= 22{,}722$$

so that

$$(\mathbf{X'X})^{-1} = \frac{1}{22{,}722} \begin{bmatrix} 10{,}193 & -299 \\ -299 & 11 \end{bmatrix}$$

and

$$\mathbf{b} = \frac{1}{22{,}722} \begin{bmatrix} 10{,}193 & -299 \\ -299 & 11 \end{bmatrix} \begin{bmatrix} 36 \\ 1{,}180 \end{bmatrix}$$

$$= \frac{1}{22{,}722} \begin{bmatrix} 14{,}128 \\ 2{,}216 \end{bmatrix}$$

$$\cong \begin{bmatrix} .6218 \\ .0975 \end{bmatrix}$$

This result suggests that, as before, $b_0 \cong .622$ and $b_1 \cong .098$.

Summarizing this section, we find that the linear regression model can be expressed by:

$$\mathbf{y} = \mathbf{Xb} + \epsilon$$

where $\mathbf{y}$ is a vector of n observations of the independent variable and $\mathbf{X}$ is an $n \times 2$ matrix consisting of a column vector of 1s and a column vector of the observed values for the independent (or predictor) variable. The vector $\mathbf{b}$ consists of the regression constants, b_0 and b_1, which are estimated using the least squares method, as expressed by the formula:

$$\mathbf{b} = (\mathbf{X'X})^{-1}\mathbf{X'y}$$

Once the regression constants have been estimated, the regression equation:

$$\hat{\mathbf{y}} = \mathbf{Xb}$$

yields the best estimate of the dependent variable for any value of the independent variable. Here, $\hat{\mathbf{y}}$ is a vector of estimated or predicted values of the dependent variable. It follows that the deviations of the actual or observed values of $\mathbf{y}$ from the predicted values of the dependent variable may be expressed by:

$$\boldsymbol{\epsilon} = \mathbf{y} - \hat{\mathbf{y}}$$

where $\boldsymbol{\epsilon}$ is a column vector consisting of the error terms e_i for $i = 1, \ldots, n$.

9.5 THE VARIANCE EXPLAINED BY THE REGRESSION LINE[B]

One of the primary reasons for performing regression analysis is to *explain* the variation exhibited by the dependent variable in terms of the different values of the independent variable. In this regard, observe that the purposes of regression analysis and the analysis of variance discussed in chapters 4 through 7 are quite similar. In fact, the objective of this section is to develop an analysis of variance table that allows us to examine the proportion of the variance of the dependent variable that is explained by the regression equation, relative to the unexplained proportion of this variance, represented by the residual error, e_i.

We saw previously that a second reason for performing regression analysis is to predict the value of the dependent variable from known or assumed values of the independent variable. The *goodness* of the prediction depends on the scatter of the observed values of y about the regression line. It seems intuitively plausible to argue that the larger the errors, the less accurate the resulting estimates. In measuring the predictive capabilities of a given regression line, we shall have occasion to refer to the *standard error of the estimate*, s_{yx}. The standard error of the estimate, which is sometimes called the *standard error of prediction*, is defined as:

$$s_{yx} = \sqrt{\frac{\Sigma(y_i - \hat{y}_i)^2}{n - (k + 1)}} \tag{9.16}$$

where n is the sample size and $(k + 1)$ is the number of constants in the regression equation. Here, the term $n - (k + 1)$ refers to the number of degrees of freedom around the regression line and, in the case of simple linear regression, $k + 1 = 2$. The selection of a straight line from which we measure dispersion uses up 2 degrees of freedom; 1 in requiring that the line pass through the point $(\bar{x}, \bar{y})$ [i.e., in determining b_0 as in Equation 9.7] and $k = 1$ in determining the slope of the line (i.e., b_1). When we consider multiple regression, in Chapter 10, k will be larger than 1.

Recalling that $e_i = y_i - \hat{y}_i$, we may also express Equation 9.16 in the form:

$$s_{yx} = \sqrt{\frac{\Sigma e_i^2}{n - (k + 1)}} \qquad (9.17)$$

If we then square Equation 9.17 we obtain:

$$s_{yx}^2 = \frac{\Sigma e_i^2}{n - (k + 1)} \qquad (9.18)$$

which is simply the sum of the squared error terms divided by the number of degrees of freedom given by the term $n - (k + 1)$. Henceforth, we shall refer to s_{yx}^2 as the *mean square due to errors*, which will be symbolized by $MS(E)$.

In further specifying variation about the regression equation, consider Figure 9-3 where we divide the vertical distance ac, which represents the deviation $(y_i - \bar{y})$, into two components, namely, the vertical distance ab, which represents $(y_i - \hat{y}_i)$, and bc, which represents $(\hat{y}_i - \bar{y})$. The partitioning of $(y_i - \bar{y})$ into these two components may be represented by:

$$(y_i - \bar{y}) = (y_i - \hat{y}_i) + (\hat{y}_i - \bar{y}) \qquad (9.19)$$

where we observe that $y_i - \hat{y}_i$ is the error term associated with observation i. Now, if we square both sides of Equation 9.19 and sum over all i, we obtain:

$$\sum_{i=1}^{n} (y_i - \bar{y})^2 = \sum_{i=1}^{n} (y_i - \hat{y}_i)^2 + \sum_{i=1}^{n} (\hat{y}_i - \bar{y})^2 \qquad (9.20)$$

Observe that the left-hand side of Equation 9.20 is the sum of squared deviations of y_i about the mean $\bar{y}$, which is referred to as the *sum of squares*

Figure 9-3 Components of the Deviation from the Mean

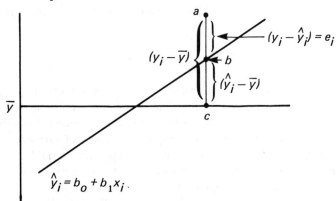

about the mean. The term $\Sigma^n_{i=1} (y_i - \bar{y})^2$ is also the *corrected* sum of squares of the observed y values. We may express Equation 9.20 in words as follows:

$$\left\{\begin{array}{c}\text{Sum of Squares}\\ \textit{about the}\\ \textit{Mean}\end{array}\right\} = \left\{\begin{array}{c}\text{Sum of Squares}\\ \textit{about the}\\ \textit{Regression}\end{array}\right\} + \left\{\begin{array}{c}\text{Sum of Squares}\\ \textit{due to the}\\ \textit{Regression}\end{array}\right\}$$

Thus, the variation of the y values about the mean has been partitioned into two components: (1) variation in the observed values of y that may be attributed to regression, which is represented by $\Sigma^n_{i=1} (\hat{y}_i - \bar{y})^2$, and (2) variation related to the fact that *not all* points lie on the line, which is represented by $\Sigma^n_{i=1} (y_i - \hat{y}_i)^2$. Obviously, if all points appeared on the line we would find that $\Sigma^n_{i=1} (y_i - \hat{y}_i)^2$ would be zero and $\Sigma^n_{i=1} (\hat{y}_i - \bar{y})^2$ would equal $\Sigma^n_{i=1} (y_i - \bar{y})^2$.

As was pointed out earlier, the sum of squares about the regression has $(n - 2)$ degrees of freedom. The sum of squares about the mean requires $(n - 1)$ observations since only $(n - 1)$ of the deviations $(y_1 - \bar{y})$, $(y_2 - \bar{y})$, ..., $(y_n - \bar{y})$ are independent. Recall that $\Sigma(y_i - \bar{y}) = 0$ and as a result, observation y_n is determined. Let us refer to the degrees of freedom associated with regression by the letter k. We may find the degrees of freedom associated with the sum of squares due to regression by noting:

$$df\text{ (total)} = df\text{ (error)} + df\text{ (regression)}$$

Therefore, $(n - 1) = (n - 2) + k$ and solving for k, we find that the degrees of freedom associated with the sum of squares due to regression is one.

9.5.1 The ANOVA Table in Linear Regression[B]

When evaluating whether a significant amount of the variance exhibited by the dependent variable is attributable to the regression line, we usually construct an ANOVA table and test the calculated F value for significance. Table 9-3 presents a preliminary or simplified analysis of variance table for a linear regression model involving a single independent variable.

The total sum of squares associated with the dependent variable, which is given by $\Sigma(y_i - \bar{y})^2$ is partitioned into two components. The first is the sum of squares, which is attributable to the regression line [i.e., $\Sigma(\hat{y}_i - \bar{y})^2$] and the second refers to the sum of squares about the regression (i.e., Σe_i^2), which is given by $\Sigma(y_i - \hat{y}_i)^2$. We can show that the sum of squares due to the regression line is given by:

$$\Sigma(\hat{y}_i - \bar{y})^2 = b_1 \left(\Sigma x_i y_i - \frac{\Sigma x_i \Sigma y_i}{n} \right) \qquad (9.21.1)$$

and that the sum of squares about the mean may be computed as follows:

$$\Sigma(y_i - \bar{y})^2 = \Sigma y_i^2 - \frac{(\Sigma y_i)^2}{n} \qquad (9.21.2)$$

Treating the sums of squares about the regression as a residual, Σe_i^2 can be found by subtraction as follows:

$$\Sigma e_i^2 = \Sigma(y_i - \bar{y})^2 - \Sigma(\hat{y}_i - \bar{y})^2$$

Table 9-3 Preliminary Analysis of Variance for Linear Regression

Source	SS	df	MS	F
Due to Regression	$\Sigma(\hat{y}_i - \bar{y})^2$	1	$MS(R) = \Sigma(\hat{y}_i - \bar{y})^2$	$\dfrac{MS(R)}{MS(E)}$
About Regression (Error or Residual)	$\Sigma(y_i - \hat{y}_i)^2$	$n - 2$	$MS(E) = \dfrac{\Sigma e_i^2}{n - 2}$	
	$= \Sigma e_i^2$		$= s_{yx}^2$	
About the Mean	$\Sigma(y_i - \bar{y})^2$	$n - 1$		

$$\Sigma e_i{}^2 = \Sigma y_i{}^2 - \frac{(\Sigma y_i)^2}{n} - b_1\left(\Sigma x_i y_i - \frac{\Sigma x_i \Sigma y_i}{n}\right) \qquad (9.22)$$

Presented in Table 9-4 is a summary of the ANOVA table using the computational formulas previously introduced. The format of the table is frequently used in practice for displaying the analysis of variance for a regression problem. However, one further step in the development of the ANOVA table using algebraic notation is useful before introducing the equivalent matrix notation.

Referring to Table 9-4, observe that the sum of squares due to regression has the value of b_1 as part of the expression. However, as shown in this table, no explicit recognition is given to the term b_0 when calculating the sum of squares due to regression. Rather, the regression coefficient b_0 is "hidden" in the sum of squares about the mean, which is also called the *total sum of squares, corrected for the mean*. In this regard the total sum of squares is given by $\Sigma y_i{}^2$ and the correction for the mean is $(\Sigma y_i)^2/n = n\bar{y}^2$. In order to avoid understating the calculated value of F, it is necessary to give explicit recognition to the sum of squares attributable to the coefficient b_0.

To illustrate this latter point, let us imagine a series of steps providing an increasingly more accurate understanding of the behavior of the independent variable. In this case, we might imagine:

1. a model that provides no estimate of y (i.e., no explanation of the total sum of squares, $\Sigma y_i{}^2$);
2. a model that estimates y by $\hat{y}_i = b_0 = \bar{y}$ (i.e., no account is taken of the

Table 9-4 Analysis of Variance for Linear Regression Using Computational Formulas

Source	SS	df	MS	F
Due to Regression	$b_1\left(\Sigma x_i y_i - \dfrac{\Sigma x_i \Sigma y_i}{n}\right) = SS(b_1)$	1	$\dfrac{SS(b_1)}{1}$	$\dfrac{SS(b_1)}{s_{yx}{}^2}$
About Regression (Residual)	By subtraction, $\Sigma e_i{}^2$	$n-2$	$s_{yx}{}^2 = \dfrac{\Sigma e_i{}^2}{n-2}$	
About the Mean	$\Sigma y_i{}^2 - \dfrac{(\Sigma y_i)^2}{n}$	$n-1$		

influence of specific values of x_i on y_i, and the sum of squares due to the constant b_0 is $n\bar{y}^2$;

3. a model that estimates $\hat{y}_i$ by $b_0 + b_1 x_i$ [i.e., a regression model in which more of the total sum of squares has been explained, and this extra amount is $SS(b_1)$].

Moving successively from the most simple to the most complex model, we have:

$$
\left\{ \begin{array}{c} \text{Total} \\ \text{Sum of} \\ \text{Squares} \end{array} \right\} = \left\{ \begin{array}{c} \text{Sum of Squares} \\ \text{due to} \\ \text{Constant } b_0 \end{array} \right\} + \left\{ \begin{array}{c} \text{Sum of Squares} \\ \text{due to} \\ \text{Regression Line, } b_1 \end{array} \right\}
$$

$$
+ \left\{ \begin{array}{c} \text{Residual} \\ \text{Sum of} \\ \text{Squares} \end{array} \right\} \qquad (9.23)
$$

which may be expressed symbolically as follows:

$$
\Sigma y_i^2 = n\bar{y}^2 + b_1 \left(\Sigma x_i y_i - \frac{\Sigma x_i \Sigma y_i}{n} \right) + \Sigma e_i^2 \qquad (9.24)
$$

These findings suggest that our ANOVA table should be modified to reflect the source of variance due to b_0. This modification is introduced in Table 9-5. As shown in this table, the constant b_0 has 1 degree of freedom and the sum of squares attributable to this source has been extracted from the sum of squares about the mean, which was defined previously as:

$$
\Sigma y_i^2 - \frac{(\Sigma y_i)^2}{n}
$$

9.5.2 ANOVA for Regression Analysis Using Matrix Notation[C]

Consider next the operations expressed in matrix notation that are equivalent to the algebraic expressions presented in Table 9-5. First, we develop the expressions for $SS(b_1)$ and $SS(b_0)$. Recall:

$$
SS(b_1) = b_1 \left\{ \Sigma x_i y_i - \frac{(\Sigma x_i)(\Sigma y_i)}{n} \right\}
$$

$$= b_1\{\Sigma x_i y_i - n\overline{xy}\} \tag{9.25}$$

$$SS(b_0) = \frac{(\Sigma y_i)^2}{n} = n\overline{y}^2 \tag{9.26}$$

Also observe that each of these sum of squares has 1 degree of freedom and that we can write:

$$SS(b_1) + SS(b_0) = b_1\Sigma x_i y_i - b_1 n\overline{xy} + n\overline{y}^2$$

$$= b_1\Sigma x_i y_i + n\overline{y}(\overline{y} - b_1\overline{x})$$

Since $b_0 = \overline{y} - b_1\overline{x}$ we have:

$$SS(b_1) + SS(b_0) = b_1\Sigma x_i y_i + b_0 n\overline{y}$$

$$= b_1\Sigma x_i y_i + b_0\Sigma y_i$$

Letting $\mathbf{b}' = [b_0 \quad b_1]$ we may write the last equation in the form:

$$[b_0 \quad b_1] \begin{bmatrix} \Sigma y_i \\ \Sigma x_i y_i \end{bmatrix} = b_0\Sigma y_i + b_1\Sigma x_i y_i$$

Table 9-5 Analysis of Variance for Linear Regression with Sum of Squares due to Constant

Source	SS	df	MS	F
Regression				
constant, b_0	$n\overline{y}^2$	1	$MS(b_0) = n\overline{y}^2$	$\dfrac{MS(b_0)}{s_{yx}^2}$
slope, b_1	$b_1\left(\Sigma x_i y_i - \dfrac{\Sigma x_i \Sigma y_i}{n}\right)$	1	$MS(b_1) = SS(b_1)$	$\dfrac{MS(b_1)}{s_{yx}^2}$
Error/Residual	Σe_i^2 by subtraction	$n-2$	$s_{yx}^2 = \dfrac{\Sigma e_i^2}{n-2}$	
Total	Σy_i^2	n		

where:

$$\begin{bmatrix} \Sigma y_i \\ \Sigma x_i y_i \end{bmatrix} = \mathbf{x'y}$$

Thus,

$$SS(b_1) + SS(b_0) = \mathbf{b'X'y} \qquad (9.27)$$

and we may write the analysis of variance table in matrix terms as shown in Table 9-6. In this way, we are able to partition the total variation $\mathbf{y'y}$ into two components: one due to the straight line that has been estimated, namely $\mathbf{b'X'y}$, and the other, which measures the remaining variation of the points about the regression line. In order to determine the variation that is absorbed by moving from the model $y_i = \bar{y} + e_i$ to $y_i = b_0 + b_1 x_i + e_i$, we need only subtract the factor $n\bar{y}^2$ from the sum of squares attributable to $\bar{y}$ if the model $y_i = \bar{y} + e_i$ is used. The remainder of $\mathbf{b'X'y}$ gives the extra sum of squares removed from e_i by the term b_1 when the model $y_i = b_0 + b_1 x_i + e_i$ is estimated.

9.5.3 Illustration of ANOVA Using Algebraic Expressions[B]

Returning to the example in which we were interested in the relationship between age and the use of physician services, recall:

$$\Sigma x_i y_i = 1{,}180, \qquad \Sigma x_i = 299, \qquad \Sigma y_i = 36, \qquad \text{and} \qquad n = 11.$$

Although we did not previously calculate the sum of the squared y values, we can easily verify:

$$\Sigma y_i^2 = (1^2 + 3^2 + 3^2 + \cdots) = 144$$

Table 9-6 ANOVA Table for Linear Regression with Matrix Formulas

Source	SS	df	MS
$\mathbf{b'} = [b_0 \quad b_1]$	$\mathbf{b'X'y}$	2	
Residual	$\mathbf{y'y} - \mathbf{b'X'y}$	$n - 2$	s_{yx}^2
Total (Uncorrected)	$\mathbf{y'y}$	n	

Given that b_1 was previously estimated to be .098, the sum of squares due to the regression line is:

$$SS(b_1) \cong b_1 \left(\Sigma x_i y_i - \frac{\Sigma x_i \Sigma y_i}{n} \right)$$

$$= .098 \left(1180 - \frac{299 \times 36}{11} \right)$$

$$\cong 19.7425$$

when we consider the coefficient b_1 only. The sum of squares about the mean is:

$$\Sigma y_i^2 - \frac{(\Sigma y_i)^2}{n} = 144 - \frac{(36)^2}{11}$$

$$\cong 26.1818$$

Finally, the sum of squares about the regression line is found by subtraction as follows:

$$\Sigma e_i^2 = 26.1818 - 19.7425 = 6.4393$$

with $n - 2 = 11 - 2$, or 9, degrees of freedom. After summarizing these results in an ANOVA table, we may then compute the mean square terms and compute the F ratio as shown in Table 9-7.

9.5.4 Illustration of ANOVA Using Matrix Notation[C]

As shown in Table 9-6 the sum of squares due to regression, including both b_0 and b_1, is given by $\mathbf{b'X'y}$. To calculate the estimates of the vector $\mathbf{b}$ we formed the matrix product

$$\mathbf{b} = (\mathbf{X'X})^{-1}\mathbf{X'y}$$

Table 9-7 Analysis of Variance for Doctor's Office Visits Regression

Source	SS	df	MS	F
Regression	19.7425	1	19.7425	27.59
Residual	6.4393	9	.7155	
Total, Corrected for Mean	26.1818	10		

The required values were:

$$\mathbf{X'X} = \begin{bmatrix} 11 & 299 \\ 299 & 10{,}193 \end{bmatrix}$$

$$(\mathbf{X'X})^{-1} = \frac{1}{22{,}722} \begin{bmatrix} 10{,}193 & -299 \\ -299 & 11 \end{bmatrix}$$

and

$$\mathbf{X'y} = \begin{bmatrix} 36 \\ 1{,}180 \end{bmatrix}$$

when the multiplication was carried out we obtained

$$\mathbf{b} \cong \begin{bmatrix} .6218 \\ .0975 \end{bmatrix}$$

We find $SS(b_0, b_1)$ by Equation 9.27 as follows:

$$SS(b_0, b_1) = \mathbf{b'X'y}$$

$$= [.6218 \quad .0975] \begin{bmatrix} 36 \\ 1{,}180 \end{bmatrix}$$

$$= (.6218 \times 36 + .0975 \times 1{,}180)$$

$$\cong 137.4348$$

We also saw that $SS(b_0, b_1)$ has the two components $SS(b_0)$ and $SS(b_1)$. Employing Equation 9.26, we calculate $SS(b_0)$ as follows:

$$SS(b_0) = n\bar{y}^2 = \frac{(\Sigma y_i)^2}{n} = \frac{(36)^2}{11} = 117.8182$$

while $SS(b_1)$ is given by:

$$SS(b_1) = \mathbf{b'X'y} - SS(b_0)$$

$$= 137.4348 - 117.8182$$

$$= 19.6166$$

This differs slightly from the value found in Table 9-7 because more significant digits were included in the matrix calculations.

Note that the total sum of squares (uncorrected) $\mathbf{y}'\mathbf{y} = \Sigma y_i^2$ and that the correction for b_0 (i.e., for the mean) is $SS(b_0) = n\bar{y}^2$.

As shown in Table 9-8, the results of these matrix operations also provide the basis for performing an analysis of variance. An inspection of this table will reveal that the sum of squares due to regression have been expanded to show $SS(b_0,b_1)$, $SS(b_0)$ and $SS(b_1)$. Also note that an F ratio has been calculated for b_1 only and that the total sum of squares (i.e., $\Sigma y_i^2 = 144$) has been partitioned to take account of the correction for b_0. Note that when a different number of significant digits is used in calculating b_0 and b_1, differences in the sums of squares for the residual, $SS(\text{Res})$, and for b_1 result. For example, if we based our calculations on seven significant digits, our estimates of b_0 and b_1 would have been .0975266 and .6217762, respectively. As a result, the values appearing in Table 9-8 would become:

$$SS(b_0,b_1) = 137.46535$$

$$SS(b_0) = 117.81818$$

$$SS(b_1) = 19.64717$$

$$SS(\text{Res}) = 6.53465 \qquad MS(\text{Res}) = .7260722$$

$$F = 27.059525 \cong 27.06$$

Table 9-8 Analysis of Variance for Doctor's Office Visits Using Matrix Calculation Results

Source	SS	df	MS	F
Regression				
(b_0,b_1)	137.4348	2		
(b_0)	117.8182	1		
(b_1)	19.6166	1	19.6166	26.89
Residual	6.5652	9	.7295	
Total				
Uncorrected	144	11		
Corrected for b_0	26.1818	10		

9.6 THE MEANING OF THE F STATISTIC[B]

When we hypothesize a linear model of the form:

$$y_i = b_0 + b_1 x_i + e_i \qquad (9.28)$$

it is necessary to distinguish between the true, but unknown, population value for the regression constant and the estimated coefficients that are derived by the least squares method. For the purpose of discussing the meaning of the F statistic, we shall designate the estimated values of the regression constants by $\hat{b}_0$ and $\hat{b}_1$, while the true, but unknown, population regression coefficients will be represented by b_0 and b_1. In a similar fashion, we estimate the value of the true population variance

$$\sigma_{yx}^2 \quad \text{by} \quad s_{yx}^2.$$

Statistical theory shows that the mean squares have the expected values:

$$E[MS(b_1)] = \sigma_{yx}^2 + b_1^2 \Sigma(x_i - \bar{x})^2 \qquad (9.29)$$

and

$$E(x_{yx}^2) = \sigma_{yx}^2 \qquad (9.30)$$

If the null hypothesis that $b_1 = 0$ is correct, the expected value of the F ratio is 1.0.

$$E(F) = [\sigma_{yx}^2 + \hat{b}_1^2 \, \Sigma(x_i - \bar{x})^2] / \sigma_{yx}^2$$

If the calculated F ratio is significantly larger than 1.0, we reject the null hypothesis $H_0 : b_1 = 0$ and accept the alternate hypothesis $H_a : b_1 \neq 0$.

Referring to Table 9-8, we find that the calculated value of F is 26.89. Comparing $F = 26.89$ with $F_{.01} = 10.6$ for 1 and 9 degrees of freedom, we conclude that the null hypothesis can be rejected and the hypothesis $H_a : b_1 \neq 0$ is accepted. The probability of committing a Type I error is less than .01 when we say that $b_1 \neq 0$.

We might interpret this F statistic in a slightly different way. Rather than evaluating the null hypothesis $H_0 : b_1 = 0$ directly, the F ratio of 26.89 as compared with $F_{.01}$ for 1 and 9 degrees of freedom might be interpreted to mean that a significant amount of variation in the dependent variable has been explained by the regression line, when only the sum of squares *in excess* of $SS(b_0)$ is considered.

In the next chapter, when we examine multiple regression, there will be two distinct points of view to be considered. One perspective is that of the individual regression coefficients $(b_1, b_2, \ldots, b_k)$. Each individual coefficient can be examined to determine whether or not it is significantly different from zero.

The second point of view will be that of the variation explained by the entire regression equation consisting of the total effects of all the regression coefficients $(b_1, b_2, \ldots, b_k)$ simultaneously. Again, the sum of squares to be considered will be that *in excess of* $SS(b_0)$.

9.7 FURTHER ANALYSIS OF THE REGRESSION EQUATION[B]

Once the basic ideas of regression analysis, estimation of coefficients, and significance testing have been mastered, it is necessary to examine:

1. the proportion of variation that is attributable to the regression equation,
2. standardized regression coefficients,
3. standard errors and confidence intervals.

These additional topics allow us to evaluate the *goodness* of the regression equation and to illustrate the interrelationships among several of the concepts discussed earlier.

9.7.1 The Proportion of Variation Accounted for by the Equation[B,C]

The *coefficient of determination* measures the proportion of the total variance in the dependent variable y, which is attributable to the regression line. The definitional form is given by:

$$R^2 = \frac{SS(\text{Reg}) - SS(b_0)}{SS(T) - SS(b_0)} \tag{9.31}$$

Using conventional algebraic notation, the computational equation by which R^2 is computed is as follows:

$$R^2 = \frac{SS(b_1)}{SS(T) - SS(b_0)} = \frac{b_1\left(\Sigma x_i y_i - \dfrac{\Sigma x_i \Sigma y_i}{n}\right)}{\Sigma y_i^2 - \dfrac{(\Sigma y_i)^2}{n}} \tag{9.32.1}$$

$$= \frac{b_1 \operatorname{Cov}(x, y)}{\operatorname{Var}(y)} \qquad (9.32.2)$$

When expressed in matrix notation, Equation 9.32 becomes:

$$R^2 = \frac{\mathbf{b'X'y} - n\bar{y}^2}{\mathbf{y'y} - n\bar{y}^2} \qquad (9.33)$$

When calculating R^2, the relevant sums of squares may be obtained directly from the ANOVA table and, returning to our example, an inspection of Table 9-8 reveals:

$$SS(b_1) = 19.6166 \quad \text{and} \quad SS(T) - SS(b_0) = 26.1816$$

Hence, we may calculate R^2 directly as:

$$R^2 = \frac{19.6166}{26.1816} = .7492$$

This finding indicates that approximately 74.9 percent of the variation of the number of doctor's office visits is *explained* or *accounted for* by the regression line relating age and the number of visits.

In the case of simple linear regression, the coefficient of determination is very closely related to the coefficient of correlation between the dependent and independent variables. It can be shown algebraically that:

$$R^2 = r_{yx}^2$$

for linear regression. Therefore, in terms of our example, we find that

$$R = \sqrt{.7492} \cong .866$$

We have previously calculated all of the appropriate matrix components to calculate the correlation directly:

$$r_{yx} = \frac{\begin{vmatrix} 11 & 36 \\ 299 & 1{,}180 \end{vmatrix}}{\sqrt{\begin{vmatrix} 11 & 299 \\ 299 & 10{,}193 \end{vmatrix} \cdot \begin{vmatrix} 11 & 36 \\ 36 & 144 \end{vmatrix}}}$$

$$= \frac{12,980 - 10,764}{\sqrt{(112,123 - 89,401) \times (1,584 - 1,296)}} = \frac{2,216}{\sqrt{22,722 \times 288}}$$

After performing these calculations we find:

$$r_{yx} \cong \frac{2216}{2558.1118} \cong .86626$$

which agrees with $\sqrt{R^2}$.

The minimum value of R^2 is 0, and the maximum value is 1.0. Values from 0 to .10 are usually regarded as extremely low; values from .10 to .20 are low; values from .2 to .4 are moderate; values from .4 to .6 are high; values from .6 to .8 are very high; and lastly, values above .8 are exceptionally high.

9.7.2 Standardized Regression Coefficients[B]

The regression coefficients discussed to this point are known as *ordinary* (or unstandardized) *regression coefficients.* In the next chapter when dealing with multiple regression we will change this name to *ordinary partial regression coefficients* to reflect the presence of several predictor variables. In most cases, the dependent and independent variables are measured in their natural (or ordinary) units. To illustrate this point, consider our example in which the ages of the patients are measured in years and their utilization is measured in numbers of visits.

Both the dependent and independent variables can be *standardized* by subtracting the mean from each observation and dividing by the standard deviation. Let us represent the standardized values by $\tilde{y}$ and $\tilde{x}$ and define them as follows:

$$\tilde{y}_i = \frac{y_i - \bar{y}}{s_y} \quad \text{and} \quad \tilde{x}_i = \frac{x_i - \bar{x}}{s_x} \quad (9.34)$$

Therefore, the new variables $\tilde{y}$ and $\tilde{x}$ are measured as standard deviations above and below the original means.

The mean and standard deviation of the standardized variables are zero and one, respectively. In addition, since the intercept has been forced to zero, our regression model now assumes the form:

$$\tilde{y}_i = \beta_1 \tilde{x}_i + \tilde{e}_i \quad (9.35)$$

where β_1 is referred to as a *Beta weight.*

To differentiate between the standardized and unstandardized regression coefficients, the standardized coefficients are usually referred to as *Beta weights,* while the unstandardized are called *b values.* In *linear regression* using standardized variables, the Beta weight is the same as the correlation between the variables. That is,

$$\beta_1 = r_{yx} \tag{9.36}$$

Most regression programs calculate and display both the *b* values and the Beta weights. The relationship between the regression coefficient b_1 and the Beta weight β_1 is as follows:

$$b_1 = \beta_1 \frac{s_y}{s_x} \quad \text{or} \quad \beta_1 = b_1 \frac{s_x}{s_y} \tag{9.37}$$

That is,

$$b_1 = r_{yx} \frac{s_y}{s_x} \quad \text{or} \quad r_{yx} = b_1 \frac{s_x}{s_y} \tag{9.38}$$

This is equivalent to:

$$b_1 = r_{yx} \sqrt{\frac{\Sigma(y_i - \bar{y})^2}{\Sigma(x_i - \bar{x})^2}} = r_{yx} \sqrt{\frac{\Sigma y_i^2 - n\bar{y}^2}{\Sigma x_i^2 - n\bar{x}^2}} \tag{9.39}$$

9.7.3 Standard Errors and Confidence Intervals[B]

When examining the regression model:

$$y_i = b_0 + b_1 x_i + e_i$$

certain assumptions concerning the error term e_i are necessary before making inferences concerning the *b* values and the estimated values of y_i. The first assumption is that the e_i have a normal distribution with zero mean and a constant variance σ_{yx}^2 (i.e., the error terms are *homoscedastic*). This assumption is summarized by:

$$e_i \sim N(0, \sigma_{yx}^2) \tag{9.40}$$

Nonuniform error variance is called *heteroscedasticity.* The second assumption required is that the values of e_i for different values of i are not related. Thus, we assume:

$$\text{Cov}(e_i, e_j) = 0 \quad \text{for} \quad i \neq j \qquad (9.41)$$

In regression analysis, we are usually interested in inferences concerning the regression coefficients as well as in the accuracy of the predicted values of the dependent variable y. In the next section, we consider the problem of testing hypotheses concerning the relationship between the two variables and return later to the question of evaluating the accuracy of predictions concerning y.

9.7.3.1 Inferences Concerning Regression Coefficients[B,C]

As observed from our example, regression coefficients are estimates of the true, but unknown parameters of the population and as such, a given set of estimates are based on a particular sample. Hence, we would expect to obtain a slightly different set of parameter estimates if we based our calculations on a different sample from the same population. Thus, similar to all statistics, the estimates of the regression coefficients exhibit sampling variability.

Given that estimates of the regression coefficients are expected to vary from sample to sample, it is necessary to examine the extent of the sampling variability. It can be shown that the standard error of the slope, b_1, of the regression line may be estimated, using algebraic notation, by:

$$s_{b_1} = \frac{s_{yx}}{\sqrt{\Sigma x_i{}^2 - (\Sigma x_i)^2/n}} \qquad (9.42)$$

or, in matrix notation:

$$s_{b_1} = \frac{s_{yx}}{\sqrt{\frac{1}{n}|\mathbf{X'X}|}} = s_{yx} \sqrt{\frac{n}{|\mathbf{X'X}|}} \qquad (9.43)$$

Also the standard error of the intercept, b_0, can be estimated, using algebraic notation, by:

$$s_{b_0} = s_{yx} \sqrt{\frac{(\Sigma x^2)/n}{\Sigma x^2 - (\Sigma x)^2/n}} \qquad (9.44)$$

or, alternatively, in matrix notation:

$$s_{b_0} = s_{yx} \sqrt{\frac{\Sigma x^2}{|X'X|}} \tag{9.45}$$

We may use these standard errors to make inferences about the regression coefficients either in the form of t-tests or in the form of confidence intervals.

Suppose we wished to test the null hypotheses:

$$H_{00}: b_0 = b_0^* \tag{9.46.1}$$

and

$$H_{01}: b_1 = b_1^* \tag{9.46.2}$$

where b_0^* and b_1^* are the values of b_0 and b_1 assumed for the null hypothesis. These values should be derived from a theoretic model or previous studies or be set to zero. In testing H_{00} and H_{01}, we calculate the t statistic:

$$t_0 = \frac{b_0 - b_0^*}{s_{b_0}} \quad \text{and} \quad t_1 = \frac{b_1 - b_1^*}{s_{b_1}} \tag{9.47}$$

The calculated values of t_0 and t_1 are then compared with the tabular value of t with $(n - 2)$ degrees of freedom and at the desired level of confidence.

In general, when testing the null hypothesis $H_{01}: b_1 = 0$, we are usually faced with a situation in which we have no prior knowledge concerning the relation between the two variables and, as a result, we set forth the null hypothesis of independence. Conversely, when testing a null hypothesis similar to $H_{01}: b_1 \geq b_1^*$, we may usually rely on previous studies or a theoretic model for the construction of such an assumption concerning the relationship between the two variables.

In order to examine these two hypotheses, we require values for s_{yx} and $X'X$. Returning to our example, recall that s_{yx} was found to be:

$$s_{yx} = \sqrt{s_{yx}^2} = \sqrt{.7260727} = .8520987$$

while

$$|X'X| = \begin{vmatrix} 11 & 299 \\ 299 & 10{,}193 \end{vmatrix} = 11 \times 10{,}193 - 299^2$$

$$= 22{,}722$$

Therefore,

$$s_{b_1} = \frac{s_{yx}}{\sqrt{\dfrac{1}{n}\,|\mathbf{X'X}|}} = \frac{.8520987}{\sqrt{\dfrac{1}{11} \times 22{,}722}}$$

$$\cong .0187483$$

Given that $b_1 = .0975266$ and we wish to test $H_{01}: b_1 = 0$, we calculate the t statistic as follows:

$$t = \frac{.0975266 - 0}{.0187483}$$

$$\cong 5.20$$

Comparing $t \cong 5.20$ with the tabulated value of $t_{.025} = 2.262$ for 9 degrees of freedom, we find that the difference between $b_1 = .0975266$ and zero is statistically significant (i.e., b_1 is positive and significantly different from zero).

Now, let us assume previous studies allow us to formulate the null hypothesis:

$$H_{01}: b_1 \geq .2 \quad \text{which implies } H_{a1}: b_1 < .2$$

We test this expectation by computing the t statistic as follows:

$$t = \frac{.0975266 - .2}{.0187483} \cong -5.466$$

We then compare the calculated value of $t = -5.466$ with the tabular value of $t_{.05} = 1.833$ for 9 degrees of freedom. This comparison reveals that the calculated value of t is significant and, as a consequence, these findings indicate that the slope of the regression line in the study setting was below the lower limit suggested by the previous studies. Thus, we can conclude from the test of these hypotheses that the number of visits to a doctor's office per person per year increases by .098 for every year of age.

The interest in the value of the y-intercept is not usually as great as the concern expressed about the value of the slope of the regression line. In terms of our example, the y-intercept should be interpreted as the annual number of visits to a physician's office by a patient between the ages of 0 and .5 years. Recall that the value of b_0 was found to be .6217762, while the standard error of the y-intercept is given by:

$$s_{b_0} = s_{yx} \sqrt{\frac{\Sigma x^2}{|\mathbf{X}'\mathbf{X}|}}$$

$$= .8520987 \sqrt{\frac{10{,}193}{22{,}722}}$$

$$\cong .5707128$$

When testing the null hypothesis:

$$H_{00}: b_0 = b_0{}^* = 0$$

we calculate the t statistic as follows:

$$t = \frac{.6217762 - 0}{.5707128} \cong 1.089$$

Comparing the calculated value of $t = 1.089$ with $t_{.025} = 2.262$ for 9 degrees of freedom reveals that the y-intercept, b_0, does not differ significantly from zero.

Observe that, thus far in this section, we have only examined the use of the t statistic in reaching inferences concerning b_0 and b_1. It is also possible to construct confidence intervals for b_0 and b_1 which may be employed to evaluate hypotheses concerning the value of the corresponding parameters. Following the general procedure outlined earlier, we define the two-sided $1\text{-}\alpha$ confidence interval for b_0 and b_1 as:

$$b_0 \pm t_{\alpha/2, n-2} \times s_{b_0} \tag{9.48}$$

and

$$b_1 \pm t_{\alpha/2, n-2} \times s_{b_1} \tag{9.49}$$

respectively.

Returning to our example, if we wished to calculate a .99 confidence interval for b_0, then

$$t_{\alpha/2, n-2} = t_{.005, 9} = 3.250$$

and using Equation 9.48 with data from the preceding calculation yields:

$$.6217762 \pm 3.25 \times .5707128$$

or

$$.6217762 \pm 1.8548166$$

which defines a .99 confidence interval with a lower confidence limit of -1.2330404 and an upper confidence limit of 2.4765928. On the basis of this finding, we conclude that b_0 is not significantly different from zero since zero lies within the bounds defined by the lower and upper confidence limits.

Referring to the calculation indicated in Equation 9.49, we can also calculate a .99 confidence interval for b_1 in our example as follows:

$$.0975266 \pm 3.25 \times .0187483$$

These calculations lead to a confidence interval that has the lower confidence limit of $.0365946$ and an upper confidence limit of $.1584585$. Observe that since the lower confidence limit is greater than zero, we conclude that b_1 is positive and significantly different from zero.

9.7.3.2 Regression Coefficient Inferences Expressed in Matrix Notation[C]

Having described the basic statistical tests concerning b_0 and b_1, we now wish to express the standard errors of b_0 and b_1 using matrix notation. A more general formulation of s_{b_0} and s_{b_1} uses the variance-covariance matrix of the b values. It can be shown that:

$$\mathbf{V}(b_0, b_1) = s_{yx}^2 (\mathbf{X'X})^{-1} = \begin{bmatrix} \text{Var}(b_0) & \text{Cov}(b_0, b_1) \\ \text{Cov}(b_0, b_1) & \text{Var}(b_1) \end{bmatrix} \qquad (9.50)$$

The standard errors of b_0 and b_1 are:

$$s_{b_0} = \sqrt{\text{Var}(b_0)} \quad \text{and} \quad s_{b_1} = \sqrt{\text{Var}(b_1)} \qquad (9.51)$$

If

$$\mathbf{X'X} = \begin{bmatrix} n & \Sigma x \\ \Sigma x & \Sigma x^2 \end{bmatrix} \qquad (9.52)$$

then

$$(\mathbf{X'X})^{-1} = \frac{1}{|\mathbf{X'X}|} \begin{bmatrix} \Sigma x^2 & -\Sigma x \\ -\Sigma x & n \end{bmatrix} \qquad (9.53)$$

and

$$V(b_0, b_1) = \frac{s_{yx}^2}{|\mathbf{X}'\mathbf{X}|} \begin{bmatrix} \Sigma x^2 & -\Sigma x \\ -\Sigma x & n \end{bmatrix} \qquad (9.54)$$

Note that

$$\mathrm{Var}(b_0) = s_{yx}^2 \frac{\Sigma x^2}{|\mathbf{X}'\mathbf{X}|} \qquad (9.55)$$

which is identical to Equation 9.45, while

$$\mathrm{Var}(b_1) = s_{yx}^2 \frac{n}{|\mathbf{X}'\mathbf{X}|} \qquad (9.56)$$

is identical to Equation 9.43.
    Also observe that

$$\mathrm{Cov}(b_0, b_1) = s_{yx}^2 \frac{-\Sigma x}{|\mathbf{X}'\mathbf{X}|} \neq 0 \qquad (9.57)$$

In our example, $\mathrm{Cov}(b_0, b_1)$ is *less than zero* and this means that the estimates of b_0 and b_1 are *inversely* related. If the estimate of b_1 is too *high*, then the estimate of b_0 is automatically too *low*.

This result leads to several problems that are encountered when performing the t-tests or constructing the confidence intervals previously described. If $|\mathbf{X}'\mathbf{X}|$ is very small, the confidence intervals for b_0 and b_1 are not independent of each other. This may be seen in Figure 9-4(a) which is based on $|\mathbf{X}'\mathbf{X}|$ being relatively small as compared with Σx. Observe that the confidence interval for b_1 depends on which value of b_0 is selected. For example, the lower level of b_1 with value b_0' is about the same as the upper level for b_1 when b_0'' is used. We shall refer to this situation in the next chapter when we discuss the problem of *multicollinearity*. On the other hand, when $|\mathbf{X}'\mathbf{X}|$ is relatively large, as in Figure 9-4(b), the estimates of b_0 and b_1 are relatively independent. We see in this figure that the joint confidence region is nearly circular, which implies that the t-test and confidence intervals for these coefficients are easily calculated.

9.7.3.3 Inferences Concerning y and ŷ[B,C]

Recall that we employed the symbol $\hat{y}$ to designate the estimated value of y. As in the case of b_0 and b_1, the estimated value of y differs from the actual value of y, and in order to perform t-tests and construct confidence

Figure 9-4 Joint Confidence Regions for Regression Coefficient Estimates

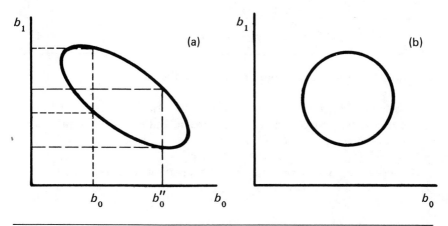

intervals concerning predicted values of y we require the standard error. For any specific value of x_i, say x_q, we could have one observation on y_q, several observations on y_q, or many observations on y_q. The standard error (Std Err) for the mean of $\hat{y}_q$ of all possible observations having value x_q is:

$$\text{Std Err}(\hat{y}_q) = s_{yx} \sqrt{\frac{1}{n} + \frac{(x_q - \bar{x})^2}{\Sigma(x_i - \bar{x})^2}} \qquad (9.58)$$

This leads to

$$\text{Std Err}(\hat{y}_q) = s_{yx} \sqrt{\frac{1}{n} + \frac{(x_q - \bar{x})^2}{\Sigma x_i^2 - (\Sigma x_i)^2/n}} \qquad (9.59)$$

and finally

$$\text{Std Err}(\hat{y}_q) = s_{yx} \sqrt{\frac{\Sigma x_i^2 - (2x_q \Sigma x_i) + n x_q^2}{n \Sigma x_i^2 - (\Sigma x_i)^2}} \qquad (9.60)$$

If matrix notation is used, the preceding expressions can be simplified substantially. Let us define a row vector of the observation as:

$$\mathbf{x}_q' = [1 \quad x_q]$$

Then we find:

$$\text{Std Err}(\hat{y}_q) = s_{yx}\ \sqrt{\mathbf{x}_q{}'(\mathbf{X}'\mathbf{X})^{-1}\mathbf{x}_q} \qquad (9.61)$$

This is an important result and holds true in the next chapter on multiple regression.

Equations 9.58 through 9.61 all express the variability of the position of the *regression line*, that is the expected (mean) value of $\hat{y}_q$. The individual observation, however, does not usually fall on the regression line but has variance $s_{yx}{}^2$.

The error variance of the individual observation must be added to the error variance of the mean value $\hat{y}$ (the line). This gives us the following:

$$\text{Var}(y_q) = s_{yx}{}^2 + \text{Std Err}^2(\hat{y}_q)$$

$$= s_{yx}{}^2 + s_{yx}{}^2\left(\frac{1}{n} + \frac{(x_q - \bar{x})^2}{\Sigma(x_i - \bar{x})^2}\right)$$

$$= s_{yx}{}^2\left(1 + \frac{1}{n} + \frac{(x_q - \bar{x})^2}{\Sigma(x_i - \bar{x})^2}\right)$$

Taking the square root of this expression, we obtain

$$\text{Std Err}(y_q) = s_{yx}\ \sqrt{1 + \frac{1}{n} + \frac{(x_q - \bar{x})^2}{\Sigma(x_i - \bar{x})^2}} \qquad (9.62)$$

which, when expressed in matrix notation, becomes:

$$\text{Std Err}(y_q) = s_{yx}\ \sqrt{1 + \mathbf{x}_q{}'(\mathbf{X}'\mathbf{X})^{-1}\mathbf{x}_q} \qquad (6.63)$$

Thus, the standard error of the value of y is larger than that for $\hat{y}$ by the addition of 1 under the square root sign. This result is intuitively sensible since the location of the *expected value* of a point should be more precisely estimated than the position of the point itself, and this is similar to the concept of the sampling distribution of the mean.

As before, the standard errors in the preceding equations can be used either to perform t-tests or to construct confidence intervals for values of $\hat{y}$

and y. It is useful to understand the behavior of these confidence intervals (and t-tests) when values of x close to $\bar{x}$ and those far from $\bar{x}$ are chosen. In Equations 9.58 and 9.62 the term $(x_q - \bar{x})^2$ is the only one that depends on the particular value of x_q. When $x_q = \bar{x}$, we find that $(x_q - \bar{x})^2 = 0$. However, as x_q is located further and further from $\bar{x}$, $(x_q - \bar{x})^2$ increases more and more rapidly. As a result, the confidence intervals for $\hat{y}$ and y may be represented by curves that gradually move away from the regression line as the difference between x_q and $\bar{x}$ increases. This situation is diagrammed in Figure 9-5.

9.8 SUMMARY OF LINEAR REGRESSION IN MATRIX NOTATION[C]

The basic structural model of linear regression is:

$$y = Xb + \epsilon$$

where:

y is a column vector of n observations of the dependent variable;
X is a matrix of a column of n ones and a column of n observations of the independent variable;
b is a column vector of regression coefficients to be estimated;

$$b = \begin{bmatrix} b_0 \\ b_1 \end{bmatrix} ;$$

ϵ is a column vector of errors that are independent of each other, and distributed normally, with a mean of zero, and constant variance σ_{yx}^2. This is represented by $\epsilon \sim N(0, \sigma_{yx}^2)$.

The results of the least squares method of estimation can be expressed as:

$$b = (X'X)^{-1}X'y$$

and the variance-covariance matrix of the b's is:

$$\text{Cov}(b_0, b_1) = s_{yx}^2(X'X)^{-1}$$

where s_{yx}^2 is drawn from the analysis of variance table as the mean square of the residuals. The analysis of variance table for linear regression takes its most general form as Table 9-9.

Figure 9-5 Confidence Intervals for $\hat{y}$ and y

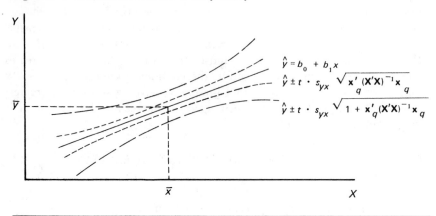

The standard errors for b_0 and b_1 are:

$$\text{Std Err}(b_0) = s_{yx} \sqrt{\frac{\Sigma x_i^2}{|\mathbf{X'X}|}}$$

$$\text{Std Err}(b_1) = s_{yx} \sqrt{\frac{n}{|\mathbf{X'X}|}}$$

The standard errors for $\hat{y}_q$ and y_q are:

$$\text{Std Err}(\hat{y}_q) = s_{yx} \sqrt{\mathbf{x}_q{}'(\mathbf{X'X})^{-1}\mathbf{x}_q}$$

$$\text{Std Err}(y_q) = s_{yx} \sqrt{1 + \mathbf{x}_q{}'(\mathbf{X'X})^{-1}\mathbf{x}_q}$$

The cross products matrix and its inverse are:

$$\mathbf{X'X} = \begin{bmatrix} n & \Sigma x_i \\ \Sigma x_i & \Sigma x_i^2 \end{bmatrix} \qquad (\mathbf{X'X})^{-1} = \frac{1}{|\mathbf{X'X}|} \begin{bmatrix} \Sigma x^2 & -\Sigma x_i \\ -\Sigma x_i & n \end{bmatrix}$$

The proportion of variation accounted for by the regression equation is called the *coefficient of determination,* and is defined as:

$$R^2 = \frac{\mathbf{b'X'y} - n\bar{y}^2}{\mathbf{y'y} - n\bar{y}^2}$$

Table 9-9 Analysis of Variance for Linear Regression

Source	SS	df	MS	F
Regression				
(b_0, b_1)	$\mathbf{b'X'y}$	2		
b_0	$n\bar{y}^2$	1		
b_1	$\mathbf{b'X'y} - n\bar{y}^2$	1	$MS(b_1)$	$\dfrac{MS(b_1)}{s_{yx}^2}$
Residual	$\mathbf{y'y} - \mathbf{b'X'y}$	$n-2$	s_{yx}^2	
Total				
Uncorrected	$\mathbf{y'y}$	n		
Corrected for				
the Mean	$\mathbf{y'y} - n\bar{y}^2$	$n-1$		

The criteria used to judge the goodness of fit of the equation to the data are R^2, s_{yx} and F. Each gives a different and complementary view of the goodness of fit. When raw (unstandardized) data (y's and x's) are used, there are two regression coefficients to be estimated, b_0 and b_1. These are often referred to as b *values*. When standardized data are used, the axes of the system are shifted so that the origin is at the original $(\bar{x}, \bar{y})$ point, which eliminates the regression coefficient for the intercept. When standardized data are used, the regression coefficient, which is given by

$$\beta_1 = r_{yx} = b_1 \frac{s_x}{s_y}$$

is referred to as a *Beta weight*.

BIBLIOGRAPHY

Draper, N. R. and Smith, H. *Applied Regression Analysis*. New York: Wiley, 1966.
Johnston, J. *Econometric Methods*. 2nd Ed. New York: McGraw-Hill, 1972.

Problems for Solution[G]

1. From the data in Table 8-1, use Age as the independent variable to predict Height.
   a. Estimate the **b** vector.
   b. Calculate the sums of squares and fill in all components of the analysis of variance table.
   c. Calculate the standard error of estimate.
   d. Calculate the variance-covariance matrix of the b values.
   e. Calculate the values of the standard errors of b_0 and b_1, assuming that the covariance of b_0 and b_1 can be ignored. Test the null hypotheses $H_{00}: b_0 = 0$ and $H_{01}: b_1 = 0$.
   f. Calculate the value of β_1.
   g. Calculate the value of R^2 and interpret it in words.
   h. Calculate $\hat{y}_q$ and the standard errors of $\hat{y}_q$ and y_q for a child of age 15 years, and one of age 9 years.
   i. Can the equation estimated be used validly to predict the height of a person of age 50 years? Explain your reason(s).

2. A researcher examined the relationship between family income level and family use of physicians' services (measured by visits), for families who had actually visited physicians during a given year. Family income levels were classified from 1 (lowest) to 5 (highest). The following data are extracted from the researcher's sample:

Family	1	2	3	4	5	6	7	8	9	10	11	12	13	14	15	16
Income	1	2	5	3	4	1	3	4	5	3	4	2	1	5	4	3
Visits	2	3	6	5	7	1	4	2	1	6	5	1	3	7	5	2

   a. From this data derive a regression equation predicting visits from income. Calculate the b values, ANOVA table, R^2, the covariance matrix of the b's, and the standard errors of the b's.
   b. Explain whether or not there is a significant relationship.

3. A laboratory director has collected statistics about the variable costs of operation and the volume of tests in the past 15 months. Linear regression is to be used to predict cost in the future from the volume of tests. The data are:

Costs ($00)	12.8	16.1	15.0	12.0	18.3	19.0	19.0	22.0
Tests (000)	4.9	3.8	5.1	3.0	6.8	5.5	4.9	6.9

Cost ($00)	15.5	21.0	19.2	16.3	11.2	16.1	13.2
Tests (000)	6.3	5.9	6.4	4.7	3.9	5.8	4.2

a. From the data construct $\mathbf{X}'$ and $\mathbf{y}'$.

b. Given:

$$\mathbf{X}'\mathbf{X} = \begin{bmatrix} 15 & 78.1 \\ 78.1 & 425.61 \end{bmatrix}$$

What is $(\mathbf{X}'\mathbf{X})^{-1}$?

c. Given:

$$\mathbf{X}'\mathbf{y} = \begin{bmatrix} 246.7 \\ 1323.78 \end{bmatrix} \quad \text{and} \quad \mathbf{y}'\mathbf{y} = 4207.41$$

What is the value of b?

d. Fill in the ANOVA table, and test for significance.

e. Plot the data and the regression line on graph paper.

Chapter 10

The Basic Multiple
Regression Model

Objectives

After completing this chapter, you should be able to:
1. Recognize the need for several predictor variables.
2. Understand the basic regression model and the methods of calculating regression coefficients.
3. Understand and interpret ANOVA for multiple regression analysis.
4. Understand and interpret the coefficient of multiple determination, and the standard error of estimate.
5. Perform inferences concerning $\mathbf{b}$ and $\hat{y}$.
6. Perform multiple regression analysis using APL.

Chapter Map

The material presented in this chapter *requires* a basic understanding of matrix algebra as well as the previous discussion of APL and SPSS. No attempt is made to develop formulas in ordinary algebra, which could be studied to the exclusion of matrix algebra.

Sections 10.1 and 10.4 contain introductory material and have been assigned the letter code A.

Section 10.2 presents the basic statement of the multiple regression model in ordinary algebra and then restates it in matrix algebra, and the section has been assigned the codes B and C.

Section 10.3, the subsections of 10.4 and all parts of Section 10.5 deal with the solution of the multiple regression model, the ANOVA table, multiple correlation, the standard error of estimate and inferences about $\mathbf{b}$ and $\hat{y}$ using matrix algebra and have been assigned the letter code C.

Section 10.6 translates all of the above matrix algebra into APL, and has been assigned both codes E and C.

Section 10.7 presents an APL program which does not require explicit knowledge of matrix algebra, and has been assigned the code E.

10.1 THE NEED FOR SEVERAL PREDICTOR VARIABLES[A]

As computing equipment has become more available and as experience with advanced estimation techniques has been accumulated, it has become increasingly well recognized that it is often very useful to measure and investigate the effects of several independent variables on a dependent variable. In many situations, the phenomenon of interest is related to several factors and in these cases, our objective is to measure the value of a dependent variable in terms of the values of a set of independent variables that we believe will be useful in explaining the variability exhibited by the dependent variable.

Ideally, we would like to establish a causal relationship so that we may view the independent variables as instrumental factors over which we may exert control and thereby influence the value assumed by the dependent variable. In the physical sciences, such as chemistry and physics, much more is known about cause and effect than in the soft sciences usually associated with health administration. For example, in chemistry enough is known about electrical and physical forces as well as electrochemical reactions to enable us to construct devices that are able to perform useful work and to be controlled within limits acceptable for the desired uses. The health care industry makes extensive use of such equipment. Often the equipment permits us to control several inputs to obtain the desired results.

Understanding of the normal state of the human body and the causes of disease states is much less well advanced. However, in pharmacology it is known that certain combinations of drugs may be very dangerous to a patient suffering from a particular problem or a set of related problems. For other combinations of drugs, each drug acts independently of the others without increasing or reducing the effectiveness of the remaining drugs in the combination. In still others, a combination of drugs may have an effectiveness that is much greater than the individual effects would suggest.

As an example of a phenomenon of interest influenced by several factors, many studies have suggested that the incidence of several categories of illness is associated with such factors as genetic predisposition, the consumption of alcohol, smoking and diet, as well as lack of exercise. The exact nature of the relationship is not known, but it is believed that, in some cases, a combination of factors leads to a much greater probability of the person contracting the disease.

The health administrator is also confronted with problems in which the relationships of interest involve several independent variables. In these cases, we are frequently interested in examining the impact of the independent variables on the dependent variable. For example, the amount of nursing care required by a group of patients depends on whether they required surgery, whether they acquired an infection, whether they require special nursing service, whether a large portion of the patients may perform normal activities of daily living and so forth. Similarly, the number of laboratory tests required by a patient depends on the presenting condition, its severity, the presence of coexisting conditions, as well as such factors as the patient's age, sex, income, education and so on. As a final example, most would recognize that staff morale depends on a number of factors such as wages and salaries, work conditions, fringe benefits, supervisor/employee relationships and so forth. Many other situations may be easily identified in which several factors operate to produce a result of interest.

Measuring and analyzing these factors may make it possible to predict or control the results or outcomes in a given situation. Multiple regression is one tool for performing this analysis. Factorial analysis of variance is another technique, which may be treated as a special case using multiple regression. The use of regression analysis allows greater flexibility, in that cell sizes (n's) need not all be equal. In both analysis of variance and multiple regression, the dependent variable is assumed to be measured on an interval or ratio scale. In analysis of variance the independent variables are measured on nominal or ordinal scales, while regression analysis is more flexible in that independent variables may be measured in terms of nominal or ordinal scales as well as in terms of ratio or interval scales. Both analysis of variance and regression analysis are used to examine the extent to which variation exhibited by the dependent variable is explained or absorbed by the set of independent variables. Observe that when these statistical tools are employed, we usually assume the independent variables are measured accurately, which implies that ANOVA and regression analysis are not used to predict the values assumed by the independent variables.

There are also other kinds of techniques, which are known collectively as *cluster analysis,* that may be used for analyzing the same kinds of data treated by ANOVA and regression analysis. ANOVA and regression analysis have been selected for detailed study because these techniques have been the subjects of greater statistical development than alternate approaches. However, several other approaches have been developed in response to the shortcomings of the techniques we shall study, and the tradeoffs among the different statistical methods are discussed in appropriate sections.

10.2 THE BASIC MULTIPLE REGRESSION MODEL[B,C]

We saw previously that the general relationship between the dependent variable y and the single independent or predictor variable x may be expressed by:

$$y = f(x) \qquad (10.1.1)$$

The corresponding linear equation that expresses the relationship between these two variables is:

$$y_i = b_0 + b_1 x_i + e_i \qquad (10.1.2)$$

In multiple regression we simply extend the basic regression model described earlier so that we are able to accommodate several independent variables. Thus, the general functional relationship between the dependent variable y and the set of independent variables $x_1, x_2, \ldots, x_k$ is given by:

$$y = f(x_1, x_2, \ldots, x_k) \qquad (10.2.1)$$

In multiple linear regression, this general functional relationship assumes the form:

$$y_i = b_0 + b_1 x_{1i} + b_2 x_{2i} + \cdots + b_k x_{ki} + e_i \qquad (10.2.2)$$

where the b's are the regression coefficients, the x's are the independent variables, and e_i is the error term. Thus, the dependent variable y is expressed as a linear combination of the independent variables and the error term e_i. Similar to our earlier discussion, the error term represents the difference between the actual value of the dependent variable and the value that is predicted from the linear combination of independent variables. As before, we may employ the notation and operations of matrix algebra to express the basic model assumed under multiple linear regression. As a matter of fact, the expression of multiple linear regression analysis in matrix terms is identical in form to the approach used in Chapter 9. The only change is that the matrix X and the vector b are expanded slightly. As before, we define y as a column vector consisting of n observations concerning the dependent variable. However, in multiple regression analysis the matrix X consists of $k + 1$ columns. The first column consists of n ones (1's) and each of the other columns contains n measurements of one of the independent variables. Each row of the matrix X represents data concerning one *observation* or *case* that is included in our sample. The vector b contains the regression coefficients that are to be estimated from the given values of the dependent and independent variables. Thus, the vector b has $k + 1$ elements corresponding to:

$$[b_0 \quad b_1 \quad b_2 \quad \cdots \quad b_k]$$

As before, the vector ϵ represents the error of the estimate for each observation. Similar to our earlier work, we may express the multiple linear regression model by:

$$y = Xb + \epsilon \qquad (10.3)$$

which is identical to Equation 9.11, Section 9.4.

To illustrate, let us return to the data pertaining to the physiological development of children, which we introduced in Chapter 8. In this situation, we could define mass as the dependent variable and age, height, and sex as the independent or predictor variables. Following the procedures outlined previously, we postulate:

$$mass = f(age, height, sex)$$

or

$$y = f(x_1, x_2, x_3)$$

The system of linear equations:

$$y_i = b_0 + b_1 x_{1i} + b_2 x_{2i} + b_3 x_{3i} + e_i \qquad (10.4)$$

expresses the relationship between the dependent variable y and the set of independent variables x_1, x_2, and x_3. Referring to the data presented in Table 8-1, we let

$$
y = \begin{bmatrix} 40 \\ 20 \\ 16 \\ 20 \\ \cdot \\ \cdot \\ \cdot \\ 30 \\ 23 \\ 57 \end{bmatrix}
\qquad
X = \begin{bmatrix}
1 & 10 & 145 & 1 \\
1 & 5 & 105 & 0 \\
1 & 3 & 105 & 0 \\
1 & 6 & 95 & 1 \\
\cdot & \cdot & \cdot & \cdot \\
\cdot & \cdot & \cdot & \cdot \\
\cdot & \cdot & \cdot & \cdot \\
1 & 8 & 130 & 1 \\
1 & 7 & 100 & 0 \\
1 & 13 & 160 & 1
\end{bmatrix}
$$

Similar to our earlier work, we also let

$$\mathbf{b} = \begin{bmatrix} b_0 \\ b_1 \\ b_2 \\ b_3 \end{bmatrix} \qquad \mathbf{\epsilon} = \begin{bmatrix} \epsilon_1 \\ \epsilon_2 \\ \epsilon_3 \\ \cdot \\ \cdot \\ \cdot \\ \epsilon_{21} \end{bmatrix}$$

Observe that a series of zeros and ones appear in the last column of the matrix $\mathbf{X}$. These values indicate whether the corresponding child was male or female. Given that sex is a dichotomous variable, we have assigned the value of zero to males and a value of one to females. As can be easily verified, the system of linear equations given by Equation 10.4 is equivalent to Equation 10.3 when the matrix $\mathbf{X}$ and the vectors $\mathbf{y}$, $\mathbf{b}$, and $\mathbf{\epsilon}$ are defined as seen above.

10.3 MULTIPLE REGRESSION SOLUTION IN MATRIX NOTATION[C]

Using the least squares criterion introduced earlier, we can show that the solution for the column vector:

$$\mathbf{b} = \begin{bmatrix} b_0 \\ b_1 \\ \cdot \\ \cdot \\ \cdot \\ b_k \end{bmatrix}$$

is found by:

$$\mathbf{b} = (\mathbf{X'X})^{-1}\mathbf{X'y} \qquad (10.5)$$

Observe that this solution is identical in form to the method of estimating the regression coefficients for the simple linear model.

10.4 GOODNESS OF FIT[A]

After estimating the regression coefficients, one of the primary areas of inquiry involves the extent to which the resulting regression equation provides a good fit to the actual values of the dependent variable. In this regard, the F ratio obtained from the ANOVA table, the coefficient of determination, and the standard error of the estimate may be used to examine the goodness of the regression equation. We consider each of these approaches in this section.

10.4.1 ANOVA[C]

We saw previously that the solution for the column vector $\mathbf{b}$ is identical to the methods we employed when finding the coefficients associated with the simple linear regression equation. Similarly, when developing the analysis of variance table for multiple regression analysis, the sums of squares are also calculated as before. Thus, we find:

$$SS(\text{total: uncorrected}) = \mathbf{y}'\mathbf{y} \qquad (10.6)$$

$$SS(\text{all } b \text{ values}) = \mathbf{b}'\mathbf{X}'\mathbf{y} \qquad (10.7)$$

$$SS(b_0) = n\bar{y}^2$$

$$= (\Sigma y)^2/n \qquad (10.8)$$

$$SS(\text{residuals}) = \mathbf{y}'\mathbf{y} - \mathbf{b}'\mathbf{X}'\mathbf{y} \qquad (10.9)$$

Similar to our earlier work, we may summarize our calculations by constructing a complete ANOVA for multiple regression as in Table 10-1. An inspection of this table will reveal that there are k degrees of freedom for the regression coefficients, representing 1 degree of freedom for each coefficient.

The most usual form of the ANOVA table is an abridged version of Table 10-1, which shows the lines for: (a) the k regression coefficients, (b) the residuals, and (c) the total corrected sums of squares. This is shown in Table 10-2.

One of the primary purposes of the ANOVA table is to examine whether any of the regression coefficients $b_1, b_2, \ldots, b_k$ are statistically different from zero. The F ratio of the ANOVA table allows us to test the null hypothesis:

$$H_0: b_1 = b_2 = \cdots = b_k = 0$$

Table 10-1 Complete ANOVA Table for Multiple Regression Using Matrix Notation

Source	SS	df	MS	F
Regression				
all b's	$SS(\mathbf{b}) = \mathbf{b'X'y}$	$k + 1$		
b_0	$SS(b_0) = n\bar{y}^2$ $= (\Sigma y)^2/n$			
b_1 to b_k	$SS(\text{Reg}) = \mathbf{b'X'y} - n\bar{y}^2$	k	$MS(\text{Reg}) = \dfrac{SS(\text{Reg})}{k}$	$\dfrac{MS(\text{Reg})}{MS(\text{Res})}$
Residuals	$SS(\text{Res}) = \mathbf{y'y} - \mathbf{b'X'y}$	$n - k - 1$	$MS(\text{Res}) = \dfrac{SS(\text{Res})}{n - k - 1}$	
Total				
Uncorrected	$\mathbf{y'y}$	n		
Corrected	$\mathbf{y'y} - n\bar{y}^2$	$n - 1$		

Table 10-2 Abridged ANOVA Table for Multiple Regression Using Matrix Notation

Source	SS	df	MS	F
Regression				
$(b_1$ to $b_k)$	$SS(\text{Reg}) = \mathbf{b}'\mathbf{X}'\mathbf{y} - n\bar{y}^2$	k	$MS(\text{Reg}) = \dfrac{SS(\text{Reg})}{k}$	$\dfrac{MS(\text{Reg})}{MS(\text{Res})}$
Residuals	$SS(\text{Res}) = \mathbf{y}'\mathbf{y} - \mathbf{b}'\mathbf{X}'\mathbf{y}$	$n - k - 1$	$MS(\text{Res}) = \dfrac{SS(\text{Res})}{n - k - 1}$	
Total, Corrected for Mean	$SS(\text{Tot}) = \mathbf{y}'\mathbf{y} - n\bar{y}^2$	$n - 1$		

against the alternate hypothesis that at least one of the regression coefficients is not equal to zero. This hypothesis may be expressed in the form:

$$H_a: b_i \neq 0$$

for at least one of the independent variables.

10.4.2 Multiple Correlation[C]

After correcting for the mean, the proportion of the total sum of squares which is explained or absorbed by the regression equation is given by the ratio:

$$R^2 = \frac{SS(\text{Reg})}{SS(\text{Tot})} = \frac{\mathbf{b}'\mathbf{X}'\mathbf{y} - n\bar{y}^2}{\mathbf{y}'\mathbf{y} - n\bar{y}^2} \qquad (10.10)$$

The term R^2, which is referred to as the *coefficient of multiple determination*, ranges from zero to one. A value of zero indicates that none of the sum of squares is absorbed by the regression coefficients b_1 to b_k. Such a finding would indicate that the only explanation provided is by the mean of the dependent variable. This is evident by observing that when $R^2 = 0$,

$$\mathbf{b}'\mathbf{X}'\mathbf{y} = n\bar{y}^2 \qquad (10.11.1)$$

which implies that only b_0 is different from zero. Conversely, when $R^2 = 1.0$, all of the total sum of squares is absorbed by the regression coefficients, after correcting for the mean. Hence, when $R^2 = 1.0$, the actual and predicted values of y are identical and as a consequence,

$$\epsilon = \mathbf{y} - \hat{\mathbf{y}} = 0 \qquad (10.11.2)$$

Recall that the predicted values of $\mathbf{y}$, which we symbolize by $\hat{\mathbf{y}}$, can be calculated by:

$$\hat{\mathbf{y}} = \mathbf{X}\mathbf{b} \qquad (10.11.3)$$

Therefore, when $R^2 = 1.0$, we have:

$$\mathbf{b}'\mathbf{X}' = \hat{\mathbf{y}}' = \mathbf{y}' \qquad (10.11.4)$$

and as a consequence,

$$\mathbf{b}'\mathbf{X}'\mathbf{y} = \mathbf{y}'\mathbf{y} \qquad (10.11.5)$$

This result implies that the numerator and the denominator of Equation 10.10 are equal when $R^2 = 1.0$.

If we take the square root of Equation 10.10, we obtain R, which is called the *coefficient of multiple correlation*. The coefficient R is a measure of the correlation between the actual and predicted values of $\mathbf{y}$. As such, R is always positive and ranges between 0 and 1.

Summarizing this section, it is important to remember that R^2 is the second overall indicator of the extent to which multiple regression analysis explains variation in the dependent variable. In this regard, we found that R^2 ranges from 0 to 1, which indicate no explanation and perfect explanation, respectively. Informal guidelines for the interpretation of R^2 in simple linear regression were presented in Section 9.7.1. The same interpretations apply to multiple regression analysis.

As might be surmised from the foregoing discussion, the addition of one or more independent variables tends to cause R^2 to increase. In fact, if $n - 1$ truly independent variables are employed in the regression model, R^2 will be 1.0. This becomes obvious by observing that a regression model characterized by two independent variables perfectly fits a data set composed of three observations of the dependent variable. However, in this case, the residuals have 0 degrees of freedom and the relationship is statistically meaningless. When faced with a limited number of observations, we have to decide which independent variables to include in the regression analysis and this important question is addressed further in Chapter 15 (Section 15.8.1 and its subsections).

10.4.3 The Standard Error of Estimate[C]

The standard error of estimate of the regression equation is defined as the square root of the mean squares of the residuals and is usually obtained directly from the calculations required when constructing the ANOVA table. Thus, using the notation developed in Chapter 9, we define the standard error of the estimate, s_{yx}, as:

$$s_{yx} = \sqrt{s^2_{yx}} \qquad (10.12.1)$$

where:

$$s^2_{yx} = MS(\text{Res}) \qquad (10.12.2)$$

$$s^2_{yx} = \frac{\mathbf{y'y} - \mathbf{b'X'y}}{n - k - 1} \qquad (10.12.3)$$

$$s^2_{yx} = \frac{\mathbf{\epsilon'\epsilon}}{n - k - 1} = \frac{(\mathbf{y} - \hat{\mathbf{y}})' \, (\mathbf{y} - \hat{\mathbf{y}})}{n - k - 1} \qquad (10.12.4)$$

As mentioned earlier, the standard error of estimate is the third major criterion by which we judge the goodness of the regression equation. A small standard error indicates that there is little uncertainty concerning the predicted value of the dependent variable for any one case. As the standard error increases, we may be less certain concerning the predicted value of the dependent variable. As a consequence, a small standard error is more desirable than a large standard error.

The standard error of the equation can be compared with the standard deviation of the dependent variable to obtain a *crude* indication of the predictive power of the regression equation. In the next section, the standard error also plays a central role when testing hypotheses concerning the significance of the relation between the dependent variable and an independent variable as well as in constructing confidence intervals for estimates of predicted values of the dependent variable and estimates of the *b* values.

10.5 INFERENCES CONCERNING *b* AND $\hat{y}^{(C)}$

In addition to its use in predicting values of the dependent variable for known or assumed values of the independent variables, multiple regression analysis may also be used to examine hypotheses concerning the estimates of the regression coefficients and to construct confidence intervals for the predicted value of the dependent variable, $\hat{y}$. We consider each of these aspects in this section.

10.5.1 Inferences Concerning the *b* Values[C]

We already know the equation

$$\mathbf{b} = (\mathbf{X'X})^{-1}\mathbf{X'y}$$

provides us with an estimate of the coefficients of the regression equation. The **b** vector can be shown to have a variance-covariance matrix of the form

$$\text{Cov}(\mathbf{b}) = \mathbf{B} = s^2_{yx}(\mathbf{X}'\mathbf{X})^{-1} \qquad (10.13)$$

The variances of the b values appear as the diagonal elements of the matrix and the standard errors of the estimates of the regression equation are obtained by taking the square root of these elements.

When examining the statistical significance of individual b values, we construct a t-test in the normal fashion. For example, if we were interested in testing the null hypothesis:

$$H_0: b_i = b_i*$$

the statistic:

$$t = \frac{b_i - b_i*}{\text{Std Err}(b_i)} \qquad (10.14.1)$$

is compared with the tabular value of t for $(n - k - 1)$ degrees of freedom. If, in particular, the null hypothesis is given by:

$$H_0: b_i = 0$$

we compare

$$t = \frac{b_i}{\text{Std Err}(b_i)} \qquad (10.14.2)$$

with the tabular value of t for $(n - k - 1)$ degrees of freedom.

As in Figure 9-11, problems arise with this form of t-test if the b values have a relatively large covariance or if the b values are highly correlated. The correlation matrix of the b values can be derived by pre- and postmultiplying $\mathbf{B}$ by a diagonal matrix containing the inverses of the standard errors. Representing the diagonal matrix by $(\mathbf{SE})^{-1}$ and the correlation matrix as $\mathbf{RB}$, we find:

$$\mathbf{RB} = (\mathbf{SE})^{-1} \mathbf{B}(\mathbf{SE})^{-1} \qquad (10.15)$$

By inspecting the $\mathbf{RB}$ matrix it is possible to identify the presence of highly correlated b values as well as the corresponding problems.

10.5.2 Inferences Concerning Predicted Values of $y^{(C)}$

In Section 9.7.3.3 inferences concerning the predicted value of the dependent variable $\hat{y}$ (one observation at a time), and concerning the actual value of the dependent variable, y, were discussed, and their standard errors were given in Equations 9.58 through 9.63. With suitable redefinition for the multiple regression situation, the matrix forms of these formulas may be used without further modification when dealing with more than one predictor variable.

In Chapter 9 the matrix $\mathbf{X}$, which consisted of observations on the independent variable was of order n by 2. However, in multiple regression, the matrix $\mathbf{X}$ has $k + 1$ columns since we now have k independent variables rather than only one. In our previous work, we defined $\mathbf{x}_q{}'$ as a row vector consisting of a single new observation. In the case of multiple regression, we define $\mathbf{x}_q{}'$ as the row vector (again representing a single new observation):

$$\mathbf{x}_q{}' = [1 \ x_{q1} \ x_{q2} \cdots x_{qk}] \tag{10.16}$$

which has $k + 1$ elements.

Employing this notation, the standard error of $\hat{y}_q$ is defined by:

$$\text{Std Err}(\hat{y}_q) = s_{yx}\sqrt{\mathbf{x}_q{}'(\mathbf{X}'\mathbf{X})^{-1}\mathbf{x}_q} \tag{10.17}$$

which is the same as Equation 9.61. Similar to Equation 9.63, the formula for the standard error of y_q is given by:

$$\text{Std Err}(y_q) = s_{yx}\sqrt{1 + \mathbf{x}_q{}'(\mathbf{X}'\mathbf{X})^{-1}\mathbf{x}_q} \tag{10.18}$$

Unlike simple linear regression, the multidimensional nature of multiple regression makes it extremely difficult to construct a single diagram that represents the meaning of these equations. However, the same general behavior of the standard errors is observed. That is, the further a new observation lies from the mean of the observations initially used to create $\mathbf{X}'\mathbf{X}$, the greater will be the two standard errors defined above. This applies whether "far" is defined in one dimension only, several dimensions, or all of the dimensions.

When performing a t-test for a newly observed point, y_q, the statistic:

$$t = \frac{y_q - \hat{y}_q}{\text{Std Err}(y_q)} \qquad (10.19)$$

is compared with the tabular value of t for $n - k - 1$ degrees of freedom. If we are now concerned about whether or not the new point is close to the expected value, then the statistic:

$$t = \frac{y_q - \hat{y}_q}{\text{Std Err}(\hat{y}_q)} \qquad (10.20)$$

is computed.

Occasionally, it is desirable to construct a confidence interval for estimated values of the dependent variable. The limits of the confidence interval are calculated from:

$$\text{Conf Lim}(\hat{y}_q) = \hat{y}_q \pm t_{\alpha/2, n-k-1} \text{ Std Err}(\hat{y}_q) \qquad (10.21.1)$$

and from

$$\text{Conf Lim}(y_q) = \hat{y} \pm t_{\alpha/2, n-k-1} \text{ Std Err}(y_q) \qquad (10.21.2)$$

Strictly speaking, these expressions must be used only for new observations that are made independently of the values contained in **X**. The quantity $(y_q - \hat{y}_q)$ is the residual for the new observation. Dividing by the standard error of y_q gives a *standardized residual*, which is a t-statistic. Observations with large standardized residuals are often referred to as *outliers*.

In some situations it is desirable to know whether or not any of the original observations in **X** are anomalous (i.e., outliers), and whether their removal would change the results of the regression substantially. Theory to allow testing this situation has been developed (Welsch and Kuh 1977) and was used (Lay 1978) in the development of disease profiles. In these disease profiles, regression models were developed explaining treatment cost (for patients with various types of gastrointestinal diseases) by groups of patient-related and problem-related factors. They were refined by using the Welsch and Kuh methodology to detect and then remove outlier patients from the original samples. The refined disease profiles can be used to test new patients, and detect outliers. This aspect is discussed further in Chapter 14, in the section on advanced tests for bias (Section 14.6).

10.6 MULTIPLE REGRESSION USING APL AS A MATRIX CALCULATOR[E,C]

Although multiple regression programs have been developed in APL, and are extremely easy to develop using matrix notation, we leave the major discussion of the use of programmed packages to Chapters 11 through 15, where we discuss the use of SPSS. Here we concentrate instead on the matrix notation, using APL as a calculator to do the arithmetic. We use the example of the physiological development study (Sections 10.2 and following) to develop the regression equation:

$$mass = f(constant, age, height, sex)$$

The study data have been stored in workspace CORRPRAC in library 3176 (Appendix F) in the matrix **Y**. In **Y** the four columns contain age, height, mass, and sex, respectively. In Exhibit 10-1 we first load CORRPRAC into our active workspace and then print the transpose of **Y** (across the page, to save space). **Y** is shown to be a 21 by 4 matrix, that is, there are 21 observations of 4 variables. Next we create **XT** (i.e., **X**′) from a vector of 1s and the age (1), height (2), and sex (4) columns of **Y**. (Remember that omitting the first subscript of a matrix specifies that *all* rows are to be used.) **XT** is then printed to verify that our work is correct. Next we replace the working copy of the 21 by 4 matrix **Y** by specifying that the third column (mass) is to be called **Y**. Then the new **Y** is printed to verify our work. Finally, we create two character string variables DEPVAR (which we use to denote the dependent variable), and INDVARS (which we use to denote the list of independent variables). Having these available to print whenever we feel the need helps later to avoid confusion about which numbers are associated with which variables.

In Exhibit 10-2, first **XTX** (i.e., **X**′**X**) is created, printed, and then its inverse is stored as **XTXI**. Next, **X**′**y** is calculated and stored as **XTY** and then B (**b** = $(X'X)^{-1}X'y$) is calculated and printed giving the *b* values, and their names are printed as well for reference purposes.

In Exhibit 10-3, a number of sums of squares are calculated:

1. **YTY**($y'y$) is the total sum of squares, uncorrected;
2. *SSB* (**b**′**X**′**y**) gives the sum of squares for all regression coefficients, including b_0.

Exhibit 10-1

```
      )LOAD CORRPRAC,3176
SAVED 15.24/ 79.107/ 6824
      )DIGITS 4
WAS 10
      Y
 5 105  20  0
 3 100  16  0
 6  95  20  1
 4  95  17  1
 3  80  15  0
15 170  64  0
12 150  45  0
10 135  40  1
 9 145  45  0
14 140  50  0
15 150  66  0
10 120  39  1
 6 115  27  0
 3  90  13  1
11 125  42  1
 9 125  31  1
 7 120  25  0
 8 130  30  1
 7 100  23  0
13 160  57  1
10 145  40  1
      ⍴Y
21 4

      XT←4 21 ⍴ (21⍴1),Y[;1],Y[;2],Y[;4]
      XT
 1   1   1   1   1   1   1   1   1   1   1   1   1   1   1   1   1   1   1   1   1
 5   3   6   4   3  15  12  10   9  14  15  10   6   3  11   9   7   8   7  13  10
105 100 95 95 80 170 150 135 145 140 150 120 115 90 125 125 120 130 100 160 145
 0   0   1   1   0   0   0   1   0   0   0   1   0   1   1   1   0   1   0   1   1

      Y←Y[;3]
      '99990'⍕Y
40  20  17  15  64  45  40  45  39  66  50  45  40  27  13  42  31  25  30  23  57

      DEPVAR← 'MASS'
      INDVARS←'CONSTANT  AGE  HEIGHT  SEX'
      )DIGITS 10
WAS 4
```

Exhibit 10-2

```
XTX←  XT +.x (⊠XT)
XTX
    21         180        2595          10
   180        1844       24000          84
  2595       24000      333125        1220
    10          84        1220          10

XTXI←  ⊟ XTX
'9990.9999999' ⊛ XTXI
 2.8443700    0.1675371   ‾0.0337248   ‾0.1372532
 0.1675371    0.0187826   ‾0.0026516   ‾0.0018079
‾0.0337248   ‾0.0026516    0.0004549    0.0004969
‾0.1372532   ‾0.0018079    0.0004969    0.1918083

XTY←  XT+.xY
B←XTXI+.xXTY
B
‾12.6936218   2.933406991   .1847438318   ‾1.585744399
INDVARS
CONSTANT     AGE        HEIGHT       SEX
```

3. *SSBO* $((\Sigma y)^2/n = n\bar{y}^2)$ is the correction for b_0.
4. *SSBREG* $(b'X'y - n\bar{y}^2)$ is the regression sum of squares, excluding b_0.
5. *MSREG* (*SSBREG* $\div k$, where k is the number of regression coefficients, excluding b_0) is the regression mean square.
6. *F* is the regression *F* ratio.
7. *SSTCOR* is the total sum of squares corrected for b_0.
8. *RSQ* is R^2.
9. *SE* is the standard error of the equation.

Quantities 1 through 7 are sufficient for filling in the ANOVA table, in either the pattern of Table 10-1 or of 10-2. The reader should do this as an exercise and compare it with the SPSS output shown in Chapter 11, Figure 11-2.

In Exhibit 10-4, the first calculation gives the covariance matrix of the *b* values (*COVB*) and prints it out. Next the main diagonal elements are extracted, by (1 1 ⊠ COVB), and their square roots taken to give *SEB*, which is the vector of standard errors of the *b* values. Dividing *B* by the vector **SEB** gives **T**, which is the vector of *t* values, that can each be tested against *t* with $[n - (k + 1)]$ degrees of freedom. Note in Figure 11-2 that SPSS prints out *F* values, which are the squares of the *t* values calculated here.

Exhibit 10-3

```
        □←YTY←Y+.×Y
30219
        □←SSB←B +.× XTY
29989.04494
        □←SSBO← ((+/Y)*2)÷21
25029.7619
        □←SSBREG ← SSB - SSBO
4959.28304
        □←MSREG←SSBREG÷3
1653.094347
        □←SSRES←YTY-SSB
229.9550557

        □←MSRES←SSRES÷(21-(3+1))
13.52676798
        □←F←MSREG÷MSRES
122.2091152
        □←SSTCOR←YTY-SSBO
5189.238095

        □←RSQ←SSBREG÷SSTCOR
.9556861621
        □←SE←MSRES*÷2
3.677875471
```

Exhibit 10-4

```
     '99990.999999' $ COVB← MSRES × XTXI
38.475133    2.266236   ¯0.456187   ¯1.856592
 2.266236    0.254068   ¯0.035868   ¯0.024455
¯0.456187   ¯0.035868    0.006153    0.006722
¯1.856592   ¯0.024455    0.006722    2.594546


     □← SEB← (1 1 ⍀ COVB)*÷2
6.202832687  .5040520434  7.844600703E¯2  1.610759732
     □← T← B÷SEB
¯2.046423374  5.819651024  2.355044428  ¯.9844698541

     INDVARS
CONSTANT    AGE     HEIGHT     SEX
```

In Exhibit 10-5, a function called DIAG is used to create a diagonal matrix from the vector **SEB** and this is inverted and called **SEBI**. It is

Exhibit 10-5

```
    □←SEBI ← ⊟ DIAG SEB
 .1612166651              0           0           0
        0    1.983922123           0           0
        0              0    12.74762143           0
        0              0           0    .6208250553



    '99990.9999' $ .00005 + RB ← SEBI +.× COVB +.× SEBI
 1.0000      0.7248    ‾0.9374    ‾0.1857
 0.7248      1.0000    ‾0.9070    ‾0.0300
‾0.9374     ‾0.9070     1.0000     0.0532
‾0.1857     ‾0.0300     0.0532     1.0000

    INDVARS
CONSTANT     AGE        HEIGHT        SEX
```

equivalent to SE^{-1} in Equation 10.15, and in Exhibit 10-5 that equation is performed. The result is called **RB** and is printed out. This is the correlation matrix of the **b** values and it can be inspected for problems of multicollinearity as described in Section 10.5.1. It can be used to supplement the Chapter 14 discussion of multicollinearity (Section 14.5.6) using the routine tests for bias. Inspection of **RB** shows that the *b* values for age and height are strongly negatively correlated, and this in turn implies that their *b* values are biased.

Finally, in Exhibit 10-6, we calculate the confidence intervals (using Equations 10.17 and 10.18) for the mass of a 12-year-old girl 140 centimeters high (**XQ1**), and for the mass of a 9-year-old boy 120 centimeters in height (**XQ2**).

SEYQ1H and *SEYQ2H* represent the standard errors of (the expected values) $\hat{y}_{q1}$ and $\hat{y}_{q2}$, respectively; while *SEYQ1* and *SEYQ2* represent the standard errors of the actual values of y_{q1} and y_{q2}, respectively.

Exhibit 10-6

```
    XQ1← 1   12   140   1
    XQ2← 1    9   120   0

    □←YQ1← B +.× XQ1
46.78565414

    □←SEYQ1H← SE × (Q1← XQ1 +.× XTXI +.× XQ1)*÷2
1.410911532
    □←SEYQ1←  SE × (1+Q1)*÷2
3.939218112


    □←YQ2← B +.× XQ2
35.87630093
    □←SEYQ2H← SE × (Q2←XQ2 +.× XTXI +.× XQ2)*÷2
1.224855659
    □←SEYQ2←  SE × (1+Q2)*÷2
3.876472542
```

10.7 MULTIPLE REGRESSION USING A PREPROGRAMMED APL PACKAGE[E]

The matrix algebra steps of Exhibits 10-1 to 10-5 have been programmed in APL and named MREG. (The listing of MREG is found in Appendix F.) MREG requires as input a dependent variable vector (left-side operand), and a vector or matrix of predictor variables. Each predictor variable should be a column in the right-side operand. In the workspace CORRPRAC, the matrix **Y** contains the physiological study data. The third column represents MASS, while columns 1, 2, and 4 represent AGE, HEIGHT, and SEX, respectively. The regression of MASS on AGE, HEIGHT, and SEX, using MREG is shown in Figure 10-1.

The output consists of:

1. the correlation matrix of the raw data.
2. the ANOVA table.
3. the b values, with their t values.
4. R^2 and standard error.
5. the correlation matrix of the b values.

Figure 10-1 Use of Preprogrammed APL Package for Multiple Regression

```
 )LOAD CORRPRAC, 3176
SAVED 15.24/ 79.107/ 6824

    YE;3]   MREG   YE;1 2 4]


MULTIPLE REGRESSION ANALYSIS

DATE:  4/18/79   TIME: 11:55:47


CORRELATION MATRIX OF RAW DATA - DEPENDENT VARIABLE FIRST


CORRELATION MATRIX
   1.000    0.969    0.930   ⁻0.097
   0.969    1.000    0.907   ⁻0.042
   0.930    0.907    1.000   ⁻0.061
  ⁻0.097   ⁻0.042   ⁻0.061    1.000

T-VALUES   FOR DF= 19
   0.000   16.956   11.066   ⁻0.430
  16.956    0.000    9.401   ⁻0.187
  11.066    9.401    0.000   ⁻0.268
  ⁻0.430   ⁻0.187   ⁻0.268    0.000

VALUES OF R AND T ARE ALSO AVAILABLE WITH FULL PRECISION
```

REGRESSION ANALYSIS OF VARIANCE TABLE

SOURCE	SUM OF SQUARES	D.F.	MEAN SQUARES	F
REGRESSION:	29,989.04494			
B0	25,029.76190			
B1 TO B3	4,959.28303	3	1,653.09434	122.2091
RESIDUALS	229.95505	17	13.52676	
TOTAL (CORR)	5,189.23809			

```
-------------------------------------------------------------------
```

BVALUES:	⁻12.6936	2.9334	0.1847	⁻1.5857
TVALUES:	⁻2.0464	5.8196	2.3550	⁻0.9844

```
R SQUARED:   0.9556
STD.ERR.:             3.67787

CORRELATION MATRIX OF BVALUES

   1.0000    0.7248   ⁻0.9374   ⁻0.1857
   0.7248    1.0000   ⁻0.9070   ⁻0.0300
  ⁻0.9374   ⁻0.9070    1.0000    0.0532
  ⁻0.1857   ⁻0.0300    0.0532    1.0000

FINISHED
```

BIBLIOGRAPHY

Lay, C. M. "Disease Costing in an Ambulatory Clinic: Disease and Physician Profiles and the Selection of Patients for Review." Ph.D. Dissertation, Alfred P. Sloan School of Management, Massachusetts Institute of Technology. Cambridge, Mass.: May 1978.

Welsch, R. E., and Kuh, E. "Linear Regression Diagnostics," Working paper WP923-77, Alfred P. Sloan School of Management, Massachusetts Institute of Technology. Cambridge, Mass.: April 1977.

Problem for Solution (G)

1. Radiology Department

    The Manager of the Radiology Department has maintained records of the volume of examinations (types A, B, and C) produced over the past 25 months, the number of overtime hours, and the variable cost for labor and supplies charged against the department. The question is raised whether or not cost can be explained as a function of the other variables. Use multiple regression to answer the question.
    a. What are the b values? Do they seem to be reasonable?
    b. How much of the variance is explained by the equation?
    c. Is the equation significant?
    d. Are the b values significant?
    e. What is the standard error of the equation?
    The data are as follows:

X-Ray Examinations

Cost	A	B	C	Overtime Hours
		(00)		
9407.5	13.0	3.5	12.2	5.0
9756.0	21.0	7.1	8.9	9.0
7785.5	7.0	2.9	9.0	10.0
10649.5	21.0	4.8	12.5	20.0
10215.5	28.0	5.1	6.8	25.0
7881.0	21.0	6.3	7.9	7.0
7589.5	13.0	4.8	8.5	15.0
7061.0	14.0	3.7	6.9	5.0
10422.5	31.0	4.1	10.4	19.0
10054.5	20.0	4.3	9.2	25.0
10680.5	28.0	4.5	9.0	27.0
8955.5	18.0	3.8	7.9	16.0

X-Ray Examinations

Cost				Overtime Hours
	A	B	C	
		(00)		
9463.5	24.0	4.6	8.3	20.0
9230.5	13.0	3.9	8.2	9.0
9603.0	12.0	6.5	11.1	12.0
8911.0	9.0	6.9	10.3	15.0
9847.0	12.0	5.8	9.8	20.0
12061.0	36.0	5.9	12.1	25.0
12210.0	25.0	6.0	11.4	18.0
10121.0	29.0	5.3	7.1	5.0
9817.5	24.0	4.6	8.3	10.0
7797.0	9.0	6.4	8.0	6.0
9937.5	25.0	5.5	8.8	12.0
9673.5	16.0	5.3	8.2	25.0
10449.0	20.0	5.7	9.1	20.0

Basic Multiple Regression Using the SPSS Batch System

Objectives

After completing this chapter you should be able to:
1. Use SPSS to perform multiple regression, entering all independent variables in a single step.
2. Interpret SPSS output, including: means and standard deviations of variables, the correlation matrix, the regression ANOVA, R^2, standard error, b values and standard errors, beta values, and plots of residuals.
3. Perform significance testing on the overall regression and the individual b values.

Chapter Map

This chapter is entirely devoted to expanding concepts from the previous chapter, using SPSS as a tool. All sections have been assigned the letter code D, except for Section 11.1, which is introductory and has been assigned the letter code A.

11.1 INTRODUCTION[A]

Although an understanding of the concepts of multiple regression is important when calculating regression coefficients, constructing the ANOVA table, and developing inferences concerning the b and y values, regression analysis frequently requires the use of a standard computer package such as SPSS. In this regard, the use of regression analysis in most real world situations requires an ability to:

1. prepare data for processing,
2. specify which procedures are to analyze the data, and
3. interpret the results obtained from computer processing.

This chapter introduces the use of SPSS to perform regression analysis, while Chapters 12 through 14 develop important concepts required for performing more extensive regression studies. SPSS is used as a teaching vehicle throughout.

11.2 MULTIPLE REGRESSION—INCLUSION
OF ALL VARIABLES[D]

Performing multiple regression analysis with SPSS is no more difficult than performing most other procedures. The cards shown in Figure 11-1 include the data for the physiological study and the necessary control cards for carrying out several different forms of regression analysis.

The first regression on the three cards immediately following the DATA LIST card is typical. The SPSS procedure name REGRESSION in columns 1 through 15 of a card identifies the beginning of the procedure. The specification of what regression is to be performed consists of two major parts. The first part specifies the set of variables (including both the dependent and predictor variables). Its format is:

VARIABLES = Variable list /

Referring to Figure 11-1 we find that the variable list calls for the four variables MASS, AGE, HEIGHT, and SEX to be included in the regression problem.

The second part of the statement specifies the dependent variable, the set of predictor variables, an *inclusion level,* and calls for calculation of the residuals. The format for this specification is:

REGRESSION = dependent variable WITH predictor list (inclusion level)
RESID=0

Figure 11-1 SPSS Cards for Carrying Out Various Forms of Multiple Regression

```
//UUCC2068    JOB    (HD123456,
///   E.*COLIN M. LAY',MSGLEVEL=2,CLASS=K
//    EXEC   SPSSH
//FT08F001   DD   *
10 145 40 1
 5 105 20 0
 3 100 16 0
 6  95 20 1
 4  95 17 1
 3  80 15 0
15 170 64 0
12 150 45 0
 9 135 40 1
 9 145 45 0
14 140 50 0
15 150 66 0
10 120 39 1
 6 115 27 0
 3  90 13 1
11 125 42 1
 9 125 31 0
 7 120 25 0
 8 130 30 0
 7 100 23 1
13 160 57 1
//SYSIN DD    *
RUN NAME         MULTIPLE REGRESSION DEMONSTRATION - PHYSIOLOGICAL STUDY
INPUT MEDIUM     DISK
N OF CASES       UNKNOWN
DATA LIST        FIXED/ 1 AGE 1-2, HEIGHT 5-7, MASS 9-10, SEX 12
REGRESSION       VARIABLES = MASS AGE HEIGHT SEX/
                 REGRESSION = MASS WITH AGE TO SEX (2) RESID = 0
STATISTICS       1,2,4,6
COMMENT          STATISTIC 1 CALLS FOR A PRINTOUT OF THE CORRELATION MATRIX
                 STATISTIC 2 CALLS FOR A PRINTOUT OF THE MEANS, STANDARD
                 DEVIATIONS, AND NUMBER OF VALID CASES OF EACH
                 STATISTIC 4 CALLS FOR A PLOT OF STANDARDIZED RESIDUALS AGAINST
                 THE SEQUENCE OF CASES IN THE FILE
                 STATISTIC 6 CALLS FOR A PLOT OF STANDARDIZED RESIDUALS AGAINST
                 STANDARDIZED Y' VALUES WITH RESIDUALS ON THE Y AXIS
READ INPUT DATA
REGRESSION       VARIABLES = MASS AGE HEIGHT SEX/
                 REGRESSION = MASS WITH AGE (6) HEIGHT(4) SEX(2)
REGRESSION       VARIABLES = MASS AGE HEIGHT SEX/
                 REGRESSION = MASS WITH AGE TO SEX (1)
REGRESSION       VARIABLES = MASS AGE HEIGHT SEX/
                 REGRESSION = MASS (10.3..4) WITH AGE TO SEX (1)
                 RESID = 0
STATISTICS       4,6
FINISH
/*
```

In the example presented in Figure 11-1, MASS is the dependent variable while AGE, HEIGHT, and SEX are the predictor (independent) variables. The inclusion level value 2 specifies that all variables in the predictor list are to be entered into the equation at the same time. (This 2 leads to the chosen title for Section 11.2, *Inclusion of all Variables.*) The keyword RESID indicates that residual statistics are to be calculated, while the 0 (zero) value indicates a particular handling of missing values (*SPSS*, Section 20.2.2.4, p. 347). The issue of missing values is discussed later and can be ignored for the time being.

The STATISTICS card calls for optional output, which is described by the COMMENT cards immediately following in the figure.

11.3 INTERPRETING THE OUTPUT—ALL VARIABLES INCLUDED[D]

The SPSS output for the first regression is shown in Figure 11-2; the printout requires eight pages in SPSS, but this has been compressed for this book by eliminating most of the blank paper left when the printer spaces to the top of a new page after each major section of the printout. Also, the Job Control Language (JCL) has been omitted, since it is irrelevant to the regression.

11.4 THE SPSS PRELIMINARIES[D]

The first page of the SPSS output lists the cards from RUN NAME to READ INPUT DATA and gives information messages about actions taken. The most important of these is that there were 21 cases read from the input data file.

11.5 MEANS AND STANDARD DEVIATIONS[D]

The second page of the SPSS output, in response to STATISTIC 2, shows a table of all the variables in the problem, their mean values, standard deviations, and numbers of cases. SEX, as a *dummy* (0,1) variable, has a mean value that gives the proportion of cases with value = 1 (female, in this case).

11.6 THE CORRELATION MATRIX[D]

SPSS performs most of its calculations on the basis of the initial correlation matrix, which is shown on the third page of the SPSS output. The corre-

Figure 11-2 SPSS Output for First Regression

```
STATISTICAL PACKAGE FOR THE SOCIAL SCIENCES                                    04/04/78        PAGE   1

SPSS FOR OS/360, VERSION H, RELEASE 7.0, MARCH 1977

DEFAULT SPACE ALLOCATION.          ALLOWS FOR..      75 TRANSFORMATIONS
WORKSPACE  52500 BYTES                              300 RECODE VALUES + LAG VARIABLES
TRANSPACE   7500 BYTES                             1200 IF/COMPUTE OPERATIONS

       RUN NAME        MULTIPLE REGRESSION DEMONSTRATION - PHYSIOLOGICAL STUDY
       INPUT MEDIUM    DISK
       N OF CASES      UNKNOWN
       DATA LIST       FIXED/ 1 AGE 1-2, HEIGHT 5-7, MASS 9-10, SEX 12

THE DATA LIST PROVIDES FOR    4 VARIABLES AND  1 RECORDS ('CARDS') PER CASE. A MAXIMUM OF    12 COLUMNS ARE USED ON A RECORD.

LIST OF THE CONSTRUCTED FORMAT STATEMENT..
(F2.0,2X,F3.0,1X,F2.0,1X,F1.0)

       REGRESSION      VARIABLES = MASS AGE HEIGHT SEX/
                       REGRESSION = MASS WITH AGE TO SEX (2) RESID = 0
       STATISTICS      1,2,4,6
       COMMENT         STATISTIC 1 CALLS FOR A PRINTOUT OF THE CORRELATION MATRIX
                       STATISTIC 2 CALLS FOR A PRINTOUT OF THE MEANS, STANDARD
                       DEVIATIONS, AND NUMBER OF VALID CASES OF EACH
                       STATISTIC 4 CALLS FOR A PLOT OF STANDARDIZED RESIDUALS AGAINST
                       THE SEQUENCE OF CASES IN THE FILE
                       STATISTIC 6 CALLS FOR A PLOT OF STANDARDIZED RESIDUALS AGAINST
                       STANDARDIZED Y* VALUES WITH RESIDUALS ON THE Y AXIS

***** REGRESSION PROBLEM REQUIRES     512 BYTES WORKSPACE, NOT INCLUDING RESIDUALS *****

       READ INPUT DATA

AFTER READING    21 CASES FROM SUBFILE NONAME  .  END OF FILE WAS ENCOUNTERED ON LOGICAL UNIT # 8
```

Figure 11-2 Continued

```
MULTIPLE REGRESSION DEMONSTRATION - PHYSIOLOGICAL STUDY                04/04/78        PAGE  2

FILE   NONAME    (CREATION DATE = 04/04/78)


VARIABLE           MEAN          STANDARD DEV      CASES

MASS             34.5238           16.1078          21
AGE               8.5714            3.8804          21
HEIGHT          123.5714           24.9571          21
SEX               0.4762            0.5118          21
```

```
MULTIPLE REGRESSION DEMONSTRATION - PHYSIOLOGICAL STUDY                04/04/78        PAGE  3

FILE   NONAME    (CREATION DATE = 04/04/78)


CORRELATION COEFFICIENTS

A VALUE OF 99.00000 IS PRINTED
IF A COEFFICIENT CANNOT BE COMPUTED.


                MASS          AGE         HEIGHT         SEX

MASS          1.00000      0.96851      0.93043      -0.09849
AGE           0.96851      1.00000      0.90722      -0.04316
HEIGHT        0.93043      0.90722      1.00000      -0.06152
SEX          -0.09849     -0.04316     -0.06152       1.00000
```

Figure 11-2 Continued

```
MULTIPLE REGRESSION DEMONSTRATION - PHYSIOLOGICAL STUDY                    04/04/78          PAGE   4

FILE   NONAME    (CREATION DATE = 04/04/78)

* * * * * * * * * * * * * * * * * * * *   M U L T I P L E   R E G R E S S I O N   * * * * * * * * * * * * * * * * * * * *

DEPENDENT VARIABLE..     MASS                                                                       VARIABLE LIST   1
                                                                                                   REGRESSION LIST  1
VARIABLE(S) ENTERED ON STEP NUMBER  1..    SEX
                                           AGE
                                           HEIGHT

MULTIPLE R          0.97759           ANALYSIS OF VARIANCE      DF      SUM OF SQUARES     MEAN SQUARE          F
R SQUARE            0.95569           REGRESSION                3.        4959.28304       1653.09435      122.20912
ADJUSTED R SQUARE   0.94787           RESIDUAL                 17.         229.95506         13.52677
STANDARD ERROR      3.67788

------------- VARIABLES IN THE EQUATION -------------         -------- VARIABLES NOT IN THE EQUATION --------

VARIABLE          B         BETA      STD ERROR B      F         VARIABLE       BETA IN      PARTIAL     TOLERANCE       F

SEX         -1.585744    -0.05038      1.61076       0.969
AGE          2.933407     0.70665      0.50405      33.868
HEIGHT       0.1847438    0.28624      0.07845       5.546
(CONSTANT) -12.69362

ALL VARIABLES ARE IN THE EQUATION


MULTIPLE REGRESSION DEMONSTRATION - PHYSIOLOGICAL STUDY                    04/04/78          PAGE   5

FILE   NONAME    (CREATION DATE = 04/04/78)

* * * * * * * * * * * * * * * * * * * *   M U L T I P L E   R E G R E S S I O N   * * * * * * * * * * * * * * * * * * * *

DEPENDENT VARIABLE..     MASS                                                                       VARIABLE LIST   1
                                                                                                   REGRESSION LIST  1
                                             SUMMARY TABLE

VARIABLE      MULTIPLE R    R SQUARE    RSQ CHANGE     SIMPLE R          B            BETA

SEX            0.09849      0.00970      0.00970      -0.09849      -1.585744      -0.05038
AGE            0.97017      0.94123      0.93153       0.96851       2.933407       0.70665
HEIGHT         0.97759      0.95569      0.01446       0.93043       0.1847438      0.28624
(CONSTANT)                                                        -12.69362


MULTIPLE REGRESSION DEMONSTRATION - PHYSIOLOGICAL STUDY                    04/04/78          PAGE   6

***** REGRESSION PROBLEM REQUIRES    2264 BYTES WORKSPACE INCLUDING RESIDUALS *****
```

Figure 11-2 Continued

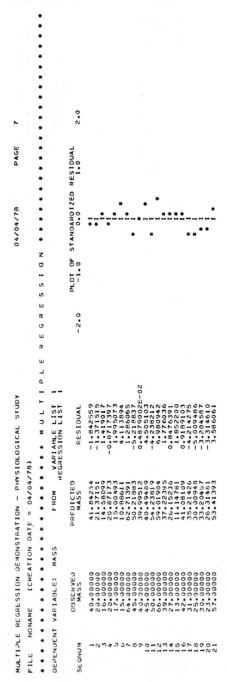

Figure 11-2 Continued

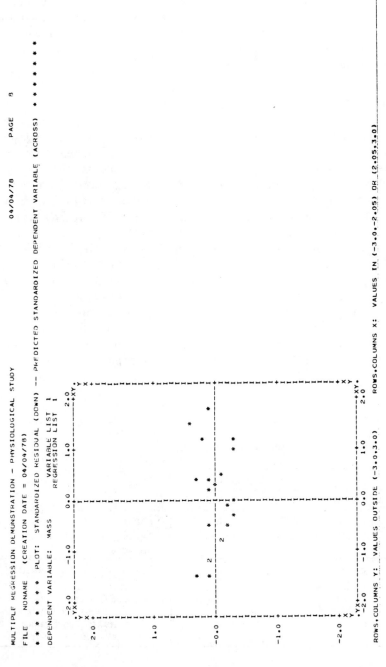

lation matrix is calculated for all variables in the VARIABLES list, in the order in which they are specified. The authors' preference is to specify the dependent variable first so that its correlations with the predictor variables are displayed in the first row (and column). Subject to the limitations of the numbers of digits printed, the values of the correlation coefficients are identical to those computed when dealing with these data in Chapter 8.

11.7 THE REGRESSION STEP OUTPUT[D]

The fourth page of the SPSS output shows the heart of the regression output. Here we find: the overall ANOVA table for the regression, R, R^2, the standard error, and the b values for the variables in the equation. The SPSS system produces this output in a standard format with which the student should become familiar. Figure 11-3 shows that the regression format has six major sections, labeled A through F. Section A gives the name of the dependent variable, which in this case is MASS.

Section B gives the name(s) of the predictor variable(s) entering on this step of the regression. Because an inclusion level of 2 was specified in the regression statement, all of the variables are brought in at once (SEX, AGE, and HEIGHT). When an even inclusion level forces all the variables to enter the equation at once, an idiosyncracy of the program causes the last variable (SEX) in the regression predictor list to appear first in Sections B and E of the regression step printout. (The original order in the regression statement was AGE, HEIGHT, and SEX, but the new order places SEX first.)

Figure 11-3 SPSS Regression Step Format

A	DEPENDENT VARIABLE name

B	VARIABLE(S) ENTERING name(s)

C	MEASURES OF GOODNESS OF FIT R, R^2, Standard Error	D	ANOVA TABLE Regression Residuals
E	VARIABLES IN EQUATION Variable names b values, β values Standard errors of b values Variable partial F values	F	VARIABLES NOT IN EQUATION Variable names Prospective β values Prospective partial correlations Computed tolerance values Prospective partial F values

11.7.1 Summary Measures—Multiple Correlation, Standard Error, and ANOVA Table (D)

Section C gives the value of the multiple correlation coefficient, R, the coefficient of multiple determination, R^2, the adjusted R^2, and the standard error of the equation. In this example, the value of R indicates that actual mass and predicted mass have a correlation of approximately .978, which when squared indicates that almost 95.6 percent (i.e., .956) of the total sum of squares is explained by the regression equation. The adjusted R^2 is a more conservative (but biased) criterion that adjusts for the number of cases and the number of predictor variables (*SPSS*, p. 358). The standard deviation of the residuals is approximately 3.68 kilograms, which agrees with the value found using APL in Exhibit 10-3, Section 10.6.

Section D gives the ANOVA table for the overall significance testing of the regression equation. In this case, the regression has 3 degrees of freedom, and the residuals have 17. The overall F value of 122.2 is highly significant, and indicates that one or more of the b values for the predictor variables is/are different from zero.

11.7.2 Variables in the Equation—b, β, Standard Error, and F (D)

Section E shows the solution values for the variables in the equation (all variables, in this case), including b values, β values, standard errors of the b values, and the partial F values for the variables. The interpretation of the b values is that 2 children (in this case), who differ only by 1 unit on the value of one of the predictor variables, have predicted masses that differ by the amount of the b value. Thus, for a boy (SEX = 0) and a girl (SEX = 1) who have the same age and height, the girl is expected to have a lower mass by a difference of 1.59 kilograms. Similarly, 2 boys (or 2 girls) of the same height, differing in age by 1 year would be expected to have a mass difference of 2.93 kilograms. Note that the CONSTANT has previously been called b_0. The negative value of the constant indicates that when predicted on the basis of AGE, SEX, and HEIGHT, MASS is, on the average, overestimated by 12.69 kilograms. This difference on one variable only is often referred to as *other things being equal* or *ceteris paribus*.

The *standardized partial regression coefficients* (β values) allow comparison of the relative impact of each of the predictor variables. The largest absolute value of β identifies the variable having the largest relative impact on the value of the dependent variable. In this case, AGE has the greatest impact, followed by HEIGHT, and then SEX. The meaning of each β value is that a difference of 1 standard deviation on a given variable is expected to be associated with β standard deviations difference in MASS (other things being equal). For example: 1 standard deviation of AGE is 3.88 years (from Figure 11-2, page 2 of SPSS output); two children differing (only) in age by this amount would be expected to differ by β (AGE) $\times$ standard deviation (MASS) kilograms = .70665 $\times$ 16.1078 $\cong$ 11.38 kilograms.

The standard errors of the b values and the partial F values allow significance testing and confidence interval estimation for the b values. For example, the b value for age is 2.933407, with a standard error of .50405. To test the significance of this b value, one approach is to form the usual t statistic:

$$t = \frac{b}{\text{Std Err } (b)} = \frac{2.933407}{.50405} \cong 5.82$$

which is the same value as found in Chapter 9. It can be compared with tabulated values of t with 17 degrees of freedom. SPSS also prints an F value for each variable, and this F value may also be used for significance testing. There is a simple relationship between the t value just calculated and the F value, in that for each variable, $F = t^2$. The values printed by SPSS have fewer significant digits printed than are used internally by the computer, but if the student performs the preceding t value computation and then squares the result, the value should be approximately 33.868. This should be compared with a critical F value with 1 and $(n - k - 1 = 17)$ degrees of freedom ($F_{.05} = 4.45$).

A confidence interval can be calculated for the b value by following the usual pattern:

$$\text{Confidence Interval}(b) = b \pm t_{\alpha/2} [\text{Std Err}(b)]$$

Then the confidence interval for the b value for age is:

$$2.933407 \pm 2.110 \times .50405 = 2.933407 \pm 1.0635455$$

giving a low value of 1.8698615 and a high value of 3.9969525. This is usually expressed in the form of a range statement:

$$1.870 \le b \le 3.997 \quad \text{(rounded to 3 decimal places)}$$

11.7.3 Variables Not in the Equation[D]

Section F gives prospective statistics for variables not yet entered into the equation. In the example used thus far, all variables have been entered into the equation in one step and no variables are shown in Section F. Therefore, discussion of Section F is deferred to Section 12.6 where the use of the information first becomes relevant in describing the forward inclusion procedure.

11.8 THE SUMMARY TABLE[D]

The final step of a regression ends with one of the following messages: "ALL VARIABLES ARE IN THE EQUATION" or "MAXIMUM STEP REACHED" or "F-LEVEL OR TOLERANCE-LEVEL INSUFFICIENT FOR FURTHER COMPUTATION." In the example of Figure 11-2 (SPSS, page 4), the first of these messages is given because, when we assigned the value 2 to the inclusion level, all variables were entered in one step.

On page 5 of the SPSS printout, a summary table provides information about the sequence in which variables were entered, the values of R and R^2 at each step, the b and β values for the variables in the final step, and each variable's simple correlation with the dependent variable (from the correlation matrix).

11.9 PLOTS OF RESIDUALS[D]

If the appropriate statistics (4 and 6) have been requested, SPSS prints, first, a case-by-case plot of the standardized residuals, which are defined as:

$$r_i^* = \frac{y_i - \hat{y}_i}{\text{Std Dev}(y)} \qquad (11.1)$$

For the example, this plot is shown on page 7 of the SPSS printout. The center line of I's represents the predicted value for each child's mass. Each asterisk represents the actual value. Values to the left indicate that the child's actual mass was lower than predicted (a negative residual), and values to the right indicate that the actual mass was greater than predicted (a positive residual).

The table on the left-hand side gives y, $\hat{y}$, and $(y - \hat{y})$ for each case (up to a maximum of 500 cases), and each line corresponds to the plot on the right-hand side. The tabulated values are in the original units of y, but the plotted values are standardized. Note that for case 9, the residual is very small and is printed in exponential notation, where E-02 means $\times 10^{-2}$. (.4879002E-02 = .004879002).

The plot on page 8 of the SPSS printout shows cases plotted with the predicted standardized dependent variable $[(\hat{y}_i - \bar{y}/\text{Std Dev}(y)]$ values on the X-axis and standardized residual (r_i*) values on the Y-axis. This plot is referred to in later portions of this chapter as the *predicted versus residual* plot.

In both of these plots the standardized scales are shown with a range of ± 2 standard deviations. From 2 to 3 standard deviations, the variables are plotted in the next position beyond 2 standard deviations. In the case-by-case analysis, they are plotted as X's, while in the predicted versus residual plots the rows and columns are labeled X. For 3 standard deviations and beyond, the letter Y is used, and this notation appears in the next position after the X's.

The examination of residuals is important in evaluating the goodness of a regression model, and is discussed in Section 14.5.5 and Figures 14-1 and 14-2.

Problems for Solution[(G)]

1. Solve the radiology department problem at the end of Chapter 10 using SPSS.
2. Life Cycle Savings
   Exhibit 11-1 shows an SPSS printout that deals with a test of an economic model, known as the Life Cycle Savings hypothesis. According to this hypothesis, savings rates should be negatively affected if nonmembers of the labor force constitute a large portion of the population.

   SAVERATE: the savings ratio is the aggregate personal saving divided by disposable income. It is expected to be explained by:

   INCOME: The level of per capita disposable income measured in constant U.S. dollars

   INGROWTH: The percentage rate of change of per capita disposable income

   and, two population variables:

   POPLT15: Percent less than 15 years of age
   POPGT75: Percent greater than 75 years of age

   The last three are the central variables in the hypothesis, and INCOME is expected to be relatively unimportant.

   To test this model, Professor Sterling of MIT collected data on 50 countries (averaged over the decade 1960–1970 to remove the effect of the business cycle and other short-term fluctuations).
   a. What are the *b* values; are they in accord with the hypothesis?
   b. How much of the variance is explained by the equation?
   c. Is the equation significant?
   d. Are the *b* values significant?
   e. Which is the most important variable, and why?

Exhibit 11-1 Data for Test of Life Cycle Savings Hypothesis

AUSTRALIA	11.43	29.35	2.87	2329.68	2.87
AUSTRIA	12.07	23.32	4.41	1507.99	3.93
BELGIUM	13.17	23.80	4.43	2108.47	3.82
BOLIVIA	5.75	41.89	1.67	189.13	.22
BRAZIL	12.88	42.19	.83	728.47	4.56
CANADA	8.79	31.72	2.85	2982.88	2.43
CHILE	.60	39.74	1.34	662.86	2.67
CHINA(TAIWAN)	11.90	44.75	.67	289.52	6.51
COLOMBIA	4.98	46.64	1.06	276.65	3.08
COSTA RICA	10.78	47.64	1.14	471.24	2.80
DENMARK	16.85	24.42	3.93	2496.53	3.99
ECUADOR	3.59	46.31	1.19	287.77	2.19
FINLAND	11.24	27.84	2.37	1681.25	4.32
FRANCE	12.64	25.06	4.70	2213.82	4.52
GERMANY F.R.	12.55	23.31	3.35	2457.12	3.44
GREECE	10.67	25.62	3.10	870.85	6.28
GUATEMALA	3.01	46.05	.87	289.71	1.48
HONDURAS	7.70	47.32	.58	232.44	3.19
ICELAND	1.27	34.03	3.08	1900.10	1.12
INDIA	9.00	41.31	.96	88.94	1.54
IRELAND	11.34	31.16	4.19	1139.95	2.99
ITALY	14.28	24.52	3.48	1390.00	3.54
JAPAN	21.10	27.01	1.91	1257.28	8.21
KOREA	3.98	41.74	.91	207.68	5.81
LUXEMBOURG	10.35	21.80	3.73	2449.39	1.57
MALTA	15.48	32.54	2.47	601.05	8.12
NORWAY	10.25	25.95	3.67	2231.03	3.62
NETHERLANDS	14.65	24.71	3.25	1740.70	7.66
NEW ZEALAND	10.67	32.61	3.17	1487.52	1.76
NICARAGUA	7.30	45.04	1.21	325.54	2.48
PANAMA	4.44	43.56	1.20	568.56	3.61
PARAGUAY	2.02	41.18	1.05	220.56	1.03
PERU	12.70	44.19	1.28	400.06	.67
PHILLIPINES	12.78	46.26	1.12	152.01	2.00
PORTUGAL	12.49	28.96	2.85	579.51	7.48
SOUTH AFRICA	11.14	31.94	2.28	651.11	2.19
SOUTH RHODESIA	13.30	31.92	1.52	250.96	2.00
SPAIN	11.77	27.74	2.87	768.79	4.35
SWEDEN	6.86	21.44	4.54	3299.49	3.01
SWITZERLAND	14.13	23.49	3.73	2630.96	2.70
TURKEY	5.13	43.42	1.08	389.66	2.96
TUNISIA	2.81	46.12	1.21	249.87	1.13
UNITED KINGDOM	7.81	23.27	4.46	1813.93	2.01
UNITED STATES	7.56	29.81	3.43	4001.89	2.45
VENEZUELA	9.22	46.40	.90	813.39	.53
ZAMBIA	18.56	45.25	.56	138.33	5.14
JAMAICA	7.72	41.12	1.73	380.47	10.23
URUGUAY	9.24	28.13	2.72	766.54	1.88
LIBYA	8.89	43.69	2.07	123.58	16.71
MALAYSIA	4.71	47.20	.66	242.69	5.08

Exhibit 11-1 Continued

```
STATISTICAL PACKAGE FOR THE SOCIAL SCIENCES                                    04/18/79        PAGE    1

SPSS FOR OS/360, VERSION H, RELEASE 8A, AUGUST 1978


DEFAULT SPACE ALLOCATION..          ALLOWS FOR..     64 TRANSFORMATIONS
WORKSPACE    44800 BYTES                            250 RECODE VALUES + LAG VARIABLES
TRANSPACE     5400 BYTES                           1024 IF/COMPUTE OPERATIONS

          1  RUN NAME        TEST SAVINGS RATE MODEL
          2  INPUT MEDIUM    DISK
          3  N OF CASES      UNKNOWN
          4  DATA LIST       FIXED/1 SAVERATE 20-24, POPLT15 30-34, POPGT75 40-44
          5                  INCOME 50-58, INGROWTH 59-63

THE DATA LIST PROVIDES FOR  5 VARIABLES AND  1 RECORDS ('CARDS') PER CASE.  A MAXIMUM OF  63 COLUMNS ARE USED ON A RECORD.

LIST OF THE CONSTRUCTED FORMAT STATEMENT..
          (19X,F5.0,5X,F5.0,5X,F4.0,6X,F7.0,2X,F5.0)

          6  REGRESSION      VARIABLES = SAVERATE POPLT15 POPGT75 INCOME INGROWTH /
          7                  REGRESSION = SAVERATE WITH POPLT15 TO INGROWTH (2) RESID=0
          8  STATISTICS      1,2,4,6

***** REGRESSION PROBLEM REQUIRES    720 BYTES WORKSPACE, NOT INCLUDING RESIDUALS *****

          9  READ INPUT DATA

AFTER READING   50 CASES FROM SUBFILE NONAME  .  END OF DATA WAS ENCOUNTERED ON LOGICAL UNIT # 9

TEST SAVINGS RATE MODEL                                                         04/18/79        PAGE    2

FILE   NONAME   (CREATION DATE = 04/18/79)


VARIABLE      MEAN       STANDARD DEV       CASES

SAVERATE      9.6710       4.4804            50
POPLT15      35.0896       9.1517            50
POPGT75       2.2930       2.2908            50
INCOME     1106.7583     990.8689            50
INGROWTH      3.7576       2.8699            50
```

Exhibit 11-1 Continued

```
TEST SAVINGS RATE MODEL

FILE   NONAME   (CREATION DATE = 04/18/79)                    04/18/79    PAGE   3

CORRELATION COEFFICIENTS

A VALUE OF 99.00000 IS PRINTED
IF A COEFFICIENT CANNOT BE COMPUTED.

              SAVERATE   POPLT15   POPGT75   INCOME   INGROWTH
SAVERATE      1.00000   -0.45554   0.31052   0.22036   0.30479
POPLT15      -0.45554    1.00000  -0.30848  -0.73700  -0.30783
POPGT75       0.31052   -0.30848   1.00000   0.78700  -0.02232
INCOME        0.22036   -0.73700   0.78700   1.00000  -0.12940
INGROWTH      0.30479   -0.30783  -0.02232  -0.12940   1.00000

TEST SAVINGS RATE MODEL

FILE   NONAME   (CREATION DATE = 04/18/79)                    04/18/79    PAGE   4

* * * * * * * * * * * * * * * * * *   M U L T I P L E   R E G R E S S I O N   * * * * * * * * * * * * * * * * * *

DEPENDENT VARIABLE..    SAVERATE                                              VARIABLE LIST   1
                                                                             REGRESSION LIST  1
VARIABLE(S) ENTERED ON STEP NUMBER   1..    INGROWTH
                                            POPLT15
                                            POPGT75
                                            INCOME

MULTIPLE R          0.58177          ANALYSIS OF VARIANCE   DF      SUM OF SQUARES    MEAN SQUARE        F
R SQUARE            0.33846          REGRESSION              4.      352.91500        88.22875        0.73203
ADJUSTED R SQUARE   0.27965          RESIDUAL               45.      650.71203        14.46029
STANDARD ERROR      3.90267

------------------ VARIABLES IN THE EQUATION ------------------               ----- VARIABLES NOT IN THE EQUATION -----

VARIABLE          B         BETA      STD ERROR B      F              VARIABLE        BETA IN    PARTIAL    TOLERANCE      F

INGROWTH     0.4996950    0.26243     0.12624       4.003
POPLT15     -0.4601028   -0.34204     0.14464      12.107
POPGT75     -1.6631496   -0.48731     1.08390       2.437
INCOME      -0.33690180-03 -0.07451   0.00003       0.131
(CONSTANT)  28.56607

ALL VARIABLES ARE IN THE EQUATION

STATISTICS WHICH CANNOT BE COMPUTED ARE PRINTED AS ALL NINES.
```

Chapter 12

Control of the Regression Analysis

After completing this chapter you should be able to:

1. Use the SPSS Batch System inclusion level parameter with even values to establish the order in which variables will enter the equation.
2. Describe the changes in the regression equation and the various criteria of *goodness* from step to step.
3. Evaluate the significance of each *b* value at each step of the equation, using the standard regression approach.
4. Evaluate the significance of the added explanation at each step of the regression analysis using the hierarchical approach.
5. Explain the basic difference in meaning of part and partial correlation coefficients.
6. Calculate the part and partial correlations for two independent variables and a dependent variable, given the correlation matrix.
7. Use SPSS odd-valued inclusion levels for forward inclusion control of the regression analysis.
8. Explain the difference between forward inclusion and stepwise regression.
9. Name and describe the function of the SPSS regression control parameters.
10. Use the regression control parameters to control the forward inclusion mode of operation.

Chapter Map

All sections use SPSS and have been assigned the letter code D. Additionally, Sections 12.3, 12.4, and 12.5 also use ordinary algebra and have been assigned the letter code B.

315

12.1 PURPOSE OF THE REGRESSION DESIGN STATEMENT[(D)]

The initial discussion of multiple regression using SPSS has focused on bringing in all variables in one step. However, there are many situations in the social sciences where a sequence of progressively more complex regression models are desirable. For instance, in our example we have seen that age is the most important variable (with the largest absolute value of β), and it might be desirable to know how good age is as a predictor of MASS, by itself, and how much improvement can be achieved by adding HEIGHT, and then by adding SEX as predictor variables. The same question can be posed from a different point of view by rephrasing it: "Controlling for AGE, how much extra explanation of variation is provided by HEIGHT; and then, controlling for AGE and HEIGHT how much more explanatory power is added by SEX?" An alternative kind of question merely asks, "What is the best sequence of variables?"

SPSS provides the inclusion level parameter for precise control of the sequence in which variables are entered into the regression model. Every variable in the predictor list must have an associated inclusion level number, assigned either individually or as part of a group. The inclusion level number must be in the range 0 to 99. It follows the variable or group of variables to which it refers, and is enclosed in parentheses. Larger inclusion level numbers indicate higher priority for selection. The order of entry (selection) is also controlled by the parity (odd/even) of the inclusion level and, for odd-valued levels, by the partial F and tolerance parameters.

12.2 EVEN-VALUED INCLUSION LEVELS[(D)]

The selection of variables to enter the equation at each step proceeds from the highest level to the lowest level. The second regression in Figure 11-1 (reproduced in Figure 12-1) shows the predictor variables with all even inclusion levels, in the following order:

AGE (6),   HEIGHT (4),   SEX (2)

Therefore, the variables are entered into the equation in the order AGE, HEIGHT, and SEX. Figure 12-1 shows the regression results in the sequence of steps.

In Step 1 (page 10 of the SPSS output) AGE is the first variable to be entered. As a single variable it accounts for about 93.8 percent of the total sum of squares of MASS (corrected for the mean, as usual). It is highly significant, with an F value of approximately 287 with 1 and 19 degrees of freedom. Since it is a single-variable equation, in this step the F values for the overall equation and for the b value are identical. The b value is interpreted as meaning that, for every year increase in age, an increase of 4.02 kilograms mass is expected. Notice that the constant is very small and positive. The D-01 is an exponential notation as was E before, with the difference being that D indicates that the number is stored in double precision internally.

12.3 CHANGES FROM STEP TO STEP[B,D]

The basic difference between Step 1 and Step 2 is the introduction of HEIGHT into the regression equation. With the entry of height into the regression equation several important changes occur. In the situation in which the most highly correlated variable enters first, these changes reflect typical behavior:

1. The values of R and R^2 increase.
2. The overall F value decreases.
3. The standard error decreases.
4. The b values and the β values change (there is no typical direction for this change).
5. The F values for the individual variables change. Here the F value for AGE has dropped dramatically, and this is typical in going from Step 1 to Step 2, when the first variable has the highest simple correlation.

In moving from Step 2 to Step 3, the same five changes can be examined, and the following exceptions to the previous pattern should be noted:

1. The increases in R and R^2 are smaller.
2. The standard error *increases* slightly.
3. The F values for AGE and HEIGHT change slightly but remain statistically significant, while that for SEX is devoid of significance.

The F value for the variable b_i in each step is called a *partial F* value, which is defined as:

$$F(b_i) = \frac{SS(b_i)/df(b_i)}{SS(\text{Res})/(n - k - 1)} = \frac{SS(b_i)/1}{SS(\text{Res})/(n - k - 1)} \quad \text{(12.1.1)}$$

Figure 12-1 Sequence of Steps with Even Inclusion Levels

```
MULTIPLE REGRESSION DEMONSTRATION - PHYSIOLOGICAL STUDY                           04/04/78                              PAGE     9

CPU TIME REQUIRED..    0.93 SECONDS

         REGRESSION        VARIABLES =   MASS AGE HEIGHT SEX/
                           REGRESSION =  MASS WITH AGE (6) HEIGHT(4) SEX(2)

***** REGRESSION PROBLEM REQUIRES    512 BYTES WORKSPACE, NOT INCLUDING RESIDUALS *****


MULTIPLE REGRESSION DEMONSTRATION - PHYSIOLOGICAL STUDY                           04/04/78                              PAGE    10

FILE   NONAME    (CREATION DATE = 04/04/78)
* * * * * * * * * * * * * * * * * * * * * *   M U L T I P L E   R E G R E S S I O N   * * * * * * * * * * * * * * * * * * * * * *
DEPENDENT VARIABLE..    MASS                                                                                 VARIABLE LIST   1
VARIABLE(S) ENTERED ON STEP NUMBER   1..    AGE                                                              REGRESSION LIST  1

                                       ANALYSIS OF VARIANCE        DF.     SUM OF SQUARES      MEAN SQUARE          F
MULTIPLE R           0.96851           REGRESSION                   1.      4867.55388         4867.55388       287.49786
R SQUARE             0.93801           RESIDUAL                    19.       321.68422           16.93075
ADJUSTED R SQUARE    0.93475
STANDARD ERROR       4.11470

-------- VARIABLES IN THE EQUATION --------                          ------------- VARIABLES NOT IN THE EQUATION --------------
VARIABLE          B           BETA       STD ERROR B       F          VARIABLE      BETA IN      PARTIAL      TOLERANCE      F

AGE            4.020398     0.96851       0.23711      287.498        HEIGHT        0.29260      0.49437      0.17696      5.822
(CONSTANT)     0.03251110-01                                          SEX          -0.05679     -0.22789      0.99814      0.986

* * * * * * * * * * * * * * * * * * * * * *   H E I G H T   * * * * * * * * * * * * * * * * * * * * * * * * * * * * * * * * * * *
VARIABLE(S) ENTERED ON STEP NUMBER   2..    HEIGHT

                                       ANALYSIS OF VARIANCE        DF.     SUM OF SQUARES      MEAN SQUARE          F
MULTIPLE R           0.97630           REGRESSION                   2.      4946.17315         2473.08658       183.14265
R SQUARE             0.95316           RESIDUAL                    18.       243.06494          13.50361
ADJUSTED R SQUARE    0.94796
STANDARD ERROR       3.67473

-------- VARIABLES IN THE EQUATION --------                          ------------- VARIABLES NOT IN THE EQUATION --------------
VARIABLE          B           BETA       STD ERROR B       F          VARIABLE      BETA IN      PARTIAL      TOLERANCE      F

AGE            2.918460     0.70305       0.50339       33.612        SEX          -0.05038     -0.23224      0.99531      0.969
HEIGHT         0.188525     0.29260       0.07827        5.822
(CONSTANT)    -13.82834
```

Figure 12-1 Continued

```
MULTIPLE REGRESSION DEMONSTRATION - PHYSIOLOGICAL STUDY                                    04/04/78                    PAGE  11

FILE   NONAME    (CREATION DATE = 04/04/78)

* * * * * * * * * * * * * * * * * * * * * * * * *   M U L T I P L E   R E G R E S S I O N   * * * * * * * * * * * * * * * * * * *   VARIABLE LIST    1
                                                                                                                                 REGRESSION LIST  1
DEPENDENT VARIABLE..      MASS

VARIABLE(S) ENTERED ON STEP NUMBER  3..     SEX


MULTIPLE R            0.97759                        ANALYSIS OF VARIANCE        DF.       SUM OF SQUARES        MEAN SQUARE            F
R SQUARE             0.95569                        REGRESSION                   3.         4959.28304          1653.09435        122.20912
ADJUSTED R SQUARE    0.94787                        RESIDUAL                    17.          229.95506            13.52677
STANDARD ERROR       3.67788


----------- VARIABLES IN THE EQUATION -----------                        ------------- VARIABLES NOT IN THE EQUATION -------------

VARIABLE          B          BETA      STD ERROR B        F                VARIABLE      BETA IN      PARTIAL      TOLERANCE        F

AGE           2.933407     0.70665      0.50405        33.868
HEIGHT        0.1847438    0.28624      0.07845         5.546
SEX          -1.585744    -0.05038      1.61076         0.969
(CONSTANT)  -12.69362


MAXIMUM STEP REACHED




MULTIPLE REGRESSION DEMONSTRATION - PHYSIOLOGICAL STUDY                                    04/04/78                    PAGE  12

FILE   NONAME    (CREATION DATE = 04/04/78)

* * * * * * * * * * * * * * * * * * * * * * * * *   M U L T I P L E   R E G R E S S I O N   * * * * * * * * * * * * * * * * * * *   VARIABLE LIST    1
                                                                                                                                 REGRESSION LIST  1
DEPENDENT VARIABLE..      MASS

                                          SUMMARY TABLE

VARIABLE      MULTIPLE R    R SQUARE    RSQ CHANGE    SIMPLE R            B              BETA

AGE            0.96851      0.93801      0.93801      0.96851        2.933407         0.70665
HEIGHT         0.97630      0.95316      0.01515      0.93043        0.1847438        0.28624
SEX            0.97759      0.95569      0.00253     -0.09849       -1.585744        -0.05038
(CONSTANT)                                                         -12.69362
```

where k is the number of variables included in that step, and n is the total number of cases. The F value for a variable and the t value are intimately related:

$$F(b_i) = t_i^2 = \left(\frac{b_i}{\text{Std Err}(b_i)}\right)^2 \qquad (12.1.2)$$

In this definition the effect of *each* variable is assessed as if it were the last one to be entered into the equation. That means that the effects of all the other variables are controlled while looking at any one of these partial F values. This approach to testing the significance of the variable coefficients is called the *standard regression approach* in the SPSS manual.

12.4 SIGNIFICANCE OF THE ADDED EXPLANATION AT EACH STEP[B,D]

The original questions leading to this example were, "How good is AGE by itself, and how much do HEIGHT and SEX add to the explanatory power of the regression equation?" To answer this question a *sequential, incremental,* or *hierarchical* approach is required, and the test is performed by calculating an F value for the change in R^2 at each step in which the test is to be performed.
We can show that for the overall equation:

$$F = \frac{[SS(b) - SS(b_0)]/k}{SS(\text{Res})/(n - k - 1)} = \frac{MS(\text{Reg})}{MS(\text{Res})} \qquad (12.2.1)$$

or

$$F = \frac{R^2/k}{(1 - R^2)/(n - k - 1)} \qquad (12.2.2)$$

The significance of each single variable or group of variables added in each step, i, can be tested by the incremental approach as follows:

$$F^*(b_i) = \frac{\text{Incremental } SS(b_i)/\Delta k}{SS(\text{Res})/(n - k - 1)} \qquad (12.3.1)$$

or

$$F^*(b_i) = \frac{\Delta R_i^2/\Delta k}{(1 - R^2)/(n - k - 1)} \qquad (12.3.2)$$

where Δ (the Greek letter delta) means *the change in* and ΔR_i^2 means *the change in R^2 due to adding variable i.* Each of these F values is tested at Δk and $(n - k - 1)$ degrees of freedom. Note that k increases from step to step by the number of variables added, namely Δk. In our example, Δk = 1 in each step.

This hierarchical testing of the effect of adding each variable sequentially has been performed, and the results are presented in Table 12-1. The ΔR^2 values are drawn from the summary table on page 12 of the SPSS output in Figure 12-1. The hierarchical F values are compared to the partial F values of the final regression step. Note the large differences. $F_{.05,1,17} = 4.45$, so that AGE and HEIGHT are both significant, using both approaches. When only one variable is added in a given step, the partial F calculated by SPSS, for that variable in that step, is F^*.

The order in which the variables are entered and tested in the hierarchical approach will make a very great difference in the apparent importance of a given variable. In this regard, the researcher's expectations play a crucial role in determining the order in which the variables enter the equation. If, for example, the researcher believes HEIGHT to be more important than AGE, and the variables were entered in that order, the results would have been quite different as shown in Table 12-2.

The apparent importances of HEIGHT and AGE have been nearly interchanged by a simple alteration in the initial assumption concerning the structure of the factors affecting MASS.

In summary, it is important to note that there are different approaches to testing the statistical significance of the variables in a regression model; the standard regression approach and the hierarchical approach lead to results that may differ substantially. The nature of the hypothesis being tested dictates the choice of the testing approach.

Table 12-1 Comparison of Hierarchical and Partial F Values

Variable	R^2	ΔR^2	df	Hierarchical F Value	Partial F Value (last step)
AGE	.93801	.93801	19	287.50	33.868
HEIGHT	.95316	.01515	18	5.822	5.546
SEX	.95569	.00253	17	0.971	0.969

Table 12-2 Effects of a Different Order of Importance on Hierarchical F Test

Variable	R^2	ΔR^2	df	Hierarchical F Value
HEIGHT	.86570	.86570	19	122.47
AGE	.95316	.08746	18	33.61
SEX	.95569	.00253	17	0.971

12.5 PARTIAL REGRESSION COEFFICIENTS AND PARTIAL CORRELATIONS[B,D]

Before considering odd-valued inclusion levels, a few terms must be defined for use in discussing selection criteria for variables to be included in the regression equation.

In previous sections we have called the b values *partial regression coefficients* and have given the interpretation of each coefficient based on *other things equal*. We have also described the other variables as being *controlled*. The basic regression model assumes that each predictor variable accounts for part of the variation in the dependent variable, and that the effects of the variables are additive. A difference between two cases of one unit each on two or three different variables leads to an expected difference in the dependent variable which is the sum of the b values. For example, a girl who is 1 year older and 1 centimeter taller than a boy is expected to have a mass that is $2.933 + .185 - 1.586 = 1.532$ kilograms greater than the mass associated with the male.

Alternatively, we might visualize the estimates and the regression coefficient as being derived from a series of simple linear regressions. In the first step, we might regress the dependent variable y on a predictor variable (let us call it x_1) and obtain an estimate of the simple linear function:

$$\hat{y} = b_{10} + b_{11} x_1 \tag{12.4.1}$$

To introduce a second variable, say x_2, it is necessary to regress the unexplained portion of y (i.e., $y - \hat{y}$) on the portion of x_2 that is unrelated to x_1. To determine the portion of the variable x_2 that is unrelated to x_1, we regress x_2 on x_1 and obtain:

$$\hat{x}_2 = b_{20} + b_{21} x_1 \tag{12.4.2}$$

Thus, $(x_2 - \hat{x}_2)$ is the portion of x_2 that is unrelated to x_1. We can now regress $(y - \hat{y})$ on $(x_2 - \hat{x}_2)$ and obtain a relationship of the form:

$$\overparen{(y - \hat{y})} = b_{22}(x_2 - \hat{x}_2) \qquad (12.4.3)$$

Observe that Equation (12.4.3) has a zero intercept term because both $(y - \hat{y})$ and $(x_2 - \hat{x}_2)$ are residuals with means of zero. The larger carat $(\frown)$ over $(y - \hat{y})$ in Equation (12.4.3) signifies that an unexplained residual remains. In this case, the residual is given by $[(y - \hat{y}) - \overparen{(y - \hat{y})}]$. To obtain the partial regression coefficients for x_1 and x_2 we substitute the values of $\hat{y}$ and $\hat{x}_2$ from Equations 12.4.1 and 12.4.2 into Equation 12.4.3.[1] Observe that we might repeat these steps by introducing a third independent variable, but the process becomes extremely cumbersome.

Returning to our example, we have been using the sequence of linear regressions to express MASS as a function of AGE, HEIGHT, and SEX. Such a solution might assume the form:

$$MASS = f_1 (AGE)$$
$$HEIGHT = f_2 (AGE)$$
$$MASS (1) \text{ RESIDUALS} = f_3 (HEIGHT (2) \text{ RESIDUALS})$$
$$MASS = f_4 (AGE, HEIGHT)$$
$$SEX = f_5 (AGE)$$
$$SEX (5) \text{ RESIDUALS} = f_6 (HEIGHT (2) \text{ RESIDUALS})$$
$$SEX = f_7 (AGE, HEIGHT)$$
$$MASS (4) \text{ RESIDUALS} = f_8 (SEX (7) \text{ RESIDUALS})$$
$$MASS = f_9 (AGE, HEIGHT, SEX)$$

The partial regression coefficients are frequently presented in a format emphasizing that the coefficient expresses the relationship between the dependent variable and a given predictor variable while controlling for other factors included in the regression equation. For example, $b_{y2.13}$ emphasizes that we are looking at the partial effect of variable 2 on y controlling for the effects of variables 1 and 3. The equation could be written as:

$$y = b_0 + b_{y1.23}\,x_1 + b_{y2.13}\,x_2 + b_{y3.12}\,x_3 + e \qquad (12.5)$$

Note that these partial regression coefficients are usually different from the simple linear coefficients of y on x_1, y on x_2, and y on x_3. This is so because the independent variables are seldom found to be completely uncorrelated with one another, and, as a result, the effects of x_1, x_2, and x_3 on the dependent variables usually overlap to some extent. In these cases, the effect of a given independent variable is said to be *confounded* by the effects of other predictor variables included in the equation. Only when x_1, x_2, and x_3 are *completely uncorrelated* will the multiple regression coefficient relating one of these independent variables to the dependent variable equal the corresponding estimate of the regression coefficient relating y to x_1, y to x_2, and y to x_3.

The correlation matrix with which we have dealt so far contains the simple (Pearson) correlation coefficients of each pair of variables. We reproduce the MASS/AGE/HEIGHT/SEX correlation matrix as Figure 12-2. Two other types of correlation are defined to take account of the overlapping partial effects discussed previously. These are the *part* and *partial* correlation coefficients. Let us call the variables y, x_1, x_2, and x_3, respectively. We focus on the relationships between y on the one hand, and x_1, x_2, and x_3 on the other. Observe that, by simply renaming the factors, y could be any of the variables.

After controlling for x_1, the PART correlation of x_2 with y yields the relationship of the residuals of x_2 with y. Thus, the influence of x_1 has been removed from only x_2, and the PART correlation of x_2 for y is given by:

$$r_{y(2.1)} = \frac{r_{y2} - r_{y1} r_{12}}{\sqrt{1 - r_{12}^2}} \qquad (12.6)$$

Controlling for x_1, the PARTIAL correlation of x_2 with y_1 removes the influence of x_1 from both x_2 and y. The PARTIAL correlation of x_2 with y, controlling for x_1, is defined as:

$$r_{y2.1} = \frac{r_{y2} - r_{y1} r_{12}}{\sqrt{1 - r_{y1}^2} \sqrt{1 - r_{12}^2}} \qquad (12.7.1)$$

or:

$$r_{y2.1} = \frac{r_{y(2.1)}}{\sqrt{1 - r_{y1}^2}} \qquad (12.7.2)$$

Letting AGE and HEIGHT be represented by x_1 and x_2, respectively, the PART correlation of HEIGHT with MASS, after controlling for AGE, is

Figure 12-2 Correlation Matrix of Physiological Study

	MASS	AGE	HEIGHT	SEX
MASS	1.00000	0.96851	0.93043	−0.09849
AGE	0.96851	1.00000	0.90722	−0.04316
HEIGHT	0.93043	0.90722	1.00000	−0.06152
SEX	−0.09849	−0.04316	−0.06152	1.00000

obtained by substituting $r_{y2} = .93043$, $r_{y1} = .96851$, and $r_{12} = .90722$ into Equation 12.6 and solving for $r_{y(2.1)}$. Thus, we find:

$$r_{y(2.1)} = \frac{.93043 - (.96851 \times .90722)}{\sqrt{1 - .90722^2}}$$

$$= \frac{.93043 - .8786516}{\sqrt{1 - .8230481}}$$

$$= \frac{.0517783}{\sqrt{.1769518}} = \frac{.0517783}{.4206564}$$

$$= .1230894 \qquad (12.8)$$

Using this finding and recognizing that $r_{y1}^2 = .96851^2$, the PARTIAL correlation of HEIGHT with MASS, after controlling for AGE is calculated by substituting appropriately into Equation 12.7.2 and solving for $r_{y2.1}$. Thus, we obtain:

$$r_{y2.1} = \frac{r_{y(2.1)}}{\sqrt{1 - r_{y1}^2}} = \frac{.1230894}{\sqrt{1 - .96851^2}}$$

$$= \frac{.1230894}{.2489746} = .4943853 \qquad (12.9)$$

12.6 ODD-VALUED INCLUSION LEVELS—FORWARD INCLUSION[D]

The use of even-valued inclusion levels in the regression design statement allows precise control over the number and sequence of variables entering the equation. The use of odd-valued levels implies a very different mode of operation—one in which the selection of variables depends on their changing statistical significance from step to step. This mode of operation is called FORWARD INCLUSION. Basically the idea is that the *best* variable is entered first, followed by the *second best*, after controlling for the first, and the next best controlling for the first two, and so on.

At each step of the regression, all of the remaining variables that are *not included* in the equation thus far are examined in order to determine the next factor that is considered for inclusion in the regression equation. The criterion for selection is the value of the *squared partial correlations* of the remaining variables with the *unexplained* portion of the dependent variable. The variable selected for entry on the next step is the one that explains the greatest amount of the remaining unexplained variation (i.e., the variable computed with the highest squared partial correlation coefficient).

At each step of the process, the program calculates the information required to make this choice, and the appropriate statistics are presented in Section F of the regression step format (Figure 11-3). Only the remaining variables not in the equation at each step are included in this section of the printout. For each, prospective information is shown, including *b* values, partial correlations, and *F* values. Also included is a *tolerance* value, which is discussed next in the sections dealing with the tolerance parameter and multicollinearity.

The third regression in Figure 11-1 calls for forward inclusion at inclusion level 1. Reproduced here, the regression design statement is:

REGRESSION = MASS WITH AGE TO SEX (1)

The first variable to enter is the one with the highest simple correlation, which is AGE ($r_{y1} = .96851$ in Figure 12-2). The sequence of entering variables happens (by accident) to be the same as that for the second regression, as shown in Figure 12-1. The partial correlations at each step are reproduced in Table 12-3, and the sequence of entering variables is indicated.

12.7 STEPWISE REGRESSION[D]

The forward inclusion mode of SPSS is similar to but not the same as a selection process called *stepwise regression*. In stepwise regression, a minimum level of significance, as evidenced by the partial *F* values, is required before a variable is allowed to enter the equation. In addition, a minimum level of significance is required to retain a variable in the equation after it has been entered. The introduction of an additional variable may cause

Table 12-3 Partial Correlations with MASS at Each Step
of Third Regression

Variable	Pearson Correlation	Partial Correlations	
		Step 1	Step 2
AGE	.96851*	—	—
HEIGHT	.93043	.49437*	—
SEX	−.09849	−.22789	−.23224*

*Variable Selected for Next Step

one or more of the variables entered previously to be eliminated from the equation. Thus, the selection procedure requires the identification of any variables that have dropped below the minimum level of significance. If any of the variables fail to achieve the specified level of significance, they are removed before proceeding to introduce a new variable into the equation. This variable must have the highest squared partial correlation and exceeds the required level of significance.

The objective of stepwise regression is to select all, but only, those variables which exceed the specified level of statistical significance as evidenced by the partial F test. SPSS has not implemented stepwise regression (in version H, release 7-0, which corresponds to the second edition of the SPSS manual). However, it has implemented control parameters for the forward inclusion mode of operation (with odd inclusion levels), which enable the researcher to achieve the same effect through a series of regression runs.

12.8 SPSS REGRESSION CONTROL PARAMETERS[D]

The regression control parameters are provided as part of the regression design statement. These parameters allow us to control the process by which variables are selected for inclusion in the regression equation. These control parameters operate in conjunction with the odd inclusion levels only. The primary purpose of the parameters is to control the forward inclusion mode of operation. The parameters are n, F, and T where:

n = the maximum number of variables to be selected under forward inclusion. (This is set to 80 as a *default* value, if not specified by the researcher.)

F = the minimum partial F value for a variable to be entered into the equation. (The partial F values of variables not yet in the equation are tested, after selection according to the partial correlation criterion. The default value is .01, but this is far too small. The researcher should normally choose an F *value close to the desired level of significance* (α), *and 1 and* $(n - k - 1)$ *degrees of freedom.*)

T = the minimum acceptable level of computed tolerance for an entering variable. Tolerance is given by $(1 - R_x^2)$ where R_x is the multiple correlation between the entering variable and the set of predictor variables that have already been included in the equation. If R_x^2 is high, and the tolerance is low, most of the variability in the new variable is accounted for by the other predictor variables. Such a situation is called *multicollinearity* and when two, three, or more variables are multicollinear, the resulting regression coefficients will be biased. In addition, if the variables are multicollinear in the extreme, it may not be possible to compute the coefficient. The default value for the tolerance parameter is .001 but, after considering the discussion of multicollinearity presented in Section 14.5.6, the researcher may wish to select a somewhat higher value. The authors use a tolerance value of .4 as a rule of thumb.

The three regression control parameters are placed in parentheses immediately following the name of the dependent variable. The user may specify either (n), or (n,F), or (n,F,T). If nothing is specified, the default values are $(80,.01,.001)$. Any of these three specifications overrides the default values, for as many of the parameters as the user specifies.

The fourth regression in Figure 11-1 uses the three parameters, and the regression design statement is reproduced here:

REGRESSION = MASS (10,3,.4) WITH AGE TO SEX (1)

This statement specifies that: No more than 10 variables are to be entered (any number equal to or greater than 3 would have worked in this case), each variable entered must have an F value of at least 3 (for $\alpha = .05$, $F_{1,17} = 4.45$), and, with a tolerance of .4, at least 40 percent of the sum of squares of each entering variable must be independent of the previously entered predictor variables.

Figure 12-3 shows the results of this regression. AGE was the first variable to enter the equation, with an extremely high F value, 287. In attempting to select another variable for entry, the program tests the variable, HEIGHT, which has the highest squared partial correlation $(.49^2)$, for acceptability on both F and tolerance criteria. It has high enough signifi-

Figure 12-3 SPSS Forward Inclusion Example for Physiological Study

```
MULTIPLE REGRESSION DEMONSTRATION - PHYSIOLOGICAL STUDY                04/04/78          PAGE  17

CPU TIME REQUIRED..    0.30 SECONDS

     REGRESSION    VARIABLES = MASS AGE HEIGHT SEX/
                   REGRESSION = MASS (10,3,.4) WITH AGE TO SEX (1)
                   RESID = 0
     STATISTICS    4,6

***** REGRESSION PROBLEM REQUIRES    512 BYTES WORKSPACE. NOT INCLUDING RESIDUALS *****


MULTIPLE REGRESSION DEMONSTRATION - PHYSIOLOGICAL STUDY                04/04/78          PAGE  18

FILE  NONAME   (CREATION DATE = 04/04/78)

* * * * * * * * * * * * * * * * * * * * * *  M U L T I P L E   R E G R E S S I O N  * * * * * * * * * * * * * * * * *    VARIABLE LIST   1
                                                                                                                       REGRESSION LIST 1
DEPENDENT VARIABLE..    MASS

VARIABLE(S) ENTERED ON STEP NUMBER  1..    AGE

MULTIPLE R           0.96851       ANALYSIS OF VARIANCE     DF     SUM OF SQUARES     MEAN SQUARE          F
R SQUARE            0.93801        REGRESSION               1.      4867.55388        4867.55388      287.49786
ADJUSTED R SQUARE   0.93475        RESIDUAL                19.       321.68422          16.93075
STANDARD ERROR      4.11470

-------------- VARIABLES IN THE EQUATION --------------     ----------- VARIABLES NOT IN THE EQUATION ----------
VARIABLE        B         BETA     STD ERROR B      F        VARIABLE     BETA IN     PARTIAL    TOLERANCE      F
AGE         4.020398    0.96851     0.23711      287.498     HEIGHT       0.29260     0.49437     0.17696     5.822
(CONSTANT)  0.6325111D-01                                    SEX         -0.05679    -0.22789     0.99814     0.986

F-LEVEL OR TOLERANCE-LEVEL INSUFFICIENT FOR FURTHER COMPUTATION
```

cance, but its tolerance is too low. Therefore, HEIGHT is rejected, and the next best variable, SEX, is tested. SEX has an adequately high tolerance, but it is not significant enough to enter the equation. There being no other variables for testing, the program stops and prints the message indicating why it stopped with variables left over.

The choice of the F value as a criterion is usually set at a value lower than that required for the desired level of confidence, because the F values of variables often fluctuate from step to step. An after-the-fact analysis of variables included in the equation will indicate which variables are statistically significant and which should be removed from the regression. If any variables should be removed they may be examined on subsequent runs by manipulating the inclusion level numbers.

As mentioned earlier, a variable that is assigned a high number when specifying the inclusion level is given a higher priority in the selection process. Therefore, if some variables have been selected for entry into the model, but later prove to be insignificant, this set of variables can be examined on a subsequent run in which the apparently good variables are assigned a high odd number and the apparently insignificant variables are assigned a low odd number when specifying the inclusion level. Here, it would be observed that all of the high level variables that pass the selection criteria specified by F and T will be entered into the model before any of the lower level variables are considered. If several variables that originally entered the model have become insignificant because of the confounding effects among that set of variables, they can be retested with a lower priority inclusion level. One or more of these factors might prove to be significant on a subsequent analysis of the data.

An inclusion level of 0 (zero) can be used to exclude variables from entry while computing all of the prospective statistics at each step. This is another way of subsequently testing variables that become insignificant during a run. If on the second run any of the variables at level 0 show significance, they can be entered on a third regression run with a level above 0.

NOTES

1. For an example of this process see Draper and Smith, pp. 107-112.

BIBLIOGRAPHY

Draper, N. R., and Smith, H. *Applied Regression Analysis*. New York: Wiley, 1966.

Problems for Solution[G]

1. OASIS

The Ontario Ambulance Service Information System (OASIS) records every ambulance trip made in the province. For each call, many factors are noted; among these factors are the pickup and destination location codes of each call. Between 1/3 and 1/2 of all trips are between a community location (where the patient lives, or became ill/injured) and a hospital. (The others are between hospitals and/or other health care institutions.) The whole province has been divided into a grid of squares (1/2 mile to the side) to enable coding of community locations. Each square is called an *ambulance sector*.

A study of ambulance calls in Kingston hypothesizes that there are sociodemographic factors that are related to the total number of calls originating or terminating in any sector. The number of calls for each sector for 1974 has been determined from the OASIS records. The sociodemographic factors have been determined from Statistics Canada 1971 Census records. In Kingston, 33 sectors had usable data (sectors with total population greater than 100).

A sample SPSS regression run is provided in Exhibit 12-1. The meanings of the variable names used in the regression are as follows:

TOTCALLS = total calls in each sector (for 11 1/2 months) per 100 population

LOWINC = proportion of total population in each sector with income below $3000

UNDER25 = proportion of total population in each sector of age 25 years or under

WIDOWED = proportion widowed (total pop.)

PLUS55 = proportion of age 55 or greater (total pop.)

LABOUR = proportion with occupations classified as *labour* (total pop.)

MGMT = proportion with occupations classified as *management* (total pop.)

FEMALE = proportion female (total pop.)

Exhibit 12-1

```
REGRESSION        VARIABLES=TCTCALLS,LCWINC,UNDER25,WIDOWED,PLUSS5,LABOUR,
                  MGMT,FEMALE
                  REGRESSION=TOTCALLS WITH LCWINC TO FEMALE (1)

                                                                    04/13/76    PAGE  6

STEPWISE MULTIPLE REGRESSION ANALYSIS <33 CASES>
            STATISTICS    ALL

***** REGRESSION PROBLEM REQUIRES   1536 BYTES WORKSPACE, NOT INCLUDING RESIDUALS *****

            READ INPUT DATA

AFTER READING   47 CASES FROM SUBFILE AMISTDY ,  END OF FILE WAS ENCOUNTERED ON LOGICAL UNIT # 8


STEPWISE MULTIPLE REGRESSION ANALYSIS <33 CASES>              04/13/76    PAGE  7
FILE   AMISTDY (CREATION DATE = 04/13/76)

VARIABLE         MEAN       STANDARD DEV     CASES
TOTCALLS       45.8293       35.1651          33
LCWINC          0.5726        0.0479          33
UNDER25         0.4607        0.0695          33
WIDOWED         0.0451        0.0295          33
PLUSS5          0.1577        0.0379          33
LABOUR          0.1356        0.0479          33
MGMT            0.1996        0.0499          33
FEMALE          0.5096        0.0258          33


STEPWISE MULTIPLE REGRESSION ANALYSIS <33 CASES>              04/13/76    PAGE  8
FILE   AMISTDY (CREATION DATE = 04/13/76)

CORRELATION COEFFICIENTS

A VALUE OF 99.00000 IS PRINTED
IF A COEFFICIENT CANNOT BE COMPUTED.

           TOTCALLS   LCWINC    UNDER25   WIDOWED   PLUSS5    LABOUR    MGMT      FEMALE
TOTCALLS   1.00000    0.52266  -0.38430   0.44314   0.40888   0.26335  -0.36622  -0.01177
LCWINC     0.52266    1.00000   0.20342   0.06084  -0.02247   0.54451  -0.27754  -0.04431
UNDER25   -0.38430    0.20342   1.00000  -0.02796  -0.41330   0.07108  -0.21905  -0.07897
WIDOWED    0.44314    0.06084  -0.02796   1.00000   1.01062   0.14488   0.20323   0.67722
PLUSS5     0.40888   -0.02247  -0.41330   1.01062   1.00000   0.10481   0.18632   0.07639
LABOUR     0.26335    0.54451   0.07108   0.14488   0.10481   1.00000   1.00000   0.31624
MGMT      -0.36622   -0.27754  -0.21905   0.20323   0.18632   0.18632   1.00000   1.00000
FEMALE    -0.01177   -0.04431  -0.07897   0.67722   0.67722   0.31624   0.31624   1.00000
```

Exhibit 12-1 Continued

```
STEPWISE MULTIPLE REGRESSION ANALYSIS (33 CASES)

FILE  AMPSDY  (CREATION DATE = 04/13/76)

* * * * * * * * * * * * * *  M U L T I P L E   R E G R E S S I O N  * * * * * * * *    04/13/76   PAGE  9
                                                                                      VARIABLE LIST   1
                                                                                      REGRESSION LIST  1
DEPENDENT VARIABLE..    TOTCALLS

VARIABLE(S) ENTERED ON STEP NUMBER  1..    LOWINC

MULTIPLE R          0.52266            ANALYSIS OF VARIANCE    DF    SUM OF SQUARES    MEAN SQUARE        F
R SQUARE            0.27317            REGRESSION               1.      10809.55566    10809.55566    11.65097
ADJUSTED R SQUARE   0.24972            RESIDUAL                31.      28761.23343      927.78172
STANDARD ERROR     30.45951

------ VARIABLES IN THE EQUATION ------                  ------------- VARIABLES NOT IN THE EQUATION -------------
VARIABLE      B          BETA      STD ERROR B      F      VARIABLE     BETA IN     PARTIAL    TOLERANCE      F
LOWINC    183.70854    0.52266     112.49018    11.651     UNDER25     -0.51180    -0.58777     0.95862    15.834
(CONSTANT) 17.89047                                        WIDOWED      0.41287     0.48339     0.99630     9.147
                                                           PLUS55      -0.39232     0.45993     0.99995     8.049
                                                           LABOUR      -0.03620    -0.02701     0.70551     0.027
                                                           MGMT        -0.23962     0.27297     0.92297     2.359
                                                           FEMALE       0.01141     0.01337     0.99804     0.005

* * * * * * * * * * * * * * * * * * * * * * * * * * * * * * * * * * * * * * * * * * * * * * * * * * * * * *

VARIABLE(S) ENTERED ON STEP NUMBER  2..    UNDER25

MULTIPLE R          0.72406            ANALYSIS OF VARIANCE    DF    SUM OF SQUARES    MEAN SQUARE        F
R SQUARE            0.52427            REGRESSION               2.      20745.65615    10372.82907    16.53029
ADJUSTED R SQUARE   0.49255            RESIDUAL                30.      18825.13294      627.50443
STANDARD ERROR     25.05004

------ VARIABLES IN THE EQUATION ------                  ------------- VARIABLES NOT IN THE EQUATION -------------
VARIABLE      B          BETA      STD ERROR B      F      VARIABLE     BETA IN     PARTIAL    TOLERANCE      F
LOWINC    460.45285    0.62077      94.48805    23.747     WIDOWED      0.14708     0.16079     0.56857     0.770
UNDER25  -259.12653   -0.51180      65.11943    15.834     PLUS55      -0.09311    -0.07366     0.29768     0.158
(CONSTANT)133.72290                                        LABOUR      -0.05921    -0.07192     0.70186     0.151
                                                           MGMT        -0.33994    -0.46636     0.89539     8.061
                                                           FEMALE      -0.20806    -0.27898     0.85526     2.447
```

Exhibit 12-1 Continued

```
STEPWISE MULTIPLE REGRESSION ANALYSIS <33 CASES>

FILE  AMBSIDY  (CREATION DATE = 04/13/76)                        04/13/76        PAGE  10

* * * * * * * * * * * * * * * *    M U L T I P L E    R E G R E S S I O N    * * * * * * * * * * * * * * * *    VARIABLE LIST 1
                                                                                                            REGRESSION LIST 1
DEPENDENT VARIABLE..    TLTCALLS

VARIABLE(S) ENTERED ON STEP NUMBER  3..    MGMT

MULTIPLE R        0.73230                   ANALYSIS OF VARIANCE      DF      SUM OF SQUARES      MEAN SQUARE        F
R SQUARE          0.72774                   REGRESSION                3.       24840.05154       8280.01718     16.30064
ADJUSTED R SQUARE 0.68923                   RESIDUAL                 29.       14730.73755        507.95647
STANDARD ERROR   22.53789
```

```
------------- VARIABLES IN THE EQUATION -------------            --------- VARIABLES NOT IN THE EQUATION ---------

VARIABLE          B          BETA      STD ERROR B       F        VARIABLE      BETA IN      PARTIAL      TOLERANCE        F

LOWINC       399.75835    0.54415      87.95904      20.797       WIDOWED       0.18775      0.23106      0.56380        1.579
UNDER25     -238.31125   -0.56045      59.48435      23.493       PLUS55       -0.00975     -0.00863      0.29170        0.002
MGMT        -239.33922   -0.33594      84.30090       8.061       LABOUR        0.12224      0.15255      0.57971        0.667
(CONSTANT)   199.00058                                            FEMALE       -0.12142     -0.17692      0.79029        0.905
```

```
* * * * * * * * * * * * * * * *   WIDOWED   * * * * * * * * * * * * * * * * * * * * * * * * * * * * * * * * * * *

VARIABLE(S) ENTERED ON STEP NUMBER  4..    WIDOWED

MULTIPLE R        0.80474                   ANALYSIS OF VARIANCE      DF      SUM OF SQUARES      MEAN SQUARE        F
R SQUARE          0.64761                   REGRESSION                4.       25626.51095       6406.62774     12.86446
ADJUSTED R SQUARE 0.59727                   RESIDUAL                 28.       13944.27814        498.00993
STANDARD ERROR   22.31614
```

```
------------- VARIABLES IN THE EQUATION -------------            --------- VARIABLES NOT IN THE EQUATION ---------

VARIABLE          B          BETA      STD ERROR B       F        VARIABLE      BETA IN      PARTIAL      TOLERANCE        F

LOWINC       370.17922    0.50388      89.93214      16.943       PLUS55       -1.06018     -0.45838      0.06587        7.182
UNDER25     -225.99739   -0.44037      76.94643       8.615       LABOUR        0.10364      0.13217      0.57309        0.480
MGMT        -239.23922   -0.33565      83.54423       8.323       FEMALE       -0.29269     -0.36875      0.55932        4.249
WIDOWED      -72.68870   -0.18775     178.02200       1.579
(CONSTANT)   163.71679
```

Exhibit 12-1 Continued

```
STEPWISE MULTIPLE REGRESSION ANALYSIS <33 CASES>                                       04/13/76        PAGE  11

FILE   AMSTDY  (CREATION DATE = 04/13/76)

* * * * * * * * * * * * * * * * * *   M U L T I P L E   R E G R E S S I O N   * * * * * * * * * * * * * * *   VARIABLE LIST   1
                                                                                                             REGRESSION LIST 1
DEPENDENT VARIABLE..    TOTCALLS

VARIABLE(S) ENTERED ON STEP NUMBER  5..    PLUS55


MULTIPLE R          0.84950         ANALYSIS OF VARIANCE      DF      SUM OF SQUARES    MEAN SQUARE       F
R SQUARE            0.72165           REGRESSION               5.       28556.38848      5711.27690     14.00026
ADJUSTED R SQUARE   0.67011           RESIDUAL                27.       11014.40460       407.94091
STANDARD ERROR     20.19755


------------- VARIABLES IN THE EQUATION -------------        ------------- VARIABLES NOT IN THE EQUATION -------------
VARIABLE         B          BETA       STD ERROR B      F     VARIABLE       BETA IN      PARTIAL      TOLERANCE      F

LOWINC        440.72987     0.59992     85.54611     26.543   LABOUR        0.08083      0.11575      0.57072      0.353
UNDER25      -454.94263    -0.98855    110.24699     17.029   FEMALE       -0.11810     -0.13460      0.36155      0.480
MGMT         -222.44902    -0.31601     76.50810      8.457
WIDOWED      1023.09012     0.69873    335.01530      9.107
PLUS55       -456.63343    -1.06018    174.08332      7.132
(CONSTANT)    295.73930


* * * * * * * * * * * * * * * * * * * * * * * * * * * * * * * * * * * * * * * * * * * * * * * * * * * * * * * * * * *

VARIABLE(S) ENTERED ON STEP NUMBER  6..    FEMALE


MULTIPLE R          0.85246         ANALYSIS OF VARIANCE      DF      SUM OF SQUARES    MEAN SQUARE       F
R SQUARE            0.72670           REGRESSION               6.       28755.94266      4792.65711     11.52204
ADJUSTED R SQUARE   0.66363           RESIDUAL                26.       10814.84643       415.95563
STANDARD ERROR     20.39495


------------- VARIABLES IN THE EQUATION -------------        ------------- VARIABLES NOT IN THE EQUATION -------------
VARIABLE         B          BETA       STD ERROR B      F     VARIABLE       BETA IN      PARTIAL      TOLERANCE      F

LOWINC        423.04810     0.57694     89.75492     22.300   LABOUR        0.05252      0.07010      0.48689      0.123
UNDER25      -460.00411    -0.99190    131.85328      9.483
MGMT         -207.09500    -0.29668    354.67240      7.309
WIDOWED      958.04501     0.65411    218.64687      2.965
PLUS55       -376.18647    -0.85834    200.94896      2.490
FEMALE       -331.17221    -0.11810
(CONSTANT)
```

Exhibit 12-1 Continued

```
STEPWISE MULTIPLE REGRSSION ANALYSIS <33 CASES>

FILE  AMBSTDY  (CREATION DATE = 04/13/76)                      04/13/76          PAGE  12

* * * * * * * * * * * * * * * * * *   M U L T I P L E   R E G R E S S I O N   * * * * * * * * * * * * * * * * * *

DEPENDENT VARIABLE..   TOTCALLS

VARIABLE(S) ENTERED ON STEP NUMBER  7..   LABOUR                                 VARIABLE LIST   1
                                                                                 REGRESSION LIST 1

MULTIPLE R          0.85325                 ANALYSIS OF VARIANCE     DF    SUM OF SQUARES    MEAN SQUARE      F
R SQUARE            0.72804                 REGRESSION               7.      28809.09340     4115.58477    9.56073
ADJUSTED R SQUARE   0.65189                 RESIDUAL                25.      10761.69569      430.46783
STANDARD ERROR     20.74772

------- VARIABLES IN THE EQUATION -------              ------- VARIABLES NOT IN THE EQUATION -------

VARIABLE        B         BETA    STD ERROR B     F       VARIABLE   BETA IN   PARTIAL   TOLERANCE    F

LOWINC       402.89689   0.54842   109.05096   13.650
UNDER25     -416.78399  -0.82319   137.59720    9.175
MGMT        -225.57910  -0.32039    93.61926    5.806
WIDOWED      958.30109   0.80435   360.80973    7.054
PLUSS5      -391.37508  -0.88939   226.32526    2.988
FEMALE      -109.38151  -0.09281   221.32316    0.244
LABOUR        49.76349   0.05252   141.62064    0.123
(CONSTANT)   32:.51051

MAXIMUM STEP REACHED

STEPWISE MULTIPLE REGRESSION ANALYSIS <33 CASES>

FILE  AMBSTDY  (CREATION DATE = 04/13/76)                      04/13/76          PAGE  13

* * * * * * * * * * * * * * * * * *   M U L T I P L E   R E G R E S S I O N   * * * * * * * * * * * * * * * * * *

DEPENDENT VARIABLE..   TOTCALLS                                                  VARIABLE LIST   1
                                                                                 REGRESSION LIST 1
                                     SUMMARY TABLE

VARIABLE     MULTIPLE R   R SQUARE   RSQ CHANGE   SIMPLE R        B          BETA

LOWINC        0.52266     0.27317     0.27317    -0.52266    402.89689    0.54842
UNDER25       0.72406     0.52427     0.25110    -0.38430   -416.78399   -0.82319
MGMT          0.79230     0.62774     0.10347    -0.36622   -225.57910   -0.32039
WIDOWED       0.84950     0.72161     0.09387     0.40888    958.30109    0.80435
PLUSS5        0.84950     0.72165     0.07404    -0.01177   -391.37508   -0.88939
FEMALE        0.85246     0.72670     0.00504     0.26335   -109.38151   -0.09281
LABOUR        0.85325     0.72804     0.00134                 49.76349    0.05252
(CONSTANT)                                                   321.51051
```

For the following questions state whatever assumptions you may consider necessary:

a. For Steps 1-3 of the regression what percentage of the total sum of squares is explained? How much explanation is added by the second variable and then by the third?

b. How can the significance of the regression be tested at any step? Answer this by explaining what ratio is formed (and why), what its components are and how it is tested. Explain the number of *tails* this test has. Is the regression significant in Step 5?

c. For Step 3, what is the confidence interval for the *b* value for MGMT? Is it significant?

d. How can the significance of the added explanation for the variable(s) entering at any step be tested? Does MGMT add a significant amount in Step 3? Is the total contribution of PLUS55 and FEMALE in Steps 5 and 6 significant in combination?

e. What is the last step in which all variables are significant? How could a regression control parameter have been used to prevent the regression procedure from proceeding to further steps?

f. If the tolerance parameter were set as suggested in the text, what change would have been observed in the regression?

2. Family Size

A study was carried out to assess the psychological factors that might be influential in a person's decision about family size, timing of births, and use of birth control.

The study design was as follows: The selected subjects (married graduate students) filled out a questionnaire, which among other things, asked about their decisions regarding family size and timing (postponement), and their certainty about and happiness with the decision. At the same time, other questions were aimed at the psychological concept of internal/external *locus of control* (i.e., primarily motivated by personal considerations, or primarily motivated by perceptions of other people's approval or disapproval). Internals and externals were randomly assigned to four *reward* groups: no reward, verbal reward, $1.00, and $5.00. (Psychological theory suggests that internally oriented people react negatively to tangible rewards, while externally oriented people react positively.)

Two weeks later the subjects were given their reward for filling out the first questionnaire, and filled out a second, apparently unrelated, questionnaire which (among other things) asked about the postponement decision and certainty and happiness.

One question that was investigated was the impact of psychological type and reward on the change in happiness between the two questionnaires while controlling for the levels of these variables on the first questionnaire.

The SPSS printout shown in Exhibit 12-2 is a portion of the analysis performed. The meanings of the variables are:

Dependent Variable:
CHNGHAPP = change in happiness
Independent Variables:
PREHAPPY = happiness on pretest
  PRECERT = certainty on pretest
 PREPSTPN = postponement on pretest
  CHGPSTP = change in postponement
 CHNGCERT = change in certainty
   REWARD = reward (none, verbal, $1, $5)
     IECAT = internal or external orientation
  INTRIERC = interaction of psychological type of reward

Note that the correlation matrix contains other variables, used in other analyses.

a. For each step of the regression, how much of the total sum of squares of the dependent variable is explained?
b. Is the regression equation significant in all steps? Explain.
c. What is the number of the last step where all *b* values are significant? Explain why. Call this Step S in the remaining parts of the question.
d. For Step S, what is the β value of the first variable? What is its meaning?
e. In Step S, which independent variable, when changing by 1 standard deviation, has the largest impact upon the dependent variable?
f. For Step S what is the *b* value for the second variable entered in the equation? Does it differ significantly from its value in Step 2 (5% level of confidence)? What does this imply about bias? Are there any other actual or potential problems of bias?
g. What are the values of the standard error of the regression equation from the first step to the last step? Comment on its behavior. Which step would be indicated as the "best" step of the regression? Explain.
h. What is the partial correlation of PREPSTPN with PRECERT, controlling for PREHAPPY?

Exhibit 12-2

SIXTH RUN WITH JABES' DATA - MARCH 5, 1974   03/05/74   PAGE 2

REGRESSION   VARIABLES = IECAT TO INTRIERS/
              REGRESSION = CHNGHAPP WITH IECAT,REWARD, PREPSTPN TO CHNGCERT.
              INTRIERC(3) RESID=0/
OPTIONS   2
STATISTICS   1,2,4,6

SIXTH RUN WITH JABES' DATA - MARCH 5, 1974   03/05/74   PAGE 16

FILE NONAME (CREATION DATE = 03/05/74)

VARIABLE	MEAN	STANDARD DEV	CASES
IECAT	1.5000	0.5029	88
REWARD	2.6250	0.6861	88
SEX12	1.5227	0.5023	88
IESCALE	1.8230	0.5552	88
PREPSTPN	27.1136	4.2916	88
PRECERT	26.5725	5.9591	88
PREHAPPY	0.1477	5.0459	88
CHNGCERT	0.0227	4.7826	88
CHNGHAPP	-0.0795	4.4236	88
INTRIERC	-3.9432	2.1675	88
INTRIERS	4.8955	2.5892	88

SIXTH RUN WITH JABES' DATA - MARCH 5, 1974   03/05/74   PAGE 17

FILE NONAME (CREATION DATE = 03/05/74)

CORRELATION COEFFICIENTS

A VALUE OF 99.00000 IS PRINTED
IF A COEFFICIENT CANNOT BE COMPUTED.

	IECAT	REWARD	SEX12	IESCALE	PREPSTPN	PRECERT	PREHAPPY	CHNGPSTP	CHNGCERT	CHNGHAPP	INTRIERC	INTRIERS
IECAT	1.00000	-0.00052	-0.31851	0.81727	-0.18220	-0.11237	-0.39700	0.13816	0.05257	0.18343	0.61693	0.44316
REWARD	-0.00052	1.00000	0.11060	0.14083	-0.10357	-0.03097	-0.02642	0.07524	0.03928	-0.00867	0.75255	0.82463
SEX12	-0.31851	0.11060	1.00000	-0.27680	0.11846	-0.11005	-0.04739	0.08255	-0.10025	0.00176	-0.09909	-0.05559
IESCALE	0.81727	0.14083	-0.27680	1.00000	0.29936	0.18390	0.44986	0.04420	0.07591	0.00485	0.57662	0.62277
PREPSTPN	-0.18220	-0.10357	0.11846	0.29936	1.00000	0.42901	0.46010	0.20397	0.07596	0.00462	0.57982	0.23453
PRECERT	-0.11237	-0.03097	-0.11005	0.18390	0.42901	1.00000	0.31997	0.26973	0.49880	-0.00405	-0.13052	-0.13935
PREHAPPY	-0.39700	-0.02642	-0.04739	0.44986	0.46010	0.31997	1.00000	-0.01997	-0.01626	0.02696	-0.30477	-0.28351
CHNGPSTP	0.13816	0.07524	0.08255	0.04420	0.20397	0.26973	-0.01997	1.00000	0.19657	0.40014	0.14476	0.08205
CHNGCERT	0.05257	0.03928	-0.10025	0.07591	0.07596	0.49880	-0.01626	0.19657	1.00000	0.37931	0.08662	0.07677
CHNGHAPP	0.18343	-0.00867	0.00176	0.00485	0.00462	-0.00405	0.02696	0.40014	0.37931	1.00000	0.13730	0.03830
INTRIERC	0.61693	0.75255	-0.09909	0.57662	0.57982	-0.13052	-0.30477	0.14476	0.08662	0.13730	1.00000	0.92100
INTRIERS	0.44316	0.82463	-0.05559	0.62277	0.23453	-0.13935	-0.28351	0.08205	0.07677	0.03830	0.92100	1.00000

Exhibit 12-2 Continued

```
SIXTH RUN WITH JABES' DATA - MARCH 5, 1974
FILE  NCNAME  (CREATION DATE = 03/05/74)                                   03/05/74        PAGE 18
* * * * * * * * * * * * * * * * * * *  M U L T I P L E   R E G R E S S I O N  * * * * * * * * * * * * * * * * * *
DEPENDENT VARIABLE..    CHNGPAPP    CHANGE IN HAPPINESS
VARIABLE(S) ENTERED ON STEP NUMBER  1..    CHNGPSTP    CHANGE IN POSTPONEMENT            VARIABLE LIST   1
                                                                                        REGRESSION LIST 1

MULTIPLE R         0.40014            ANALYSIS OF VARIANCE    DF      SUM OF SQUARES     MEAN SQUARE         F
R SQUARE           0.16011            REGRESSION              1.         272.57801       272.57801       16.39435
STANDARD ERROR     4.07754            RESIDUAL               86.        1429.86517        16.62634

-------------- VARIABLES IN THE EQUATION --------------       ------------- VARIABLES NOT IN THE EQUATION -------------
VARIABLE         B        BETA    STD ERROR B       F          VARIABLE      BETA IN    PARTIAL    TOLERANCE       F
CHNGPSTP     0.35079    0.40014     0.08664      16.394        IECAT         0.13064    0.14119    0.98091      1.729
(CONSTANT)  -0.13137                                           REWARD       -0.03900   -0.04244    0.99434      0.153
                                                              PREPSTPN     -0.12076   -0.12689    0.92725      1.391
                                                              PRECERT      -0.04672   -0.05071    0.98974      0.272
                                                              CREHAPPY     -0.02934   -0.03359    0.96916     10.716
                                                              CHNGCERT     -0.31274   -0.09616    0.97904      0.658
                                                              INTRIERC      0.08116    0.08763

* * * * * * * * * * * * * * * * * * * * * * * * * *  CHNGCERT  CHANGE IN CERTAINTY  * * * * * * * * * * * * * * * * * * * *
VARIABLE(S) ENTERED ON STEP NUMBER  2..    CHNGCERT    CHANGE IN CERTAINTY

MULTIPLE R         0.50412            ANALYSIS OF VARIANCE    DF      SUM OF SQUARES     MEAN SQUARE         F
R SQUARE           0.25414            REGRESSION              2.         432.65406       216.32703       14.48099
STANDARD ERROR     3.86506            RESIDUAL               85.        1269.78912        14.93870

-------------- VARIABLES IN THE EQUATION --------------       ------------- VARIABLES NOT IN THE EQUATION -------------
VARIABLE         B        BETA    STD ERROR B       F          VARIABLE      BETA IN    PARTIAL    TOLERANCE       F
CHNGPSTP     0.29690    0.33866     0.08376      12.565        IECAT         0.12253    0.14058    0.98024      1.693
CHNGCERT     0.28927    0.31274     0.08837      10.716        REWARD       -0.04673   -0.05358    0.99371      0.245
(CONSTANT)  -0.12998                                           PREPSTPN     -0.09702   -0.10786    0.92184      0.989
                                                              PRECERT       0.16391    0.15978    0.70875      2.201
                                                              PREHAPPY     -0.30806   -0.35649    0.99879     12.229
                                                              INTRIERC      0.06281    0.07183    0.97553      0.436
```

Exhibit 12-2 Continued

```
SIXTH RUN WITH JABES' DATA - MARCH 5, 1974                                03/05/74        PAGE   19

FILE   NCNAME   (CREATION DATE = 03/05/74)

* * * * * * * * * * * * * * * * * *  M U L T I P L E   R E G R E S S I O N  * * * * * * * * * * * * * * *   VARIABLE LIST   1
                                                                                                          REGRESSION LIST  1
DEPENDENT VARIABLE..   CHNGHAPP   CHANGE IN HAPPINESS

VARIABLE(S) ENTERED ON STEP NUMBER   3..     PREHAPPY   HAPPINESS ON PRETEST

MULTIPLE R            C.59970                ANALYSIS OF VARIANCE      DF.       SUM OF SQUARES     MEAN SQUARE           F
R SQUARE             C.34892                 REGRESSION                 3.         59.02454          198.00818        15.00578
STANDARD ERROR       3.63256                 RESIDUAL                  84.       1108.41864           13.19546

---------- VARIABLES IN THE EQUATION ----------              ------ VARIABLES NOT IN THE EQUATION ------

VARIABLE         B          BETA        STD ERROR B      F         VARIABLE      BETA IN     PARTIAL    TOLERANCE      F

CHNGFSTP      0.29084     0.33175        0.07874      13.644       IECAT        -0.00201    -0.00226    0.82359     0.000
CHNGCERT      0.29820     0.32240        0.08309      12.880       REWARD       -0.05482    -0.06770    0.99304     0.382
PREHAPPY     -0.22868    -0.30806        0.06539      12.229       PREPSTPN      0.33338     0.34917    0.69741    11.525
(CONSTANT)    5.94902                                             PRECERT       0.37059     0.35409    0.59440    11.898
                                                                  INTRIERC     -0.02621    -0.03081    0.89957     0.079

* * * * * * * * * * * * * * * * * * * * * * * * * * * * * * * * * * * * * * * * * * * * * * * * * * * * * * * *

VARIABLE(S) ENTERED ON STEP NUMBER   4..     PRECERT    CERTAINTY ON PRETEST

MULTIPLE R            C.65617                ANALYSIS OF VARIANCE      DF.       SUM OF SQUARES     MEAN SQUARE           F
R SQUARE             C.43056                 REGRESSION                 4.        732.99780          183.24945        15.68908
STANDARD ERROR       3.41761                 RESIDUAL                  83.       969.44538           11.68006

---------- VARIABLES IN THE EQUATION ----------              ------ VARIABLES NOT IN THE EQUATION ------

VARIABLE         B          BETA        STD ERROR B      F         VARIABLE      BETA IN     PARTIAL    TOLERANCE      F

CHNGFSTP      0.22011     0.25107        0.07686       8.200       IECAT        -0.01139    -0.01369    0.82286     0.015
CHNGCERT      0.48698     0.52649        0.09543      26.042       REWARD       -0.04858    -0.06414    0.99257     0.339
PREHAPPY     -0.32176    -0.43345        0.06718      22.939       PREPSTPN      0.24493     0.25223    0.50368     5.571
PRECERT      -0.38377     0.37059        0.11126      11.898       INTRIERC     -0.01759    -0.02209    0.89883     0.040
(CONSTANT)   -2.22925
```

Exhibit 12-2 Continued

```
SIXTH RUN WITH JABES' DATA - MARCH 5, 1974                                        03/05/74        PAGE  20

FILE  NONAME   (CREATION DATE = 03/05/74)

* * * * * * * * * * * * * * * * * *   M U L T I P L E   R E G R E S S I O N   * * * * * * * * * * * * * * * * * *
                                                                                              VARIABLE LIST   1
                                                                                              REGRESSION LIST   1
DEPENDENT VARIABLE..   CHNGHAPP    CHANGE IN HAPPINESS

VARIABLE(S) ENTERED ON STEP NUMBER  5..      PREPSTPN   POSTPONEMENT ON PRETEST

                                   ANALYSIS OF VARIANCE      DF      SUM OF SQUARES      MEAN SQUARE         F
MULTIPLE R       0.68322           REGRESSION                5.       794.67360          158.93472       14.35678
R SQUARE         0.46678           RESIDUAL                 82.       907.76958           11.07036
STANDARD ERROR   3.32722

------- VARIABLES IN THE EQUATION -------                    ------- VARIABLES NOT IN THE EQUATION -------
VARIABLE      B         BETA      STD ERROR B      F          VARIABLE    BETA IN     PARTIAL    TOLERANCE      F
CHNGFSTP    0.29745    0.39929    0.08169       13.258        IECAT      -0.02108    -0.02616    0.82112      0.055
CHNGCERT    0.42387    0.45826    0.09667       19.224        REWARD     -0.03249    -0.04417    0.98532      0.158
PREHAPPY   -0.28355   -0.51568    0.07045       29.641        INTRIERC   -0.01588    -0.02062    0.89876      0.034
PRECERT     0.28316    0.27343    0.11640        5.917
PREFSTPN    0.19192    0.24493    0.08131        5.571
(CONSTANT) -3.00624

* * * * * * * * * * * * * * * * * * * * * * * * * * * * * * * * * * * * * * * * * * * * * * * * * * * * * * * * *

VARIABLE(S) ENTERED ON STEP NUMBER  6..      REWARD     REWARD

                                   ANALYSIS OF VARIANCE      DF      SUM OF SQUARES      MEAN SQUARE         F
MULTIPLE R       0.68398           REGRESSION                6.       796.44457          132.74076       11.86757
R SQUARE         0.46782           RESIDUAL                 81.       905.99861           11.18517
STANDARD ERROR   3.34442

------- VARIABLES IN THE EQUATION -------                    ------- VARIABLES NOT IN THE EQUATION -------
VARIABLE      B         BETA      STD ERROR B      F          VARIABLE    BETA IN     PARTIAL    TOLERANCE      F
CHNGFSTP    0.29649    0.34047    0.08216       13.200        IECAT      -0.02134    -0.02651    0.82108      0.056
CHNGCERT    0.42451    0.45960    0.09721       19.019        INTRIERC    0.02674     0.02185    0.35534      0.038
PREHAPPY   -0.38305   -0.51601    0.07082       29.251
PRECERT     0.28367    0.27392    0.11701        5.877
PREFSTPN    0.18913    0.24137    0.08203        5.316
REWARD     -0.13234   -0.03249    0.33259        0.158
(CONSTANT) -2.61096
```

Exhibit 12-2 Continued

```
SIXTH RUN WITH JABES' DATA - MARCH 5, 1974                              03/05/74        PAGE  21

FILE  NONAME   (CREATION DATE = 03/05/74)

* * * * * * * * * * * * * * *  M U L T I P L E   R E G R E S S I O N  * * * * * * * * * * * * *     VARIABLE LIST  1
                                                                                                  REGRESSION LIST 1
DEPENDENT VARIABLE..     CHNGHAPP    CHANGE IN HAPPINESS

VARIABLE(S) ENTERED ON STEP NUMBER  7..    IECAT      INTERNAL-EXTERNAL CATEGORIES

MULTIPLE R          0.68425           ANALYSIS OF VARIANCE    DF      SUM OF SQUARES       MEAN SQUARE         F
R SQUARE            0.46820           REGRESSION              7.        797.08126          113.86875       10.06172
STANDARD ERROR      2.36408           RESIDUAL               80.        905.36192           11.31702

--------- VARIABLES IN THE EQUATION ---------          --------- VARIABLES NOT IN THE EQUATION ---------

VARIABLE        B          BETA      STD ERROR B      F       VARIABLE     BETA IN    PARTIAL   TOLERANCE      F

CHNGFSTP     0.30103     0.34338      0.08333     13.050      INTRIERC     0.33271    0.11188    0.06014     1.001
CHNGCERT     0.42596     0.46053      0.09786     18.946
PREHAPPY    -0.38980    -0.52510      0.07691     25.820
PRECERT      0.22397     0.24422      0.11771      5.821
REWARD       0.24002     0.24250      0.08260      5.292
PRE-FSTPN   -0.13293    -0.03264      0.33555      0.158
IECAT       -0.18774    -0.02134      0.79152      0.056
(CONSTANT)  -2.18132

* * * * * * * * * * * * * * * * * * * * * * * * * * * * * * * * * * * * * * * * * * * * * * * * * * * * * *

VARIABLE(S) ENTERED ON STEP NUMBER  8..    INTRIERC    INTERACTION INT-EXT CATEG BY REWARD

MULTIPLE R          0.68910           ANALYSIS OF VARIANCE    DF      SUM OF SQUARES       MEAN SQUARE         F
R SQUARE            0.47486           REGRESSION              8.        808.41404          101.05175        8.92934
STANDARD ERROR      2.36405           RESIDUAL               79.        894.02915           11.31682

--------- VARIABLES IN THE EQUATION ---------          --------- VARIABLES NOT IN THE EQUATION ---------

VARIABLE        B          BETA      STD ERROR B      F       VARIABLE     BETA IN    PARTIAL   TOLERANCE      F

CHNGFSTP     0.29459     0.33603      0.08358     12.424
CHNGCERT     0.42723     0.46190      0.09787     19.056
PREHAPPY    -0.38478    -0.51834      0.07688     25.052
PRECERT      0.30147     0.29111      0.18323      4.666
PRE-FSTFN    0.17978     0.28107      1.06504      1.155
REWARD      -1.54266    -0.22064      1.92403      1.019
INTRIERC     0.67902     0.33271      0.68855      1.001
(CONSTANT)   0.08876

MAXIMUM STEP REACHED
```

Exhibit 12-2 Continued

```
SIXTH RUN WITH JABES' DATA - MARCH 5, 1974                                    03/05/74        PAGE  22

FILE   NONAME   (CREATION DATE = 03/05/74)

* * * * * * * * * * * * * * * * * * * *  M U L T I P L E   R E G R E S S I O N  * * * * * * * * * * * * * * * *
DEPENDENT VARIABLE..   CHNGHAPP    CHANGE IN HAPPINESS                                          VARIABLE LIST   1
                                                                                               REGRESSION LIST 1
```

SUMMARY TABLE

VARIABLE		MULTIPLE R	R SQUARE	RSQ CHANGE	SIMPLE R	B	BETA
CHNGFSTP	CHANGE IN FCSTPONEMENT	0.40014	0.16011	0.16011	0.40014	0.29459	0.33603
CHNGCERT	CHANGE N CERTAINTY	0.50412	0.25414	0.09403	0.37331	-0.42723	-0.41190
PREHPRY	HAPPINESS CN PRETEST	0.59017	0.34892	0.09479	-0.30977	-0.38478	-0.51834
PRECERT	CERTAINTY CN PRETEST	0.65617	0.43056	0.08163	-0.00462	0.30147	0.29111
PREPSTPN	POSTPONEMENT ON PRETEST	0.68322	0.46678	0.03623	-0.00405	0.17978	0.22944
REWARD	REWARD	0.68398	0.46782	0.00104	-0.00867	-1.14477	-0.28107
IECAT	INTERNAL-EXTERNAL CATEGORIES	0.68425	0.46820	0.00037	0.18343	-1.94266	-0.22084
INTRIERC	INTERACTICN INT-EXT CATEG BY REWARD	0.68910	0.47486	0.00666	0.13739	0.67902	0.33271
(CONSTANT)						0.08876	

Chapter 13

Transformed Variables in the Regression Equation

Objectives

After completing this chapter you should be able to:
1. Describe and draw the general shape of simple functions involving powers of x (e.g., $1/x$, $\sqrt{x}$, x, x^2, x^3).
2. Describe and draw the general shape of simple exponential functions of x (e.g., 10^x and e^x).
3. Write the appropriate SPSS statements to create the functions named in objectives 1 and 2.
4. Explain the concept of dummy variables.
5. Construct dummy variables using SPSS.
6. Explain the concept of interaction, relating analysis of variance and multiple regression.
7. Construct interaction variables for two nominal variables.
8. Construct interaction variables for a nominal and an interval or ratio variable.

Chapter Map

This chapter relates aspects of basic mathematics to SPSS and most sections have been assigned the letter codes B or D, or both B and D.

Introductory material is presented in Sections 13.1, 13.2.3 and 13.4 and these have been assigned the letter code A.

13.1 INTRODUCTION [A]

Many situations arise in multiple regression where one or more variables are in one form and should be transformed into another. For example, growth processes may be characterized by an exponential curve that may be transformed into a linear function by simply using the logarithm of the dependent variable rather than the original scale of measurement. For other nonlinear functions to be fitted by regression methods, we can use transformed predictor variables to express the curve in linear form. In other cases, categorical predictor variables with k categories must be transformed to $(k - 1)$ dichotomous *dummy variables*. In still other cases, interactions between two variables may be hypothesized and, as a result, it is necessary to create one or more interactive variables.

13.2 SIMPLE VARIABLE TRANSFORMATIONS [B]

Presented in Figures 13-1(a) and (b) are several common shapes of curves that may be considered when reaching a decision about the types of transformations that should be used.

Illustrated in Figure 13-1(a) are the shapes and relative positions of various common functions of x for the range of x values from -9 to $+9$, while Figure 13-1(b) has an expanded scale with x ranging from -1.8 to $+1.8$.

13.2.1 Exponential Functions [B,D]

Note that the exponential functions 10^x and e^x are similar in shape, but that the value of 10^x rises much more steeply as x increases. For values of x less than zero these two functions asymptotically approach zero. They are so close to zero that an expanded scale of Figure 13-1(b) is required to see the difference between the curves and the negative x-axis. These two curves are used in the study of growth phenomena. The equations representing growth usually are expressed by:

$$y = 10^{a+bx}$$

or

$$y = e^{a+bx}$$

Figure 13-1(a) Curves showing x and Common Functions of x (x ranging
from -9 to $+9$)

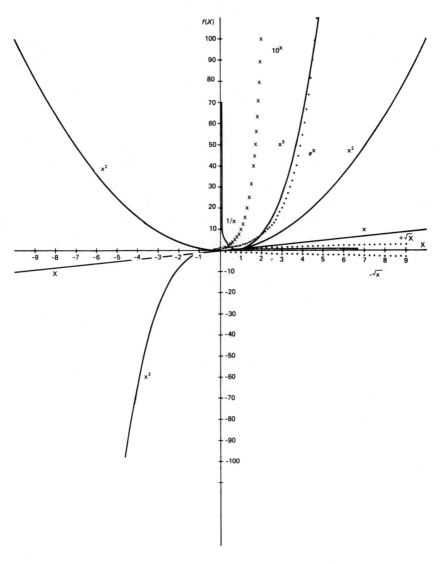

Figure 13-1(b) Curves Showing x and Common Functions of x (x ranging from -1.8 to $+1.8$)

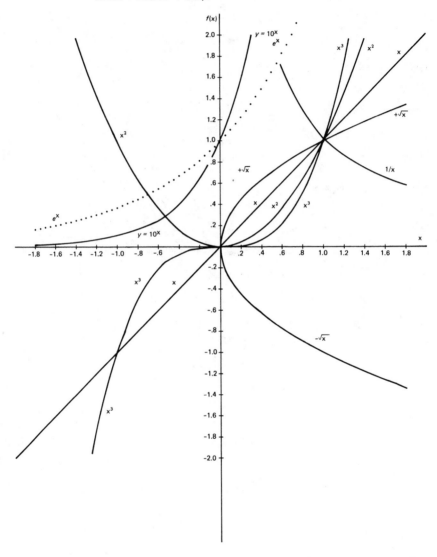

and the corresponding transformations have the form:

$$\log (y) = a + bx \quad \text{(logarithm with base 10)}$$

$$\ln (y) = a + bx \quad \text{(logarithm with base } e)$$

The a and b of these equations can be estimated by linear regression because they have a linear form.

Growth processes are often plotted on semilogarithmic (semilog) graph paper where the vertical scale is expressed in logarithmic form. Figure 13-2 shows population estimates for the United States and Canada for a number of years. Note the tremendous range of values that can be plotted on semilog graph paper. Straight lines indicate constant growth rates. Curves with increasing slopes indicate increasing growth rates, and curves with decreasing slopes represent decreasing growth rates.

The SPSS statements used to obtain either of these transformations are:

$$\text{COMPUTE} \quad \text{LOGY} = \text{LG10(Y)}$$

or

$$\text{COMPUTE} \quad \text{LNY} = \text{LN(Y)}$$

The transformed variables could be used in regression design statements as follows:

$$\text{REGRESSION} = \text{LOGY WITH X(2)}$$

or

$$\text{REGRESSION} = \text{LNY WITH X(2)}$$

13.2.2 Powers of x [B,D]

Various powers of x have shapes and behaviors that can be useful in fitting curves using regression. In addition, the response variable may be proportional to some power of the independent variable. The first power of x is a straight line of constant slope. Powers of x higher than 1 are curves with increasing slope, and the greater the power, the greater the rate of increase in the slope of the function. Returning to Figure 13-1(b), let us consider the behavior of x^2 and x^3 for values of x greater than 1. Here, $x^3 > x^2$ and, by differentiation, the slopes of the curves are $3x^2$ and $2x$ respectively, which shows that the slope of x^3 is always greater than that of x^2 for any value of x greater than 1.

Figure 13-2 The Population of the United States and Canada from 1850/51 to 1970/71

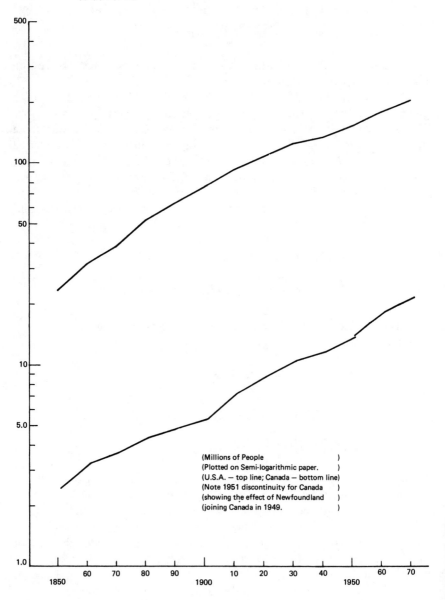

(Millions of People   )
(Plotted on Semi-logarithmic paper.   )
(U.S.A. — top line; Canada — bottom line)
(Note 1951 discontinuity for Canada   )
(showing the effect of Newfoundland   )
(joining Canada in 1949.   )

When x is less than 0, only integer powers are defined, and odd powers of x are negative. This is evident by observing the behavior of x^3 with respect to x^2 in Figure 13-1(a).

An inspection of Figure 13-1(b) will reveal that when x is between 0 and 1, $y = x^3$ lies below $y = x^2$. Also, observe that slopes of the two functions are equal when $x = 2/3$. When x is less than $2/3$, the slope of $y = x^3$ is lower than the slope of $y = x^2$, while for values of x greater than $2/3$ the reverse is true.

Consider next the general function $y = x^a$ where a is between 0 and 1. Here, for example, we might assign the value of $1/2$ to the index a, which implies that $y = \sqrt{x}$. As shown in Figure 13-1(b), when the powers of x are between 0 and 1, the function $y = x^a$ for $0 < a < 1$ exhibits a different behavior than $y = x^a$ for $a > 1$. Also, observe that for *real numbers*, fractional powers of x require x to assume only positive values. The $\sqrt{-1}$ is undefined in the real number system, and, as a result, we ignore negative values of x for the purposes of transformation.

SPSS statements for these transformations would be:

COMPUTE   XSQUARE = X**2

COMPUTE   XCUBE   = X**3

COMPUTE   SQROOTX = SQRT(X)

These transformations are of value when estimating a nonlinear cost function in which total cost is the dependent variable and a measure of output represents the independent or predictor variable. Here, for example, we might estimate the *total cost function* by a curve of the quadratic form:

$$y = b_0 + b_1 x + b_2 x^2$$

If we differentiate y with respect to x, we find that this expression yields a linear *marginal cost curve*. In this case, the regression design statement would be:

REGRESSION = Y WITH X, XSQUARE

On the other hand, if we suspected that the marginal cost curve was non-linear, we might estimate the total cost function by fitting an equation of the cubic form:

$$y = b_0 + b_1 x + b_2 x^2 + b_3 x^3$$

Observe that, if coefficient b_2 is negative, and b_3 is positive, differentiating the total cost function results in a U-shaped marginal cost curve. In this case, the regression design statement is:

REGRESSION = Y WITH X, XSQUARE, XCUBE

13.2.3 Trigonometric Functions [A]

The trigonometric functions (sine, cosine, and tangent) as well as the inverse trigonometric functions (arc sine, arc cosine, and arc tangent) can be used as well, but their use is beyond the scope of this text.

13.3 DUMMY VARIABLES [D]

In analysis of variance (Chapters 4-7) we used independent variables that were nominal (i.e., categorical) in nature. There is no order implicit in nominal variables. An example is the male/female dichotomous sex variable. Another example is the trial of several drugs (one variable) on several types of illnesses (another variable).

To use nominal variables in multiple regression, each category of the variable must be represented by a *dummy variable*. A dummy variable represents the members of its category by 1s, and all others as 0. For example, marital status could be represented by the dummy variables SINGLE, MARRIED, DIVORCED, WIDOW, WIDOWER, OTHER. Each person would be represented by a 1 in the appropriate dummy variable, and by a 0 in all the others.

For a nominal variable with k categories it is possible to create k dummy variables. However, one of these is redundant, because it is a perfect linear combination of the others. For SEX it is necessary to have only 1 dummy variable MALE (or FEMALE if one prefers). For other situations it is often difficult to decide ahead of time which dummy variable to omit. Fortunately in multiple regression the use of the tolerance parameter with the forward inclusion mode can select the most useful $(k - 1)$ dummies, while eliminating the kth variable which would otherwise cause multicollinearity.

In SPSS the creation of dummy variables is simple. If SEX is coded 0 for males and 1 for females, then SEX is the dummy variable for FEMALE. In this case, the required dummy variable is created by the statement:

COMPUTE   FEMALE = SEX

If, however, the coding were 2 for males and 3 for females then one could create MALE by the statement:

IF   (SEX EQ 2) MALE = 1

If marital status categories were coded 1, 2, 3, 4, 5, and 6 for single, married, divorced, widow, widower, and other respectively, then SPSS would require a series of statements:

IF   (MARITAL EQ 1) SINGLE = 1
IF   (MARITAL EQ 2) MARRIED = 1
IF   (MARITAL EQ 3) DIVORCED = 1
IF   (MARITAL EQ 4) WIDOW = 1
IF   (MARITAL EQ 5) WIDOWER = 1
IF   (MARITAL EQ 6) OTHER = 1

(Note that one can use the variable name OTHER only once in any given analysis. If another nominal variable were being transformed to dummy variables, the catchall category would require a different name.)

13.4 INTERACTIVE VARIABLES [A]

We have already discussed the situations in which interactions might occur among predictor variables. Two types of interactions can be considered:

1. between two or more nominal variables
2. between an interval or ratio scale variable and either nominal or interval/ratio scale variables.

13.4.1 Interactions With Nominal Variables [D]

Let us assume a design in which sex and marital status are believed to interact in their effects on patient satisfaction. Assume that we are able to measure the patient's satisfaction on a scale which ranges from 0 to 100. Also, suppose that we know the individual's sex and marital status. In this case, we may wish to examine the main effects of sex and marital status as well as their interactions. Assume we have the predictor variables MALE, SINGLE, MARRIED, DIVORCED, OTHER. (Note that we have collapsed WIDOW and WIDOWER into OTHER.) In the sex by marital

status matrix there are eight cells, and we can create eight dummy variables
by the following SPSS statements:

IF	(MALE EQ 1 AND SINGLE EQ 1) MSING = 1
IF	(MALE EQ 1 AND MARRIED EQ 1) MMARR = 1
IF	(MALE EQ 1 AND DIVORCED EQ 1) MDIVOR = 1
IF	(MALE EQ 1 AND OTHER EQ 1) MALEOTH = 1
IF	(MALE EQ 0 AND SINGLE EQ 1) FSING = 1
IF	(MALE EQ 0 AND MARRIED EQ 1) FMARR = 1
IF	(MALE EQ 0 AND DIVORCED EQ 1) FDIVOR = 1
IF	(MALE EQ 0 AND OTHER EQ 1) FEMOTHR = 1

The complete regression statement would be:

REGRESSION   VARIABLES = SATIS, MALE,
                  SINGLE TO OTHER, MSING
                  TO FEMOTHR/
                  REGRESSION = SATIS (20, .001,
                  .4) WITH MALE (4), SINGLE TO
                  OTHER (2), MSING TO
                  FEMOTHR (1)

In this case we introduce the MALE variable first followed by the marital
status variables as a group and finally, under forward inclusion, up to seven
out of the eight interactive variables. If each of the eight cells of the interactive portion of the design matrix has a large number of observations,
seven interactive variables would enter the equation. However, if any of the
cells have no patients, the corresponding variables would be excluded by
the tolerance test. This may be seen by observing that we assigned a value
of .4 to the tolerance parameter, T.

Another type of interactive test involves the situation in which one cell
of the matrix is expected to have a different response from any of the others.
For example, assume that male patients over age 40 are expected to have a
different level of satisfaction from all others. We can dichotomize age by:

IF   (AGE GT 40) OVER40 = 1

and the interactive variable can be specified as:

COMPUTE   MALE4OPL = MALE*OVER40

The same effect could be achieved by:

IF   (AGE GT 40 AND MALE EQ 1) MALE40PL = 1

In both cases, only males over age 40 will have a value of 1 in the interactive variable. The other three categories will have a value of 0. This type of interactive term is known as a *multiplicative interaction*.

13.4.2 Interactions With Interval/Ratio Variables [D]

The second type of interaction might be typified by an experiment concerning the effectiveness of warewashing equipment designed for use in dietetic departments. Assume that the two factors of interest are the wash-water temperature (in degrees above or below 150°F) and the length of the wash cycle (in minutes). Here a multiplicative variable can be created by:

COMPUTE   TEMPMIN = TEMP * MIN

In this situation, both variables in the interaction are ratio variables, but one could be a categorical variable, as in the case of a hypothesized difference in the age relationship to length of stay for males and females. The two distributions of ages could be obtained by:

IF   (MALE EQ 1) MALEAGE = AGE
IF   (MALE EQ 0) FEMAGE = AGE

Problem for Solution (G)

1. Days off Work

   A researcher expects to find that a respondent's age, sex, occupation, and general happiness will affect the number of days the respondent has been off work in a year because of illness.

   a. Construct a data collection table for a model to be tested using *factorial analysis of variance*, to show how to test for the main effects and interactions of the first three independent variables upon the dependent variable.

   b. How would each of the variables be defined and measured in order to fit the ANOVA model properly? Give an example for each variable, and use the example for the rest of the problem.

   c. Assuming that the researcher wants 20 observations per cell, how many completed interviews are required? What problems can arise in trying to get the required number of completed interviews? What sampling strategy can be used to minimize these problems?

   d. Construct a dummy analysis of variance table using assumed numbers. How many degrees of freedom are there for each of the main effects and interactions? State how you would test for the significance of *one* of the main effects and *one* of the interactions.

   e. Construct a multiple regression model (equation) that hypothesizes the main effects only for the four independent variables onto the dependent variable. (i.e., the dependent variable as a function of the independent variables.)

   f. Contrast the measurement of the variables for a multiple regression model, with measurement for the ANOVA model (Part b). Does the use of a multiple regression model change the method of measuring any of the variables? If so, which one(s) and why? If not, why not?

   g. How would interaction effects be tested in a multiple regression model for this problem? Give an example.

   h. Assuming that you have constructed two equivalent models for this problem, how do ANOVA and multiple regression formulations differ in the information they provide about main effects and interactions? (Which allows you to say more, and why?)

   i. Why might we want to use a stepwise regression procedure to test the model rather than testing all variables at once?

Chapter 14

Unbiased Estimates of Regression Coefficients

Objectives

After completing this chapter you should be able to:
1. State the crucial assumptions of the regression model.
2. Name and describe the common problems leading to biased estimates.
3. Describe and perform the routine tests for bias.
4. Name the advanced tests for bias.
5. Name and describe the methods for eliminating problems of biased estimators.

Chapter Map

This chapter contains a large amount of descriptive material and most sections have been assigned the letter code A, although many have second or third codes as well.

Ordinary algebraic formulas are included in Sections 14.3, 14.5.4, 14.5.5 and 14.5.6 and they are assigned the code B.

Matrix algebra is added to Sections 14.2, 14.3, 14.5.3 and 14.6 and they are assigned the code C.

SPSS is used in Sections 14.5.5 and 14.5.6 and they are assigned the letter code D.

14.1 CORRECT AND INCORRECT b VALUES[A]

One of the major purposes of regression analysis is to obtain estimates of the regression coefficients. The coefficients are used in predicting the value of the dependent variable for given or assumed values of the predictor variables. Needless to say, if the b values are not *correct*, the predicted value of the dependent variable may not be correct, and it may be extremely inaccurate. The predicted value is used as a point of reference for an observed value of the dependent variable and may be used to decide whether the observed value is within an appropriate confidence interval, or whether the observation must be considered an outlier. There may be some penalty associated with being an outlier, especially if the regression equation is being used for the purposes of controlling operational activity.

Estimated b values that do not have the true population value as their expected value are called *biased*. Biased b estimates then are incorrect. They yield incorrect estimates of the dependent variable, as well as incorrect confidence intervals. This may lead to incorrect control decisions. Penalties may be inflicted unfairly on those whose performance is acceptable, and those who should be corrected may escape detection.

Unfortunately, the possibility of obtaining biased estimates is ever present. Too often the problems are not recognized, and incorrect decisions are made. The objective of this chapter is to discuss the assumptions of the regression model, the problems that may arise, and methods of detecting and avoiding the problems.

14.2 ASSUMPTIONS OF THE REGRESSION MODEL[A,C]

The coefficients of the regression model are estimated from a sample of all possible observations. A specific form of the relationship between the predictor and dependent variables is assumed, and either the dependent or the predictor variables, or both, may have to be transformed before the model fits the assumptions of a regression model. If the postulated model is correct, the sampling was random, the observations are independent and representative of the population, and no errors were made in recording the data, then the ordinary least squares estimation procedure produces unbiased estimates of the b values and of the statistics based on the coefficients.

The regression model, in matrix notation, is:

$$y = Xb + \epsilon$$

The **Xb** term gives a linear transformation of the **X** values to produce estimates of **y**. The effects of each predictor variable can be added to the effects for all the other variables, and the error can be added to ŷ to obtain **y**. The regression model is often called *linear and additive*.

The distribution of the error terms (the vector ϵ) is assumed to be normal with a zero mean, a constant variance σ^2, and no covariance among errors. Symbolically this is written:

$$\epsilon \sim N(0, \sigma^2 I)$$

The variance/covariance matrix of the errors is represented by a diagonal matrix with an expected value of σ^2 for each element of the diagonal (i.e., $\sigma^2 I$). Constant variance is called *homoscedasticity* and its opposite (a nonconstant variance) is referred to as *heteroscedasticity*.

No assumptions are made about the *statistical distributions* of the predictor variables. The usual assumption is that the predictor variable can be measured *exactly*, and that there is no (statistical) uncertainty about any value in the **X** matrix. The observed values of **y** have a statistical distribution with means and standard errors.

14.3 PROBLEMS LEADING TO BIASED ESTIMATES[A,B,C]

A number of problems that can lead to incorrect estimates of the regression coefficients have been identified. These are:

- heteroscedasticity
- specification error
- bad observations
- lack of independence of observations
- insufficient range of variability in the predictors
- multicollinearity of predictor variables
- changing relationships as time passes

The problem of heteroscedasticity is the violation of the assumption of constant variance for the error terms. Heteroscedasticity is usually detected through examination of a plot of the residuals. When it is detected, heteroscedasticity usually indicates that a specification error has been committed, or that a nonlinear model should be used. In either case, the estimates are biased.

Specification errors occur when the wrong **X** variables are used or the assumption of the form of the relationship is incorrect. Important variables may be omitted from the model while irrelevant ones may be included. The first problem is difficult to correct because there is no positive indication of whether any variable is really missing, and if so which one(s). The second is more easily corrected, because an inspection of the t or F values of the regression coefficients indicates which coefficients are statistically insignificant. However, statistical insignificance may result from other problems as well—in particular, an insufficient range of values in the observed predictor variable.

The third type of specification error is an incorrect form of hypothesized relationship. The relationship may be tested as:

$$y = b_0 + b_1 x_1 + b_2 x_2 + \cdots + e$$

but perhaps a multiplicative model of the form:

$$y = c x_1^{b_1} x_2^{b_2} x_3^{b_3} \cdots \epsilon \qquad (14.5)$$

is appropriate. This expression is linear if both sides of the equation are expressed in logarithms as follows:

$$\log y = b_0 + b_1 \log x_1 + b_2 \log x_2 + \cdots + \log \epsilon$$

Consideration of the underlying physical relationships and their theoretical expression may lead to an alteration of the form of a hypothesized relationship.

Errors in recording the data or in original measurement may also lead to bias through the leverage that is exerted on regression coefficients by an observation that, by error, is quite different from the rest of the observations. In perverse cases, a single erroneous observation can lead to extremely large and highly significant regression coefficients associated with a variable that cannot logically be included in the model. Lay (1978) documents cases where patients with cancers of the bowel or pancreas were incorrectly recorded as having *irritable bowel*, which is a relatively minor problem. The treatment costs associated with these patients were found to be quite high relative to the costs associated with those patients who were correctly classified. As a result, the coefficients pertaining to such variables as surgery and death were found to have high dollar values and proved to be highly significant. However, because of the influence exerted by incorrectly identified patients on the regression coefficients, the relationships proved to be spurious.

Lack of independence of the observations in a study also leads to bias. The interdependence of the observations means that they are related to each other in some unrecognized way. If the mechanism by which they are related can be recognized and measured, then it can be included as a variable in the model. If the cases or observations in a study are sequenced in some fashion (usually time, in time series studies) the Durbin-Watson test may be used to detect this interdependence.

A predictor variable may have an influence in the real life situation but may have only been measured over a portion of the range of values that it may assume. In such a case, the error variance of the response may swamp the systematic variation due to the variable in question, and result in a regression coefficient that is not significantly different from zero. Sometimes there will be a significant coefficient, but it may have a value that is significantly different from the population value.

Multicollinearity is a problem for regression when two or more predictor variables are strongly related to each other. Large simple (Pearson) correlation coefficients are indicative of two variable multicollinear relationships. However, sets of three or more predictor variables may exhibit large multiple correlations without large simple correlations. Since no statistical assumptions are made about the variables in the X matrix, multicollinearity has not been handled as a statistical problem. However, multicollinearity leads to problems of bias and to problems of computability.

In the case of a perfect *linearly dependent* set of predictors (either $r_x = 1.0$ or $R_x = 1.0$), the matrix $X'X$ is *singular*. Singularity means that there is *no* inverse, and that the determinant of $X'X$ is 0. Therefore, there is no solution for the regression coefficients.

However, when r_x or R_x is only *close* to 1 the inverse *does* exist and the b values can be computed. Computer arithmetic works with a limited number of digits of accuracy. With $X'X$ of order 2, the origin of the computational problem can be demonstrated in that large and nearly equal cross-products are subtracted. The difference is often very small compared to the numbers, and, if it is small enough, the limits of the computer may have been such as to leave only 4, 3, 2, 1, or 0 digits of accuracy in the result. Many computer programs use *double precision* arithmetic in order to retain 12 or 13 decimal digits of accuracy, which usually leads to at least 6 to 8 digits of accuracy in the results.

Nearly perfect multicollinearity leads to strong correlations among the b value estimates. Small changes in the observed y and X values lead to large changes in estimated b values, and the correlated b values change simultaneously. Therefore both b values in a correlated pair are computationally unstable and may be biased.

Finally, there is a possible problem of a changing relationship as time passes. If a hypothetical model is cross-sectional (i.e., taken at one point, or period, of time) and estimates of b values are obtained for one year, they may not be correct a few years later, if the underlying physical processes have changed substantially.

14.4 DETECTION OF PROBLEMS[A]

The existence of some of the problems discussed in the preceding section can be detected by a combination of approaches. Some of the detection methods are easy to perform and should be employed on a routine basis for every regression model developed. Some, however, are at the leading edge of the state of the art and are not generally available as of early 1979. For large or important projects these more advanced techniques should be employed.

14.5 ROUTINE TESTS FOR BIAS[A]

The most important test of all is the one of reasonableness, and it involves the least amount of statistics. The questions that must be asked are:

- Do the results appear reasonable?
- Are the variables the appropriate ones?
- Are there any obvious omissions?
- Do the regression coefficients have the right sign and approximately the right value?
- Is there any circularity of definition in the model? (Sometimes the dependent variable may appear in a disguised fashion as a predictor variable, leading to an exceedingly high R^2 value).
- Does the formulation of the model make sense?
- Is there a good theoretical basis for the model?
- Are the results comparable with those of previous similar studies, and if not, are the reasons for the differences fairly clear?
- Are any of the predictor variables so closely related to each other that they must lead to problems of multicollinearity?
- Are the variables, as defined, really meaningful or do they bear no meaning in real life?
- Are good measurements available for the variables or are they so full of errors as to be useless?
- If the model is intended to be used for management purposes in either predicting or controlling, are the variables ones that can be measured ahead of time (for predicting) or ones that can be influenced in an appropriate direction (for control purposes)?

If the model fails to obtain a clean bill of health on the preceding questions, then the model builders either have to start over again or give up. The following more technical considerations need to be undertaken for models that appear basically reasonable.

14.5.1 Significance Tests—F and t[A]

Initial statistical tests of the overall regression and the individual regression coefficients include the F ratio for the regression with k and $(n - k - 1)$ degrees of freedom, and the F ratio or t value for each regression coefficient. If the overall regression is not significant, then the coefficients are all insignificant. If the regression is significant, each coefficient must be evaluated for statistical significance. Insignificant coefficients may indicate that irrelevant variables and resulting bias in the other coefficients are present in the regression equation. Insignificant coefficients for reasonable variables may result from errors of measurement, insufficient range of values of the predictor variable, or multicollinearity.

14.5.2 Step by Step—R Squared[A]

If a multistep regression analysis is used, the next step is to examine the behavior of the R^2 value, the standard error of estimate, and the regression coefficient significance levels from step to step. If a stepwise or a forward inclusion regression is used, the value of R^2 should increase at each step, with the first step representing the largest increase and succeeding steps becoming progressively smaller. The summary table in Figure 12-1 illustrates this point. Here, we observe a sequence of R^2 changes of .938, .015, and .0025. The significance of the additional R^2 at each step can be tested as described in Section 12.4 where we introduce the incremental or hierarchical approach.

If the final value of R^2 is extremely high (say .9 or greater), it may indicate that there is a predictor variable which is merely a transformation of the dependent variable. Such a finding indicates that the model may have been defined using a circular logic. If the final value of R^2 is extremely low (say below .25), so much of the variation is left unexplained that the model is not very useful in prediction.

14.5.3 Step by Step—Standard Error of Estimate[A,C]

In the same series of steps the standard error of estimate (s_{yx}) should be decreasing if there is significant additional explanation of variation at each step. If insignificant variables are added, the standard error will either begin to rise again or to fluctuate. In the example presented in Figures 11-2 and 12-1, the standard deviation of mass, before developing the equation, is 16.1 kilograms. The standard errors for the three steps are: 4.11 kilograms, 3.67 kilograms, and 3.68 kilograms. In this case, the minimum standard error was reached on the second step, and this corresponds with the fact that the third variable was insignificant. The ratio of the minimum standard error to the standard deviation of y gives a rough indication of the amount of improvement in the error with which a prediction is made. In this case, the standard error is roughly 23 percent of the standard deviation, which indicates a substantial gain in accuracy of prediction. In fact, Equation 10.18 presented in Section 10.5.2 shows that the standard error of any one observation is slightly larger than the standard error of the equation. Depending on the value of $x_q{}'$; which corresponds to the new observation, the inflation factor normally ranges from 0 percent to about 5 percent, although in the case of extreme $x_q{}'$ values it has been observed as high as 17 percent.

14.5.4 Step by Step—b Values[B]

The values of the regression coefficients and their standard errors may be examined over the sequence of steps. Fluctuations from step to step are to be expected. However, major changes are automatically cause for suspicion. Such changes are likely to be accompanied by an increase in standard error. A simple t-test may be performed for any regression coefficient to determine the presence of potential bias, as shown in Equation 14.1.

$$t = \frac{b\ \text{initial} - b\ \text{final}}{\text{Std Err}(b\ \text{initial})} \tag{14.1}$$

This test has $(n - k - 1)$ degrees of freedom, where k is the number of variables included in the initial step during which b was estimated.

14.5.5 Residuals[A,B,C]

Following the first simple examinations of the regularly provided statistics, the user should shift attention to plots of the residuals. SPSS provides: (1) a case-sequence plot of standardized residuals and (2) a plot of standardized residuals (the Y-axis) versus the standardized predicted values (the X-axis). Standardized values are obtained by dividing residuals and predicted values by the original standard deviation of the dependent variable.

An inspection of the case-sequence plot of residuals is most useful if the cases have some inherent order. For example, in time series analyses, the cases usually represent consecutive months or years. Patterns (if any) of these residuals can be related to the basic sequence. The desired situation is one in which the residuals are evenly distributed with few or none of the observations being more than 1 or 2 standard deviations from the predicted value. Examination of page 7 of the SPSS printout in Figure 11-2 shows that there is a fairly even distribution with the maximum residual being about .4 standard deviation. In this example, the residuals are exceptionally small.

Figure 14-1 shows the basic desired pattern of residuals in the first plot (a), while the other three plots are representative of typical problems. In plot (b) the residuals gradually change from negative to positive with increasing values of x_s, the sequencing variable (usually time). This indicates that x_s should be added to the set of predictor variables. The third plot shows that the residuals form a quadratic curve, indicating that x_s^2 should be added as a predictor variable. Plot (d) represents the problem of heteroscedasticity, where the variance is obviously changing. The method for correcting this last situation is less apparent. Possibly a multiplicative model should be used by taking the logarithms of both the dependent and predictor variables. Possibly an approach to regression entitled weighted least squares (as opposed to ordinary least squares) should be used, but its use is beyond the scope of this book.

Presented in Figure 14-2 are patterns of standardized residuals (plotted vertically) versus the standardized predicted values (plotted horizontally). The first plot illustrates the desired situation in which the residuals have equal variance regardless of the predicted value and the predictions are evenly distributed about the mean.

The second plot shows a situation where a few cases have extremely high predicted values compared to the majority of cases, which are clustered to the left of the Y-axis. This indicates a highly skewed distribution of the dependent variable. The nature of and the reasons for these high predicted values (skewed) cases should be investigated. They may be anomalous in some way or they may convey special information about rare or special cases. They may be identified by some particular variable, which would serve to separate the cases into two separate groups that could be modelled by separate regressions.

Plot (c) shows a situation of increasing variance, which exhibits unmistakable heteroscedasticity. The possible cures for heteroscedasticity have

Figure 14-1 Patterns of Residuals on a Case-Sequence Plot

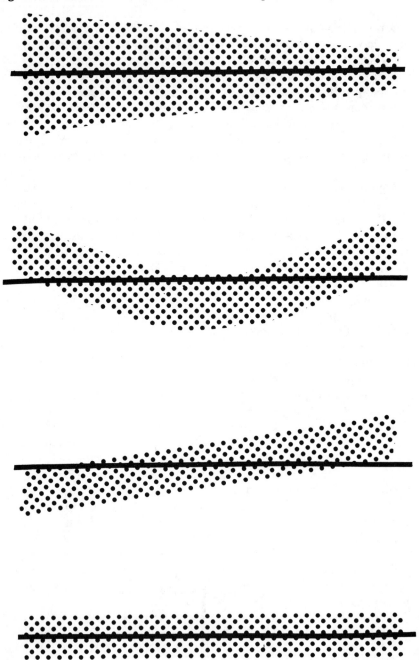

Figure 14-2 Patterns of Residuals versus Predicted Values

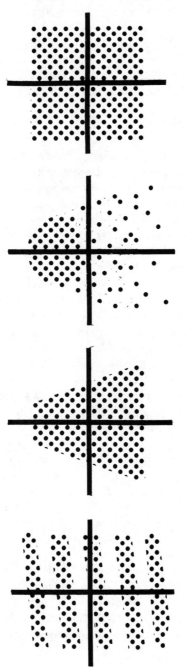

been discussed previously. The last plot (d) shows bars of residuals, which demonstrate the effect of a dominant variable that is probably of an ordinal level of measurement. Its pattern could result from a categorical variable represented by dummy variables, from a ranking (ordinal) variable, or from a higher level of measurement restricted to a few distinct values. In such a situation, an analysis of covariance (again, beyond the scope of this work) may be appropriate for obtaining a set of more even distributions.

14.5.6 Multicollinearity[A,B,D]

The last group of routine tests to be performed deals with the assessment of the possibility that serious multicollinearity exists. Simple tests for multicollinearity are described here, and recent advances in diagnosing the problem are covered in the next subsection.

The first test for multicollinearity is to examine the correlation matrix (of the raw data) looking for high ($|r| > .8$) correlations between pairs of predictor (x) variables. Since SPSS gives the correlation matrix with the dependent (y) variable as well, its row and column must be ignored. To simplify the search for multicollinearity, the authors make it a habit to specify the dependent variable as the first one in the VARIABLES-list. Thus the first row and column refer to the dependent variable, and all others to the predictor variables. Referring to Figure 12-2, we see the first row and column are for MASS, while the others are for AGE, HEIGHT, and SEX. The high correlations in the top row give no cause for concern, because high correlations with the dependent variable are desirable. However, the correlation of .90722 between AGE and HEIGHT does indicate the presence of multicollinearity. This indicates that their b values are highly and negatively correlated as can be verified in Exhibit 10-5 of Section 10.6. A high negative correlation means that an overestimate of one of the coefficients is accompanied by an underestimate of the other. Both b values may be biased, but in opposite directions.

A second test, and prevention mechanism, for multicollinearity is the tolerance value for a variable and the tolerance parameter (discussed in Section 12.8). As discussed in that section, tolerance of a predictor variable is defined as $(1 - R_x^2)$ and is the proportion of the variable's sum of squares not explained by other predictor variables. A small tolerance indicates that the variable is a member of a highly related set, and indicates a problem of multicollinearity. A tolerance of zero would indicate a perfectly related set of variables. The problem is: "How small is small?" The view taken by those who have developed the major statistical packages has been that low tolerance of a variable causes computational problems, and very little attention has been paid to the problem of bias. From the point of view of computability, severe instability arises when tolerance is less than .001, which is the default value used by SPSS. From the point of view of bias, however, problems arise for a pair of variables if $r > .8$ and therefore $r^2 > .64$. By extension to multiple variable collinearity, $R_x^2 > .64$ seems a reasonable maximum, and therefore a tolerance limit of approximately .36 is appropriate. The authors habitually use a tolerance parameter setting of .4 in SPSS that is slightly more conservative. Some authors have argued that it should be set as low as .2 to correspond to $r = .9$, but the following demonstration provides a counter argument.

In the example used thus far, there is a small empirical demonstration of the problem. Figure 12-3 showed a regression of MASS with AGE to SEX chosen in a forward inclusion mode under the control of the F and tolerance parameters, with values 3 and .4, respectively. On the first step AGE was selected with a b value of 4.020 and standard error .237. This is highly significant. No second step is permitted, because HEIGHT with an acceptable F value fails the tolerance test, while the opposite is true for SEX. HEIGHT would be significant if included, but what would be the effect on the regression coefficients? Part of the answer was found in Figure 12-1 where AGE, HEIGHT and SEX were entered, in that order under control of even inclusion levels. To illustrate the bias introduced by collinearity the results are summarized in Table 14-1.

Inspection of the changes for AGE from the first to the second step shows a highly significant decrease in the b value as well as an increase in the standard error for which the F ratio is $.503^2 / .237^2 \cong 4.5$ which is significant at the .05 level. HEIGHT was not entered on the first step. However,

Table 14-1 Effects of Collinearity on AGE and HEIGHT Regression Coefficients

Variable	First Step		Second Step		Third Step	
	b	Std Err(b)	b	Std Err(b)	b	Std Err(b)
AGE	4.020	0.237	2.918	0.503	2.933	0.504
HEIGHT	—	—	0.189	0.078	0.185	0.078
SEX	—	—	—	—	−1.586	1.611

if we had entered HEIGHT on the first step, the corresponding b value would have been

$$b_{y2} = r_{y2} \frac{s_y}{s_2} = .93043 \times \frac{16.1078}{24.9571}$$

$$\cong .601$$

This is again very different from the regression coefficient for HEIGHT, derived in the second step of the analysis. This finding indicates the bias which is introduced when highly related variables are included as independent variables in the regression equation.

Two separate points are to be drawn from the preceding discussion of tolerance and the changing b values. First, the tolerance of HEIGHT on the second step was .19, which is close to the .2 level suggested previously as being arguable for the tolerance limit. Substantial differences are observed in the b values obtained in the sequential steps of the example. Significant bias may be found with tolerance values in the range of .2, and therefore a higher tolerance limit seems reasonable.

The second point is that examination of the changes in b values from step to step will disclose significant differences. These differences may be due to multicollinearity and the resulting bias. Therefore, examination of changes in the b values from step to step is one of the tests that should routinely be performed to detect bias resulting from the presence of multicollinearity.

In summary, then, the routine tests for multicollinearity should include:

- examination of the correlation matrix for large pairwise correlations ($r > .8$)
- setting the tolerance parameter to approximately .4 or inspecting the tolerance level of variables for values of less than .4
- inspection of changes in the b values for significant differences from step to step

Evidence from two or more of these should be sought in order to demonstrate the presence of bias which results from multicollinearity.

In addition to the tests for multicollinearity, the model should be assessed on a routine basis for:

- reasonableness
- statistical tests on the overall regression and regression coefficients

- the behavior of R^2 and s_{yx}^2
- pattern of residuals

Any of these tests may reveal that the model is inadequate and that the regression coefficient estimates are biased.

14.6 ADVANCED TESTS FOR BIAS[A,C]

The tests discussed in the preceding section are simple and should be applied routinely. In addition, there are also other more powerful tests that have been developed recently. Moreover, there are other methods that have been known for some time, which are beyond the scope of this text, but can be described in general terms. Included in the more advanced techniques are an improvement of the tolerance test described previously, the use of *factor analysis* to determine which predictor variables are highly correlated, the use of a *singular value decomposition* method to detect multicollinearity and diagnose its degrading effects, and the detection of influential observations, or cases, which when deleted would modify the regression results substantially.

The tolerance test previously mentioned operates at the time a variable is being considered for entry into the regression model. However, the practice has been questioned recently. It is evident that a variable entering the equation during a later stage may share sufficient common variability with other variables introduced into the equation at earlier steps so that a linearly dependent set is formed without the entering variable exhibiting a low tolerance. Because of this problem, the Biomedical Computer Programs (BMDP)—Series P have recently instituted a recomputation of the tolerance for all included variables at each step. A variable that fails on the basis of its recomputed tolerance is removed from the regression.

Factor analysis is a well-known technique but beyond the scope of this work. Its purpose is to detect groupings of related variables among a large set of variables. Each group is called a *factor*, and each factor is chosen to be as independent of other factors as possible. Each factor is a linear combination of the original variables, and the combinations are chosen to be relatively orthogonal to or uncorrelated with each other. Recall from our discussion of *contrasts* in analysis of variance, that a contrast, c, was defined as a linear combination of the cell means, and that two contrasts c_1 and c_2 were orthogonal to each other if $c_1 'c_2 = 0$. The definition is equivalent to the definition of zero covariance and correlation. In regression analysis the orthogonal factors developed from the set of predictor variables can be used to detect whether there are highly multicollinear variables. If two or more variables are found to be highly collinear, a single factor that combines the related variables can be used as a predictor in the regression analysis. Alternatively, it is possible to drop all but one of the variables in a factor and thus avoid the problem.

The *singular value decomposition* method (Belsley 1976) is related to the initial steps of factor analysis but uses a method of computation that produces more numerically reliable results. These are referred to as *singular values* and correspond to *eigenvalues* in factor analysis. There are k singular values for k predictor variables, and those with small or zero values indicate strong or perfect dependencies. Smallness is defined in terms of the ratio of the largest singular value, to each of the others, giving $(k - 1)$ *condition indexes*. Condition indexes ranging from 10 to 1000 represent progressively stronger and more degrading dependencies. This method not only permits the identification of situations in which multicollinearity exists but it also identifies which variables are involved and which are not. Some regression estimates may be severely biased, while others may be immune to the effects. As of early 1979 the software implementing Belsley's work has not become widely available, but when it becomes more widespread it appears to provide a more satisfactory approach to the diagnosis of multicollinearity than any previously published approach.

Recent interest has also focused on the detection of individual observations which, if removed from the matrix X would result in: changed regression coefficients; changed variances of the b values; or large studentized residuals, which are relatively distant from the center of mass of the other observations in terms of the predictor variables only (Cook 1977; Welsch and Kuh 1977). The idea of deleting an observation row from the X matrix is important. All of the inferences about y values discussed in Section 10.5.2 deal with new, independent, single observations. They do not strictly apply to observations used in estimating the b values. The thrust of the two articles is to judge the differences that would be observed, for each observation in turn, if that observation had not been included originally.

All of the methods described in this section are relatively advanced approaches to the detection and/or correction of problems in the use of multiple regression. As time passes and the software becomes more generally available, these techniques will move into the realm of routine tests. Some of them are already being programmed in the set of statistical analysis programs known as the Biomedical Computer Programs (BMDP), which *are* widely distributed, but are more difficult than SPSS for novices to use.

14.7 METHODS FOR THE ELIMINATION OF PROBLEMS OF BIASED ESTIMATORS IN REGRESSION[A]

The preceding methods have been primarily oriented to detection and diagnosis of problems leading to biased estimates of the regression coefficients. In passing, methods of eliminating the problems have been discussed, and we now summarize these techniques in this section.

The problem of including irrelevant variables can be resolved in some cases by discarding those variables which do not make significant contribution either in terms of the standard regression test of the t or F statistics based on the standard errors of the coefficients, or in terms of the hierarchical approach measured by the change in R^2. Also multicollinear variables may be excluded by the use of a critical tolerance level.

In much sociological and management research the use of multiple regression is often exploratory without a strongly developed body of theory dictating exactly which variables must (or must not) be included in a given model. In such a situation there is relative freedom to add or delete variables that seem appropriate or inappropriate respectively. In much economic theory and its testing via econometrics there is little freedom to do so. In this case, the theoretical specification of the model precedes empirical examination. Thus, the determination of which variables are significant, or are multicollinear, and so on, leaves the researcher in a quandry because deletion of variables, and trying again, are not allowed.

Another approach (where allowable) is to use factor analysis to determine which original variables are redundant, or which can be combined to create relatively independent factors. The use of factor analysis leads to some difficulties of interpretation beyond the scope of this book.

The approach of dropping apparently anomalous cases appears promising. However, there is an important decision to be made for each case dropped. Here, we must decide whether a case is truly anomalous or whether it is providing valuable information about the behavior of the system from which it was drawn.

Lastly, if there are problems not easily resolved by other methods, it may be necessary to determine whether or not a different form of model is required. Perhaps a multiplicative form may be necessary, with linearity of form restored by transforming both the dependent and predictor variables into logarithms.

Substantial emphasis has been placed in this section of Chapter 14 on the problems inherent in the use of multiple regression, their diagnosis, and possible correction. The tool is powerful but easily misused, misapplied, and misunderstood, especially since little guidance has heretofore been provided to novices about the pitfalls and how to avoid them. We hope that this presentation will help to overcome this problem.

BIBLIOGRAPHY

Belsley, D. A. "Multicollinearity: Diagnosing Its Presence and Assessing the Potential Damage It Causes Least-Squares Estimation." Unpublished Working Paper #154, National Bureau of Economic Research, Inc. Cambridge, Mass., October 1976.

Cook, R. D. "Detection of Influential Observation in Linear Regression." *Technometrics,* vol. 19, no. 1, February 1977, pp. 15–18.

Lay, C. M. "Disease Costing in an Ambulatory Clinic: Disease and Physician Profiles and the Selection of Patients for Review." Unpublished Ph.D. Dissertation, Alfred P. Sloan School of Management, Massachusetts Institute of Technology, May 1978.

Welsch, R. E. and Kuh, E. "Linear Regression Diagnostics." Working Paper WP923-77, Alfred P. Sloan School of Management, Massachusetts Institute of Technology, Cambridge, Mass., April 1977.

Problems for Solution[(G)]

1. Disease Costing

In a disease costing study at a large clinic a regression equation was developed to predict the total cost of treating patients (with specific diseases).

The *dependent* variable was:

COST99 = total episode cost in $

The *independent* variables were:

AGE = the patient's age in years
SEX = female = 0; male = 1
PROXIM = patient's residence proximity to the clinic (categories 1-9 ranging from the same city to 1,000s of miles)
REFER = not referred = 0; referred to the clinic = 1
TOPMD1 = number of physicians seen at clinic
TWEIGHT = total diagnoses weighted for severity
NUMDIAG = total number of diagnoses

It is hypothesized that some combination of the demographic variables (AGE, SEX, and PROXIM) and the *need* variables (REFER to NUMDIAG) will explain a substantial amount of variability in the cost of treatment. Cases of patients whose costs are much higher or lower than the predicted value are to be reviewed by the Utilization Review Committee. The SPSS regression run is provided in Exhibit 14-1.

In answering the following questions, state whatever assumptions you may consider necessary.

a. By itself which variable explains the most variance in COST99 and which the least? How much does each explain?

b. For each of the first three steps of the regression equation, what percentage of the variance of COST99 is explained? How much explanation is added by the second variable and then by the third?

375

Exhibit 14-1 Disease Costing

```
***** REGRESSION PROBLEM REQUIRES   1536 BYTES WORKSPACE, NOT INCLUDING RESIDUALS *****

                RUN SUBFILES      (IDBL,ULCR,LIVR,GALL)
                REGRESSION        VARIABLES = COST99,AGE,SEX,PROXIM,REFER,TOPMD1,TWEIGHT,NUMDIAG/
                                  REGRESSION = COST99 WITH AGE TO NUMDIAG (1)
                STATISTICS        1,2

HAH5141 FINAL EXAM - AUGUST 1976                                                         09/22/76       PAGE   2

FILE   ALLGI2    (CREATION DATE = 27/27/76)   PATIENTS WITH GI PRIMARY PROB WITH SUBFILE BY DIAG GROUP
SUBFILE  IDBL          ULCR        LIVR        GALL

VARIABLE       MEAN        STANDARD DEV        CASES

COST99      514.6974        443.8074          1026
AGE          44.7466         15.1617          1026
SEX           1.5955          0.4910          1026
PROXIM        3.4263          1.7317          1026
REFER         0.4346          0.4965          1026
TOPMD1        7.7593          5.3452          1026
TWEIGHT       1.7218          1.0466          1026
NUMDIAG


HAH5141 FINAL EXAM - AUGUST 1976                                                         04/22/76       PAGE   3

FILE   ALLGI2    (CREATION DATE = 27/27/76)   PATIENTS WITH GI PRIMARY PROB WITH SUBFILE BY DIAG GROUP
SUBFILE  IDBL          ULCR        LIVR        GALL

CORRELATION COEFFICIENTS

A VALUE OF 99.00000 IS PRINTED
IF A COEFFICIENT CANNOT BE COMPUTED.

           COST99      AGE       SEX       PROXIM    REFER     TOPMD1    TWEIGHT   NUMDIAG
COST99    1.00000    0.19109   -0.00192    0.03443   0.07535   0.63779   0.41474   0.32546
AGE       0.19109    1.00000    0.00173    0.14195   0.12223   0.10361  -0.27281   0.30910
SEX      -0.00192    0.00173    1.00000    0.02695   0.04407   0.01475   0.11256  -0.05082
PROXIM    0.03443    0.14195    0.02695    1.00000   0.21728   0.11843   0.08279   0.07801
REFER     0.07535    0.12223    0.04407    0.21728   1.00000   0.03304   0.04326  -0.03301
TOPMD1    0.63779    0.10361    0.01475    0.11843   0.03304   1.00000   0.28939   0.25361
TWEIGHT   0.41474   -0.27281    0.11256    0.08279   0.04326   0.28939   1.00000   0.85550
NUMDIAG   0.32546    0.30910   -0.05082    0.07801  -0.03301   0.25361   0.85550   1.00000
```

Exhibit 14-1 Continued

```
MAHS141 FINAL EXAM - AUGUST 1976                                           08/22/76        PAGE   4

FILE   ALLG12   (CREATION DATE = 07/27/76)   PATIENTS WITH GI PRIMARY PROB WITH SUBFILE BY DIAG GROUP
SUBFILE  TRBL            ULCR           GALL           LIVR
* * * * * * * * * * * * * * * * * * * * *   M U L T I P L E   R E G R E S S I O N   * * * * * * * * * * * * * *   VARIABLE LIST   1
                                                                                                           REGRESSION LIST  1
DEPENDENT VARIABLE..      COST02     TOTAL $ - TOTAL EPISODE
VARIABLE(S) ENTERED ON STEP NUMBER   1..    TOPM01      NUMBER OF DIFFERENT PHYSICIANS VISITED

MULTIPLE R        .63779             ANALYSIS OF VARIANCE       DF        SUM OF SQUARES      MEAN SQUARE        F
R SQUARE          .40677             REGRESSION                 1.       82122854.70392     82122854.70392   702.14900
ADJUSTED R SQUARE .40619             RESIDUAL                1024.      119766321.57898       116959.29842
STANDARD ERROR  341.99313

------------ VARIABLES IN THE EQUATION ------------           ----------- VARIABLES NOT IN THE EQUATION -----------

VARIABLE           B          BETA     STD ERROR B      F           VARIABLE      BETA IN      PARTIAL     TOLERANCE      F

TOPM01        210.41562    .63779      7.94078       702.149         AGE          0.12635      0.16317     0.93326     27.980
(CONSTANT)    193.92505                                              SEX         -0.01134     -0.01417     0.99978      0.222
                                                                    PROXIM        0.02268      0.02945     0.99966      0.888
                                                                    REFER         0.05434      0.07052     0.99891      5.112
                                                                    TWEIGHT       0.25121      0.31220     0.91625    110.479
                                                                    NUMDIAG       0.17496      0.21973     0.93568     51.898

* * * * * * * * * * * * * * * * * * * * * * * * * * * *   TWEIGHT   WEIGHT ACROSS ALL DIAGNOSES   * * * * * * * * * * * * * * * * *

VARIABLE(S) ENTERED ON STEP NUMBER   2..    TWEIGHT

MULTIPLE R        .69161             ANALYSIS OF VARIANCE       DF        SUM OF SQUARES      MEAN SQUARE        F
R SQUARE          .47832             REGRESSION                 2.       93796356.67115     46898178.33558   443.84851
ADJUSTED R SQUARE .46735             RESIDUAL                1023.     108092819.61174       105662.58227
STANDARD ERROR  325.05781

------------ VARIABLES IN THE EQUATION ------------           ----------- VARIABLES NOT IN THE EQUATION -----------

VARIABLE           B          BETA     STD ERROR B      F           VARIABLE      BETA IN      PARTIAL     TOLERANCE      F

TOPM01        186.43165    .56502      7.88494       559.039         AGE          0.06919      0.09094     0.92491      8.523
TWEIGHT        20.28996    .25121      1.93029       110.479         SEX          0.01829      0.02481     0.99488      0.629
(CONSTANT)     -7.03600                                              PROXIM        0.00324      0.00441     0.99311      0.020
                                                                    REFER         0.03355      0.04565     0.99316      2.134
                                                                    NUMDIAG      -0.12223     -0.08649     0.25807      7.703
```

Exhibit 14-1 Continued

```
HAM141 FINAL EXAM - AUGUST 1976                                                          04/22/76      PAGE   5

FILE   ALLGI2   (CREATION DATE = 07/27/76)   PATIENTS WITH GI PRIMARY PROB WITH SUBFILE BY DIAG GROUP
SUBFILE THRU   ULCR   LIVR   GALL

* * * * * * * * * * * * *   M U L T I P L E   R E G R E S S I O N   * * * * * * * * * * * * *   VARIABLE LIST   1
DEPENDENT VARIABLE..   COST99      TOTAL % - TOTAL EPISODE                                     REGRESSION LIST  1

VARIABLE(S) ENTERED ON STEP NUMBER   7..   AGE

MULTIPLE R          0.68805                    ANALYSIS OF VARIANCE      DF          SUM OF SQUARES     MEAN SQUARE         F
R SQUARE            0.46922                    REGRESSION                 3.         94690317.18868    31563439.06289    300.91584
ADJUSTED R SQUARE   0.46746                    RESIDUAL                1072.        107719385.09422      100489.25156
STANDARD ERROR    323.86319

-------------- VARIABLES IN THE EQUATION --------------         ------------ VARIABLES NOT IN THE EQUATION ------------
VARIABLE          B         BETA    STD ERROR B        F         VARIABLE      BETA IN    PARTIAL    TOLERANCE       F
TOPMD1      145.81718     0.56323     7.45903      552.042        SEX          0.01636    0.02227    0.99405       0.507
TWEIGHT      14.88005     0.27287     1.24901       49.415        PROXIM      -0.00810   -0.01292    0.96500       0.182
AGE           2.02535     0.06919     0.69376        8.523        REFER       -0.02708   -0.03681    0.99117       1.386
(CONSTANT)  -84.92746                                             NUMDIAG     -0.14507   -0.10148    0.26190      10.710

* * * * * * * * * * * * * * * * * * * * * * * * * * * * * * * * * * * * * * * * * * * * * * * * * * * * *

VARIABLE(S) ENTERED ON STEP NUMBER   4..   NUMDIAG     TOTAL NUMBER OF DIAGNOSES

MULTIPLE R          0.68846                    ANALYSIS OF VARIANCE      DF          SUM OF SQUARES     MEAN SQUARE         F
R SQUARE            0.47453                    REGRESSION                 4.         95803095.45511    23950773.86129    230.50847
ADJUSTED R SQUARE   0.47247                    RESIDUAL                1021.       106606380.43379      103904.39445
STANDARD ERROR    322.34159

-------------- VARIABLES IN THE EQUATION --------------         ------------ VARIABLES NOT IN THE EQUATION ------------
VARIABLE          B         BETA    STD ERROR B        F         VARIABLE      BETA IN    PARTIAL    TOLERANCE       F
TOPMD1      136.02727     0.56386     7.42213      559.592        SEX          0.02245    0.03115    0.97703       0.991
TWEIGHT      28.55675     0.35356     3.57646       63.750        PROXIM      -0.00994   -0.01198    0.96551       0.146
NUMDIAG     -51.47726    -0.14507     0.69858        1.531        REFER        0.02639    0.03606    0.99108       1.328
(CONSTANT)  -71.83970
```

Exhibit 14-1 Continued

```
HAHS141 FINAL EXAM - AUGUST 1976                                              03/22/76     PAGE  6
FILE  ALLIG12   (CREATION DATE = 07/27/76)   PATIENTS WITH GI PRIMARY PROB WITH SUBFILE BY DIAG GROUP
SUBFILE  IPHL    ULCR    LIVR   (ALL

* * * * * * * * * * * * * *   M U L T I P L E   R E G R E S S I O N   * * * * * * * * * * * * *
                                                                                VARIABLE LIST  1
                                                                                REGRESSION LIST 1
DEPENDENT VARIABLE..   COST99      TOTAL $ - TOTAL EPISODE

VARIABLE(S) ENTERED ON STEP NUMBER  5..   REFER

                                  ANALYSIS OF VARIANCE
MULTIPLE R          0.68936                          DF      SUM OF SQUARES     MEAN SQUARE          F
R SQUARE            0.47522       REGRESSION          5.    95941028.26358    19188205.65262    184.73159
ADJUSTED R SQUARE   0.47364       RESIDUAL         1020.   105948148.01382      103870.73335
STANDARD ERROR    322.29983
```

```
---------- VARIABLES IN THE EQUATION ----------        ---------- VARIABLES NOT IN THE EQUATION ----------
VARIABLE          B        STD ERROR B       F          VARIABLE     BETA IN     PARTIAL    TOLERANCE      F
TCPMD1       195.91361        7.82093     565.561        SEX          0.02252     0.03073     0.97688     0.963
TWEIGHT       29.34423        3.71834      62.920        PROXIM      -0.01468    -0.01942     0.92760     0.388
AGE           -2.22017        0.72205      10.642
NUMDIAG      -61.31624       18.73564       1.128
REFER        -23.52045
(CONSTANT)   -77.56124
```

```
* * * * * * * * * * * * * *   M U L T I P L E   R E G R E S S I O N   * * * * * * * * * * * * *

VARIABLE(S) ENTERED ON STEP NUMBER  6..   SEX

                                  ANALYSIS OF VARIANCE
MULTIPLE R          0.68972                          DF      SUM OF SQUARES     MEAN SQUARE          F
R SQUARE            0.47571       REGRESSION          6.    96041075.18645    16006845.86447    154.09796
ADJUSTED R SQUARE   0.47262       RESIDUAL         1019.   105848101.09605      103974.43386
STANDARD ERROR    322.22565
```

```
---------- VARIABLES IN THE EQUATION ----------        ---------- VARIABLES NOT IN THE EQUATION ----------
VARIABLE          B        STD ERROR B       F          VARIABLE     BETA IN     PARTIAL    TOLERANCE      F
TCPMD1       195.62147        7.43025     561.959        PROXIM      -0.01412    -0.01877     0.92703     0.359
TWEIGHT       28.89428        3.61442      63.862
AGE           -2.28330        0.72215      10.547
NUMDIAG      -61.49364       18.49364       1.113
REFER        -23.34745
SEX           20.74626
(CONSTANT) -109.87879
```

Exhibit 14-1 Continued

MAHS141 FINAL EXAM - AUGUST 1976   04/22/76   PAGE 7

FILE ALLG12 (CREATION DATE = 3/22/76) PATIENTS WITH GI PRIMARY PROB WITH SUBFILE BY DIAG GROUP
SUBFILE INAL   ULCR   LIV3   GALL

* * * * * * * * * * * * * * * * * M U L T I P L E R E G R E S S I O N * * * * * * * * * * * * * * * *

DEPENDENT VARIABLE..   COST99   TOTAL $ - TOTAL EPISODE

VARIABLE(S) ENTERED ON STEP NUMBER 7..   PROXIM

MULTIPLE R	0.68995	
R SQUARE	0.47590	
ADJUSTED R SQUARE	0.47229	
STANDARD ERROR	322.33710	

ANALYSIS OF VARIANCE

	DF	SUM OF SQUARES	MEAN SQUARE	F
REGRESSION	7.	9627317130 9515	13725841.42734	132.05211
RESIDUAL	1018.	105813904.88774	103939.49692	

---------- VARIABLES IN THE EQUATION ----------   ---------- VARIABLES NOT IN THE EQUATION ----------

VARIABLE	B	BETA	STD ERROR B	F		VARIABLE	BETA IN	PARTIAL	TOLERANCE	F
TOPMD1	185.57424	0.56242	7.83311	561.263						
TWEIGHT	24.92113	0.35939	3.61603	47.557						
AGE	2.94174	0.04407	0.74621	15.483						
NUMDIAG	-62.35378	-0.09579	18.46091	11.402						
REFRO	22.04578	0.02440	20.49562	1.129						
SEX	-1.64157	0.02219	2.75557	0.933						
PROXIM	-102.24926	-0.01412	6.14594	0.359						
(CONSTANT)										

MAXIMUM STEP REACHED

MAHS141 FINAL EXAM - AUGUST 1976   04/22/76   PAGE 8

FILE ALLG12 (CREATION DATE = 3/22/76) PATIENTS WITH GI PRIMARY PROB WITH SUBFILE BY DIAG GROUP
SUBFILE INAL   ULCR   LIV3   GALL

* * * * * * * * * * * * * * * * * M U L T I P L E R E G R E S S I O N * * * * * * * * * * * * * * * *

DEPENDENT VARIABLE..   COST99   TOTAL $ - TOTAL EPISODE

SUMMARY TABLE

VARIABLE	MULTIPLE R	R SQUARE	RSQ CHANGE	SIMPLE R	B	BETA
TOPMD1 NUMBER OF DIFFERENT PHYSICIANS VISITED	0.63779	0.40677	0.40677	0.63779	185.57424	0.56242
TWEIGHT WEIGHT ACROSS ALL DIAGNOSES	0.64151	0.46459	0.05782	0.41474	24.92113	0.35939
AGE	0.68485	0.46902	0.00441	0.29441	-62.35374	0.04407
NUMDIAG TOTAL NUMBER OF DIAGNOSES	0.68436	0.47453	0.00551	-0.19316	-62.35374	-0.09579
REFRO	0.68972	0.47522	0.00068	0.07535	22.04731	0.02489
SEX	0.68972	0.47571	0.00050	-0.00192	-1.64157	-0.02218
PROXIM	0.68995	0.47590	0.00018	0.03443	-102.24926	-0.01412
(CONSTANT)						

c. How can the significance of the equation be tested at any step? Answer this by explaining what ratio is formed, what it means, what its components are, and how it is tested. Explain the number of tails this test has. Is the equation significant at Step 5? (Show your work.)

d. For Step 3, what is the 95% confidence interval for the *b* value for AGE? Is it significant? Show your work.

e. For this regression, are there any problems of multicollinearity? Give a detailed reason for your answer. What effect does multicollinearity have on calculated *b* values? What can be done to avoid the problem?

2. **Ontario Per Case**

In a study of the average cost per patient (case) in Ontario hospitals, a regression equation approach was used. The objective was to predict, for any one hospital, the expected average cost per patient, based on a number of variables associated with the hospital's operations. Hospitals with predicted cost very different from the actual could be investigated to determine the reasons for the differences.

A sample SPSS run is shown in Exhibit 14-2 using a forward selection multiple regression approach. The meanings of the variable names are as follows:

PERCASE = average cost per case (dependent variable)
LABUNITS = lab units per case (based on number of separations)
RADIOLGY = radiological examinations per case (separations)
PHYSIOTH = physiotherapy patient attendances per case (")
EXPALOS = expected average length of stay weighted for patient age, sex and diagnosis as drawn from the Ontario Relative Stay Index Report
FTEMPLOY = full-time equivalent employees per 1000 patient days
OCCUPNCY = deviation of average occupancy rate from 77.59% (percentage points)
OCCUPSQ = OCCUPNCY squared
OVRUNDR = days over or under ALSEXP (per case)

a. For each step of the regression, how much variance is explained?

b. Is the regression equation significant in all steps? Explain.

c. Are there any problems with multicollinearity? Explain.

d. Are there any nonsignificant *b* values in the final step? Interpret the meanings of the *b* values, taking into account their direction and practical importance.

e. Interpret the printouts of residuals.

Exhibit 14-2 Ontario PER Case

```
STATISTICAL PACKAGE FOR THE SOCIAL SCIENCES                                        04/16/79          PAGE   1
SPSS FOR OS/360, VERSION H, RELEASE 8A, AUGUST 1978

DEFAULT SPACE ALLOCATION..         ALLOWS FOR..          64 TRANSFORMATIONS
WORKSPACE     44300 BYTES                               256 RECODE VALUES + LAG VARIABLES
TRANSPACE      5400 BYTES                              1024 IF/COMPUTE OPERATIONS

     1  RUN NAME        ONTARIO PER CASE COST
     2  DATA LIST       FIXED / HOSP34 1-2, PERCASE 6-11, LABUNITS 12-19,
     3                  RADIOLGY 20-29, PHYSIOTH 27-33, EXPALOS 34-39,
     4                  FTEMPLOY 39-46, OCCUPNCY 47-55, OVRUNDR 56-59

THE DATA LIST PROVIDES FOR  9 VARIABLES AND 1 RECORDS ('CARDS') PER CASE. A MAXIMUM OF    59 COLUMNS ARE USED ON A RECORD.

WARNING - A NUMERIC VARIABLE HAS A WIDTH GREATER THAN 7. SMALL ROUNDING/TRUNCATION ERRORS MAY RESULT.

LIST OF THE CONSTRUCTED FORMAT STATEMENT..
     (F2.0,F3.0,F8.0,2F7.0,F5.0,F8.0,F9.0,F4.0)

     5  INPUT MEDIUM     DISK
     6  N OF CASES       UNKNOWN
     7  COMPUTE          OCCUPSQ   = OCCUPNCY**2
     8  VAR LABELS       PERCASE,  HOSPITAL AVERAGE COST PER CASE/
     9                   LABUNITS, AVERAGE LAB UNITS PER CASE/
    10                   RADIOLGY  AVG. XRAY EXAMS PER CASE/
    11                   PHYSIOTH  AVG. PHYSIOTHERAPY ATTENDANCES PER CASE/
    12                   EXPALOS   HOSP. MATCHED AVG. LENGTH OF STAY IN MSJ/
    13                   FTEMPLOY  FULL-TIME EMPLOYEES PER 1000 PAT.DAYS/
    14                   OVRUNDR   DAYS PER CASE +OR- FROM MATCHED AVG LOS/
    15                   OCCUPNCY  PERCENTAGE POINTS +OR- FROM GROUP AVG./
    16                   OCCUPSQ   SQUARE OF OCCUPANCY DEVIATION/
    17  REGRESSION       VARIABLES = PERCASE TO OCCUPSQ/
    18                   REGRESSION = PERCASE WITH LABUNITS TO OCCUPSQ (1) OCCUPSQ (1) RESID = 0
    19  STATISTICS       1,2,4,6

***** REGRESSION PROBLEM REQUIRES  1872 BYTES WORKSPACE, NOT INCLUDING RESIDUALS *****

    20  READ INPUT DATA

    92 CASES FROM SUBFILE NONAME  .  END OF DATA WAS ENCOUNTERED ON LOGICAL UNIT # 8

AFTER READING
```

Exhibit 14-2 Continued

```
ONTARIO PER CASE COST                                                04/18/79      PAGE    2
FILE    NONAME    (CREATION DATE = 04/18/79)
```

VARIABLE	MEAN	STANDARD DEV	CASES
PERCASE	678.7408	128.5055	92
LABUNITS	353.4996	110.7756	92
RADIOLGY	3.2460	0.3937	92
PHYSIOTH	2.3450	0.8965	92
EXPALOS	8.0337	0.6394	92
FTEMPLOY	5.0471	0.8772	92
OCCUPNCY	0.4734	8.7329	92
OVRUNDR	0.0587	0.7956	92
OCCUPSQ	75.6584	120.4199	92

```
ONTARIO PER CASE COST                                                04/18/79      PAGE    3
FILE    NONAME    (CREATION DATE = 04/18/79)
```

CORRELATION COEFFICIENTS

A VALUE OF 99.00000 IS PRINTED
IF A COEFFICIENT CANNOT BE COMPUTED.

	PERCASE	LABUNITS	RADIOLGY	PHYSIOTH	EXPALOS	FTEMPLOY	OCCUPNCY	OVRUNDR	OCCUPSQ
PERCASE	1.00000	0.47863	0.35095	0.33025	0.56169	0.40209	0.15687	0.48916	-0.00852
LABUNITS	0.47863	1.00000	0.22773	0.15178	0.16379	0.19905	0.08269	0.19657	-0.12230
RADIOLGY	0.35095	0.22773	1.00000	0.31167	0.10813	0.00407	-0.14119	0.21955	-0.16795
PHYSIOTH	0.33025	0.15178	0.31167	1.00000	0.21036	0.02191	0.05025	0.16445	-0.01231
EXPALOS	0.56169	0.16379	0.10813	0.21036	1.00000	0.06933	0.21301	0.24059	-0.13568
FTEMPLOY	0.40209	0.19905	0.00407	0.02191	0.06933	1.00000	0.02889	0.11203	0.01429
OCCUPNCY	0.15687	0.08269	-0.14119	0.05025	0.21301	0.02889	1.00000	0.17776	-0.35657
OVRUNDR	0.48916	0.19657	0.21955	0.16445	0.24059	0.11203	0.17776	1.00000	-0.04739
OCCUPSQ	-0.00852	-0.12230	-0.16795	-0.01231	-0.13568	0.01429	-0.35657	-0.04739	1.00000

Exhibit 14-2 Continued

```
ONTARIO PER CASE COST

FILE   NONAME   (CREATION DATE = 04/18/79)                      04/18/79        PAGE   4

* * * * * * * * * * * * * * * * * * * *   M U L T I P L E   R E G R E S S I O N   * * * * * * * * * * * * * * * * * * * * * *

DEPENDENT VARIABLE..    PERCASE   HOSPITAL AVERAGE COST PER CASE                              VARIABLE LIST   1
                                                                                             REGRESSION LIST  1

VARIABLE(S) ENTERED ON STEP NUMBER  1..   EXPALOS   HOSP. MATCHED AVG. LOS BASED ON RSI

MULTIPLE R              0.55169             ANALYSIS OF VARIANCE      DF      SUM OF SQUARES      MEAN SQUARE        F
R SQUARE               0.31550             REGRESSION                 1.     474107.50630       474107.50630     41.48193
ADJUSTED R SQUARE      0.30789             RESIDUAL                  90.    1028032.28964       11429.24766
STANDARD ERROR        106.90766

---------- VARIABLES IN THE EQUATION ----------            ------------ VARIABLES NOT IN THE EQUATION ------------

VARIABLE          B           BETA      STD ERROR B        F        VARIABLE      BETA IN      PARTIAL      TOLERANCE        F

EXPALOS       112.9846      0.56169      17.52689      41.482       LABUNITS     0.39729     0.47371     0.97317      25.750
(CONSTANT)   -225.1394                                              RADIOLGY     0.23505     0.35230     0.98331      12.037
                                                                   PHYSIOTH    -0.27399     0.23504     0.95524      10.419
                                                                   FTEMPLOY     0.36490     0.43998     0.93519      21.365
                                                                   OCCUPNCY     0.03999     0.04605     0.95963      0.189
                                                                   OVRUNDR      0.37578     0.44085     0.94212     21.470
                                                                   OCCUPSO      0.06955     0.08327     0.96132      0.621

* * * * * * * * * * * * * * * * * * * * * * * * * * * * * * * * * * * * * * * * * * * * * * * * * * * * * * * * * * * * * *

VARIABLE(S) ENTERED ON STEP NUMBER  2..   LABUNITS   AVERAGE LAB UNITS PER CASE

MULTIPLE R              0.64491             ANALYSIS OF VARIANCE      DF      SUM OF SQUARES      MEAN SQUARE        F
R SQUARE               0.46917             REGRESSION                 2.     704596.27621       352498.13811     39.52994
ADJUSTED R SQUARE      0.45719             RESIDUAL                  89.     797803.51972         8964.08449
STANDARD ERROR         94.67885

---------- VARIABLES IN THE EQUATION ----------            ------------ VARIABLES NOT IN THE EQUATION ------------

VARIABLE          B           BETA      STD ERROR B        F        VARIABLE      BETA IN      PARTIAL      TOLERANCE        F

EXPALOS        99.80686      0.49652      15.73404      40.259      RADIOLGY     0.21928     0.29225     0.94269      8.643
LABUNITS        0.4609770     0.39729      0.09729      25.750      PHYSIOTH    -0.22863     0.30445     0.94141     9.025
(CONSTANT)   -288.3013                                              FTEMPLOY     0.30091     0.24564     0.52228     7.372
                                                                   OCCUPNCY     0.01743     0.02564     0.96228     0.058
                                                                   OVRUNDR      0.21697     0.41697     0.91638    18.520
                                                                   OCCUPSO      0.11133     0.15902     0.97096     2.043
```

Exhibit 14-2 Continued

```
ONTARIO PER CASE COST
FILE   NONAME   (CREATION DATE = 04/18/79)                                              04/18/79        PAGE   5
* * * * * * * * * * * * * * * * * * * *   M U L T I P L E   R E G R E S S I O N   * * * * * * * * * * * * * * * * * *
DEPENDENT VARIABLE..     PERCASE    HOSPITAL AVERAGE COST PER CASE                                    VARIABLE LIST   1
                                                                                                     REGRESSION LIST  1
VARIABLE(S) ENTERED ON STEP NUMBER  3..    OVRUNDR    DAYS PER CASE +OR- FROM MATCHED AVG LOS

MULTIPLE R           0.74927                   ANALYSIS OF VARIANCE      DF       SUM OF SQUARES        MEAN SQUARE          F
R SQUARE             0.56141                   REGRESSION                 3.      84647.76079       28215.92693        37.54711
ADJUSTED R SQUARE    0.54645                   RESIDUAL                  38.      69092.01515         749.68179
STANDARD ERROR      86.54295

-------- VARIABLES IN THE EQUATION --------                      ----- VARIABLES NOT IN THE EQUATION -----
VARIABLE         B        BETA      STD ERROR B         F       VARIABLE     BETA IN      PARTIAL    TOLERANCE        F
EXPA_US     86.16724    0.42975    14.72752         34.231      RADIOLOGY    0.17071      0.24661    0.71592       0.032
LABUNITS    30.30522    0.34537     6.38419         22.648      PHYSIOTH     0.19861      0.29976    0.93105       7.974
OVRUNDR     51.27031    0.31743    11.91555         18.320      FTEMPLOY    -0.23085      0.04530    0.93443      18.027
(CONSTANT) -160.1436                                            OCCUPSQ     -0.11073      0.10679    0.97025       2.420

* * * * * * * * * * * * * * * * * * * * * * * * * * * * * * * * * * * * * * * * * * * * * * * * * * * * * * * * * *
VARIABLE(S) ENTERED ON STEP NUMBER  4..    FTEMPLOY    FULL-TIME EMPLOYEES PER 1000 PAT.DAYS

MULTIPLE R           0.79733                   ANALYSIS OF VARIANCE      DF       SUM OF SQUARES        MEAN SQUARE          F
R SQUARE             0.63573                   REGRESSION                 4.      95777.01305       23944.25408        36.11507
ADJUSTED R SQUARE    0.59693                   RESIDUAL                  37.      54596.77728         827.43422
STANDARD ERROR      79.21764

-------- VARIABLES IN THE EQUATION --------                      ----- VARIABLES NOT IN THE EQUATION -----
VARIABLE         B        BETA      STD ERROR B         F       VARIABLE     BETA IN      PARTIAL    TOLERANCE        F
EXPA_US     84.88892    0.42339    13.49429         39.632      RADIOLOGY    0.13429      0.29534    0.21214       0.493
LABUNITS    31.34575    0.29945     3.07631         19.026      PHYSIOTH     0.23355      0.32327    0.93105       1.644
OVRUNDR     48.06884    0.29761    10.93118         19.337      OCCUPNCY    -0.01771      0.00160    0.93443       0.086
FTEMPLOY    41.14445    0.28095     9.69049         18.027      OCCUPSQ      0.03831      0.13038    0.95992       2.230
(CONSTANT)-373.1948
```

Exhibit 14-2 Continued

```
ONTARIO PER CASE COST

FILE  NONAME   (CREATION DATE = 04/18/79)                                          04/18/79          PAGE   5

* * * * * * * * * * * * * * * * * * * * * *  M U L T I P L E   R E G R E S S I O N  * * * * * * * * * * * * * * * * * * * * *
                                                                                                    VARIABLE LIST  1
DEPENDENT VARIABLE..   PERCASE   HOSPITAL AVERAGE COST PER CASE                                      REGRESSION LIST  1

VARIABLE(S) ENTERED ON STEP NUMBER  5..   PHYSIOTH  AVG. PHYSIOTHERAPY ATTENDANCES PER CASE

MULTIPLE R          0.32221            ANALYSIS OF VARIANCE      DF      SUM OF SQUARES      MEAN SQUARE          F
R SQUARE            0.55633                  REGRESSION          5.    191689.76003       20317.75001        35.09151
ADJUSTED R SQUARE   0.55720                  RESIDUAL           80.    450041.01391      30003.94205
STANDARD ERROR     75.23923

------------------- VARIABLES IN THE EQUATION -------------------        ------------ VARIABLES NOT IN THE EQUATION ------------

VARIABLE              B           STD ERROR B        F            VARIABLE    BETA IN    PARTIAL    TOLERANCE       F

EXPALOS          77.88297        12.98928        35.951          RADIOLGY    0.14300    0.24125    0.94752      4.897
LABUNITS          0.31 58760      0.07430        17.833          OCCUPNCY   -0.05092   -0.03577    0.93672      2.370
OVRUNDR          44.58868        10.43791        18.248          OCCUPSQ     0.09236    0.13966    0.90803      2.223
FTEMPLOY         41.43842         9.12093        20.643
PHYSIOTH         29.45561         9.11774        10.444
(CONSTANT)     -380.71988

* * * * * * * * * * * * * * * * * * * * * * * * * * * *  RADIOLGY  AVG. XRAY EXAMS PER CASE  * * * * * * * * * * * * * * * * *

VARIABLE(S) ENTERED ON STEP NUMBER  6..   RADIOLGY  AVG. XRAY EXAMS PER CASE

MULTIPLE R          0.83269            ANALYSIS OF VARIANCE      DF      SUM OF SQUARES      MEAN SQUARE          F
R SQUARE            0.69337                  REGRESSION          6.    194795.68509       17309.94806        36.03471
ADJUSTED R SQUARE   0.67173                  RESIDUAL           85.    455785.10755      3420.37774
STANDARD ERROR     73.62729

------------------- VARIABLES IN THE EQUATION -------------------        ------------ VARIABLES NOT IN THE EQUATION ------------

VARIABLE              B           STD ERROR B        F            VARIABLE    BETA IN    PARTIAL    TOLERANCE       F

EXPALOS          78.19850        12.71141        37.758          OCCUPNCY    0.01301    0.02221    0.69320      0.041
LABUNITS          0.35770950      0.07431        14.995          OCCUPSQ     0.11527    0.20245    0.94590      3.590
OVRUNDR          41.11972        10.33617        15.820
FTEMPLOY         42.92231         9.02204        22.031
PHYSIOTH         24.05061         9.25794         6.749
RADIOLGY         20.63514         0.32006         4.807
(CONSTANT)     -433.32771
```

Exhibit 14-2 Continued

```
ONTARIO PER CASE COST
FILE   NONAME   (CREATION DATE = 04/18/79)

* * * * * * * * * * * * * * *   M U L T I P L E   R E G R E S S I O N   * * * * * * * * * * * * * * *        04/18/79            PAGE   7
DEPENDENT VARIABLE..   PERCASE    HOSPITAL AVERAGE COST PER CASE                                                                VARIABLE LIST   1
VARIABLE(S) ENTERED ON STEP NUMBER   7..     OCCUPSQ   SQUARE OF OCCUPANCY DEVIATION                                            REGRESSION LIST  1

MULTIPLE R            0.84020          ANALYSIS OF VARIANCE       DF.      SUM OF SQUARES        MEAN SQUARE          F
R SQUARE             0.70594          REGRESSION                  7.     1030842.46390      151343.91340         26.90784
ADJUSTED R SQUARE    0.68143          RESIDUAL                   84.      441097.36714       5200408.34
STANDARD ERROR      72.53057

------------ VARIABLES IN THE EQUATION ------------            ------------ VARIABLES NOT IN THE EQUATION ------------
VARIABLE           BETA          STD ERROR B          F              VARIABLE         BETA IN      PARTIAL      TOLERANCE          F
EXPALOS           81.07059         1.61928          41.272           OCCUPNCY         0.00976      0.11003      0.76125          1.023
LABUNITS          0.2994849        0.07337          16.016
FTEMPDY          49.74823         10.18409          16.005
PHYSIOTH          22.42057         22.007           16.005
RADIOLGY          23.03974          0.14312           0.231
OCCUPSQ           0.12330058        2.88770           0.164
(CONSTANT)       -471.6247          0.06472           3.590


ONTARIO PER CASE COST
FILE   NONAME   (CREATION DATE = 04/18/79)

* * * * * * * * * * * * * * *   M U L T I P L E   R E G R E S S I O N   * * * * * * * * * * * * * * *        04/18/79            PAGE   3
DEPENDENT VARIABLE..   PERCASE    HOSPITAL AVERAGE COST PER CASE                                                                VARIABLE LIST   1
VARIABLE(S) ENTERED ON STEP NUMBER   8..     OCCUPANCY   PERCENTAGE POINTS +OR- FROM GROUP AVG.                                 REGRESSION LIST  1

MULTIPLE R            0.84234          ANALYSIS OF VARIANCE       DF.      SUM OF SQUARES        MEAN SQUARE          F
R SQUARE             0.79954          REGRESSION                  8.     1030251.14035      132281.37251         25.39437
ADJUSTED R SQUARE    0.68154          RESIDUAL                   33.      430498.05509       5205637947
STANDARD ERROR      72.51827

------------ VARIABLES IN THE EQUATION ------------            ------------ VARIABLES NOT IN THE EQUATION ------------
VARIABLE           BETA          STD ERROR B          F              VARIABLE         BETA IN      PARTIAL      TOLERANCE          F
EXPALOS           79.27231         12.74113          36.710
LABUNITS          0.2966362        0.07331          16.295
FTEMPDY          48.33072         10.35005          14.057
PHYSIOTH          22.39432          2.29879          22.033
RADIOLGY          25.31926          0.18146           7.140
OCCUPSQ           0.1504122         0.14095           4.576
OCCUPNCY          1.011823         0.07031           1.023
(CONSTANT)       -466.1426          0.99771

MAXIMUM STEP REACHED

STATISTICS WHICH CANNOT BE COMPUTED ARE PRINTED AS ALL NINES.
```

Exhibit 14-2 Continued

```
ONTARIO PER CASE COST

FILE   NONAME   (CREATION DATE = 04/18/79)
* * * * * * * * * * * * * * * * * * * * * *   M U L T I P L E   R E G R E S S I O N   * * * * * * * * * * * * * * * * *   04/18/79        PAGE  3

DEPENDENT VARIABLE..   PERCASE   HOSPITAL AVERAGE COST PER CASE

                                         SUMMARY TABLE

VARIABLE                                  MULTIPLE R   R SQUARE   RSQ CHANGE   SIMPLE R           B

EXPALOS    HOSP. MATCHED AVG. LOS BASED ON RSI    0.50169    0.31550    0.31550    0.50169     79.27231
LABUNITS   AVERAGE LAB UNITS PER CASE             0.68491    0.46910    0.15361    0.47600     0.29000304
PYRADIO    DAYS PER CASE +DR- FROM MATCHED AVG LOS 0.74927   0.56141    0.09231    0.43916    33.33022
PHYSEMP    FULL-TIME EMPLOYEES PER 1000 PAT.DAYS   0.79793    0.63669    0.07523    0.03209    42.30771
PHYSIOTH   AVG. PHYSIOTHERAPY ATTENDANCES PER CASE 0.82221    0.67603    0.03934    0.38024    25.07424
RADIOLGY   AVG. XRAY EXAMS PER CASE                0.83257    0.69337    0.01734    0.30909    20.24122
OCCUP SQ   SQUARE OF OCCUPANCY DEVIATION           0.84020    0.70594    0.01257    0.10807     1.1311022
OCCUPNCY   PERCENTAGE POINTS +OR- FROM GROUP AVG.  0.84234    0.70954    0.00000    0.13887  -400.14020
(CONSTANT)

                                                                                     VARIABLE LIST    1
                                                                                     REGRESSION LIST  1

                                                                                                 BETA
                                                                                              0.39444
                                                                                              0.25571
                                                                                              0.24041
                                                                                              0.28879
                                                                                              0.19410
                                                                                              0.15445
                                                                                              0.14035
                                                                                              0.06076
```

Exhibit 14-2 Continued

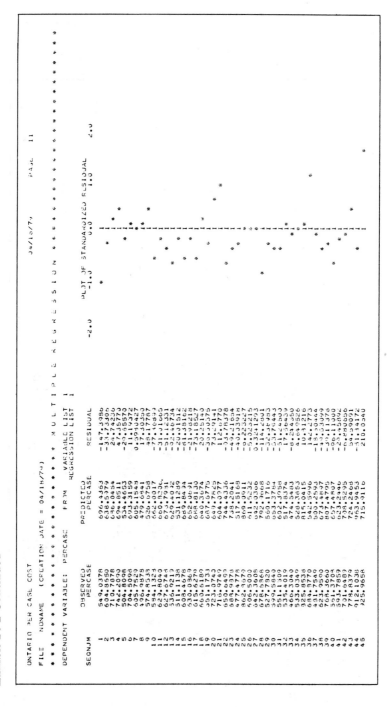

Exhibit 14-2 Continued

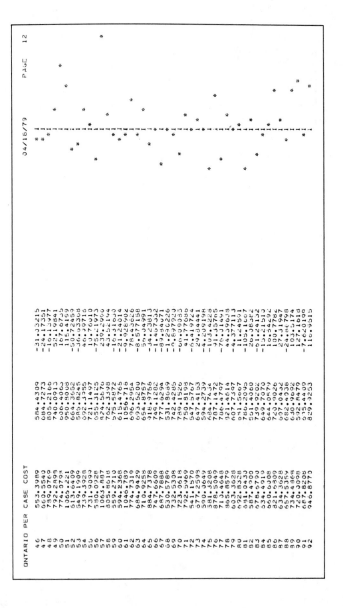

Exhibit 14-2 Continued

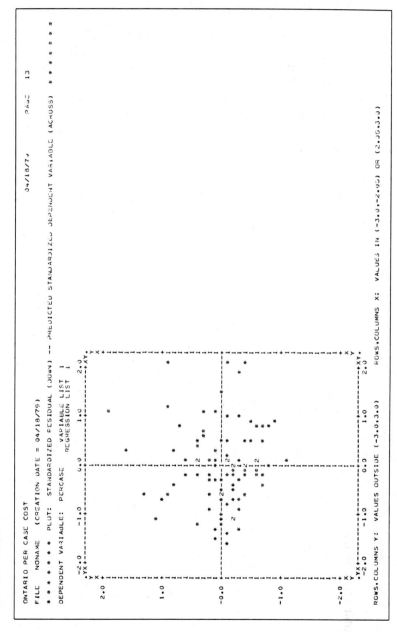

f. For the last step in which all variables are significant, interpret the meanings of the *b* values. Do they make sense? Are there any incongruous values?

g. The people doing the study decide that OCCUPNCY and OCCUPSQ cannot be separated. Either both are included, or neither is to be included. Do they, as a pair, add a significant extra explanation (and therefore qualify for inclusion)?

h. What is the estimated *b* value for the first variable entering: in the first step, in the last step? What is the 95% confidence interval for the *b* value of this variable in the last step? Does this show the final estimate to be significantly different from the initial estimate? What are the causes of *bias* in regression coefficient estimates? Comment on bias in this case.

i. Comment on the behavior of the standard error of the equation from the first step to the last. How does it compare to the standard deviation of the dependent variable?

Part IV

Statistical Modeling

Chapter 15

Statistical Models and Problem Solving

Objectives

After completing this chapter, you should be able to:
1. Describe the methods and process of problem solving.
2. Understand the problems of selecting an appropriate statistical methodology, study design, and sampling techniques.
3. Describe the process of collecting data, as well as the process of preparing data for analysis.
4. Describe the major difficulties inherent in multiple regression analysis.
5. Identify major problems in multiple regression analysis, and employ techniques to avoid identified difficulties.

Chapter Map

Sections 15.1 through 15.7 discuss the basic process of empirical research, and these sections have been assigned the letter code A.

Section 15.8 requires an understanding of Chapters 10 through 14. However, the material is largely descriptive, dealing with the application of the tools and techniques covered in those chapters. This section and its subsections have also been assigned the letter code A.

Section 15.9 provides references to selected health care management research studies using regression analysis. The section has been assigned the letter code A.

15.1 APPROPRIATE USE OF STATISTICAL MODELS[A]

An important difficulty confronting practitioners and students alike involves the appropriate use of the statistical tools that have been described in this text and its companion, Volume I. It almost goes without saying that acquiring a skill in the use of any tool requires practice. Only with repeated use is it easy to determine when a given technique is appropriate for a specific situation. It is possible to gain statistical experience by reading reports that use the tools and techniques of statistics. However, it is best to limit such a review to the area of one's own interest.

It is also important to realize that an ability to manipulate numbers and to perform statistical tests is not the only attribute of a good manager and problem solver. It is necessary to be able to identify the essential aspects of any problem, most of which may not be numerical or statistical in any sense. As a consequence, good insight and a firm conceptual understanding of the situation are required in order to isolate a problem area and develop a remedial course of action. Numbers without such an understanding are sterile, and understanding the dimensions of a problem need not depend on, or even require, quantitative data. However, when viewed from the perspective of this work, we seek to examine the contribution of numbers and statistics to the solution of an underlying problem.

15.2 THE PROBLEM-SOLVING PROCESS[A]

Managers at all levels of responsibility in the health care system continually face problems for which they must find solutions. Frequently, the problems are small and well enough understood that the process of developing a solution may be short and informal. Occasionally, however, a problem is of such magnitude, complexity, and importance that it requires a more formal approach to the development of possible solutions. The resources required for a formal examination of many difficult and complex problems are frequently not available, and the manager must allocate the organization's resources in accordance with the importance of the problems facing the institution. Whether problems are solved formally or informally, a careful and orderly approach is required if management is to discharge the function of problem solving efficiently and effectively.

In general, the problem-solving process consists of the following phases:

- problem identification
- problem analysis
- data collection

- data analysis
- development of tentative solutions
- solution verification with new data
- interpretation and presentation of results
- application of the results to the problem situation

Observe that these phases may be overlapping, repeated or performed in a different sequence. The discussion that follows addresses each of these phases.

15.2.1   Problem Identification[A]

In the initial phase of the problem-solving process, management recognizes that a problem area exists and that a solution is required. A study of the methods used by managers to isolate problems (Pounds 1969) revealed that a number of rules of thumb are employed by administrators to identify problem areas. A problem was defined as a difference between management's perception of an actual situation and the desired situation (Newell and Simon 1963). On the other hand, a solution may be defined as a course of action that will reduce or eliminate the imbalance between the actual and the desired situation. The most frequently employed method of detecting a problem area involves a comparison of the current situation with the situation which existed in the recent past. Unfavorable trends in the length of stay, supply costs, the time required to report the results of various laboratory tests and so forth, are examples of the historical method of identifying problem areas in the health care industry. Planning and budgeting models have been found to be the next most frequently used methods of identifying problem areas. In this regard, the actual financial or operational performance of the institution might be compared with the expected or planned performance which, in turn, may reveal problem areas requiring managerial attention. For example, costs in excess of the budget, fewer x-rays than planned, and a lower occupancy rate than planned would all identify problem areas to hospital administrators. Pounds also reported that the application of standards, criteria, and theory developed outside of the organization was the least commonly employed method of identifying problem areas. Examples of externally developed methods of identifying problem areas in the health care industry involve the previous use of patient scheduling systems based on queuing theory and job shop scheduling systems. Admittedly, administrators must carefully evaluate the validity and applicability of externally developed standards and systems to their own situations. However, management should not reject the possibility of implementing such a system or standard simply because it has been developed elsewhere.

15.2.2   Problem Analysis (A)

The problem analysis or problem specification phase of the problem-solving process requires the manager to identify the most important aspects of the differences that serve to define the problem. Usually, the problem exists within the context of an organization that has established a reasonably well defined set of goals and objectives. For example, the organization could be a physician's office, a meals-on-wheels service, a laboratory, a hospital, a ward, and so on. Frequently, organizations such as these have one or more goals, and the identified problem area may be analyzed in terms of the extent to which it constitutes an obstacle to the attainment of the organizational objectives. When analyzed in these terms, it is possible to define the nature, extent, and importance of the problem.

Once the relationship of the problem to the attainment of organizational goals is understood, management should examine the problem area in greater detail. Such an investigation should be designed to identify specific aspects of organizational activity which are operating improperly or the discovery of relationships that are not adequately understood. As an example of this latter point, suppose that one of the major objectives of management is to preserve the financial viability of the institution and in order to achieve this goal the occupancy rate must be maintained at some specified level. Now, suppose the occupancy rate falls below the specified level which, of course, serves to identify the problem area of interest. In this case, a low occupancy rate could be the result of a poorly functioning admission and discharge system or it could be the result of concurrent changes in the incidence of illness, a change in the size of the population served by the institution, or the mode of treating patients with specific illnesses. In this situation, a formal research effort is required to establish the relationship between the declining occupancy rate and the set of underlying factors. Such an analysis provides the basis for distinguishing between the effects of the various factors on the occupancy rate, which allows management to identify the most important aspects of the problem. This example also serves to illustrate a situation in which data collection and data analysis will not suffice to solve the problem. In this situation, the collection and analysis of data only serve to contribute information about the problem, and these phases of the problem-solving process should not be relied upon to provide guidance in formulating corrective action.

A research problem can usually be stated in terms of a relationship to be examined. Insight into the problem can only be demonstrated by describing the nature of the relationship in words. In section 12.4 of Volume I we saw that a relationship constitutes the linkage between two or more ideas, concepts or variables of interest. When examining the dimensions of a relationship, it is necessary to specify not only the direction of association, but also the reasons for believing that a change in one variable will lead to changes in the others. Before proceeding with the empirical investigation, the researcher must be able to define the variables in operational terms as well as indicate the methods by which the variables are to be measured. An operational definition specifies the actions and instruments required to arrive at a numeric value or measurement of the variable that embodies the concept of interest. When considering the operational statement of the relationship, the researcher must decide whether a statistical study is possible, useful, valid, and warranted.

15.2.3 Analysis of Previous Work Related to the Problem [A]

In our discussion of problem identification, we found that managers tend to rely least of all on standards, criteria, or theories that have been developed by sources external to the organization. However, previous research should be accorded much more importance in the formal problem-solving process. There are many journals devoted to publishing articles and research of interest to managers, and health administrators should be receptive to systems of evaluation that have been developed for use in the health field as well as in other areas of endeavor. When reviewing previous work, the administrator should focus on those studies which have examined:

- issues or relationships dealing with the same or similar problems
- methodologies that have been used to address the same or similar problems
- the concepts and variables that are central to the problem
- the problems of measurement
- the problems of analysis
- the applicability of results to the underlying problem

The analysis of individual articles should be focused on reaching conclusions concerning the strengths and the weaknesses of previous work. In this regard, particular attention should be paid to the adequacy of the formulation and analysis of the problem, to the adequacy of the methodologies and statistical techniques employed, and to the plausibility of the results of the analysis, including a comparison of the expected and the actual results. Such an evaluation provides the basis for avoiding difficulties that have been experienced previously as well as improving the research design of the present study. In this regard, the final phase of the literature review should be devoted to an examination of the relationship of previous studies to the present research and to a specification of how previous work supports or guides the current study.

At this stage of development, a formal proposal should be prepared addressing the following issues. First, the research proposal should specify the problem to be studied as well as the relationships to be examined. Further, the proposal should specify the overall approach that will characterize the study and it should provide an indication of the differences between methodologies employed previously and the approach that will be employed in the present study. In addition, the proposal should include a specification of the operational definitions that will be employed in the study as well as the contribution of the study to the identification of a solution to the underlying problem.

Moreover, the data collection procedures, measurement problems, and methods of overcoming them should be proposed and justified by reference to previous work. Since many variables cannot be measured directly, surrogates or proxy variables should be developed and justified at this stage of the project. Finally, the researcher should specify: (1) methods of analyzing the data; (2) the types of tables and graphs that will be used in the study; (3) the statistical techniques to be employed; (4) where appropriate, the hypotheses to be tested; and (5) the expected results as related to the major problem confronting management.

Care should be exercised when formulating the study so as to select only those variables that are important to the problem and for which data will be collected and analyzed. In this regard, there must be a well-specified reason for the inclusion of each variable to be examined in the project. The selection of too many variables results in two kinds of problems. The first problem involves the inordinately large amount of data required when many variables are selected for analysis, and the second involves the problem of reaching a decision concerning the use of these data once they have been collected. In addition, the researcher must avoid the tendency of collecting an insufficient amount of information as well as the tendency to aggregate data (i.e., to condense several variables into one, or to condense categories of variables) while collecting the data. This is of importance because it is impossible to reconstruct data after they have been collected in an improper form, but statistical packages such as the SPSS Batch System can be used to condense or collapse information as desired. For example, the ages of patients should always be measured in years (or hours or days, for babies) and, if desired, these data can be recoded later into appropriate age ranges.

15.3 SELECTION OF THE APPROPRIATE TYPE OF ANALYSIS[A]

As implied earlier, many of the problems confronting the administrator of a health care facility have quantitative dimensions as well as qualitative nonnumerical components. As a result, both nonnumerical or nonstatistical, and statistical models will be appropriate for various kinds of studies. An understanding of the problem as well as the ability to express that understanding in writing is of the utmost importance when reaching decisions concerning the appropriate type of analysis that should be employed in a given situation. Here, then, it is important to distinguish between those portions of the problem which can, and those aspects which cannot, be expressed numerically and analyzed statistically. When differentiating between these two aspects, it is necessary to develop a clear specification of the problem as well as a clear description of the components of the problem that will be the subject of empirical investigation. With regard to those components which will be investigated empirically, it is usually necessary to specify the relationships to be examined in mathematical or statistical terms, as well as in words.

Concerning those portions of the problem which will be subjected to numerical or empirical examination, the most useful kind of analysis will depend on the hypotheses to be tested, the nature of the relationships, the type of data available for dependent and predictor variables, and whether the study is cross-sectional or longitudinal in design. Statistics based on proportions, including chi-square and other similar statistics, should be employed when analyzing data that are based on counts or frequencies. In these situations, the dependent variable is the number or frequency of cases that exhibit a given attribute such as the number of males, the number of unacceptable laboratory tests, the number of patients requiring a given procedure, the number of patients in various disease categories, or the number of patients experiencing various lengths of stay. On the other hand, statistics based on the t distribution, the normal distribution, or other parametric and nonparametric tests beyond the scope of this work should be used when examining data that arise when we *measure* the attributes associated with a given observation. In this case, the dependent variable is the value assumed by the attribute of each case. Examples of such variables include the mass of a child, as measured in kilograms; the height of an individual, as measured in centimeters; the cost of treating a patient, as measured in dollars; the length of time spent in the operating room, as measured in minutes or fractions of an hour; expenditures in excess of the budget, as expressed in dollars or percentages; the amount of laundry processed, as measured in terms of pounds; and patient satisfaction, as measured on a scale ranging from 1 to 10.

Studies in which a single predictor variable is examined should use simple statistics that are similar to the techniques described in Volume I. Whether used in a descriptive or an inferential mode, distributions, measures of location, measures of variability, and proportions are the simplest statistical tools that may be used appropriately in almost all situations where the analysis of numerical information is required. In addition, a number of nonparametric statistics are also available, but an examination of these methods is beyond the scope of this text. The basic reference in this field (Siegel 1956) is highly recommended to the interested reader. This text is written at a level that makes it easy for nonmathematicians to understand and to use nonparametric methods in a research or problem-solving setting. The more advanced statistical techniques such as analysis of variance and regression analysis are also applicable when examining the relationship between a dependent variable and a single predictor variable. Given that ANOVA and regression analysis are techniques by which we may partition the variability exhibited by the dependent variable into the variation associated with the predictor variable and the error term, these tools represent more powerful tools than the simpler statistical tests. We have seen previously that these techniques allow us to assess the relationship between the dependent variable and the predictor variable by examining the portion of the variation exhibited by the dependent variable that is explained by variability in the independent variable. In many situations, managers are faced with the problem of understanding variability as well as the factors contributing to observed variation. For example, the administrator may be frustrated by the fact that the overall average cost is a very poor predictor of cost in a particular situation. Understanding and the use of the concept of *treatment effects* in analysis of variance may permit a much closer and more accurate prediction of cost than previous methods of forecasting costs.

Many problems confronting the manager are quite complex and require an examination of multiple predictor variables. In this work we have limited our discussion of the more sophisticated statistical techniques to two-way and factorial analysis of variance, as well as multiple regression techniques. It should be noted, however, that techniques that are more sophisticated than the methods described in this work have been developed in recent years and the student or administrator should seek expert assistance before undertaking large or complex projects requiring more sophisticated techniques to ensure that appropriate statistical tools are chosen and applied properly.

The power of multivariate techniques is derived from their ability to measure the partial predictive usefulness of individual variables and their joint effect, which often results in better predictions than is possible when a single predictor variable is used. In this regard, the concept of main effects and interactive effects is extremely important. Because there is usually a confounding influence exerted by the independent variables, it is only possible to assess the joint effects and partial effects of the multiple variables by the use of multivariate techniques. As implied earlier, the simpler statistics that are limited to a single predictor variable are simply inappropriate when dealing with situations in which it is necessary to examine several factors that may influence the phenomenon of interest.

15.4 THE STUDY DESIGN MATRIX [A]

An important tool that may be used when designing a project that will employ either univariate or multivariate techniques is the study design matrix referred to in earlier chapters. Each dimension of the matrix represents one predictor variable. When dealing with predictor variables that are measured in terms of nominal data, the subdivision of a dimension of the matrix represents a specific value of the variable. On the other hand, when dealing with variables that are measured in terms of an interval or ratio scale, the number of potential values associated with the variable is so large that it is not useful to provide for such subdivisions. The cells of the matrix represent unique combinations of the predictor variables, which assist the researcher in determining the number and the types of observations which must be made in order to detect the effects that are expected. Each cell represents a unique combination of variables, and the minimum number of cases required to detect the effect is between 10 and 30. It almost goes without saying that we prefer to have more than 30 observations per cell, but the costs of obtaining these data may be prohibitive. Here, observe that the minimum number of cases required in a study is obtained by the product of the number of cells and the number of observations per cell. The natural joint distribution of cases across the predictor variables should be assessed to determine whether special sampling techniques will be required to obtain the minimum number of cases in any cell.

15.5 SAMPLING AND THE STUDY DESIGN [A]

Once the objectives of the study have been stated clearly and the relationships as well as the variables have been operationally defined, the study population must be specified. When defining the study population, the researcher must specify the units of analysis that will characterize the study, since this specification indicates the nature of the data which must be collected. Prior to the selection of the sample on which the data base of the study will rest, it is necessary to develop a *sampling frame*. A sampling frame either lists or operationally defines every eligible member of the population from which a sample of observations will be selected randomly. For a study designed to examine the costs of treatment, the sampling frame would consist of all patients treated for the illnesses to be analyzed. For a study involving the prescribing behavior of physicians, the sampling frame would consist of all patient encounters with physicians during the study period. In many situations, it is not feasible to physically list the entire sampling frame, in which case two or more stages might be required. For example, from a list of hospitals or physicians, a sample might be selected, and then a listing of only the patients associated with the selected institutions or physicians would constitute the sampling frame.

Once the sampling frame has been developed, individual cases must be selected randomly so that members of the population appearing in the individual cells of the study design matrix have equal probabilities of being chosen. When the joint distribution of cases in the population across the design matrix is even, simple random sampling is appropriate. However, in other situations, stratification and unequal probabilities of selection may be required in order to obtain sufficient cases for each cell. The text by Moser and Kalton (1971) describes practical techniques of sampling and should be consulted for the details of constructing sampling frames and drawing samples.

15.6 DATA COLLECTION[A]

Data for a study may be derived from primary, secondary, or tertiary sources and each of these sources has its own characteristics, benefits, and problems. A primary source of data is usually associated with the direct observation of a phenomenon or individuals included in a survey. Primary sources are the most direct and, in many situations, the only means of obtaining required information. On the other hand, the collection of data from primary sources is likely to be more costly than obtaining the information from secondary or tertiary sources. Secondary sources consist of records that were originally collected for some purpose other than the current research project. For example, data for a study may be abstracted from such secondary sources as patient medical records, departmental activity logs, clinic appointment logs, accounting records, administrative records, correspondence files, and incident or accident reports. While secondary sources are perhaps more accessible to the researcher, the data as originally recorded may not meet the researcher's requirements, and this fact may not be recognized. For example, problems may exist in the definition and completeness of previous data collection efforts. Tertiary sources consist of data collected and summarized by organizations that are external to the institution. Hospital associations, the U.S. Bureau of the Census, Statistics Canada, and many other organizations publish special-purpose summaries of health care information. Data developed by these tertiary sources may appear to be the easiest to collect and to be in the appropriate format, but differences among the underlying secondary sources may not have been resolved adequately, resulting possibly in an undetected error constituting an important potential problem.

Most statistical analyses use computers for processing collected information, but the raw data are seldom in a form suitable for computer processing. In these situations, the information on which the study is based will require one or several modifications and transcriptions. Each time data are transcribed, the probability of committing an error increases and, as a result, the number of transcriptions should be minimized. Many studies concerning the health care industry are based on data that are derived from responses to a questionnaire and are recorded by an interviewer or by the respondent and later recoded into a numerical score by a research assistant. Once the recoding has been verified, the data are key punched into cards, which may then be used to read the information into the computer.

One of the primary difficulties associated with questionnaires and survey samples involves the possibility that the questions will be misinterpreted or that information will be recorded incorrectly. Errors in interpreting questions and recording responses can be partially overcome by a careful wording of the questionnaire and design of the format. Coding can be built into the questionnaire or coding and keypunching can be eliminated by using a well-developed mark sensing form. Computer reading of cards or forms seldom causes any problems since most systems have built in error-detecting mechanisms. However, these mechanisms cannot detect errors in the original recording of data.

Once the data have been collected and read by the computer, preliminary data screening should be performed to ensure that all forms have been processed and that each form contains all the required data. In addition, the information should be assessed to ensure that the data assume seemingly appropriate values. For example, males and females may be assigned the numeric codes 0 and 1, respectively, while the age of the individual should assume a value between 0 and a reasonable upper limit of, say, 120 years. For all variables collected, ranges of acceptable values should be determined and the data should be compared with these ranges to detect obvious errors.

15.7 PRELIMINARY DATA ANALYSIS[A]

Once the data have been collected and verified, the distributional properties of the dependent and predictor variables, including ranges, percentiles, frequency distributions, measures of location and variation, should
be examined by the use of the descriptive statistics discussed in Volume I.
This analysis may be employed in a search for possible errors, as the final
analysis, or as a preliminary analysis prior to proceeding to further multivariate analysis. For nominal variables such as sex and marital status, it may
be desirable to check the proportion of individuals appearing in the various
categories. Graphical presentation of simple statistics should be employed.
Pie charts, histograms, cumulative frequency graphs, and scattergrams are
all appropriate.

Before employing analysis of variance or multiple regression techniques,
the researcher should examine scattergrams, which may reveal problems of
unequal variance (heteroscedasticity) and possible interactions among
predictor variables. In addition, the matrix containing the zero order
correlation coefficients should also be examined for problems of multicollinearity and the need to construct multiplicative variables or eliminate
existing variables in order to overcome these problems.

15.8 SPECIAL CONSIDERATIONS FOR MULTIPLE REGRESSION MODELS[A]

The material discussed thus far deals with statistical models in general,
and we now shift our focus to concentrate specifically on multiple regression models. Special considerations are required for multivariate models,
since they are more complicated than models based on simpler statistics.
Even though multivariate methods are more powerful than the simpler
approaches, these techniques are more susceptible to misuse and misinter-
pretation. In addition, there is the very real problem of selecting the variables that will be incorporated in the model and, in this regard, the results
of the model can be altered substantially by a poor choice. A related
question that also must be resolved involves the form to be assumed by the
regression equation and whether transformed variables or interactive terms
should be included in the model. Moreover, the assumptions concerning
the distributional properties relative to the predictor variables as well as
the assumptions concerning the error term (i.e., zero mean, constant
variance, and zero covariance) should be examined empirically. Recall that
the term *heteroscedasticity* refers to the problem arising when the error
term exhibits a variance that is not constant, and a simple test for heteroscedasticity is an examination of plots of residuals. The problem that

arises when residuals exhibit positive or negative covariance is often manifested in serial autocorrelation and may be examined empirically as well. These problems are usually present in models employing time series data.

No explicit assumptions are made about the distributional properties of the independent variables, but problems of bias and computability arise if any of the predictors are highly correlated (i.e., the problem of multicollinearity). These problems and their solutions have been discussed previously in Chapter 14. The important point is to recognize the potential existence of these problems so that they may be investigated and corrected.

15.8.1 Selection of the Best Regression Equation[A]

The objective of constructing a multiple regression model is to obtain an equation that correctly expresses the relationship between the dependent and all relevant predictor variables. In achieving this goal, it is necessary to include all of the relevant variables and to exclude all of the irrelevant factors. Observe that these two considerations refer to the problem of selecting the best combination of predictor variables in a given situation.

The identification of all relevant variables requires a careful analysis of the problem and its context. Sections 15.2.2 and 15.2.3 describe the process of problem identification and analysis as well as an examination of previous work related to the current problem. The identification and measurement of variables are key concerns when specifying the parameters of the model to be employed in a given situation. In this regard, insight and understanding of the problem are the only guidelines that assist management in this aspect of developing the research problem. Given that the researcher's insights and understanding of the problem are likely to be imperfect, the first round of model building usually provides information leading to improvements in the second round, and so on. In addition, the development of knowledge in any field is always iterative and the researcher should rely on previous work when specifying the model to be employed.

The rounds of model modification, data collection, model estimation, and evaluation serve to identify variables that have either been omitted or are irrelevant. Variables that were initially expected to be important, but later proved to have insignificant coefficients, a low contribution to R^2, or are redundant (i.e., collinear with other predictor variables) may be regarded as irrelevant factors.

15.8.1.1 Econometric Models[A]

A number of methods may be employed to identify those variables which are relevant and those which are irrelevant. The simplest but most rigorous approach is found in econometric studies where the primary emphasis is to examine theoretical models specifying the variables to be included. In these studies, great faith is placed in the underlying theoretical model, and variables are not usually eliminated from the analysis merely because of insignificant coefficients. In addition, multicollinearity is a problem that occurs in many econometric studies, but the econometrician would prefer to improve the estimates of the regression coefficients by means of independent estimates rather than discard a variable that is highly correlated with other predictor variables. The student should reexamine the "Life Cycle Savings Hypothesis" problem of Chapter 11 for an example of this model testing situation, and estimation problems resulting from multicollinearity.

15.8.1.2 Exploratory Model Building[A]

The approaches taken by other social scientists and health care researchers tend to be guided but not bound by theoretical models. In these cases, if a variable is found to be insignificant, the researcher simply eliminates the factor from further study. The emphasis in these studies is usually on maximizing the value of R^2, subject to the constraint that all variables retained for examination are significant. The tests for significance include the partial F test, as well as the hierarchical contribution to R^2 described in Section 12.4. Another criterion used frequently when examining the variables included in the model is the standard error of the equation. Here, the objective is to select those factors which minimize the value assumed by the standard error of the equation.

The equation that maximizes R^2 or minimizes s_{yx} may be found by using several different methods. One of these methods is to employ all possible combinations of the independent variables in estimating the regression equation, and, on the basis of these results, to select that combination of predictor variables which results in a maximum R^2 or a minimum s_{yx}. This approach is almost never used, because the amount of computation is prohibitive when the researcher wishes to examine a large number of independent variables.

To avoid the computational tasks associated with this approach, several alternatives, including forward selection, backward elimination, and stepwise regression, have been suggested. Forward selection permits the addition of the most useful variable at each step of the computation, while backward elimination deletes the least useful variable at each step. Both of these approaches require that we specify the critical value of F for the selection or elimination of variables. When forward selection procedures are employed, a variable that has been found to be significant at one step may become insignificant at a later step. The obverse may be true when backward elimination procedures are employed. The stepwise method is designed to avoid both problems by operating forward and backward algorithms at each step. Thus, when stepwise regression techniques are employed, the result of a single data run is that all, and only, significant variables in the set of predictors are included in the equation. Only forward selection is available in SPSS, while BMDP provides the researcher with access to stepwise regression. Also observe that the equivalent to stepwise regression can be performed using SPSS by simply employing the hierarchical control that is available through the odd and even inclusion level numbers that were discussed in Chapters 11 and 12.

The major difficulty with the approaches by which we may identify the best regression equation is that they permit the investigator to examine a large number of independent variables without thinking seriously about the real relation of these variables to the dependent variable. Further, when a large number of independent variables are included in the examination, there is a relatively great chance of finding a statistically significant relationship by accident. The fact that a partial regression coefficient is found to be statistically significant is not a sufficient reason for accepting it as being a necessary part of the regression equation that relates the set of predictor variables to the dependent variable. Rather, the decision to include a given predictor in the final regression model must be based on prior reasoning, which suggests a plausible relationship between the dependent and the independent variable.

Another problem that frequently emerges in constructing regression models and searching for high R^2 values is that of defining independent variables so that they are mere transformations of the dependent variable. In these cases, the independent variable is closely, but not causally related with the dependent variable. The presence of circularly defined variables may be detected by their extremely high correlations with the dependent variable and by their conceptual interchangeability with the phenomenon of interest. Regarding the latter point, conceptual interchangeability refers to those situations in which the independent variable could be used as an alternative to the factor actually being predicted. For example, in trying to predict *total salary costs* for each institution in a group of hospitals, we might be tempted to use *total paid hours* and *total full-time equivalents* (FTE) as predictor variables. Unless there are tremendous disparities in the wage rates paid by the hospitals, *total paid hours* is almost a perfect linear transformation of *total salary costs*. For similar reasons, the variable *FTE employees* should not be included as a predictor variable when examining the total salary costs of these institutions. When specifying the model, then, it is important not to be deceived by high R^2 values. In the preceding example, a set of factors representing the demand for hospital services constitutes much better predictor variables when examining total costs. In this case, we might use such variables as the number of patient days by diagnosis, deviations of length of stay from the national average length of stay by major diagnostic grouping, outpatient visits, provision of specialty care by type of service, and so forth. Such a set of predictor variables would lead to a relatively low value of R^2, but the validity of the study would be much greater than one using circularly defined variables.

These considerations suggest that the selection of the best regression equation is not merely a mechanical procedure. Instead, the process should be viewed as an integral part of the search for improved understanding of the problem situation. The investigation of the variables should include all aspects of the difficulties mentioned in this chapter and in Chapter 14. Multicollinearity, heteroscedasticity, and problems leading to biased regression estimates should be carefully assessed. In addition, each variable included in the analysis should be justified by prior reasoning and by reference to published research. Both the direction and the strength of the regression coefficients should be predicted prior to performing regression analysis. These expectations should then be assessed in terms of the results of the analysis. Moreover, the anomalies should be investigated to avoid obvious errors of bad data. The process will probably require the researcher to perform several regression runs and to assess the results before arriving at a final set of regression equations that constitute *the model*.

Model validation is an issue related to the selection of the best regression equation. Here, the issue is whether or not the data are truly represented by the model or whether the relationship is partially or completely spurious. One approach to validation is to divide the available data randomly into two halves. One-half of the data may be used to estimate the parameters of the regression equation, and the other half may be used to test the model by reestimating the coefficients. Significant differences among the coefficients of the two resulting equations indicate that one or both of the expressions are wrong. Should this situation arise, it is frustrating since there are no automatic mechanisms indicating the reasons for the observed disparity. A nonrandom split of the data may represent one explanation of significant differences among the coefficients of the two equations, since some of the variables used to estimate the parameters may be distributed in a markedly different manner. If the two halves of the data are not equivalent, there is no reason to expect the results to be the same. Nonequivalence is most likely to occur when data are originally gathered without an adequate sampling design or when all available data are used. One possible solution to this problem is to calculate $\hat{y}$ values for the second half of the sample using the b values, which were derived using the first half of the data and compare the two R values using a t-test. Another alternative is to select a new independent sample at a later time and use the resulting data for purposes of validation.

15.8.2 Presentation, Analysis, and Interpretation of Results[A]

The final report on the research project should include the analysis of the problem, previous work related to the problem, the variables chosen for analysis, the methods of collecting data, preliminary data analysis, the final methods of statistical examination, a presentation and interpretation of the results, a discussion of the potential problems, and an explanation of how the results of the study can be applied to the underlying problem situation. During this phase of the project, it is important to describe the raw data as well as the derived variables. To provide an indication of the accuracy of the data on which the study is based, the researcher should also indicate the methods employed in verifying the raw information.

Concerning the statistical component of the report, the researcher should present the correlation matrix, paying special attention to anomalies regarding correlation among the predictor variables and potential problems of multicollinearity. In this regard, tests for multicollinearity should be described, including step-to-step shifts or changes in b values. Moreover, plots of residuals should be presented and the potential problems associated with outliers and heteroscedasticity should be analyzed. In addition, the ordinary and standardized partial regression coefficients along with their significance should be reported and interpreted. The procedure for selecting variables should be described, and the variables that were either included or omitted from the analysis should be listed.

The meaningfulness and plausibility of the results should be discussed, and their contribution to understanding the underlying problem should be presented. This presentation is the most important aspect of an applied study. The preceding statistical material is necessary to demonstrate that the research project has technical validity, but a discussion of the insight and understanding provided by the study is necessary to assure managerial acceptability and validity. Use of the model in attempting to solve the problem confronting management requires that the application of the results be demonstrated.

Finally, areas of potential future improvement in the model should be outlined to indicate areas in which the results are less than conclusive. Once the study has been completed, its results should be subjected to both technical and managerial peer review in order to ensure that if any important aspects of the problem may have been overlooked, then they may be evaluated in terms of their impact on the results of the study. At the very

least, an external review of the final report should be solicited and, optimally, the results should be published in both technical and managerial
form.

15.9 MODEL BUILDING EXAMPLES DRAWN FROM HEALTH CARE RESEARCH LITERATURE[A]

In order for the student or manager using this text to obtain an in-depth
appreciation of the model building process, it is necessary to look at major
studies that have been published. An early major work investigating the
cost of health care is found in the book *Economic Analysis for Health
Service Efficiency,* by Martin Feldstein, published in 1967 by North Holland
Publishing Company of Amsterdam. A more recent major study entitled
"Evaluation of the New Mexico Peer Review System: 1971 to 1973", by
R. H. Brook and K. N. Williams was published as a supplement to *Medical
Care,* volume 14, number 12, December 1976. It was jointly published by
Medical Care and the Rand Corporation. Both studies should be considered
required reading for serious students of health care economics and research.

As well, there are a number of journals publishing health care related
research. The most important of those publishing studies relevant to
statistical model building are:

Health Services Research
Inquiry (Blue Cross)
International Journal of Health Services
Medical Care

It is difficult to make a selection among the many articles published over
the past 20 years that are relevant to a discussion of model building using
statistical techniques. The authors have selected a few that offer a useful
starting point, but are by no means an exhaustive listing. In alphabetical
order by author they are:

Berki, S. E. and Kobashigawa, B., "Socioeconomic and Need Determinants
of Ambulatory Care Use: Path Analysis of the 1970 Health Interview
Survey Data." *Medical Care,* May 1976, vol. XIV, no. 5, pp. 405–421.

The proof of causality is impossible, but a network of causal relationships can be hypothesized, and can be represented by a series of
regression equations. This leads the reader beyond the scope of this
book, and a good basic reference is the book by Blalock (listed next).

Blalock, H. M., ed. *Causal Models in the Social Sciences.* Chicago: Aldine Publishing Co., 1971.

Hershey, J. C., Luft, H. S., and Gianaris, J. M., "Making Sense Out of Utilization Data." *Medical Care,* October 1975, vol. XIII, no. 10, pp. 838-854.

The analysis of utilization data often has led to contradictory conclusions, because the analyses were too simple-minded in their use of statistics. This paper suggests that need, accessibility, attitudes, and demographic characteristics are all required to be considered in multiple regression models in order to determine their true relationship to utilization.

Lave, J. R., and Leinhardt, S., "The Cost and Length of a Hospital Stay." *Inquiry,* vol. XIII, no. 12, December 1976, pp. 327-343.

This work is similar in nature to that by Lay (1978) discussed previously in this work. The authors develop a behavioral model of the treatment of patients and then estimate the relationships among the variables using multiple regression. The patient's diagnosis is viewed as being of substantial importance in predicting utilization of resources.

Lave, L. B. and Seskin, E. P., "Epidemiology, Causality, and Public Policy." *American Scientist,* vol. 67, no. 2, March-April 1979, pp. 178-186.

This is a good discussion of the problems of unambiguous proof of causal relationships from environmental factors such as air pollution, personal habits such as smoking, and other possible causes to health disorders. Scientists are prone to pointing out both sides of the argument ("On the one hand ..., but on the other ...") leaving decision makers well informed, but perhaps more confused. The authors report a remark by Senator Edmund Muskie that he wished that there were more "one-armed scientists."

Reinke, W. A., "Analysis of Multiple Sources of Variation: Comparison of Three Techniques." *Health Services Research,* vol. 8, no. 4, Winter 1973, pp. 309-321.

This article branches out in another direction, examining two similar methods of *pattern analysis,* namely *automatic interaction detector* (AID) and *multisort,* a variation of ANOVA, and comparing their results to those achievable using regression. These techniques are similar in intent to the AUTOGRP system developed at Yale University, reported in the article by Thompson et al, below. There are a large number of techniques extending beyond these articles. These techniques include Factor Analysis, Discriminant Analysis, and many others based on *information theory.*

Ro, K., "Interactions among Variables Affecting Hospital Utilization." *Health Services Research,* vol. 8, no. 4, Winter 1973, pp. 298–308.

This is a good article detailing the use of the dummy variables representing age, sex, and race, and two-way and three-way interactions among them. It is strongly recommended for reading in conjunction with Chapter 13 of this text.

Ruchlin, H. S. and Leveson, I., "Measuring Hospital Productivity." *Health Services Research,* vol. 9, no. 4, Winter 1974, pp. 308–323.

The authors propose that hospital output be defined as a weighted sum of different types of inpatient and outpatient care services, education of various types of health care personnel, and research. Hospital inputs are to be measured as the sum of labor cost, supplies (nonpayroll operating expenses) cost and capital assets (plant and equipment, but this is not depreciation as calculated for third party payers). These can all be measured in the form of indexes based on local, regional, or national averages and can be combined into a productivity index that is output/input. Some of the regressions reported have exceptionally high R^2 values.

Thompson, J. D., Fetter, R. B., and Mross, C. D., "Case Mix and Resource Use." *Inquiry,* vol. XII, no. 6, December 1975, pp. 300–312.

The use of the AUTOGRP system has enabled the authors to differentiate among a very large number of diagnostic groupings of patients. Each grouping is determined by a number of predictor variables. Each group is unique, and is based on a heuristic selection of variables, guided by an overall criterion of minimizing within-group variance. It is very similar in concept to factorial analysis of variance, with many empty or undefined cells in the data collection matrix. The method proceeds by splitting large groups into successively smaller more homogeneous groups on the basis of the categories of predictor variables. The splitting process stops when no further splits can result in smaller within-group variance. The resulting groups have extremely different variances. Attempting to perform regressions combining different groups in a single regression would obviously encounter severe problems of heteroscedasticity. This problem was not recognized by Lave and Leinhardt in the study referenced earlier in the list.

The study of articles such as the ones mentioned previously is very important in obtaining a thorough understanding of the complexities and problems in model building using statistical techniques. Although most of these studies are aimed at extremely important policy issues, the results are ambiguous and conflicting. It should be no surprise that attempts to draw clear-cut policy implications from such studies are fraught with difficulty. The concluding chapter of this work consists of a case study of an attempt to apply multiple regression to hospital budget control.

BIBLIOGRAPHY

Moser, C. A. and Kalton, G., *Survey Methods in Social Investigation,* 2nd ed. New York: Basic Books, 1971.

Newell, A. and Simon, H. A., "GPS: A Program that Simulates Human Thought." In E. A. Feigenbaum and J. Feldman, *Computers and Thought.* New York: McGraw-Hill, 1963, pp. 279-293.

Pounds, W. F., "The Process of Problem Finding." *Industrial Management Review* (now the *Sloan Management Review*), vol. 11, no. 1, Fall 1969, pp. 1-19.

Siegel, S., *Non-Parametric Statistics.* New York: McGraw-Hill, 1956.

Chapter 16

The Identification of Potential Hospital Budget Cuts: A Case Study in the Use of Multiple Regression Analysis*

Objectives

When reviewing this chapter, you should emphasize two major requirements of the use of sophisticated analysis. The first is that of the correct technical application of a complex tool. The second is the appropriate managerial use of the results of such analysis. The first is necessary, but it does not automatically lead to success in the second.

---

*This case study has been abstracted from an actual situation. It is presented neither as good nor bad management of the situation, but rather as a stimulation for classroom discussion of the technical material presented in this text and its application in problem solving.

PART A: THE REGRESSION STUDY AND ITS EVALUATION

In January 197X the Provincial Ministry of Health was attempting to determine how to restrain the growth of hospital budgets in the province. A number of approaches had been considered in the past and some had been tried, including across-the-board fixed percentage cuts and percentages based on type of hospital and size of city (town, etc.). There were always objections that such budget cuts were not based on an analysis of the situations facing individual hospitals, and some individual hospitals were able to mount enough political pressure to have their budget cuts reduced or rescinded. This resulted in the government being unable to achieve its targets for budget restraints.

Ministry officials had heard and read that multiple regression is able to account for individual differences, and they decided that budgetary cuts based on multiple regression might be able to overcome objections concerning the lack of analysis and consideration of individual differences.

A small group of analysts in the Ministry was asked to develop an equation to assist in identifying high cost hospitals that could be asked to cut their budgets. Only limited time was available to carry out the study, but extensive data were available from the statistical reporting systems of the government.

The group decided that a physical measure of workload was more appropriate for study than total expenditures. Therefore, *total paid hours* was chosen as the *dependent* variable. Once total paid hours were predicted for a hospital, then the average wage rate for the individual hospital could be used to determine the predicted budget, and differences could be used to indicate required budget cuts. The predictor (independent) variables were chosen from the available statistics and are listed in the left hand column of Table 16-1. The remainder of Table 16-1 is a summary of the regression results as presented to the higher officials in the Ministry. Exhibit 16-1 is a partial copy of the report presented by the group to the higher officials.

The Ministry decided that the report achieved the objectives and recommended that a policy of budget cuts be based on it. The minister and the provincial cabinet accepted the recommendations. The affected hospitals were informed about the intended cuts.

Most hospital administrators felt inadequately prepared to understand the methodology used and were unable to respond. However, one hospital hired a consultant to analyze and respond to the study.

The hospital's consultant felt that a number of questions needed to be considered in interpreting and evaluating the study, and implementing the results. These included:

1. *The variables used*:
   a. the meaning of and interrelationships among the dependent and independent variables
   b. the comparability of measurement of the variables, using the hospitals' accounting systems (alleged incompatibilities)
   c. the exclusion of potentially important variables
2. *The meaningfulness of the regression equation*:
   a. the appropriateness of the dependent variable
   b. the significance of the equation
   c. the significance of the regression coefficients
   d. the possibility of technical problems in carrying out the regression (multicollinearity and heteroscedasticity)
   e. the meaning and interpretation of the regression coefficients both within groups of hospitals and across all the groups
3. *The use of the results to identify high cost hospitals*:
   a. the standard error of estimate for the equation
   b. the significance of any hospital's deviation
   c. the effect of removing any one hospital from the sample and rerunning the regression

Discussion Questions

1. Using the hospital's consultant's criteria, what problem areas can you see, and what information could or should have been provided by the Ministry analysts to allow proper interpretation and evaluation of the study?
2. What approach(es) could (or should) have been considered for identification of high cost hospitals?
3. Evaluate the hospital's consultant's criteria. Were they appropriate? Sufficient?

PART B: REACTION TO THE STUDY AND RECOMMENDATIONS

The hospitals of the province objected to the intended application of the study results, and in the resulting discussions the government decided to use a different approach to determining budget cuts.

In retrospect, the Ministry decided that it needed to evaluate the process and problems of using the multiple regression technique and asked another consultant to investigate and report. The Ministry consultant's report is contained in Exhibit 16-2.

TABLE 16-1 Annualized (i.e., × 12/10) Regression Equations for Paid Hours (Annual) Active Treatment Hospitals 10 Months (January-October) ($n = 20$ to 25 in Each Group)

	Group 1 A 100+ Teaching	Group 2 B 400+ Non-teaching	Group 3 B 250-399 Non-teaching	Group 4 B 150-249 Non-teaching	Group 5 B 100-149 Non-teaching	Group 6 C 50-99 Non-teaching	Group 7 C 1-49 Non-teaching
Active Patient Days	8.38	6.79	7.79	10.42	3.17	3.14	7.76
Emergency Visits	-5.73	-1.96	1.48	2.69	-0.66		0.34
Total Patient Meal Days	3.03	1.64					
Lab Units (minutes of time)	0.04	0.05		-0.002			
Ambulatory Visits	2.13						
Separations	10.24	38.43	-1.88	-13.44	48.23	27.15	-0.36
Radiology Exams	1.00	-6.82	-0.39	4.84	0.84	0.96	
Physiotherapy Visits	0.03	0.24	0.05	0.09	-0.18		
Operations	-2.05	3.81	26.37	15.87	16.94	4.34	1.98
Square Feet		0.70		0.03	0.57	1.34	0.77
Constant	111,355	-174,319	116,407	10,629	10,407	-8,766	-4,029

Discussion Questions

1. Evaluate the Ministry consultant's report.
2. Summarize the recommendations made to the Ministry.
3. What recommendations would you add, delete, or modify?
4. What are the strengths and weaknesses of the multiple regression approach to this type of problem?
5. How could this approach be used in the future with greater probability of acceptance by hospitals in the province?
6. What, if any, other things need to be accomplished before another attempt to use such a control mechanism?

Exhibit 16-1 Regression Result Presentation

INTRODUCTION

The purpose of this presentation is to examine various indices of activity in a hospital and how they are related to the level of paid hours. Once the relationship is formulated, it should be possible to predict the level of paid hours of a hospital given the values of the activity indices. Hence, the number of excess hours that a hospital has, based on their activity, can be determined.

THE DATA

The data used in the analysis came from two sources. The following variables, along with their source, were used as indices of activity:

Paid Hours	(OS)
Active Patient Days	(OS)
Chronic Patient Days	(OS)
Number of Separations	(OS)
Number of Emergency Visits	(OS)
Number of Operations	(OS)
Number of Lab Units	(OS)
Number of Radiology Exams	(OS)
Total Patient Meal Days	(OS)
Square Feet (Housekeeping)	(HSI)
Ambulatory Care	(HSI)
Laundry	(HSI)
Physiotherapy	(HSI)
Occupational Therapy	(HSI)

(OS)   Operating Statement
(HSI)   Hospital Statistics 1.

The indices of activity noted above were arrived at in the manner described below. The data for Active Patient Days, Chronic Patient Days, Number of Separations, Number of Emergency Visits, Number of Operations, Number of Laboratory Units, and Number of Radiology Examinations was for a nine-month period. These activities were adjusted to a twelve-month period. Ambulatory Care, Physiotherapy, and Occupational Therapy were determined from the sum of their respective inpatient and outpatient activities. Total Patient Meal Days were determined from the difference between the total Meal Days and Non-Patient Meal Days, where these were adjusted to the twelve-month period from nine months. Laundry and Square Feet were used as reported on the HSI form.

The Paid Hours were initially adjusted to an annual basis from a ten-month basis. Since Non-Patient Meal Days were excluded, their related hours had to be subtracted from the Paid Hours adjusted for twelve months. The ratio of Non-Patient Meal Days to Total Meal Days was multiplied by Dietary Hours adjusted to twelve months from ten months, to determine the hours to be excluded. Total paid hours were adjusted for any activity index which was fully purchased or partially purchased.

The adjustments made to an annual basis may introduce other variables which change with the passage of time and influence the activity indices used in the study. These other variables are virtually impossible to include in the analysis and hopefully do not bias the results. One assumes that the quality remains constant over the full twelve months.

Since the study is cross-sectional, the institutions covered should be reasonably homogeneous. Generally speaking, hospitals provide similar services. However, the organizational structure may be somewhat different. The hospitals were grouped according to the groupings in Hospital Statistics 197X provided by the Ministry Information System Division of the Provincial Ministry of Health with exceptions noted below.

Differences in accounting practices may be a reason for differences in hospitals. How significant this factor may be is unknown and therefore it is assumed that accounting is performed in a like manner at all hospitals.

REGRESSION ANALYSIS

A regression analysis was performed on each of the following groups of hospitals:

Group A   (rated beds (100+) Teaching)
Group B   (rated beds (400+) Non-Teaching)
Group B   (rated beds 250–399)
Group B   (rated beds 200–249)

Group B   (rated beds 150-199)
Group B   (rated beds 100-149)
Group C   (rated beds 50-99)
Group C   (rated beds   1-49)

Note: Western Royal was placed in Group B (rated beds 200-249)
      Northern (Jamestown Unit) was placed in Group B (rated beds
      100-149)
      Northern (Newton Unit) was placed in Group C (rated beds
      1-49).

For each group, as much of the information was used as possible. Hence, a subset of the thirteen activity indices was used in each group, with the paid hours adjusted for indices not used because of institutions not having that particular function. That is, hospitals having values for indices not used had their paid hours adjusted accordingly. Some hospitals were excluded from group consideration because their inclusion would have necessitated a further reduction in the activity subset. These hospitals were considered individually.

Multiple regression is a general statistical technique used to analyze the relationship between a dependent or criterion variable (Paid Hours of Work) and a set of independent or predictor variables (13 indices of activity). Through regression techniques, an equation can be determined which indicates how scores on the independent variables could be weighted and summed to obtain the best possible prediction of Paid Hours for the group. At the same time, the amount of variation in paid hours, between the hospitals, is accounted for by the joint linear influences of the activity indices. Once an equation has been determined for each group considered, it is possible to estimate the total paid hours for each hospital given the data used. These estimated values for paid hours based on the regression line, which is an average for that group, can be compared with the actual paid hours. Hence, one can calculate whether an institution has paid hours which are more or less than the average and how large the difference is.

A dollar value could then be placed on each institution with "surplus" paid hours. To determine the average hourly rate for each hospital the following procedure was followed: Salaries and wages were adjusted to twelve months from ten. Supplemental salaries were adjusted to twelve months from six and hence, the total salaries and wages were the sum of the above. Fringe benefits were taken to be 8.5% of total wages and salaries. From this figure and the total paid hours, an average cost by hour was determined. This resulted in the assignment of a dollar amount to the surplus hours associated with a given institution.

EQUATIONS FOR PEER GROUP COMPARISONS

GROUP A

PAIDHOUR = 111354.68271 + 8.37901 Active Patient Days
− 5.73012 Emer. Visits + 3.02953 Total Patient Meal Days
+ .04068 Lab Units + 2.1315 Ambulatory Care
+ 10.23706 Separations + .99863 Radiology Exams
+ .03469 Physiotherapy − 2.04952 Operations

GROUP B (400+)

PAIDHOUR = − 174319.09705 + 6.79219 Active Patient Days
+ .69764 Square Feet + 38.42808 Separations
+ .23641 Physiotherapy − 1.96322 Emergency Visits
+ .04609 Lab Units − 6.82306 Radiology Exams
+ 1.64048 Total Patient Meal Days + 3.81292 Operations

GROUP B (250-399)

PAIDHOUR =   116407.40250 + 7.7897 Active Patient Days
+ 26.3727 Operations + 1.47577 Emergency Visits
+ .05107 Physiotherapy − .38749 Radiology Exams
− 1.87518 Separations

GROUP B (150-249)

PAIDHOUR =   10628.76714 + 10.41688 Active Patient Days
+ 2.69399 Emergency Visits + .03384 Square Feet
+ 15.86932 Operations + 4.84469 Radiology Exams
+ .09286 Physiotherapy − 13.43755 Separations
− .00208 Lab Units

GROUP B (100-149)

PAIDHOUR =   10406.68213 + 48.23333 Separations + .57134 Square
Feet
+ 3.17224 Active Patient Days + .8421 Radiology Exams
− .17701 Physiotherapy + 16.9411 Operations
− .66266 Emergency Visits

GROUP C (50-99)

PAIDHOUR = − 8766.23306 + 27.15335 Separations + 1.34601 Square
Feet
+ 3.13586 Active Patient Days + .95904 Radiology
Exams
+ 4.34411 Operations

GROUP C (1-49)
PAIDHOUR = − 4028.87758 + 7.75682 Active Patient Days
+ .76504 Square Feet + 1.97955 Operations
+ .33618 Emergency Visits − .36055 Separations

Exhibit 16-2 Ministry Consultant's Report

 PROVINCIAL HOSPITAL ASSOCIATION

50 Capital Drive, Provincetown   Tel: 123-4567

October 22nd, 197X

To: Chief Executive Officers of Member Institutions
Subject: Regression Analysis—An Evaluation

Mr. J. B. Williams, Deputy Minister of Health, has provided me with a copy of a July, 197X report on "An Evaluation of the Use of Regression Analysis in the Determination of Hospital Budget Cuts." After what happened earlier this year, I believe you will find it interesting to read the views of Health Consulting Associates Ltd. on the use of regression analysis in determining hospital budget cuts. Mr. Williams kindly agreed, with my suggestion, that copies should be sent to members of the Association.

A. James Rodger
Executive Director

Encl.

THE USE OF REGRESSION ANALYSIS IN DETERMINING HOSPITAL BUDGET CUTS

This report will be presented in five sections. In Section 1, I will make some general remarks about the relevance of statistical analysis to the determination of hospital budget cuts. In Section II, the specific application of regression analysis will be discussed with particular attention paid to the problem that can be encountered and potential solutions through a somewhat sophisticated use of the technique. Section III will contain a specification of the resources needed to accomplish a satisfactory application of regression analysis in this context. Section IV will deal with my subjective evaluation of the resources currently in place in the Ministry of Health, as well as with an assessment of the availability of these resources outside the Ministry. Finally, I will make recommendations in Section V about how the development of statistical analyses of hospital costs might be structured within the Ministry of Health.

1. Multivariate Analyses of Hospital Costs

The use of regression analysis in establishing hospital budget cuts in Province last spring was at least partly motivated by the Ministry's eagerness to comply with the Provincial Hospital Association's suggestion of differential budget cuts across hospitals. In other words, it represented an attempt to discriminate between efficient and inefficient hospitals when establishing funding levels, with the largest relative budget cuts assigned to supposedly inefficient hospitals. This is, of course, a sound strategy, both from the point of view of fairness and in terms of providing incentives toward efficient operation of the hospital sector.

The task of identifying efficient and inefficient hospitals is enormously complex, and can be addressed only in part by the use of statistical tools. In other words, to the extent that very inefficient hospitals are *deviantly* inefficient with respect to a peer group norm, statistical analyses can identify these cases. On the other hand, statistical analysis of any sort is powerless to determine whether or not the norm itself reflects efficient operation.

To some extent the average performance will always be somewhat inefficient if we define efficiency in terms of lowest-cost performance for a given level of service. Unless all hospitals operate at optimal efficiency, the average will reflect the performance of the inefficient hospitals as well as the efficient ones, and therefore diverge from the efficient ideal. But the extent of this divergence is crucial, and it cannot be revealed by even the most sophisticated analysis unless one is willing to simply identify efficiency with low-cost performance, even in the absence of reliable output measures. The problem of sectorwide efficiency must, in general, be addressed by restructuring the incentives that face decision makers in the hospital; it cannot be solved by insisting that all hospitals behave as efficiently (or *inefficiently*) as the norm.

What statistical analyses can do, however, is identify those hospitals that are deviantly inefficient even with respect to a supposedly inefficient norm (in other words, those hospitals which are most responsible for the norm being inefficient!) And, to the extent that pressuring those deviant cases back to the norm is accomplished, this will yield financial dividends.*

Multivariate statistical analysis can identify deviantly "expensive" hospitals by comparing the standardized cost performance of each hospital with its peer group average. By "standardization" I mean adjustment for the particular circumstances of each hospital along all the dimensions which are relevant in determining cost performance. This does *not* mean taking all of the hospital's idiosyncrasies into account, but only all the idiosyncrasies that "count", i.e., those that are significant determining factors. Statistical analysis can determine which factors are in fact significant determinants of hospital cost behaviour, and one can then proceed to standardize for these variables in deciding whether or not a particular hospital is deviant.

2. Regression Analysis

Basically, multivariate analysis accomplishes this task by relating the variation in hospital costs to variation in each potentially significant explanatory factor. In other words, the cost performances of hospitals are related to their descriptive characteristics, to identify which characteristics are important determining factors. Since a number of variables are considered, the analysis is "multivariate". There are several multivariate techniques that could be used in this context, but the one that recommends itself is regression analysis.

Regression analysis describes the relation between the "dependent" variable (in this case, some measure of hospital cost performance) and a set of "independent" explanatory variables in terms of an equation. In the case of a linear regression the equation calculates the expected value

---

*It should be noted that forcing high deviants down to the norm will also progressively lower the norm itself. This strategy can therefore, over time, move the whole sector towards lower-cost operation.

of the dependent variable as a weighted sum of the explanatory variables, where the weights are the coefficients generated by the regression analysis. The analysis not only computes the weights, but provides estimates of the explanatory significance of each independent variable, and of the equation as a whole. Thus it provides not only an expected value of the dependent variable for any hospital, given its characteristics as defined by the explanatory variables, but also an indication of the credibility of that estimate.

The success of the regression equation in standardizing for all the relevant variables in generating expected values for the dependent variables depends on many things. First and foremost, it depends on correct specification of the variables. One must have some sense about which variables to include and in which form they are to be quantified. Thus, for example, in terms of the dependent variable, should we be concerned about number of staff, paid hours, total wages and salaries, total costs, costs per patient, cost per bed-day etc., etc.? Which explanatory variables should be quantified? What is the expected relation between the dependent and independent variables—additive? multiplicative? exponential? These questions must be addressed if the regression equation is to achieve significant explanatory power. And to address these questions, one must draw on a theoretical, intuitive and pragmatic understanding of the functioning of hospitals. One cannot arbitrarily specify the form of the dependent variable, and randomly select explanatory variables (or worse, make these decisions simply on the basis of data availability) and expect sensible results. Statistical analysis must be *informed* by an understanding of the behaviour of the institutions and the sector as a whole.

Even a well-specified regression analysis must be interpreted carefully and applied with caution. It is not a panacea; it is simply a guide to intelligent decision making. And it is always imperfect. Fortunately regression analysis is "self-consciously" imperfect; it provides a quantitative indication of how believable its estimates are. Thus, along with the expected value of the dependent variable, it provides an estimate of the error "range".

A powerful explanatory equation, one with a "good fit", has a relatively narrow error range and vice versa, but there is always some margin. Thus one can say that the expected value of cost performance for hospital X, with its particular characteristics, is, say 100 plus or minus 20, meaning that one is 95% certain that the expected value for that hospital should fall between 80 and 120, given its characteristics. If the regression equation had a worse "fit" (lower R^2), the margin of error on the estimated expected value would be larger, perhaps ± 50.

This estimate of the error range is particularly useful in applying the regression results to the determination of hospital budget cuts. If one uses as a decision criterion the reduction of budgets to a non-deviant level, one cannot justify cutting funding levels down to the expected performance, but only down to the expected value plus the margin of error. Thus, if we have a hospital with an observed level of 130 and the expected value is 100 ± 20, we should reduce the funding level to 120 by our decision criterion, *not* down to 100. If the expected value is 100 ± 50, we should not reduce the funding level at all, because the observed performance is not demonstrably deviant.

This is one example of a somewhat more cautious application of the regression results than the straightforward approach, but it highlights the increased defensibility of the technique, and the results of its application, if some sophistication is brought to bear. In an area as politically sensitive as hospital budget determination, one can ill-afford to place a greater load on any decision technique than it can reasonably bear.

3. Resource Requirements

To successfully develop the use of regression analysis, or in fact of any sophisticated statistical techniques, in the examination of hospital costs, one requires at least four different kinds of resources. (These are not presented in any particular order of importance since all are essential).

First, one needs some human resources, and of a very particular kind. I emphasized above that a correctly specified regression equation had to be informed by an understanding of the behaviour of individual hospitals and of the sector as a whole. In other words, technical statistical knowledge must be merged with practical knowledge of the field. In some contexts, this integration can be accomplished by the "team approach"; one can put statisticians together with practitioners, and hope that their skills will complement each other in a productive way. What this generally involves is getting the statistician to understand something about the field, and the practitioner to master some basic statistics. For some kinds of problems this partial overlap is sufficient. I would suggest, however, that in this context something more is required. It is necessary to bring to bear not only a basic understanding of statistics and of hospital behaviour, but an appreciation of the subtleties of each. In this context, it is the nuances of regression analysis and the intuitive appreciation of the hospital sector that are important, given the politically sensitive nature of the application. But these subtleties are very difficult to communicate to those who have not mastered the basics.

What one needs then are multi-disciplinary individuals, rather than an interdisciplinary team. One needs health statisticians, health economists and statistically-trained hospital administrators. One does need a team (this kind of understanding is far too large to be a single-person project), but a team composed of individuals who have some knowledge of both the hospital sector and statistical techniques. Hopefully there would be a mix of specialization, but a common core in both areas is essential.

Second, one needs data, data that are comprehensive, accurate and up-to-date. The outputs of any regression analysis are of no better quality than the inputs. The data must be made available in an appropriate form, both in terms of categorization and in the way they are quantitatively defined. Finally, the data must be presented in computer-readable form.

Third, one needs time. It is impossible to intelligently proceed with this kind of research project under pressing deadlines. The data must be collected, in some cases from scratch. Different forms of equations must be tried; the results must be tested. Unfortunately, in this context, to get it right one has to get it fairly slowly. I would guess that the order of magnitude required would be about 1–2 years, rather than a few months.

Finally, one needs the co-operation of the field itself. I suggest that this would be extremely useful from the point of view of informing the preliminary stages of the analysis and the specification of the variables and the equation. It is probably even more important in making the application of the results to the determination of hospital budget cuts politically acceptable. Some input from the hospital community would therefore be both useful and politic.

4. Available Resources

I am afraid that this section of my report will be the least enthusiastic. Let me proceed to give you my subjective evaluation of the Ministry's resources in each area I have described above.*

I did not discover anywhere in the Ministry the kind of multidisciplinary capability that I suggested is required. To be sure there are some individuals with a good understanding of hospitals, and some with statistical capabilities; but I did not come across any with both. There is some expertise in the Ministry in the use of regression analysis in the health sector, but this is on the medical side in the Professional Services Monitoring Branch. In many ways, the Physician Monitoring System being developed by that branch is analogous to the project under discussion here.**

---

*It should be noted that these impressions are based on a very quick and sketchy survey of the Ministry.

**I should alert the reader to the fact that I have had some input into the development of that system, and therefore may be rendering a biased opinion.

I was quite surprised to find the hospital data base in as poor shape as it is at present. The data that were used for the regression analysis last spring had to be drawn from different sources, for different time periods, and in manual form only. An integreted computerized information system on the hospital side is an essential prerequisite for any sophisticated analysis of the sector, statistical or otherwise.

Finally, with respect to cooperation from the field, I was pleasantly surprised to find some modicum of goodwill still in existence. There remains a willingness to try to sophisticate the budgeting process, though I would doubt that this positive attitude could weather another storm.

In summary, the available resources currently within the Ministry of Health fall considerably short of those required to successfully undertake a regression analysis project, in my estimation.

There are some resources outside the Ministry that can and should be tapped. Much progress has been made by academic researchers, mainly health economists and operations researchers, in the statistical analysis of hospital costs. One of the prominent names in the field is that of Prof. Able Jones of University of Otherplace, and his most recent Ph.D. student James Capable has just joined the Provincial Economic Council. There are others, though somewhat more remote geographically. With respect to data, my impression is that raw data do exist at the hospital level, so that the major problem is data organization rather than data collection. If the Ministry does proceed with this project, efforts should be made to tap these outside resources and avoid unnecessary duplication.

5. Recommendations

I believe that the Ministry should undertake a project to statistically research hospital costs in Province. Indeed, the complexity of the sector makes it almost mandatory that some sophisticated quantitative analysis be done on a continuing basis. The Ministry cannot afford to have a lesser capacity in this area than some of the large hospitals with which it must negotiate funding levels. It is therefore necessary to put human resources in place, and give them sufficient data and time to conduct a proper analysis.

The data should optimally be a by-product of a generalized hospital information system. As an inferior alternative, one could institute a special-purpose data collection project, whereby specific information on a set of pre-determined variables could be requested from the hospitals.

In terms of human resources, I would suggest that the Ministry put together a team of researchers with the capabilities described above. Such individuals are in short supply especially in Canada, but one can with effort attract them to a project as important and interesting as this one.

Optimally such a team should be constituted as a project group with clearly specified objectives, and no regular operational responsibilities. These individuals should not, in general, be viewed as resource personnel for other projects, and should therefore be insulated as much as possible from the regular workings of the Ministry. For this reason, and also in recognition of the importance of this endeavour, they should probably report at a very senior level. Finally, I would suggest that the use of outside resources, both from the government and from outside consultants, be minimized as far as possible. The Ministry of Health must develop internal capabilities in an area such as this, which is far too sensitive to contract out.

I would suggest that the residual goodwill of the hospital community be tapped by striking an advisory committee, both to provide practical input into the project group's work, and to communicate with the field at large.

In conclusion, I would urge you not to be overly jaundiced by the initial experience with regression analysis. One can do much better than that first pass, and well enough, I believe, to warrant a sizeable investment in its development.

The Standard Normal Distribution

Table A-1 The Standard Normal Distribution*

z	.00	.01	.02	.03	.04	.05	.06	.07	.08	.09
0.0	.0000	.0040	.0080	.0120	.0160	.0199	.0239	.0279	.0319	.0359
0.1	.0398	.0438	.0478	.0517	.0557	.0596	.0636	.0675	.0714	.0753
0.2	.0793	.0832	.0871	.0910	.0948	.0987	.1026	.1064	.1103	.1141
0.3	.1179	.1217	.1255	.1293	.1331	.1368	.1406	.1443	.1480	.1517
0.4	.1554	.1591	.1628	.1664	.1700	.1736	.1772	.1808	.1844	.1879
0.5	.1915	.1950	.1985	.2019	.2054	.2088	.2123	.2157	.2190	.2224
0.6	.2257	.2291	.2324	.2357	.2389	.2422	.2454	.2486	.2517	.2549
0.7	.2580	.2611	.2642	.2673	.2704	.2734	.2764	.2794	.2823	.2852
0.8	.2881	.2910	.2939	.2967	.2995	.3023	.3051	.3078	.3106	.3133
0.9	.3159	.3186	.3212	.3238	.3264	.3289	.3315	.3340	.3365	.3389
1.0	.3413	.3438	.3461	.3485	.3508	.3531	.3554	.3577	.3599	.3621
1.1	.3643	.3665	.3686	.3708	.3729	.3749	.3770	.3790	.3810	.3830
1.2	.3849	.3869	.3888	.3907	.3925	.3944	.3962	.3980	.3997	.4015
1.3	.4032	.4049	.4066	.4082	.4099	.4115	.4131	.4147	.4162	.4177
1.4	.4192	.4207	.4222	.4236	.4251	.4265	.4279	.4292	.4306	.4319
1.5	.4332	.4345	.4357	.4370	.4382	.4394	.4406	.4418	.4429	.4441
1.6	.4452	.4463	.4474	.4484	.4495	.4505	.4515	.4525	.4535	.4545
1.7	.4554	.4564	.4573	.4582	.4591	.4599	.4608	.4616	.4625	.4633
1.8	.4641	.4649	.4656	.4664	.4671	.4678	.4686	.4693	.4699	.4706
1.9	.4713	.4719	.4726	.4732	.4738	.4744	.4750	.4756	.4761	.4767
2.0	.4772	.4778	.4783	.4788	.4793	.4798	.4803	.4808	.4812	.4817
2.1	.4821	.4826	.4830	.4834	.4838	.4842	.4846	.4850	.4854	.4857
2.2	.4861	.4864	.4868	.4871	.4875	.4878	.4881	.4884	.4887	.4890
2.3	.4893	.4896	.4898	.4901	.4904	.4906	.4909	.4911	.4913	.4916
2.4	.4918	.4920	.4922	.4925	.4927	.4929	.4931	.4932	.4934	.4936
2.5	.4938	.4940	.4941	.4943	.4945	.4946	.4948	.4949	.4951	.4952
2.6	.4953	.4955	.4956	.4957	.4959	.4960	.4961	.4962	.4963	.4964
2.7	.4965	.4966	.4967	.4968	.4969	.4970	.4971	.4972	.4973	.4974
2.8	.4974	.4975	.4976	.4977	.4977	.4978	.4979	.4979	.4980	.4981
2.9	.4981	.4982	.4982	.4983	.4984	.4984	.4985	.4985	.4986	.4986
3.0	.4987	.4987	.4987	.4988	.4988	.4989	.4989	.4989	.4990	.4990

*This table is based on Table 1 of *Biometrika Tables for Statisticians. Volume I,* 3rd ed., Cambridge: University Press, 1966, by permission of the *Biometrika* trustees.

The *t* Distribution

Table B-1 The *t* Distribution (Values of t_α—One-Tailed Test)*

d.f.	$t_{.100}$	$t_{.050}$	$t_{.025}$	$t_{.010}$	$t_{.005}$	d.f.
1	3.078	6.314	12.706	31.821	63.657	1
2	1.886	2.920	4.303	6.965	9.925	2
3	1.638	2.353	3.182	4.541	5.841	3
4	1.533	2.132	2.776	3.747	4.604	4
5	1.476	2.015	2.571	3.365	4.032	5
6	1.440	1.943	2.447	3.143	3.707	6
7	1.415	1.895	2.365	2.998	3.499	7
8	1.397	1.860	2.306	2.896	3.355	8
9	1.383	1.833	2.262	2.821	3.250	9
10	1.372	1.812	2.228	2.764	3.169	10
11	1.363	1.796	2.201	2.718	3.106	11
12	1.356	1.782	2.179	2.681	3.055	12
13	1.350	1.771	2.160	2.650	3.012	13
14	1.345	1.761	2.145	2.624	2.977	14
15	1.341	1.753	2.131	2.602	2.947	15
16	1.337	1.746	2.120	2.583	2.921	16
17	1.333	1.740	2.110	2.567	2.898	17
18	1.330	1.734	2.101	2.552	2.878	18
19	1.328	1.729	2.093	2.539	2.861	19
20	1.325	1.725	2.086	2.528	2.845	20
21	1.323	1.721	2.080	2.518	2.831	21
22	1.321	1.717	2.074	2.508	2.819	22
23	1.319	1.714	2.069	2.500	2.807	23
24	1.318	1.711	2.064	2.492	2.797	24
25	1.316	1.708	2.060	2.485	2.787	25
26	1.315	1.706	2.056	2.479	2.779	26
27	1.314	1.703	2.052	2.473	2.771	27
28	1.313	1.701	2.048	2.467	2.763	28
29	1.311	1.699	2.045	2.462	2.756	29
inf.	1.282	1.645	1.960	2.326	2.576	inf.

*Abridged with permission of Macmillan Publishing Co., Inc. from *Statistical Methods for Research Workers*, 14th Edition, by R. A. Fisher. Copyright © 1970 University of Adelaide.

The F Distribution

The concept of the F distribution arises from taking repeated pairs of random samples from a large population and taking the ratios of the variances (usually called *mean squares* in analysis of variance). Since the samples are from the same population, their variances should be roughly equal, and their ratio, F, should be approximately 1.0. That is,

$$F = \frac{s_1^2}{s_2^2} \cong 1.0$$

The sampling variability results in a probability distribution that is unimodal and positively skewed (i.e., it has a long tail to the right). There are, in fact, many distributions depending on the number of degrees of freedom in each sample, where the number of degrees of freedom is 1 less than the number of observations. Let us call the degrees of freedom df_1 (numerator) and df_2 (denominator).

By random chance, s_1^2 can be greater than s_2^2 and the F ratio will be greater than 1. Since the F distribution is a probability distribution, the probability, α, of exceeding a particular value of F can be calculated. Figure C-1 shows a typical F distribution, with the portion of the curve beyond F_α indicated. It is common to use α values of .10, .05, .01, .005, and .001.

Because there is a different F distribution curve for each possible combination of n_1 and n_2, only the values of F_α are tabulated. For the purposes of this text we include only tables for $\alpha = .05$ and .01, and they are Tables

437

Figure C-1 The F Distribution

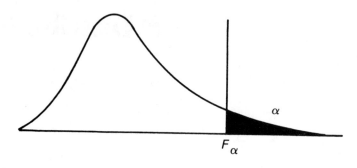

C-1 and C-2, respectively. The α level critical value of F is found at the intersection of the df_1 column and the df_2 row.

Notice that df_1 takes on the values (1, 2, 3, 4, 5, 6, 7, 8, 9, 10, 12, 15, 20, 24, 30, 40, 60, and ∞) while df_2 has all the integers from 1 to 25, as well as 30, 40, 60, 120, and ∞. If the degrees of freedom for a particular problem are not in the table, then the critical value of F can be found by linear interpolation between the surrounding values in the table. Of course, if the calculated value of F is large, then it is not necessary to perform the interpolation to find the exact critical value.

Examples of Interpolation

1. Required to test calculated F versus $F_{.01}$ for 3 and 26 degrees of freedom. Note that $F_{.01}$ values are tabulated for $df_2 = 25$ and 30 but not 26.

$df_1 = 3$	
$df_2 = 25$	4.68
26	?
30	4.51

Thus, we can state the range within which the critical value is found as:

$$4.51 < F_{.01} < 4.68$$

Case A:

Calculated value of F = 7.41

No interpolation is needed because $7.41 > 4.68$ and $4.68 > F$ for 3 and 26 *df*.

Case B:

Calculated value of F = 4.63

$$F_{.01} = 4.68 - \left(\frac{26\text{-}25}{30\text{-}25}\right)(4.68 - 4.51)$$

$$= 4.68 - \frac{1}{5}(.17)$$

$$\cong 4.68 - .03$$

$$= 4.65$$

$\therefore F < F_{.01}$ and H_0 must be retained.

2. Required to test calculated F versus $F_{.01}$ for 17 and 45 degrees of freedom.

	$df_1 = 15$	17	20
df_2			
40	2.52		2.37
45		?	
60	2.35		2.20

Three interpolations are required. First find $F_{.01}$ for $df_1 = 17$ and $df_2 = 40$ and 60.

a. $df_2 = 40$: $F_{.01} = 2.52 - \frac{2}{5}(.15) = 2.46$

b. $df_2 = 60$: $F_{.01} = 2.35 - \frac{2}{5}(.15) = 2.29$

Then find $F_{.01}$ for $df_1 = 17$ and $df_2 = 45$

c. $df_2 = 45$: $F_{.01} = 2.46 - \frac{5}{20}(.17) \cong 2.42$

Table C-1 The F Distribution (Values of $F_{.05}$)*

Degrees of freedom for numerator

Degrees of freedom for denominator	1	2	3	4	5	6	7	8	9	10	12	15	20	24	30	40	60	120	∞
1	161	200	216	225	230	234	237	239	241	242	244	246	248	249	250	251	252	253	254
2	18.5	19.0	19.2	19.2	19.3	19.3	19.4	19.4	19.4	19.4	19.4	19.4	19.4	19.5	19.5	19.5	19.5	19.5	19.5
3	10.1	9.55	9.28	9.12	9.01	8.94	8.89	8.85	8.81	8.79	8.74	8.70	8.66	8.64	8.62	8.59	8.57	8.55	8.53
4	7.71	6.94	6.59	6.39	6.26	6.16	6.09	6.04	6.00	5.96	5.91	5.86	5.80	5.77	5.75	5.72	5.69	5.66	5.63
5	6.61	5.79	5.41	5.19	5.05	4.95	4.88	4.82	4.77	4.74	4.68	4.62	4.56	4.53	4.50	4.46	4.43	4.40	4.37
6	5.99	5.14	4.76	4.53	4.39	4.28	4.21	4.15	4.10	4.06	4.00	3.94	3.87	3.84	3.81	3.77	3.74	3.70	3.67
7	5.59	4.74	4.35	4.12	3.97	3.87	3.79	3.73	3.68	3.64	3.57	3.51	3.44	3.41	3.38	3.34	3.30	3.27	3.23
8	5.32	4.46	4.07	3.84	3.69	3.58	3.50	3.44	3.39	3.35	3.28	3.22	3.15	3.12	3.08	3.04	3.01	2.97	2.93
9	5.12	4.26	3.86	3.63	3.48	3.37	3.29	3.23	3.18	3.14	3.07	3.01	2.94	2.90	2.86	2.83	2.79	2.75	2.71
10	4.96	4.10	3.71	3.48	3.33	3.22	3.14	3.07	3.02	2.98	2.91	2.85	2.77	2.74	2.70	2.66	2.62	2.58	2.54
11	4.84	3.98	3.59	3.36	3.20	3.09	3.01	2.95	2.90	2.85	2.79	2.72	2.65	2.61	2.57	2.53	2.49	2.45	2.40
12	4.75	3.89	3.49	3.26	3.11	3.00	2.91	2.85	2.80	2.75	2.69	2.62	2.54	2.51	2.47	2.43	2.38	2.34	2.30
13	4.67	3.81	3.41	3.18	3.03	2.92	2.83	2.77	2.71	2.67	2.60	2.53	2.46	2.42	2.38	2.34	2.30	2.25	2.21
14	4.60	3.74	3.34	3.11	2.96	2.85	2.76	2.70	2.65	2.60	2.53	2.46	2.39	2.35	2.31	2.27	2.22	2.18	2.13
15	4.54	3.68	3.29	3.06	2.90	2.79	2.71	2.64	2.59	2.54	2.48	2.40	2.33	2.29	2.25	2.20	2.16	2.11	2.07
16	4.49	3.63	3.24	3.01	2.85	2.74	2.66	2.59	2.54	2.49	2.42	2.35	2.28	2.24	2.19	2.15	2.11	2.06	2.01
17	4.45	3.59	3.20	2.96	2.81	2.70	2.61	2.55	2.49	2.45	2.38	2.31	2.23	2.19	2.15	2.10	2.06	2.01	1.96
18	4.41	3.55	3.16	2.93	2.77	2.66	2.58	2.51	2.46	2.41	2.34	2.27	2.19	2.15	2.11	2.06	2.02	1.97	1.92
19	4.38	3.52	3.13	2.90	2.74	2.63	2.54	2.48	2.42	2.38	2.31	2.23	2.16	2.11	2.07	2.03	1.98	1.93	1.88
20	4.35	3.49	3.10	2.87	2.71	2.60	2.51	2.45	2.39	2.35	2.28	2.20	2.12	2.08	2.04	1.99	1.95	1.90	1.84
21	4.32	3.47	3.07	2.84	2.68	2.57	2.49	2.42	2.37	2.32	2.25	2.18	2.10	2.05	2.01	1.96	1.92	1.87	1.81
22	4.30	3.44	3.05	2.82	2.66	2.55	2.46	2.40	2.34	2.30	2.23	2.15	2.07	2.03	1.98	1.94	1.89	1.84	1.78
23	4.28	3.42	3.03	2.80	2.64	2.53	2.44	2.37	2.32	2.27	2.20	2.13	2.05	2.01	1.96	1.91	1.86	1.81	1.76
24	4.26	3.40	3.01	2.78	2.62	2.51	2.42	2.36	2.30	2.25	2.18	2.11	2.03	1.98	1.94	1.89	1.84	1.79	1.73
25	4.24	3.39	2.99	2.76	2.60	2.49	2.40	2.34	2.28	2.24	2.16	2.09	2.01	1.96	1.92	1.87	1.82	1.77	1.71
30	4.17	3.32	2.92	2.69	2.53	2.42	2.33	2.27	2.21	2.16	2.09	2.01	1.93	1.89	1.84	1.79	1.74	1.68	1.62
40	4.08	3.23	2.84	2.61	2.45	2.34	2.25	2.18	2.12	2.08	2.00	1.92	1.84	1.79	1.74	1.69	1.64	1.58	1.51
60	4.00	3.15	2.76	2.53	2.37	2.25	2.17	2.10	2.04	1.99	1.92	1.84	1.75	1.70	1.65	1.59	1.53	1.47	1.39
120	3.92	3.07	2.68	2.45	2.29	2.18	2.09	2.02	1.96	1.91	1.83	1.75	1.66	1.61	1.55	1.50	1.43	1.35	1.25
∞	3.84	3.00	2.60	2.37	2.21	2.10	2.01	1.94	1.88	1.83	1.75	1.67	1.57	1.52	1.46	1.39	1.32	1.22	1.00

*This table reproduced from M. Merrington and C. M. Thompson. "Tables of percentage points of the inverted beta (F) distribution." *Biometrika.* Vol. 33 (1943). by permission of the *Biometrika* Trustees.

Table C-2 The *F* Distribution (Values of $F_{.01}$)*

	\multicolumn{19}{c}{Degrees of freedom for numerator}
Degrees of freedom for denominator	1	2	3	4	5	6	7	8	9	10	12	15	20	24	30	40	60	120	∞
1	4,052	5,000	5,403	5,625	5,764	5,859	5,928	5,982	6,023	6,056	6,106	6,157	6,209	6,235	6,261	6,287	6,313	6,339	6,366
2	98.5	99.0	99.2	99.2	99.3	99.3	99.4	99.4	99.4	99.4	99.4	99.4	99.4	99.5	99.5	99.5	99.5	99.5	99.5
3	34.1	30.8	29.5	28.7	28.2	27.9	27.7	27.5	27.3	27.2	27.1	26.9	26.7	26.6	26.5	26.4	26.3	26.2	26.1
4	21.2	18.0	16.7	16.0	15.5	15.2	15.0	14.8	14.7	14.5	14.4	14.2	14.0	13.9	13.8	13.7	13.7	13.6	13.5
5	16.3	13.3	12.1	11.4	11.0	10.7	10.5	10.3	10.2	10.1	9.89	9.72	9.55	9.47	9.38	9.29	9.20	9.11	9.02
6	13.7	10.9	9.78	9.15	8.75	8.47	8.26	8.10	7.98	7.87	7.72	7.56	7.40	7.31	7.23	7.14	7.06	6.97	6.88
7	12.2	9.55	8.45	7.85	7.46	7.19	6.99	6.84	6.72	6.62	6.47	6.31	6.16	6.07	5.99	5.91	5.82	5.74	5.65
8	11.3	8.65	7.59	7.01	6.63	6.37	6.18	6.03	5.91	5.81	5.67	5.52	5.36	5.28	5.20	5.12	5.03	4.95	4.86
9	10.6	8.02	6.99	6.42	6.06	5.80	5.61	5.47	5.35	5.26	5.11	4.96	4.81	4.73	4.65	4.57	4.48	4.40	4.31
10	10.0	7.56	6.55	5.99	5.64	5.39	5.20	5.06	4.94	4.85	4.71	4.56	4.41	4.33	4.25	4.17	4.08	4.00	3.91
11	9.65	7.21	6.22	5.67	5.32	5.07	4.89	4.74	4.63	4.54	4.40	4.25	4.10	4.02	3.94	3.86	3.78	3.69	3.60
12	9.33	6.93	5.95	5.41	5.06	4.82	4.64	4.50	4.39	4.30	4.16	4.01	3.86	3.78	3.70	3.62	3.54	3.45	3.36
13	9.07	6.70	5.74	5.21	4.86	4.62	4.44	4.30	4.19	4.10	3.96	3.82	3.66	3.59	3.51	3.43	3.34	3.25	3.17
14	8.86	6.51	5.56	5.04	4.70	4.46	4.28	4.14	4.03	3.94	3.80	3.66	3.51	3.43	3.35	3.27	3.18	3.09	3.00
15	8.68	6.36	5.42	4.89	4.56	4.32	4.14	4.00	3.89	3.80	3.67	3.52	3.37	3.29	3.21	3.13	3.05	2.96	2.87
16	8.53	6.23	5.29	4.77	4.44	4.20	4.03	3.89	3.78	3.69	3.55	3.41	3.26	3.18	3.10	3.02	2.93	2.84	2.75
17	8.40	6.11	5.19	4.67	4.34	4.10	3.93	3.79	3.68	3.59	3.46	3.31	3.16	3.08	3.00	2.92	2.83	2.75	2.65
18	8.29	6.01	5.09	4.58	4.25	4.01	3.84	3.71	3.60	3.51	3.37	3.23	3.08	3.00	2.92	2.84	2.75	2.66	2.57
19	8.19	5.93	5.01	4.50	4.17	3.94	3.77	3.63	3.52	3.43	3.30	3.15	3.00	2.92	2.84	2.76	2.67	2.58	2.49
20	8.10	5.85	4.94	4.43	4.10	3.87	3.70	3.56	3.46	3.37	3.23	3.09	2.94	2.86	2.78	2.69	2.61	2.52	2.42
21	8.02	5.78	4.87	4.37	4.04	3.81	3.64	3.51	3.40	3.31	3.17	3.03	2.88	2.80	2.72	2.64	2.55	2.46	2.36
22	7.95	5.72	4.82	4.31	3.99	3.76	3.59	3.45	3.35	3.26	3.12	2.98	2.83	2.75	2.67	2.58	2.50	2.40	2.31
23	7.88	5.66	4.76	4.26	3.94	3.71	3.54	3.41	3.30	3.21	3.07	2.93	2.78	2.70	2.62	2.54	2.45	2.35	2.26
24	7.82	5.61	4.72	4.22	3.90	3.67	3.50	3.36	3.26	3.17	3.03	2.89	2.74	2.66	2.58	2.49	2.40	2.31	2.21
25	7.77	5.57	4.68	4.18	3.86	3.63	3.46	3.32	3.22	3.13	2.99	2.85	2.70	2.62	2.53	2.45	2.36	2.27	2.17
30	7.56	5.39	4.51	4.02	3.70	3.47	3.30	3.17	3.07	2.98	2.84	2.70	2.55	2.47	2.39	2.30	2.21	2.11	2.01
40	7.31	5.18	4.31	3.83	3.51	3.29	3.12	2.99	2.89	2.80	2.66	2.52	2.37	2.29	2.20	2.11	2.02	1.92	1.80
60	7.08	4.98	4.13	3.65	3.34	3.12	2.95	2.82	2.72	2.63	2.50	2.35	2.20	2.12	2.03	1.94	1.84	1.73	1.60
120	6.85	4.79	3.95	3.48	3.17	2.96	2.79	2.66	2.56	2.47	2.34	2.19	2.03	1.95	1.86	1.76	1.66	1.53	1.38
∞	6.63	4.61	3.78	3.32	3.02	2.80	2.64	2.51	2.41	2.32	2.18	2.04	1.88	1.79	1.70	1.59	1.47	1.32	1.00

Quadrant Test for Associations

Significance Levels for Number of Points Falling in Any Quadrant

Number of points	Lower limit 0.05	0.01	Upper limit 0.05	0.01	Number of points	Lower limit 0.05	0.01	Upper limit 0.05	0.01
8-9	0	—	4	—	74-75	13	12	24	25
10-11	0	0	5	5	76-77	14	12	24	26
12-13	0	0	6	6	78-79	14	13	25	26
14-15	1	0	6	7	80-81	15	13	25	27
16-17	1	0	7	8	82-83	15	14	26	27
18-19	1	1	8	8	84-85	16	14	26	28
20-21	2	1	8	9	86-87	16	15	27	28
22-23	2	2	9	9	88-89	16	15	28	29
24-25	3	2	9	10	90-91	17	15	28	30
26-27	3	2	10	11	92-93	17	16	29	30
28-29	3	3	11	11	94-95	18	16	29	31
30-31	4	3	11	12	96-97	18	17	30	31
32-33	4	3	12	13	98-99	19	17	30	32
34-35	5	4	12	13	100-101	19	18	31	32
36-37	5	4	13	14	110-111	21	20	34	35
38-39	6	5	13	14	120-121	24	22	36	38
40-41	6	5	14	15	130-131	26	24	39	41
42-43	6	5	15	16	140-141	28	26	42	44
44-45	7	6	15	16	150-151	31	29	44	46
46-47	7	6	16	17	160-161	33	31	47	49
48-49	8	7	16	17	170-171	35	33	50	52
50-51	8	7	17	18	180-181	37	35	53	55
52-53	8	7	18	19	200-201	42	40	58	60
54-55	9	8	18	19	220-221	47	44	63	66
56-57	9	8	19	20	240-241	51	49	69	71
58-59	10	9	19	20	260-261	56	54	74	76
60-61	10	9	20	21	280-281	61	58	79	82
62-63	11	9	20	22	300-301	66	63	84	87
64-65	11	10	21	22	320-321	70	67	90	93
66-67	12	10	21	23	340-341	75	72	95	98
68-69	12	11	22	23	360-361	80	77	100	103
70-71	12	11	23	24	380-381	84	81	106	109
72-73	13	12	23	24	400-401*	89	86	111	114

*For N large, use $\dfrac{N}{4} \pm \left(\dfrac{1}{2} + \dfrac{d\sqrt{N}}{4} \right)$

where $d = 1.96$ for 5 per cent significance.

$= 2.58$ for 1 per cent significance.

Reprinted with permission from M. H. Quenouille, *Associated Measurements* (England, Butterworths Publishers, Ltd., 1952), Table I, page 225.

Workspace ANOVPRAC

```
        )WSID
ANOVPRAC

        )FNS
R+ANOVA2 D
AN2WAYIN DATA
DATETIME
C+DET Z
T+MVSD X


        )VARS
AA ABSENTEE ABSNAME AMBULANC FCTINFCT INFECT LABTESTS ORTIME ORTNAME
PRESCRIP REFERRAL REFNAME TECHMACH TECHNICS XRAYS

        DATETIME
DATE:  4/18/79     TIME: 10:54:50
```

```
      )FNS ANOVA2
 ∇ R←ANOVA2 D;T;N;CT;A
 [1]  R←((3+T←(ρD)[2]),4)ρ0
 [2]  R[(ιT);13]←⍉(3,T)ρ(ιT),N,(+/D)÷N←+/D>0
 [3]  R[(T+3);12]←(¯1++/N),(+/+/D*2)-CT←((+/+/D)*2)÷+/N
 [4]  R[(T+1);13]←(T-1),A,(A←(+/((+/D)*2)÷N)-CT)÷T-1
 [5]  R[(T+2);12]←R[(T+3);12]-R[(T+1);12]
 [6]  R[(T+2);3]←R[(T+2);2]÷R[(T+2);1]
 [7]  R[(T+1);4]←R[(T+1);3]÷R[(T+2);3]
 [8]  R[(T+3);3]←R[(T+2);3]*0.5
 ∇


      )FNS DATETIME
 ∇ DATETIME;H
 [1]  H←(24 60 60 60)⊤TI20
 [2]  ('DATE: ';'99/99/99'⍕I25);'
      TIME: ';H[1];':';H[2];':';H[3]
 ∇


      )FNS DET
 ∇ C←DET Z;J;Q
 [1]  →(1=ρ,Z)ρ0,C←,Z
 [2]  →L2×ι(2=ρρZ)∧=/ρZ
 [3]  →0,ρ⎕←'ILLEGAL STRUCTURE'
 [4]  L2:→0×ι(1↑ρZ)<J←(Z[1;]=0)ιC←,0
 [5]  Z←(J-1)⌽Z
 [6]  L6:Z←Z-Z[;1]∘.×Z[1;]÷C←Z[1;1]
 [7]  C←(¯1*J-1)×C×DET 1 1 ↓Z
 ∇


      )FNS MVSD
 ∇ T←MVSD X;N;M;VAR;SD
 [1]  SD←(VAR←(+/(X-(ρX)ρM←(+/X)÷N)*2)÷(N←(ρX)[1])-1)*0.5
 [2]  T←⍉(3,ρM,10)ρM,VAR,SD
 ∇
```

```
)FNS AN2WAYIN

∇ AN2WAYIN DATA;X;XT;XTX;Y;YT;YTY;Z;ZT;ZTZ;W;WT;WTW;N;P;Q;NPQ;DXTX;DYTY;DZTZ;DWTW;SST;SSTR;SSB;SSTRB;SSE
[1]   LF←'COCO'I30
[2]   □←LF;'TWO WAY ANALYSIS OF VARIANCE WITH INTERACTION';LF
[3]   ⍝ USES FUNCTIONS DET (DETERMINANT OF MATRIX) AND DATETIME (DATE AND TIME)
[4]   ⍝ LF IS 2 'LINE FEED'S
[5]   DATETIME
[6]   LF
[7]   M1←'999,999,999,990.9999999'
[8]   M2←'999990'
[9]   M3←'999,999,999,990.9999999'
[10]  M4←'99,990.999'
[11]  M5←'9990'
[12]  M1A←M3A←.00000005∘M4A←.0005
[13]  →(3=ρN÷ρDATA)/SIZEOK
[14]  →((2>ρN)∨(3<ρN))/BADDATA
[15]  □←'INPUT MATRIX WAS ONLY 2 DIMENSIONED (';(M5$N);')', NO INTERACTION CAN BE TESTED'
[16]  N←N,1
[17]  DATA←N⍴,DATA
[18]  →SIZEOK
[19]  BADDATA:□←'INPUT MATRIX WAS INCORRECTLY DIMENSIONED (';(M5$N);')', NO CALCULATIONS ARE PERFORMED'
[20]  →0
[21]  SIZEOK:N←N[3]-Q←N[2]-P←N[1]
[22]  PQ←P×Q
[23]  □←(;P);' TREATMENTS (ROWS IN DESIGN MATRIX)'
[24]  □←(;Q);' BLOCKS (COLUMNS IN DESIGN MATRIX)'
[25]  □←(;PQ);' CELLS IN DESIGN MATRIX'
[26]  □←(;N);' CASES PER CELL'
[27]  NPQ←N×PQ
[28]  ⍝ CALCULATE TOTAL SUM OF SQUARES
[29]  XTX←XT+.×X←⍀XT←(2,NPQ)ρ(NPQρ1),(,DATA)
[30]  SST←(÷NPQ)× DET XTX
[31]  ⍝ CALCULATE TREATMENTS SUM OF SQUARES
[32]  YTY←YT+.×Y←⍀YT←(2,P)ρ(Pρ1),(+/+/DATA)÷N×Q
[33]  SSTR←(Q×N÷P)× DET YTY
[34]  ⍝ CALCULATE BLOCKS SUM OF SQUARES
[35]  ZTZ←ZT+.×Z←⍀ZT←(2,Q)ρ(Qρ1),(+/+/DATA)÷N×P
[36]  SSB←(P×N÷Q)×DET ZTZ
[37]  ⍝ CALCULATE INTERACTION SUM OF SQUARES
```

```
[38]  XBIJ+(+/DATA)÷N
[39]  XBAR+(÷PQ)×+/+/XBIJ
[40]  MSTRB+SSTRB+DFTRB+0
[41]  +(N=1)/CALSSE
[42]  XBI+(÷Q)×+/XBIJ
[43]  XBI+XBI∘.×(QP1)
[44]  XBJ+(PP1)∘.×(÷P)×+/XBIJ
[45]  WTW+WT+.×W+QWT+(2,PQ)ρ(PQP1),(,XBIJ-(XBI+XBJ-XBAR))
[46]  SSTRB+(N÷PQ)× DET WTW
[47]  ⍝ CALCULATE ERROR SUM OF SQUARES
[48]  CALSSE:SSE+SST-(SSTR+SSB+SSTRB)
[49]  ⍝ DEGREES OF FREEDOM
[50]  DFTR+P-1
[51]  DFB+Q-1
[52]  DFTRB+DFTR×DFB∘+(N=1)/CALDFE
[53]  CALDFE:DFE+(NPQ-1)-(DFTR+DFB+DFTRB)
[54]  ⍝ MEAN SQUARES
[55]  MSTR+SSTR÷DFTR
[56]  MSB+SSB÷DFB
[57]  MSTRB+SSTRB÷DFTRB∘+(N=1)/CALMSE
[58]  CALMSE:MSE+SSE÷DFE
[59]  ⍝ PRINT OUT RESULTS
[60]  ☐+LF;'CELL MEANS'
[61]  M4$M4+XBIJ
[62]  ☐+LF;'GRAND MEAN  ';XBAR
[63]  ☐+LF;'ANOVA TABLE WITHOUT F-VALUES'
[64]  ☐+'SOURCE';(16ρ' '),'SUMS OF SQUARES       DF       MEAN SQUARES';LF
[65]  ☐+'TREATMENT   ';(M1$M1A+SSTR);(M2$DFTR);M3$M3A+MSTR
[66]  ☐+'BLOCK       ';(M1$M1A+SSB);(M2$DFB);M3$M3A+MSB
[67]  ☐+'INTERACTION ';(M1$M1A+SSTRB);(M2$DFTRB);M3$M3A+MSTRB
[68]  ☐+'ERROR       ';(M1$M1A+SSE);(M2$DFE);M3$M3A+MSE
[69]  ☐+'TOTAL       ';(M1$M1A+SST);M2$NPQ-1
[70]  ☐+LF;'CALCULATE APPROPRIATE F-VALUES'
[71]  ☐+'DEPENDING ON INTERACTION SIGNIFICANCE '
[72]  ☐+'AND DATA MODEL OF FIXED, RANDOM OR MIXED EFFECTS'
[73]  ☐+LF;LF
[74]  ◊')ERASE LF M1 M2 M3 M4 MSB MSE MSTR MSTRB PQ XBAR XBI XBIJ XBJ'
[75]  ◊')ERASE DFB DFE DFTR DFTRB'
[76]  ◊')ERASE M5 M1A M3A M4A'
```

AA

```
10   9   8   9
14  13  12   9
 6   5   4   6
```

ABSENTEE

```
3  2  4  5  4
2  4  5  6  3
4  3  6  4  3
1  2
2  2
```

ABSNAME

RADIOL   LABOR   HOUSEKEEP

AMBULANC

```
4  3  5  6  7  3
3  4  4  3  5  4
2  3  4  2  4  4
2  2  3  4  5  3
```

FCTINFCT

```
558.63   602.82    634.96    657.2     681.72   686.78   694.13   694.24   699.76   700.13   718.36
743.37   744.41    805.45    807.13    724.75   788.6    802.34   899.09   914.42   918.77   928
609.58   629.06    642.45    701.18    708.79   782.91   787.41   789.41   804.34   862.8    912.9
928.68   935.95   1196.31   1245.47    707.01   708.69   750.34   776.6    915.15   993.42  1043.17

582.3    606.44    649.9     652.25
919.09   959.02    984.28   1229.99
610.51   675.28    682.24    690.7
1144.93 1259.49   1475.71   1786.01
```

```
INFECT
558.63     609.58      582.3     610.51
602.82     629.06     606.44     675.28
634.96     642.45      649.9     682.24
657.2      701.18     652.25      690.7
681.72     724.75     708.79     707.01
686.78      788.6     782.91     708.69
694.13     802.34     787.41     750.34
694.24     899.09     789.41      776.6
699.76     914.42     804.34     915.15
700.13     918.77      862.8     993.42
718.36        928      912.9    1043.17
743.37     928.68     919.09    1144.93
744.41     935.95     959.02    1259.49
805.45    1196.31     984.28    1475.71
807.13    1245.47    1229.99    1786.01
```

```
LABTESTS

    1          3          5
    6          4          7
    8          9         10

    4          7          5
    7          8          9
    2          5          6

    1          2          4
    3          7          6
    1          4          5

    2          1          5
    1          2          4
    8          9         11
```

```
ORTIME

   35         42         29         48         28
   30         47         32         46         33
   39         41         37         42         39
   32         38         30         44         34
```

```
ORTNAME
HOSP I    HOSP II    HOSP III    HOSP IV    HOSP V
```

```
PRESCRIP
    11       7       3
    12      10       8
     8       6       4
    10       6       2

    12       8       4
     6       4       2
    17      14      11
     3       1       0


REFERRAL
    13      17      10       8
    15      16      14       6
    12      19      12       9
    14      19      11      10

  REFNAME
  CITY A   CITY B   CITY C   CITY D


    )DIGITS 4
WAS 10

    TECHMACH
91  80  71  74  85  85  72  79  95  86  95  71  82  80  73
86  84  93  86  84  87  90  82  90  76  88  99  80  85  92
71  77  71  77  79  79  71  82  87  88  70  76  88  88  89

79  62  71  81  78  66  65  63  71  80  67  74  62  61  82
58  70  80  77  79  71  58  79  62  79  72  67  73  75  74
81  86  87  87  78  81  69  85  73  76  69  73  71  82  76

    )DIGITS 10
WAS 4

    TECHNICS
        91      58
        80      70
        71      80
        74      77
        85      79
        85      71
        72      58


    XRAYS

     3       4       2       4       7
     2       4       1       5       5
     4       5       2       6       9
```

Workspace CORRPRAC

```
A   LIBRARY FOR   CORRELATION, COVARIANCE AND
    MULTIPLE REGRESSION PRACTICE

      )WSID
CORRPRAC

      )FNS
CMRT X
CMRTHOW
C+COV X
DATETIME
C+DET Z
X+DIAG A
MRCLEAN
Y MREG X
T+MVSD X

      )VARS
A COST COSTEST RAD X5 X6 X6NAMES Y YNAMES

      DATETIME
DATE:   4/17/79      TIME: 15:8:6
```

```
      )FNS CMRT
∇ CMRT X;V;C;N;LF;I
 [1]  D←LF←'CO'I30
 [2]  N←1↑N∘C←1↓N←ρX
 [3]  'CORRELATION MATRIX'
 [4]  '9990.999' $.0005+R←R÷(V∘.×V←(1 1)⍴R←(⍉R)+.×R←X-(ρX)ρ(+⌿X)÷N)*0.5
 [5]  LF
 [6]  'T-VALUES  FOR DF= ';N-2
 [7]  '9990.999' $.0005+T←R×((1-I)×(N-2)÷((I←(C,C)ρ1,CρO)+(1-R*2)))*÷2
 [8]  LF;'VALUES OF R AND T ARE ALSO AVAILABLE WITH FULL PRECISION'
 [9]  LF
 ∇
```

```
      )FNS CR
)FNS CMRTHOW

∇ CMRTHOW
 [1]  ''
 [2]  'CMRT  X'
 [3]  ''
 [4]  'CMRT FINDS THE CORRELATION MATRIX OF A SET OF VARIABLES'
 [5]  'CONTAINED IN THE MATRIX  X, WHICH IS OF SIZE N BY C,'
 [6]  'WHERE N IS THE NUMBER OF OBSERVATIONS'
 [7]  'AND    C IS THE NUMBER OF VARIABLES (COLUMNS).'
 [8]  ''
 [9]  'IT ALSO CALCULATES THE T STATISTIC FOR EACH CORRELATION COEFFICIENT,'
 [10] 'AND PRINTS THE APPROPRIATE NUMBER OF DEGREES OF FREEDOM.'
 [11] ''
 [12] 'THE RESULTS ARE PRINTED, ROUNDED OFF TO 3 DECIMAL PLACES,'
 [13] 'BUT THEY ARE ALSO STORED IN TWO MATRICES,  R AND T,'
 [14] 'WHICH REPLACE ANY VARIABLES  WHICH PREVIOUSLY HAD THOSE NAMES.'
 [15] ''
 [16] 'A MATRIX ''A'' IS STORED IN THIS WORKSPACE,'
 [17] 'WITH SIZE 6 BY 3, AS FOLLOWS:'
 [18] ''
 [19] ⍎'A'
 [20] ''
 [21] 'AND THE RESULT OF TYPING:'
 [22] '    CMRT A'
 [23] 'IS:'
 [24] ⍎'CMRT A'
 ∇
```

```
      CMRTHOW

CMRT   X

CMRT FINDS THE CORRELATION MATRIX OF A SET OF VARIABLES
CONTAINED IN THE MATRIX  X, WHICH IS OF SIZE N BY C,
WHERE N IS THE NUMBER OF OBSERVATIONS
AND    C IS THE NUMBER OF VARIABLES (COLUMNS).

IT ALSO CALCULATES THE T STATISTIC FOR EACH CORRELATION COEFFICIENT,
AND PRINTS THE APPROPRIATE NUMBER OF DEGREES OF FREEDOM.

THE RESULTS ARE PRINTED, ROUNDED OFF TO 3 DECIMAL PLACES,
BUT THEY ARE ALSO STORED IN TWO MATRICES,  R AND T,
WHICH REPLACE ANY VARIABLES  WHICH PREVIOUSLY HAD THOSE NAMES.

A MATRIX 'A' IS STORED IN THIS WORKSPACE,
WITH SIZE 6 BY 3, AS FOLLOWS:
```

```
        10          145         1
         5          105         0
         3          100         0
         6           95         1
         4           95         1
         3           80       •  0
```

AND THE RESULT OF TYPING:
      CMRT A
IS:

CORRELATION MATRIX
    1.000   0.899   0.623
    0.899   1.000   0.414
    0.623   0.414   1.000

T-VALUES   FOR DF= 4
    0.000   4.100   1.591
    4.100   0.000   0.909
    1.591   0.909   0.000

VALUES OF R AND T ARE ALSO AVAILABLE WITH FULL PRECISION

)FNS COV

▼ C←COV X;R;N
  [1] C←(÷N-1)×(⍉R)+.×R←X-(⍴X)⍴(+/X)÷N←(⍴X)[1]
▼

)FNS DATETIME

▼ DATETIME;H
  [1] H←(24 60 60 60)⊤I20
  [2] ('DATE: ';'99/99/99'⍕I25);'   TIME: ';H[1];':';H[2];':';H[3]
▼

)FNS DET

▼ C←DET Z;J;Q
  [1] →(1=⍴,Z)⍴0,C←,Z
  [2] →L2×⍳(2=⍴⍴Z)∧=/⍴Z
  [3] →0,⍴□←'ILLEGAL STRUCTURE'
  [4] L2:→0×⍳(1↑⍴Z)<J←(Z[1;]=0)⍳C←,0
  [5] Z←(J-1)⌽Z
  [6] L6:Z←Z-Z[;1]∘.×Z[1;]÷C←Z[1;1]
  [7] C←(¯1*J-1)×C×DET 1 1 ↓Z
▼

)FNS DIAG
▼ X←DIAG A;X;A;N
  [1] X←(N,N)⍴((N×N)⍴1,(N←⍴A)⍴0)\A
▼

)FNS MRCLEAN

▼ MRCLEAN
  [1] ⍕')ERASE MSS MDF MF MB MRB LF KK K N XTXINV XTY SST SSB SSBO
      SSREG SSRES MSREG MSRES F COVB SEB RB RSQ '
  [2] ⍕')ERASE SEBI B'
▼
```
```

```
      )FNS MREG
    ▽ Y MREG X
[1]   □←3ρLF←'CO'I30
[2]   MSS←'999,999,999,990,9999'◦MDF←'999990'◦MF←'99,990,9999'◦MB←'999,990,9999'◦MRB←'9990.9999'
[3]   'MULTIPLE REGRESSION ANALYSIS'
[4]   LF
[5]   DATETIME
[6]   3ρLF
[7]   N←1↑K←ρX
[8]   LINTEST:K←K,1◦→(1≠ρK)/LINFIX
[9]   LINFIX:KK←1+K+1↓K
[10]  TEST:→0◦□←'SIZE OF Y AND X NOT COMPATIBLE'◦→(N≡ρY)/OKSIZE
[11]  OKSIZE:
[12]  X←⍉(KK,N)ρY,(,⍉X)
[13]  'CORRELATION MATRIX OF RAW DATA - DEPENDENT VARIABLE FIRST'
[14]  LF
[15]  CMRT X
[16]  3ρLF
[17]  X[;1]←Nρ1
[18]  XTXINV←⊞(⍉X)+.×X
[19]  XTY←(⍉X)+.×Y
[20]  B←XTXINV+.×XTY
[21]  SST←Y+.×Y
[22]  SSB←B+.×XTY
[23]  SSB0←((+/Y)*2)÷N
[24]  SSREG←SSB-SSB0
[25]  SSRES←SST-SSB
[26]  MSREG←SSREG÷K
[27]  MSRES←SSRES÷N-K+1
[28]  F←MSREG÷MSRES
```

```
[29] COVB←MSRES×XTXINV
[30] SEB←(1 1⍉COVB)*÷2
[31] RB←SEBI+.×COVB+.×SEBI←(KK,KK)⍴((KK×KK)⍴1,(KKρO))\÷SEB
[32] RSQ←SSREG÷SST-SSB0
[33] ⎕←'REGRESSION ANALYSIS OF VARIANCE TABLE'
[34] LF
[35] 'SOURCE           SUM OF SQUARES        D.F.        MEAN SQUARES
[36] LF
[37] 'REGRESSION: ';MSS $ SSB
[38] 'B0        ';MSS $ SSB0
[39] 'B1 TO B';K;'    ';(MSS $ SSREG);(MDF $ K);(MSS $ MSREG);(MF $ F)
[40] LF
[41] 'RESIDUALS   ';(MSS $ SSRES);(MDF $ N-K+1);(MSS $ MSRES)
[42] LF
[43] 'TOTAL (CORR)';MSS $ SST-SSB0
[44] LF
[45] 80ρ'-'
[46] 2ρLF
[47] 'BVALUES: ';MB$B
[48] 'TVALUES: ';MB $B÷SEB
[49] LF;LF
[50] 'R SQUARED:';MF $ RSQ
[51] 'STD.ERR.:';MSS$ MSRES*÷2
[52] 2ρLF
[53] 'CORRELATION MATRIX OF BVALUES'
[54] LF
[55] MRB $ .00005+RB
[56] LF
[57] 'FINISHED'
[58] 3ρLF
```

RAD

19	3.5	12.2	5
17	7.1	8.9	9
13	2.9	9	10
20	4.8	12.5	20
26	5.1	6.8	25
16	6.3	7.9	7
12	4.8	8.5	15
12	3.7	6.9	5
24	4.1	10.4	19
24	4.3	9.2	25
24	4.5	9	27
17	3.8	7.9	16
22	4.6	8.3	20
17	3.9	8.2	9
15	6.5	11.1	12
10	6.9	10.3	15
15	5.8	9.8	20
30	5.9	12.1	25
27	6	11.4	18
26	5.3	7.1	5
24	4.6	8.3	10
10	6.4	8	6
24	5.5	8.8	12
21	5.3	8.2	25
23	5.7	9.1	20

25    $_4^{8}$RAD

```
      )FNS  MVSD

∇ T←MVSD X;N;M;VAR;SD
[1] SD←(VAR←(+/(X-(ρX)ρM←(+/X)÷N)*2)÷(N←(ρX)[1])-1)*0.5
[2] T←⍕(3,ρM,10)ρM,VAR,SD
∇
```

```
      A
10  145  1
 5  105  0
 3  100  0
 6   95  1
 4   95  1
 3   80  0
```

```
      COST
 9407.5   9756   7785.5  10649.5  10215.5  7881  7589.5  7061  10422.5  10054.5  10680.5  8955.5  9463.5  9230.5  9603  8911  9847
12061  12210  10121  9817.5  7797  9937.5  9673.5  10449
```

```
      25  ρCOST
```

```
      COSTEST
12.8  16.1  15    12    18.3  19   19   22   15.5  21   19   19   22   15.5  21   19.2
16.3  11.2  16.1  13.2  6.8   5.5  4.9  6.9  6.3   5.9  5.5  4.9  6.9  6.3   5.9  6.4
 4.9   3.8   5.1   3
 4.7   3.9   5.8   4.2
```

```
      )DIGITS 5
WAS 10
```

```
      COSTEST
12.8  16.1  15   12   18.3  19   22   15.5  21   19.2
 4.9   3.8   5.1   3   6.8  5.5  6.9  6.3   5.9  6.4
```

```
      )DIGITS 10
WAS 5
```

X5

21	43	76
43	56	54
34	78	86
45	34	43
25	12	52
36	45	75
21	56	65
75	67	54
34	78	45
67	35	56
89	47	34
30	24	24
21	38	78
35	15	56
36	45	34

X6

105	150	26	300
147	175	37	588
245	200	62	857
175	150	44	525
210	145	52	903
252	250	63	1008
203	200	50	709
154	160	39	473
140	120	35	495
196	150	50	983

X6NAMES

BED DAYS	LAB TESTS	HOUSEKEEPING	NURSING

YNAMES

AGE	HEIGHT	MASS	SEX

Y

AGE	HEIGHT	MASS	SEX
10	145	40	1
5	105	20	0
3	100	16	0
6	95	20	1
4	95	17	1
3	80	15	0
15	170	64	0
12	150	45	0
10	135	40	1
9	145	45	0
14	140	50	0
15	150	66	0
10	120	39	1
6	115	27	0
3	90	13	1
11	125	42	1
9	125	31	1
7	120	25	0
8	130	30	1
7	100	23	0
13	160	57	1

Solutions to Selected Problems

Chapter 1

1. (a) $\mathbf{A} + \mathbf{B} = \begin{bmatrix} 1290 & 6512 & 736 \\ 4303 & 8206 & 1020 \\ 5672 & 1927 & 2001 \end{bmatrix} + \begin{bmatrix} 926 & 5200 & 230 \\ 3000 & 9000 & 800 \\ 6260 & 1700 & 2200 \end{bmatrix}$

$= \begin{bmatrix} 2216 & 11712 & 966 \\ 7303 & 17206 & 1820 \\ 11932 & 3627 & 4201 \end{bmatrix}$

(b) $\mathbf{A} - \mathbf{B} = \begin{bmatrix} 364 & 1312 & 506 \\ 1303 & -794 & 220 \\ -588 & 227 & 199 \end{bmatrix}$

2. (a) $\mathbf{A} \cdot \mathbf{B} = \begin{bmatrix} 12 & 14 & 16 \\ 30 & 50 & 10 \\ 8 & 7 & 9 \\ 4 & 6 & 1 \end{bmatrix} \cdot \begin{bmatrix} 1 & 3 & 2 & 6 \\ 4 & 2 & 6 & 1 \\ 5 & 5 & 7 & 4 \end{bmatrix}$

463

$$= \begin{bmatrix} 148 & 144 & 220 & 150 \\ 280 & 240 & 430 & 270 \\ 81 & 83 & 121 & 91 \\ 33 & 29 & 51 & 34 \end{bmatrix}$$

(b) $\mathbf{B} \cdot \mathbf{A} = \begin{bmatrix} 142 & 214 & 70 \\ 160 & 204 & 139 \\ 282 & 393 & 197 \end{bmatrix}$

(c) $\mathbf{A} \cdot \mathbf{B} \neq \mathbf{B} \cdot \mathbf{A}$

3. (a) $\mathbf{A} \cdot \mathbf{B} = \begin{bmatrix} 1 & 3 & 6 \\ 2 & 7 & 9 \\ 8 & 3 & 4 \end{bmatrix} \cdot \begin{bmatrix} 2 & 6 \\ 12 & 10 \\ 20 & 1 \end{bmatrix} = \begin{bmatrix} 158 & 42 \\ 268 & 91 \\ 132 & 82 \end{bmatrix}$

(b) $\mathbf{B} \cdot \mathbf{A} =$ Impossible $\qquad (3 \times 2) \cdot (3 \times 3)$
$$\underset{\neq}{\underbrace{\qquad}}$$

(c) $\mathbf{A} \cdot \mathbf{B} \neq \mathbf{B} \cdot \mathbf{A}$

4. (a) $\mathbf{A} \cdot \mathbf{B} = \begin{bmatrix} 3 & 5 \\ 7 & 8 \end{bmatrix} \cdot \begin{bmatrix} 4 & 2 & 12 \\ 9 & 3 & 6 \end{bmatrix} = \begin{bmatrix} 57 & 21 & 66 \\ 100 & 38 & 132 \end{bmatrix}$

(b) $\mathbf{B} \cdot \mathbf{A} =$ Impossible

(c) $|\mathbf{A}| = 24 - 35 = -11$

(d) $\mathbf{A}'\mathbf{A} = \begin{bmatrix} 3 & 7 \\ 5 & 8 \end{bmatrix} \cdot \begin{bmatrix} 3 & 5 \\ 7 & 8 \end{bmatrix} = \begin{bmatrix} 58 & 71 \\ 71 & 89 \end{bmatrix}$

(e) $\mathbf{B}'\mathbf{B} = \begin{bmatrix} 4 & 9 \\ 2 & 3 \\ 12 & 6 \end{bmatrix} \cdot \begin{bmatrix} 4 & 2 & 12 \\ 9 & 3 & 6 \end{bmatrix} = \begin{bmatrix} 97 & 35 & 102 \\ 35 & 13 & 42 \\ 102 & 42 & 180 \end{bmatrix}$

(f) $\mathbf{BB'} = \begin{bmatrix} 4 & 2 & 12 \\ 9 & 3 & 6 \end{bmatrix} \cdot \begin{bmatrix} 4 & 9 \\ 2 & 3 \\ 12 & 6 \end{bmatrix} = \begin{bmatrix} 164 & 114 \\ 114 & 126 \end{bmatrix}$

(g) $\mathbf{x'B} = \begin{bmatrix} 1 & 6 \end{bmatrix} \cdot \begin{bmatrix} 4 & 2 & 12 \\ 9 & 3 & 6 \end{bmatrix} = \begin{bmatrix} 58 & 20 & 48 \end{bmatrix}$

(h) $\mathbf{x'Ax} = \begin{bmatrix} 1 & 6 \end{bmatrix} \cdot \begin{bmatrix} 3 & 5 \\ 7 & 8 \end{bmatrix} \cdot \begin{bmatrix} 1 \\ 6 \end{bmatrix} = \begin{bmatrix} 1 & 6 \end{bmatrix} \cdot \begin{bmatrix} 33 \\ 55 \end{bmatrix} = 363$

$\text{OR} = \begin{bmatrix} 45 & 53 \end{bmatrix} \cdot \begin{bmatrix} 1 \\ 6 \end{bmatrix} = 363$

(i) $\mathbf{A}^{-1} = \frac{1}{|\mathbf{A}|} \begin{bmatrix} 8 & -5 \\ -7 & 3 \end{bmatrix} = \frac{1}{-11} \begin{bmatrix} 8 & -5 \\ -7 & 3 \end{bmatrix}$

$= \begin{bmatrix} -\dfrac{8}{11} & \dfrac{5}{11} \\[2ex] \dfrac{7}{11} & -\dfrac{3}{11} \end{bmatrix}$

5. (a) $\mathbf{AB} = \begin{bmatrix} 4 & 6 \\ 3 & 2 \\ 7 & 1 \end{bmatrix} \cdot \begin{bmatrix} 2 & 4 & 5 & 7 \\ 3 & 2 & 7 & 5 \end{bmatrix} = \begin{bmatrix} 26 & 28 & 62 & 58 \\ 12 & 16 & 29 & 31 \\ 17 & 30 & 42 & 54 \end{bmatrix}$

(b) $\mathbf{BA} = $ Impossible

(c) $\mathbf{A'A} = \begin{bmatrix} 4 & 3 & 7 \\ 6 & 2 & 1 \end{bmatrix} \cdot \begin{bmatrix} 4 & 6 \\ 3 & 2 \\ 7 & 1 \end{bmatrix} = \begin{bmatrix} 74 & 37 \\ 37 & 41 \end{bmatrix}$

(d) $\mathbf{A}^{-1} = $ IMPOSSIBLE ($\mathbf{A}$ must be square).

(e) $(\mathbf{A}'\mathbf{A})^{-1} = \begin{bmatrix} 74 & 37 \\ 37 & 41 \end{bmatrix}^{-1}$

$$= \frac{1}{(74 \times 41) - 37^2} \begin{bmatrix} 41 & -37 \\ -37 & 74 \end{bmatrix}$$

$$= \frac{1}{1665} \begin{bmatrix} 41 & -37 \\ -37 & 74 \end{bmatrix}$$

$$= \begin{bmatrix} 0.0246246 & -0.0222222 \\ -0.0222222 & 0.0444444 \end{bmatrix}$$

6. (a) $\mathbf{X}'\mathbf{X} = \begin{bmatrix} 1 & 1 & 1 & 1 & 1 & 1 & 1 \\ 3 & 7 & 4 & 9 & 6 & 5 & 8 \end{bmatrix} \cdot \begin{bmatrix} 1 & 3 \\ 1 & 7 \\ 1 & 4 \\ 1 & 9 \\ 1 & 6 \\ 1 & 5 \\ 1 & 8 \end{bmatrix} = \begin{bmatrix} 7 & 42 \\ 42 & 280 \end{bmatrix}$

(b) $\mathbf{X}'\mathbf{y} = \begin{bmatrix} 1 & 1 & 1 & 1 & 1 & 1 & 1 \\ 3 & 7 & 4 & 9 & 6 & 5 & 8 \end{bmatrix} \cdot \begin{bmatrix} 6 \\ 3 \\ 9 \\ 10 \\ 12 \\ 8 \\ 7 \end{bmatrix} = \begin{bmatrix} 55 \\ 333 \end{bmatrix}$

(c) $(\mathbf{X}'\mathbf{X})^{-1} = \begin{bmatrix} 7 & 42 \\ 42 & 280 \end{bmatrix}^{-1}$

$$= \frac{1}{(7 \times 280) - 42^2} \begin{bmatrix} 280 & -42 \\ -42 & 7 \end{bmatrix}$$

$$= \frac{1}{196} \begin{bmatrix} 280 & -42 \\ -42 & 7 \end{bmatrix}$$

$$= \begin{bmatrix} 1.4285714 & -0.2142857 \\ -0.2142857 & 0.0357142 \end{bmatrix}$$

(d) $(\mathbf{X}'\mathbf{X})^{-1}\mathbf{X}'\mathbf{y} = \frac{1}{196} \begin{bmatrix} 280 & -42 \\ -42 & 7 \end{bmatrix} \begin{bmatrix} 55 \\ 283 \end{bmatrix}$

$$= \frac{1}{196} \begin{bmatrix} 3514 \\ -329 \end{bmatrix}$$

$$= \begin{bmatrix} 17.928571 \\ -1.6785714 \end{bmatrix}$$

7. (a) $\mathbf{X}'\mathbf{X} = \begin{bmatrix} 1 & 1 & 1 & 1 & 1 \\ 2 & 7 & 3 & 9 & 5 \\ 4 & 6 & 1 & 9 & 2 \\ 9 & 5 & 8 & 6 & 4 \end{bmatrix} \cdot \begin{bmatrix} 1 & 2 & 4 & 9 \\ 1 & 7 & 6 & 5 \\ 1 & 3 & 1 & 8 \\ 1 & 9 & 9 & 6 \\ 1 & 5 & 2 & 4 \end{bmatrix} = \begin{bmatrix} 5 & 26 & 22 & 32 \\ 26 & 168 & 144 & 151 \\ 22 & 144 & 138 & 136 \\ 32 & 151 & 136 & 222 \end{bmatrix}$

(b) $\mathbf{X}'\mathbf{y} = \begin{bmatrix} 1 & 1 & 1 & 1 & 1 \\ 2 & 7 & 3 & 9 & 5 \\ 4 & 6 & 1 & 9 & 2 \\ 9 & 5 & 8 & 6 & 4 \end{bmatrix} \cdot \begin{bmatrix} 6 \\ 3 \\ 9 \\ 10 \\ 8 \end{bmatrix} = \begin{bmatrix} 36 \\ 190 \\ 157 \\ 233 \end{bmatrix}$

8.   Let number of physicians in region I be **N1**.
Let number of physicians in region II be **N2**.

$$N1 = \begin{bmatrix} 400 & 60 & 190 \\ 800 & 240 & 30 \\ 110 & 52 & 70 \\ 30 & 3 & 6 \end{bmatrix}$$

$$N2 = \begin{bmatrix} 212 & 83 & 364 \\ 350 & 612 & 87 \\ 62 & 316 & 79 \\ 14 & 4 & 12 \end{bmatrix}$$

$$N1 + N2 = \begin{bmatrix} 612 & 143 & 554 \\ 1150 & 852 & 117 \\ 172 & 368 & 149 \\ 44 & 7 & 18 \end{bmatrix}$$

9. $$N1 - N2 = \begin{bmatrix} 188 & -23 & -174 \\ 450 & -372 & -57 \\ 48 & -264 & -9 \\ 16 & -1 & -6 \end{bmatrix}$$

Region I has more physicians in general practice than Region II for each age group. The opposite is true for surgery and internal medicine.

10.   Let male disability days be **MDD**.
Let female disability days be **FDD**.

(a) $$MDD = \begin{bmatrix} 20 & 17 & 18 \\ 35 & 29 & 21 \\ 42 & 37 & 36 \end{bmatrix} \qquad FDD = \begin{bmatrix} 12 & 9 & 3 \\ 28 & 27 & 15 \\ 37 & 25 & 27 \end{bmatrix}$$

(b) $\mathbf{MDD} - \mathbf{FDD} = \begin{bmatrix} 8 & 8 & 15 \\ 7 & 2 & 6 \\ 5 & 12 & 9 \end{bmatrix}$

11.   Let service requirements by condition be **R**.
Let labor requirements by service be **L**.

$$R = \begin{bmatrix} 1200 & 1300 & 20 \\ 800 & 600 & 400 \\ 500 & 480 & 150 \\ 0 & 370 & 230 \end{bmatrix} \qquad L = \begin{bmatrix} 1.3 & .5 & 0 & .1 \\ 2.1 & 1.2 & 2.3 & 1.0 \\ 0 & 0 & 1.5 & 2.6 \end{bmatrix}$$

Total labor requirements by diagnostic condition is

$$RL = \begin{bmatrix} 4290 & 2160 & 3020 & 1472 \\ 2300 & 1120 & 1980 & 1720 \\ 1658 & 826 & 1329 & 920 \\ 777 & 444 & 1196 & 968 \end{bmatrix}$$

Total labor requirements is $\mathbf{SRL}' = \begin{bmatrix} 1 & 1 & 1 & 1 \end{bmatrix} \cdot \mathbf{RL}$

$$= \begin{bmatrix} 9025 & 4550 & 7525 & 5080 \end{bmatrix}$$

12.   Let wage rates be $\mathbf{W} = \begin{bmatrix} 7 \\ 6 \\ 9 \\ 4 \end{bmatrix}$.

Total wage bill $= \mathbf{SRL}' \cdot \mathbf{W}$

$$= \begin{bmatrix} 9025 & 4550 & 7525 & 5080 \end{bmatrix} \cdot \begin{bmatrix} 7 \\ 6 \\ 9 \\ 4 \end{bmatrix} = \$178{,}520$$

Chapter 4

1.
Source	SS	df	MS	F	$F_{.05}$
Treatments (Departments)	11.2	2	5.6	5.09	3.89
Error	13.2	12	1.1		
Total	24.4	14			
Significant					

2.
Source	SS	df	MS	F	$F_{.01}$
Treatments (Cities)	187.1875	3	62.39583	25.60	5.95
Error	29.25	12	2.4375		
Total	216.4375	15			
Significant					

3.
Source	SS	df	MS	F	$F_{.05}$
Treatments (Hospitals)	539.2	4	134.8	9.77	3.06
Error	207	15	13.8		
Total	746.2	19			
Significant					

Chapter 5

1. $\mathbf{X}' = \begin{bmatrix} 1 & 1 & 1 & 1 & 1 & 1 & 1 & 1 & 1 & 1 & 1 & 1 & 1 & 1 & 1 \\ 3 & 4 & 2 & 4 & 7 & 2 & 4 & 1 & 5 & 5 & 4 & 5 & 2 & 6 & 9 \end{bmatrix}$

$\mathbf{X}'\mathbf{X} = \begin{bmatrix} 15 & 63 \\ 63 & 327 \end{bmatrix}$

$SS(T) = \dfrac{1}{15} \begin{vmatrix} 15 & 63 \\ 63 & 327 \end{vmatrix} = 327 - \dfrac{1}{15}(63)^2 = 327 - 264.6 = 62.4$

$\mathbf{Y}' = \begin{bmatrix} 1 & 1 & 1 \\ 4 & 4.2 & 5.2 \end{bmatrix}$

$$\mathbf{Y'Y} = \begin{bmatrix} 3 & 13.4 \\ 13.4 & 60.68 \end{bmatrix}$$

$$SS(TR) = \frac{5}{3} \begin{vmatrix} 3 & 13.4 \\ 13.4 & 60.68 \end{vmatrix} = 5 \times 60.8 - \frac{5}{3}(13.4)^2$$

$$= 304.0 - 299.2666 = 4.13334$$

$$\mathbf{Z'} = \begin{bmatrix} 1 & 1 & 1 & 1 & 1 \\ 3 & 4.333 & 1.667 & 5 & 7 \end{bmatrix}$$

$$\mathbf{Z'Z} = \begin{bmatrix} 5 & 21 \\ 21 & 104.55555 \end{bmatrix}$$

$$SS(B) = \frac{3}{5} \begin{vmatrix} 5 & 21 \\ 21 & 104.55555 \end{vmatrix} = 313.66665 - 264.6 = 49.06665$$

$$SS(E) = SS(T) - SS(TR) - SS(B)$$
$$= 62.4 - 4.13334 - 49.06665$$
$$= 9.20001$$

ANOVA Table

Source	SS	df	MS	F	$F_{.05}$
Treatment (Hospitals)	4.13334	2	2.06667	1.797	4.46
Block (Problems)	49.06665	4	12.266662	10.67	3.84
Error	9.20001	8	1.1500012		
Total	62.4	14			

The differences in utilization of radiology among the hospitals are not significant, but those among the problems are, at the $\alpha = .05$ level.

3. a) $\mathbf{X'} = \begin{bmatrix} 1 & 1 & 1 & 1 & 1 & 1 & 1 & 1 & 1 & 1 & 1 & 1 \\ 11 & 7 & 3 & 12 & 10 & 8 & 8 & 6 & 4 & 10 & 6 & 2 \end{bmatrix}$

$$\begin{bmatrix} 1 & 1 & 1 & 1 & 1 & 1 & 1 & 1 & 1 & 1 & 1 & 1 \\ 12 & 8 & 4 & 6 & 4 & 2 & 17 & 14 & 11 & 3 & 1 & 0 \end{bmatrix}$$

$$\mathbf{X'X} = \begin{bmatrix} 24 & 169 \\ 169 & 1639 \end{bmatrix}$$

$$SS(T) = \frac{1}{24} \begin{vmatrix} 24 & 169 \\ 169 & 1639 \end{vmatrix} = 1639 - \frac{1}{24}(169)^2$$

$$= 1639 - 1190.0416$$
$$= 448.9584$$

$$\mathbf{Y'} = \begin{bmatrix} 1 & 1 \\ 7.25 & 6.833333 \end{bmatrix}$$

$$\mathbf{Y'Y} = \begin{bmatrix} 2 & 14.083333 \\ 14.083333 & 99.256943 \end{bmatrix}$$

$$SS(TR) = \frac{12}{2} \begin{vmatrix} 2 & 14.083333 \\ 14.083333 & 99.256943 \end{vmatrix}$$

$$= 1191.0833 - 1190.0415 = 1.0418$$

$$SS(E) = SS(T) - SS(TR) = 448.9584 - 1.0418 = 447.9166$$

ANOVA Table

Source	SS	df	MS	F	$F_{.05}$
Treatment (Physicians)	1.0418	1	1.0418	.051	>1.0
Error	447.9166	22	20.359845		
Total	448.9584	23			

Therefore the differences between the physicians are not significant.

b) $SS(T) = 448.9584$

$$\mathbf{Z'} = \begin{bmatrix} 1 & 1 & 1 & 1 \\ 7.5 & 7 & 10 & 3.66666 \end{bmatrix}$$

$$\mathbf{Z'Z} = \begin{bmatrix} 4 & 28.166666 \\ 28.166666 & 281.69444 \end{bmatrix}$$

$$SS(B) = \frac{6}{4} \begin{vmatrix} 4 & 28.166666 \\ 28.166666 & 281.69444 \end{vmatrix}$$

$$= 1312.1666 - 1190.0416$$
$$= 122.125$$
$$SS(E) = 448.9584 - 122.125 = 326.8334$$

ONE-WAY ANOVA Table

Source	SS	df	MS	F	$F_{.05}$
Blocks (Diagnoses)	122.125	3	40.708333	2.491	3.10
Error	326.8334	20	16.34167		
Total	448.9584	23			

Therefore, the differences among the diagnoses are not significant.

c) $\mathbf{W}' = \begin{bmatrix} 1 & 1 & 1 & 1 \\ -.7083 & 2.7917 & -4.2083 & 2.1250 \end{bmatrix}$

$\begin{bmatrix} 1 & 1 & 1 & 1 \\ .7083 & -2.7917 & 4.2083 & -2.1250 \end{bmatrix}$

$$\mathbf{W}'\mathbf{W} = \begin{bmatrix} 8 & 0 \\ 0 & 61.04138 \end{bmatrix}$$

$$SS(TRB) = \frac{3}{8} \begin{vmatrix} 8 & 0 \\ 0 & 61.04138 \end{vmatrix} = 183.12414$$

$$SS(E) = 448.9584 - 1.0418 - 122.125 - 183.12414 = 142.66746$$

ANOVA Table

Source	SS	df	MS	F	$F_{.05}$
Treatments (Physicians)	1.0418	1	1.0418	.117	>1.0
Blocks (Diagnoses)	122.125	3	40.708333	4.565	3.24
Interaction	183.12414	3	61.04138	6.846	3.24
Error	142.66746	16	8.9167162		
Total	448.9584	23			

There are changes in the previous conclusions. Now the interaction is significant, and the differences among diagnoses are significant, but the differences between the physicians are still insignificant.

d) Design Matrix with Cell Means

Physician	Diagnosis				Mean
	A	B	C	D	
1	7	10	6	6	7.25
2	8	4	14	1.333	6.8333
Mean	7.5	7	10	3.6666	7.0416665

e) $\mu_{ij} = \mu + \alpha_i + \beta_j + \alpha\beta_{ij}$

Chapter 7

1. a) Chapter 5, Problem #1

Since there is no interaction component, there can be no mixed or random model testing.

b) Chapter 5, Problem #3

The ANOVA Table with only the interaction F value is reproduced here:

Source	SS	df	MS	F	$F_{.05}$
(A) Physicians	1.0418	1	1.0418		
(B) Diagnoses	122.125	3	40.708333		
(AB) Interaction	183.12414	3	61.04138	6.846	3.24
Error	142.66746	16	8.9167162		
Total	448.9584	23			

First, assume a mixed model in which there are only 2 physicians of interest and the four diagnoses represent the rest of their work. The first test is for the interaction, which was seen previously to be significant. The appropriate F test for the diagnoses is

$$F_B = \frac{MS(B)}{MS(E)} = \frac{40.708333}{8.9167162} = 4.565$$

which is significant ($F_{.05} = 3.24$).

The appropriate F test for physicians is

$$F_A = \frac{MS(A)}{MS(AB)} = \frac{1.0418}{61.04138} < 1.0$$

which is insignificant.

Thus the mixed model, as formulated, leads to the same conclusions as the fixed model. If the diagnoses factor were fixed, then both main effects would be insignificant.

Second, assume a random model, in which the physicians and diagnoses are both random factors. With significant interaction the appropriate main effect F tests are:

$$F_A = \frac{MS(A)}{MS(AB)} < 1.0$$

$$F_B = \frac{MS(B)}{MS(AB)} < 1.0$$

and both are insignificant.

2. Chapter 4, Problem #1

The average days absent in each department are:

Radiology: 2.4;   Laboratory: 2.8;   Housekeeping: 4.4

The vector of means is:

$$\bar{x} = [2.4 \quad 2.8 \quad 4.4]$$

There are 2 degrees of freedom, and the most appropriate test is the average of the two similar departments (radiology and laboratory) against housekeeping. This is given by:

$$c_1 = [.5 \quad .5 \quad -1]$$

The only test which is orthogonal is given by:

$$c_2 = [1 \quad -1 \quad 0]$$

It is easily verified that $c_1{}'c_2 = 0$

The total sum of squares is: $SS(T) = 24.4$

The sum of squares for c_1 is: $SS(c_1) = \dfrac{n(c_1{}'\bar{x})^2}{c_1{}'c_1} = \dfrac{16.2}{1.5} = 10.8$

The sums of squares are:

Treatment: $SS(Tr) = 11.2$

$$c_1: \quad SS(c_1) = \frac{n(c_1{}'\bar{x})^2}{c_1{}'c_1} = \frac{16.2}{1.5} = 10.8$$

$$c_2: \quad SS(c_2) = .4$$

$$SS(c_1) + SS(c_2) = 10.8 + .4 = 11.2 = SS(Tr)$$

ANOVA Table

Source	SS	df	MS	F	$F_{.05}$
Treatments (Departments)	11.2	2	5.6	5.09	3.89
c_1	10.8	1	10.8	9.82	4.75
c_2	.4	1	.4	.36	4.75
Error	13.2	12	1.1		
Total	24.4	14			

Therefore the housekeeping department experience is significantly different from the average of the experience of the radiology department and the laboratory. However there is no significant difference between radiology and the laboratory.

The structural model is:

$$\mu_i = \mu + \alpha_i$$

$$\bar{x}.. = 3.2$$

The estimated components of the structural model are:

$\alpha_1 = 2.4 - 3.2 = -.8$

$\alpha_2 = 2.8 - 3.2 = -.4$

$\alpha_3 = 4.4 - 3.2 = 1.2$

Chapter 8

1. (a) +ve high   (c) zero
   (d) zero   (f) −ve high
   (g) +ve low   (i) zero

5. (a) Var(a) = 422.6   Std Dev(a) = 20.557
   (b) Cov(a, c) = −135.97
   (c) r_{ab} = .1733062

Chapter 9

1. Let height be represented by **y**

$\mathbf{y}' = \begin{bmatrix} 145 & 105 & 100 & 95 & 95 & 80 & 170 & 150 & 135 & 145 & 140 & 150 \\ 120 & 115 & 90 & 125 & 125 & 120 & 130 & 100 & 160 \end{bmatrix}$

Let **X** contain the vector of ages and a vector of 1s.

$\mathbf{X}' = \begin{bmatrix} 1 & 1 & 1 & 1 & 1 & 1 & 1 & 1 & 1 & 1 & 1 & 1 & 1 & 1 & 1 \\ 10 & 5 & 3 & 6 & 4 & 3 & 15 & 12 & 10 & 9 & 14 & 15 & 10 & 6 & 3 \end{bmatrix}$

$\begin{bmatrix} 1 & 1 & 1 & 1 & 1 & 1 \\ 11 & 9 & 7 & 8 & 7 & 13 \end{bmatrix}$

$\mathbf{X}'\mathbf{X} = \begin{bmatrix} 21 & 180 \\ 180 & 1844 \end{bmatrix}$

$$(\mathbf{X'X})^{-1} = \frac{1}{21 \times 1844 - 180^2} \begin{bmatrix} 1844 & -180 \\ -180 & 21 \end{bmatrix}$$

$$= \frac{1}{6324} \begin{bmatrix} 1844 & -180 \\ -180 & 21 \end{bmatrix}$$

$$= \begin{bmatrix} .2915876 & -.0284629 \\ -.0284629 & .0033206 \end{bmatrix}$$

$$\mathbf{X'y} = \begin{bmatrix} 2595 \\ 24000 \end{bmatrix} \qquad \mathbf{y'y} = 333{,}125 \qquad \mathbf{b} = (\mathbf{X'X})^{-1}\mathbf{X'y}$$

a. $\mathbf{b'} = [73.5579 \quad 5.8349]$

b. ANOVA Table

Source	SS	df	MS	F
Regression				
constant, b_0	320,667.8571	1		
slope, b_1	10,252.7785	1	10,252.7785	88.37
Residual	2,204.3643	19	116.0192	
Total				
uncorrected	333,125	21		
corrected	12,457.1429	20		

c. $s = 10.7712$

d. $\mathrm{Cov\,(b)} = \begin{bmatrix} 33.8298 & -3.3023 \\ -3.3023 & .38526292 \end{bmatrix} = s^2\,(\mathbf{X'X})^{-1}$

e. $\mathrm{Std\,Err(b)} = [5.8163 \quad .6206955]$

t values $= [12.647 \quad 9.401] \qquad df = 19$

$t_{19,\,.05/2} = 2.093$

f. $\beta_1 = .907$

g. $R^2 = .823$

h. For $x_q = 15$, $\qquad \mathrm{Std\,Err}(\hat{y}_q) = 4.6310$

$\hat{y}_q = 161.0816$, $\mathrm{Std\,Err}(y_q) = 11.7246$

For $x_q = 9$, Std Err$(\hat{y}_q) = 2.3655$

$\hat{y}_q = 126.0721$, Std Err$(y_q) = 11.0279$

i. No. The equation is based on children at different stages of growth. People do not continue to grow. This illustrates the danger of blindly extrapolating an equation beyond the range of observed values.

2. a. $b = [1.2815 \quad .7899]$

ANOVA Table

Source	SS	df	MS	F
Regression				
constant, b_0	225.0000	1		
slope, b_1	18.5630	1	18.5630	5.150
Residual	50.4370	14	3.6026	
Total				
uncorrected	294.0000	16		
corrected	69.0000			

$R^2 = .2690$ \qquad $F_{1, 14, .05} = 4.60$

$$\text{Cov}(b) = \begin{bmatrix} 1.40775 & -.378429 \\ -.378429 & .121097 \end{bmatrix}$$

Std Err$(b) = [1.1865 \quad .34799]$

b. $t = [1.080 \quad 2.270]$

$t_{14, .05/2} = 2.145$

The relationship is significant at the .05 level, but only the slope is significantly different from zero.

Chapter 10

1. Radiology Department

```
        COST MREG RAD


MULTIPLE REGRESSION ANALYSIS

DATE:   4/17/79     TIME: 16:13:35


CORRELATION MATRIX OF RAW DATA - DEPENDENT VARIABLE FIRST


CORRELATION MATRIX
    1.000    0.840    0.219    0.524    0.590
    0.840    1.000   ⁻0.050    0.165    0.506
    0.219   ⁻0.050    1.000    0.127    0.024
    0.524    0.165    0.127    1.000    0.215
    0.590    0.506    0.024    0.215    1.000

T-VALUES  FOR DF= 23
    0.000    7.412    1.077    2.948    3.503
    7.412    0.000   ⁻0.244    0.801    2.813
    1.077   ⁻0.244    0.000    0.614    0.117
    2.948    0.801    0.614    0.000    1.057
    3.503    2.813    0.117    1.057    0.000

VALUES OF R AND T ARE ALSO AVAILABLE WITH FULL PRECISION



REGRESSION ANALYSIS OF VARIANCE TABLE

SOURCE          SUM OF SQUARES      D.F.     MEAN SQUARES           F

REGRESSION:  2,331,448,955.38782
BO           2,295,943,055.99999
B1 TO B4        35,505,899.38783     4    8,876,474.84695    55.4804

RESIDUALS        3,199,855.11217    20      159,992.75560

TOTAL (CORR)    38,705,754.50000

-------------------------------------------------------------------------


BVALUES:  2,390.3367    160.1380    236.0958    269.0537    25.6940
TVALUES:      3.9237      9.5924      3.1978      5.2186     1.9370


R SQUARED:     0.9173
STD.ERR.:          399.99094


CORRELATION MATRIX OF BVALUES

    1.0000   ⁻0.3644   ⁻0.5473   ⁻0.6078    0.0699
   ⁻0.3644    1.0000    0.0825   ⁻0.0761   ⁻0.4894
   ⁻0.5473    0.0825    1.0000   ⁻0.1301   ⁻0.0377
   ⁻0.6078   ⁻0.0761   ⁻0.1301    1.0000   ⁻0.1486
    0.0699   ⁻0.4894   ⁻0.0377   ⁻0.1486    1.0000


FINISHED
```

Chapter 11

2. Life Cycle Savings
   a. The b values and the hypotheses are:

Variable	b Value	β	Hypothesis	Agree?
INGROWTH	.4097	.26	+ve	Yes
POPLT15	−.4612	−.94	−ve	Yes
POPGT75	−1.6915	−.49	−ve	Yes
INCOME	−.00034	−.07	unimportant	Yes

   b. The proportion of variance explained is .338 (R^2).

   c. To test the significance of the equation we test the overall F value, which is 5.75 against $F_{.05}$ for 4 and 45 degrees of freedom:

   $(2.53 < F_{.05} < 2.61)$. Since $F > F_{.05}$ the equation is significant.

   d. Testing the b values for significance, for 1 and 45 degrees of freedom:

   $$4.00 < F_{.05} < 4.08$$

Variable	b Value	F	Significant?
INGROWTH	.4096	4.36	Yes
POPLT15	−.4612	10.17	Yes
POPGT75	−1.6915	2.44	No
INCOME	−.00034	.13	No

   e. The most important variable is POPLT15, because its $|\beta|$ is greatest.

Chapter 12

1. Ontario Ambulance Service Information System (OASIS)
   a. The percentage of variance explained requires R^2

Step	Variable	R^2	ΔR^2
1	LOWINC	.273	.273
2	UNDER25	.524	.251
3	MGMT	.628	.103

b. The significance of the overall equation is tested by the overall F ratio, which is defined as:

$$F = \frac{MS(\text{Reg})}{MS(\text{Res})} = \frac{SS(\text{Reg})/k}{SS(\text{Res})/(n - k - 1)} = \frac{R^2/k}{(1 - R^2)/(n - k - 1)}$$

The F ratio compares the portion of the total sum of squares that can be attributed to the regression coefficients ($b_1, b_2, \ldots b_k$) to the portion of $SS(T)$ that has not yet been explained (i.e., the residuals).

The calculated F ratio must be tested against the tabulated critical value of F for the desired confidence level (e.g., .05 or .01) and (k) and ($n - k - 1$) degrees of freedom for the numerator and denominator. The calculated F must exceed the tabulated critical value of F to show statistical significance.

This is a *one-tailed* test because the hypothesis is: $MS(\text{Reg}) > MS(\text{Res})$

In Step 5: $F = 14.00$, ($k = 5$), ($n - k - 1 = 27$)

$$2.53 < F_{.05} < 2.6$$

The calculated value of F is greater than the tabulated value; therefore, the equation is significant on Step 5.

c. The Step 3 confidence interval for MGMT b value. $b_3 = -239.33922$
Std Err(b_3) = 84.3009   ($n - k - 1 = 29$) Confidence interval:
$-239 \pm 2.045 \times 84.3009$

$$-411.73454 \leq b_3 \leq -66.94386$$

d. If one or more variables enter on a given step (or in a sequence of steps) their contribution may be tested by:

$$F = \frac{\Delta R^2/\Delta k}{(1 - R^2)/(n - k - 1)}$$

SPSS computes this automatically for single variables; so that for Step 3, for MGMT, the F value is 8.061 with (1,29) df. This is significant at the .05 level. For Steps 5 and 6, for the variables PLUS55 and FEMALE: $\Delta R^2 = .72670 - .64761 = .07909$
This gives:

$$F = \frac{.07909/2}{(1 - .72670)/26} = 3.762$$

Since $3.32 < F_{.05,\ 2,\ 32} < 3.39$, the calculated F is greater than the tabulated F, and together the two variables make a significant contribution to the explanation of the variance of ambulance calls per 1000 population.

e. The last step where all variables are significant is Step 3, because in that step all partial Fs > 4.24. Setting the F parameter to 3 would have prevented further steps.

f. If the tolerance parameter were set to .4 (with the F parameter low), then PLUS55 would have been excluded in Step 5.

2. *Family Size*

a. Proportion of variance of dependent variable explained at each step (R^2)

Step	R^2	Step	R^2
1	.1601	5	.4668
2	.2541	6	.4678
3	.3489	7	.4682
4	.4306	8	.4749

b. Significance of regression equation in all steps—test overall F (.05 level)

Step	Calc. F	df	Crit. F	Step	Calc. F	df	Crit. F
1	16.39	1,86	<4.00	5	14.36	5,82	<2.31
2	14.48	2,85	<3.15	6	11.87	6,81	<2.25
3	15.01	3,84	<2.76	7	10.06	7,80	<2.17
4	15.69	4,83	<2.53	8	8.93	8,79	<2.10

The calculated $F >$ the critical F for each step. (This is also true at the .01 level of confidence.) Therefore, the equation is significant in all steps.

c. The last step where all b values are significant (at the .05 level of confidence) is Step 5. The variable REWARD entering on Step 6 has an F value of .158, which is insignificant.

d. For Step 5, the β value for CHNGPSTP is .33929. This β value means that for every 1 standard deviation change in the value of CHNGPSTP (5.0459) the change in the expected value of CHNGHAPP is .33929 standard deviations (.33929 × 4.4236 = 1.5009) controlling for any changes in the other predictor variables.

e. In Step 5, PREHAPPY has the greatest impact with a $\beta = -.51668$.

f. In Step 5, the b_2 value for CHNGCERT is .42387. In Step 2, $b_2 =$ .28927 with Std Err(b_2) = .08837. Testing the difference between the Step 5 and Step 2 values we form the t statistic

$$t = \frac{.42387 - .28927}{.08837} = 1.523$$

and test it at 85 (or 82) degrees of freedom

$$t_{.025, \, 85} \cong 1.96$$

Since the t value is less than $t_{.05}$, the change from Step 2 to Step 5 is *not* significant. Therefore, there is no apparent bias at this step, for this variable.

For all of the variables the confidence intervals (based on their first step of entry) are:

		Low	High
CHNGPSTP =	.35079 ± 1.96 × .08664 =	.18098	.52060
	(OK on all steps)		
CHNGCERT =	.28927 ± 1.96 × .08837 =	.11606	.46248
	(violated on Step 4, but OK on 5 to 8)		
PREHAPPY =	−.22868 ± 1.96 × .06539 =	−.35684	−.10051
	(violated in Step 5, and all subsequent steps)		
PRECERT =	.38377 ± 1.96 × .11126 =	.16570	.60184
	(OK in all steps)		
PREPSTPN =	.19192 ± 1.96 × .08131 =	.03255	.35129
	(OK in all steps)		
REWARD =	−.13234 ± 1.96 × .33259 =	−.78422	.51954
	(not significant; significant difference in Step 8)		

IECAT $= -.18774 \pm 1.96 \times .79152 = -1.73912$ 1.36364
(not significant, significant difference in Step 8)
INTRIERC $=$ Not significant because F value too low.
(Final variable.)

The value of **PREHAPPY** has a problem in Step 4, but it is not terribly bad. REWARD, IECAT and INTRIERC are all insignificant when they enter, and therefore must be considered to be biased.

g. The standard error of the equation in all steps:

Step	Standard Error	Step	Standard Error
0	4.4236 (Std Dev)		
1	4.07754	5	3.32722
2	3.86506	6	3.34442
3	3.63256	7	3.36408
4	3.41761	8	3.36405

The standard error drops from Step 1 to Step 5 but goes up slightly in Steps 6 to 8. This indicates that after Step 5 the predictive ability of the equation becomes worse, and Step 5 would be best.

h. Call **PREPSTPN** x_1, **PRECERT** x_2, and **PREHAPPY** x_3
$r_{12} = .32901$ $r_{13} = .48010$ $r_{23} = .31997$

$$r_{12.3} = \frac{.32901 - .48010 \times .31997}{\sqrt{(1 - .48010^2) \times (1 - .31997^2)}} = \frac{.1753924}{\sqrt{.6907215}}$$

$$= .2110373$$

Chapter 13

1. a. Draw a 3 dimensional data collection design matrix.
   b. Each must be defined as a nominal (categorical) variable.
      e.g., Age in ranges with 10 year intervals
      15-24, 25-34, 35-44, 45-54, 55-64 (there are five categories)

Sex is dichotomous: M and F, or MALE with values 0, and 1, or similarly with FEMALE.

Occupation would be classified according to a list of appropriate categories.

e.g., nurses, physiotherapists, orderlies, aides, housekeepers, ward clerks, office staff, and others. (There are eight categories, but in practice it would probably be desirable to have fewer.)

c. The design matrix has $5 \times 2 \times 8 = 80$ cells, and for 20 observations per cell we would require interviews with 1,600 people. It is quite possible that for some cells there would be too few people available, while for others there would be more than sufficient. One way to reduce the effect of the non-randomness introduced is to redesign the study to use fewer age and occupation categories. Once an appropriate number of categories has been obtained the sampling frame should be established listing all people eligible for each cell. Then twenty people should be selected at random for each cell.

d. ANOVA Table (fictitious data)

Source	SS	df	MS	F
AGE	4,000	4	1,000	75.99
SEX	—	1	—	—
OCCUPATION	—	7	—	—
AGE, SEX	—	4	—	—
AGE, OCCUPATION	12,000	28	428.57	32.57
SEX, OCCUPATION	—	7	—	—
AGE, SEX, OCCUPATION	—	28	—	—
Error	20,000	1,520	13.16	
Total	—	1,599		

Assuming a fixed model

$F(AGE) = MS(AGE)/MS(ERROR)$
$= 1000/13.16 = 75.99$ with 4 and 1520 df
$F(AGE, OCCUPATION) = MS(AGE, OCCUPATION)/MS(ERROR)$
$= 428.57/13.16 = 32.57$ with 28 and 1520 df

Both are significant at the .05 level.

e. DAYSOFF = F(AGE, SEX, OCCUP)

f. For a regression model the independent variables *may* be measured either as continuous variables or as categorical variables. (Continuous variables include ordinal, interval and ratio scales. Categorical variables include either nominal or ordinal scales of measurement. Any variable measured on an interval or ratio scale can be arbitrarily categorized to be measured as an ordinal variable.) For an ANOVA model the independent variables *must* be measured as categorical variables. The dependent variable *must* be measured as a continuous variable in both models.

In this example AGE *may* be measured as a continuous variable for a multiple regression model, but it *must* be categorized for an ANOVA model.

Chapter 14

1. *Disease Costing Study*
   a. By itself which variable explains most variance in COST99, and which explains the least?
   Require maximum and minimum $|r_{yx}|$ and r_{yx}^2.
   With $r = .63779$, TOPMD1 explains 40.68% of the variance of COST99, which is more than any other variable.
   With $r = -.00192$, SEX explains the smallest amount, .00037%, of the variance of COST99.
   b. For first three steps what percentage is explained?

Step	$R^2 \times 100$	$\Delta R^2 \times 100$
1	40.667	
2	46.459	5.782
3	46.902	.443

   c. The testing of the significance of the equation at any step is performed by an F test of the overall equation.

$$F = \frac{MS(\text{Reg})}{MS(\text{Res})} = \frac{SS(\text{Reg})/k}{SS(\text{Res})/(n - k - 1)}$$

If the null hypothesis (that each of the regression coefficients b_1 to b_k is zero) is true then the expected value of F is 1.0. If false, then the value will be greater and can be tested against the tabulated critical value of F with level of confidence α, k degrees of freedom for the numerator and $(n - k - 1)$ degrees of freedom for the denominator. This is a one-tailed test. For Step 5 $F = 184.73$, $k = 5$, and $n - k - 1 = 1020$, $F_{.05} = 2.21$. Since $F > F_{.05}$ the equation is significant.

d. For Step 3, $b_{AGE} = 2.02535$ with $F = 8.523$. The F can be tested against $F_{.05}$ with 1 and 1022 degrees of freedom, which is 3. Since $F > F_{.05}$, b_{AGE} is significantly different from zero.

e. Problems of multicollinearity?

Examining the correlation matrix, we find that NUMDIAG and TWEIGHT have an exceptionally high correlation of .8555, which indicates a probable problem.

TWEIGHT enters the equation on Step 2, and NUMDIAG on Step 4 with a tolerance of only .2619, which is less than the suggested value of .4.

On Step 2 and b value for TWEIGHT has a .95 confidence interval of $(20.28906 \pm 1.96 \times 1.93029)$, which has a low value of 16.5057 and a high value of 24.0724. On Step 4, and b value for TWEIGHT increases to 28.55575, which is a significant change caused by the entry of NUMDIAG.

At the same step, the b value for NUMDIAG is -61.51716 and significant. A negative value *must* be incorrect since NUMDIAG is a measure of severity of the patient's problem.

Based on the high correlation and low tolerance we conclude that multicollinearity exists. The significant increase in the b value for TWEIGHT and the incorrect negative value for NUMDIAG indicate that the multicollinearity has biased the b values for those variables.

Note that only one other variable, TOPMD1, experiences a large change in b value. In Step 2, its value changes from 210.4 to 186.4. This change is highly significant ($t \cong 24/7.94 = 3.02$). It is *not* caused by multicollinearity, because the correlation of TOPMD1 and TWEIGHT is only .28939.

The problem of multicollinearity can be avoided by specifying a minimum acceptable tolerance level of .4 for any entering variable. In this case, NUMDIAG would have been excluded from the equation.

2. *Ontario PER Case*

a. How much variance is explained in each step?

Step	R^2	Step	R^2
1	.31550	5	.67603
2	.46910	6	.69337
3	.56141	7	.70594
4	.63669	8	.70954

b. Is the regression significant in all steps? The overall F value starts at 41.48 in Step 1 and gradually decreases to a final value of 25.34 in Step 8. The .05 values of F range from approximately 3.97 to 2.08. Since the calculated values are much greater than the tabulated values the equation is significant in all steps.

c. Problems of multicollinearity?
Inspection of the correlation matrix shows that no predictor variables have simple correlations approaching .8, which would be the critical level. Inspection of the tolerances of the entering variables shows them all to be acceptably high. We conclude that there is no problem of multicollinearity.

d. Final Step b values significant?

$$F_{.05} \cong 3.97$$

Only OCCUPNCY with $F = 1.028$ is insignificant.

Variable	b Value	β	Interpretation
EXPALOS	79.27	.39	A positive value of $79 per day of expected average LOS is reasonable, and the β value shows that this is the most influential variable.
LABUNITS	.29664	.26	A positive value of $.30 per lab unit per case is reasonable. The β value shows that this is the 3rd most influential variable.
OVRUNDR	38.83	.24	An increase in per case cost of $39 for each day's increase in average stay over the Ontario matched

Variable	*b* Value	β	Interpretation
			ALOS indicates that the marginal cost of an extra day of care is positive but somewhat lower than the average cost. This is reasonable and in a range of cost that raises no questions.
FTEMPLOY	42.31	.29	Each extra employee per patient day leads to an increase in per case cost and this is reasonable. The β value gives this variable a rank of 2.
PHYSIOTH	22.09	.15	Each extra physiotherapy attendance per case should be expected to lead to higher cost. The β value gives a rank of 6.
RADIOLGY	25.92	.18	Each extra radiological examination per case should lead to higher case cost. The β value gives a rank of 5.
OCCUPSQ	.15	.14	The average occupancy of these
OCCUPNCY	1.01	.07	hospitals is approximately 78%. Lower than average occupancy has OCCUPSQ partially offsetting the effect of OCCUPNCY, and higher than average occupancy has their effects adding to each other. The net effect is that of a U-shaped response to deviations from average occupancy. Hospitals with extremely high or extremely low occupancy would be expected to have higher per case costs, everything else held constant.
CONSTANT	−466.14		The other variables collectively overestimate the value of the dependent variable.

e. Interpret Residuals:
SPSS standardizes residuals by dividing by the standard deviation of the dependent variable. The standard deviation of PERCASE = 128.5053.
The standard error of the equation $s_{yx} = 72.51827$ (Step 8). The ratio of these is $128.5053/72.51827 \cong 1.772$. Therefore, in the plot of standardized residuals 1 standard deviation should be 1.772 standard errors from the equation, 2 standard deviations is approximately 3.544 standard errors, and 1.13 standard deviations is approximately 2 standard errors, close to the .05 level of confidence.

Case-by-Case Plot
The first hospital has a negative residual which is at or just beyond the .05 level. About 4 hospitals seem to have positive residuals at or beyond the .05 level. Thus, 5 out of 92 hospitals have residuals that seem to be beyond the .05 level. This is approximately the number that would have been expected. There is no apparent trend in the residuals and the variance appears constant.

Standardized Residuals Versus Standardized Predicted
The 5 hospitals with large residuals are easily visible. Apart from those hospitals the others seem to be fairly evenly distributed. No problems are apparent.

f. Number 6 is the last step in which all variables are significant, because $F_{.05} \cong 3.96$. The values and interpretation for all variables are similar to those given in Section d. Only OCCUPNCY and OCCUPSQ are excluded. All of the values appear reasonable.

g. To test OCCUPNCY and OCCUPSQ for significance, we must test the incremental R^2.

$$F = \frac{\Delta R^2/2}{(1 - R^2)/(n - k - 1)} = \frac{.01617/2}{(1 - .70954)/83} \cong 2.31$$

This is to be tested against $F_{.05}$ with 2 and 83 degrees of freedom.

$$F_{.05} \cong 3.12$$

Since $F < F_{.05}$, they do not add sufficiently to the explanation to be retained in the equation.

h. The first variable entering is EXPALOS

First Step				Last Step
b Value	Std Err	95% Conf. Int.		*b* Value
		Low	High	
112.8846	17.52689	77.73	148.03	79.27231

The final estimate of the *b* value of ALSEXP is not significantly different from that in the first step. Bias in multiple regression may be caused by problems of multicollinearity, or by inclusion of insignificant variables, or by exclusion of important ones, or by misspecification of the functional form of the equation.

In this case, there were no problems of multicollinearity. OCCUPNCY and OCCUPSQ are insignificant and should be excluded. The impact of outpatient activity on hospital costs is ignored in this study, and possibly a variable for the ratio of outpatient and emergency visits to inpatient separations could have filled this gap.

i. The standard error from step to step:

Step	Standard Error	Step	Standard Error
1	106.91	5	75.24
2	94.68	6	73.63
3	86.54	7	72.53
4	79.22	8	72.52

Standard Deviation of PERCASE = 128.5053

The standard error drops on each step from first to last, but after Step 6 there is very little further decline. Had any very insignificant variables been included in the regression the standard error would have increased, perhaps substantially, indicating that predictions would be less precise.

Glossary*

A

Absolute Deviation from the Mean—*See* Deviation from the Mean

Acceptance Region—The subset of the sample space (or the set of all values of the test statistic) for which a null hypothesis is accepted.

Accuracy— The tendency of values of an estimator to come close to the quantity they are intended to estimate. *See also* Precision

Algorithm—A well-defined procedure which, when routinely applied, leads to a solution of a particular class of mathematical problems. Various algorithms exist, for example, for solving linear programming problems.

Alienation, Coefficient of— A measure of the lack of linear association between two variables; it is given by the square root of 1 minus the square of the coefficient of correlation. Usually designated by k, its square is the coefficient of nondetermination.

Alpha, α—*See* Level of Significance; Regression Coefficient; Type I Error

Alpha-Four, α_4—*See* Kurtosis

Alpha-Three, α_3—*See* Skewness

Alternative Hypothesis—The hypothesis which one accepts when the null hypothesis (the hypothesis under test) is rejected. It is usually denoted H_A or H_1.

Analysis of Covariance—A statistical analysis which consists of the combined application of linear regression and analysis of variance techniques. It is used when treatments are compared in the presence of concomitant variables which can be neither eliminated nor controlled.

Analysis of Variance, ANOVA—(1) The analysis of the total variability of a set of data (measured by their total sum of squares) into components which can be attributed to difference sources of variation. A table which lists the various sources of variation together with the corresponding degrees of freedom, sums of squares,

---

*The Glossary printed in Volume I as well as here is abridged with permission of Macmillan Publishing Company, Inc. from *Dictionary/Outline of Basic Statistics* by John E. Freund and Frank J. Williams, © 1966. The permission of Macmillan is greatly appreciated.

493

mean squares (sometimes also expected mean squares), and values of F, is called an *analysis of variance table*. (2) Sometimes abbreviated ANOVA, the term also refers to the totality of statistical techniques based on this kind of analysis. *See also* One-Way Analysis of Variance; Two-Way Analysis of Variance

Annual Rate—A quantity designed to facilitate the reporting of month-to-month changes in data that are ordinarily (and more meaningfully) reported on an annual basis. An annual rate is calculated by multiplying a deseasonalized monthly figure by twelve. For instance, if a store's July sales were $1.4 million and the July value of the corresponding seasonal index is 0.80, it can be said that these July sales were running at an annual rate of $\frac{1.4}{0.8} \cdot 12 = \$21$ million.

Annual Trend Increment—The average year-to-year change produced in a series of data by the action of forces (such as population growth or advances in technology) which presumably exert their influence over long periods of time.

Approximate—To approximate is to obtain a result near a desired result, or to obtain a succession of results approaching a desired result. An approximate result is one that is nearly but not exactly correct.

Approximation—A result that is not exact, but sufficiently close for a given purpose. For instance, 22/7 may serve as an approximation to the value of π. In statistics, the normal distribution may be used as a large-sample approximation of the binomial distribution.

Area Sampling—A method of sampling where a geographical region is subdivided into smaller areas (counties, villages, city blocks, etc.), some of these areas are selected at random, and the chosen areas are then subsampled or surveyed 100 per cent.

Arithmetic Line Chart—A graph obtained by plotting values of a time series on arithmetic paper (graph paper with uniform subdivisions for both scales) and connecting successive points with straight lines.

Arithmetic Mean—Commonly referred to as an "average," the arithmetic mean (or simply the mean) of n numbers is given by their sum divided by n. *See also* Mean

Arithmetic Paper—A graph paper with uniform subdivisions for both scales; on either scale, equal distances represent equal amounts.

Array—A particular arrangement of observations, say, according to size. *See also* Matrix

Arrival Distribution—In queuing theory, a probability function for the number of customers arriving at a service counter during a given period of time. The Poisson distribution is often used as a model for arrival distributions. *See also* Interarrival Distribution

Assumed Mean—The origin of a scale used when coding to simplify the calculation of a mean, a standard deviation, or some other statistical description.

Asymmetrical Distribution— *See* Skewness

Average—A term lacking in precision and having different colloquial meanings (as in "batting average," "average" taste, etc.), but widely used to refer to the arithmetic mean.

Average Deviation—*See* Mean Absolute Deviation

Axioms of Probability—*See* Probability, Postulates of

B

Balanced Design—The balance of an experimental design depends on the allocation of treatments (levels of variables or factors) to blocks. A randomized block design is balanced if every treatment appears in each block the same number of times; an incomplete block design is balanced if every two treatments appear together in a block the same number of times.

Bar Chart—A chart, used to present frequency distributions or time series, which consists of bars (rectangles) of equal width, whose lengths are proportional to the frequencies (or values) they represent.

Bartlett's Test—A test for the homogeneity of variances; specifically, a test of the null hypothesis that a set of independent random samples comes from normal populations having the same variance.

Base year (or Base Period)—In index number construction, the year (or period) with reference to which a comparison is being made. It is usually denoted by the subscript "$_0$;" for example, the price of a commodity in the base year is written p_0 and the corresponding quantity produced (consumed, sold, etc.) is written q_0.

Bell-Shaped Distribution—A distribution having the over-all shape of a vertical cross section of a bell; normal distributions are among those having this characteristic.

Bernoulli Random Variable—A random variable whose values, 0 and 1, correspond to "failure" and "success" in a Bernoulli trial.

Bernoulli Trial—A mathematical model for an experiment having just two outcomes, usually referred to as "success" and "failure." It is a special case of the binomial distribution, with $n = 1$.

Best Fit—*See* Goodness of Fit; Least Squares, Method of

Beta, β—*See* Regression Coefficient; Type II Error

Between-Samples Sum of Squares—The treatment sum of squares is a one-way analysis of variance; measuring the variability among the sample means, it serves as an indication of possible differences among the corresponding population means.

Bias—(1) In problems of estimation, an estimator is said to be biased if its expected value does *not* equal the parameter it is intended to estimate. (2) In index number construction, the bias of an index is the systematic tendency to overestimate or underestimate changes. (3) In sampling, a bias is a systematic error introduced by selecting items from a wrong population, favoring some of the elements of a population, or poorly phrasing questions. (4) In hypothesis testing, a test is said to be biased when the probability of rejecting the null hypothesis is *not* a minimum when the null hypothesis is, in fact, true.

Bimodal Distribution—*See* Multimodal Distribution

Binomial Coefficient— The binomial coefficient $\binom{n}{k}$ is the coefficient of $a^k b^{n-k}$ in the expansion of $(a + b)^n$; in factorial notation it is given by $\dfrac{n!}{k!(n - k)!}$.

The calculation of binomial coefficients can be facilitated by using the following arrangement, called *Pascal's triangle:*

$$
\begin{array}{ccccccccc}
 & & & & 1 & & & & \\
 & & & 1 & & 1 & & & \\
 & & 1 & & 2 & & 1 & & \\
 & 1 & & 3 & & 3 & & 1 & \\
1 & & 4 & & 6 & & 4 & & 1 \\
\end{array}
$$

. . . .

. . . .

Each row begins and ends with a 1, each other number is the sum of the two nearest numbers in the row immediately above, and the binomial coefficient $\binom{n}{k}$ is given by the $(k + 1)$st number in the $(n + 1)$st row.

Binomial Distribution—The distribution of the number of *successes* in *n trials,* when the probability of a success remains constant from trial to trial and the trials are independent. Also, the distribution of the sum of *n* independent Bernoulli random variables, each with the same probabilities θ and $1 - \theta$ for success and failure. Values of the binomial probability function may be obtained from the National Bureau of Standards Tables.

Bio-Assay—Methods devoted to the design and analysis of tests made for the purpose of assigning limits within which the potency of such preparations as vitamins, drugs, and sera may be presumed to fall in comparison with a standard.

Bit—(1) A common abbreviation for "Binary Digit," that is, 0 or 1 in the binary system. (2) In information theory, when a message consists of some pattern of the digits 0 and 1, each digit conveys a "unit of information," and each unit of information is called a "bit." Hence, the term "bit" refers both to a two-valued variable used to represent a unit of information, and to a unit of information itself.

Bivariate Distribution—*See* Joint Density Function; Joint Distribution; Joint Distribution Function; Joint Probability Function

Bivariate Normal Distribution—The joint distribution of two random variables X and Y for which the marginal distribution of X is normal, the regression of Y on X is linear, and the conditional distribution of Y for a fixed value of X is normal with a variance which does not depend on the value of X. If X and Y are furthermore independent and have the same variance, their joint distribution is referred to as the *circular normal distribution;* it owes its name to the fact that contours of equal probability density are, in fact, circles (while in the general case they are ellipses).

Block—A homogeneous grouping of experimental units, designed to enable the experimenter to isolate (hence, eliminate) variability due to extraneous causes.

Block Effect—In analysis of variance, a quantity (usually a parameter of the model), which represents the change in response produced by a given block. The block effects are the parameters β_j.

Block Sum of Squares—In analysis of variance, that component of the total sum of squares which can be attributed to possible differences among the blocks.

BLS Seasonal Factor Method (1964)—An iterative procedure, prepared by the Bureau of Labor Statistics, for developing seasonal factors (a seasonal index) for its employment and unemployment series. The method has yielded good results when applied to various other general economic series.

Business Cycle—A business cycle consists of a repeated up-and-down movement of business activity, having a length greater than one year. The periods of prosperity, recession, depression, and recovery, which constitute the four phases of a complete cycle, are considered to be caused by much more complex factors than the weather, social customs, etc., which account for seasonal variations.

C

Categorical Distribution—A frequency distribution in which items are grouped into nonoverlapping categories according to some qualitative description. For instance, when classifying the books published in a given year, one might construct a categorical distribution showing how many were historical novels, how many were mysteries, how many were cookbooks, and so on.

Cell Frequency—In the analysis of count (or enumeration) data, the number of items falling into an individual category (classification, or subclassification) is sometimes referred to as cell frequency. The term is used mainly in connection with contingency tables.

Census—A complete enumeration of a population; partial enumerations based on samples are sometimes referred to as "sample censuses."

Centered (12-Month) Moving Average—A moving average obtained by averaging successive pairs of values of a 12-month moving average; the purpose of this adjustment is to obtain values corresponding to the midpoints (rather than the beginning or the end) of the various months.

Central Limit Theorem—In its simplest form, the theorem states that for random variables from a population with a finite variance, the sampling distribution of the standardized sample mean approaches the standard normal distribution as the sample size n becomes infinite. This theorem is of fundamental importance in probability and statistics, as it justifies the application of normal distribution theory to a great variety of statistical problems.

Central Tendencies, Measures of—A name sometimes given to "averages," that is, to statistics such as the mean, median, or mode.

Chance Variable—*See* Random Variable

Chance Variation—In general, the term applies to the fluctuations one observes between the values of a random variable. An appreciation of the fact that such fluctuations can be studied mathematically and the fact that one can make predictions about their possible size is basic to an understanding of modern statistics.

Change of Variable (or Scale)—*See* Coding; Transformation

Chebyshev's Theorem (or Inequality)—An important result in probability, which provides an upper limit to the probability that a value of a random variable differs from the mean of its distribution by more than k standard deviations. If $P(\mid X - \mu \mid > k\sigma)$ denotes the probability that the value assumed by a random variable X differs from its mean μ by more than $k\sigma$, the theorem can be expressed symbolically in the following form:

$$P(\mid X - \mu \mid > k\sigma < \frac{1}{k^2}$$

When applied to actual data, Chebyshev's Theorem correspondingly provides an upper limit to the *proportion* of the data which differs from the mean by more than k standard deviations.

Chi-Square Distribution (χ^2 Distribution)—A distribution which is of great importance in inferences concerning population variances or standard deviations. It arises in connection with the sampling distribution of the sample variance for random samples from normal populations; it is a special form of a *gamma distribution*. The parameter of this distribution is ν, the number of degrees of freedom. Table A-6 in Volume I contains values of $\chi^2_{\alpha,\nu}$, which denotes the value for which the area *to its right* under the chi-square distribution with ν degrees of freedom is equal to α.

Chi-Square Statistic—A statistic which is given by a sum of terms, where each term is the quotient of the squared difference between an observed frequency and an expected frequency divided by the expected frequency. *See also* Binomial Index of Dispersion; contingency Table; Goodness of Fit; Poisson Index of Dispersion

Circular Normal Distribution—*See* Bivariate Normal Distribution

Class Boundary—The dividing line between successive classes of a frequency distribution; to avoid ambiguities, class boundaries are usually chosen so that they represent "impossible" values, namely, values which cannot occur among the data which are to be grouped. Class boundaries are also referred to as *real class limits*. *See also* Frequency Distribution

Class Frequency—The number of items falling into a particular class of a frequency distribution. *See also* Frequency Distribution

Class Interval—The length of a class, or the range of values covered by a class of a frequency distribution. For any one class, it is given by the difference between its upper and lower boundaries; for a distribution with equal class intervals it is given by the difference between successive class marks or class boundaries. *See also* Frequency Distribution

Class Limit—The upper and lower limits of a class are, respectively, the largest and smallest values it can contain. *See also* Frequency Distribution

Class Mark—The midpoint of a class; hence, the mean of its boundaries or the mean of its limits. *See also* Frequency Distribution

Cluster Sampling—A method of sampling in which the elements of a population are arranged in groups (or clusters); some of the clusters are selected at random, and the ones chosen are then subsampled, or surveyed 100 per cent. Generally, the clusters consist of natural groupings, and if they are geographic regions the sampling is referred to as *area sampling.*

COBOL (Common Business Oriented Language)—An elaborate computer programming language, independent of any make or model of computer, which is oriented toward the solution of a wide range of business data processing problems such as, for example, the maintenance of large files of data. The COBOL system consists of a *source program* written in the COBOL language, a *compiler* to translate a *source program* into an *object program,* and a COBOL *library.*

Coding—Transforming or changing a scale of measurement; that is, converting numbers given in one scale to their equivalents in a different scale. For instance, one might code the numbers 2.12, 2.15, 2.20, 2.10, and 2.18 by subtracting 2.10 from each and multiplying the differences by 100, thus getting the numbers 2, 5, 10, 0, and 8. Usually, the purpose of coding is to simplify the numbers with which one has to work, or to facilitate the comparison of data (distributions) given in different units of measurement. *See also* Normalized Standard Scores; Standard Units

Coding (a Digital Computer)—The act of translating a sequence of well-defined operations (which specify the particular way in which a problem is to be solved) into a set of detailed instructions appropriate for a given computer. Computer coding is often called *programming* and the resulting set of instructions is called a *computer code, computer program,* or *routine.*

Coefficient—In algebra, the term "coefficient" is most commonly used for constant factors as distinguished from variables; it is in this sense that one speaks of a regression coefficient. The term is also used to denote a dimensionless description of a set of data, or a distribution; for example, a coefficient of correlation or a coefficient of variation. *See also* individual listings under subject matter; for example, for Coefficient of Variation *see* Variation, Coefficient of

Combination—A selection of one or more of a set of distinct objects without regard to order. The number of possible combinations, each containing r objects, that can be formed from a collection of n distinct objects is given by $\frac{n!}{(n-r)!r!}$ and it is denoted $\binom{n}{r}$, $_nC_r$, C_r^n, or $C(n,r)$. For instance, the number of combinations of the first ten letters of the alphabet, taken three at a time, is $\frac{10!}{7!3!} = 120$. *See also* Binomial Coefficient.

Compiler—Generally the most useful type of automatic coding system, a compiler is a computer program which translates and expands (by adding required subroutines, for example) a source program into an object program. The FORTRAN and COBOL compilers are well-known automatic compiling systems in the scientific and business data processing areas, respectively. FORTRAN, COBOL, and some other languages, are often called "compiler languages."

Complement (of a Set)—The complement of a set A relative to a sample space S, denoted A' or $\bar{A}$, is the set which consists of all elements of S that do not belong to A.

Complete Block Design—An experimental design in which every treatment appears the same number of times in each block.

Completely Randomized Design—An experimental design in which the treatments are allocated to the experimental units (plots) entirely at random.

Component Bar Chart—A bar chart in which the individual bars (rectangles) are divided into sections proportional in size to the components of the total they represent. The various components are usually shaded or colored differently to increase the over-all effectiveness of the chart.

Components of a Time Series—In time series analysis, the four basic types of movements: secular trend, seasonal variation, cyclical variation, and irregular variation. The combined effect of these components is presumed to account for the observed fluctuations and the over-all movement of a series.

Components of Variance Model—*See* Random-Effects Model

Computer—*See* Analog Computer; Digital Computer

Computer Graphics—A combination of various communication and graphic arts skills, computer equipment, and computer techniques which results in the rapid and economical production of detailed drawings by a computer of such things as price changes over time, variability in treatment costs among different types of patients, staffing ratios, surgical suite utilization by specialty, and many others.

Conditional Distribution—The distribution of a random variable (or the joint distribution of several random variables) when the values of one or more other random variables are held fixed, or some other event has occurred.

Conditional Probability—If A and B are any two events and the probability of B is not equal to zero, then the conditional probability of A relative to B is denoted $P(A \mid B)$ and given by $P(A \cap B)/P(B)$, where $P(A \cap B)$ is the probability of the joint occurrence of A and B. Informally, the conditional probability of A relative to B is the probability that A will occur *given* that B has occurred or will occur.

Confidence Interval—An interval for which one can assert with a given probability $1 - \alpha$, called the *degree of confidence* or the *confidence coefficient,* that it will contain the parameter it is intended to estimate. The endpoints of a confidence interval are referred to as the *(upper and lower) confidence limits;* they are generally values of random variables calculated on the basis of sample data. A confidence interval is said to be *one-sided* when only one of the limits is a value of a random variable, while the other limit is a constant (and often omitted) or infinite. For instance, a confidence interval for the proportion θ of defectives in a large lot may be given in the form $\theta < k$, where k is a value obtained from sample data; although it is not given explicitly, the lower limit of this confidence interval is 0.

Confidence Limits—*See* Confidence Interval

Confounding—In factorial experimentation, a process by which one foregoes some information (usually about higher-order interactions) in order to reduce an experiment to manageable size. Specifically, two effects are confounded and referred to as *aliases*, if it is impossible to differentiate between them on the basis of a given experiment; that is, the contrasts which measure one effect are the very same contrasts which measure the other effect. An effect is confounded with blocks if it is impossible to differentiate between the effect and variations caused by differences among the blocks.

Consumer Price Index—Constructed by the Bureau of Labor Statistics, this index is designed to measure the over-all change in the prices of a large collection of goods and services (called a "market basket"), which represents the greater part of the expenditures of city wage-earner and clerical-worker families. The primary source of this important index is the *Monthly Labor Review.*

Consumer's Risk—The probability β of committing Type II error; the term is used especially in problems of sampling inspection.

Contagious Distribution—If the distribution of a random variable X depends on a parameter which is actually a value of a random variable, then the *unconditional* distribution of X is referred to as a contagious distribution. For instance, the distribution of the number of persons hurt in an automobile accident may be obtained as a contagious distribution from the distributions of the number of persons hurt in one-car accidents, in two-car accidents, in three-car accidents, . . ., and a distribution for the number of cars involved in an accident.

Contingency Coefficient—A measure of the strength of the association between two variables, usually qualitative, on the basis of data tallied into a contingency table. The value of this statistic is never negative and it has a maximum less than 1, depending on the number of rows and columns in the contingency table.

Contingency Table—A table consisting of two or more rows and two or more columns, into which individuals or items are classified according to two criteria (or variables). The simplest form of contingency table, the 2 by 2 table, arises when both variables are dichotomized. The notation used in connection with contingency tables and formulas for their analysis are given in Chapter 14 in Volume I. The following is a 3 by 2 contingency table in which 237 families have been classified according to whether (1) their annual income was $5,000 or less, over $5,000 but less than $10,000, or $10,000 or more, and (2) they expected to be better off or worse off financially one year later:

	Better off	Worse off	
$5,000 or less	48 (59.2)	42 (30.8)	90
Over $5,000 but less than $10,000	63 (57.3)	24 (29.7)	87
$10,000 or more	45 (39.5)	15 (20.5	60
	156	81	

The numbers 48, 42, 63, 24, 45, and 15 are the *observed (cell) frequencies,* the numbers in parentheses are the *expected (cell) frequencies,* and the numbers at the bottom and side of the table are called the *marginal totals.*

Continuity Correction—An adjustment made when approximating the distribution of a discrete random variable with that of a continuous random variable. For instance, when approximating a binomial distribution with a normal distribution, the adjustment consists of representing each integer k (from 0 to n) by a corresponding interval from $k - 1/2$ to $k + 1/2$.

Continuous Population— It is customary to say that one is sampling from a continuous population when one observes values of a continuous random variable.

Continuous Random Variable—A random variable whose range (set of possible values) is an interval or a set of intervals on the real axis (often the entire real axis), and which possesses a probability density function. For instance, a random variable having a normal distribution is said to be continuous.

Contrast—In analysis of variance, a linear combination of observations which is designed to estimate a particular parameter of the model; the coefficients of the linear combination are subject to the restriction that their sum must equal zero. Two such contrasts are said to be *orthogonal* if the sum of the pairwise products of their coefficients is equal to zero.

Correlated Samples—Two samples consisting of paired data, such as the ages of husbands and wives, or the weights of individuals before and after a diet.

Correlation—In general, the term denotes the relationship (association or dependence) between two or more qualitative or quantitative variables. *See also* Curvilinear Correlation; Linear Correlation; Multiple Correlation Coefficient; Negative Correlation; Partial Correlation; Positive Correlation; Rank Correlation

Correlation Analysis—The analysis of paired data constituting the values of two random variables X and Y; it is referred to as *normal correlation analysis* if X and Y have the bivariate normal distribution. More generally, the term applies to the analysis of n-tuples of data constituting the values of n random variables. *See also* Regression Analysis

Correlation Coefficient—(1) For two random variables, the ratio of their covariance to the product of their standard deviations; it is designated $\varrho(rho)$. (2) A measure of the linear relationship between two quantitative variables, known also as the *Pearson product-moment coefficient of correlation.* It is denoted by the letter r and its values range from -1 to $+1$, where 0 indicates the absence of any linear relationship, while -1 and $+1$ indicate, respectively, a perfect *negative* (inverse) and a perfect *positive* (direct) relationship. *See also* Alienation, Coefficient of; Determination, Coefficient of; Negative Correlation; Nondetermination, Coefficient of; Positive Correlation; z-Transformation

Correlation Matrix—The matrix whose elements are correlation coefficients; that is, for $i \neq j$ the element a_{ij} of the matrix is the correlation coefficient for the ith and jth variables, while $a_{ii} = 1$ for all i.

Count Data—Data obtained by performing actual counts, as contrasted to data obtained by performing measurements on continuous scales. Such data are also referred to as *enumeration data.*

Covariance—The expected value of the product of the deviations of two random variables from their respective means. The covariance of two *independent* random variables is zero, but a zero covariance does not imply independence. The covariance is also referred to as the *first product-moment,* and it is analogously defined for a set of paired data as the mean of the products obtained by pairwise multiplying the deviations from the respective means. As such, it appears in the numerator of the formula for the coefficient of correlation, and it is thus indicative of the extent of the linear association between the two variables.

Covariance Analysis—*See* Analysis of Covariance

Critical Region—For a given test, the subset of the sample space which contains all outcomes for which the null hypothesis is rejected. The *size* of a critical region is the probability of obtaining an outcome belonging to the critical region when the null hypothesis is true; hence, it is the probability α of a Type I error.

Critical Values—The dividing lines of a test criterion or, more generally, the boundary of a critical region.

Cross-Section Data—Data collected on some (usually economic) variable, at the same point or period in time, from different geographical regions, organizations, institutions, etc; for instance, occupancy levels in October, 1980, in each of the hospitals in California. *See also* Time Series

Cross Stratification—Stratification of a population with respect to two or more variables. Thus, a public opinion poll might cross-stratify a population of voters with respect to income, education, age, and profession. *See also* Stratified Random Sampling

Cumulative Distribution—(1) For grouped data, a distribution showing how many of the items are "less than" or "more than" given values (usually the class limits or the class boundaries). (2) For random variables, the term "cumulative distribution" is synonymous with "distribution function." *See also* Distribution Function

Curve Fitting—(1) The process of describing (approximating) an observed frequency distribution by means of a probability function or a probability density; for example, approximating an observed distribution with a normal curve. This may involve the choice of a particular kind of probability function or probability density, the estimation of its parameters, and the calculation of probabilities corresponding to the classes of the observed distribution. (2) The process of fitting a curve to points representing paired data (or, more generally, a surface to *n*-tuples of observations). This may involve the choice of a particular kind of curve or surface as well as the estimation of the parameters (or constants) appearing in its equation. *See also* Least Squares, Method of

Cycle—In time series analysis, a periodic movement; the *period* or *length* of a cycle is the time it takes for one complete up-and-down and down-and-up movement. *See also* Business Cycle

Cyclical Irregulars—In time series analysis, estimates of the cyclical and irregular components; they are usually obtained by eliminating from a series components attributed to trend and seasonal patterns.

Cyclical Relatives—In time series analysis, quantities (in percentage form) arrived at by removing the trend, and seasonal variation, as well as irregular variations from a series of data.

Cyclical Variation—In time series analysis, that component in a series which presumably results from the action of forces connected with business cycles. *See also* Business Cycle

D

Data—The results of an experiment, census, survey, and any kind of process or operation. *See also* Deseasonalized Data; External Data; Internal Data; Primary Data; Raw Data; Secondary Data

Data Reduction—The process of summarizing large masses of data by the methods of descriptive statistics, namely, by grouping them into tables or representing them by means of statistics such as the mean, a quartile, or the standard deviation.

Debugging—The process of locating and correcting errors in a computer routine, or of isolating and eliminating malfunctions of a computer itself.

Deciles—The deciles $D_1, D_2, \ldots$, and D_9 are values at or below which lie, respectively, the lowest 10, 20, $\ldots$, and 90 per cent of a set of data.

Deflating—In time series analysis, a general term applied to the process of adjusting a value series (reflecting changes in both quantity and price) for changes in price. This is usually done by dividing each number in the value series by an appropriate price index number. For instance, if an index of retail sales (a value series) and an index of retail prices, both with 1959 as base, stood at 124 and 110, respectively, in 1965, then the index of deflated sales, $124/1.10 = 112.7$, is an estimate of the ratio of the quantity of goods sold at retail in 1965 to the quantity sold in 1959.

Degree of Confidence—*See* Confidence Interval

Degrees of Freedom—(1) A random sample of size *n* is said to have $n - 1$ degrees of freedom for estimating the population variance, in the sense that there are $n - 1$ independent deviations from the mean on which to base such an estimate. (2) The parameter *v(nu)* of the chi-square distribution is referred to as its degree of freedom. (3) The parameter *v* of the *t* distribution is referred to as its degrees of freedom. (4) The parameters v_1 and v_2 of the *F* distribution are referred to as the numerator and denominator degrees of freedom. (5) In applications of a chi-square statistic, the number of degrees of freedom is given by the number of terms in the formula for the statistic *minus* the number of independent restrictions imposed on the expected frequencies; for instance, in the analysis of an r by k contingency table there are $rk - (r + k - 1) = (r - 1)(k - 1)$ degrees of freedom. (6) In an analysis of variance table, the degrees of freedom listed for the various sources of variation are the degrees of freedom of the chi-square distributions of the corresponding mean squares (divided by suitable constants).

Dependent Variable—If the value of a function f is given by $y = f(x_1, x_2, \ldots, x_k)$ as the *independent variables* and to y as the *dependent variable*. The major objective of many statistical investigations is to predict values (or expected values) of dependent variables in terms of known or assumed values of independent variables.

Descriptive Statistics—Although this term has been used to refer only to tabular and graphical presentations of statistical data, nowadays it is used more broadly to refer to any treatment of data which does not involve generalizations.

Deseasonalized Data—In time series analysis, monthly (weekly, daily, or hourly) data from which the seasonal variations have been eliminated, as far as possible, by dividing the actual data by corresponding values of a seasonal index (expressed as proportions). For instance, if a store's sales for July, 1965, were \$1.4 million and the July seasonal index is 80.0, then the deseasonalized (or *seasonally adjusted*) July, 1965, sales were 1.4/0.80 = \$1.75 million. *See also* Annual Rate; Seasonal Index

Design of Experiments—*See* Experimental Design

Determinant—A square array of numbers, called the *elements* of the determinant, symbolizing the sum of certain products of these elements, which arises in the solution of simultaneous linear equations. The number of rows (or columns) is called the *order* of the determinant. For instance, a determinant of order 2 is a square array of the form

$$\begin{vmatrix} a & b \\ c & d \end{vmatrix}$$

and its value is $ad - bc$. Using determinants, the solution of the system of equations

$$ax + by = e$$

$$cx + dy = f$$

can be written

$$x = \frac{\begin{vmatrix} e & b \\ f & d \end{vmatrix}}{\begin{vmatrix} a & b \\ c & d \end{vmatrix}} \qquad y = \frac{\begin{vmatrix} a & e \\ c & f \end{vmatrix}}{\begin{vmatrix} a & b \\ c & d \end{vmatrix}}$$

provided $ad - bc \neq 0$. A determinant of order 3 is a square array of the form

$$\begin{vmatrix} a & b & c \\ d & e & f \\ g & h & i \end{vmatrix}$$

and its value is $aei + bfg + cdh - ceg - bdi - afh$.

Determination, Coefficient of—The square of the correlation coefficient; it gives the proportion of the total variation of the dependent variable which is accounted for by the linear relationship with the independent variable. The term has also been applied to the square of the multiple correlation coefficient.

Deviation from the Mean—For a given set of data, the amount by which an individual observation differs from the mean; thus, the deviation of the ith observation x_i from the mean $\bar{x}$ is given by $x_i - \bar{x}$. An important property of deviations from the mean is that, for any set of data, their sum is always equal to zero. The absolute value of $x_i - \bar{x}$, namely, $|x_i - \bar{x}|$, is referred to as an *absolute deviation* from the mean.

Dichotomy—A classification which devides the elements of a population (or sample) into two categories. For example, a dichotomy may be a classification into which one groups items as defective or nondefective, or a classification into which one groups individuals as being married or single. A two-way classification where each variable divides the elements of a population (or sample) into two categories is called a *double dichotomy*. For example, a double dichotomy may be a classification in which one groups persons into single males, married males, single females, and married females.

Difference Between Proportions, Standard Error of—The standard deviation of the sampling distribution of the difference between two sample proportions.

Discrete Distribution—The distribution of a discrete random variable. *See also* Probability Function

Digital Computer—A computer which, unlike an analog computer, performs the ordinary operations of arithmetic on numbers as such. The main difference between a digital desk calculator and an electronic digital computer is that the latter has an extensive memory for storing information, that it performs long sequences of arithmetical and logical operations without human intervention, and that it operates at a very high speed. Since most formulas, even complex scientific ones, can be reduced to sequences of basic arithmetical operations (at least to any desired degree of approximation), digital computers have a very wide range of applicability. The five *major* components of a computer are: (1) The *input section* which takes information stored externally (as in punched cards or magnetic tape) and "reads" (transfers) it into the internal storage (or memory) of the computer. (2) The *storage* (or *memory*) *section* into which information can be introduced, in which it can be retained, and from which it can be extracted when needed. At present, the most widely used type of internal storage is magnetic core storage, a unit built of many small magnetic cores. Substantial progress has been made recently in developing semiconductor, integrated circuit memories. (3) The *arithmetic-logic section* in which the arithmetical and logical operations necessary to the solution of a problem are actually performed. (4) The *control section* which causes the various units of the computer to function in such a way that each instruction in storage is sensed at the proper time and executed in the proper manner. (5) The *output section* which transfers information from the internal storage (memory) of the computer to some suitable or desirable external form (punches it in cards, for example, or records it on magnetic tape). The input and output sections are often collectively called the *I/0 units*.

Discrete Density Function—*See* Probability Function

Discrete Distribution—The distribution of a discrete random variable. *See also* Probability Function

Discrete Random Variable—A random variable whose range is finite or countably infinite. For example, random variables having the binomial or the Poisson distribution are referred to as discrete.

Dispersion—The extent to which the elements of a sample or the elements of a population are not all alike in size, are spread out, or vary from one another. Measures of this characteristic are usually called *measures of variation*. *See also* Mean Deviation; Standard Deviation

Distribution—(1) For observed data, the term is used to refer to their over-all scattering and also as a synonym for "frequency distribution." (2) The distribution of a random variable is its *probability structure* as described, for example, by its probability function or its probability density function. It is in this sense that one speaks, for example, of a binomial distribution or a normal distribution. *See also* Distribution Function; Frequency Distribution; Probability Density Function; Probability Distribution; Probability Function

Distribution-Free Methods—This term is applied to methods of inference in which no assumptions whatsoever are made about the nature, shape, or form of the populations from which the data are obtained. *See also* Nonparametric Tests

Distribution Function—A function whose values $F(t)$ are the probabilities that a random variable assumes a value less than or equal to t for $-\infty < t < \infty$. *See also* Joint Distribution Function

Duncan's Multiple Range Test—*See* Multiple Comparisons Tests

E

Econometrics—That area of economic science in which modern mathematical and statistical techniques are used to analyze economic situations for the purpose of predicting future behavior, or to test the validity of economic theory formulated in mathematical terms.

Effect—(1) In factorial experimentation, a quantity (usually a parameter of the model) which represents a change in response produced by a change in level of one or more of the factors. (2) In analysis of variance, a parameter of the so-called fixed-effects model. *See also* Block Effect; Interaction; Main Effect; Treatment Effect

Equal Allocation—In stratified sampling, the allocation of equal parts of the total sample to the individual strata. For instance, if a stratified sample of 100 students is to be taken from among the 400 freshmen, 300 sophomores, 200 juniors, and 100

seniors attending an undergraduate school, equal allocation requires that 25 students be taken from each of the classes (regardless of their differences in size). *See also* Proportional Allocation

Error Mean Square—In analysis of variance, the error sum of squares divided by its degrees of freedom; it provides an estimate of the (supposedly) common error variance of the populations. In the analysis of variance tables it is denoted MSE.

Error Sum of Squares—In analysis of variance, that component of the total sum of squares which is attributed to experimental error.

Error Variance—The variance of a random (or chance) component of a model; the term is used mainly in the presence of other sources of variation, as for example in regression analysis or in analysis of variance. It is referred to as σ^2.

Estimate—A number or an interval, based on a sample, which is intended to match a parameter of a mathematical model. *See also* Interval Estimation; Point Estimation

Estimator—*See* Point Estimation

Event—In probability theory, an event is a subset of a sample space. Thus "event" is the nontechnical term and "subset of a sample space" is the corresponding mathemetical counterpart. For example, the event of rolling a ten with a pair of dice is the subset which consists of the outcomes where the first die comes up four and the other six, where both dice come up five, and where the first die comes up six and the other four.

Expectation—*See* Mathematical Expectation

Expected Frequency—(1) In the analysis of count (or enumeration) data, a cell frequency calculated on the basis of appropriate theory or assumptions; for example, the frequencies calculated according to formula for a contingency table. (2) In curve fitting, a class frequency obtained by approximating an observed frequency distribution with a probability function or a probability density function.

Expected Mean Square—In analysis of variance, the expected value of a mean square under a given set of assumptions; that is, for a given model. Expected mean squares serve an important function in setting up significance tests and confidence intervals for the various parameters of the model.

Expected Value—The expected value of a random variable is the mean of its distribution.

Experimental Condition—In factorial experimentation, the levels at which the individual factors are applied to a given experimental unit. In analysis of variance, the term is used synonymously with "treatment."

Experimental Design—The statistical aspects of the design (or planning) of an experiment are: (a) Selecting the treatments (factors, and levels of factors) whose effects are to be studied; (b) Specifying a layout for the experimental units (plots) to which the treatments are to be applied; (c) Providing rules according to which the treatments are to be distributed among the experimental units; (d) Specifying what measurements are to be made for each experimental unit. All these things must be accomplished in such a way that the techniques to be used in the analysis of the results are clear prior to the conduct of the experiment.

Experimental Error—The errors, or variations, not accounted for by hypothesis; in analysis of variance, their magnitude is estimated by the error sum of squares. Presumed to be caused by extraneous variables, such errors are often combined under the general heading of "chance variation." Note that in this sense the word "error" does not mean "mistake." *See also* Sampling Error

Experimental Sampling Distribution—A distribution of the values of a statistic obtained by simulating repeated samples from a given population by means of random numbers or other Monte Carlo techniques. For example, if the means of repeated samples from a given population are grouped, the resulting distribution is referred to as an experimental sampling distribution of the mean.

Experimental Unit—In experimental design, an experimental unit is the subject, object, area, grouping, or subdivision to which a treatment is applied. thus, an experimental unit might be a plot of land, a student taking a given course, several pigs in a pen, a piece of wood, or a batch of seed. Since much of the theory of experimental design was originally developed for agricultural experiments, experimental units are often referred to simply as *plots*. Experimental units have also been described as the smallest divisions of experimental material which are such that any two experimental units may receive different treatments. Also called Unit of Observation or Unit of Analysis.

Exponential Distribution—Also referred to as the *negative exponential distribution,* this distribution has important applications in engineering to reliability studies and life testing, in queuing theory, and in other areas. The exponential distribution also arises as the distribution of the waiting times between successive occurrences (arrivals) in a Poisson process.

Exponential Smoothing—A method of forecasting which makes use of exponentially weighted moving averages; it continuously corrects for the amount by which the actual and estimated figures for a just completed period fail to agree.

Exponential Trend—A trend in a time series which is adequately described by an equation of the form $y = ab^x$. On semilogarithmic graph paper such trends appear as straight lines.

External Data—Statistical data gathered by an organization from sources outside the organization itself (as by a business firm from government or trade publications).

Extrapolation—The process of estimating (or predicting) a value which lies beyond the range of values on the basis of which the predicting equation was obtained; for example, in estimating 1980 sales from a trend equation fit to sales for the years 1960-1976.

Extreme Values—The smallest and largest values of a sample. These values form the basis of a number of estimation and hypothesis testing procedures. Sometimes, extreme values are analyzed to decide whether values which differ considerably from the bulk of the data can be discarded from the data. *See also* Modified Mean; Outliers

F

F **Distribution**—A distribution which is of fundamental importance in analysis of variance. It arises as the sampling distribution of the ratio of the values of two independent random variables having chi-square distributions, each divided by its degrees of freedom; for example, the ratio of the variances of two random samples from normal populations having the same variance. Correspondingly, the parameters v_1 and v_2 of the F distribution are referred to as its *numerator* and *denominator degrees of freedom.* The F distribution is also known as the *variance-ratio* distribution. The appendices contain values of F α, v_1, v_2 for which the area *to their right* under the F distribution with v_1 and v_2 degrees of freedom is equal to α.

F Test—A test based on a statistic which (under an appropriate null hypothesis) has an F distribution; for example, a test concerning the equality of two population variances, and the test in analysis of variance and regression.

Factor—(1) In experimentation, a factor is a variable, or a quantity (a possible source of variation) under investigation. (2) In factor analysis, a factor is a linear combination of (observable) variables to which one attributes a special relevance.

Factor Analysis—In multivariate analysis (especially in psychological applications), a method of expressing data linearly in terms of factors which are of special relevance so far as the construction of appropriate models is concerned. For example, the scores n individuals obtained on k tests may be related linearly to such relevant factors as arithmetic or verbal facility.

Factorial Experiment—A *complete* factorial experiment is an experiment in which all levels of each factor (variable) are investigated in combination with all levels of every other factor. It is customary to denote complete factorial experiments by indicating the number of levels for each factor; thus, a 3 × 4 factorial experiment is a two-factor experiment where one factor has three levels and the other has four levels. Similarly, a 2^3 factorial is a three-factor experiment where each factor has two levels. If certain properly chosen levels of factors are omitted, the experiment is referred to as a *fractional factorial experiment*, or as a *fractional replicate* of a factorial experiment. Usually, the experimental conditions included in a fractional replicate of a factorial experiment are chosen in such a way that main effects and some of the lower-order interactions can be estimated, while higher-order interactions are confounded with each other. Many of the methods of *response surface analysis* (for example, methods utilizing rotatable designs) are also included under the general heading of factorial experiments. *See also* Confounding; Defining Contrast

Factorial Notation—In mathematics, the product of all positive integers less than or equal to the positive integer n is referred to as *"n factorial"* and it is denoted $n!$. Thus, $3! = 3 \cdot 2 \cdot 1 = 6$, $4! = 4 \cdot 3 \cdot 2 \cdot 1 = 24$, $5! = 5 \cdot 4 \cdot 3 \cdot 2 \cdot 1 = 120$, and so on. Also, by definition $0! = 1$.

Finite Population—A well-defined set consisting of a finite number of elements. The term is used mainly when a sample of some of these elements forms the basis of an inference concerning the entire set.

Fisher's Ideal Index—An index number which meets various mathematical tests of quality and attempts to eliminate the upward bias of the Laspeyres' index and the downward bias of the Paasche Index by taking the geometric mean of the two.

Fixed-Base Index—An index number series in which all comparisons are made to the same base year (or period).

Fixed-Effects Model—The model used in analysis of variance when the treatment effects, block effects, etc., are looked upon as parameters, namely, as constants. This model is also referred to as Model I. *See also* Mixed Model; Random-Effects Model

Fixed-Weight Aggregative Index—An index number (currently in favor) in which the prices are weighted by corresponding quantities referring to some (fixed) period other than the base year or the given year.

Forecasting—Predictions that involve explaining events which will occur at some future time are called *forecasts*, and the process of arriving at such explanations is called *forecasting*. In so-called *intrinsic* methods of prediction, predictions of the future values of variables are based on their past values; this includes most of the standard statistical methods used in time series analysis.

FORTRAN (FORmula TRANslation System)—A computer programming system, consisting of a mathematically oriented language, largely independent of the computer on which a FORTRAN program is to be executed, together with a compiler for converting a source program written in the FORTRAN language into an object program which can be executed by a particular computer. The mathematical nature of the FORTRAN language is clear from the following two statements, instructing a computer to find the roots of the quadratic equation $A\chi^2 + B\chi + C = 0$:

$$ROOT1 = (-B + SQRTF(B**2 - 4.*A*C)) / (2.*A)$$

$$ROOT2 = (-B - SQRTF(B**2 - 4.*A*C)) / (2.*A)$$

Fractile—A value, also called a *quantile,* at or below which lies a given fraction (1/10, fifty per cent, ¾, etc.) of a set of data. *See also* Deciles; Median; Percentiles; Quartiles

Frequency—The number of items, or cases, falling (or expected to fall) into a category or classification. *See also* Expected Frequency; Observed Frequency

Frequency Distribution—A table (or other kind of arrangement) which shows the classes into which a set of data has been grouped together with the corresponding frequencies, that is, the number of items falling into each class. The following is a frequency distribution of the weights of fifty boxes of diapers taken from the production of a machine:

Weight (pounds)	Number of Boxes
15.60 - 15.79	1
15.80 - 15.99	5
16.00 - 16.19	10
16.20 - 16.39	14
16.40 - 16.59	10
16.60 - 16.79	5
16.80 - 16.99	2
17.00 - 17.19	2
17.20 - 17.39	1
	50

Other items of interest in connection with this frequency distribution (see the individual listings) are: (1) the *class limits,* which are 15.60 and 15.79, 15.80 and 15.99,..., and 17.20 and 17.39; (2) the *class boundaries,* which are 15.595, 15.795, 15.995,..., 17.195, and 17.395; (3) the *class marks,* 15.695, 15.895,..., and 17.295; and (4) the *class interval,* 0.20. *See also* Cumulative Distribution; Frequency Polygon; Histogram; Ogive; Percentage Distribution

Frequency Interpretation of Probability—A theory in which the probability of an event is interpreted as the proportion of the time the event will occur in the long run. Accordingly, probabilities are estimated by sample proportions; for instance, the probability that a patient will survive a given sickness is estimated by the proportion of recoveries from the sickness that have been observed in the past.

Frequency Polygon—The graph of a frequency distribution obtained by drawing straight lines joining successive points representing the class frequencies, plotted at the corresponding class marks. To complete the picture, classes with zero frequencies are usually added at both ends of a distribution.

Frequency Table—A tabular presentation of a frequency distribution; this term is often used interchangeably with "frequency distribution."

G

Gauss-Markov Theorem—An important theorem in the theory of estimation; in its simplest form, the theorem asserts that (under certain general conditions) among all unbiased linear estimates of regression coefficients the ones obtained by the method of least squares have a minimum variance.

General Purpose Index—An index number which attempts to measure changes in such broad and complicated phenomena as production, wholesale prices, or consumer prices. Index numbers which measure changes in somewhat more limited phenomena are sometimes called *special purpose indices.*

General Rule of Addition—In probability theory, a formula for calculating the probability that at least one of two events will occur. When the two events are mutually exclusive, the corresponding formula is sometimes referred to as the *Special Rule of Addition*, which is, in fact, a postulate.

General Rule of Multiplication—In probability theory, a formula for calculating the probability that two events will both occur. When the two events are independent, the corresponding formula is sometimes referred to as the *Special Rule of Multiplication.*

Geometric Mean—A special kind of "average;" for a set of n positive numbers it is given by the nth root of their product and, unless the numbers are all alike, it is always less than their arithmetic mean. The geometric mean of the numbers 4, 6, and 9, for example, is $(4 \cdot 6 \cdot 9)^{1/3} = 6$. Geometric means are used mainly for averaging rates of change (for instance, index numbers); in practice, their calculation is facilitated by the fact that the logarithm of a geometric mean equals the corresponding arithmetic mean of the logarithms of the numbers.

Given Year (or Given Period)—In index number construction, the year (or period) one wants to compare. It is usually denoted by the subscript "n;" for example, the price of a commodity in the given year is written p_n and the corresponding quantity produced (consumed, sold, etc.) is written q_n.

Goodness of Fit—(1) In the comparison of observed frequencies and expected frequencies, the closeness of the agreement between the two sets of frequencies; it is usually measured by an appropriate chi-squate statistic. (2) In fitting a curve to paired data (or a surface to triples of numbers, etc.), the closeness of the points to the curve (surface, etc.); it is measured by various criteria, including the correlation coefficient when fitting a straight line to paired data. *See also* Kolmogorov-Smirnov Tests; Least Squares, Method of

Grand Mean—In analysis of variance models, the parameter μ which is estimated by the mean of all the observations in an experiment. The term has also been used to denote the mean of all the observations in an experiment itself, and the over-all mean of several sets of data.

Graphical Presentation—The presentation of statistical data in graphical form, including line charts, bar charts, pie charts, pictograms, maps, and the like.

Grouped Data—A set of data which has been grouped, or classified, according to some quantitative or qualitative characteristic; that is, data which have been put into a frequency distribution.

H

Hardware (of a Computer)—The various mechanical, electrical, electronic, and magnetic devices (wires, resistors, relays, transistors, connectors, frames, etc.) with which a computer is built. *See also* Software

Higher-Order Interaction—*See* Interaction

Histogram—A graph of a frequency distribution obtained by drawing rectangles whose bases coincide with the class intervals and whose areas are proportional to the class frequencies. In a histogram representing a distribution with *equal* classes, the *heights* of the rectangles are also proportional to the class frequencies.

Homogeneity of Variances—*See* Bartlett's Test

Homoscedasticity—In regression analysis, the property that the conditional distributions of Y for fixed values of the independent variable all have the same variance.

Hypergeometric Distribution—A distribution which applies to sampling without replacement from a finite population. If a population consists of a elements of one kind and $N - a$ elements of another kind, the probability function of the hypergeometric distribution gives the probability of getting χ elements of the first kind in a random sample of size n. When N is large and n is small compared to N, the hypergeometric distribution is usually approximated by means of the binomial distribution. Hypergeometric distributions are widely used in quality control and sample survey analysis.

Hypothesis—In statistics, an assertion about the parameter (or parameters) of a population or an assertion about the functional form of a population. For example, one might formulate and test the hypothesis that a sample comes from a population with the mean μ_o, or one might assert and test the hypothesis that a sample comes from a normal population. *See also* Alternative Hypothesis; Composite Hypothesis; Null Hypothesis; Simple Hypothesis

Hypothesis Testing—*See* Hypothesis; Neyman-Pearson Theory; Significance Test; Tests of Hypotheses

I

Ideal Index—*See* Fisher's Ideal Index

Independent Events—In probability theory, two events are said to be independent if, and only if, the probability that they will both occur equals the product of the probabilities that each one, individually, will occur. If two events are not independent, they are said to be *dependent*.

Independent Random Variables—Two or more random variables are independent if, and only if, the values of their joint distribution function are given by the products of the corresponding values of their individual (marginal) distribution functions. If random variables are not independent, they are said to be dependent.

Independent Samples—Two samples are independent if the selection of one in no way affects the selection of the other. More rigorously, two samples of size n_1 and n_2 are independent if they consist of the values of $n_1 + n_2$ independent random variables, with the first n_1, and the other n_2 having, respectively, identical distributions. For example, two random samples of the IQs of students selected separately at two universities are independent, whereas the IQs of husbands and their wives do not constitute independent random samples. Samples which are not independent are referred to as *correlated, paired,* or *matched*.

Independent Variable—*See* Dependent Variable

Index Number—A statistical measure which reflects a comparison of prices, quantities, or values pertaining to two different periods of time, two different locations, etc. Many important index numbers which reflect changes in various economic variables are published *in series*, that is, at regular intervals of time, by Federal government and other organizations.

Inference—*See* Statistical Inference

Infinite Population—(1) the infinite set of values which can be assumed by a continuous random variable. (2) the phrase "sampling from an infinite population" refers to the process of obtaining a sample which consists of the values of independent random variables having the same (population) distribution. In contrast to sampling *without replacement* from a finite population, the composition of an infinite population is *not* affected by values previously drawn.

Interaction—In general, a joint effect of several variables or factors. In factorial experimentation, it is a measure of the extent to which a change in response produced by changes in the levels of one or more factors depends on the levels of the other factors. Interactions involving at least three factors (at least four, as the case may be, etc.) are referred to as *higher-order interactions*, while the others are referred to as *lower-order interactions*.

Interarrival Distribution—In queuing theory, the distribution of the time lapses between successive arrivals at a service "counter." The exponential distribution is often used as a model for interarrival distributions. *See also* Arrival Distribution

Internal Data—Data taken by an organization from its own private records (as by a business firm from its stock status reports, order book, personnel sheets, etc.) for its own use in statistical studies.

Interpolation—The process of determining a value of a function between two known values without using the equation of the function itself. *See also* Extrapolation

Interquartile Range—A measure of variation given by the difference between the values of the third and first quartiles of a set of data; it represents the length of the interval which contains the middle 50 per cent of the data. *See also* Quartile Deviation

Intersection (of Two Sets)—The intersection of two sets A and B, denoted $A \cap B$, is the set which consists of all elements that belong to both A and B.

Interval Estimate—*See* Interval Estimation

Interval Estimation—The estimation of a parameter in terms of an interval, called an *interval estimate,* for which one can assert with a given probability (or degree of confidence) that it contains the actual value of the parameter. Note that in connection with confidence intervals the endpoints of the intervals are the random variables, but in the theory of fiducial intervals the probability applies to the parameter. *See also* Confidence Interval.

Inverse Matrix—*See* Matrix

Irregular Variation—In time series analysis, a term used to describe all fluctuations other then those systematic ones attributed to trend, seasonal, and cyclical influences. Thus, irregular variations are the ever-present, more or less random, movements which, though individually unpredictable, tend to average out in the long run.

J

J-Shaped Distribution—A frequency distribution having the general shape of a letter J (lying on its side).

Joint Density Function—An extension of the concept of a probability density function to two or more continuous random variables. Joint density functions are also referred to as joint probability densities and as *multivariate density functions.* In the case of two continuous random variables, probabilities are given by appropriate volumes under the surface representing their *bivariate density function.*

Joint Distribution—An extension of the concept of the distribution of a random variable to that of two or more random variables. Joint distributions are also referred to as *multivariate distributions,* and in the case of two random variables, as *bivariate distributions.*

Joint Distribution Function—An extension of the concept of a distribution function to two or more random variables. Joint distribution functions are also referred to as *multivariate distribution functions.* In the case of two random variables X_1 and X_2, the values $F(t_1, t_2)$ of their *bivariate distribution function* are the probabilities that X_1 assumes a value less than or equal to t_1 while, at the same time, X_2 assumes a value less than or equal to t_2.

Joint Probability Function—An extension of the concept of a probability function to two or more discrete random variables. Joint probability functions are also referred to as *multivariate probability functions*, and in the case of two random variables, as *bivariate probability functions*.

Judgment Sample—Unlike a probability sample, a sample in whose selection personal judgment plays a significant part. Though judgment samples are sometimes required by practical considerations, and may lead to satisfactory results, they do not lend themselves to analysis by standard statistical methods.

K

Kolmogorov-Smirnov Tests—Tests for significant differences between two cumulative distributions. The one-sample test is a test of *goodness of fit*, and it concerns the agreement between an observed cumulative distribution and an assumed distribution function of a continuous random variable; the two-sample test concerns the agreement between two observed cumulative distributions.

Kurtosis—The relative peakedness or flatness of a distribution; it is usually measured by the statistic α_4 (*alpha-four*), whose value is equal to three for the normal distribution. A distribution which is more peaked and has relatively wider tails than the normal distribution is said to be *leptokurtic,* and for such a distribution α_4 exceeds three. A distribution which is less peaked and has relatively narrower tails than the normal distribution is said to be *platykurtic*, and for such a distribution α_4 is less than three.

L

Laspeyres' Index—A weighted aggregative index in which the prices are weighted by the corresponding quantities produced (consumed, sold, etc.) in the base year.

Law of Large Numbers—Informally, the *weak* law of large numbers states that if an experiment is repeated again and again, one can assert with a probability close to 1 that the proportion of the time a given event occurs will come arbitrarily close to the probability of the event (on an individual trial); the *strong* law of large numbers states that for an infinite number of trials the corresponding probability is actually equal to 1.

Least Squares Estimate—An estimate obtained by the method of least squares; such estimates are used extensively in regression analysis and in analysis of variance. *See also* Gauss-Markov Theorem

Least Squares, Method of—A method of curve fitting and, hence, a method of estimating the parameters appearing in the corresponding equations. It consists of minimizing the sum of the squares of the differences between observed values and the corresponding values calculated by means of a model equation. For example, when fitting a straight line $y = a + bx$ to a set of paired data by this method, one minimizes (with respect to a and b) the sum of the squares of the differences between the observed y's and the corresponding values obtained by substituting the given x's into the expression $a + bx$.

Leptokurtic Distribution—*See* Kurtosis

Level (of a Factor)—In factorial experimentation, the values at which a factor (variable) is held fixed in an experiment are referred to as its levels. For example, if certain measurements are made at temperatures of 120°, 150°, and 180°, these three values are referred to as the three levels of temperature; similarly, if persons are classified as employed and unemployed in a certain study, these are the two levels of employment considered in the investigation.

Level of Significance—In a significance test, the probability of erroneously rejecting a true null hypothesis, namely the probability α of committing a Type I error.

Linear Combination—In mathematics, a linear combination of $\chi_1, \chi_2, \ldots$, and χ_k is an expression of the form $a_1\chi_1 + a_2\chi_2 + \ldots + a_k\chi_k$, where $a_1, a_2, \ldots$, and a_k are constants.

Linear Correlation—The relationship between two or more random variables for which the regression equations are linear.

Linear Equation—An equation of the form $y = b_0 + b_1\chi_1 + b_2\chi_2 + \ldots + b_k\chi_k$, where y is the dependent variable, $\chi_1, \chi_2, \ldots$, and χ_k are the independent variables, and $b_0, b_1, \ldots$, and b_k are constants. Such equations can be written in various alternate (through equivalent) forms. When a common solution is to be obtained for several linear equations, one refers to these equations as a system of *simultaneous linear equations*. *See also* Determinant

Linear Estimate—An estimate which is given by a linear combination of observed values of random variables. Examples of linear estimates are those of the regression coefficients when fitting a straight line by the method of least squares.

Linear Hypothesis—*See* Linear Model

Linear Model—A mathematical model in which the equations relating the random variables and parameters are linear. In analysis of variance, for example, where the assumption of this kind of model is referred to as a *linear hypothesis,* it is assumed that an observed value is given by the sum of terms representing different effects (main effects, treatment effects, block effects, interactions, etc.) and a value of a random variable.

Linear Regression—*See* Regression

Linear Trend—In time series analysis, a secular trend which is represented (that is, reasonably well fit) by a straight line. The constants appearing in the trend equation are usually estimated by the method of least squares.

Location, Measures of—Statistical descriptions, such as the mean, median, or a quartile, which have the following property: if the same constant is added to each observation, this constant must also be added to the measure of location.

Logarithmic Line Chart—A graph obtained by plotting the values of a series on semilogarithmic paper and connecting successive points by means of straight lines.

Logit—In dosage problems (bio-assay), a transformed value of the probability of obtaining a particular response to a given dosage.

Lower-Order Interaction—*See* Interaction

M

Main Effect—In factorial experimentation, the *average* change in response produced by changing the level of *one* factor; the changes in response are averaged over all possible combinations of the levels of the other factors.

Marginal Distribution—The distribution of a random variable (or a set of random variables) obtained from a joint distribution by summing out, or integrating out, all the other variables.

Master Sample—A sample drawn for repeated use, perhaps for subsequent subsampling. Such samples are used, for example, in obtaining periodic ratings of television programs.

Mathematical Expectation—The mathematical expectation of a random variable, or simply its *expected value*, is given by the mean of its distribution. Originally, the concept of a mathematical expectation was introduced with reference to games of chance where, if a player stood to win an amount a with the probability p, his mathematical expectation was defined as the product $a \cdot p$.

Matrix—An m by n matrix is a rectangular array having m rows, each containing n numbers, called its *elements*. If the element of the ith row and jth column is denoted a_{ij}, the corresponding 3 by 3 matrix is

$$\begin{pmatrix} a_{11} & a_{12} & a_{13} \\ a_{21} & a_{22} & a_{23} \\ a_{31} & a_{32} & a_{33} \end{pmatrix}$$

A matrix such as the above which has $m = n$ is called a *square matrix* of *order n*. A matrix A^{-1} is called the *inverse* of the square matrix A (with elements a_{ij}) if the product of the two matrices is a matrix, called the *identity matrix* and denoted by I, having 1 s on the main diagonal running from upper left to lower right and 0s elsewhere.

Mean—(1) The mean of n numbers is their sum divided by n. Technically referred to as the *arithmetic mean* and commonly referred to as the "average," the mean is by far the most widely used measure of the middle, or center, of a set of data. It is usually denoted by symbols such as $\bar{\chi}$ or $\bar{y}$, depending on whether the observations themselves are represented by the letters χ or y. (2) The mean of a finite population of size N is given by the sum of its elements divided by N. Population means are usually denoted by the Greek letter μ (*mu*). The mean of the distribution of a random variable is its *expected value*, and it is usually denoted by μ. *See also* Geometric Mean; Harmonic Mean; Modified Mean: Weighted Mean

Mean Absolute Deviation—A measure of the variation of a set of data, also called the *average deviation*, which is given by the (arithmetic) mean of the absolute deviations from the mean.

Mean Square—In analysis of variance, a sum of squares divided by the corresponding number of degrees of freedom. *See also* Error Mean Square; Expected Mean Square

Mean Square Error—A measure of the error to which one is exposed by the use of an estimator, which is given by the expected value of the squared difference between the estimator and a (theoretically) correct value. For unbiased estimators, the mean square error equals the variance. The square root of the mean square error is referred to as the *root-mean-square error.*

Median—(1) For ungrouped data, the value of the middle item (or, by convention, the mean of the values of the two middle items) when the items in a set are arranged according to size. (2) For a frequency distribution, the number corresponding to the point of the horizontal scale through which a vertical line divides the total area of the histogram of the distribution into two equal parts. (3) For the distribution of a random variable, the value (or any one of the set of values) for which the distribution function equals $\frac{1}{2}$, or a point of discontinuity, say χ_0, such that the value of the distribution function is less than $\frac{1}{2}$ for $\chi < \chi_0$ and greater than $\frac{1}{2}$ for $\chi > \chi_0$.

Minimum-Variance Estimator—An estimator having the smallest possible variance within a given class of estimators, usually unbiased estimators. *See also* Gauss-Markov Theorem

Mixed Model—In analysis of variance, the model used when some, but not all, of the parameters of the fixed-effects model are themselves values of random variables. *See also* Fixed-Effects Model; Random-Effects Model

Mixed Sampling—Multi-stage sampling, where different sampling procedures are used in the different stages; for instance, when cluster sampling is used first to select certain geographic regions and simple random samples are then selected from each of these regions.

Modal Class—That class of a frequency distribution which has the highest frequency; sometimes a class of a frequency distribution which has a higher frequency than both adjacent classes.

Mode—(1) A measure of location defined simply as the value (or, in the case of qualitative data, the attribute) which occurs with the highest frequency, namely, most often. Note that a set of data (or a distribution) can have more than one mode, or no mode at all when no two values are alike. (2) For the distribution of a random variable, a mode is a value of the random variable for which the probability function or the probability density has a relative maximum. *See also* Multi-Modal distribution

Model—A theory, usually expressed mathematically, which attempts to describe the inherent structure of selected aspects of a phenomenon, or process, which generates observed data. An equation which expresses a relationship among pertinent variables of a model is referred to as a *model equation. See also* Linear Model; Multiplicative Model

Modified Mean—When one or more of the items (usually lying at the extremes of the data) are omitted because they are judged to be atypical of the data, the mean of the remaining values is referred to as a modified mean.

Monthly Trend Increment—the typical month-to-month change in monthly data (for example, the average monthly increase in monthly sales). It is usually obtained by converting the corresponding annual trend increment for annual data to a form reflecting the monthly increment for monthly data.

Moving Average—An artificially constructed time series in which each actual value in a series is replaced by the mean of itself and some of the values immediately preceding it and directly following it. Such series are often used to describe the "general sweep" of the development of a time series when a mathematical equation is not wanted; they also form the basis for the most widely used method of constructing a seasonal index. *See also* Smoothing

Mu, μ—*See* Mean

Multicollinearity—A term used mainly in econometrics to describe a common situation in multiple regression analysis of economic data where there is such a high degree of correlation between two or more explanatory (independent) variables that it is impossible to measure accurately their individual effects on the explained (dependent) variable. For instance, if income and prices are used to explain demand, these two explanatory variables are often highly correlated.

Multinomial Distribution—An extension of the binomial distribution which applies when each trial permits k possible outcomes, the trials are independent, and the probability for each possible outcome remains constant from trial to trial.

Multi-Modal Distribution—A distribution with several modes, that is, with several relative maxima; such distributions often result from the mixing of several non-homogeneous sets of data.

Multi-Phase Sampling—A kind of sampling in which certain items of information are collected from all the units in a sample, then other items of information (often more detailed) are collected from a subsample. Sometimes, further phases are added beyond this kind of *two-phase process*. Multi-phase sampling differs from multistage sampling in that the *same* sampling units are used throughout in the former, while the elements of the subsample(s) are of an inherently different nature in the latter.

Multiple Comparisons Tests—Tests designed to show which mean (or set of means) differs significantly from which other mean (or set of means). They are used, for example, as a follow-up to F tests in analysis of variance which have yielded significant results. *See also* Contrast

Multiple Correlation Coefficient—A measure of the closeness of the fit of a regression plane (or hyperplane) and, hense, an indication of how well one variable can be predicted in terms of a linear combination of the others. The multiple correlation coefficient is given by the *maximum* correlation coefficient between the dependent variable and any linear combination of the independent variables.

Multiple Linear Regression—A linear regression involving two or more independent variables.

Multiple Stratification—This term is synonymous with "cross stratification," namely, stratification of a population with respect to two or more variables.

Multiplicative Model—In time series analysis, the model which assumes that each value of a series is the *product* of factors that can be attributed to the individual components (secular trend, seasonal variation, cyclical variation, and irregular variation).

Multi-Stage Sampling—In this kind of sampling, a population is divided into a number of primary (first-stage) units, which are sampled in some appropriate way;

then the selected primary units are subdivided into smaller secondary (second-stage) units and a sample is taken from these units; further stages may follow. For example, one might first select from a given population a random sample of n_1 counties (the primary units), then randomly select a subsample of n_2 townships (the secondary units) from each of these counties.

Multivariate Analysis—The analysis of data consisting of n-tuples (pairs, triples, etc.) of observations or, in other words, values of random vectors. It included regression and correlation analysis, analysis of variance and covariance, linear discriminant analysis, and other techniques.

Mutually Exclusive Events—In probability theory, two events are mutually exclusive if, and only if, they are represented by *disjoint* subsets of the sample space, namely, by subsets which have no elements in common. An alternative definition is that two events are mutually exclusive if, and only if, their intersection has a zero probability.

N

Negative Correlation—Two variables are said to be negatively correlated when the larger values of either variable tend to go with the smaller values of the other variable, and their correlation coefficient is, in fact, negative.

Neyman-Pearson Theory—A general theory of hypothesis testing based on the concepts of Type I and Type II errors, and in particular on the concept of a power function.

Noise—In information theory, the term refers to a random disturbance which is superimposed on a signal. The term *random noise* is often used in connection with artificially generated continuous random processes.

Nondetermination, Coefficient of—One minus the square of the correlation coefficient; it gives the proportion of the total variation of the dependent variable which is *not* accounted for by the linear relationship with the independent variable.

Nonparametric Tests—Tests which do not involve hypotheses concerning specific values of parameters. Such tests are used when the assumptions underlying so-called "standard" tests cannot be met, and they are often used as computational shortcuts. Many statisticians use the terms "nonparametric" and "distribution-free" interchangeably. *See also* Distribution-Free Methods and listings of individual tests

Normal Curve—The graph of a normal distribution; it has the shape of a vertical cross section of a bell. Theoretically speaking, it extends from $-\infty$ to ∞, having the horizontal axis as an asymptote.

Normal Distribution—A distribution which was first studied in connection with errors of measurement and, thus, referred to as the "normal curve of errors." Nowadays, the normal distribution forms the cornerstone of a very large portion of statistical theory. Sometimes referred to also as the *Gaussian distribution*, the normal distribution has the two parameters μ and σ; when $\mu = 0$ and $\sigma = 1$ it is said to be in its *standard form,* and it is referred to as the *standard normal distribution.* Some probabilities related to the normal distribution are given in Tables in the Appendices.

Normal Equations—In applications of the method of least squares, a system of equations whose solution gives the least squares estimates of the parameters. For example, when fitting a straight line to a set of paired data, the normal equations are the two linear equations whose solution provides values for the regression coefficients.

n-Tuple—In mathematics, an ordered set of n numbers; it is a generalization of such terms as "pair," "triple," etc.

Null Hypothesis—Nowadays, the term is used for any hypothesis H_0 which is to be tested against an alternative hypothesis H_1 (or H_A), and whose erroneous rejection is looked upon as a Type I error. Originally, the term was used in connection with hypotheses of "no difference" in tests of significance.

Numerical Distribution—A frequency distribution, also called a *quantitative distribution,* in which data are grouped according to numerical size and not according to a qualitative description.

O

Objective Probability—In contrast to subjective probabilities, this term is applied to probabilities interpreted in the frequency sense. *See also* Frequency Interpretation of Probability

Observed Frequency—The actual number of sample values (items) falling into a class of a distribution or into a cell of a contingency table.

Ogive—The graph of a cumulative (frequency or percentage) distribution, obtained by plotting the cumulative frequencies or percentages corresponding to the class boundaries and connecting successive points with straight lines. Since most ogives met in practice have the general shape of an elongated letter S, they are also referred to as *sigmoids.*

One-Sided Alternative—In hypothesis testing, a composite alternative hypothesis is said to be *one-sided* if the values of the parameter assumed under the alternative hypothesis are all larger or all smaller than the value (or values) assumed under the null hypothesis. Correspondingly, a composite alternative hypothesis is said to be *two-sided* if some of the values of the parameter assumed under the alternative hypothesis are larger and some are smaller than the value (or values) assumed under the null hypothesis. For example, when testing the null hypothesis $\mu = \mu_0$, the two alternative hypotheses $\mu < \mu_0$ and $\mu > \mu_0$ are both one-sided, while the alternative hypothesis $\mu \neq \mu_0$ is two-sided.

One-Tail Test (One-Sided Test)—A test of a statistical hypothesis in which the region of rejection (the critical region) consists of either the right-hand tail or the left-hand tail (but not both) of the sampling distribution of the test statistic. Correspondingly, a test is referred to as a *two-tail test* (or a *two-sided test*) when the region of rejection consists of both tails of the sampling distribution of the test statistic. For example, when testing a hypothesis concerning the mean of a population, $\bar{x} < k$ (where k is an appropriate constant) represents a one-tail test, and $\bar{x} < k_1$ or $\bar{x} < k_2$ (where k_1 and k_2 are appropriate constants) represents a two-tail test.

One-Way Analysis of Variance—An analysis of variance where the total sum of squares is expressed as the sum of the treatment sum of squares, the error sum of squares, and no others.

One-Way Classification—A classification of a set of observations according to one characteristic (or the values of one variable). Thus, the term is used in analysis of variance when the data are grouped only according to treatments (and not according to blocks or other characteristics).

Open Class—A class at the lower or upper end of a frequency distribution having no stated lower or upper limit. For instance, classes such as "less than $100" or "$1,000 or more" are open classes.

Operating Characteristic Curve (OC-Curve)—In hypothesis testing (especially in sampling inspection), the graph of a function whose values are the probabilities of accepting the null hypothesis for various values of the parameter under considera-tion. Thus, for all values of the parameter other than those assumed under the null hypothesis, the OC-curve gives the probability β of committing a Type II error; for the values of the parameter assumed under the null hypothesis it gives the probability of *not* committing a Type I error (the probability $1 - \alpha$ when the parameter assumes only one value under the null hypothesis). *See also* Power Function

Operations Research—The application of modern scientific techniques to problems involving the operation of a "system" looked upon as a whole, say, the conduct of a war; the management of a firm; the manufacture of a product; the planning of an economy; and so on.

Orthogonal Contrast—*See* Contrast

Outliers—Observations at either extreme (small or large) of a sample which are so far removed from the main body of the data that the appropriateness of including them in the sample is questionable. Sources of outliers are gross errors in the recording of or calculations with data, malfunctions of equipment, or contamination. *See also* Modified Mean

P

Paasche's Index—A weighted aggregative index in which the prices are weighted by the corresponding quantities produced (consumed, sold, etc.) in the given year.

Parabolic Trend—In time series analysis, a trend which is best described by a parabola, that is, by a curve having an equation of the form $y = b_0 + b_1 x + b_2 x^2$.

Parameter—In statistics, a numerical quantity (such as the mean or the standard deviation) which characterizes the distribution of a random variable or a population. Parameters are usually denoted by Greek letters to distinguish them from the cor-responding descriptions of samples.

Partial Correlation—In multivariate problems, a measure of the strength of the rela-tionship (correlation) between any two of the variables for fixed values of the others.

Partition (of a Sample Space)—The sets $B_1, B_2, \ldots$, and B_k constitute a partition of a sample space S, if they have pairwise no elements in common and $B_1 \cup B_2 \cup \ldots \cup B_k = S$.

Peakedness—*See* Kurtosis

Pearson Product-Moment Coefficient of Correlation—*See* Correlation Coefficient

Pearsonian Coefficient of Skewness—*See* Skewness

Percentage Distribution—A converted frequency distribution in which the class frequencies are replaced by the corresponding percentages of the total number of items grouped.

Percentiles—The percentiles P_1, P_2, ..., and P_{99} are values at or below which lie, respectively, the lowest 1, 2, ..., and 99 per cent of a set of data.

Periodic Movement—In time series analysis, any movement which occurs more or less regularly within a prescribed period; for example, within a day, a week, a month, or a year. The main interest in the study of such phenomena has been in those movements called "seasonal variation," which recur year after year in the same months and with about the same intensity. *See* Seasonal Variation

Permutation—Any ordered subset of a collection of n distinct objects. The number of possible permutations, each containing r objects, that can be formed from a collection of n distinct objects is given by $n(n - 1) \cdot \ldots \cdot (n - r + 1) = n!/(n - r)!$, and denoted $_nP_r$, P_r^n, $P(n,r)$, or $(n)_r$. For instance, the number of permutations of the first ten letters of the alphabet, taken three at a time, is $10!/7! = 720$.

Point Estimation—The estimation of a parameter by assigning it a unique value, called a *point estimate*. The merits of a method of point estimation are assessed in terms of the properties of the estimator which gives rise to the particular estimate; for example, unbiasedness, consistency, sufficiency, relative efficiency, and minimum variance.

Poisson Distribution—A distribution which may be introduced as a limiting form of the binomial distribution when the probability of a success on an individual trial approaches zero, the number of trials becomes infinite, and the product of these two quantities remains constant. More generally, the Poisson distribution serves as a model for situations where one is concerned with the number of "successes" per unit of observation, say, the number of imperfections per roll of cloth, the number of telephone calls arriving at a switchboard during a fixed period of time, or the daily number of automobile accidents occurring at a given intersection.

Poisson Process—A random process, continuous in time, for which the probability of the occurrence of a certain kind of event during a small time interval Δ is approximately $\alpha\Delta$, the probability of the occurrence of more than one such event during the time interval Δ is negligible, and the probability of what happens during such a small time interval does not depend on what happened before. It can be shown that under these assumptions the probability for the occurrence of x such events during a time interval of length t is given by the Poisson distribution with the parameter αt.

Polynomial Function—A function given by an equation of the form $y = b_0 + b_1x + b_2x^2 + \ldots + b_kx^k$. The highest power of x with a nonzero coefficient is referred to as the *degree* of the polynomial function.

Polynomial Trend—In time series analysis, a trend which is best described by a polynomial function. *See* Polynomial Function; Parabolic Trend

Pooled Estimate—An estimate of a parameter obtained by pooling (combining) two or more sets of data. For example, in the two-sample t test the squared deviations from the means of the two samples are pooled to obtain an estimate of the presumed common population variance.

Pooling of Error—In analysis of variance, sums of squares attributed to (supposedly nonexisting) higher-order interactions or other sources of variation are sometimes combined (pooled) with the error sum of squares to obtain more degrees of freedom for estimating the experimental error.

Population—*See* Finite Population; Infinite Population

Population Mean—*See* Mean

Population Parameter—*See* Parameter

Population Size—The number of elements in a finite population; it is usually denoted by the letter N.

Population Standard Deviation (or Variance)—*See* Standard Deviation

Positive Correlation—Two variables are said to be *positively correlated,* or have a *positive correlation,* when the larger values of either variable tend to go with the larger values of the other variable, the smaller values of either variable, and their correlation coefficient is, in fact, positive.

Positive Skewness—*See* Skewness

Postulates of Probability—*See* Probability, Postulates of

Power—For a given alternative (that is, a specific alternative value of the parameter under consideration), the probability $1 - \beta$ of not committing a Type II error with a given test. Correspondingly, one test is said to be *more powerful* than another for a given alternative if its power exceeds that of the other test. *See also* Power Function

Power Efficiency—This concept concerns the increase in sample size required to make a test as powerful as the most powerful known test of its type (when used with data which meet its assumptions). It is given by the percentage $n_1/n \cdot 100$, where n_1 is the sample size required with test T_1 to make it as powerful as test T with a sample of size n. Generally, the power efficiency of a test will depend on n and also the value of the parameter assumed under the alternative hypothesis.

Power Function—In hypothesis testing, a function whose values are the probabilities of rejecting a given null hypothesis (and accepting the alternative hypothesis) for various values of the parameter under consideration. Thus, for all values of the parameter other than those assumed under the null hypothesis the power function gives the probability $1 - \beta$ of *not* committing a Type II error; for the values of the parameter assumed under the null hypothesis it gives the probability of committing a Type I error (the probability α when the parameter assumes only one value under the null hypothesis). Observe that the values of the power function are given by 1 *minus* the corresponding values of the *operating characteristic curve.*

Precision—(1) The precision of an estimator is its tendency to have its values cluster closely about the mean of its sampling distribution; thus, it is related inversely to the variance of this sampling distribution—the smaller the variance, the greater the precision. (2) The term "precision" has been used to denote the parameter $h = 1/\sigma\sqrt{2}$ of the normal distribution.

Prediction, Limits of—In regression analysis, a pair of values for which one can assert with a given probability that they will contain a future observation of the dependent variable for a given value of the independent variable.

Price Index—An index number intended to estimate changes in the prices of certain goods or services; for example, wholesale food prices or consumer prices.

Price Relative—The ratio of the price of an individual item in the given year to its price in the base year.

Primary Data—Statistical data which are published by the same organization by which they are collected (and often processed).

Probability—*See* Frequency Interpretation of Probability; Probability, Postulates of; Subjective Probability

Probability Density—This term is used as an abbreviation for "probability density function," and also to denote a *value* of such a function. *See* Probability Density Function

Probability Density Function—A function with non-negative values, whose integral from a to b ($a \leq b$) gives the probability that a corresponding random variable assumes a value on the interval from a to b. Most of the probability density functions used in basic statistics may be represented by continuous curves, and probabilities are given by appropriate areas under these curves. Probability density functions are also referred to in the literature as *continuous densities, continuous distributions, densities, density functions, frequency functions,* and *probability densities.*

Probability Distribution—(1) A synonym for "probability function." (2) The probability distribution (or simply the distribution) of a random variable is its *probability structure* as described, for example, by a probability function or a probability density function. *See also* Probability Density Function; Probability Function

Probability Function—A function which assigns a probability to each value within the range of a discrete random variable. Probability functions are also referred to in the literature as *densities, discrete density functions, discrete densities, frequency functions, probability distributions,* and *probability distribution functions.*

Probability, Postulates of—Basic rules, or axioms, which form the foundation of the mathematical theory of probability. These rules apply regardless of whether probabilities are interpreted as frequencies, as degrees of belief, or as logical relationships.

Probability Sample—A sample obtained by a method in which every element of a finite population has a known (not necessarily equal) chance of being included in the sample.

Probit—In dosage problems (Bio-Assay), a transformed value of the probability of obtaining a certain response to a given dosage. This transformation consists of adding five (to avoid negative values) to the values of a random variable having the standard normal distribution, and for which the area under the curve to its left equals the probability of the response to the dosage.

Program—A complete plan for solving a problem with an automatic computer. However, the term is often used to refer only to that part of the computer plan which consists of the detailed written instructions to the machine itself. *See also* Programming (a Digital Computer); Coding (a Digital Computer)

Programming (a Digital Computer)—Specifying precisely how a problem is to be solved on a digital computer. Although the terms "programming" and "coding" are often used synonymously, strictly speaking, programming includes the following: problem recognition, definition, and analysis; flowcharting; coding; testing and debugging; documentation (describing the problem, the results, and the process by which they are obtained); and program maintenance. The two major types of programming are (1) *applications programming,* namely, writing programs to solve specific scientific or commercial data processing problems by utilizing the computing resources of a particular computer or computer facility. A regression analysis program written for execution on one of the IBM System/360 computers, for example, is an applications program. The other type is (2) *systems programming,* namely, writing programs which facilitate operating, and writing applications programs for, (often) a wide range of computers. Among the various products of this extremely complex and difficult work are operating systems, programming languages and compilers, and testing programs to detect mechanical and electrical equipment malfunctions.

Programming Language/One (PL/1)—A high-level computer programming language, announced in 1964, and developed for use initially with the IBM System/360 family of computers. Intended as a more or less universal language to meet most business and scientific needs, PL/1 incorporates some features of the FORTRAN, COBOL, and ALGOL languages, as well as a number of others found in none of these languages.

Proportional Allocation—In stratified sampling, the allocation of portions of the total sample to the individual strata so that the sizes of these subsamples are porportional to the sizes of the corresponding strata. For instance, if a stratified sample of 100 students is to be taken from among the 400 freshmen, 300 sophomores, 200 juniors, and 100 seniors attending an undergraduate school, proportional allocation requires that 40, 30, 20, and 10 students be chosen from these four classes.

Pseudorandom Numbers—*See* Random Numbers

Q

Qualitative Distribution—*See* Categorical Distribution

Quantitative Distribution—*See* Frequency Distribution; Numerical Distribution

Quantity Index—An index number intended to estimate changes in the physical volume or quantity produced, consumed, sold, etc., of certain goods or services.

Quantity Relative—The ratio of the quantity produced, consumed, sold, etc., of an individual item in the given year to the corresponding quantity in the base year.

Quartile Deviation—A measure of variation, also called the *semi-interquartile range,* which is given by half the difference between the third and first quartiles; hence, the average amount by which the first and third quartiles differ from the median.

Quartiles—The quartiles Q_1, Q_2, and Q_3 are values at or below which lie, respectively, the lowest 25, 50, and 75 per cent of a set of data.

Questionnaire—A list of questions sent (or given) to a subject in a statistical investigation which, it is hoped, he will answer completely and truthfully, and promptly return to the source.

Queue—Also called a waiting line, a line formed by the arrival of persons, items, or units seeking service of some sort at a facility which serves and subsequently releases them; for instance, trucks waiting to be unloaded at a dock, aircraft waiting to land, court cases waiting to be heard, relief cases waiting to be processed, and customers waiting to be served at a ticket office or market checkout stand all form queues. Except in special circumstances, queues eventually develop whenever units arrive at a servicing facility. *See also* Queuing Theory

Queuing Theory—Sometimes called *congestion theory, trunking theory,* or *waiting-line theory,* queuing theory is a (largely) mathematical theory concerned with the study of such factors of interest in queuing problems as the distribution of arrivals, the distribution of the lengths of service times, the average time a unit spends in the system (waiting to be served and being served), the average length of the queue, and the probability distribution for the number of units waiting to be served. *See also* Arrival Distribution; Interarrival Distribution; Mean

Quota Sampling—A type of judgment sampling, in which an interviewer is given a quota to be filled (for example, three American-born shopkeepers in the over-65 age bracket living in a certain area, etc.); such quotas are usually filled as quickly and simply as possible, without much consideration to questions of randomizing the selection.

R

Random-Effects Model—The model used in analysis of variance when the parameters of the fixed-effects model are, themselves, values of random variables; this model is also referred to as *Model II,* the *variance-components model,* and the *components of variance model. See also* Fixed-Effects Model; Mixed Model

Random Numbers—Published tables of random numbers (or *random digits*) consisting of pages on which the digits 0, 1, 2, ..., 9 are set down in much the order as they would appear if they had been generated by a gambling device which gives each digit a probability of 1/10. Before publishing tables of this sort, the numbers are usually required to "pass" various statistical tests intended (insofar as this is possible) to insure their randomness. In computer work it is generally convenient to generate sequences of random numbers as they are needed by following some calculational rule, which is devised in such a way that the numbers generated would meet various statistical tests of randomness although they are never actually tested; such numbers are called *pseudorandom numbers*. Sometimes, it is convenient in such work to use sequences of *quasirandom numbers,* that is, "more or less" random numbers which, though failing to satisfy some statistical criterion, are nevertheless valid for use in particular situations.

Random Order—An ordering of a set of objects which is such that every possible order has the same probability. The process of arranging a set of objects in random order is referred to as *randomization;* it is used, for example, when allocating treatments to the experimental units (plots) as part of the design of an experiment.

Random Process—A random process, or *stochastic process,* is (1) a physical process which is governed at least in part by some random mechanism, and (2) a corresponding mathematical model. In the study of random processes one is generally concerned with sequences of random variables with special reference to their interdependence and limiting behavior. Examples of random processes are provided by the growth of populations such as bacterial colonies, and the fluctuating throughput in successive runs of an oil-refining mechanism. A random process can be discrete or continuous in time, and its value at any given time can be a value of a discrete or a continuous random variable. For instance, a continuous graph having the values 1 or 0, depending on whether or not a computer is in use, is continuous in time while the random variable (with values 0 and 1) observed at any given time is discrete; on the other hand, if, in quality control, one takes hourly samples from normal populations and records their means, the process is discrete in time while the random variable observed at any given time is continuous.

Random Sample—(1) A sample of size *n* from a *finite* population of size *N* is said to be random if it is chosen so that each of the $\binom{N}{n}$ possible samples has the same probability of being selected; such samples are also referred to as *simple,* or *unrestricted,* random samples. (2) A set of observations constitutes a random sample of size *n* from an *infinite* population, if the *n* observations are values of independent random variables having the same (population) distribution.

Random Variable—Also called a *chance variable*, a *stochastic variable,* or a *variate,* a random variable is a real-valued function defined over a sample space. The number of heads obtained in five flips of a coin, the height of a person chosen for an experiment, and the number of traffic accidents in Phoenix during the month of April, are all examples of random variables. In order to distinguish between random variables (functions) and their values, it has become customary to use capital letters (as in this book) or boldface type, say X or **x**, to denote random variables, and the corresponding lower case letters, x, to denote their values. *See also* Continuous Random Variable; Discrete Random Variable

Range—A simple and easily obtained measure of the variation of a set of data given by the difference between the largest value and the smallest. For instance, the range of the five lengths 3.09, 3.14, 3.07, 3.10, and 3.12 is $3.14 - 3.07 = 0.07$. As an estimator of a population standard deviation, its efficiency, relative to the sample standard deviation, decreases as the sample size is increased.

Raw Data—Data which have not been subjected to any sort of statistical treatment (such as grouping, coding, censoring, etc.).

Raw (Test) Scores—The first recorded numerical result of a test, such as the number of correct answers. Since raw scores generally are not comparable from one test to another and have no "standard" meaning, they usually are subjected to some sort of statistical treatment or analysis; for example, converted into standard scores or normalized standard scores.

Real Time (Computer) Systems—Information processing systems (such as are found in process control, in many military applications, and elsewhere) in which subsequent control of the system depends entirely, or almost so, on the output of the computer. In such time-critical situations, solutions are required almost immediately after the input data are entered into the computer. When a computer *simulation* is performed in the same time it takes to perform the actual operation being simulated, it is said to be performed in *real time;* simulations are performed in "slow time" or "fast time" when they are performed slower or faster than the actual operations.

Regression—The relationship between the (conditional) mean of a random variable and one or more independent variables; a mathematical equation expressing this kind of relationship is called a *regression equation.* When the regression equation is a linear equation, the regression is also referred to as *linear;* when the regression equation represents some other kind of curve or surface, the regression is referred to as *curvilinear.* The term "regression" is due to Francis Galton, who employed it first in connection with a study of the heights of fathers and sons, observing a regression (or turning back) from the heights of sons to the heights of their fathers.

Regression Analysis—The analysis of paired data (x_1,y_1), (x_2,y_2), ..., and (x_n,y_n), where the x's are constants and the y's are values of random variables; it is referred to as *normal regression analysis* if the y's are values of independent random variables having normal distributions with the respective means $\alpha + \beta x_i$ and the common variance σ^2. The term "regression" is also applied to the analysis of n-tuples of data, where the values of the independent variables are looked upon as constants and the values of the dependent variable are values of random variables. *See also* Correlation Analysis

Regression Coefficient—A coefficient in a regression equation; for example the parameters α and β in the linear regression equation $y = \alpha + \beta x$. The term is also used for corresponding estimates, but it is preferable to refer to these specifically as *estimated regression coefficients.*

Rejection, Region of—*See* Critical Region

Relative Frequency—If an event occurs x times in n trials, the relative frequency of its occurrence is x/n; relative frequencies are also referred to as *sample proportions.*

Relative Variation—The variation of a set of measurements relative to the size of whatever object (or quantity) is being measured. The most widely used measure of relative variation is the coefficient of variation, which is given by the ratio of the standard deviation to the mean (multiplied by 100 to express the coefficient as a percentage). For instance, if the mean and the standard deviation of a sample are 2.00 in. and 0.10 in., respectively, the coefficient of variation is $(0.10/2.00)100 = 5$ per cent.

Reliability—(1) In statistics, the term "reliability" is often used interchangeably with "consistency;" thus, when speaking of the reliability of an estimator, one is referring to the possible size of chance errors. (2) In engineering, the reliability of a product (component, unit, etc.) is the probability that it will perform within specified limits for at least a specified length of time under given environmental conditions. (3) In educational and psychological testing, the reliability of a test is the consistency with which it measures whatever trait it does measure.

Replacement, Sampling With and Without—If an element is drawn from a finite population, its distribution (or composition) for the next drawing is disturbed unless the element is replaced. When elements are not replaced, sampling is said to be *without replacement,* successive drawings are dependent, and the probability of getting x elements of a certain kind in n drawings is given by the hypergeometric distribution. When each element is replaced before the next one is drawn, sampling is said to be *with replacement,* successive drawings are independent, and the probability of getting x elements of a certain kind in n drawings is given by the binomial distribution. If the sample size is small compared to the size of the population (less than 5 per cent), the binomial distribution is often used as an approximation to the hypergeometric distribution when sampling is *without replacement.*

Replication—In experimental design, the performance of an experiment (or parts of an experiment) more than once; the purpose of replication is to obtain more information (more degrees of freedom) for estimating and assessing the experimental error and to obtain estimates of effects with smaller standard errors. The individual repetition of an experiment (or part of an experiment) is referred to as a *replicate.*

Residual Method—In time series analysis, a classical method of estimating cyclical components by first eliminating the trend, seasonal variations, and irregular variations, thus leaving the cyclical relatives as residuals.

Residual Variance—In regression analysis and analysis of variance, that part of the variability of the dependent variable which is attributed to chance or experimental error, namely, that part of the variability of the dependent variable which is not attributed to specific sources of variation.

Risk, Producer's and Consumer's—In hypothesis testing, especially in acceptance sampling, the respective probabilities of committing Type I and Type II errors.

Root-Mean-Square Deviation—*See* Standard Deviation

Root-Mean-Square Error—*See* Mean Square Error

S

Sample—*See* Judgment Sample; Probability Sample; Random Sample; Sample Design

Sample Census—A detailed census, or examination, of individuals, households, businesses, etc., selected in a sample from some population.

Sample Design—A definite plan, completely specified before any data are actually collected, for obtaining a sample from a given population. Alternate terms are "sampling plan" and "survey design." *See also* Area Sampling; Cluster Sampling; Judgment Sample; Multi-Phase Sampling; Multi-Stage Sampling; Probability Sample; Quota Sampling; Random Sample; Stratified Random Sampling

Sample Mean—*See* Mean

Sample Proportion—*See* Relative Frequency

Sample Size—The number of observations in a sample; it is usually denoted by the letter n.

Sample Space—In probability, a set of points (elements) which represent all possible outcomes of an experiment.

Sample Standard Deviation—*See* Standard Deviation

Sample Survey—A survey of human populations, businesses, social institutions, etc., which is based on samples. *See also* Sample Census; Sample Design

Sample Variance—*See* Standard Deviation

Sampling—The process of obtaining a sample. *See also* the various kinds of samples and methods of sampling referred to under Sample Design

Sampling Distribution—The distribution of a statistic; for example, the distribution of the sample mean for random samples from normal populations, or the distribution of the coefficient of correlation under the assumptions of normal correlation analysis. *See also* Experimental Sampling Distribution

Sampling Error—(1) In general, the difference between an observed value of a statistic and the quantity it is intended to estimate. (2) In analysis of variance, the following distinction is made between *sampling error* and *experimental error:* if there are several observations per cell, namely, if several observations are made on *one* experimental unit, their variation is referred to as *sampling error;* on the other hand, differences not attributed to specific sources of variation among observations made on *different* experimental units are referred to as *experimental error.*

Scale Parameter—A parameter of a distribution having the following property: if each value x of a random variable having a given distribution is replaced by $ax + b$, then the parameter must be multiplied by the constant a. For example, a population standard deviation is a scale parameter, whereas a population mean is not. Generally, parameters which are given by powers of scale parameters are also referred to as scale parameters; in this sense, a population variance would be considered a scale parameter.

Scaling—In general, scaling is a process of measuring. In particular, *nominal scaling,* or *categorical scaling,* is the process of grouping individual observations into qualitative categories, or classes; for example, classifying hospital patients according to their disorders. *Ordinal scaling* is a measuring procedure which assigns one object a greater number, the same number, or a smaller number than a second object only if the first object possesses, respectively, more, the same amount, or less of the characteristic being measured than the second object; for example, rating the hardness of five minerals by means of scratch tests, assigning the number one to the softest (which is scratched by all and scratches no others) and the number five to the hardest (which scratches all and is scratched by no others). *Interval scaling* is a special kind of ordinal scaling where the measurement assigned to an object is linearly related to its true magnitude; in other words, in interval scaling the scale of measurement has an arbitrary origin and a fixed, though arbitrary, unit of measurement (as, for example, when finding temperatures in Fahrenheit units). *Ratio scaling* is a special kind of interval scaling where the measurement assigned to an object is proportional to its true magnitude; in other words, the scale of measurement has an absolute zero and a fixed, though arbitrary, unit of measurement (as, for example, when measuring length or weight).

Scatter Diagram—A set of points obtained by plotting paired measurements, as points in a plane. The visual inspection of such diagrams aids in analyzing the general nature of the relationship between the two variables.

Schedule—A form on which an agent, enumerator, or interviewer enters the answer to questions asked directly of a subject; hence, a kind of questionnaire.

Scheffe's Test—*See* Multiple Comparisons Tests

Scientific Notation—A widely used scheme for writing numbers in scientific work. In such notation, numbers are written as a number between 1 and 10 multiplied by a power of 10. For instance, 530,000,000,000 is written $5.3 \cdot 10^{11}$ and 0.00000072 is written $7.2 \cdot 10^{-7}$.

Seasonal Index—For monthly data, a set of twelve numbers (one for each month), in which each month's activity is expressed as a percentage of that of the average month. For example, a January index of 71 means that January figures are typically 71 per cent of those of the average month. Correspondingly, a seasonal index may also be identified for weekly or daily data. *See also* BLS Seasonal Factor Method (1964)

Seasonal Variation—Strictly speaking, the movements in a time series which recur year after year in the same months with more or less the same intensity. Although the name implies a connection with the seasons of the year, the term is often used somewhat loosely to indicate other periodic movements; for example, those occurring within a day, week, or month. *See also* Periodic Movement

Secondary Data—Statistical data which are published by some organization other than the one by which the data are collected (and often processed).

Secular Trend—Sometimes called a *long-term trend,* the secular trend of a time series ordinarily is the underlying smooth (or regular) movement of the series over a fairly long period of time. This underlying movement is thought to result from persistent forces slowly affecting growth or decline (changes in population, income and wealth, changes in the level of education and technology, etc.).

Semi-Averages, Method of—A simple, though very crude, method of fitting a straight line trend to a time series.

Semi-Logarithmic Paper—Graph paper, also called *ratio paper,* which is so constructed that equal intervals on the vertical scale represent equal rates of change, while equal intervals on the horizontal scale represent equal amounts of change. For instance, the series 1, 2, 4, 8, 16, and 32 would plot as points on a straight line.

Set—A collection, class, or aggregate of objects, real or abstract; the objects which constitute a set are referred to as its *elements.*

Sigma, σ—*See* Standard Deviation

Sigma, Σ—**Summation sign;** $\displaystyle\sum_{i=1}^{n} x_i$ (or simply Σx) represents the sum $x_1 + x_2 + \ldots + x_n$.

Significance Level—*See* Level of Significance

Significance Test—In hypothesis testing, a test which provides a criterion for deciding whether a difference between theory and practice (a difference between observations and corresponding expectations, or a difference between an observed value of a statistic and an assumed value of a parameter) can reasonably be attributed to chance. If the difference is so small that it can be attributed to chance, one has the option of accepting the hypothesis on which the theoretical value (or values) was based, or of *reserving judgment* (when feasible) by merely stating that the data do not permit the rejection of the null hypothesis.

Simple Hypothesis—A hypothesis is said to be simple if it completely specifies the distribution of a random variable. For example, the hypothesis that the mean and the standard deviation of a normal population are, respectively, $\mu = \mu_0$ and $\sigma = \sigma_0$ is a simple hypothesis.

Single-Tail Test—*See* One-Tail Test (One-Sided Test)

Size of Critical Region—The probability α of committing a Type I error. *See also* Critical Region

Size of a Population—The number of elements in a finite population; it is usually denoted by the letter N.

Size of a Sample—The number of observations in a sample; it is usually denoted by the letter n.

Skewness—The lack of symmetry in a distribution; it is usually measured by the statistic α_3 (*alpha-three*), whose value is zero for a symmetrical distribution, or by the *Pearsonian Coefficient of Skewness,* whose value is zero when the median of a distribution coincides with its mean. A distribution is said to have *positive skewness* (or be *positively skewed*) when it has a long thin tail at the right, and α_3 as well as the Pearsonian coefficient of skewness are, in fact, positive. A distribution is said to have *negative skewness* (or be *negatively skewed*) when it has a long thin tail at the left, and α_3 as well as the Pearsonian coefficient of skewness are, in fact, negative.

Smoothing—In time series analysis, the removal of minor fluctuations or erratic fluctuations from a series of data. This is often accomplished by use of a moving average.

Software—All of the programming aids (such as programming languages and various operating routines), usually supplied by computer manufacturers, intended to help users make the most efficient use of their computer hardware. For example, the FORTRAN system is a part of the software package supplied by many manufacturers. *See also* Hardware (of a Computer)

Spurious Correlation—(1) This term is sometimes used when a high positive or negative value obtained for the coefficient of correlation can be attributed entirely to chance. (2) The term is also used to describe the inflated correlation which results from an overlap of two variables that are being correlated (for example, when scores on two tests consisting partly of the same items are correlated).

Square Root Transformation—The transformation $y = \sqrt{x}$ or $y = \sqrt{x + 1/2}$ is often used to make data consisting of values of random variables having Poisson distributions amenable to analysis of variance techniques.

Standard Deviation—(1) The standard deviation of a sample of size n (usually called a "sample standard deviation") is given by the square root of the sum of the squared deviations from the mean divided by $n - 1$. It is by far the most widely used measure of the variation of a set of data and it is generally denoted by the letter s. Some statisticians prefer to divide by n (rather than by $n - 1$) in the definition of the standard deviation, in which case it has also been referred to as the *root-mean-square deviation* and it may be described as the square root of the second moment about the mean. The square of the sample standard deviation is called the *sample variance.* (2) The standard deviation of a finite population is defined in the same way as the standard deviation of a sample; it is generally denoted by the Greek letter σ (*sigma*) when division is by the population size N, and by S when division is by $N - 1$. The square of the population standard deviation is called the *population variance.* (3) The standard deviation of the distribution of a random variable is given by the square root of the second moment about the mean and it is generally denoted by the Greek letter σ; such a standard deviation is usually referred to as a *population standard deviation,* and its square as a *population variance.*

Standard Error—The standard deviation of the sampling distribution of a statistic.

Standard Error of Estimate—In regression analysis, the square root of the residual variance.

Standard Normal Distribution—*See* Normal Distribution

Standard Score—A standard score, *z-score,* or *standard measure* is a score converted into standard units.

Standard Units—A set of data is converted into standard units by subtracting from each value the mean of the data and then dividing by their standard deviation. Note that in standard units the mean of any set of data is zero and its standard deviation is equal to 1.

Standardized Random Variable—A random variable which has been transformed linearly so that its mean is 0 and its standard deviation is 1. If X and Y are a random variable and the corresponding standardized random variable, then $Y = (X - \mu)/\sigma$, where μ and σ are, respectively, the mean and the standard deviation of the distribution of X.

Standardized Test—A test whose items have been carefully selected and evaluated, and which is accompanied by such things as directions for its administration and scoring, tables of norms, and suggestions for interpreting the results.

Statistic—A quantity (such as a mean or a standard deviation) calculated on the basis of a sample. In practice, the term is used for values of such random variables as well as the random variables themselves.

Statistical Inference—Also called inductive statistics, a form of reasoning from sample data to population parameters; that is, any generalization, prediction, estimate, or decision based on a sample. It is customary to refer to the Neyman-Pearson theory of testing hypotheses and the method of confidence intervals as classical statistical inference.

Statistics—(1) The totality of methods employed in the collection and analysis of any kind of data and, more broadly, that branch of mathematics which deals with all aspects of the science of decision making in the face of uncertainty. (2) A collection of numerical data such as those found in the financial pages of newspapers, the *Statistical Abstract of the United States,* Census Reports, and the like. The word "statistics" comes from the Latin word *status,* meaning a political state.

Stochastic Independence—This term is synonymous with "independence," as defined in probability theory. *See also* Independent Events; Independent Random Variables

Stochastic Process—*See* Random Process

Stochastic Variable—*See* Random Variable

Stratified Random Sampling—A method of sampling in which portions of the total sample are allocated to individual subpopulations and randomly selected from these *strata*. The principal purpose of this kind of sampling is to guarantee that population subdivisions of interest are represented in the sample and to improve the precision of whatever estimates are to be made from the sample data. *See also* Equal Allocation; Proportional Allocation

Student-*t* Distribution—*See t* Distribution

Subjective Probability—A point of view which is currently gaining in favor is to interpret probabilities (particularly those relating to single, nonrepetitive events) as subjective, or *personal*, probabilities; namely, as measures of the strength of a person's belief concerning the occurrence or nonoccurrence of events.

Subset—Set A is a subset of set B if and only if each element of A is also an element of B. Thus, each set is a subset of itself and, by definition, the empty set ϕ which has no elements at all is a subset of every set. *See also* Event

Sum of Squares—In analysis of variance, a sum of the squared deviations of observed quantities from appropriate means. *See also* Between-Samples Sum of Squares; Block Sum of Squares; Error Sum of Squares; Total Sum of Squares; Treatment Sum of Squares; Within-Samples Sum of Squares

Summation Sign—*See* Sigma, Σ

Symmetrical Distribution—A distribution is symmetrical if values equi-distant from the mean have identical frequencies, probabilities, or probability densities.

System of Equations—A set of equations to be solved for values of the variables which satisfy all of the equations. *See also* Determinant; Linear Equation; Normal Equations

Systematic Error—A nonrandom error which introduces a bias into all the observations; such an error might be caused by faulty, or poorly adjusted, measuring instruments.

Systematic Sample—A sample obtained by selecting every kth item on a list, every kth voucher in a file, every kth house on a street, every kth piece coming off an assembly line, and so on. An element of randomness may be introduced into this kind of sampling by randomly selecting from the first k units the unit with which to start. This is referred to as a *random start,* and a sample so chosen is sometimes called an "every kth" systematic sample.

T

***t* Distribution**—A distribution which is used largely for inferences concerning the mean (or means) of normal distributions whose variances are unknown. It is also referred to as the *Student-t distribution,* after W.S. Gossett, who used the pen name "Student." The parameter of this distribution is ν, the number of degrees of freedom. A table in the Appendices contains values of $t_{\alpha,\nu}$, which denotes the value for which the area *to its right* under the t distribution with ν degrees of freedom is equal to α.

***t* Tests**—Tests based on statistics having the t distribution. The *one-sample t test* is a test of the null hypothesis that a random sample comes from a normal population with the mean $\mu = \mu_0$; it is used when the population standard deviation is unknown. The *two-sample t test* is a test concerning the difference between the means of two normal populations having the same standard deviation; it is based on independent random samples from the two populations. The *paired-samples t test* is an application of the one-sample *t* test to differences between paired data; it is used when the data are actually given as *matched pairs* or when they are *randomly matched* because the assumption of equal standard deviations in the two-sample *t* test cannot be met.

Test—(1) A decision procedure for accepting or rejecting a statistical hypothesis. (2) An examination. *See also* Hypothesis; Neyman-Pearson Theory; Significance Test

Test of Significance—*See* Significance Test

Test Statistic—A statistic on which the decision whether to accept or reject a given hypothesis is based.

Tests of Hypotheses—Rules, or procedures, for deciding whether to accept or reject a hypothesis. *See also* Hypothesis; Neyman-Pearson Theory; Significance Test

Theoretical Distribution—A general term used to denote the distribution of a random variable, as contrasted with a distribution of observed data.

Theoretical Frequency—In some applications, an alternate term for "expected frequency."

Time Series—Any series of data collected, observed, or recorded at regular intervals of time; for instance, the monthly occupancy rates for California hospitals from 1960 to 1976. Though usually applied to economic and business data, the term and the techniques developed for analyzing such data apply also to the treatment of data from any of the social and natural sciences.

Time Series Analysis—The study of time series, or more specifically, the separation or decomposition of a time series into its individual components according to some model (or some set of assumptions). The ultimate goal of most analyses of time series is to make predictions or forecasts. *See also* Multiplicative Model

Tolerance Limits—In industrial applications, values between which one can expect to find a given proportion of a population. Whenever such values are determined on the basis of samples, one can only assert with a specified probability (or degree of confidence) that *at least* a given proportion of the population falls between the limits.

Total Sum of Squares—In analysis of variance, the sum of the squared deviations of all the observations (in a given experiment) from their mean. The foremost objective of an analysis of variance is to divide the total sum of squares into components which can be attributed to various specific sources of variation.

Transformation—A change of variable. Sometimes, transformations are performed to simplify calculations; sometimes, random variables are transformed so that one can meet the assumptions underlying "standard" methods; and sometimes random variables are transformed so that their distributions are of a certain well-known type.

Treatment—A treatment is an experimental condition; for example, different treatments can be different levels of a factor (or different values of a variable), or they can be different combinations of the levels of several factors. In other words, the term "treatment" may denote, literally, two fertilizer treatments for corn or four diets for animals, but also three machines operated at the same speed or the nine combinations possible when a machine is operated by each of three persons at each of three speeds.

Treatment Effect—In analysis of variance, a quantity (usually a parameter) which represents the change in response produced by a given treatment. The treatment effects are the parameters α_i.

Treatment Sum of Squares—In analysis of variance, that component of the total sum of squares which can be attributed to possible differences among the treatments.

Tree Diagram—A diagram in which the individual paths (all emanating from one point) represent all possible outcomes of an experiment. Such diagrams are of special value in situations where the end-result is attained through various intermediate steps.

Trend—*See* Secular Trend

Trend Cycle Component—When treated as a single component in time series analysis, it is considered to be the combination of the underlying long-term trend, the periodic movements that accompany economic cycles, and the short-term subcycles that have occurred in a series.

Trend Increment—*See* Annual Trend Increment; Monthly Trend Increment

Trial—This term is used to designate one of a series of repeated experiments, such as repeated flips of a coin, where one is interested, for instance, in the probability of getting x "successes" in n "trials." *See also* Bernoulli Trial

True Mean—The mean of a population; the term is meant to emphasize the distinction between a sample mean and the constant (though unknown) mean of a population.

Tukey's Test—*See* Multiple Comparisons Tests

Two-Tail Test—*See* One-Tail Test (One-Sided Test)

Two-Way Analysis of Variance—An analysis of variance, where the total sum of squares is expressed as the sum of the treatment sum of squares, the block sum of squares, the error sum of squares, and no others.

Two-Way Classification—A classification of a set of observations according to two characteristics (or two variables). Thus, the term is used in analysis of variance when the data are grouped according to treatments as well as blocks. *See also* Dichotomy

Type I Error—In hypothesis testing, the erroneous rejection of a null hypothesis; the probability of committing a Type I error is usually denoted by α.

Type II Error—In hypothesis testing, the erroneous rejection of a null hypothesis; the probability of committing a Type II error is usually denoted by β. *See also* Consumer's Risk; Power; Power Function

Typical Seasonal Pattern—A pattern obtained by averaging in some way the specific seasonal patterns observed (or calculated) for a number of years. The twelve numbers which result from averaging the specific Januaries together, and so on through the specific Decembers, are called a "seasonal index." *See also* Seasonal Index

U

U-Shaped Distribution—A frequency distribution having the general shape of the letter U.

Unbiased Estimator—An estimator whose expected value (namely, the mean of its sampling distribution) equals the parameter it is intended to estimate. *See also* Bias

Uniform Distribution—A distribution which in the *discrete case* assigns the same probability to each value within its domain; in the *continuous case* it has a constant probability density over a given interval. Uniform distributions are also referred to as *rectangular distributions.*

Unimodal—A set of data or a distribution is said to be unimodal if it has only one mode or modal class. *See also* Multi-Modal Distribution

Union (of Two Sets)—The union of two sets A and B, denoted $A \cup B$, is the set which consists of all elements that belong to A, to B, or to both.

Univariate Distribution—The distribution of one random variable.

Universe—A synonym for "population."

V

Value Index—An index number reflecting changes in both physical volume and prices; for example, changes in total sales, inventories, or wages.

Variance—*See* Standard Deviation

Variance-Components Model—*See* Random-Effects Model

Variance-Covariance Matrix—In multivariate analysis, a matrix for which the element a_{ij} is given by the covariance of the ith and jth random variables when $i \neq j$, and by the variance of the ith random variable when $i = j$.

Variance Ratio—An alternate name for a statistic having the F distribution; specifically, the ratio of two independent estimates of a population variance.

Variation—The extent to which observations or distributions are spread out, or dispersed. *See also* Chance Variation

Variation, Coefficient of—A widely used measure of *relative variation* which is given by the ratio of the standard deviation of a set of data to their mean, thus expressing the magnitude of their variation relative to their average size. This ratio is often multiplied by 100 to express the measure of relative variation as a percentage.

Variation, Measures—Statistical descriptions such as the standard deviation, the mean deviation, or the range, which are indicative of the spread, or dispersion, of a set of data or distribution.

Vector—A matrix having only one row or one column, for example, $x = (x_1, x_2, \ldots, x_n)$; its elements are referred to as the *components* of the vector, and the integer n is called the *dimension* of the vector.

Venn Diagram—A diagram in which sets are represented by circular regions, parts of circular regions, or their complements with respect to a rectangle representing the sample space which, in this connection, is also referred to as a "universal set" or a "universe of discourse." Venn diagrams are often used to verify relationships among sets and subsets (or events).

W

Waiting Line—*See* Queue

Weighted Aggregative Index—An index number constructed for an aggregate, or collection, of items which have been weighted in some way so as to reflect their relative importance with regard to the overall phenomenon the index is designed to describe. In a price index the weights are usually the corresponding quantities produced, consumed, sold, etc. *See also* Fixed-Weight Aggregative Index; Laspeyres' Index; Paasche's Index

Weighted Mean—The average of a set of numbers obtained by multiplying each number by a weight expressing its relative importance, and then dividing the sum of these products by the sum of the weights. For instance, if one buys five boxes of berries at 49 cents a box and two more boxes at 70 cents a box, the (weighted) mean price per box is $(49 \cdot 5 + 70 \cdot 2)/7 = 55$ cents.

Weighted Moving Average—A moving average in which the individual terms are explicitly weighted so as best to accomplish the purpose for which the moving average is calculated (usually to eliminate irregular variations). Any number of weighting systems are in use (or have been tried) in connection with the smoothing of economic time series, including weights based on binomial coefficients, parabolic weights, exponential weights, and many others.

Wholesale Price Index—Constructed by the Bureau of Labor Statistics, the Wholesale Price Index is intended to measure changes in the prices of large lots of commodities in primary markets; that is, at their first important commercial transaction. The primary source of this important index is the *Monthly Labor Review.*

Within-Samples Sum of Squares—Another name for the error sum of squares in a one-way analysis of variance.

Z

z-Scores—An alternate name for standard scores, that is, scores converted into standard units.

z-Transformation—A transformation of the sample correlation coefficient by means of the formula $z = 1/2 \ln(1 + r)/(1 - r)$. This transformation is used to perform significance tests and construct confidence limits for correlation coefficients.

Index